HEINRICH HIMMLER

ROLF MICHAELIS

HEINRICH HIMMLER

A DETAILED HISTORY OF HIS OFFICES, COMMANDS, AND ORGANIZATIONS IN NAZI GERMANY

Schiffer Publishing Ltd

4880 Lower Valley Road • Atglen, PA 19310

Other Schiffer Books by the Author:

Cavalry Divisions of the Waffen-SS (978-07643-3661-4)
The Kaminski Brigade (978-0-7643-3765-9)
Panzer Division of the Waffen-SS (978-0-7643-4477-0)

Other Schiffer Books on Related Subjects:

The Cruel Hunters: SS-Sonderkommando Dirlewanger by French MacLean (978-0-7643-0483-5)
Police Battalions of the Third Reich by Stephen Campbell (978-0-7643-2771-1)
Commanders of Auschwitz by Jeremy Dixon (0-7643-2175-7)

Copyright © 2017 by Schiffer Publishing Ltd.

Originally published as *Heinrich Himmler: Die Konzentration der Exekutivgewalt im Nationalsozialismus*, © 2014 by Rolf Michaelis, Berlin, Germany.

Translated from the German by David Johnston

Library of Congress Control Number: 2016959493

Type set in Minion and Trade Gothic

ISBN: 978-0-7643-5259-1

Printed in China

Published by Schiffer Publishing, Ltd.
4880 Lower Valley Road
Atglen, PA 19310
Phone: (610) 593-1777; Fax: (610) 593-2002
E-mail: Info@schifferbooks.com
Web: www.schifferbooks.com

For our complete selection of fine books on this and related subjects, please visit our website at www.schifferbooks.com. You may also write for a free catalog.

Schiffer Publishing's titles are available at special discounts for bulk purchases for sales promotions or premiums. Special editions, including personalized covers, corporate imprints, and excerpts, can be created in large quantities for special needs. For more information, contact the publisher.

We are always looking for people to write books on new and related subjects. If you have an idea for a book, please contact us at proposals@schifferbooks.com.

CONTENTS

FOREWORD

When Heinrich Himmler became *Reichsführer-SS* at the age of twenty-eight, he had about 280 members of the SS under his command. By the time the National-Socialist German Worker's Party (NSDAP) took power in 1933, that number had grown to approximately 52,000 men, and just before the German surrender the forty-five-year-old was the superior of about 3.3 million members of the *Wehrmacht*, *Waffen-SS,* and police.

In the twelve years of National–Socialist rule he concentrated within himself almost the entire executive power of the Third Reich. In addition to his original function as *Reichsführer-SS*, he was ultimately commander of the German police, Reich Commissar for the Consolidation of German Nationhood, Reich Minister of the Interior, commander of the Replacement Army, and Commander-in-Chief of Army Group Vistula. In the process many positions overlapped and thus formed the executive bodies of National–Socialism and the basis for an "SS state"[1] he strove for.

In this book these offices and functions will be described clearly and understandably, beginning with a description of National-Socialism, which represented the basis for the ominous developments in Germany that began in 1933. Without it, Himmler would probably have become—to use a modern term—an organic farmer. In addition to a brief biography of Himmler and a description of all his offices, several of his speeches are contained in the appendix. They give an impressive insight into his thinking and for this reason make this publication a useful addition to the existing literature.

I hope that my work contributes to the understanding of recent German history and gives new information and perspectives both to the interested layman and the historian.

The suffering that this one man brought over Europe is reflected in the fates of millions of Germans and foreigners. Not only political opponents became victims in accordance with the understanding of the National–Socialist system, but our own people as well. Himmler's orders to send sixteen-year-old students to the front in 1945, while at the same time sending feelers to the western Allies to negotiate a separate peace, for example, show that he tried tooth and nail to delay his own downfall and that of the NSDAP. Totally divorced from reality, he saw himself as the negotiating partner of the western Allies.

This book cannot delve into the millions of individual fates that can be attributed to Heinrich Himmler's actions. Instead the outline data relates to quantitatively more extensive processes and therefore only contingently reflect the smaller scale tragedies. The reader should be aware of this.

Rolf Michaelis
Berlin, November 1, 2014

CHAPTER 1
THE NATIONAL–SOCIALIST GERMAN WORKERS PARTY (NSDAP)

Within a few days of Kaiser Wilhelm II's abdication in November 1918, a multitude of political parties formed themselves, some of which—with the horror of the First World War and the terrible misery of the population in view—wanted to offer radical alternatives to the existing parties. One of them was the German Workers Party (DAP) founded by Anton Drexler (June 13, 1884 – February 24, 1942) and Karl Harrer (November 8, 1890 – September 5, 1926) in Munich on January 5, 1919—just before the *Landtag* elections in Bavaria. Like most small parties of its kind, it initially had little support. Most of its members came from the Munich railway, where Anton Drexler worked as a tool fitter. In the late summer of 1919, when Adolf Hitler joined, it had just fifty-four members. Thanks to his demagogic speaking ability and organizational skill, Hitler not only became an outstanding propagandist, but also one of the movement's leading functionaries. On February 24, 1920, at a large gathering in the Munich *Hofbräuhaus* organized by him, Hitler announced that the DAP had been renamed the NSDAP. The addition of "NS" to the party, which was now called the National–Socialist German Workers Party, was Hitler's idea. He wanted to show to the outside the strict nationalist views of its members as well as the then still strongly socialist direction of the party.

The NSDAP's 25-point program published that day openly revealed its objectives. If one compares the later history of the Third Reich with the party program of 1920, one can see that, apart from various socialist ideas (for example the nationalization of and profit sharing in major companies) the points were absolutely adhered to even just under twenty-five years later.[1] As the 25-point program had enormous importance for subsequent history after 1933, it will be repeated here in its entirety:

1. We demand the unification of all Germans in the Greater Germany on the basis of the people's right to self-determination.
2. We demand equality of rights for the German people in respect to the other nations; abrogation of the peace treaties of Versailles and St. Germain.
3. We demand land and territory (colonies) for the sustenance of our people, and colonization for our surplus population.
4. Only a member of the race can be a citizen. A member of the race can only be one who is of German blood, without consideration of creed. Consequently no Jew can be a member of the race.
5. Whoever has no citizenship shall only be able to live in Germany as a guest, and must be under the authority of legislation for foreigners.
6. The right to determine matters concerning administration and law belongs only to the citizen. Therefore we demand that every public office, of any sort whatsoever, whether in the Reich, state or municipality, be filled only by citizens. We combat the corrupting parliamentary economy, office-holding only according to party inclinations without consideration of character or abilities.
7. We demand that the state be charged first with providing the opportunity for a livelihood and way of life for the citizens. If it is impossible to sustain the total population of the State, then the members of foreign nations (non-citizens) are to be expelled from the Reich.
8. Any further immigration of non-citizens is to be prevented. We demand that all non-Germans, who have immigrated to Germany since August 2, 1914, be forced immediately to leave the Reich.
9. All citizens must have equal rights and obligations.
10. The first obligation of every citizen must be to work both spiritually and physically. The activity of individuals is not to counteract the interests of the community, but must have its result within the framework of the whole for the benefit of all. Consequently we demand:
11. Abolition of unearned (work and labor) incomes. Breaking of debt (interest)-slavery.
12. In consideration of the monstrous sacrifice in property and blood that each war demands of the people, personal enrichment through a war must be designated as a crime against the people. Therefore we demand the total confiscation of all war profits.
13. We demand the nationalization of all (previous) associated industries (trusts).
14. We demand a division of profits of all heavy industries.
15. We demand an expansion on a large scale of old age welfare.
16. We demand the creation of a healthy middle class and its conservation, immediate communalization of the great warehouses and their being leased at low cost to small firms, the utmost consideration of all small firms in contracts with the State, county or municipality.
17. We demand a land reform suitable to our needs, provision of a law for the free expropriation of land for the purposes of public utility, abolition of taxes on land and prevention of all speculation in land.
18. We demand struggle without consideration against those whose activity is injurious to the general interest. Common national criminals, usurers, profiteers and so forth are to be punished with death, without consideration of confession or race.
19. We demand substitution of a German common law in place of the Roman Law serving a materialistic world-order.

20. The state is to be responsible for a fundamental reconstruction of our whole national education program, to enable every capable and industrious German to obtain higher education and subsequently introduction into leading positions. The plans of instruction of all educational institutions are to conform with the experiences of practical life. The comprehension of the concept of the State must be striven for by the school [civics] as early as the beginning of understanding. We demand the education at the expense of the State of outstanding intellectually gifted children of poor parents without consideration of position or profession.

21. The State is to care for elevating national health by protecting the mother and child, by outlawing child-labor, by the encouragement of physical fitness, by means of the legal establishment of a gymnastic and sport obligation, by the utmost support of all organizations concerned with the physical instruction of the young.

22. We demand abolition of mercenary troops and formation of a national army.

23. We demand legal opposition to known lies and their promulgation through the press. In order to enable the provision of a German press, we demand, that: a.) All writers and employees of the newspapers appearing in the German language be members of the race; b.) Non-German newspapers be required to have the express permission of the State to be published. They may not be printed in the German language; c.) Non-Germans are forbidden by law any financial interest in German publications, or any influence on them, and as punishment for violations the closing of such a publication as well as the immediate expulsion from the Reich of the non-German concerned. Publications which are counter to the general good are to be forbidden. We demand legal prosecution of artistic and literary forms which exert a destructive influence on our national life, and the closure of organizations opposing the above made demands.

24. We demand freedom of religion for all religious denominations within the state so long as they do not endanger its existence or oppose the moral senses of the Germanic race. The Party as such advocates the standpoint of a positive Christianity without binding itself confessionally to any one denomination. It combats the Jewish-materialistic spirit within and around us, and is convinced that a lasting recovery of our nation can only succeed from within on the framework: The good of the state before the good of the individual.

25. For the execution of all of this we demand the formation of a strong central power in the Reich. Unlimited authority of the central parliament over the whole Reich and its organizations in general. The forming of state and profession chambers for the execution of the laws made by the Reich within the various states of the confederation. The leaders of the Party promise, if necessary by sacrificing their own lives, to support by the execution of the points set forth above without consideration.

As there were justified doubts about the party's democratic conformity because of the actions of party members (from the coercion of political opponents to participation in street battles) and public agitation by functionaries, in combination with a critical examination of the party's program, as a result of the Law for the Protection of the Republic, the NSDAP was banned in several German *Länder* (states), but surprisingly not throughout all of the Reich. In Bavaria the National–Socialist movement was able to register a steadily-growing number of members and sympathizers.

When, on November 8, 1923, Hitler took Mussolini's march on Rome as an example for his march on the Feldherrnhalle, Reich President Friedrich Ebert (February 4, 1871 – February 28, 1925) gave executive authority to *Generaloberst* Hans von Seeckt (April 22, 1866 – December 27, 1936), commander-in-chief of the army. He subsequently imposed a Reich-wide ban on the NSDAP with its 55,797 members, as well as the German National Freedom Party (DVFP), which also took part in the putsch under its leader *General der Infanterie* Erich Ludendorff (April 9, 1865 – December 20, 1937). Also considered an extremist party, the Communist Party of Germany (KPD), which a few weeks earlier in Hamburg had called for street battles, was also banned.

Various party functionaries—in particular Adolf Hitler—were subsequently convicted of high treason and furthermore the NSDAP was outlawed. New "*Völkisch*" movements were immediately established to pick up the party members, including for example the "*Großdeutsche Volksgemeinschaft*" (Greater German Folk Community). When, in 1924, Ludendorff was released and the DVFP was again allowed, it merged with followers of the still-banned NSDAP and was renamed the "*Nationalsozialistische Freiheitspartei*" (National–Socialist Freedom Party). As in other countries (France, for example), at frequent intervals there were short-lived alliances and disagreements between, in particular, *völkisch* and nationalist splinter groups.

Hitler was released from Landsberg prison in December 1924, after serving half a year of his sentence, and he immediately set about reorganizing the NSDAP. He recentralized its former members and in February 1925, he refounded the party. With 27,117 members, at the end of the year the party had just under 50% of the members it had had before the ban on November 23, 1923.

The economic situation in Germany after the hyper-inflation of 1923, and the slowly improving situation after the introduction of the *Rentenmark* brought the NSDAP many new members. Surprisingly there was a change in the social background of the new members. Because of Hitler's rapprochement with the capitalist market organization, these were no longer mainly workers, but also farmers, craftsmen, and merchants, who feared that they would be dispossessed and collectivized if the communists took power in Germany.

Hitler's rapprochement with capital led to a split in the party, however. While Gregor Strasser (May 31, 1892 – June 30, 1934) wanted to achieve socialism in Germany, contrary to original party thought Hitler now planned to reach all social strata—including big and heavy industries, and therefore founded various working groups which pursued exactly the goals of the various levels of society and recruited among them for the NSDAP.

With respect to the industrialists in particular, to many "National Bolsheviks" Hitler's agitation seemed like a breach of promise, however if Hitler had implemented the original party program, a confrontation with them would have been inevitable. It was clear to Hitler that taking power would be impossible without the support of big industry.

By the end of 1926, the membership of the NSDAP had risen to 49,523 men and women and by the end of 1927, it stood at 72,590. One year later there were 108,717 party members, and by the end of 1929, 176,426. Just one year later the NSDAP had about 389,000 members, and by the end of 1931, this number had risen to 806,294.

As one can assume that not only party members will select a certain party, by that time the NSDAP already represented a political force that could not be underestimated. Discussions with national-conservative parties about the formation of a coalition began in early 1932, however Hitler made it a condition that he be named Reich Chancellor if a government was formed. As this was vehemently rejected, the sixth Reichstag election on July 31, 1931, failed to produce a majority capable of governing. In consequence, during the seventh Reichstag election which followed on November 6, 1932, former Reich Chancellor Franz von Papen (October 29, 1879 – May 2, 1969) finally agreed that Reich President Paul von Hindenburg (October 2, 1847 – August 2, 1934) should name Hitler the new Reich Chancellor if he won. Hitler's huge gamble had paid off.

When Hitler was named Reich Chancellor on January 30, 1933, the NSDAP had about 849,009 members. The next day, however, the Reichstag was again dissolved, as no government could be formed. The eighth Reichstag election followed on March 5, 1933:

NSDAP .... 17,277,180 votes (43.9%)
SPD .... 7,181,629 votes (18.3%)
KPD .... 4,848,058 votes (12.3%)
Center Party .... 4,424,905 votes (11.3%)
Black-White-Red Battle Front[2] .... 3,136,760 votes (8%)
Bavarian People's Party .... 1,073,552 votes (2.7%)
German People's Party .... 432,312 votes (1.1%)

The KPD's votes were annulled, giving the NSDAP an absolute majority. Hitler now planned to have the Reichstag transfer its law-making authority to the government—meaning him. The so-called Enabling Act of March 23, 1923—the Law to Remove the Stress of People and State—was passed with the required two-thirds majority with the help of the Black-White-Red Battle Front and the Center Party. With it the Reichstag became almost irrelevant. Hitler could now pass decrees and laws independently and conclude treaties with foreign countries, even if this was not in accordance with the Weimar constitution.

On July 14, 1933, Hitler passed the law against the formation of new parties, one of the most important laws on the path to dictatorship. The law was worded succinctly:

The Reich government has passed the following law, which is hereby announced:
1. The National–Socialist German Workers Party exists as the only political party in Germany.
2. Anyone who undertakes to maintain the organizational cohesion of another political party or form a new political party will, provided the act is not punished by a more severe sentence as per other laws, be punished with penal servitude up to three years or with imprisonment from six months to three years.

All existing parties—except the NSDAP—thus had to disband, provided they had not already been forcibly abolished by special bans (for example the KPD or SPD). And so in the ninth Reichstag election on November 12, 1933, the only candidates were fielded by the NSDAP, plus a number of "guests" who were not affiliated with any party and who had belonged mainly to the DNVP or Bavarian People's Party. Hitler had created the one-party state, in which all members of the opposition were silenced or declared enemies of the state and could be sent to a concentration camp. The Reichstag election also included a referendum on Germany's recently-announced departure from the League of Nations. As with the banning of the German Communist Party—and in part also of the Social-Democratic Party—the referendum produced a not-insignificant majority among the people.

On the surface, the banning of political parties was also followed by the closure of private associations and clubs, with most members integrated into the corresponding—some newly created—National–Socialist organizations. This was intended to bring all of German society under National–Socialist command and control and indoctrinate its body of thought into the population. Through the ultimately compulsory disbandment of private associations and organizations and the transition to state organizations, social individualism for the most part fell victim to a National–Socialist mass movement. The people were surprised by this and the state order gave them no chance to object. The new organizations and sub-organizations of the NSDAP, some of which had existed since the late 1920s, included, for example:

- the *Sturmabteilungen* (SA) and the *Schutzstaffel* (SS),
- the National–Socialist Motor Corps (NSKK),
- the Hitler Youth (HJ),

- the National–Socialist German Students' League (NSDStB),
- the National–Socialist Women's Groups (NSF),
- the National–Socialist Lecturers' Alliance (NSDD),
- the German Labor Front (DAF),
- the National–Socialist People's Welfare Association (NSV),
- the National–Socialist War Victim's Care (NSKOV),
- the National–Socialist German Doctors' Alliance (NSDÄB),
- the National–Socialist Teachers' Alliance (NSLB),
- the German National Association of Breeders of Small Animals

While this resulted in the population being guided but also controlled, the NSDAP also saw as another of its primary tasks the maintenance of power, in part through constant propaganda. The Reich leadership including all its attached departments, ultimately formed a governing body which contained an unbelievable bureaucracy and had an extraordinary volume of personnel.

Within the NSDAP followed the elimination of all those who did not or no longer appeared to conform to Hitler's objectives. On the one hand there was the extreme socialist-oriented left wing under Gregor Strasser, as well as the likewise socialist-oriented SA command under Ernst Röhm (November 28, 1887 – July 1, 1934). Both groups were liquidated without trial in an internal housecleaning action in the summer of 1934 which, it was declared, had been carried out to prevent a putsch. Hitler's position was thus secured for the next ten years.

The so-called *Reichskristallnacht* took place in November 1938. Officially it was triggered by the assassination attempt against German legation secretary Ernst Eduard vom Rath (June 3, 1909 – November 9, 1938) in Paris on November 7, 1938. Shot by a seventeen-year-old Jew, he died of his wounds two days later. Portrayed by German propaganda as a political act, the two men had in fact met previously in Paris' homosexual scene, making it unlikely that this was a "political act." The Reich Minister for Public Enlightenment and Propaganda, Dr. Josef Goebbels (October 29, 1897 – May 1, 1945), took the incident as a welcome opportunity to encourage senior SA and party functionaries to show, "the fury of the German people against this assassination attempt." This resulted in actions against Jewish businesses, synagogues, and private citizens on the night of November 10, 1938. The pogrom ended with the deaths of about 400 German Jews, the arrest of about 30,000 Jews and the destruction of more than 1,400 synagogues and temples. The material damages were in the millions. Viewed socially, this pogrom was a tragedy. It showed the level of the SA in particular, but also how elements of the population were drawn into this group dynamic.

While there was an enormous increase in membership, especially after the assumption of power in 1933, during the course of the Second World War it became apparent that growing numbers of the German people were growing tired of the NSDAP. While the NSDAP still had great support among the population on account of its political and military successes until 1940, the steadily-lengthening death notices in the newspapers and the feeling that, after the defeats in Stalingrad and Africa, the war could not be won caused a growing number of Germans to wish for an end to the war. They did not see it as "their" war but as the specific war of Hitler and the NSDAP.

The attempt on Hitler's life on July 20, 1944, showed that elements of the *Wehrmacht* command wanted to put an end to the bloody regime and with it a war that could not be won. After this failed, more German soldiers and civilians were killed in the remaining approximately ten months until the unconditional surrender than had died in the previous just under five years of war.

The collapse of the Third Reich also ended the activities of the NSDAP. The Allied Control Council's Law of October 2, 1945, banned the party with all its organizations and attached units. In 1946, during the Nuremberg Trials, it was labeled a "criminal organization" because of its drastic party program and the terrible actions it had carried out.

The majority of those who were most guilty escaped punishment by committing suicide. What Hitler thought of "his" German people, however, sounded like mockery. On November 7, 1941, when it became apparent that the USSR was not going to be defeated in a blitzkrieg and Hitler obviously began thinking that the war could no longer be ended victoriously, he declared:[3]

> I am ice-cold here too. If the German race is no longer sufficiently strong and willing to make sacrifices, to shed its own blood for its existence, then it will die and be destroyed by another, stronger power […] In this case I will shed no tears for the German people.

And he repeated these thoughts on March 19, 1945:

> If the war is lost, the people will also be lost. It is not necessary to pay any attention to the basis of what the German people needs for its most primitive existence. On the contrary, it is better to destroy even these things. For the people has proved to be the weaker, and the future belongs exclusively to the stronger eastern people. What remains after this struggle will be the inferior anyway, for the good will have fallen.

Significant words, which show that the German population was nothing more than a host for Hitler's visions of a National–Socialist social order.

Agitation by NSDAP functionaries resulted in about eight million Germans joining the party. A further significant number belonged to party organizations without being members of the NSDAP. These included the *Waffen-SS*, in which almost a million men served, of which probably not even a quarter were members of the party. Especially in the prewar period, most members joined because of the party's real or propagandized (economic) successes. Later, pressure was also exerted on individuals or professions to join the party. The reason behind this was, on the one hand, to raise the number of party members, as well as the fact that a party member basically could or would offer less to no opposition. Not least, however, the contributions of eight million members represented a not-inconsiderable source of income. Ulla Wilm, born in Berlin in 1924, described how the average German felt about Hitler and the NSDAP:

> On special political occasions—anniversaries and birthdays—my colleagues and I stood in a huge crowd of people and waved swastika flags that had been handed out. Our places of work gave us time off and after the event, during which Hitler once drove past us in his open Mercedes, we were allowed to go home. We therefore had almost the whole day off. I believe that almost no one went to these "turbulent" homages if we had to take a day's vacation or go after work, at least my colleagues and I didn't. Now, watching the old films on television, one gets the impression that they were all convinced National–Socialists. We weren't and it certainly wasn't very much different with many others.

The "national revolution" intended by Hitler could have led to a longer-lasting social order if it hadn't been brought to collapse by the war he himself started.

CHAPTER 2
HEINRICH HIMMLER: A BRIEF BIOGRAPHY

Heinrich Luitpold Himmler was born at Hildgardstrasse 2 in Munich on October 7, 1900, the son of school principal Joseph Gebhard Himmler (May 17, 1865 – October 29, 1936) and Anna Maria, nee Heyder (January 16, 1866 – September 10, 1941).

His paternal grandparents were Johann Conrad Clemens Matthus Himmler and Agathe Rosine, nee Kiene. Born in Ansbach in 1809, his grandfather initially became a weaver and later served for several years in the Bavarian Army. This was followed by years of police service, after which Himmler worked in administration in Lindau on Lake Constance. While his grandfather had profited from the societal conditions in the Kingdom of Bavaria, Himmler's father had an even more worry-free career.

After his father Johann died in 1872, Joseph Himmler received state scholarships to attend the classical grammar school in Neuburg/Donau and from 1884 to attend the Royal Bavarian Maximilian University. After graduation he worked as a tutor for various titled families, and his students included Prince Heinrich of Bavaria (June 24, 1884 – November 8, 1916).

Joseph Himmler and his wife Anna had three sons. Gebhard Ludwig was born on July 29, 1898. Heinrich Luitpold followed two years later and on December 23, 1905, Ernst Hermann entered the world.

Joseph Himmler showed his gratitude to the Bavarian royal house, which had made it possible for him, a half-orphan, to study, by naming his second son Heinrich Luitpold. His first given name Heinrich was an expression of his gratitude to Prince Heinrich of Bavaria, who became godfather of his second-born at the age of sixteen.[1] His second name Luitpold was dedicated to the prince regent of the Kingdom of Bavaria, Luitpold Karl Joseph Wilhelm von Bayern (March 12, 1821 – December 12, 1912).

The young Heinrich Himmler was enrolled in the Munich cathedral school at the age of six. Because of missing vaccinations—in Germany vaccinations against measles, for example, did not begin until the mid-1970s—he suffered repeatedly from infections and childhood diseases, which kept him away from school. While this was not unusual, he obviously had a weaker physical constitution than his two brothers and fellow students. Two years later he moved to the *Amalienschule* and two years after that to the Wilhelm Grammar School in Munich. After his father obtained a position in Landshut, the family moved there. Heinrich Himmler attended the humanist grammar school there, with good to very good marks.

The fourteen-year-old Himmler was enthusiastic when the German Reich declared war on Russia on August 1, 1914, and two days later France. The initial successes—especially by Bavarian troops—in France caused euphoria similar to that produced by the victory over France in 1871. Like many other grammar students, Himmler also recreated great historical battles in games of strategy and like many of his fellow students he wanted to become an officer in the Bavarian Army as quickly as possible. That this desire was influenced by the First World War is shown by the fact that Heinrich Himmler did not apply to the Bavarian Cadet Institute in Munich, which was equivalent to a secondary school and was seen as a school that produced candidates for the Bavarian officer corps.

It was also not until he was seventeen that his father gave his permission for him to volunteer, and on January 2, 1918, he joined the replacement battalion of the 11th Royal Bavarian Infantry Regiment "von der Thann" in Regensburg. Coming from a good home, where in the afternoons he was "invited to tea with pastries" and where value was placed on good manners and meaningful topics of discussion, he suddenly found himself in a very different environment. Social differences, poor food and quarters, plus intimidating drill by Bavarian sergeants caused him to seek an extraordinarily close relationship with his parental home. Surviving letters reveal that he was proud to be a soldier but that he missed his family terribly.

After half a year of basic training, on June 15, 1918, Heinrich Himmler was sent to Freising for officer candidate training and on September 15, he began a two-week course with the 17th Machinegun-Company in Bayreuth.

By that time the situation in Germany was catastrophic. The German civilian population, in particular, was suffering from inadequate nutrition and medical care—the so-called Spanish influenza was spreading quickly, becoming a pandemic, ultimately claiming 50,000 lives in Germany. After Germany's allies asked for ceasefire talks, efforts also began in Germany to bring about political change. On October 3, 1918, Max von Baden (July 10, 1867 – November 6, 1929) became the new Reich Chancellor, and on November 9, 1918, he arbitrarily announced the abdication of German Kaiser Wilhelm II (January 27, 1859 – June 4, 1941). A few days earlier German sailors in Kiel had mutinied against further war service, beginning a revolution that, because of the terrible living conditions, soon gripped all of Germany.

Just eighteen years old, Heinrich Himmler experienced the collapse of the monarchy which he so respected. The Bavarian King Ludwig III (January 7, 1845 – October 18, 1921) abdicated on November 7, 1918, and the German Kaiser fled in exile to the Netherlands.[2] The ceasefire was signed in Compiègne on November 11, 1918. The young Heinrich was demobilized on December 18, 1918, before he had completed his officer training or ever got to the front.

As in all of Germany, in Bavaria there began a period of political unrest and constant power struggles between left, right, and moderate political movements. When a Soviet republic was declared in Munich on April 7, 1919, Heinrich Himmler joined the *Freikorps Oberland*. Made up of nationalist volunteers, it eliminated the Soviet republic in early May 1919. As a member of a reserve company, however, Himmler had taken no part in the action.

After joining the military in 1918 before completing high school, like many his age in 1919 he received a distress graduation—a certificate of matriculation standard without actually having graduated. At the same time he moved from Landshut to Ingolstadt, where his father was principal of the local grammar school. With his certificate of matriculation standard, in mid-October 1919 Heinrich Himmler enrolled at the Technical University of Munich in the field of agriculture. He rented a room near the university at Amalienstrasse 28. It was obvious that he harbored no compelling desire to become an officer and instead saw his future in agriculture.

On November 22, 1919, he joined the Apollo fencing fraternity in Munich. His selection of this student league was probably due to his brother Gebhard Ludwig, who had joined this very nationalist-leaning fraternity a year and a half earlier. Joining the fraternity was usual for nationalistic students and the contacts made there could later prove useful career-wise. As he had done when he joined the military in 1918, he accepted the, for him, unpleasant side effects. This included the heavy consumption of alcohol by his fellow students, which the nineteen-year-old avoided by obtaining a doctor's certificate for his stomach problem. One can assume that this did not exactly lead to the reputation he desired among the student body.

In May 1920, he and his brother Gebhard joined the Munich *Einwohnerwehr*, or civil defense guards, as volunteer *Reichswehr* reservists and were assigned to the 14th Alert Company within the 21st Rifle Brigade. There, at the age of twenty-one, the *Reichswehr* named Himmler *Fähnrich*[3] *der Reserve* on December 1, 1921, and in January of 1922 he met the thirty-four-year-old *Hauptmann* Ernst Röhm, who obviously impressed him with his characteristic style and political mindset.

His study time also included grappling with themes that would later ultimately help shape his later actions. Heinrich Himmler read numerous treatises on Jews, Russia, and sexuality. In all cases, the interest of an inquisitive mind whose thinking was, however, significantly influenced by the books—often of doubtful objectivity—must have been decisive. As he had no girlfriend or female partner, even though there were women his age among his acquaintances, the by then twenty-two-year-old possibly also sublimated this with thoughts of abstinence, comradeship, and loyalty to one's own people.

After Heinrich Himmler earned his farmer's diploma at the Technical University of Munich, as an agriculturalist, he obtained the position of agricultural assistant with the Stickstoff-Land GmbH in Schleissheim on 1 September 1922. He later wrote of his activities there:[4]

> Dear Pohl,
> Attached you will find a treatise on biological-dynamic fertilization. I have added several notes. I can very well imagine the IG-Farben reports, for nineteen years ago when I was a young assistant in the Stickstoff company, they wanted me to come up with similarly-fudged reports, in which I was supposed to prove that a certain large use of calcium cyanamide would be best for agriculture, which I obviously didn't do.

The almost twenty-three-year-old Heinrich Himmler's employment in the free economy ended a year later, at the end of September 1923. Perhaps the termination of his working relationship with the Stickstoff-Land GmbH was connected to his "refusal to work," which he mentioned in his 1941 letter. It is also possible, however, that he wanted time in the NSDAP, which he joined on August 2, 1923, receiving membership number 42,404. The party program was obviously completely in step with his political thinking.

In addition to his membership in the NSDAP, since October 17, 1923—by then living at Marktplatz 8/1—he had been a member of the Munich Command of the "*Reichs-Kriegsflagge*," which was led by Ernst Röhm. There the intellectual *Fähnrich der Reserve* Himmler advanced to flag bearer. As the flag was the most important outward symbol of the movement, he surely carried out this task given to him by Röhm with special pride. Himmler subsequently took part in the failed Hitler putsch in Munich on November 8–9, 1923 at his mentor's side.

Initially inactive because of the subsequent ban on the NSDAP, at the beginning of July 1924, he became secretary to the later *Gauleiter* of Lower Bavaria and Head of Reich Propaganda Gregor Strasser.[5] When the NSDAP was reestablished in February 1925, when he rejoined (membership number 14,303) he was named Deputy *Gauleiter* of Lower Bavaria. Within about half a year, the secretary became the *Gauleiter*'s deputy. In this capacity he spoke, often at brief intervals, about the NSDAP's objectives and its fundamental political views—with respect to Free Masonry, the Jews, and Bolshevism.

Heinrich Himmler joined the *Schutz-Staffeln*, which Hitler created because of the ban on the *Sturm-Abteilungen* (SA) that was still in place, on August 8, 1925. With membership number

168, he became leader of the SS in the *Gau* of Lower Bavaria with the rank of *Truppführer*. He had under his command about fifteen members of the SS out of a total strength of 200 SS men in Germany. Himmler remained commander of the SS in the *Gau* of Lower Bavaria until 1930, ultimately as an *SS-Oberführer*.

As a well-known speaker, Himmler took over another position, that of deputy head of Reich Propaganda, in September 1926.[6] In the course of this his office was moved to Munich. When named deputy *Gauleiter* of Upper Bavaria and Swabia, Heinrich Himmler was representatively responsible for half of Bavaria (except for Franconia and the Upper Pfalz) with approximately 15,000 NSDAP members.

In the private sphere, at the end of 1926, he met Margarete Boden (September 9, 1893 – August 25, 1967) in Bad Reichenhall. They married about a year and a half later, on July 3, 1928. His wife gave up her career—running a small care home in Berlin—and moved with him to the Waltrudering colony in Trudering near Munich. Heinrich Himmler, who in 1927, had become deputy *Reichsführer* over about 250 SS men, immediately established two new NSDAP *Ortsgruppen* in the area. This was in keeping with his nature, to actively engage for the party without regard for his personal interests. While he concentrated on being politically active, his wife Margarete bred small animals. That the former nurse was now breeding chickens and rabbits was obviously in keeping with Himmler's desires as an agriculturalist. Their daughter Gudrun was born on August 8, 1929.

While the world was grappling with its greatest economic crisis— in Germany alone there were more than three million out of work at the beginning of 1929—on January 6, 1929, *SS-Oberführer* Heinrich Himmler was named as Erhard Heiden's successor as *Reichsführer-SS*. This placed him over about 280 SS men Germany-wide, but organizationally they were part of the SA, which had been reestablished in 1926.

While in previous years there had been conflicts between the SA leadership and Hitler with respect to political objectives, in 1929–30 there were further disagreements, including to what degree the SA should be carried or supported financially by the NSDAP. After Hitler wanted to use the available financial resources primarily for the election campaign, there was a revolt by the Berlin SA, in which the SS opposed the SA. Heinrich Himmler's men thus demonstrated their absolute loyalty toward Hitler and toward their own comrades.

The catastrophic economic situation in Germany after the world economic crisis led to great success by the NSDAP in the Reichstag election on September 14, 1930. It received 18.3% of the votes and a total of 107 seats in the Reichstag. Heinrich Himmler stood for the Weser–Ems electoral district and was elected to the Reichstag. In doing so he not only gained immunity but also many monetary advantages.[7] While previously he had increased the number of offices he held, he now gave up his position as deputy head of propaganda.

Because of the numerous quarrels with the SA, Hitler, as SA supreme commander, personally assumed command of the SA and on January 5, 1931, replaced Ernst Röhm as chief of staff. He also gave Himmler permission to recruit volunteers for the SS from among the approximately 80,000 SA men. The disputes between the Supreme Commander of the SA East (*SA-Oberführer* Stennes), who viewed the SA as a people's army—in accordance with Point 22 of the NSDAP bylaws—which should replace the *Reichswehr* and also act sovereignly against the party, were aggravated even further, however. On March 31, 1931, Hitler, fearing that the party would be banned again, ordered Ernst Röhm to replace Walther Stennes (April 12, 1895 – May 18, 1989). The next day Stennes, who after the 1930 Reichstag election had accused the NSDAP of falangism, ordered the party headquarters in Berlin occupied. This resulted in brawls between SA and SS men. The police cleared party headquarters and Paul Schulz (February 5, 1898 – August 31, 1963) took over as acting commander of the SA in Berlin.

After this so-called "Stennes revolt," on June 13, 1931, there was a gathering of party functionaries at party headquarters. Heinrich Himmler not only took the opportunity to report the basic loyalty of the SS to Hitler, but also for the first time spoke at length about the racial look he expected of his SS members. Former frontline soldiers of the First World War, who had already proved their bravery, were held to a different standard than was the case for the young SS applicants. To Himmler the appearance—the ethnogenic characteristics of his SS men (especially the shape of the head)—was the guarantee that the young volunteers would remain faithful to National–Socialism. He explained his strange-sounding ideas on this in 1935:

> Like a research breeder wishing to purify an old, good variety which has been mixed and degraded, we first go over the field to the so-called choice perennials, in order to weed out those that we believe we cannot use for the *Schutzstaffel*. [...] I first set about demanding a certain height. I took no one under one meter seventy, because I know that people whose height is over a certain number of centimeters somehow must have the desired blood. [...] I looked at photos of all of them, and wondered, are there traces of foreign blood here? Why did I do that? Please remember the soldier rat types of 1918 and 1919. You will find that by and large they were people who looked rather strange to our German eye, who had somehow strange features. They were the type of men who, at the moment that the ultimate pressure test of character and nerve comes, must somehow fail because of their blood.

Ideally, the SS men should have an athletic, slim, and tall physique with striking, rather narrow facial features, a type that, paradoxically, the often rather ill-looking Himmler himself little corresponded to. Concerning this, the later *Gauleiter* of Danzig–West Prussia, Albert Forster (July 26, 1902 – February 28, 1952), said in 1940:

> If I looked like Himmler, I wouldn't talk so much about race.

On this premise, after the Stennes revolt Himmler became particularly active in recruiting SA men for the SS. Almost 15,000 SA men were taken into the SS by the end of 1931. When the SA leadership protested, Himmler—the actual initiator of this action—issued a not very believable directive that was supposed to appease the SA:

> To put an end once and for all to the nonsense about recruiting in the SA, effective January 20, 1932, I will not be taking any more SA men into the SS, unless this SA man has voluntarily received his deregistration notice after applying directly to his responsible *SA-Gruppenführer*.

This directive was obviously not implemented, however, for one year later the SS already had 52,000 members. Even though many of the new members came from the army of the unemployed, by then eight million strong, more than a few others transferred from the ranks of the SA to the SS.

On January 25, 1932, Hitler commissioned Himmler with providing security at party headquarters in the Braun Haus at Brienner Strasse 45 in Munich. The Reich High Command of the SS with the SS senior staff was also housed there. In addition, Hitler also gave Himmler the task of creating a Study Group for Economic Questions. The latter was supposed to cultivate contacts with businessmen who could support the NSDAP in the election. Created at the same time was the institution of the Supporting Member of the SS.[8]

After the so-called "assumption of power" by the National–Socialists on January 30, 1933, the functionaries of the NSDAP were immediately given new fields of responsibility. Himmler—recently promoted to *SS-Obergruppenführer*[9]—was named provisional police chief of Munich and finally held the office of the Political Police Commander in Bavaria. By 1934, he succeeded

Reichsführer-SS, *SS-Obergruppenführer* Heinrich Himmler, with Ernst Röhm and *SS-Gruppenführer* Siegfried Seidel-Dittmarsch in the summer of 1933.

Since the summer of 1934, the designation *Reichsführer-SS* was also the highest rank within the SS.

Hitler with Himmler and Dietrich during Berlin's 700 Year Celebration in the summer of 1937.

in taking over the political police of the various federal states, as well as the Secret State Police in Prussia.

Aware of the latent danger of the SA, one year later Hitler decided to eliminate the SA leadership. Himmler was given the task of carrying this out in June 1934. The murder of the about 200 SA leaders and other opponents (like Gregor Strasser, for example) was publicly declared to be necessary for the maintenance of internal security. Defacto there was no court judgment of any kind, and this showed the legal understanding the leader of the NSDAP had, even against former so-called "*Alte Kämpfer*" (old fighters).

With its SA's leadership eliminated, the organization lost its effectiveness, which favored Himmler. On August 23, 1934, "in recognition of his loyalty towards the *Führer*" he was elevated to the position of "*Reichsleiter der NSDAP*" (official designation *Reichsleiter SS*) and the SS was separated from the superior-ranked SA. Himmler thus became one of eighteen *Reichsleiter* in the NSDAP. His function as *Reichsführer-SS* simultaneously became the highest official rank within the SS. From then on he was no longer an *SS-Obergruppenführer*, instead as *Reichsführer-SS* he was personally only bound by instructions from Hitler.

Heinrich Himmler moved his office to Berlin and was initially separated from his wife and daughter, who had been joined by foster child Gerhard von der Ahé[10] on March 1933. The settlement house in Waldtrudering was sold in 1934, and Margarete Himmler and her two children moved to the Lindenfycht country home in Gmund am Tegernsee. The separation was proof that the marriage was failing.

On July 1, 1935, Himmler, together with *Reichsbauernführer* (Minister of Agriculture) Richard Walther Darré (July 14, 1895 – September 5, 1953), and Dutch private scholar Herman Wirth (May 6, 1885 – February 16, 1981) formed the Study Society for Primordial Intellectual History, German Ancestral Heritage (*Das Ahnenerbe*). It was subsequently renamed the Research and Teaching Community of the Ancestral Heritage.[11]

One year later—on June 17, 1936—the thirty-five-year-old Himmler received his greatest gain in power. He was named Chief of German Police. Three years after the assumption of power by the NSDAP he was the superior of more than 100,000 policemen.

At the end of 1938, Himmler's secretary Hedwig Potthast, with whom he would have two children, entered his private life.[12]

In the course of the NSDAP's folklore policy, on September 10, 1939, Heinrich Himmler was named Reich Commissar for the Consolidation of German Nationhood. It was an office with which he would come to have an unbelievable influence on the living conditions of millions of people in Europe through the numerous settlement and resettlement plans. In this capacity he changed more than he did as Reich Minister of the Interior, to which position he was appointed by Hitler on August 25, 1943.

Himmler again lived up to his comradely understanding in October 1943, when he took over guardianship of the minor Jürgen Pleiss, son of fallen Knight's Cross holder *SS-Hauptsturmführer* Gerd Pleiss (April 20, 1915 – November 17, 1941). Himmler thus had a total of three children of his own and was guardian of two more.

On June 21, 1944, Himmler was named Commander of the Replacement Army (BdE) and Chief of Army Equipment. As a result of this, more than two-million soldiers were placed under his command. On July 1, 1944, the German armed service (*Wehrmacht*) had a total strength of about 9,750,000 troops, of which 24.3% were in the Replacement Army. As well, approximately 460,000 members of the *Waffen-SS* and about 260,000 members of the *Allgemeine-SS* were subordinate to him as *Reichsführer-SS*. The members of the *Allgemeine-SS* however, served in part in the *Wehrmacht*, the *Waffen-SS*, or the German Police. In addition, as Chief of the German Police he was the highest superior of more than 350,000 German and foreign police members, so that by the summer of 1944, he had power over approximately 3.3 million bearers of arms.

Himmler, together with Dr. Joseph Goebbels and Reich Minister Hans Frank, in conversation with Benito Mussolini during the state visit to Italy on May 8, 1938.

September 11, 1938: During the Reich Party Congress, Himmler reports 20,000 assembled SS men and members of the German Police to Hitler.

On April 17, 1944, Himmler took part in a walk of condolence for Adolf Wagner, the late *Gauleiter* of Munich.

At the end of 1944, Himmler's organizational talent led him to the Western Front. On December 2, 1944, Hitler tasked him with stabilizing the front on the Upper Rhine. As BdE, Himmler ordered all available replacement units at the front to march, and ultimately assumed command of the Nineteenth Army (*19. Armee*). The *Fähnrich der Reserve* of 1921, had risen to command an army without having completed officer's tactical training or having received general staff training. After having committed at least no fundamental errors, in January 1945, he was committed on the broken Eastern Front. As a skilled organizer he was to form Army Group Vistula, mainly using troops of the Replacement Army, and he also took over as the army group's commander-in-chief.

The concentration of all these executive positions showed, on the one hand, the trust Hitler had in Himmler, but, on the other, that he also had no one else to turn to. So an ever smaller group of NSDAP functionaries governed the German people, which was growing increasingly tired of National–Socialism and the war. As early as October 10, 1943, *SS-Obergruppenführer* Berger warned Himmler:[13]

> The mood of the population is for the most part good. The middle and working classes are holding up well. The farmers and the so-called Haute volé [high society] are doing most of the complaining, whether in the small towns of Württemberg, Bavaria or East Prussia. The population in Munich is hostile as nowhere else. For years already I have been doing all I could to prevent the emergence one day of the thought: this war is the war of the *Schutzstaffel* or the NSDAP, which at the present time—I say this without any exaggeration—means the same thing. [...]
>
> *Reichsminister* Dr. Goebbels believes that he has the people in his hand. He thinks himself a fakir, to whose whistles and calls the viper and the cobra dance. In my opinion, this creates for us a tremendous responsibility to ensure that the war is always portrayed as a war for the Reich, never as a war for the Führer, the NSDAP and the SS.

While war weariness in the homeland was already apparent, the Allied offensives in the west and the east in the summer of 1944, showed that the war was going to end in a defeat for Germany in the foreseeable future. To prevent this, various functionaries advised Himmler to look into the possibility of a separate peace. The fact that this happened just after July 20, 1944, seems, like so much else, paradoxical. On September 26, 1944, *SS-Obergruppenführer* Berger wrote:[14]

> As one of your most faithful, with two graves (his sons) in areas now occupied by the Russians, please allow me to propose the following:
>
> *Reichsführer*, advocate that we bail out our back in the east. I believe that if we act quickly, the possibility and opportunity still exist. Perhaps we can hold the Russian border at the Carpathian hills, buy ourselves out with possession of Poland and the general Warsaw line. If we can attack in the west next spring, it will be no problem not only to reach the Somme River line quickly but also to hold it and then in my opinion to secure the last-named area for the next ten years. [...] When Frederick the Great concluded the Peace of Hubertusburg, he kept what he already had and nevertheless he won the war. It was the rise and the foundation of the Prussian state.

One could scarcely define the wish that power should remain in the hands of National-Socialism and the SS—obviously with Heinrich Himmler at its head—in the coming years any more unrealistically. Hitler, who probably had no knowledge of these thoughts, as he fundamentally ruled out a separate peace, simultaneously mobilized the last reserves by ordering the formation of the German *Volkssturm* on September 25, 1944.

As commander of the Replacement Army, Himmler would assume responsibility for training the 16- to 60-year-old *Volkssturm* people, while *Reichsleiter* Martin Bormann (June 17, 1900 – May 2, 1945) was to handle the organizational questions. As the party leadership quite obviously wanted the *Volkssturm* to be trained and committed to the party line, on October 31, 1944, Bormann turned explicitly to his old friend Himmler:[15]

Dear Heinrich,

I ask that you not resent the following statement. As the BdE, you are supposed to see to the military training of the *Volkssturm* people. In fact, so far *SS-Obergruppenführer* Berger[16] has concerned himself with organizational matters, for which I am responsible, while directives about military training have not been issued. Most of the men can handle a rifle. The supreme command of the SA could have been placed in charge of this rifle training, whether it was a priority or not.

In fact, however, as commander of the Replacement Army, the *Reichsführer-SS* was tasked with training the *Volkssturm* soldiers on modern equipment, especially anti-tank weapons, using all the weapons and resources of the Replacement Army.

If the necessary orders are not issued immediately, there is no doubt that certain *Gauleiters* will make the necessary agreements with *Herr Generaloberst* Guderian for the purpose of achieving the necessary training with the replacement units. If things begin in this direction, there will be no changing them. [...] The agreements in the districts [Gauen] should actually only be made between the heads of service of the BdE and the *Gauleiters*. I ask that you understand me properly. I do not want to meddle in your responsibilities. In the current situation, however, things must take a completely wrong direction. Because the necessary initiative from the BdE is lacking, training in the districts is going over to the panzer arm's replacement units.

One can see that the resentment towards the *Wehrmacht*, which existed even before the attempt on Hitler's life on July 20, 1944, was constantly present among the leaders of the NSDAP. Aware of the opposition by many *Wehrmacht* officers and generals, they tried to keep manpower under the control of National–Socialist leaders.

Interestingly it was none other than Himmler who, in February 1945, tried to negotiate a separate peace, not with Stalin—as urged by *SS-Obergruppenführer* Berger in September 1944—but with the western allies. With Hitler giving the impression of a broken man, both physically and psychologically, and probably having told his closest circle of his plans to commit suicide, Himmler felt himself to be his legitimate successor. And so on April 21, 1945, one day after Hitler's birthday, he met with Norbert Masur (1901–1971), the Stockholm representative of the World Jewish Congress, at the Hartzwalde estate (about seventy kilometers north of Berlin), which belonged to his Swedish masseur Felix Kersten (September 30, 1898 – April 16, 1960). The next day Himmler received Folke Bernadotte Count von Wisborg (January 2, 1895 – September 17, 1948), vice-president of the Swedish Red Cross, in Hohenlychen, and once again in Lübeck on April 23–24, 1945. The subsequent release of 20,000 concentration camp prisoners to the Swedish Red Cross was probably supposed to initiate the negotiations with the western allies about a one-sided capitulation.

Hitler learned of these unauthorized negotiations from a BBC broadcast on April 28, 1945, and the next day expelled Himmler from the party and all his official offices. In the second part of his political testament on April 29, 1945, he declared:

Before my death I expel the former *Reichsführer-SS* and Minister of the Interior, Heinrich Himmler, from the party and from all offices of State. In his place I appoint *Gauleiter* Karl Hanke as *Reichsführer-SS* and Chief of the German Police, and *Gauleiter* Paul Giesler as Reich Minister of the Interior. Göring and Himmler, quite apart from their disloyalty to my person, have done immeasurable harm to the nation and the entire people by secret negotiations with the enemy, which they conducted without my knowledge and against my wishes, and by illegally attempting to seize power in the nation for themselves.

The formulation that Himmler had done, "immeasurable harm to the people and the whole nation" through his attempt to negotiate with the western allies, shows how distanced from reality Hitler was ten days before the end of the war and one day before his suicide—Germany was in ashes and had been almost completely conquered by Allied forces because of his policies. Less this direct reference, however, Hitler was correct: Himmler's actions in the previous twelve years had, "done immeasurable harm to the nation and the entire people."

In his political testament, Hitler named *Großadmiral* Dönitz (September 16, 1891 – December 24, 1980) as his successor. When, on the afternoon of April 30, it was announced that Hitler had committed suicide, Dönitz began forming a new government. Contrary to Hitler's order, Dönitz did not arrest Himmler, who had been staying in the Flensburg area since the end of April, and the former *Reichsführer-SS* tried to participate in the new government. The astute Dönitz understandably had no interest in this and finally officially dismissed Himmler on May 6, 1945.

It suddenly became apparent that even German representatives—just like the Allied politicians and military, with whom Himmler had tried to establish contact—had no interest in the former *Reichsführer-SS*. In Flensburg on May 3, 1945, Johann Ludwig Count Schwerin von Krosigk (August 22, 1887 – March 4, 1977), the newly-appointed "leading minister" of the so-called "acting national government," even advised Himmler, "to drive straight to General Montgomery's headquarters and to say that he was Heinrich Himmler and bore full responsibility for what the SS had done."

After his embarrassing dismissal, Himmler and his inner circle[17] stayed at a farm in Satrup (approximately twelve kilometers southeast of Flensburg) until May 10, 1945. After an attempt to obtain asylum in Sweden failed, he wanted to try to reach his old homeland of Bavaria. He had a pay book made for himself at police headquarters in Flensburg in the name "Heinrich Hitzinger," *Feldwebel* in the Secret Field Police. A poorly thought out attempt at deception, for one must have assumed that the Allies would be looking for members of the secret field police among the prisoners of war. A pay book made out for a member of a home defense unit would surely have been less noticeable. *SS-Untersturmführer* Fritz Bohrer met the former *Reichsführer-SS* in police headquarters in Flensburg:

> When I returned to the Zollschule hospital after a walk with *Sturmbannführer* Schiller of the LAH, a package with cigarettes and sweets was lying on my bed, along with the news that I should immediately proceed to police headquarters via the shortest route. I received the news from my best friend, *Hauptsturmführer* Walter Linnemayr, then adjutant to *Obergruppenführer* von Herff of the personnel office.
>
> On two crutches (in Vogelsang on the Oder Front, a bullet had fractured my lower right leg on February 7, 1945) I hurried to police headquarters, where I knew the secretary of the troop care organization well. I told her why I was there and she fetched *Hauptsturmführer* Linnemayr from the briefing room and we two friends hugged each other for a few seconds. Then Linnemayr told me that our *Reichsführer* and several members of his escort detachment had just telephoned Sweden (Count Folke Bernadotte) to seek asylum. I was so outraged by this that I said to Linnemayr: the *Reichsführer* demanded of us loyalty unto death and more and now he wants to run away?

At that moment the *Reichsführer* emerged from the consultation room and walked along the corridor on the first floor to the toilets. When he returned he stood by us. Linnemayr introduced me and as he did so Himmler looked at me critically and observed that I had lost all of my upper front teeth. His question: "Where did you lose your teeth?" I replied truthfully: "In the fighting in Normandy after the invasion!" Then Himmler clapped me on the shoulder and said paternally, "Comrade Bohrer, we'll get your teeth back." I replied: "*Reichsführer*, I can't imagine that for the life of me." He replied: "Yes, yes!" and after a handshake disappeared into the consulting room. After a long while Himmler and his escort left police headquarters. The secretary told us that he had been issued a German military pay book.

The men left Flensburg by car on May 10, 1945, and drove via Delve to Brunsbüttel, where a fisherman took them across the Elbe on May 12. From there the group proceeded on foot south in the direction of Bremervörde, about sixty kilometers away. Covering about ten kilometers per day, they reached the city on May 18. They then spent three days in a farmhouse on Waldstrasse. Parts of the group—not including Himmler—planned to cross the Oste over a bridge in the town and were captured by British soldiers trying to doing so. After the failure of one such attempt, Himmler and his adjutants *SS-Obersturmbannführer* Grothmann and *SS-Sturmbannführer* Macher walked some distance to the south and crossed the Oste near Minstedt (approximately six kilometers south of Bremervörde) on May 21, 1945. There the three men were caught by former Soviet prisoners of war and initially returned to Bremervörde. One of the two Russians, Ivan Sidorov, stated for the record on June 7, 1945:[18]

I was liberated by Allied troops in the Sandbostel camp [Stalag XB, the author] on April 29, 1945. After I was freed I found myself in Collection Point 619 and voluntarily joined the Russian camp's garrison company. We guarded the camp and every second day we went on patrol with English soldiers on the streets and in the surrounding villages.

At nine in the morning on May 21, 1945, we—an English and Russian patrol—arrived in the village of Minstedt. [...] With the corporal's approval, we—Gubarev and I—went on our rounds. At ten in the morning we returned for coffee, at one in the afternoon we had our lunch and then the two of us went on our rounds again. At seven in the evening we returned to the house where English soldiers were, smoking, talking and drinking coffee. They said to us: "It's still too early, we're leaving at 1930. You can rest if you want or walk your beat again." We decided to walk to the outskirts of the village again. I soon saw three Germans emerging from the bushes. Shielded by the bushes, they were trying to cross the street and reenter the forest. We called to them, but they kept walking. We ran after them. Gubarev fired into the air. One German stopped, but the other two continued into the forest. Gubarev again shouted to them commandingly and made the sign: "Stop! Everyone come here!" We took aim at the Germans. Then they stopped. We walked towards them. One of the detainees, who later turned out to be Himmler, was wearing a grey coat of officer's cut, civilian trousers, military boots and a black hat, and he had a black bandage over his left eye. In his hands he held a stick, which served as a crutch. The coat was buttoned up to the top. On his wrist he had a watch with a compass. The other two were wearing similar coats and boots but nothing on their head. Their German garrison caps were stuck in their coat pockets. [...] We brought all three to the village, to the house where the English soldiers were. [...] With gestures and single words, the detainees tried to explain that they had come from a hospital. Himmler pointed at his bandaged eye and left leg, at his crutch, and tried to convince the soldiers that he was ill.

The English soldiers said to us: "You should let them go, they're sick." But we, Gubarev and I, signaled them: "No. We have to take them to the camp." In the camp we handed

On October 18, 1944, Himmler announced the formation of the German *Volkssturm* in East Prussia. Beside him on the left: *SS-Obergruppenführer* Lammers, chief of the Reich Chancellory, and *Generaloberst* Guderian.

The training given members of the *Volkssturm* included how to destroy enemy tanks from close range.

SS-Untersturmführer Fritz Bohrer was wounded in action while serving on the Oder Front with the *32. Freiwilligen-Grenadier-Division "30. Januar."* When the war ended, he was in a military hospital in Flensburg.

the three over to an English officer and an interpreter. […] About three days later we were again sent out on patrol. Sixteen Russians assembled in the square, waiting for a truck. [An] English officer also arrived, along with the interpreter. The interpreter asked: "Who brought in the three Germans on the 21st of May?" I answered: "I did." Gubarev also answered: "I did." He wrote down our family, first and surnames, as well as both our birthplaces. Then he asked: "Do you know who you captured?" We replied, "no." "The one with the eye patch was Himmler, head of the Gestapo. They took him to another town, he took poison while being interrogated and has died." Afterwards, in the camp there was much talk among the Russians and English about who had captured Himmler.

Himmler and his party were taken to the civil internment camp in Westertimke, about thirty kilometers to the south, on the morning of May 22, 1945. From there he was transferred to Barnstedt (approximately fifteen kilometers south of Lüneburg). There, at about 1900, Himmler identified himself to the camp commander, Capt. Thomas Selvester. He later remembered:

The first man who entered my office was short, sickly-looking and shabbily dressed, but he was immediately followed by two other men (Grothmann and Macher), both of whom were tall and soldierly-looking, one slim and well-built. The well-built man was limping. I sensed something unusual and ordered my sergeant to detain the two men so that they could not speak to each other without my permission. Then they were taken out of the office, whereupon the small man, who had a patch over his left eye, removed it and put on a pair of glasses. I immediately recognized him and he said "Heinrich Himmler" in a very soft voice.

Capt. Selvester subsequently informed the headquarters of the British Second Army in Lüneburg, which ordered a major of the British Security Service to confirm Himmler's identity by checking his signature. Then he was strip-searched. Selvester remembered:

In his jacket I found a small brass case, similar to a cartridge case, which contained a glass phial. I realized what the item was for, but I nevertheless asked Himmler what it contained. He said that it was his medicine, for stomach cramps. I found another, similar brass case, this one without a phial, and came to the conclusion that the phial must be hidden somewhere on the prisoner. When all of Himmler's clothing had been removed and inspected, all of his body cavities were examined, his hair was combed and every possible hiding place was inspected, but no phial was found. Himmler was not asked to open his mouth at that time, because I thought that a phial hidden in his mouth might initiate a regrettable action if we should attempt to remove it. I ordered cheese sandwiches and tea, which I offered to Himmler, expecting that I would be able to see Himmler removing anything from his mouth. I watched him closely as he ate but was unable to see anything unusual.

The next day (May 23, 1945), Himmler was taken to British Security Service headquarters, located at Uelzener Strasse 31a in Lüneburg. He was forced to disrobe and Capt. Wells, a military doctor, again examined him for the missing phial. The doctor spotted a dark object in a cavity in Himmler's lower jaw. He told him to step closer to the light and then tried to remove the phial. Himmler bit it, however, and died a short time later at about eleven in the evening.

After a Soviet delegation examined Himmler's body on May 24, 1945, it was probably buried in a wood near Melbeck on May 26. Himmler's death ended a life which, through concentrated power, had influenced millions of people and also ended the lives of countless millions. Many historians pursue the question, what kind of man must Himmler have been to be capable of something like that. The psyche of the *Reichsführer-SS* is studied and researched, hoping to find the reason, perhaps in his childhood. This overlooks one basic fact: Heinrich Himmler found his political direction in National–Socialism and pursued the objectives of the NSDAP pragmatically and meticulously. He had the vision that the German people should lead and that National–Socialist Germany would assume leadership in Europe. He felt responsible for achieving these goals and as Hitler bit by bit transferred almost all executive power to him, Himmler ultimately represented the "executor of National–Socialist policy." In this role he fought against all those who were declared enemies of the Reich. Those who could be seized were at best sent to a concentration camp or pragmatically murdered. He and his circle forbade compassion, as he felt himself to be the powerful engine of the National–Socialist ideology.

If one examines his surviving speeches (see the appendix) and the countless documents that have survived, the resulting picture is similar to what the former NSDAP *Gauleiter* Albert Krebs (March 3, 1889 – June 26, 1974) wrote about Heinrich Himmler. To him, he was a, "curious mixture of warlike bombast, the regulars' table twaddle of a petty bourgeois, and the enthusiastic prophecies of a sectarian preacher."

That this "bombastic militarist" ultimately became the second most powerful man in National–Socialist Germany, became a tragedy for millions of people in Germany and Europe.

CHAPTER 3
REICHSFÜHRER-SS

The *Allgemeine-SS*

The roots of the *Schutzstaffel* (SS) are linked to those of the *Sturmabteilung* (SA). The latter was created on October 5, 1921, by renaming the so-called Gymnastics and Sport Division of the NSDAP which had been in existence since November 12, 1920. From the beginning, the members of this "Sport Division" acted as an internal security service at party meetings. When street fights with political opponents (mostly the KPD) became more frequent, this order service ultimately developed into the party's general protection force. The first approximately 300 men of the SA were frequently members of the *Einwohnerwehren* (citizen's militias),[1] which had been disbanded in June 1921.

With membership numbers steadily growing, there also followed parades and public demonstrations of power aimed at the population and political opponents. On the NSDAP Party Day on January 27–28, 1923, Hitler for the first time awarded flags to SA battalions that had "proved themselves." Hermann Göring assumed command and began organizing the SA along military lines, into *Stürme* (companies), *Sturmbanne* (battalions) and *Standarten* (regiments). Victor Lutze (December 28, 1890 – May 2, 1943), later chief of staff of the SA, described the conception of the SA:[2]

> Born in the time of disgrace and defeat, grown out of an epoch of dishonor and corruption, the SA today is an unshakeable rock, against which enemies of all shades will smash open their skulls. For the will and the faith of the German people is with us, because we are from and with this people. Because German blood flows in our veins, because we were born of a German mother, have grown up on German soil. Our mission is therefore determined by fate, because the calling through blood underlies it. Our struggle therefore is one desired by fate and God, because we wage it for the community of the German people created by God. That is the unshakeable faith that the *Führer* has given us and which we are called to carry from generation to generation in the National–Socialist ideal. Bolshevism, Jewry, reaction, and whatever our enemies are called or call themselves, have lost their right to exist wherever the SA marches. Where the storm banners of the SA lead the way in a new age, there is nothing left for them to seek. We are shaping Germany without all their doings. We, the political soldiers, according to the orders and will of our leader.

These statements not only show the National–Socialist world of ideas, which also repeatedly invoke God, but also how the NSDAP received encouragement from the population. The majority of Germans regarded the Treaty of Versailles as a "disgrace," the "roaring twenties" were for many an "epoch of dishonor," and the world economic crisis that spread from the USA was a synonym for corruption and capitalism. The propaganda calling on the people to oppose this was very effective and ultimately resulted in the SA reaching a membership of about four million.

A *Stabswache* (staff guard) was formed in March 1923, its purpose to guard the NSDAP offices at Corneliusstrasse 12 in Munich and provide personal protection for Hitler. Its members were specially chosen for their reliability and physical strength and were commanded by Josef Berchtold (March 6, 1897 – August 23, 1962). Two months later it was renamed *Stoßtrupp Hitler*. Organizationally attached to the *SA-Standarte* Munich, the special unit also accompanied its party leader on his propaganda trips all over Germany.

Initially about twenty men strong, within a few weeks the *Stoßtrupp* (shock troop) grew to about 100 members. After Hitler's failed putsch attempt in early November 1923, the NSDAP and all its organizations, including the Hitler Shock Troop, were banned. While the NSDAP was allowed to reestablish itself on February 27, 1925, the SA as a party force remained banned. Despite this a new staff guard was formed under Julius Schreck (July 13, 1898 – May 16, 1936) in April 1925 and was called the *Schutzstaffel* (defense corps). It was seen publicly for the first time on April 16, 1925 at the funeral for Ernst Pöhner (January 11, 1870 – April 11, 1925), former chief of police in Munich and participant in the march on the Feldherrnhalle.

Through the practice of forming *Schutzstaffeln* with eight to ten men and one officer in all larger local branches of the NSDAP, the SS expanded relatively quickly. Heinrich Himmler joined the SS on August 8, 1925, becoming member number 168. Like the earlier staff guard and shock troop, the *Schutzstaffeln* were supposed to protect Hitler and other prominent party functionaries and also recruit new members. Recruits were to be between 25 and 33 years old, strong and healthy, and have unconditional loyalty to Hitler.

Joseph Berchtold, who had emigrated to Austria after the NSDAP was banned, returned to Munich in April 1926, and assumed command of the *Schutzstaffeln*. When the SA was finally allowed to reform in November 1926, these *Schutzstaffeln* were placed under Franz Pfeffer von Saloman (February 19, 1888 – April 12, 1968), the SA Supreme Commander (OSAF). In the process, Berchtold, who like Schreck was initially designated *Oberleiter der SS*, received the title *Reichsführer-SS*. With a strength of only about 200 members, this formulation seemed rather exaggerated.

Nevertheless, by the summer of 1926 Berchtold was able to raise a total of seventy-five *Schutzstaffeln* with about 1,000 men. The SA supreme command, however, rejected his plan to add further units. As a result, in March 1927, he stepped down from his position as *Reichsführer-SS*. His successor was *SS-Sturmbannführer* Erhard Heiden (February 23, 1901 – April 1933), who like Berchtold had been a member of the Hitler Shock Troop.

Surprisingly Heiden released more than 700 members back to the SA. As a result the *Schutzstaffeln* lost much of their importance and it is likely that this happened at the urging of the SA leadership. When Hitler replaced him with Heinrich Himmler on January 6, 1929, Heiden again became active in the SA. A further indicator of a "conspirative" link to the oppositional SA leadership, which resulted in a reduction in the size of the SS, which it regarded with skepticism, is the fact that Erhard Heiden was arrested by Himmler in the Café Orlando di Lasso in Munich and died shortly thereafter for reasons that were unexplained.

Heinrich Himmler, who was situated at Schellingstrasse 50 in Munich together with the SA supreme command, immediately began expanding the *Schutzstaffeln*, with the majority of candidates again recruited from the SA. Himmler stressed outward appearance in the selection of volunteers. If someone had a striking face, light hair and blue eyes, as well as an athletic build without much body fat, Himmler assumed that he basically came from "good blood" and was therefore honest and loyal. By the end of 1929, the SS membership had again reached 1,000 and one year later it was 2,700, including 1,640 in southern Germany. By August 1932, the SS had 25,853 members, and at the end of 1932 approximately 52,000.

In addition to protecting the offices of the NSDAP and party functionaries, the principle tasks of the SS included extensive propaganda work. To recruit new members for the NSDAP, leaflets and brochures were distributed on the street, posters were put up, subscriptions to the *Völkische Beobachter* (Racial Observer) were sold and donations were collected. Basically, SS men were supposed to spend about two hours working for the SS two nights per week, plus from three to six hours on two Sundays of the month. Half the number of hours sufficed for members over the age of thirty-five who were in the SS reserve, and comradeship evenings were held for those over the age of forty-five who were still with their home unit.

In August 1930, the *Schutzstaffeln* were forced to defend the party offices against their own "comrades" for the first time when the Berlin SA under Walter Stennes (April 12, 1895 – May 18, 1989) demonstrated its displeasure towards Hitler's policies by occupying the NSDAP headquarters there. The Berlin SS lacked the numbers to prevent it, however it did "come to blows" with its SA comrades, thus demonstrating its loyalty to Hitler.

Following this, on November 7, 1930, Hitler expressly transferred all (security) police functions within the NSDAP to the SS. In the course of this, on February 5, 1931, he tasked Himmler with the protection of all future party gatherings against internal and external threats.

Whereas in the past there had been only small *Schutzstaffeln* with about eight to fifteen men, mainly in the larger towns, as a result of the expansion that had taken place these were reorganized effective February 20, 1931. The smallest unit was the *Schar* (squad) with a strength of about eight men under the command of an *SS-Scharführer*. Three *Scharen* formed a *Trupp* (platoon), which was about 25 to 40 men strong, commanded by an *SS-Truppführer*. Three *Trupps* with a total of about 100 to 120 men formed a *Sturm* (company) with an *SS-Sturmführer* at its head. Four *Stürme* in turn constituted a *Sturmbann* (battalion), whose *SS-Sturmbannführer* commanded a total of about 460 men. Three to four *Sturmbanne* were supposed to result in an *SS-Standarte* (regiment), which was commanded by an *SS-Standartenführer*. The *SS-Standarten* were initially attached to fourteen *SS-Abschnitten* (brigades), which in turn were attached to *SS-Gruppen* (divisions). At the beginning of 1934, the *SS-Gruppen* were renamed *SS-Oberabschnitte*.

Until the summer of 1931, the *Reichsführung-SS* was organized in divisions and departments, resembling the headquarters of a division.[3] On August 10, 1931, Himmler formed *Abteilung I c* in the *SS-Oberstab*. This intelligence service was supposed to monitor opponents inside the NSDAP (for example, gauge opinion within the SA) and outside the party and inform itself as to the actual state of affairs. When, on April 13, 1932, Reich Defense Minister Wilhelm Groener (November 22, 1867 – May 3, 1939) banned the SA, including the SS, as per the Emergency Decree to Safeguard the Authority of the State, under the command of *SS-Sturmführer* Heydrich *Abteilung Ic* acted as a "press information service" for two months. On July 19, 1932, after the readmission of the SA/SS, Heydrich was named leader of the NSDAP's *Sicherheitsdienst* (security service) and with his new agency moved into Zuccalistrasse 4 in Munich.

The *SS-Rassenamt* (SS Racial Office) was also established in late December 1931, under *SS-Standartenführer* Walter Darré (July 14, 1895 – September 5, 1953). It was supposed to prove and document that, "blood alone determines history, civilization, law and economy." It also assumed responsibility for standardized acceptance inspection of SS recruits and the training of advisors attached to the various units.

In the summer of 1932, there was a reorganization of the *Reichsführung-SS* as a result of the organization's growth. The former divisions and departments became the *SS-Amt* (SS Office) and the SS Racial Office was renamed the SS Race and Resettlement Office. On July 15, 1932,

Himmler also ordered the formation of an *SS-Verwaltungsamt* (SS Administration Office) under the command of *SS-Sturmbannführer* Gerhard Schneider. *Referate I d* (clothing, rations and accommodations) and *IV a* (finance management) had existed previously and now they were merged. The *SS-Verwaltungsamt* was thus responsible for SS housekeeping as well as securing food, quarters, and uniforms. Funds initially came from so-called "supporting members." Not until passage of the Law to Safeguard the Unity of Party and State on December 1, 1933, did the SA and with it the SS receive state funds from the Reich budget.[4]

When Hitler took power on January 30, 1933, Heinrich Himmler had been a member of the NSDAP for scarcely ten years. Through his extraordinarily agile and loyal manner he had already made a career in the party. In about four years he had succeeded in increasing the SS by more than 51,000 men. This was an extraordinary growth in power, although it was only a small percentage of that of the SA, which by then had about half a million members.[5]

When the NSDAP took steps to disband private societies and organizations, Himmler tried to convince all the exclusive riding clubs to join the SS. The elitist principles of the SS were stressed in keeping with the thinking of many riders: many of the socially established and respected members were given honorary SS ranks without having to be further active in the organization. A cavalry *Standarte* and a central riding school were established in Munich in *SS-Oberabschnitt Süd*.

The SA also profited from this policy and through the transfer of the *Stahlhelm* paramilitary organization, the *Kyffhäuser* veterans organization and many non-organized veterans groups it achieved a strength of about 4.5 million members. It thus had more members than the NSDAP.

In June 1933—ten years after the formation of a *Stabswache* in Munich—another *Stabswache* was formed in Berlin. Under the command of *SS-Gruppenführer* Josef Dietrich (May 28, 1892 – April 21, 1966), approximately 120 SS men undertook guard duty inside the Reich Chancellery.[6]

Because of the diverging political views, the enormous increase in the size of the SA was not only a threat to Hitler. Because of the SA's enormous numerical superiority, the army also saw it as a potential opponent. Hitler subsequently decided to eliminate this element of uncertainty by eliminating the SA leadership. The basis for this action was supposed preparations by Ernst Röhm for a putsch. Himmler was given a central role and ordered elements of the *Leibstandarte-SS Adolf Hitler* from Berlin to Bavaria. In Munich, SS men shot the SA leaders who had been arrested by the Bavarian Political Police the same day. Two days later Röhm refused to commit suicide in his prison cell in Munich–Stadelheim and was subsequently shot through the hatch in the door of his cell by *SS-Oberführer* Theodor Eicke, the commander of Dachau concentration camp (October 17, 1892 – February 26, 1943), and *SS-Obersturmbannführer* Michael Lippert, the leader of the camp guard (April 24, 1897 – September 1, 1969). Finally numerous, in some cases prominent, opponents of the party, who were no "party comrades," were also murdered in the course of this action against dissidents within the party.

This renewed proof of Himmler's loyalty to Hitler resulted in the elevation of the SS to an independent organization within the NSDAP on July 20, 1934. This ended its longtime subordination to the SA. Himmler took advantage of the situation and recruited extensively within the SA, adding several thousand more members of the SA to the SS. The strength achieved as a result led to a reorganization of the *Reichsführung-SS* in early 1935. The *SS-Amt*,[7] *SS-Sicherheitsamt* and *SS-Rasse- und Siedlungsamt* were elevated to *Hauptämter* (main offices).

In the course of further expansion of the SS, which in January 1935, had just under 165,000 members and just two years later encompassed about 210,000 men, on November 13, 1937, a decree by the Minister of the Interior created the position of Senior SS and Police Commander. These were installed in all defense districts and in the event of mobilization they would lead the combined forces of the SS and the police. Under them were the Inspectors of the Security Police and the Order Police with coordination, supervisory, and disciplinary authority.[8]

Whereas the primary tasks of the SS had been to protect party functionaries and conduct active propaganda for the NSDAP, in 1936, Himmler described his *Schutzstaffel* as an "anti-Bolshevist battle formation:"

> We have formed ranks and, obeying immutable laws, march as a National–Socialist, soldierly order[9] of Nordic-infused men and a sworn community of their tribe into a distant future. We wish and believe that we might not only be the grandchildren who fought more resolutely, but beyond that the forebears of later generations necessary for the eternal life of the German people.

Himmler was clearly stating how he saw the SS seven years after he assumed command of the organization as *Reichsführer-SS*. Himmler's mythic ideas alternate with phrases, whose message—as, for example, his own coinage "Nordic-infused"—are difficult to define. What are "nordic-infused" men?

SS-Standartenführer Gunther d'Alquen (October 24, 1910 – May 15, 1998), executive editor of the SS' journal *Das Schwarze Korps* (The Black Corps), described the contemporary scope and organization of the SS in the publication *Die SS: Geschichte, Aufgabe und Organisation der Schutzstaffeln der NSDAP* at the turn of the year 1938–39. His statements provide a good insight and overview:

Organization of the *Allgemeine-SS*

With a strength of 240,000 men, the *Allgemeine-SS* today is organized into fourteen division-strength commands (*Oberabschnitte*), thirty-eight brigade-strength commands (*Abschnitte*), 104 foot regiments (*Fußstandarten*), nineteen cavalry regiments (*Reiterstandarten*), fourteen signals battalions (*Nachrichtensturmbanne*), and nine pioneer battalions (*Pioniersturmbanne*), plus motor transport and medical units. As during the time of struggle, the *Allgemeine-SS* is fully involved in careers, with the exception of a small number of full-time officers and men.

The division-strength commands, each of which is under an *SS-Obergruppenführer* or *SS-Gruppenführer*, are likewise organized into brigades, regiments, battalions and companies.

The Career Path to *SS-Mann*

The career path to *SS-Mann* is as follows: after confirmation of suitability for service in the SS, at the age of eighteen a member of the Hitler Youth becomes an SS candidate. On Reich Party Day of that same year, he is then accepted into the *Schutzstaffel* as an SS candidate and is issued his SS identity card. After a short proving period he takes the oath of allegiance to the leader on November 9.

During his first year of service in the *Schutzstaffel*, the SS candidate earns the Defense Sports Badge and the Defense Sports Badge in Bronze. Then, either at the age of 19 or 19½—depending on how his age class is called up—he begins his labor service and then enters the *Wehrmacht*.

After another two years he returns from the *Wehrmacht*, provided he does not want to remain there as a non-commissioned officer candidate or long-service soldier. The one who returns to the SS is initially still an SS candidate. In the subsequent period until his acceptance, he is again specially schooled in ideology, during which he is taught the basic laws of the SS, especially the marriage order and the honor code of the SS. If all other conditions are met, the SS candidate is accepted into the *Schutzstaffel* on the next 9th of November after his release from the *Wehrmacht*.

At the same time, on that 9th of November he receives the right to wear the SS dagger and on this occasion swears that he and his kin will obey the basic laws of the SS at all times. From that day on, he has the right and obligation to defend the honor of the Black Corps according to its honor code.

As an *SS-Mann* he then remains in the active *Allgemeine-SS* until the age of thirty-five. On application he is subsequently transferred to the SS reserve, and after age forty-five is assigned to the *Stammabteilung* (parent battalion).

The *SS-Verfügungstruppen* (VT)

After the seizure of power, for considerations cited elsewhere, the *SS-Verfügungstruppen* were created from the *Allgemeine-SS*, the foundation of the entire *Schutzstaffel*, in a slow and organized process. Its bases and organization are also described elsewhere.

The *Verfügungstruppen* are built up based on the experiences of the *Schutzstaffel*, on the fundamental basis of National–Socialist knowledge of selection, command and education. In their clearly-proven form, the *SS-Verfügungstruppen* are an actively-garrisoned and armed component of the SS. The men, who are selected and tested by the standards of the *Schutzstaffel*, have signed up for at least a four-year period of service. After reaching the status of *SS-Mann*, these troops receive full military training. Service in the *Verfügungstruppen* is also considered to meet the requirements of compulsory military service. After completion of their service obligation in the *Verfügungstruppen*, the SS men obviously return to the *Allgemeine-SS*, from which they came.

The Death's Head Units (*Totenkopfverbände*)

Part of the barracked SS forms the SS Death's Head units. They were created from the volunteers of the *Allgemeine-SS* conscripted to guard the concentration camps in 1933. In addition to educating the armed political soldiers, their role is to guard enemies of the state in concentration camps. The SS Death's Head units sign up their members for twelve years. Most are recruited from men who have completed their obligatory service in the *Wehrmacht*. This service time is fully taken into account. In organization and equipment, the Death's Head units are largely similar to the *SS-Verfügungstruppen*. They consist of four *Standarten*.

Internal Security

After the external conclusion of the revolution of our world view, in possession of power and with it completely, utterly responsible for the principles and subsets of our ideal, began the greater, though externally less heroic phase of permeation.

All subsections of the internal and external positions of the concept of the state and the nature of the state must now be convincingly and permanently filled by our new body of thought or through it redefined. We must carry the revolution, the living body of a comprehensive movement, with and against statutes, into the rigor of hardened institutions and concepts with all means. We must overthrow that which, after this process, does not seem viable, fill it anew with living spirit, which proves itself useful and usable.

Few subsections of the conquered state must from the outset appear to be so charged with resistance against the life and expression of the new power as the police. All our hate and all our rebellion have come together with it as the most pronounced symbol of the power of the system.

Rubber truncheons, house searches, prison, terror, tracking, all the countless expressions of the difficulty and cruelty of that time behind us, seem to crystallize and flow together in the term police. Quite inevitably the word police was itself a term of the hated and cursed, and therefore at the outset it seemed almost impossible to realize the idea of achieving the identity of National–Socialist law, of National–Socialist community authority with the term and the institution of the police. Within the movement itself it naturally required a considerable authority to make this compelling desire a reality.

As a formation, a community of officers, men and family of strict National–Socialists, the SS had this authority throughout its history and the development of the party. From its original role within the party, it has now been given the same expanded role in the entire people and the state occupied by them: internal security, the internal protection of the National–Socialist people, the consistent defense against its internal enemies in all areas of public life.

Seen from this principle, insurmountable resistance seemed to rise when, as per the leader's order to the *Schutzstaffel*, the *Reichsführer-SS* was given the task of concentrating all German police in his hands and thereby as per to the very special concept of the SS.

This takeover took place, contrary not only to old ideas but often enough contrary to existing rules, under the sole valid law, the right to life of the German people.

In few areas of state and people has such a revolutionary and thoroughly comprehensive approach been taken to the solving the biggest problems of the party and state, and scarcely anywhere has it been demonstrated that the leader's will should determine the idea of the state than on this difficult ground.

The personal authority of the *Reichsführer-SS* and his dedicated team is responsible for the start of this new formation, and its subsequent course will guarantee the success of the National–Socialist measures that have been taken.

The traditional concept of the police has become the new idea of a defense corps of the German people. And as the old term for the lackey, as it were, has found its expression in the word type, the new term also demands the new man.

We need more than an official, and likewise we do not consider the apolitical soldier suitable. The new type will correspond to the SS man, who grows from the principle of the orientation and the path of the SS and who has clearly evolved before the people. The people shall and must have a political soldier in this post in the best interpretation of this National–Socialist concept.

Against the deceit of liberal police law, the policeman was given the power of life and death, clear principles, and through the National–Socialist authority of the *Schutzstaffel* took the hate and contempt of the best part of our people. The police were thus again borne into the midst of the people as an important link for the protection and defense of the community.

It is clear and natural that the new type of policeman and his young, clear ideal should result in a reinterpretation of the term enemy of the state. The restriction in the general defense must result in far-reaching prevention, the clear interpretation of the term state concept a clarification of the term state parasite, a formulation which assigns an historic mission of unheard-of scope in the healthy development of the people to the National–Socialist defense corps.

The spirit of discipline and comradeship, recognition of the sources of our existence and their unique lessons, this broad body of SS thought as an expression of the comprehensive factor of a National–Socialist internal consolidation and security over any possible development that might come, all this is ever more content and inspiration of all new large formations in this sector of internal security.

Guaranteeing the internal security of this new Reich is the biggest task of the *Schutz-staffel* and with it and, within its framework, also the police at every level. This is the comprehensive mission which the Leader has given the SS. It goes about this work each day anew, with the utmost seriousness, clearly aware that it is a tremendous National–Socialist task, and in the firm conviction that the best ideological upbringing of its men and their careful selection enables it to carry out this task to the fullest.

It is obvious that the SS saw itself as the guarantor of the existence of the National–Socialist movement. And its strength and influence continued to grow. Police officials now also joined its ranks. No doubt many did so in the hope of making a career in the "new" society. The further increase in the size of the SS resulted in offices that had previously been under the *SS-Hauptamt* or *Reichsführung-SS* being elevated to independent *Hauptämter* or main offices. Ultimately, there were twelve of these powerful posts:

- *SS-Hauptamt* (SS Headquarters)
- *SS-Führungshauptamt* (SS Operational Headquarters)
- Personal Staff *Reichsführer-SS*
- *Rasse- und Siedlungshauptamt-SS* (SS Central Office for Race and Resettlement)
- *Hauptamt Dienststelle SS-Obergruppenführer Heißmeyer* (Heißmeyer Office)
- *Reichssicherheitshauptamt* (Reich Security Main Office)
- *Hauptamt SS-Gericht* (SS Main Legal Department)
- *SS-Personalhauptamt* (SS Main Office for Personnel)
- *Hauptamt Ordnungspolizei* (Order Police Main Office)
- *SS-Wirtschafts- Verwaltungshauptamt* (Economic and Administrative Main Office)
- *Hauptamt Volksdeutscher Mittelstelle* (German Racial Assistance Main Office)
- *Stabshauptamt des Reichkommissars für die Festigung deutschen Volkstums* (Office of the Reich Commissar for the Consolidation of German Nationhood)

With its use in the role of auxiliary police beginning in 1933 (the later SS concentration camp guards) and the armed *Verfügungstruppe* (which later became the *Waffen-SS*), the essentially unarmed SS had received important responsibilities.

The outbreak of war in 1939, ultimately led to a restructuring of the SS. While the *Allgemeine-SS* lost much of its importance with its members in service (for example in the *Wehrmacht* or police),[10] the armed SS (*Waffen-SS*) steadily grew in influence. It is interesting that less than half of the approximately 300,000 who joined the *Allgemeine-SS* until 1945 served in the *Waffen-SS*, the central offices or the police: approximately 35,000 were drafted into the *Waffen-SS* in the first months of the war and about 115,000 serves as reservists in the *Wehrmacht*. As well, about 67,000 members worked in the twelve central offices during the war. A further approximately 19,000 men were attached to offices and units of the Security Police and the SD. The rest of the roughly 64,000 members were not mobilized because of age, their "war-vital" indispensability at home or other reasons.

The *Waffen-SS*

Introduction

While the *Allgemeine-SS* had about 300,000 members, the *Waffen-SS* reached a total membership of about one million. More than a few, however, were not German nationals, had not joined the service voluntarily, or certainly did not meet the SS' exacting physical requirements.

Auszeichnungen

Name	Rank	Unit	Award
Dr. Ferch Bruno	ϟϟ-Ostuf.	Stab XXXIX	Erdkampfabz. der Luftwaffe
Dr. Günther Walter	ϟϟ-Ustuf.	Stab XXXIX	Krimschild, Rum. Med. „Kreuzzug g. d. Bolschewismus"
Opländer Walter	ϟϟ-Brigf.	Stab XXXIX	KVK I o. Schw.
Dr. Czihal Erich	ϟϟ-Bew.	San.-Sturm XXXIX	KVK II m. Schw.
Dr. Schram Franz	ϟϟ-Uscha.	San.-Sturm XXXIX	EK II
Dr. Worzfeld Karl	ϟϟ-Hscha.	San.-Sturm XXXIX	Verw.-Abz. Schw.
Sladek Emanuel	ϟϟ-Staf.	Stab 107	Volkspflegemed., KVK II m. Schw.
Broßmann Irmfried	ϟϟ-Hscha.	2/107 XXXIX	EK I und II
Hertel Wilhelm	ϟϟ-Strm.	2/107	EK II
Malirsch Gerhard	ϟϟ-Mann	2/107	EK II
Ehrfurt Rudolf	ϟϟ-Uscha.	4/107	KVK II m. Schw.
Hückel Erhard	ϟϟ-Strm.	4/107	EK II
Faldik Hubert	ϟϟ-Scha.	5/107	KVK II m. Schw.
Baier Alfred	ϟϟ-Mann	6/107	EK II
Legner Walter	ϟϟ-Mann	7/107	Verw.-Abz. Silber
Penischka Richard	ϟϟ-Rttf.	7/107	Ostmed., KVK II m. Schw., EK I und II
Seubert Ernst	ϟϟ-Scha.	1/108	EK I und II
Dr. Nowy Herbert	ϟϟ-Hscha.	7/108	KVK II m. Schw., Inf.-Sturmabz.
Basler Alex	ϟϟ-Mann	11/108	KVK II m. Schw.

BEFÖRDERUNGEN

Name	Rank	Unit	Promotion
Dr. Günther Walter	ϟϟ-Ustuf.	Stab XXXIX	zum Stabsarzt
Dr. Gladisch Karl	ϟϟ-Uscha.	San.-Sturm XXXIX	zum Unterarzt
Dr. Schram Franz	ϟϟ-Uscha.	San.-Sturm XXXIX	zum Stabsarzt
Dr. Umlauf Alfred	ϟϟ-Mann	San.-Sturm XXXIX	zum ϟϟ-Ustuf. d. R.
Hain Kurt	ϟϟ-Strm.	1/107	zum ϟϟ-Strm. d. R.
Dahnel Hans	ϟϟ-Mann	2/107	zum ϟϟ-Oscha. d.R.
Hetmanek Kurt	ϟϟ-Strm.	2/107	zum ϟϟ-Uscha. d.R.
Drdla Erhard	ϟϟ-Scha.	5/107	zum Leutnant
Sebera Wilhelm	ϟϟ-Rttf.	5/107	zum Uffz.
Baier Alfred	ϟϟ-Mann	6/107	zum ϟϟ-Ustuf. d. R.
Berger Herbert	ϟϟ-Rttf.	7/107	zum Oberleutnant
Fibich Hubert	ϟϟ-Bew.	7/107	zum ϟϟ-Strm. d. R.
Glückselig Kurt	ϟϟ-Mann	7/107	zum Uffz.
Herrmann Herwig	ϟϟ-Strm.	7/107	zum Uffz.
Hlavka Hans	ϟϟ-Mann	7/107	zum Obergefreiten
Hückel Robert	ϟϟ-Strm.	7/107	zum Uffz.
Raschendorfer Kurt	ϟϟ-Strm.	7/107	zum Obergefreiten
Schletz Leonhard	ϟϟ-Bew.	7/107	zum Gefreiten
Steinbrecher Walter	ϟϟ-Oscha.	7/107	zum Obergefreiten
Seubert Ernst	ϟϟ-Scha.	1/108	zum Feldwebel
Eschler Hans	ϟϟ-Strm.	2/108	zum Uffz.
Foehr Wilhelm	ϟϟ-Mann	2/108	zum Uffz.
Hartung Hans	ϟϟ-Scha.	2/108	zum ϟϟ-Strm. d. R.
Spaček-Streer Hans	ϟϟ-Oscha.	2/108	zum ϟϟ-Ustuf. d. R.
Dr. Nowy Herbert	ϟϟ-Hscha.	7/108	zum Unterarzt
Maier Herbert	ϟϟ-Bew.	9/108	zum Uffz.
Basler Alex	ϟϟ-Mann	11/108	zum Feldwebel
Rieß Jakob	ϟϟ-Scha.	11/108	zum Gefreiten

oder später, bestimmt aber nach Kriegsende, doch wieder nach Pilsen zurück. Bei der vielen Arbeit hier habe ich für private Dinge kaum Zeit.

Ansonsten geht es mir aber ganz gut — ich bin froh, daß ich auf diese Weise meine fachlichen Kenntnisse verwerten und so dem großen Ganzen vielleicht mehr nützen kann.

Es wird mich sehr freuen, mal wieder etwas von Euch und von Pilsen zu hören. Brem ist so schreibfaul, daß man von ihm höchstens jedes halbe Jahr eine Karte erhält!

Mit herzlichen Grüßen und besten Wünschen für alle Kameraden bleibe ich Euer

Hans Sommer, ϟϟ-Mann 10/108.

Aus Sippe und Familie

HOCHZEITEN

Name	Rank	Unit	Date
Plöckinger Edbert Leichsenring Marianne	ϟϟ-Rttf.	San.-Sturm XXXIX	17. 8. 43
Kerpes Franz Kunschak Katharina	ϟϟ-Rttf.	13/107	5. 10. 43

GEBURTEN

Söhne:

Name	Rank	Unit	Date	Details
Dr. Link Rudolf	ϟϟ-Oscha.	San.-Sturm XXXIX	14. 7.43	2. Kind Z.
Seipel Walter	ϟϟ-Strm.	3/107	21.10.43	1. Kind
Uhl Franz	ϟϟ-Ustuf.	Stab II/107	25. 9.43	1. Kind
Karl Emil	ϟϟ-Uscha.	Stabst. 108	15.10.43	4.u.5.K. Z.
Eschler Hans	ϟϟ-Strm.	2/108	2.10.43	1. Kind
Tackenberg Alfred	ϟϟ-Hscha.	11/108	28. 9.43	2. Kind

Töchter:

Name	Rank	Unit	Date	Details
Dr. Link Rudolf	ϟϟ-Oscha.	San.-Sturm XXXIX	14. 7.43	3. Kind Z.
Schenk Karl	ϟϟ-Uscha.	1/107	17. 9.43	3. Kind
Hanak Erhard	ϟϟ-Mann	San III/107	10. 9.43	1. Kind
Dr. Wildhage Kurt	Sta.-Oscha.	Stab III/107	25. 9.43	1. Kind
Kastner Karl	ϟϟ-Strm.	12/107	31. 8.43	4. Kind
Modl Sepp	ϟϟ-Mann	13/107	19. 6.43	1. Kind
Stärz Eduard	ϟϟ-Oscha.	2/108	3.10.43	4. Kind
Vicenec Anton	ϟϟ-Scha.	8/108	23. 9.43	2. Kind

Quellennachweis: Bild auf S. 1 und 5 von E. Schmachtenberger, Ochsenfurt; übrige Bilder und Vignetten Archiv ϟϟ-Abschnitt; Erzählung „Auf der Flucht" von E. Dwinger abgedruckt mit Erlaubnis des Verlages E. Diederichs, Jena; Herausgeber: ϟϟ-Abschnitt XXXIX, Prag. / Schriftleitung: ϟϟ-Abschnitt XXXIX. / Druck: Böhmisch-Mährische Verlags- und Druckerei-Gesellschaft m. b. H., Prag II.

42942

In the SS Sector XXXIX (Prague) bulletin under "Promotions" in December 1943, it was obvious that the majority of the members of the *Allgemeine-SS* in the sector were serving in the armed forces.

After the *Stabswache* was officially armed in Berlin in 1933, across Germany so-called political alert squads (*Politische Bereitschaften*), also formed from members of the SS, were also armed. These were supposed to secure the NSDAP's position within Germany. In May 1939, however, Hitler declared that the armed SS units, by then renamed the *SS-Verfügungstruppe* (SS-VT), should not exceed a maximum strength of 20,000 men. This was in response to an express wish by the *Wehrmacht*, which saw the SS not only as a competitor but also a—political—threat. Through the skillful use of different designations and classifications, within a year the head of the replacement office was able to increase the number of men in the armed SS units to almost 125,000. The breakdown of personnel was as follows:

SS-Verfügungs-Division 21,005
SS-VT Replacement Units..15,692
SS-Totenkopf-Division 21,311
SS-Totenkopf-Division replacement units/
Reinforced *SS-Totenkopf-Standarten* 32,630
SS-Polizei-Division and replacement unit 33,561

Internally, these armed SS formations were already being referred to as the *Waffen-SS* in the autumn of 1939. Hitler first used this formulation in a speech on July 19, 1940 after the Western Campaign.

German casualties—including those of the *Waffen-SS*—during the early campaigns had been manageable, however this changed in the war against the Soviet Union. The enormous casualties that resulted led Himmler and the *SS-Hauptamt* to begin looking for other sources of manpower in 1942. As the *Wehrmacht* was opposed to higher quota among draft-eligible Reich-Germans, initially they fixed their gaze on ethnic Germans living abroad and foreign volunteers.

As a result, the strict physical requirements for the *Waffen-SS* were steadily lowered. When, after the heavy losses at Stalingrad and in Africa, so-called "*Waffen-Verbände der SS*" were formed using, "from the racial point of view an on average lower quality [...] of human resources," on May 28, 1944, Himmler wrote to the Commander of Security Police and the SD in Berlin:

> The Reich Security Headquarters criminal report of May 26, 1944 speaks of a Ukrainian SS man under Number 2. It should read: a Ukrainian serving in the *Waffenverbände* of the SS. I ask that you see to it that you avoid using the designation "SS man," which is so dear and superior to us, when referring to the many members of foreign peoples which we are organizing under the command of the SS, in all reports and in official and unofficial statements.

The centralization of all foreign volunteer units in German service under the *Waffen-SS* began in the summer of 1944. In addition to the Guidance Office for Germanic Volunteers, Volunteer Guidance Office East was set up in the *SS-Hauptamt* as Office III in Office Group D.

In keeping with Himmler's ideas, the SS units were designated according to the so-called racial classification of their members. The *SS-Hauptamt* fell back on five categories:[11]

I .... pure Nordic
II... predominantly Nordic or Phalian
III ....Nordic or Phalian with slight Alpine, Dinaric or Mediterranean admixture
IV .... crossbreeds, primarily eastern or Alpine origin
V...crossbreeds, non-European

SS Divisions were for the most part made up of members from racial groups I and II with the draft registration class kv-SS.

SS Volunteer Divisions were for the most part made up of members from racial groups I, II and III with the draft registration class: kv-Heer.

Waffen Divisions of the SS were for the most part made up of members from racial groups III, IV and V.

While it proved impossible to achieve a homogenous outward appearance in the *Waffen-SS*, its leaders were at least able to ensure a common ideology. While commander of the *10. SS-Panzer-Division "Frundsberg,"* *SS-Brigadeführer* von Treuenfeld (March 31, 1885 – June 6, 1946) gave the following instructions for ideological instruction on November 25, 1943:

> Lectures about the great periods of German history shall be given to awaken in each man pride in being a member of the German race. He does not need to know any details, it is sufficient that as a result of this training [he knows that] there were struggles against external and internal enemies in every century of the German past, until the Leader was able to complete the unification of all Germans. He must know that how the Leader shapes the future of the German Reich lies with every single one of us.
>
> Lectures about enemy should turn every man into a fanatic hater. […] It makes no difference on which front our division sees action: the boundless hate for any enemy, be he English, American, Jew or Bolshevik, must make every one of our men capable of mighty deeds.

This psychological conditioning was also to lead to actions that were contrary to international law. These were orders that resulted from "the ultimate struggle between two opposing political systems." While the *Waffen-SS* was fundamentally subordinate to the Army High Command during military operations, "within the scope of these actions […] the *Reichsführer-SS*" acted "independently and on his own responsibility." Primarily affected were units attached to the *Einsatzgruppen* of the Security Police and SD or ordered to undertake comparable missions.

Fitness Requirements

The requirements for joining the SS frequently varied. Whereas in 1932, the maximum age for volunteers was fixed at thirty years and minimum height set at 1.70 meters, this changed for men volunteering for the *SS-Verfügungstruppen*. The maximum age was lowered to twenty-three, and the minimum height modified to 1.74 meters. Because the heavy casualties in the war however, volunteers were ultimately accepted until they reached the end of their forty-fifth year.

In addition to strict physical requirements—wearers of glasses were initially considered unsuitable, for example—the candidate had to:

- be worthy to bear arms,
- produce Aryan certification back to the eighteenth century,
- have no court or police record,
- if underage produce authorization from person with parental authority,
- if an apprentice, must have completed apprenticeship on the day of joining.

Outward appearance was an important component of SS suitability, which was determined by the five previously cited racial groups. To meet the further increases in requirements for personnel, in November 1940, the *Waffen-SS* gazette announced that in future:

… that only Army Regulation 252/1, "Regulation Concerning Wehrmacht Military Medical Examinations" [is] valid for determining fitness.

Among the changes that resulted was the elimination of bad teeth as grounds for rejection, provided that at least five teeth were present! Defective vision was permitted provided it could be corrected by glasses of up to four diopters even if astigmatism was also present. Minimum height for SS candidates was set as follows:[12]

for the 17th year	1.68 meters
for the 18th year	1.69 meters
for the 19th year	1.70 meters
for the 20th year	1.71 meters
for the 21st year	1.72 meters

Although selection was to be based solely on army fitness levels, the draft class remained SS suitable, resulting in a total of six categories:

- fit for active service in the SS (*kv-SS*)
- fit for active service in the Army (*kv-Heer*)
- fit for limited service in the field (*g.v.F.*)
- fit for limited service in the homeland (*g.v.H.*)
- fit for labor duty only (*a.v.*)
- unfit for military service (*w.u.*)

Kv-SS were those who met the original selection criteria. Sometimes suffixes were added which contained certain restrictions. *Kv-Heer mot.Truppe*, for example, meant that the man met the army's fitness requirements for motorized units.[13]

As a result of the constantly-growing need for personnel, regulations were also issued for the use of "less fit for war service." The *Waffen-SS* gazette published the following:

I. General

1. In wartime, use must also be made of foreign volunteers who are less than fit for war service. Unrestricted peacetime requirements with respect to the quality of replacements can therefore not be made by the units.

On the other hand the units must not be encumbered with men for whom there is no prospect of employment (see No. 2) and whose remaining in service would constitute a unbearable burden on the unit.

All volunteers who are less than fit for war duty, who can not be used appropriately by their unit, are to be reported to the *Waffen-SS* command office (convalescent exchange post) with the prescribed strength reports for other employment.

2. Men who are less fit for war service can be used:
A) with degree of fitness "g.v.H."
    a) guard duty with the concentration camp Sturmbannen,
      the guard companies,
      radio security companies etc.
    b) conditionally fit for guard duty as above, in positions according to their
      physical defects, etc.
    c) Other g.v.H. personnel:
I. as telephone/teletype operator in permanent signals installations.

II. with all units, headquarters and other offices in the homeland in duty stations, kitchens, workshops, storerooms, stables, in administration as aides-de-camp etc.

B) with degree of fitness "a.v." labor service with all units, headquarters and other duty stations in the homeland.

3. Volunteers with the degree of fitness "w.u." may also not be used in the *Waffen-SS* during wartime.

II. Conscriptions

4. Volunteers with the degree of fitness "g.v.H." can also be conscripted in wartime for the uses listed in paragraph I 2.

5. On the other hand conscription of volunteers with the degree of fitness "a.v." is to be avoided, with the exception of drivers, specialists etc.

6. Volunteers who prove to be unfit for war duty during their recruitment should be thoroughly checked to determine if they can be used to relieve k.v. [fit for active service] personnel and positions listed in paragraph I 2.

In September 1942, the categorization was simplified:

Effective immediately, only the following levels of fitness are permissible for the *Waffen-SS*:

k.v. – g.v.F. – g.v.H. – a.v. – w.u.

Use of previously common additions such as "*mot.*" [motorized], "*mech. Einheiten*" [mechanized units], "nicht Fußtruppe' [not infantry] etc. must stop. As most *Waffen-SS* field units are fully motorized, these are superfluous in any case.

In the majority of cases, z.B. SS members previously assessed as fit for active service (motorized) can be assessed as fit for active service, while the remaining cases can be assessed as g.v.F. or g.v.H.

In the end, the relaxation of draft requirements, which were so restrictive in the beginning, resulted in a *Waffen-SS* in which only about 15% of its members met the ideal of the, "tall, racially-outstanding SS man." With the recruitment of eastern- and southeastern-European volunteers, even Himmler's guiding principle of "Nordic-infused" men was watered down.

Personnel Composition

The composition of the *Waffen-SS* changed rapidly during the course of the war. Initially considered for Germans only, beginning in 1940, "Germanic" volunteers in particular could and were supposed to strengthen the armed units of the SS. There followed umpteen thousands of ethnic Germans, at first voluntarily, later forcefully conscripted. When even these men no longer sufficed, Rumanians, Slavs, and even Asiatics were signed up for the *Waffen-SS*.

The strength report submitted by the Statistical-Scientific Institute of the *Reichsführer-SS* on June 30, 1944, will be used as a basis of calculation in order to obtain an approximate total number of members who served in the *Waffen-SS* until 1945. Approximately 600,000 members were reported on that key date, broken down as follows:

Field units	368,654
Replacement army	21,365
Replacement and training units	127,643
Schools	10,822

As head of the *SS-Hauptamt, SS-Obergruppen-führer Berger* was particularly responsible for all personnel replacements for the *Waffen-SS*.

As the war went on, the heavy losses ...

... were also made good with older age classes, children, and foreigners.

Volunteers of the British Free Corps.

Walter Gengelbach was killed before his seventeenth birthday.

Directly attached to the SS-FHA 26,544
SS-Hauptämter 39,415

The fallen, plus those discharged on account of severe wounds, plus the new recruits and those transferred from other services, must be added to this total.

Casualties until the summer of 1944, totaled approximately 150,000 killed, missing and captured or discharged from military service on account of wounds, as well as the foreign legionnaires who left the service after their one- to two-year terms of service were completed. About 25,000 ethnic Germans, 100,000 members of the *Wehrmacht* and 70,000 Reich Germans eligible for military service were conscripted into or transferred to the *Waffen-SS* as of the summer of 1944.

Taking into account these arrivals and departures, this results in a total figure of approximately 945,000 members in the *Waffen-SS*. Of these, there were approximately:

- 470,000 Reich Germans (approx. 50%), 270,000 volunteers and 200,000 who were conscripted or transferred
- 210,000 ethnic Germans (approx. 22%), 80,000 volunteers and 130,000 conscripts
- 35,000 "Germanic" volunteers (approx. 3%)
- 230,000 "foreign" members (approx. 25%), 100,000 volunteers and 130 who were transferred

On May 8, 1945, the *Waffen-SS* had an actual strength of approximately 650,000 men. Given a total membership of about 945,000, wartime losses were thus approximately 295,000 killed, missing, and seriously wounded. Over time these personnel losses resulted in a mixture of personnel in the SS divisions. Divisions which were initially Reich German (RD) or foreign (A), were repeatedly brought up to strength using ethnic Germans (VD) or transferred *Wehrmacht* members (W), and as a result the divisions had the following composition in 1944–45:

1. SS-Panzer-Division .... RD/W/VD
2. SS-Panzer-Division ....RD/W
3. SS-Panzer-Division .... RD/W/VD
4. SS-Polizei-Panzergrenadier-Division ....RD/VD/W
5. SS-Panzer-Division .... RD/A/W
6. SS-Gebirgs-Division ....RD/VD
7. SS-Freiwilligen-Gebirgs-Division .... VD
8. SS-Kavallerie-Division .... VD/RD
9. SS-Panzer-Division .... RD/W/VD
10. SS-Panzer-Division .... RD/W/VD
11. SS-Polizei-Panzergrenadier-Division .... VD/A/RD
12. SS-Panzer-Division ....RD/W
13. Waffen-Gebirgs-Division der SS ....A/VD/W
14. Waffen-Grenadier-Division der SS ....A/W
15. Waffen-Grenadier-Division der SS .... A
16. SS-Panzergrenadier-Division ....VD/RD/W
17. SS-Panzergrenadier-Division ....RD/VD/W
18. SS-Freiwilligen-Panzergrenadier-Division .... VD/W
19. Waffen-Grenadier-Division der SS .... A
20. Waffen-Grenadier-Division der SS .... A
21. Waffen-Gebirgs-Division der SS ....A/W*

Reich Germans

Approximately 470,000 citizens of the Greater German Reich (including South Styria and Carniola), the Sudetenland, and the district of Wartheland and Elsass–Lothringen (Alsace–Lorraine) served in the *Waffen-SS*. Of these, approximately 270,000 were volunteers and 200,000 were conscripted or transferred without volunteering.

Until 1942, men entered the service only after volunteering. For many the deciding factors were surely a National–Socialist education, the propagandized free choice of branch of service, including modern training and equipment, and the possibility of becoming an officer without a high school diploma.

In 1943, the *Waffen-SS* began actively recruiting in the RAD, which used peer pressure to promote "voluntary" joining of the *Waffen-SS*. Late in the war, committees from the SS replacement centers subjectively selected which Hitler Youth and Reich Labor Service members should be drafted into the *Waffen-SS*. As these were, as a rule, sixteen-year-old youths, there were few objections. Claude Wever, an Alsatian, described one standard practice:

> In the spring of 1945, a committee came to our RAD camp and we were ordered to fall in. All of us who had volunteered for the army, air force or navy were then ordered to fall out to the right. We who remained were ordered to step forward one or three paces and the SS committee went through the ranks: "you," "you," "you" and so on. With my height of almost 1.80 meters and my blonde hair, I was among them. Fortunately, the war ended before I was called up. Then in 1947, I did my compulsory military service in the French army as the driver of an American [-made] M-47 tank.

After the losses at Stalingrad, in the spring of 1943, many members of the *Luftwaffe* flak battalions in the homeland were transferred to the *Waffen-SS*. Anti-aircraft auxiliaries or Russian POWs took their place. Of the approximately 100,000 members of the *Wehrmacht* who were taken into the *Waffen-SS* en masse or individually, beginning in the summer of 1944, about 10,000 joined the concentration camp *Sturmbanne*, approximately 60,000 were sent to the divisions as replacements, while about 30,000 formed new SS units. Former *Obergefreite* Karl Schneider remembered:

Because of a shortage of experienced officers, the National–Socialist Reichskriegerbund asked veterans of the First World War to join the *Waffen-SS*. They were told that they could serve in the *Waffen-SS* instead of the *Wehrmacht*.

Hauptmann Behr underlined his aversion to the SS by writing "no" in the margin of the letter.

Nationalsozialistischer Reichskriegerbund
(Kyffhäuserbund)

Berlin W 30, den .... April 1940
Geisbergstraße 2
Fernsprecher: 25 97 81
Postscheckkonto: Berlin Nr. 2292
Bank-Konten: Preuß. Staatsbank, Berlin W 8
Dresdner Bank, Dep.-Kasse 9, Berlin
Thür. Staatsbank, Bad Frankenhausen (Kyffh.)

Abtlg. Ib 2004/40

Betrifft: Verwendung als Artille-
rieoffizier

Bezug:

Anlage: 1   Vertraulich!

Herrn

Hauptmann B e h r

B a m b e r g

Wildensorgerstr. 8

Durch Ihre Offizierkameradschaft sind Sie auf Grund eines
Rundschreibens der Reichskriegerführung dieser für eine artille-
ristische Verwendung zur Weitergabe an das Oberkommando des Heeres
namhaft gemacht worden.

Es wird darauf hingewiesen, dass ausser einer etwaigen
Verwendung im Heere auch für einige Artillerieoffiziere die Möglichkeit der artilleristischen Verwendung in der ℋ-Verfügungstruppe besteht. Diese wird voraussichtlich eher erfolgen können als
eine Verwendung im Heere und gilt ebenfalls als Wehrdienst.

Es wird um gefl. umgehende Mitteilung an die Reichskriegerführung unmittelbat gebeten, ob Sie gegebenenfalls zu einer Verwendung in der ℋ-Verfügungstruppe bereit wären, damit sodann die
Weitergabe Ihrer Meldung an die zuständige ℋ-Dienststelle erfolgen
kann. Das ℋ-Personalamt würde sich dann voraussichtlich mit Ihnen
in Verbindung setzen.

Bejahendenfalls wird gebeten, beiliegendes Formular ausgefüllt der Reichskriegerführung einsenden zu wollen.

Mit kameradschaftlichem Gruss !
Heil Hitler !
I.A.des Reichskriegerführers.

ℋ-Oberführer, Major a.D.

Nationalsozialistischer Reichskriegerbund
(Kyffhäuserbund)

Berlin W 30, den 22. Mai 1940
Geisbergstraße 2
Fernsprecher: 25 97 81
Postscheckkonto: Berlin Nr. 2292
Bank-Konten: Preuß. Staatsbank, Berlin W 8
Dresdner Bank, Dep.-Kasse 9, Berlin
Thür. Staatsbank, Bad Frankenhausen (Kyffh.)

Abtlg. Ib 2004/40 Vertraulich

Betrifft: Verwendung als Artille-
rieoffizier

Bezug:

Anlage:

Herrn

Hauptmann B e h r

B a m b e r g

Wildensorgerstr. 8

Die Reichskriegerführung hatte mit ihrem Schreiben vom
20. April ds.Js., unter obiger Nummer, Sie um umgehende Mitteilung
gebeten, ob Sie gegebenenfalls zu einer Verwendung als Artillerie-
offizier in der ℋ-Verfügungstruppe bereit wären. Eine Antwort ist
auf diese Frage bisher nicht eingegangen.

Da es sich hierbei um eine eilige Mob-Sache handelt, wird
nochmals um umgehende Rückäusserung gebeten.

Mit kameradschaftlichem Gruss !
Heil Hitler !
I.A.des Reichskriegerführers.

ℋ-Oberführer, Major a.D.

Karl Behr, born on December 15, 1884, joined *Feld-Artillerie-Regiment 69* as a *Fahnenjunker* on August 7, 1906. Until he left the service as a *Hauptmann* on August 30, 1919, he served in several artillery formations. On October 1, 1939, he was reactivated—because of his age as a *Hauptmann z.V.* Initially employed as adjutant in leichte *Artillerie-Ersatz-Abteilung 17*, he served in various military administration headquarters. On June 19, 1944, the z.V. position was lifted and Behr was released from military service as a *Major*.

I was born in Rheinbischofsheim (Kehl District) on July 19, 1925, and on October 5, 1942, I was conscripted into RAD *Feld-Abteilung K 1/322* (Military Postal Code 19 573) in Lubeln, Westmark. After deployments in southern France (Camarque/Bay of Biscay) and the Saar region, in April 1943, I was discharged in Karlsruhe. There I was called up to join *4./Grenadier-Ausbildungs- und Ersatz-Bataillon 111*. In December 1943, we moved to the Eastern Front into the area south of Mogilev. There I was assigned to *4./Grena-dier-Regiment 111 of the 35. Infanterie-Division* (Fish Division). Initially we fought east of the Dniepr and from the beginning of January 1944, in the Pripet Marshes (appro-imately thirty kilometers south of Bobruisk).

On March 2, 1944, I was wounded by shell fragments in the left leg and foot. I was initially sent to the military hospital in Minsk and then to the field hospital in Thorn and finally to the auxiliary hospital in Brussels. From there, in mid-June 1944, I joined the convalescent company of *Grenadier-Ersatz-Bataillon 111* in Vlissingen/Walcheren. When the Allies advanced out of Normandy, at the beginning of August our company with other units was sent into action against British armored spearheads west of Antwerp. The company was almost completely wiped out near Beveren. On August 3, 1944, I was wounded again, by shell fragments in the left knee. Separated from my unit, while re-treating across the Schelde, I was seized by members of *SS-Panzer-Grenadier-Ausbil-dungs- und Ersatz-Bataillon 4* near Gorinchem, Holland. They had set up a blocking position in Gorinchem and had their headquarters in a nearby sugar factory. My previous rank was crossed out in my pay book and replaced with *SS-Rottenführer*—that's how easy it was in those days to become a soldier of the *Waffen-SS*!

Some of those posted away were openly opposed to the *Waffen-SS*, while others had no objec-tions to the transfer. Wilhelm Müller, who, with *Korps-Nachrichten-Abteilung 435* (corps signals battalion) was transferred to the *Waffen-SS* for the formation of corps headquarters, *XIII. SS-Armee-Korps*, remembered:

That was my best time as a soldier. The comradeship there was much better than in the army. There was no "*Herr Hauptmann*" there, instead simply *Hauptsturmführer*!

The expansion of the *Waffen-SS* through the use of Reich Germans subject to military service[14] was achieved using an OKW allocation key. The *Waffen-SS* contingent grew as the war went on, in part because the number of personnel needed by the air force and navy dropped steadily. The OKW war diary noted for the first time on September 6, 1940:

By order of the OKW, according to which the distribution of the draft-eligible recruits from age classes 1919 (last third) and 1920 to the three *Wehrmacht* elements and the *Waffen-SS* is to be based on the strength of the wartime armed forces on May 1, 1941, the AHA[15] submits speaking notes concerning recruit adjustment in autumn 1944 for presentation to the commander of the OKW.

Based on the status quo of May 1, 1941, the wartime armed services will have a total strength of 6,764,000 men, specifically:

the army ....4,900,000 men = 72.5%
the navy ....298,000 men = 4.4%
the air force ....1,485,000 men = 22%
the *Waffen-SS* ....80,000 men = 1.1%

These percentages result in the following recruit quotas:

Birth year 1919 (last third)	
Physical examinations	208,500
Found unfit	16,424
	192,076

Birth year 1920	
Physical examinations	613,264
Found unfit	92,525
	520,739

	Quota	Volunteers	Still available	Quota	Volunteers	Still available
Army	139,255	85,300	53,935	377,536	102,108	275,428
Navy	8,451	4,000	4,451	22,913	12,232	10,681
Air force	42,257	33,000	9,257	114,562	71,924	41,638
Total	192,076	124,300	67,776	520,739	201,982	

In the first third of 1941, the 15,718 volunteers from the 1920 age class were called up by the *Waffen-SS*. As this was about 10,000 more than the original OKW quota, the number who joined the *Wehrmacht* was reduced by 7,322 recruits for the army, 445 for the navy and 2,223 for the air force.

In the second third of 1941, the 1921 age class was called up. Once again about 15,000 volunteers joined the *Waffen-SS*. One of them was Willi Wild, who later rose to the rank of *SS-Rottenführer*. On May 27, 1941, he wrote to his mother about his experiences during his first days with *SS-Ersatz-Bataillon "Ost"* in Breslau:

> Now I would like to tell you how I got here and how I am getting along. I arrived at 1330 on Sunday. They were waiting with a board, so that we could report immediately. We waited until forty men had assembled there, then we were led to a barracks. Dear mother, so far I like it here very much. The food is excellent. There is therefore no need for you to worry—I am getting along magnificently and we have to be sharp. No one dominates in our room—open comradeship, there is just one thing to emphasize: conversation is of a very low level, for there are representatives from every district. There are very few Swabians in the barracks, but 3/4 Prussians. That's not the worst, however. We are forbidden to smoke in the company, which I personally welcome. In our company there is a strict ban on smoking for those under twenty.

The 522,000 men[16] of the 1923 age class were called up in the first third of 1942. Among them were about 15,000 volunteers for the *Waffen-SS*. The 1924 age class was called up in the last third of 1942. Once again approximately 15,000 men joined the *Waffen-SS*.

In 1943, the 1925 age class was called up, the first time that eighteen-year-olds had been conscripted in large numbers. The number of men called up by the *Waffen-SS* changed dramatically. On December 29, 1942, Himmler planned with *SS-Gruppenführer* Berger, chief of the *SS-Hauptamt*, to take 25,000 members of the 1925 age class from the RAD. This included the conscription of 17-year-olds—15,000 youths of the Hitler Youth from the 1926 age class. The increase in the *Waffen-SS* contingent of military conscripts was in part achieved by reducing that of the air force (*Luftwaffe* field divisions) by 20,000 men. On January 5, 1943 the OKW noted:

> Orders are further issued for the securing of replacements for the two new SS divisions, formation of which has been prescribed by the *Führer* by February 1, 1943. For this purpose 27,000 men from the 1925 age class are to be secured by recruiting in the RAD,

10,000 men from *Aktion Rü 43* (armaments workers), and 5,000 ethnic Germans; if the last-mentioned 15,000 do not materialize, the 1925 age class shall provide a correspondingly higher number. The Reich Labor Leader is asked for his assistance in recruiting the 1925 age class.

In the last third of 1943, the quota for the *Waffen-SS* was raised once again and a further approximately 15,000 draftees from the 1925 age class were inducted into the *Waffen-SS*. Concerning this the OKW war diary recorded on September 3, 1943:

> The Chief of the OKW advises the *Reichsführer-SS* that the general replacements emergency makes it necessary to finally regulate the distribution of volunteers from the 1926 age class, which represents almost all of the replacements for the fighting troops. The *Waffen-SS* was allocated 15,000 men [*Author*: 1924 age class] on October 1, 1942. This number has since been far surpassed. According to Defense Replacement Office files, the *Waffen-SS* has so far received about 44,000 volunteers [*Author*: 1925 age class]. Based on the authority given him by the Defense Act, the Chief of the OKW now sets the *Waffen-SS* contingent for the 1925 age class at 60,000, although the 1926 age class remains behind that of 1925.

The 1926 age class was called up in the first half of 1944. As approximately 15,000 volunteers from this age class had been called up to serve in the *Waffen-SS* in the previous year, only about 45,000 17- and 18-year-old draftees reached the *Waffen-SS*. The 1927 age class—likewise a contingent of approximately 60,000 men—was called up in the second half of 1944, some of whom were only sixteen years old.

The *Waffen-SS* contingent of draftees was raised to 95,000 for the year 1945. On February 19, the OKW war diary documented the planned use of the 1928 age class. The *Wehrmacht* Operations Staff assumed that 550,000 youths (1928 age class) could be conscripted in the first half of the year. 266,400 of these would be discharged from the RAD by March 26, 1945. The entire age class was to be distributed as follows:

		1945	1940
Army	412,500 men =	75%	72.5%
Navy	12,500 men =	2.3%	4.4%
Air force	30,000 men =	5.4%	22%
Waffen-SS	95,000 men =	17.3%	1.1%

If one compares the percentages assigned to the *Wehrmacht* elements and the *Waffen-SS* in 1940 and 1945, one sees that the allocation to the army remained almost the same. That of the navy was almost halved and that of the air force was only about a quarter, while that of the *Waffen-SS* rose from 1.1% to 17.3%! The land forces thus received more than 92% of an entire draftee age class. It is a clear indication that the navy and air force were no longer viable services.

Discussions about calling up the 1929 age class in the second half of 1945 began in February of that year. *SS-Obersturmbannführer* Grothmann, Himmler's adjutant, remarked in Himmler's *Feld-Kommandostelle* on February 16, 1945:

> The *Reichsführer-SS* has also rejected the planned formation of ten Hitler Youth divisions from the 1929 age class. This age class is to be better fed and trained and will be used later to bring the old SS divisions up to strength.

Assuming that the *Waffen-SS* was supposed to be assigned the contingent for ten divisions from the 1929 age class, one can suppose that between 95,000 and 120,000 sixteen-year-olds would have been drafted for service in the *Waffen-SS*. To realize this increase, the already low quotas for the navy and air force would probably have fallen even further, likely to near zero.

Ethnic Germans

Because of the heavy losses suffered by the *Wehrmacht* and the *Waffen-SS*, an ever greater importance fell to the military potential of the ethnic Germans from 1941.[17] In total, approximately 650,000 of them served in German formations—including about 210,000 in the *Waffen-SS*.

While the latter initially tried to recruit volunteers from among the returnees—mainly in the returnee camps in the German Reich—*before* they received German citizenship[18] and then came under military monitoring,[19] the foreign Germans (for example Transylvanian Saxons and Swabians from the Banat) were liable to military service, for example in Rumania or Hungary. After discussions with the Rumanian government, in June 1940, it for the first time released 1,000 ethnic Germans from military service so that they could join the *Waffen-SS*. Hungary made a similar agreement in 1941. This was done less to make good losses that had been suffered to date than to promote the propagandized common bond between Reich and ethnic Germans.

The first large scale intake of ethnic Germans into the *Waffen-SS* took place in 1942 in Serbia—which was under German military administration. Further agreements with southern European states followed. Himmler's intentions were no longer restricted to volunteers suitable for the SS, instead they turned pragmatically towards quantity. It generally expected that the foreign Germans would do their compulsory military service on the German side.[20] On July 13, 1942 he commented:

> The German ethnic groups in the entire southeast must understand that compulsory military service exists for them not by law, but from the iron law of their national values, from age 17 to 50, and if need be until their fifty-fifth year.

Of the roughly 210,000 ethnic Germans who served the *Waffen-SS*—in the end reminding them with appropriate pressure of the "iron law of their national values"—about 40% were volunteers, while the remaining 60% had to be more or less forcibly mobilized. These figures will be broken down in more detail in the subsequent text.

Denmark

Of the total of approximately 60,000 ethnic Germans who lived in Denmark and in part were organized in the ethnic minority under Jens Moeller (July 2, 1894 – November 28, 1951), about 100 voluntarily joined the *SS-Verfügungstruppe* before the war. Following the occupation of Denmark in 1940, the *Waffen-SS* began actively recruiting among the approximately 5,000 men between 17 and 35. About every third one volunteered and ultimately about 600 joined the *Waffen-SS*.

Another recruiting campaign among two new age classes in the spring of 1942, brought in another roughly 600 volunteers. The next age class was called up in 1943, and the age limit was raised to forty-five. This resulted in a total of 1,292 volunteers for the *Waffen-SS* by the end of the year.

A total of approximately 1,500 ethnic Germans from Denmark served in the *Waffen-SS* by the end of the war—most in the *Freikorps "Danmark"* or later in *SS-Freiwilligen-Panzergrenadier-Division 24 "Danmark."* This was equivalent to about 3.75% of the ethnic group.

Reichsführer-SS Heinrich Himmler inspects the *17. SS-Panzer-Grenadier-Division "Götz von Berlichingen."*

Division commander *SS-Brigadeführer* Ostendorff.

With the inspection: *SS-Gruppenführer* Oberg, and *SS-Obergruppenführer* Dietrich.

Himmler in conversation with men and officers of the division.

Heinrich Himmler

After the Yugoslavian campaign, Southern Styria was incorporated into *Wehrkreis* XVIII and with it compulsory military service was introduced for the local population.

August Jelen received German citizenship "until revoked" and as a seventeen-year-old joined the *Waffen-SS*. From June 1, 1943, he was a member of the *6. SS-Gebirgs-Division*. Tragically, during the retreat from Finland Jelen was killed in a battle with Finnish troops, former allies, on October 29, 1944.

Croatia

Approximately 200,000 foreign Germans lived in Croatia, the majority of them in the German ethnic minority group under Branimir Altgayer (November 8, 1897 – May 15, 1950). The first German-Croatian agreement was reached on September 16, 1941, according to which 90% of the ethnic Germans would do their compulsory military service in the Croatian Army and 10% in the German armed services.

Like all leaders of ethnic minority groups, however, Altgayer tried to keep the military potential in his own area. Realizing that recruiting by the *Waffen-SS* would mean the young men of his minority group leaving their homeland, he even endorsed the attachment of his 3,000-man-strong *Einsatzstaffel der Deutsche Mannschaft* (paramilitary militia) to the Croatian *Ustascha*.[21] The militia had been formed in August 1942, of 17- to 20-year-old volunteers and was organized in a headquarters guard in Essig and the "*Prinz Eugen*" Duty Bataillon with a total of 1,500 men. There were also three Standby Battalions—"*Ludwig von Baden*," "*General Laudon*," and "*Emanuel von Bayern*"—with a total of 1,500 men. The volunteers' service time was recognized as active duty time in the Croatian army.

In September 1942, however, *SS-Obergruppenführer* Berger, chief of the *SS-Hauptamt*, was able to initiate a German-Croatian agreement which gave the *Waffen-SS* permission to recruit 17- to 30-year-old ethnic Germans in Croatia. By the end of November 1942, approximately 6,529 volunteers were taken in for the *Waffen-SS* from the fourteen age classes (a total of about 20,000 draft eligible men). Beginning in 1943, increasing pressure was put on the ethnic German men and the *Einsatzstaffel* was simply incorporated into the *Waffen-SS*. In addition to age class 1925, which was eligible for military service, recruiting was also extended to the 1903 to 1913 age classes. On December 28, 1943, there was a total of 32,158 ethnic Germans from Croatia in active service. This was equivalent to about 16.1% of the minority group. Roughly half of these—17,538—served in the *Waffen-SS*.

In 1944, the 1926–27 age classes were examined for fitness and the 41- to 50-year-olds were also included. In total, by 1945, approximately 25,000 members of the ethnic German group in Croatia were taken into the *Waffen-SS*, equivalent to 12.5% of the population. The majority of them served in the *7. SS-Freiwilligen-Gebirgs-Division "Prinz Eugen."* Older age classes and younger men unfit for active service were often employed as guards in the concentration camps. Zvonimier Bernwald joined the *Waffen-SS* as a volunteer at the age of eighteen:

I was born in Brod on the Save River in 1924. My grandparents were still called Brenwald, but this became Bernwald in Croatian. Roman Catholics, we had the status of ethnic Germans. Several changes took place in eastern Croatia in 1938. Previously dominated by the Serbs, only Croatian flags could be flown and only Croatian spoken and written. When Croatia became an independent state, the Serbs and Jews disappeared from public life.

In May 1941, the *Leibstandarte Adolf Hitler* came to our city and distributed Greek Papastratos cigarettes. We were thrilled. In 1942, it was announced in our school that anyone who volunteered would be taken into the *Leibstandarte*. As we all feared that the war would be over before we could take part, we all volunteered. Then in October 1942 I was in fact called up by the *Leibstandarte* in Berlin. At the end of the year I was transferred to northern France for the formation of the *SS-Panzer-Grenadier-Division "Das Reich"* and trained on the 37 mm anti-tank gun. We ethnic Germans were not treated badly, but the drill and harassment were generally so great that some of us were sent back to Croatia. In January 1943, I joined the *SS-Kradschützen-Ersatz-Abteilung* (motorcycle replacement battalion) in Ellwangen, then in March, I was sent to the SS Interpreter Replacement and Training Company in Oranienburg. From there I was transferred to Department VI of the division headquarters of the new Croatian SS volunteer mountain division being formed. I worked on the division newspaper *Handzar*, which was printed in Zagreb.

Poland

Recruiting of ethnic Germans in Poland began after the conquest of the country in 1939. before they were given German nationality, as a rule they were Poles and thus not obliged to serve in the German military. The *Waffen-SS* was therefore particularly interested particularly in recruiting among the ethnic Germans who still did not have German citizenship. As the legal age in Poland was twenty-one, however, youths had to have their parents' permission to enlist. On December 3, 1941, the head of SS Replacement Center Vistula (XX) wrote to the father of a volunteer:

> Your son Johann has volunteered to serve in the *Waffen-SS* and informed the Replacement Center Vistula (XX) that you do not wish to give your consent. By volunteering, your son, like thousands of other volunteers, has demonstrated the need to fight against our greatest enemy for a great, strong Germany.
>
> I therefore ask you to reconsider your decision and to authorize the attached form and the declaration of commitment (which is still in your son's possession) with your signature.
>
> Should you, however, deny your consent as before, I request that you provide an explanation of the reason. Please note that, as a member of the 1921 age class, your son must soon expect to be called up by the *Wehrmacht*.

Parents were not always impressed by such letters. The father of the volunteer—Johann Chynacki—from Gotenhafen replied succinctly:

> Concerning your letter of December 3, 1941, the reason is that we have not yet been recognized as ethnic Germans, even though I have been trying without success since 1939.

The bulk of the ethnic Germans from Poland served after being called up by the *Wehrmacht*. The majority of the volunteers for the *Waffen-SS*, estimated at about 8,500 men, served in the *SS-Polizei-Division* or as concentration camp guards—often in Auschwitz.

Rumania

Most of the ethnic Germans in Rumania were organized in the German minority group under Andreas Schmitt (May 24, 1912 – 1948). In contrast to Hungary, the relationship with the Rumanian state was without problems and the ethnic German zones were also permitted to develop freely economically.

Out of youthful enthusiasm, 1,000 volunteers joined the *Waffen-SS* in 1940—the Rumanian government officially authorized their travel as labor forces going to work in Germany. At the end of April, during the campaign in the Balkans, a further 600 ethnic Germans took the opportunity to avoid Rumanian military service and spontaneously joined the *SS-Division "Reich."* They were taken by truck to the SS Schönbrunn Barracks in Vienna and there formed into a battalion.

As service in the antiquated Rumanian Army had little appeal for the ethnic Germans eligible for military service, there was great desire to serve in modern German units. Initially disinterested in transferring ethnic Germans serving in the Rumanian Army to the *Wehrmacht*, in early 1943, Rumanian Prime Minister Ion Antonescu (June 15, 1882 – June 1, 1946) acceded to Hitler's wishes. In order to be allowed to withdraw his troops from the front after the

Otto Kalmbach was born in Bessarabia on April 26, 1923, and in September 1940, he resettled in West Prussia.

In 1942, he joined the *Waffen-SS* as a volunteer and served in the *SS-Kraft-fahr-Ausbildungs-und Ersatz-Regiment*. At the beginning of 1945, he was transferred to the *17. SS-Pan-zergrenadier-Division "Götz von Berlichingen."*

Christian Kreter was born in Bescjka, Croatia on December 10, 1900. After the campaign in the Balkans the area belonged to Hungary. At the beginning of 1942, he joined the *Waffen-SS* as a volunteer and on May 7, 1942, he was called up with orders to report to the *Waffen-SS* recruiting depot in Debica.

Kreter served briefly in the field recruiting depot of the *1. SS-Infanterie-Brigade* and in 1943, he was transferred to the *SS-Funkschutz-Bataillon*. Kreter saw action in Danzig in February 1945, and he died on March 31 from wounds sustained in fighting in the Danzig–Gotenhafen area.

SS-Gruppenführer tragedy, on May 13, 1943, he accepted an intergovernmental agreement concerning recruiting ethnic Germans for service in the *Waffen-SS*. The *Völkische Beobachter* reported on this on May 22, 1943 under the headline "Ethnic Germans from Rumania in the Waffen-SS":

> With great enthusiasm, the men of the Rumanian minority group are presently stepping forward in the German settlement areas of Rumania, in Transylvania, the Banat and in the mountain land, for service in the *Waffen-SS*. Minority group leader Andreas Schmidt saw off the first transport of SS recruits at Kronstadt Station, and in his speech he made reference to the fact that Rumanian Germans had already served bravely on the Eastern Front in the Rumanian Army and that most of them wear Rumanian decorations for bravery on their grey tunics.

47,580 volunteers were taken in by June 2, 1943. Of these—after the age was initially restricted to 18 to 30—17,748 were found to be fit for service in the SS, 12,743 fit for service in the army, 2,031 fit for garrison duty and 1,429 fit for labor service. The first wave of recruiting thus delivered about 33,800 ethnic Germans from Rumania to the *Waffen-SS*. Hans Hedrich was one of them:

> I was born in Mediasch (Transylvania) in 1924, and in 1943, I joined the *Waffen-SS* as a volunteer. I felt that I had to do my part in the struggle for the existence of the German people—as the war was portrayed to us in those days. There was also moral pressure from the organization of the "German Minority Group in Rumania" and society in general.

After five more age classes (31–35 years of age) were examined, an additional approximately 16,000 men were inducted, so that by the end of 1943, about 52,000 ethnic Germans[22] had joined the *Waffen-SS*. This was equal to about 10% of the minority group. Of these, about 12,000 who were classified fit to serve in the army joined the *III.SS-Panzer-Korps* then being formed. As a rule, those volunteers found fit for service in the SS were sent to the cadre units, for example to the *SS-Panzergrenadier-Division "Leibstandarte-SS Adolf Hitler."*

In contrast to the minority group in Hungary, in Rumania there was no general mobilization in the spring of 1944 with call-up of men up to the age of sixty. Nevertheless, until the summer of 1944, another roughly 6,000 ethnic Germans were called to arms. In total, about 58,000 members of the German minority in Rumania served in the *Waffen-SS*. This was equivalent to about 11% of the foreign Germans living in Rumania.

Serbia

Most of the ethnic Germans in Serbia were organized in the ethnic minority under Dr. Josef Janko (November 9, 1905 – September 25, 2001). Their military employment began in the summer of 1941, when the German military commander used volunteers to guard traffic routes against partisan ambushes. At the same time the *Waffen-SS* began planning to use the basically untapped potential of the ethnic Germans in Serbia. Completely ignoring the real possibilities, *SS-Gruppenführer* Berger, chief of the *SS-Hauptamt*, planned the formation of a roughly 26,000-man-strong SS mountain division. With a minority group of approximately 123,000 people, *every* man between the ages of 18 and 45—regardless of his fitness category—would have to join the unit.

In order to nevertheless begin the formation of an SS mountain division, Dr. Janko introduced compulsory military service for the ethnic Germans in the Banat. As the residents were

Franz Löw was born in Marpod (Rumania) on October 2, 1923, and in 1943 he joined the *Waffen-SS* as a volunteer.

Collar patch with karst thistle for the ethnic German *SS-Karstjäger.*

Initially called up to serve in *SS-Grenadier-Ersatz-Bataillon "Ost,"* he was later transferred to the *SS-Karstwehr-Bataillon.*

Serbian citizens and were not subject to German military service, this was legally complicated. Aware of this fact, he implored the men of his ethnic group to volunteer:

> The German armed services placed our villages and homes under their protection in the spring of the previous year. Germany and its soldiers are fighting a difficult battle to protect all of Europe from bolshevism. In the past weeks and months, in our country too the Bolshevik enemy has been trying to raise his head, make the roads unsafe and burn our villages. Together with us and all order-loving elements of the country, German troops have once again eradicated this danger. For us it is now a matter of honor that we, following the traditions of our fathers, assume responsibility for defending our house and home. I therefore call upon all men from the ages of 17 to 50, when the appropriate age class is called up, to report to the mayor and in Belgrade to the district leadership of the ethnic group to bear arms in defense of our homes. No one who is healthy can exclude this service. German folk comrades, show yourselves worthy to your fathers by serving bravely and by your actions!

With just under 1,000 men eligible for military service from each age class, this meant that thirty-four age classes with a total of approximately 34,000 men had to be mustered. As fifty-year-old men were ill-suited for service in an SS mountain division, initially about 15,000 members of the minority group in the fitness categories *kv-SS* and *kv-Heer*, ages 17 to 35 years, were used to form the later *7. SS-Freiwilligen-Gebirgs-Division "Prinz Eugen."* Another roughly 2,500 men up to forty-five years of age were drafted into the *Waffen-SS* by the end of 1942, so that initially about 17,500 ethnic Germans from Serbia served in the *Waffen-SS*.

Three more age classes (1925–27) were mustered by the end of the war and 46- to 50-year-olds were also called up, and another 2,500 men were integrated into the *Waffen-SS*—some as guards in the concentration camps. In total, therefore, about 20,000 ethnic Germans from Serbia served in the *Waffen-SS*. This was equivalent to about 16% of the ethnic group.

Slovakia

In Slovakia the ethnic Germans were organized in a minority group under Franz Karmasin (September 2, 1901 – June 25, 1970). On August 2, 1942, an agreement was reached between the German Reich and the Slovakian Prime Minister Vojtech Tuka (July 4, 1880 – August 20, 1946), which authorized 17- to 35-year-old ethnic Germans to volunteer for service in the *Waffen-SS*. Those already serving in the Slovakian Army were excluded. From this one can assume that the first volunteers—also referred to as Carpathian Germans—joined the *Waffen-SS* by way of SS Recruiting Office "Southeast" (VIII) before 1940 was over.

5,390 men joined the *Waffen-SS* by December 28, 1943. By that time a total of 8,367 ethnic Germans from Slovakia were serving in the war. In addition to the SS volunteers there were:

- 1,740 in the Slovakian Army
- 3,500 in the labor service in Germany
- 237 in the German armed services
- 1,000 in paramilitary units

This was equal to 6.4% of the total number of ethnic Germans in Slovakia.

Six months later, on June 7, 1944, an agreement was reached which made service in the *Waffen-SS* compulsory for the ethnic Germans. The two purely German battalions in the Slovakian Army were also affected, whose approximately 1,740 men were also transferred to the *Waffen-SS*. At the beginning of 1945, 17,175 men were in war service, equal to 19.1% of the ethnic Germans in Slovakia. They were distributed as follows:

Josef Winkler was born in Slovakia on January 23, 1914, and served in the Slovakian Army in 1937–38.

After the agreement between Hitler and Dr. Tiso of June 7, 1944, like all ethnic Germans from Slovakia fit for military service he was drafted into the *Waffen-SS*. Initially assigned to *SS-Panzergrenadier-Ausbildungs-und Ersatz-Bataillon 5*, in November 1944, he was transferred to *7./SS-Panzergrenadier-Regiment 3 "Deutschland."*

Winkler (2nd row, 3rd from left) while serving in the Slovakian Army in 1937–38.

Josef Winkler, 1936.

- 8,222 in the *Waffen-SS*
- 8,116 in home defense
- 292 in the German armed services
- 545 in paramilitary units

In total, approximately 10,000 men, roughly 8% of the German minority group in Slovakia, served in the *Waffen-SS* between August 1942 and May 1945.

Hungary

Approximately 845,000 ethnic Germans lived in Hungary, the majority of them in the minority group under Dr. Franz Basch (July 13, 1901 – April 27, 1946). The Hungarian government under Prime Minister Lazlo Bárdossy (December 10, 1890 – January 10, 1946) was not fundamentally opposed to the *Waffen-SS*' growing interest in ethnic German volunteers. It saw an opportunity to weaken the German minority, which was not especially well-liked, and the agreement reached on February 1, 1942, also included a provision that the SS volunteers would lose their Hungarian citizenship. Ethnic Germans from the 1912 to 1925 age classes (17- to 30-year-olds) were called up provided they were not serving in the Hungarian Army. With roughly 6,000 ethnic Germans eligible for military service in each age class, this totaled 84,000 men, of whom about 30,000 were already serving in the Hungarian Army. Of the remaining men, 25,709 volunteered. Of these, a total of 17,860 were found suitable and the action thus represented a major success.

From March 22, 1942, until May 3, 1943, 16,257 men left their country for the SS Heidelager Training Camp, which acted as a recruiting depot. Most of the men were used for the formation of the *SS-Kavallerie- und Gebirgs-Division "Nord."* Volunteers who met SS standards were also assigned to the cadre divisions of the *Waffen-SS*.

Recruitment among the ethnic Germans in Hungary was repeated one year later. After only the 1926 age class was affected, the second agreement reached on June 1, 1943, raised the age limit to thirty-five years. This made six more age classes available with a total of about 36,000 men. As some were already serving in the Hungarian Army, the new Hungarian Prime Minister Miklos Kallay (January 23, 1887 – January 14, 1967) agreed that should be released if they volunteered. The first trains left Hungary on September 7, 1943. The action, which lasted until February 8, 1944, resulted in about 20,000 men joining the *Waffen-SS*—often not quite voluntarily.

On December 28, 1943, there were 62,845 ethnic Germans from Hungary in war service. This was equal to about 7% of the minority group. Of these, 22,125 were serving in the *Waffen-SS*.[23] By the spring of 1944, this number grew by about 35,000 men. Adding casualties, by then just under 40,000 members of this minority group had served in the ranks of the *Waffen-SS*. Just a few weeks later, on April 14, 1944, a third agreement followed with the new Prime Minister Döme Sztójay (January 5, 1883 – August 22, 1946), which introduced compulsory service in the *Waffen-SS* for ethnic Germans from Hungary. All men from the age of 17 to 60 had become eligible for military service. With those in the 17 to 35 age class who were medically fit already in military service, at that time the German ethnic group in Hungary still numbered about 350,000 men. The 36- to 45-year-olds were now to be drafted for the *Waffen-SS*, and the 46- to 50-year-olds for the *Ordnungspolizei*. Of the first group, about 35,000 of the roughly 50,000 examined were taken into the *Waffen-SS*, while about 15,000 of the 30,000 men in the older age groups were taken into the *Ordnungspolizei*. In total, more than 75,000 ethnic Germans from Hungary served in the *Waffen-SS*. This was equivalent to about 9% of the foreign Germans.

Josef Meinzinger was born in Genna (Hungary) on July 21, 1924, and joined the *Waffen-SS* as a volunteer following the second inter-state agreement in the summer of 1943.

After initial training in the *SS-Artillerie-Ausbildungs-und Ersatz-Regiment* in Prague, in autumn 1943, he was transferred to the *4. SS-Polizei-Panzergrenadier-Division*.

Desederus Inesberger, a Satu Mare Swabian, was born in Oberwischau in 1922. In spring 1942, he joined the *Waffen-SS* in Hungary as a volunteer.

Initially trained at the *Waffen-SS* recruiting depot in Debica, he subsequently joined *SS-Gebirgs-Division "Nord."*

Inesberger was transferred to the *4. SS-Polizei-Panzergrenadier-Division* in 1944, and was killed in action in the Oxhöfter Kämpe on March 22, 1945.

"Germanic" Volunteers

The so-called "Germanic" volunteers were in Himmler's understanding members of the "Germanic" peoples. These included, first of all, the Scandinavian countries, England, the Netherlands, and the Flemings from Belgium. He saw the Swiss and finally the Walloons from Belgium somewhat differently.

When these countries—except for England—were occupied by German troops in the spring of 1940, the recruiting of volunteers began immediately and September 1940 saw the formation of the *SS-Division "Wiking,"* in which they were to serve. Recruiting success was minimal: few suitable volunteers were found, even among the right-wing movements in the countries. Service in the SS, which was National–Socialist in nature, had little appeal for Dutchmen or Scandinavians, who were generally rather liberal in nature. As only about 600 Dutchmen plus roughly 200 Danes and 250 Norwegians had volunteered by mid-January 1941, on February 22, 1941, Hitler expanded recruitment to the Finns, who were actually non-Germanic. With not even ten percent of the division made up of "Germanic" volunteers, in March 1941, Himmler established the Germanic Volunteer Central Office. Under Dr. Riedweg (April 10, 1907 – January 22, 2005), a Swiss, it was supposed to coordinate and accelerate the recruitment of volunteers. The central office later became Office VI in the *SS-Hauptamt.*

At the same times, the first plans were formulated for the formation of so-called "Germanic Legions" for the coming war against the Soviet Union. Recruitment stressed the war against bolshevism and acceptance criteria were lower than those for the *SS-Division "Wiking."* In total about 35,000 "Germanic" volunteers served in the *Waffen-SS.*

Britons

In the summer of 1942, the German leadership learned of plans by an English politician in exile who wanted to recruit from the approximately 60,000 British prisoners of war for a legion to join the fight against bolshevism. Hitler viewed the idea with skepticism and it was not until April 1943, that he authorized the recruiting of British POWs: these tended to be members of right-wing parties, such as the British Union of Fascists. Originally under the patronage of the OKW, by the end of 1943, just under thirty men volunteered to serve in the so-called Legion of St. George. This was less than .05% of the POWs.

At the beginning of 1944 the *SS-Hauptamt* took over organization of the British volunteer unit which, formed in battalion strength, was to bear the name "British Free Corps." The recruits received the same rights and obligations as all Germanic volunteers: German citizenship after two years of service and for those who signed up for four years a "farm in the east" after the final victory.

The hostile British attitude—which was rigorously enforced by the prison camp committees—was intensified by the invasion of Normandy and the general war situation. On July 8, 1944, the chief of the *SS-Hauptamt* reported to the *Reichsführer-SS*:

> Because of the attitude of the British POWs, influenced by the mood produced by the invasion, preliminary work for the recruitment of British prisoners of war for the "British Legion" had to be put on a new foundation, in which the recruitment of volunteers was reformed.

The roughly 100 volunteers who had been recruited were initially quartered in Hildesheim and in early September 1944, were sent to *SS-Pionier-Ausbildungs- und Ersatz-Bataillon 1* in Dresden. At the end of February 1945, about fifteen British SS volunteers were sent to Niemegk to attend a close-range anti-tank course. The others saw action briefly on the Oder Front with *SS-Panzer-Aufklärungs-Abteilung 11 "Nordland."*

Danes

After the German occupation of Denmark in April 1940, the democratically-elected government of the country's roughly 3,623,000 inhabitants remained in office until August 1943. The recruiting of Danish volunteers for the *SS-Standarte "Nordland"* began in April 1940. As the recruitment was for a Germanic Reich, it was mainly members of the *Dansk National Socialistik Arbejder Parti* (DNSAP) and the ethnic Germans in Northern Schleswig who joined the *Waffen-SS*. Dr. Frits Clausen (November 12, 1893 – December 5, 1947), leader of the DNSAP, issued an appeal to his then about 20,000 party members.

When only about 200 Danes volunteered by January 1941, in February Himmler eased the criteria. Married men up to the age of twenty-nine could now volunteer. Employed within the *SS-Division "Wiking,"* the number of Danes in the unit—repeatedly augmented—never exceeded about 200 volunteers.

After the attack on the Soviet Union, the *Waffen-SS* also began recruiting in Denmark for a national legion for the struggle against bolshevism. In contrast to other occupied countries under German occupation, in this case the legion was designated a Freikorps. Without emphasizing a "Germanic Reich" and reduced entrance criteria, by the end of 1941 almost 1,100 Danes and men from Northern Schleswig volunteered to fight in the war against the Soviet Union.

In selecting volunteers, preference was given to men who had completed their military service after 1931, meaning the 1910 to 1918 age classes. Active soldiers in the Danish Army, which still existed, could also volunteer. The government placed them on leave for the duration of their service in the *Freikorps Danmark*.

As some of the men came from the ranks of the DNSAP and NSDAP in Northern Schleswig and their muster criteria kept them from being accepted in the *SS-Standarte "Nordland,"* there were frequent confrontations between them and other, less political, volunteers from Denmark.

After more than a few young DNSAP party members were taken into the *Waffen-SS*, on February 19, 1942, Dr. Clausen asked that no more recruits be accepted from Denmark. He did not wish to further weaken his position in Denmark. Himmler was much less concerned about the concerns of the politically insignificant DNSAP, however, than he was about the country's human resources. A new recruiting effort brought in 1,402 Danes, however just 450 of them were found suitable. A majority of them were again members of the German ethnic minority in Northern Schleswig. They replaced the volunteers who had completed their year of service in the *Freikorps Danmark*.

In May 1943, after the end of the second one-year service commitment, the Freikorps, about 700 men strong, was used as a cadre for the formation of the new *SS-Panzergrenadier-Regiment "Danmark"* of the *11. SS-Freiwilligen-Panzergrenadier-Division "Nordland."* Service commitments were no longer of limited duration, instead they lasted until the end of the war.

On January 15, 1943, Dr. Werner Best (July 10, 1903 – June 23, 1989), the Reich Plenipotentiary in Denmark, reported that 4,777 Danes—1,254 of the from Northern Schleswig—had served in the *Waffen-SS* since 1940. In total, by 1945, just under 6,000 Danish citizens had served in the *Waffen-SS*. About 4,500 of these were native Danes.

Flemings

In 1940, just under 5,000,000 Dutch-speaking Flemings lived in Belgium. Discriminated against in their own land, in the nineteenth century Flemish politicians began seeking union with the Netherlands or sovereignty. After the campaign in the west, in June 1940, *General der Infanterie* Alexander von Falkenhausen (October 29, 1878 – July 31, 1966) was named military commander in Belgium and northern France. The *Vlaamsch Nationaal Verbond* (VNV) under Staf de Clerq (September 16, 1884 – October 22, 1942), which wanted to unit Flanders with the Netherlands, and the *Duitsch-Vlaamische Arbeidsgemeenschap (DeVlag)* under Jef van de Wiele (July 20, 1903 – September 4, 1979) became collaborationist forces, seeking to incorporate Flanders into the German Reich.

The *Waffen-SS* began recruiting among the Flemings in May 1940, but with very limited success. In September 1940, not even fifty volunteers had joined the *SS-Standarte "Westland"* (*SS-Division "Wiking"*). As there was obviously little interest in the *"Germanic" SS-Division "Wiking,"* in April 1941, recruiting began for the *SS-Freiwilligen-Standarte "Nordwest."* With a service commitment of just one year and the possibility of serving at home, this suited the objectives of the VNV, which urged its members to join. Consequently approximately 450 Flemish volunteers were taken in by the end of May 1941.

Following the start of the campaign against the Soviet Union, another recruiting campaign was launched, this time for an anti-Bolshevik *Freiwilligen-Legion "Flandern."* In addition to about 400 new recruits, in September 1941, the *SS-Freiwilligen-Standarte "Nordwest"* was disbanded with no warning and its personnel were also used to form the legion. As a result it had a total of about 900 men.

The behavior of the German core personnel towards the Flemish volunteers showed, however, that the propaganda about a "European struggle against bolshevism" was nothing more than waste paper. The leader of the *Vlaamsch Nationaal Verbond*, Staf de Clerq, voiced his anger over the treatment of the Flemish to Himmler in March 1942:

> In the 1st Company the company commander did nothing to hide his disdain towards the Flemish. In his unfair approach to the Flemish he was surpassed only by the senior non-commissioned officer. The boys were abused with the coarsest words for the most minor offenses, even beaten with sticks.
>
> [...] about 140 soldiers had been recruited from among the workers in Northern France, with promises that they would work in Germany and receive more pay [...]
>
> I am even more angry about the statements made by officers of the Flemish Legion about our people. In the 1st Company, for example, the Flemings are regularly criticized as "dirty people," "filthy people," "stupid people," "gypsies," etc. And to the Flemish officers: "Translate that into your Russian language." Even worse: these insults were made in front of the population of the occupied territories. When the 1st Company was quartered in Zapol, the legionnaires were called together in the local square, where in the presence of 100 Latvians they were called "gypsy people" and told "that you are mistaken if you thought that you came here to get fat, for you are going to work for your pay." Afterwards the Latvians came to us and asked if we really were soldiers who were paid to fight. The boys' morale has been destroyed.

In May 1943, the formation of a Flemish *SS-Sturmbrigade* was planned as part of the *III. (germanischen) SS-Panzer-Korps* then being created. In addition to about 400 new recruits from Belgium, approximately 1,000 Flemish armament workers were recruited in Germany. At the end of 1943, there were roughly 2,000 Flemish troops in the *SS-Freiwilligen-Sturmbrigade "Langemarck."* In the summer of 1940, volunteers were recruited from organizations that had been collaborationist since 1940. Approximately 2,000 Flemings—in part from the *Vlaamse Wacht*, the NSKK and the *Organisation Todt*—reinforced the former volunteers of the Legion and *Waffen-SS*. Between 1940 and 1945, a total of about 7,000 Flemings served in the *Waffen-SS*.

Dutchmen

Approximately 8,227,000 people lived in the Netherlands in 1940. After the victorious western campaign in May 1940, Dr. Arthur Seyß-Inquart (July 22, 1892 – October 16, 1946) was installed

Heinrich Himmler

Members of the *Freiwilligen-Legion "Flandern"* at a Vlaamsch Nationaal Verbond rally in Belgium.

Jan de Vriese

Freiwilligen-Legion "Flandern" graves at the Volkhov.

The *Finnische Freiwilligen-Bataillon* of the *Waffen-SS*.

Memorial stone for the fallen Swedish SS volunteers in Estonia.

The *Freiwilligen-Legion "Norwegen"* during a parade in Oslo.

as Reich Commissar for the Occupied Netherlands. Collaborating forces were the *Nationaal Socialistische Beweging* under Adriaan Mussert (May 11, 1894 – May 7, 1946), who saw the Netherlands as an alliance partner of the German Reich, and the leader of the NSNAP Ernst Haman van Rappard (October 30, 1899 – January 11, 1953), who saw the Netherlands as part of the Greater German Reich.

The recruiting of Dutchmen for the *SS-Standarte "Westland"* was begun in May 1940. By February 1941, this succeeded in attracting roughly 600 volunteers with a two-year service commitment. This figure rose to 820 men by August 1941. After the Standarte was attached to the *SS-Division "Wiking,"* in April 1941, recruiting began for a new independent unit: the *SS-Freiwilligen-Standarte "Nordwest."* By the end of August 1941, its personnel included 1,400 Dutch, 805 Flemish, and 108 Danish troops.

The start of the war with the Soviet Union also resulted in the formation of the *Freiwilligen-Legion "Niederlande,"* which had lower muster criteria than the other two SS formations. Those accepting a one-year term of service had to be between 17 and 40 years of age and be at least 1.65 meters tall.

During the course of the creation of the *Freiwilligen-Legion "Niederlande"* the *SS-Freiwilligen-Standarte "Nordwest"* was disbanded and its 1,400 men used as a cadre for the new formation. A further 800 volunteers were recruited—most from the *Nationaal Socialistische Beweging*—by the end of 1941.

Approximately one quarter of the men left the unit when their year of service ended, however. Like the Flemish, they were discouraged by the condescending treatment they received and action on the Eastern Front in -42 degree temperatures. They were replaced by newly-recruited volunteers. The *Freiwilligen-Legion "Niederlande"* was disbanded on May 20, 1943. It formed the core of the *SS-Freiwilligen-Panzergrenadier-Brigade "Nederland,"* which was formed in Grafenwöhr using the Dutch troops and ethnic Germans from Rumania.

At the beginning of 1943, the *Landwacht Niederlande* was formed within the *Ordnungspolizei*, and at the end of 1944—by then part of the *Waffen-SS*—it was used to form the *SS-Freiwilligen-Grenadier-Brigade "Landstorm Nederland."* During the effort to expand the unit to division size, young men were recruited from among Dutch armaments workers in Germany. Despite this, the unit's strength never exceeded 6,000 men and the reason for volunteering was usually of a very pragmatic nature: the food supply for the civilian population in the Netherlands had reached a low point by late 1944.

The planned expansion of the *SS-Freiwilligen-Panzergrenadier-Brigade "Nederland"* into the *23. SS-Freiwilligen-Panzergrenadier-Division "Nederland"* remained no more than a paper exercise. The transfer of large numbers of sailors from the Kriegsmarine was insufficient even to make good losses.

A total of about 14,000 Dutchmen served in the *Waffen-SS* between 1940 and 1945.

Norwegians

Approximately 2,845,000 people lived in Norway in 1940. After the German occupation in April 1940, Reich Commissar Josef Terboven (May 23, 1898 – May 8, 1945) assumed control over the occupied areas of Norway. In February 1942, the responsibilities of government were handed over to Vidkun Quisling (July 8, 1887 – October 24, 1945), the leader of the rightist *Nasjonal Samling*.

Just as in Denmark, the *Reichsführer-SS* immediately began recruiting Norwegian volunteers for the *SS-Standarte "Nordland."* When just 246 Norwegians volunteered to serve in the "greater Germanic" combat unit by January 12, 1941, in February Himmler lowered the entrance requirements.

After the attack on the Soviet Union, a volunteer legion was also formed. Applicants only had to meet army mustering criteria to be accepted. Approximately 1,900 men volunteered by

The Dutchman Henk Ophoff joined the Replacement Battalion of the SS-Standarte "Westland" on April 26, 1941. After serving with the Feldersatz-Bataillon "Wiking," he was transferred to the SS-Freiwilligen-Panzergrenadier-Brigade "Nederland."

Dirk Groos volunteered on January 27, 1945, for service in the SS-Freiwilligen-Grenadier-Brigade "Landstorm Nederland."

the end of 1941 in the anticipation of serving in Finland. About half of these men, most of whom were members of the *Organisation Hird* of the *Nasjonal Samling* (an equivalent of the German SA), were accepted.

A replacement battalion and a Norwegian ski company were formed from the excess volunteers, and unlike the other units these were in fact deployed in Finland with the *SS-Aufklärungs-Abteilung "Nord."*

By February 1943, 1,089 Norwegians had served in the *SS-Panzergrenadier-Regiment "Nordland"* (former *SS-Standarte "Nordland"*) and 2,018 in the *Freiwilligen-Legion "Norwegen"*—with a one- or two-year service commitment. 928 legionnaires, often demotivated, left service after their one-year commitment was over. Some of the men discharged from *SS-Panzergrenadier-Regiment "Nordland"* and the Volunteer Legion did, however, join the *SS-Wach-Bataillon Oslo*, which was not used to relieve frontline units.

In May 1943, the *Freiwilligen-Legion "Norwegen,"* about 700 men strong, was merged with the Norwegian *II./SS-Panzergrenadier-Regiment "Nordland,"* and when the *11. SS-Freiwilligen-Panzergrenadier-Division "Nordland"* was formed it provided the cadre for the new *11. SS-Freiwilligen-Panzergrenadier-Regiment "Norge."* Between 1940 and 1945, approximately 3,500 Norwegians served in the *Waffen-SS*, equivalent to 0.12% of the population.

Sweden

When the *Waffen-SS* unofficially began recruiting for the *SS-Standarte "Nordland"* in Sweden in 1940, the country had 6,190,000 inhabitants. As in all the Scandinavian countries, the number of volunteers was far below expectations. Just forty Swedes volunteered!

After the start of "Operation Barbarossa," however, the *SS-Hauptamt* hoped that it would be able to form a Swedish *Freikorps*—similar to the *Freikorps "Danmark."* The Swedish government, however, was eager to avoid placing its neutrality in question and prohibited any recruiting actions.

Propaganda was therefore limited mainly to the right-wing *Svensk Socialistik Samling* under the leadership of Sven Lindholm (February 8, 1903 – April 26, 1998). Those Swedes who subsequently reported to the German embassy in Stockholm were evaluated by the *Waffen-SS* replacement detachments in Finland or Norway and, if found suitable, were assigned to the *SS-Division "Wiking."* When the *11. SS-Freiwilligen-Panzergrenadier-Division "Nordland"* was created, they formed a platoon in *3./SS-Panzer-Aufklärungs-Abteilung 11.*

Roughly 200 Swedes in total served in the *Waffen-SS* between 1940 and 1945. Former volunteer Tor Hillvärn remembered:

I was born in Göteborg, Sweden on April 2, 1920. After having volunteered for the *Svenska Frivilligkåren* (Swedish Volunteer Corps) for the Winter War in Finland in 1939–40, in the summer of 1941 nine other boys and I went to Stockholm and once again volunteered to fight against bolshevism. They told us there that a battalion of Swedish volunteers was to be formed in northern Finland and gave us train tickets to Tornio (Finland). When we arrived in Tornio on August 10, 1941, they told us that we were going to Germany for training.

We knew absolutely nothing about the SS! What it was or anything else. They told us that a Finnish battalion was being trained in Germany. Well, we finally decided that it made no difference whether we served in the north or the south.

We arrived in Klagenfurt by way of Stralsund and there we were trained by the replacement battalion of the *SS-Standarte "Westland"* from September 2–28, 1941. On October 1, I joined *10./SS-Standarte "Germania."* I remained with this unit until the end of 1943, and then after a serious illness was transferred to the *SS-Panzergrenadier-Ausbildungs- und Ersatz-Bataillon 5* in Ellwangen. My duties there included serving as an assistant armorer-artificer and instructor at the target range in Dalkingen.

In May 1944, I was transferred to Oslo to serve as an interpreter with the SD, as I spoke Norwegian like a Norwegian. Although Norwegian is similar to Swedish, one can instantly tell if one is a Swede or a Norwegian. When the war ended I became a prisoner of war in Akershus, Oslo, I was released on June 8, 1946, and returned home.

Swiss

Although the Germans imagined that all of the just under three million German-speaking residents of the confederation were ethnic Germans, efforts which began at the latest after the start of the Russian campaign to create a free corps of Swiss volunteers were unsuccessful. As the Swiss, like the Swedes, wished to maintain their neutrality, official recruiting for a German–Swiss volunteer unit was forbidden.

Despite this, propaganda, which was limited almost exclusively to word of mouth, brought in approximately 1,400 volunteers, of which about 800 were accepted by the *Waffen-SS* between 1940 and 1945. The Swiss who entered German service *de jure* illegally were initially trained at the SS Training Camp "Sennheim" and formed a relatively homogenous unit, for example in *SS-Aufklärungs-Abteilung 6*.

Walloons

Until 1943, Himmler had no interest in Wallonian war volunteers for ideological reasons—neither for the *Waffen-SS* nor for the war against bolshevism in the form of a legion. The army, however, accepted volunteers from the approximately 3.2 million French-speaking Belgians and with just under 900 men formed a Wallonian infantry battalion.

Himmler changed his mind in May 1943, and made plans to use the Walloons, who by the were characterized as "French-speaking Teutons," in the formation of the *Germanisches SS-Panzer-Korps*. At the same time, recruiting was stepped up in Belgium, especially in the rightist Rexist Movement, however this resulted in no more than 300 volunteers between the ages of 17 and 40.

When, far from reality, orders for the formation of the *28. SS-Freiwilligen-Grenadier-Division "Wallonien"* were issued in the autumn of 1944, all Walloons serving in other formations were transferred. Approximately 2,000 volunteers—including those from the Wallonian Guard Battalion and the NSKK—bolstered the ranks of the *Waffen-SS*. The additional recruiting among armaments workers contributed only marginally to the rise in the total number of Wallonian SS volunteers between May 1943 and May 1945 to more than 4,500 men.

"Foreigners"

"For every foreigner who falls, no German mother will weep!" *SS-Obergruppenführer* Berger, chief of the *SS-Hauptamt*, expressed this by then prevailing sentiment in a letter to *SS-Gruppenführer* Oberg, Senior SS and Police Commander attached to the Military Commander France, on February 8, 1944.[24] Still demanding the racial cream of the crop from among the foreign volunteers—for example Estonians and Latvians—as the war went on Himmler adopted an increasingly pragmatic approach, especially with regard to quantitative targets. It made no difference to him whether they were "Teutons," "Slavs," "Latins" or even asiatics.

On February 14, 1943, the OKW informed the Army General Staff and the Chief of Army Armaments and Commander-in-Chief of the Replacement Army that Hitler—as a result of the tragedy at Stalingrad—had tasked Himmler with the formation of three foreign divisions by the beginning of June 1943. The planned divisions were the:

Himmler inspected the Wallonian war volunteers in Meseritz on May 24, 1943.

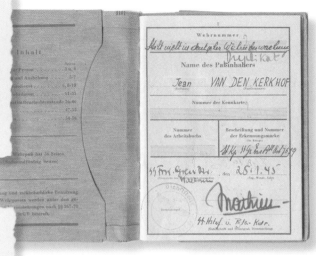

The *SS-Freiwilligen-Sturmbrigade "Wallonien"* was organized into a grenadier battalion and a heavy battalion.

Jean-Jacquet van den Kerkhof was born in France on June 26, 1925, the son of a Flemish father and French mother. He joined the *Waffen-SS* on April 18, 1943. Among the units he served with was the *SS-Freiwilligen-Sturmbrigade "Langemarck,"* until 9 May 9, 1944. He joined the *SS-Freiwilligen-Grenadier-Division "Wallonien"* on January 25, 1945.

The *SS-Freiwilligen-Sturmbrigade "Wallonien,"* part of the *XI. Armee-Korps*, was encircled by the Red Army west of Cherkassy in late January 1944.

11. Lettisches SS-Freiwilligen-Division (11th Latvian SS Volunteer Division)
12. Litauische SS-Freiwilligen-Division (12th Lithuanian SS Volunteer Division)
13. Kroatische SS-Freiwilligen-Division (13th Croatian SS Volunteer Division)

Recall in this context Hitler's words from the summer of 1941:

> We must never allow anyone to bear arms except Germans! This is particularly important; even if at first it seems easier to use any foreign subjugated peoples to bolster our military, it is wrong! One day they will absolutely and unavoidably strike out against us. Only the German may bear arms, not the Slav, not the Czech, not the Cossack or Ukrainian.

After, on the one hand, the Lithuanians displayed little interest in the *Waffen-SS'* recruiting efforts and, on the other, Himmler finally questioned the country's basic reliability, on December 2, 1943 the OKW war diary noted:

> The *Reichsführer-SS* has decided not to form a Lithuanian formation. The army has only recruited Lithuanians to serve in construction battalions.

Initially only a Croatian, plus a Ukrainian and a Latvian SS Division were formed. These were followed by an Estonian unit, and from the summer of 1944, Himmler also instructed the *SS-Hauptamt* to form mostly small units, brigades, and divisions within the *Waffen-SS* from formations previously under the *Wehrmacht* and the *Ordnungspolizei*. As well, in June 1944, the *Freiwilligen-Leitstelle "Ost"* (Volunteer Central Office "East") was formed in the *SS-Hauptamt* alongside the existing *Germanischen Freiwilligen Leitstelle* (Germanic Volunteer Central Office).

With the exception of the Baltic units, practically none of the newly-formed divisions were of use to the German command—in the form of an increase in fighting strength. With a few exceptions, all of the foreign troops failed in combat, if they actually saw action. In any case, about 230,000 foreigners were taken into the *Waffen-SS*. This represented just under a quarter of its total strength. Their number included:

6,500 Albanians	1,000 Bulgarians	20,000 Estonians
1,500 Finns	9,600 Frenchmen	3,000 Indians
6,000 Italians	5,000 Caucasians	25,000 Cossacks
23,000 Croatians	40,000 Latvians	4,000 Eastern Turks
3,000 Rumanians	15,000 Russians	5,000 Serbs
400 Spaniards	20,000 Ukrainians	42,000 Hungarians

Albania

A provisional government for the roughly one million Albanians was constituted under Imbrahim Bicaku (September 10, 1905 – January 4, 1977) following the withdrawal of Italian forces in October 1943, however it had little central authority. The economy and the military were divided in interrelated families, consequently no general development took place in the country.

After Albania decided to at least become involved in the battle against the communist partisan movement under Tito, at the beginning of 1944, the *SS-Hauptamt* made plans to form an SS mountain division which, deployed primarily in the Kosovo area, was to prevent partisans from crossing over from Montenegro.

As the provisional government was already in no position to create a functioning army, it was not opposed to these plans. Its promise that the 1922 to 1924 age classes might be drafted

Members of the *21. Waffen-Geb-irgs-Division der SS "Skanderbeg" (albanische Nr. 1)*.

Johann Zehr and Heinrich Willner, core personnel of the *23. Waffen-Geb-irgs-Division der SS "Kama" (kro-atische Nr. 2)*.

Brigadeführer Kaminski, later com-mander of the *29. Waffen-Gren-adier-Division der SS "RONA" (russische Nr. 1)*, with *Generalma-jor* Heidkämper.

Later *Waffen-Brigadeführer* Kaminski (1st row, far right).

for the formation of an SS volunteer division was, however, like many of the government's decrees, nothing but talk. The regional families remained the real decision makers.

With each age class containing about 7,000 Albanians, approximately 21,000 men were to be conscripted for the *21. Waffen-Gebirgs-Division der SS "Skanderbeg" (albanische Nr. 1)*. In fact, from the beginning only about 60% of these answered this call. Of the approximately 12,000 men examined, 9,275 were classified kv-*Heer*. In total, from mid-April 1944, about 6,500 Albanians were taken into the *Waffen-SS*. The motivation of these men was so low that most of them deserted within a few weeks. When the country was abandoned at the beginning of October 1944, efforts to create an effective unit came to an end. The entire effort must be seen as a failure for Germany.

Bulgaria

Exactly one year after Italy renounced its Axis alliance with Germany, on September 8, 1944, influenced by the parade of Soviet victories, Bulgaria, a country of roughly six-million inhabitants, declared war on the German Reich.

Two months later a Bulgarian government in exile was formed in Vienna under Prime Minister Aleksander Zankov (June 29, 1879 – July 27, 1959) to serve as a propaganda counter-pole. After discussions with Col. Kostov, the war minister in exile with no armed forces, the recruiting of volunteers for a *Waffen-Grenadier-Division der SS (bulgarische Nr. 1)* began. This was supposed to represent the core of a Bulgarian army of liberation. As recruiting was limited to Bulgarians in Germany—some of them deserters—on November 1, 1944, Himmler ordered the formation of a *Waffen-Grenadier-Regiment der SS (bulgarisches)*. Surprisingly, despite the situation some men did volunteer:

Officers	NCOs	Enlisted Men	Total
25	56	500	581
4.3%	9.6%	86.1%	100%

The regiment was formed at the "Döllersheim" Training Camp in Lower Austria (approximately ninety kilometers northwest of Vienna) under *Waffen-Standartenführer* Rogosaroff but was never committed to action. With a total of about 1,000 Bulgarian volunteers, the unit reached battalion strength and marched into western captivity.

Estonia

Approximately 1,125,000 people lived in Estonia in 1941, of which about one million were native Estonians. Soon after German forces occupied Estonia in the summer of 1941, roughly 6,000 volunteers were used to form Estonian Security Battalions 181 to 186. Then in autumn 1941, about 6,000 Estonians were used to form so-called *Schutzmannschafts-Bataillonen* (police battalions), which, under the *Ordnungspolizei*, were used mainly to fight partisans, but also to guard prisoners of war.

When the one-year commitments of the first volunteers expired in the autumn of 1942, the *Waffen-SS* recruited them for further service on the German side. While about 50% of the Estonians wanted to leave service completely, the other approximately 1,000 men signed up to fight on in an Estonian Legion.

In the course of the "total war" declared by Goebbels after Stalingrad, on February 25, 1943, the 1919 to 1924 age classes were called up for compulsory labor service. After completing their service in the war economy, the young men had the choice of joining the *Waffen-SS* or the *Wehrmacht*. Of the 42,000 Estonians affected, roughly 5,300 volunteered for the *Waffen-SS* and about 6,000 for the *Wehrmacht*. In October 1943, the 1925 age class was also called up and about 3,300 Estonians joined the SS Legion.

General mobilization followed in Estonia on February 7, 1944. Of the total of 105,000 men affected, by April 1944, about 10,000 joined the *Waffen-SS* and 22,000 volunteered to serve in the six new *Grenzschutz-Regimenter* (frontier guard regiments) being formed. Smaller contingents joined the *Luftwaffe*, the police or construction battalions. Altogether, about 20,000 Estonians were members of the *Waffen-SS*.

Finland

In 1939, Finland had approximately 3,721,000 inhabitants. In the course of general planning for the formation of the *SS-Standarte "Nordland,"* a unit made up of Scandinavian volunteers, in March 1940, discussions began between the German ambassador in Helsinki and the Finnish government regarding the potential recruitment of volunteers for the *Waffen-SS*. It is interesting to note that as a branch of the Mongolian race, the (Finno–Ugric), the Finns were not in fact "Teutons." However, as they were a Scandinavian people and the country had had political links with Germany since 1918, Himmler chose to ignore this.

Finland, which had a small peacetime army of about 25,000 soldiers, was basically not opposed to the idea of having its people trained within the German military. Interest in the *Waffen-SS* was non-existent, however. Because of Himmler's fondness for the Nordic peoples, however, the *SS-Hauptamt* played a leading role in the negotiations. In February 1941, the first Finns left their homeland for Vienna for the formation of the *SS-Freiwilligen-Bataillon "Nordost"* (SS Volunteer Battalion "Northeast"). Another roughly 400 committed themselves to two years of service in the *SS-Division "Wiking."* Former *SS-Schütze* Kurt Kubiak remembered:

> I was a member of *5./SS-Standarte "Nordland."* In Vienna we were assigned Finnish volunteers. There was not much contact between us because of the language problem. If at all, we communicated in sign language. Despite this, they were outstanding comrades whom one could trust implicitly.

The first volunteers were discharged after the end of their one-year commitment and returned to Finland in February 1942. They were replaced by fresh volunteers. The *SS-Freiwilligen-Bataillon "Nordost,"* which had been based at the Groß–Born Training Camp since September 1941 was ultimately designated the *Finnisches Freiwilligen-Bataillon der Waffen-SS* and with its approximately 1,100 men formed *III./SS-Regiment "Nordland" of the SS-Division (mot.) "Wiking."*

When their service commitments ended, in June 1943, the Finnish volunteers were discharged to return home. Because of the war situation Finland put an end to further service commitments for political reasons. In total about 1,500 Finns had served in the *Waffen-SS* during the two years.

France

After the end of the Western Campaign, a ceasefire was signed in Compiègne Forest on June 22, 1940. This led to the partitioning of France's roughly 41,880,000 inhabitants. The northern half of the country to the Spanish border was under the military administration headed by *General* von Stülpnagel (January 2, 1886 – August 30, 1944), who resided in Paris. In the south, a new French government under Marshall Philippe Pétain (April 24, 1856 – July 23, 1951) was established in Vichy. This Vichy government controlled about 40% of the country and had a 100,000-man army. In November 1942, German troops marched into the *bis dato* unoccupied south of France to prevent a potential landing by Anglo-American forces on the Mediterranean coast.

Heinrich Himmler

Estonian *Waffen-Unter-scharführer.*

Award of the War Merit Cross 2nd Class with Swords to an Estonian Red Cross sister.

Swearing-in at Debica.

SS

Soldbuch

zugleich

Personalausweis

Palgaraamat

ühtlasi

isikutunnistus

Im Namen

des

Führers

und

Obersten Befehlshabers der Wehrmacht

verleihe ich

der

Schwester Elies-Aino T o o m l a
20. Waffen-Gren.Div. der SS (estn.Nr.1)
das

Kriegsverdienstkreuz 2. Klasse
mit Schwertern

K. H. Qu. , den 20 April 19 45

General der Artillerie
u. Kommandierender General

Aleksander Ronk was draft-ed into the Estonian Border Defense Regiment and later joined the *20. Waffen-Gren-adier-Division der SS.*

Estonian SS volunteers at Debica.

While Himmler had begun recruiting volunteers for the *Waffen-SS* and volunteer legions in the "Germanic" countries in 1940–41, initially he had no interest in the "Latin" French. However the deteriorating military situation led him to decide on December 10, 1942, to form a division of, "especially racially-pure, Germanic-looking" Frenchmen.

After lengthy negotiations and the fact that presumably not enough volunteers could be recruited, Hitler initially authorized the formation of a regiment. French Prime Minister Pierre Laval (June 28, 1883 – October 15, 1945) subsequently passed a law on July 22, 1943, which officially permitted Frenchmen to join the *Waffen-SS* for the "struggle against Bolshevism." French newspapers reported the new formation on August 14, 1943:

> A French regiment of the *Waffen-SS* has now been formed as part of the struggle of European youth against the world enemy of bolshevism.
>
> The age limit for volunteers is 17 to 40, minimum height is 1.65 meters. Volunteers for the Waffen-SS are relieved of their labor obligation. French officers and non-commissioned officers retain their ranks and the non-commissioned officer and officer path is open to every volunteer from the enlisted ranks based on performance and ability. The welfare and provision of family members is governed by existing regulations. Although they are not providers, unmarried volunteers will receive an allowance that will be paid to an account which they can access in France.
>
> The first enthusiastic intakes of volunteers have shown that a significant part of the French youth has realized that the fighting youth of Germany views them as friends and comrades.

The number of volunteers from the rightist collaborationist organizations was modest. By January 1944 only about 2,500 Frenchmen had joined the *Waffen-SS*. Expansions of the French unit into a brigade and ultimately the *33. Waffen-Grenadier-Division der SS "Charlemagne" (französische Nr. 1)* led to considerable personnel problems. Only by detaching French volunteers—from the navy, the army, the NSKK and the militia—was it possible to mass about 9,600 Frenchmen in the *Waffen-SS*. The strongly divergent political views of the individual groups made it impossible to speak of a homogenous unit, however.

India

After he was named commander of the Replacement Army in the summer of 1944, Himmler began concentrating the foreign units fighting on the German side in the *Waffen-SS*. In the course of this, on August 8, 1944, *Indische Infanterie-Regiment 950* (950th Indian Infantry Regiment), which had previously been attached to the army and had about 3,000 men on strength, was taken over by the *Waffen-SS*. Already in the summer of 1942 there had been preliminary discussions between Himmler and Subhas Chandra Bose, former president of the Indian National Congress, about how they might form volunteer units from Indian prisoners of war.

As the Indische Legion in the *Waffen-SS*, the men were used primarily in work on fortifications. In November 1944, they were in the Rastatt area and in December were transferred to the "Heuberg" Training Camp. In mid-April 1945, the unit marched in the direction of Allgäu and disbanded there.

Italy

After Italy abandoned its alliance with Germany and left the war, Benito Mussolini (July 29, 1883 – April 28, 1945) proclaimed the *Republica Sociale Italia* in northern Italy in October 1943. It encompassed about 17 million Italians who, however, no longer had much enthusiasm, either for fascism or the war. This was clearly reflected in military strengths. If one assumes

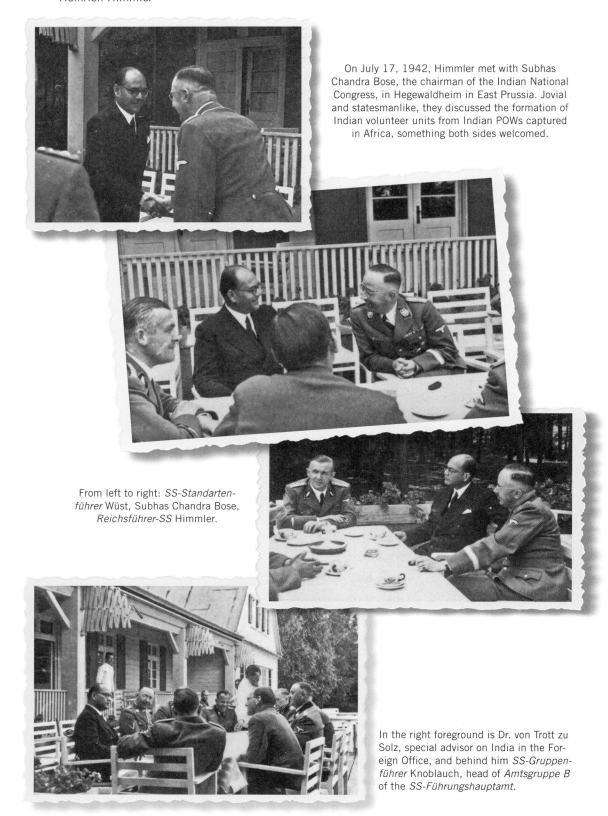

On July 17, 1942, Himmler met with Subhas Chandra Bose, the chairman of the Indian National Congress, in Hegewaldheim in East Prussia. Jovial and statesmanlike, they discussed the formation of Indian volunteer units from Indian POWs captured in Africa, something both sides welcomed.

From left to right: *SS-Standarten-führer* Wüst, Subhas Chandra Bose, *Reichsführer-SS* Himmler.

In the right foreground is Dr. von Trott zu Solz, special advisor on India in the Foreign Office, and behind him *SS-Gruppenführer* Knoblauch, head of *Amtsgruppe B* of the *SS-Führungshauptamt*.

that about ten percent of the population could see military service, 1.7 million Italians would have served in northern Italy. In fact, less than 0.1% saw active service.

The *Wehrmacht* tried to recruit volunteers from among the approximately 400,000 Italian prisoners of war for the formation of four divisions. On November 13, 1943, Mussolini declared to *Generalfeldmarschall* Wilhelm Keitel (September 22, 1882 – October 16, 1946):

> I will feel that my honor has been violated if 50,000 volunteers cannot be found among the many internees for the formation of the four divisions.

It is impossible to say if he in fact felt that his honor had been violated—fact is that there was not even that number of volunteers. And many of those who did volunteer did not wish to fight anymore, instead they simply wanted out of the internment camps.

For its part, the *Waffen-SS* wanted to form fascist militias from the approximately 50,000 members of the newly-founded *Partito Fascista Repubblicano*. Recruiting was carried out both in northern Italy and in the internment camps. On October 9, 1943, Albert Speer (March 19, 1905 – September 1, 1981), the Reich Minister for Armaments and Munitions, complained to Himmler that the propaganda for joining the *Waffen-SS* was hindering the use of Italian military internees as labor:

> It has been reported to me that before being released to industry, the prisoners of war are urged by the SS to join the newly-created militia, which I think entirely correct. I would, however, be grateful, if this action could be carried out more quickly, because to date only 70,000 Italians have been transferred to industry for this reason. Any time saved is beneficial to me.

Of the approximately 15,000 Italians who volunteered, about 9,000 were rejected as unfit at "Münsingen" Training Camp. 3,000 of these (mostly from older age glasses) were set to the *Ordnungspolizei*. The rest were assigned to labor duties. By way of the *Ordnungspolizei*, a total of about 6,000 Italians ultimately came to the later *29. Waffen-Grenadier-Division der SS (italienische Nr. 1)*. Several hundred also joined German divisions as replacements, for example the *9. SS-Panzer-Division "Hohenstaufen,"* or were employed as guards, some at the Dachau concentration camp.

Caucasians

The term "Caucasian" is not an expression of nationality, instead it is a collective name for the non-Russian and non-Slavic peoples living in the Caucasus. Numbered among them were, in particular, the Georgians, Azerbaijanis, Armenians, and Circassians, which together with others are designated so-called North Caucasians.

The *SS-Hauptamt* began making plans to take over the Caucasian volunteers serving in the *Ordnungspolizei* and the army for the *Waffen-SS* in the spring of 1944. After this was realized only with so-called East-Turkish volunteers, however, it was not until December 30, 1944 that the SS-FHA repeated the *Reichsführer-SS'* order, according to which the Caucasian *Waffen-Verband der SS* (armed unit of the SS) was to be formed. The formation order stated:

> The Caucasian armed unit of the SS serves to pool all available Caucasians (Georgians, Azerbaijanis, Armenians, etc.), their military and political training and command, their organization into useful combat units, plus the carrying out of all cultural and propagandistic tasks.

This shows that, not only was a quantitative strengthening of the German defense force being strived for, but a political use as well. The latter was surely the essential point that the *SS-Hauptamt* grappled with these tribes. By then the Caucasus had long been outside the Reich's area of influence, recruiting could only take place in the POW camps. The reason most prisoners volunteered was simply the wish to survive.

The Caucasian armed unit of the SS was to be organized into four battalion-strength *Waffen-Gruppen* with the titles "*Georgien*," "*Aserbeidschan*," "*Armenien*," and "*Nordkaukasus*." Attached to the SS and Police Commander "Adriatic West" in the area north of Tolmezzo and under the command of *SS-Standartenführer* Theuermann, the unit achieve a strength of about 5,000 men and was armed with light and heavy machine-guns and small arms. Organized into two regiments, the units were used for security purposes and were among the forces under the Supreme SS and Police Commander "Italy."

Cossacks

At the end of July 1944, discussions were held between the Volunteer Central Office "East" in *Amtsgruppe D* of the *SS-Hauptamt* and *Generalleutnant* von Pannwitz (October 14, 1898 – January 16, 1947), commander of the army's *1. Kosaken-Division*. In addition to transferring the division to the *Waffen-SS*, the topics included the formation of a second Cossack division, for which volunteers were to be recruited in the prisoner of war camps.

On August 26, 1944, there followed a meeting between the *Reichsführer-SS* and *Generalleutnant* von Pannwitz, during which the formation of a Cossack cavalry corps was discussed. It was to be formed within the *Waffen-SS*, but initially it was not to be identified as a *Waffen-SS* formation. The majority of the German cadre personnel were very opposed to joining the *Waffen-SS* and von Pannwitz also told Himmler that the majority of the Cossacks would see being forced to join the *Waffen-SS* as political bullying. So the corps was first formed and only later was it to be officially declared a unit of the *Waffen-SS*. It is interesting to note that the *SS-Hauptamt* characterized the Cossacks as a Nordic–Dinaric people.

On September 29, Himmler ordered the senior SS and police commanders to report the Cossack units deployed in their areas—mostly within the *Ordnungspolizei*—for the formation of the *2. Kosaken-Division*. Formation of the *XV. Kosaken-Kavallerie-Korps* then followed on November 30, 1944.

On February 1, 1945, the SS-FHA advised that, "all indigenous members of the Cossack units attached to the *Waffen-SS*" were considered transferred to the *Waffen-SS*. Internally, the SS-FHA simultaneously named the Cossack divisions the *1.* and *2. SS-Kosaken-Kavallerie-Division*. Outwardly the Cossacks, and the German cadre personnel, remained members of the army until the end of the war. Apart from that, as of December 1944, all SS members were transferred to the signals unit of the *XV. Kosaken-Kavallerie-Korps*.

On April 9, 1945, the *1. SS-Kosaken-Kavallerie-Division* had a strength of about 12,500 men and was organized into three infantry and one cavalry regiments plus three so-called *Volksgruppen-Regimenter*. The latter were also called *Don–Stanizen*, *Terek–Stanizen*, and *Terek–Stanizen* (*Stanizen* = Cossack settlement). Equipped with light and heavy machine-guns and small arms, the Cossacks were attached to the SS and Police Commander "Adriatic West" in the Tolmezzo area.

Technically about 25,000 Cossacks were members of the *Waffen-SS*, though the majority of them were unaware of that fact.

Croatia

After the enormous losses at Stalingrad and in Tunisia, the Germans began looking for previously unexploited human resources. In the case of the independent states, they recognized

This photo documents the composition of the *1. SS-Kosaken-Division* excellently: on the left a Cossack, right a member of the German Army from the former core personnel, and, seated, a member of the *Waffen-SS*.

Ostmuselmanische SS-Regiment 1 was formed in June 1, 1944, by taking over the Turkmens serving in the army. Khalimov, now designated a "*turkmenischer SS-Mann*," had previously served in the *Turkmenischen Bau-Bataillon 402* (construction battalion).

Heinrich Himmler

Bosnian SS volunteer.

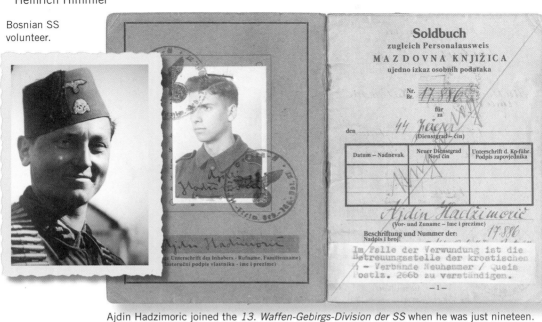

Ajdin Hadzimoric joined the *13. Waffen-Gebirgs-Division der SS* when he was just nineteen.

Members of *SS-Nachrichten-Abteilung 13.*

SS-Sturmscharführer Düll.

great potential in Croatia. Of the roughly four million Catholic and Muslim Croats, only about 80,000 were in military service at the end of 1942.

Socially the land was torn apart and the military was also in an unbelievably desolate condition. Primarily engaged in the conflict with Tito's partisans, while it committed brutal crimes just like the partisans, it had no success in pacifying the country.

Not least in the hope of scoring a propaganda success throughout the entire Islamic world, the idea ripened in the *SS-Hauptamt* of at first forming one division from the 700,000-strong Muslim population of Bosnia–Herzegovina. In doing so they recalled the Bosnian regiments of the Austro-Hungarian monarchy until 1918. Ante Pavelic (July 14, 1889 – December 28, 1959), the Croatian head of state, had little interest in such a unit because of his restrictive policies towards the Bosnian Muslims, however he was unable to close himself to the German request. He did, however, at least try to restrict the number of future new bearers of arms. Whereas the *SS-Hauptamt* planned a Muslim division with about 26,000 troops, Pavelic is known to have wanted a mixed unit of Catholic and Muslim Croats. Making up about one-fifth of the population in Croatia, the Muslims—with the Bosnians already serving in the Croatian Army—would have formed almost half the military! Although Himmler originally wanted a purely Muslim unit, he also agreed to the recruiting of about 3,000 Catholic Croats.

As the German and Croat commands had different opinions in many matters, many complications also arose when it came to recruiting: rigorous German action on the one hand and at times a complete boycott on the Croatian side. The Muslim volunteer Sahibbegović wrote the following on September 25, 1943, in a report about the situation in Croatia:

> In Travnik, for example, conscription of recruits for the division was carried out during prayers in the mosques, and those fit for military service were led away. The next morning a number of them fled into the forest. In this way the division lost the sympathy of the entire population, because the enemy propaganda endeavored to inform all of Bosnia about these events.

In order to bring order to the process, from the draft-eligible 1924 and 1925 age classes only one-third were to be conscripted by the Croatian Army and two-thirds released for the *Waffen-SS*. This was, without taking fitness into account, 3,400 of approximately 5,000 draft-eligible men per age class. As well, the *SS-Hauptamt* was also allowed to recruit older age classes which had not served and reservists. Of the Bosnians serving in the Croatian military, about 3,000 men were to be discharged to serve in the new division.

Despite various modifications, it did not prove possible to form the division with 26,000 men. At first the division strength was lowered to 20,000 men and ultimately the unit was made up of 15% (ethnic) German cadre personnel, 15% Catholic Croats and 70% Muslims.

After only about 14,000 Bosnians served in the *13. Waffen-Gebirgs-Division der SS "Handschar" (kroatische Nr. 1)*, the *SS-Hauptamt* planned—despite the problems in forming the first division—to create a second. The entire 1926 and 1927 age classes were to be inducted into the *Waffen-SS* and additional volunteers recruited. When, despite all efforts, no more than 3,500 men could be signed up, the *23. Waffen-Gebirgs-Division der SS "Kama" (kroatische Nr. 2)* was quickly disbanded and the available recruits taken over by the first Division.

In total, approximately 18,000 Muslim and 3,000 Catholic Croats served in the ranks of the *Waffen-SS*.

Latvia

Approximately 1,800,000 people lived in Latvia in 1941, of which about 1,500,000 were native Latvians. Autumn 1941 saw 15,000 Latvian volunteers recruited for the formation of so-called "police battalions," which were attached to the *Ordnungspolizei*. These were employed at the

Draft registration notice.

Latvian war volunteers.

Administering the oath in front of Latvian and German flags.

Romans Riekstins was just twenty-five when he was drafted into the *15. Waffen-Grenadier-Division der SS* in August 1944.

front or against partisans, and to guard Jewish ghettos. In some cases they were attached to the *Einsatzgruppen* of the Security Police.

When the one-year commitments of the first police battalions expired in autumn 1942, the *Waffen-SS* recruited for continued service on the German side. About 2,500 men declared themselves ready to fight on in the *Lettische SS-Freiwilligen-Legion* (Latvian SS Volunteer Legion). When, approximately three months later—on February 25, 1943—compulsory labor service was introduced for Latvians of age classes 1919 to 1924, the young men could decide whether they wanted to serve in the armaments industry or in the Latvian SS Volunteer Legion or *Wehrmacht*. Of the about 70,000 Latvians, approximately 30,700 of those found fit volunteered for military service. Of these, about 18,000 were used to form the *Lettische SS-Freiwilligen-Division*. In October 1943, a further approximately 5,600 men were signed up by the *Waffen-SS* from age classes 1919 to 1924, and 1912 to 1918. Just one month later the 1925 age class was called up.

> The OKW war diary noted on December 2, 1943:
> Ten age classes have been called up in Latvia following a registration effort based on the compulsory work law; but the successes have remained below expectations, as the Latvian draft system is itself ineffective and many eligible for military service try to avoid serving, their personal motives the effect of enemy propaganda. Fifty recruiting offices had been set up to exploit Latvia's manpower, each of which included a member of the *Wehrmacht*. The SS, the GBA, the Reichsbahn, the indigenous economy and other participating offices reported their requirements. What use will be made of the Latvians brought in by the new measures has not yet been completely clarified.
> In general, it can be said that the Estonians have proved themselves very well, the Latvians well and the Lithuanians poorly, the White Russians very poorly.
> The OKW now advises the participating offices that the *Führer* has passed responsibility for conscription of Estonians and Latvians fit for military service to the *Reichsführer-SS*, who has set up SS replacement training detachments in Reval and Riga. These have been given the authority of a German recruiting district headquarters.

General mobilization was declared in Latvia on February 7, 1944, affecting the 1908 to 1914 age classes. Of the total of about 70,000 men called up, by April 1944, about 10,000 voluntarily joined the *Waffen-SS* and another 17,000 joined six new Frontier Guard Regiments. Smaller contingents reached the *Luftwaffe*, the police, or construction battalions.

In August 1944, the 1926 and 1927 age classes were mobilized and older age classes, some of whom had previously been classified unfit, were also called up. All of those fit for military service from the 1927 age class were drafted into the *Luftwaffe* to serve as flak auxiliaries. In total about 124,000 Latvians saw action in the war, about 40,000 of them in the *Waffen-SS*.

Eastern Turks

Like the Caucasians, the term "Eastern Turk" was a collective designation in the parlance of the *SS-Hauptamt*. It mainly encompassed Turkestanis, Volga, and Ural Tatars, and Crimean Turks (Crimean Tatars).

Crimean Tatar volunteers serving in the so-called Police Battalions in the area of the Senior SS and Police Commander "Black Sea" were supposed to be used to form the *Waffen-Gebirgsjäger-Regiment der SS (tatarische Nr. 1)* in the summer of 1944. On July 8, 1944, however, the SS-FHA announced that, "by order of the *Reichsführer-SS*, Muslim Tatars evacuated from the Crimea are to be used to form the *Waffen-Gebirgs-Brigade der SS (tatarische Nr. 1)* in Hungary."

Under the command of *SS-Standartenführer* Fortenbacher, formation began in the area of the *Wehrmacht*'s commanding general in Hungary. The brigade submitted the following strength report on September 30, 1944:

Officers	NCOs	Enlisted Men	Total
11	191	2,219	2,421
0.5%	7.9%	91.6%	100%

After it proved impossible to achieve the planned formation with Crimean Tatars alone, approximately 1,100 ethnic Germans were attached to the unit. As a result, about thee months after the start of formation only about 1,300 Tatars were in the unit. As there was little prospect of adding to these numbers, the formation of a *Waffen-Gebirgs-Brigade der SS (tatarische Nr. 1)* must rather be seen from a propaganda point of view.

When the Russians reached the Danube near Apatin and Batina in October 1944, a battle group was formed from the approximately 800 ethnic German members and sent to *Divisionsgruppe "Lombard" (31. SS-Freiwilligen-Grenadier-Division)*. After it became apparent that the formation of the *Waffen-Gebirgs-Brigade der SS (tatarische Nr. 1)* could not be carried out due to shortages of materiel and manpower, the order for its disbandment was issued on December 31, 1944. The Crimean Tatars were incorporated into the *Osttürkischen Waffen-Verband der SS* (Eastern Turkish Armed SS Unit)—a catchment basin for Muslim volunteers from the USSR—as *Waffengruppe Krim*.

The order for its formation had been issued on October 1, 1944. Its predecessor was *Ostmuselmanische SS-Regiment 1* (East Muslim SS Regiment 1) formed in June 1944. It was formed from Turkmens working in Germany and Norway following negotiations between the *SS-Hauptamt, Dienststelle Sauckel*, and the *Wehrmacht* in June 1944 assisted by the commander of *SS-Sonderregiment "Dirlewanger"* in White Russia. With the formation order of October 1, 1944, the *SS-Hauptamt* announced:

> The Eastern Turkish armed unit of the SS serves to pool all available Eastern Turks (Turkestanis, Volga and Ural Tatars, Crimean Turks, Azerbaijanis, etc.), their military and political training and command, their organization into useful combat units, plus the carrying out of all cultural and propagandistic tasks.

Effective December 15, 1944, the *Osttürkische Waffen-Verband der SS* under the command of *SS-Standartenführer* Harun-el-Rashid Bey[25] (May 26, 1886 – March 29, 1963) was initially to be organized into three *Waffen-Gruppen*:

> *Waffen-Gruppe "Idel-Ural"* from *III./Ostmuselmanische SS-Regiment 1*
> *Waffen-Gruppe "Turkestan"* from *I.* and *II./ Ostmuselmanische SS-Regiment 1*
> *Waffen-Gruppe "Krim"* from *Waffen-Gebirgs-Brigade der SS (tatarische Nr. 1)*

Formed in Slovakia in December 1944, *II./Waffen-Gruppe "Turkestan" (Nr. 1)* deserted to the partisans. This still left the *Waffen-Gruppe* with three battalions. To make further desertions more difficult, the units were subsequently moved into the area north of Bergamo and placed under *SS-Brigadeführer und Generalmajor der Polizei* Karl-Heinz Berger (February 16, 1904 – December 2, 1988), the SS and Police Commander "Upper Italy-Center."

In March 1945, the Caucasian *Waffen-Verband der SS* was attached to *Waffen-Gruppe "Aserbeidschan."* As a result, near the end of the war the unit was again organized into four battalions with a total of about 3,800 men.

Rumania

The idea of recruiting Rumanians for service in the *Waffen-SS* came about after Rumania left the Axis alliance on August 23, 1944. The plans did not take shape, however, until large elements of the Rumanian 4th Infantry Division, by then fighting on the Russian side, were captured by the Germans on October 20, 1944, during the fighting in Hungary. The division commander, Brigadier-General Platon Chirnoaga (October 24, 1894 – March 29, 1947) immediately declared his interest in taking up the fight against the Russians with his men.

After discussions with Horia Sima (July 3, 1906 – May 25, 1993), leader of the Rumanian Iron Guard, who had been in exile in Germany since the spring of 1941, on November 1, 1944, Himmler ordered the formation of a *Waffen-Grenadier-Regiment der SS (rumänische Nr. 1)* as the foundation for the planned formation of a *Waffen-Grenadier-Division der SS (rumänische Nr. 1)*. The unit was to be organized like a *Volksgrenadier-Division*.

Brigadier-General Chirnoaga became minister of war in the Rumanian national government in exile formed in Vienna under Sima on December 10, 1944. About 2,000 Rumanian prisoners of war, who were in the Kaisersteinbrüch camp, volunteered. Their decision was based on an anti-Soviet attitude but also pragmatism: by the end of 1944 prisoners of war were being very poorly supplied. Rumanian armaments workers in Germany (most members of the iron Guard) also volunteered.

Russia

The *Waffen-SS* was very skeptical about Russian volunteers for a long time. From 1941 to 1944, however, police battalions were formed within the *Ordnungspolizei*, and these were attached to the senior SS and police commanders to fight partisans and guard military sites. A change occurred in June 1944, when the Volunteer Central Office "East" (*SS-Obersturmbannführer* Dr. Arlt) was set up in the *SS-Hauptamt*. *SS-Obersturmführer* Dr. Kröger took over the Russia Unit, which was later renamed *Sonderkommando "Ost"* and attached to the SD.

One of the first actions was the takeover of the Russian People's Defense Brigade "RONA" which, attached to the Senior SS and Police Commander "Russia Center," was about 4,000 men strong. Initially planned as the *Waffen-Sturmbrigade der SS "RONA,"* after discussions with Himmler in mid-August 1944, formation orders were issued for the *29.* and *30. Waffen-Grenadier-Division der SS (russische Nr. 1* and *2)*. While on the one hand the *Waffen-Sturmbrigade der SS "RONA"* was supposed to be expanded into the *29. Waffen-Grenadier-Division der SS*, the *30. Waffen-Grenadier-Division der SS* was to be formed from police battalions concentrated in *Schutzmannschaft-Brigade "Siegling."*

After the nominal *29. Waffen-Grenadier-Division der SS* proved to be unfit for operations and was disbanded in October 1944, the *30. Waffen-Grenadier-Division der SS* at least saw action for a time in the west. The changing morale with the rapidly sinking motivation of the foreign volunteers is reflected in an order issued by the commander of the *30. Waffen-Grenadier-Division der SS (russische Nr. 2)* in August 1944:

The division has arrived in the temporary quartering area, on old German soil. The task of the officers and non-commissioned officers is, through intensive training, to make the men into capable SS soldiers in the shortest possible time. The human material is good, strong and robust. All of them no longer have a home. The company, battalion, regiment will become their new homes. It is up to us Germans how we shape this new home.

To do this it is necessary that we see all foreigners as equal comrades, just as the opposite should be true. It is completely unacceptable—as has happened—for foreigners to be called bandits or Bolsheviks or whatever, or to be struck. We do not need that. A soldier who fails to carry out an order will be brought before a summary court martial for failure to obey orders and is unacceptable as a soldier in the unit. Anyone who must resort to blow or verbal abuse to have his orders carried out is no non-commissioned officer.

Everyone should keep in mind that our foreigners will be fighting side by side with us in the foreseeable future. If we succeed in drawing and binding the foreigners to us, awaken and encourage their pride and offer them proof that they are equal comrades, not just externally in uniform but also internally, then we will have the most loyal fighters with us.

The doctors will conduct physical examinations to quickly identify all of those foreigners who, for physical reasons, are not suited to remain with the unit.

Battalion medics are to assist the regimental medical officer. Documentation of those found unfit is to be submitted by way of the battalions immediately.

The documentation is to also include those foreigners who are unsuited to remain with the unit for other reasons.[26]

The units are to provide regular instruction on how to behave in the quartering area. The unit commander will inform the residents of the quartering area in a suitable manner that any abuses, no matter how minor, are to be reported to the unit commanders immediately.

These directives are interesting in a number of respects. On the one hand they illustrate the attitude of the division commander, who was just thirty-two years old, and on the other make clear the problems caused by the hasty formation of the division. As later events would demonstrate, the division had about 3,000 foreign troops who had no interest in continuing in German service. The offenses and the corporal punishment by the overage German cadre personnel (some more than forty-five years of age) showed the helplessness to deal with the situation. One should note that most of the officers and NCOs had previously served in the police battalions and were familiar with the mentality of the foreigners. In total, about 15,000 Russians were members of the *Waffen-SS* for varying lengths of time.

Serbia

After the end of the Balkan campaign in April 1941, Serbia was placed under German military administration. Serbian Army General Milan Nedić (September 2, 1878 – February 4, 1946) was named prime minister and formed a government at the end of August 1941. Among the Serbian forces authorized by the Germans to maintain internal order was the Serbian Volunteer Corps founded in Belgrade on September 15, 1941.

In it served primarily anti-communist volunteers, most of whom were members of the Yugoslav National Movement (ZBOR). By the summer of 1944 the Serbian Volunteer Corps, which was under the Military Commander "Southeast," was supposed to be expanded to almost 14,000 men. Developments in the situation prevented this, however. Because of the Red Army's advance, in October 1944 the units, with a strength of barely 5,000 men, were transferred to Istria into the area of the Senior SS and Police Commander "Adriatic Coastland." Like the Cossacks, the Serbian Volunteer Corps, which had proved itself extremely well in the fighting against the Tito partisans, was transferred to the *Waffen-SS* on November 27, 1944. Again there was no external indication of the change, nor was it explicitly explained to the Serbian volunteers. The German cadre personnel were attached to the *Waffen-SS* for the duration of the war.

Spaniards

After the start of the German offensive against the Soviet Union, with Hitler's agreement General Franco (December 4, 1892 – November 20, 1975), the Spanish head of state, authorized the formation of a volunteer division. The volunteers left Spain on July 13, 1941, and the *250.*

(spanische) Infanterie-Division was formed at the "Grafenwöhr" Training Camp, its strength just under 20,000 men. Attached to the army—Himmler had no interest in the Latin Spaniards—the division fought at the front before Leningrad and at the Volkhov. The unit suffered casualties of 3,092 killed and 8,204 wounded from October 1941 until April 1943.

In the autumn of 1943, there was a change in Spanish policy: under pressure from the western allies and the general progress of the war, General Franco ordered the return of the Spanish volunteers. The men assembled in Jamburg, however in November 1943, about 1,500 Spaniards volunteered for a so-called Spanish Legion, which was roughly equal to a regiment in strength. Three months later, however, Franco also ordered these men home.

In fact, however, approximately 400 Spaniards remained in Germany despite the order and were assembled at the "Stablack" Training Camp. The troops were not committed en masse, to avoid compromising Spain. While about half continued to serve in the *Wehrmacht*, for example in the *3. Gebirgs-Division*, the other half were taken into the *Waffen-SS*.

Initially they were placed under the politically farsighted Wallonian Rexist leader Leon Degrelle (June 15, 1906 – March 31, 1994). The Spaniards formed a company in the *5. SS-Freiwilligen-Sturmbrigade "Wallonien"* formed after the fighting in the Cherkassy Pocket. At the end of April 1944, the Spanish volunteers arrived at SS Training Camp "Heidelager" near Debica and ultimately took part in the fighting in Estonia. Then, in 1945, the Spaniards were attached to the *Waffen-Gebirgs[Karstjäger]-Brigade der SS*, which was chronically short of personnel.

Ukraine

After the defeat at Stalingrad, *SS-Brigadeführer* Dr. Wächter, governor of the district of Galicia, proposed to the *SS-Hauptamt* that Ukrainian volunteers be recruited from the Generalgouvernement for military service. He was thinking primarily of the roughly 3.5 million Greek–Orthodox Ukrainians living in his district.[27] There was also a large Greek Orthodox Ukrainian population in the Lublin District. On April 14, 1943, *SS-Oberstgruppenführer und Generaloberst der Polizei* Daluege, commander of the *Ordnungspolizei*, commented on the various religious denominations of the Ukrainians in the Generalgouvernement:

> A frontline division is being formed for the *Waffen-SS* and by the *Waffen-SS* which is made up of Greek-Catholic Ukrainians and will probably be called the Galician Division; for these Ukrainians come from Galicia. The remaining Ukrainians in the Generalgouvernement, from the Lublin area, are Greek-Orthodox. They are being made available to us for the formation of police regiments.

The Ukrainians living in Galicia to be recruited were initially supposed to be between seventeen and thirty years of age and have a minimum height of 1.6 meters. With an average birth cohort of 25,000 men, the prospective number of Greek–Orthodox Ukrainian recruits was in excess of 500,000. As the majority of them were already serving in the Red Army and others were working in the German armaments industry, this number was reduced accordingly. Regardless of age restrictions, the appeal for volunteers to serve in the later *14. Waffen-Grenadier-Division der SS (galizische Nr. 1)* received an overwhelming response. The first recruiting wave brought in approximately 80,000 volunteers. Even though the physical examinations were quite liberal, only about 10% of the volunteers were found to be fit for service in the division.

After a second recruiting phase lasting until September 1943, a total of about 12,000 volunteers were taken into the *Waffen-SS* by the end of the year. In addition, about 8,000 men from older age classes, plus Greek–Orthodox Ukrainians from the Lublin District, formed Galician SS Volunteer Regiments 4 to 7. The German authorities intentionally designated these units, which were attached to the *Ordnungspolizei*, as SS volunteer regiments so as to avoid feelings of discrimination. SS volunteer Michael Werkalec remembered:

I was born in the Ukrainian Carpathians in 1922. When the German *Wehrmacht* reached the Ukraine in 1941, many young people were recruited to work in the German war industry. Regular deportations[28] began after the number of volunteers proved insufficient. Many fled into the forests, and this led to the formation of the Ukrainian Resistance Army (UPA). As this was poorly armed, our leaders told us to volunteer for the *SS-Frei-willigen-Division "Galizien."* Let them train and arm you. One day we will use you! And so in early 1943, after a physical examination, I arrived at SS Training Camp Heidelager. I was transferred for special training: I was sent to Mühlhausen in Alsace, others to Holland or to the Protectorate of Bohemia and Moravia. After about two months I returned to the division, which by then was on Neuhammer am Queiss.

As the division never achieved its authorized strength despite the relaxed physical and entrance requirements, at the end of January 1944, Galician Volunteer Regiments 6 and 7 released a total of 1,945 men to the division. A final recruiting wave began in spring 1944 and ended just a few weeks before the Red Army entered the country. In May and June 1944, SS Volunteer Regiments 4 and 5 also transferred about 1,500 men to the *14. SS-Freiwilligen-Division.* Men from older age classes were also attached to the concentration camp guard units.

Approximately 11,000 of the division's 15,000 Ukrainians took part in the first action in the summer of 1944. The remaining 4,000 were used in part to form the third battalions of the three *Waffen-Grenadier-Regiment der SS.* In addition, approximately 4,000 Ukrainians—including elements of *SS-Freiwilligen-Regimenter 4* and 5 and volunteers taken in during the first half of 1944—were in *Waffen-Grenadier-Ausbildungs- und Ersatz-Regiment der SS 14.*

After about 6,000 Ukrainians deserted to the UPA, were killed or captured by the Soviets after the fighting in the Brody Pocket, at the end of September 1944, the roughly 5,000 survivors of the first action, together with the *Waffen-Grenadier-Ausbildungs- und Ersatz-Regiment der SS 14*, totaled roughly 13,000 men. After its first action, Himmler described the unit as follows:

> [The] division consisted not of German soldiers prepared to fight to the end, but of Ukrainians from Galicia, internally weak and fickle and lacking all of the German manly and military virtues.

In fact, in two years of war the unit saw only two weeks of action and both times displayed no outstanding performance or motivation. Altogether about 20,000 Ukrainians were enlisted in the *Waffen-SS.*

Hungary

In Hungary, the year 1944 was marked by political turmoil. On October 15, 1944, this culminated in the proclamation by Reich Administrator Admiral von Horthy in which he called upon the army to lay down its weapons and asked the Allies for a ceasefire. Rudolf Rahn (March 16, 1900 – January 7, 1975), the German ambassador in Budapest, took action immediately, and an official denial was broadcast by radio just an hour later. The government and the Reich administrator stepped down and the next day the fascist Ferenc Szálasi (January 6, 1897 – March 12, 1946) formed a new government whose policies were completely aligned with Germany.

The new prime minister immediately ordered the reorganization of the desperate Hungarian Army. In cooperation with the German Reich, Colonel-General Karoly Beregfy (February 12, 1888 – March 12, 1946), Hungary's minister of war, was supposed to form eight new divisions from the existing roughly 220,000 Hungarian troops and newly-drafted Hungarians. Four of these were planned as *Waffen-SS* divisions.

Himmler inspects the *14. Galizische SS-Freiwilligen-Division* at Training Camp Heidelager.

...rigadeführer Freitaag, the division commander, presents ...

... his unit's officer corps to Himmler.

SS-Brigadeführer Freitag (left) with Heinrich Himmler (center), and *SS-Brigadeführer* Dr. Wächter, the governor of the District of Lvov.

An "*Agreement for the formation of a Hungarian Armed SS Division—based largely on volunteers*" was reached between Senior SS and Police Commander Winkelmann and Colonel-General Beregfy on October 23, 1944. This was followed by an order from the Honvéd minister to carry out the formation. It allowed career and reserve officers and recruits from age classes 1914 to 1927 to volunteer. A knowledge of German was desirable for officers and mandatory for staff officers. The volunteers came forward for different reasons. While there were probably recruits who did not know that they were volunteering for an SS division,[29] others probably came for reasons of the promises made by the *Waffen-SS*. It advertised that the recruits would be well trained for six months and be well fed and equipped. This was an incentive for many, for the alternative was being sent into action with Hungarian units virtually untrained and under-armed.

In excess of 30,000 Hungarians signed up by the end of December 1944. More volunteers were sent to the three *Waffen-Divisionen der SS* in formation until March 1945, bringing the total number of Hungarians who signed up to serve in the *Waffen-SS* to about 42,000. The only action they saw was when the Red Army approached the training camps and battle groups covered the withdrawal of their comrades.

The *Waffen-SS* in Action[30]

As previously stated, the *Waffen-SS* reached a total strength of almost a million members during the course of the war. In addition to smaller independent formations, for example *SS-Wehrgeologen-Bataillon 500*, the majority of them served in divisions, which originally consisted of about 20,000 men but by the end of the war in some cases had authorized strengths of only about 12,000 men. The following is a chronological description of operations involving the approximately forty *Waffen-SS* divisions.

The first action in which the *Waffen-SS* took part with its own divisions was the campaign in Western Europe in 1940. Always attached to *Wehrmacht* army corps at first, as the *Waffen-SS* steadily grew; the first SS army corps was formed in 1942. As a rule, these corps commanded two or three SS divisions. After Himmler took over the position of commander of the Replacement Army, army divisions were also attached to SS army corps.

The first SS panzer corps was formed in the spring of 1943 during the fighting at Kharkov and it had a total strength of more than 60,000 men. During the defensive battles in Normandy in the summer of 1944, two SS panzer corps were deployed in the same sector of front, and during the major German offensives in the Ardennes in December 1944, and Hungary in spring 1945 a total of about 100,000 SS members saw action. Both offensives were unsuccessful.

Before the Second World War, the *I.* and *II. Sturmbann* of the *Leibstandarte-SS Adolf Hitler* took part in the march into the Saarland on March 1, 1935. Three years later they participated in the march into Austria, together with the *SS-Standarten 1 "Deutschland"* and *2 "Germania."* Former *SS-Mann* Herbert Kühl remembered:

> Late on the afternoon of March 13, 1938, the LAH—attached to the *2. Panzer-Division*—entered Vienna before cheering crowds. We frequently had to stop, and people rushed the vehicles. Girls crowded into our *Kübelwagen*. Our mixed formation reached Hietzig, where our *14. Kompanie* found quarters in a school. In the days that followed, our neighbors treated us to delicious apple strudel, and as a result of many invitations we got to know the specialties of Viennese cooking. Unable to get rid of the pea soup, the senior NCO drove to the less-well-off sections of the city and distributed it there.
>
> Our uniforms and leather things, dusty after a journey of 1,000 kilometers, were cleaned and polished for the *Wehrmacht* parade on the ring road on March 15, 1938.

The *1. SS-Totenkopf-Standarte "Oberbayern"* demonstrated its military training during a parade for the Hungarian Reich Administrator Admiral Horthy on August 20, 1938.

Young recruits of the *10. SS-Totenkopf-Standarte*.

As of February 25, 1941, members of the former reinforced *SS-Totenkopf-Standarten* wore the *sig-runen* on their collar patches.

Our *14. Kompanie* formed a cordon in the area of the *Führer* stage. Infantry, artillery and tanks, plus units of the Austrian Federal Army marched past, bringing up the rear the twelve companies of the LAH. Behind me stood an elderly but lively woman who kept us entertained, and on seeing our regiment she said: "Such fine young men."

While the *SS-Verfügungstruppe*—including *SS-Standarte 3 "Der Führer"* formed in Vienna in spring 1938—together with the *2. SS-Totenkopf-Standarte "Brandenburg"* and the *3. SS-Totenkopf-Standarte "Thüringen"* marched into the Sudetenland in October 1938, the *1. SS-Totenkopf-Standarte "Oberbayern"* had been deployed in the "Ascher Zipfel" (Sudetenland) to support *Freikorps "Henlein"* in September 1938, prior to the conclusion of the Munich Agreement.

1939

In mid-March 1939, the above-named SS units, with a total strength of about 10,000 men, took part in the occupation of rump Czechoslovakia (Bohemia and Moravia). Elements of the *SS-Verfügungstruppe* subsequently undertook guard and ceremonial duties in Prague for a time—attached to the Reich Protector of Bohemia and Moravia.

At the end of August 1939, the **Leibstandarte-SS Adolf Hitler** moved to Upper Silesia, into the area of the *XIII. Armee-Korps* (*8. Armee*). Initially attached to the *17. Division*, after several days it was attached to the *4. Panzer-Division* in the *XVI. Armee-Korps*. It fought in the Bzura sector and from September 21, 1939, was part of the siege ring in front of Modlin as part of the *XV. Armee-Korps*. Before the end of the campaign in Poland it was transferred to the Protectorate of Bohemia and Moravia. After about six weeks it was moved from there into the Coblenz area and attached to the *XIX. Armee-Korps*.

The formation order for *Panzer-Verband "Ostpreußen"* was issued in July 1939. It was also called *Panzer-Division "Kempff"* after its commander. The unit was a combination of army units and elements of the **SS-Verfügungstruppe**. The reason for this lay on the one hand in the *Wehrmacht* command's desire to keep the SS units under the army's tight control, while it also wanted to form a motorized armored formation in East Prussia for the coming campaign in Poland without alerting enemy intelligence by removing an entire panzer division from the Reich. In addition to the SS troops attached to this unit, **SS-Standarte 3 "Der Führer"** was deployed in the Westwall, **SS-Standarte 2 "Germania"** was attached to AOK 14 (Headquarters, 14th Army), and the **SS-Pioneer-Sturmbann** to the *10. Armee*. *Panzer-Verband "Ostpreußen"* initially attacked the Polish fortress of Rozan on the Narev River and then advanced towards Lomza. On September 10, 1939, the division halted its advance on Lomza and rushed to Brok on the River Bug. When the ring around Warsaw was closed on September 16, 1939, the order was issued for action in front of Fortress Modlin. Sent to the area northeast of Modlin near Nasielsk, about 110 kilometers away, *Panzer-Verband "Kempff"* relieved the *228. Infanterie-Division* in the siege ring. Before the planned assault on the fortress, however, the Poles surrendered on September 29, 1939. On October 1, 1939, the SS units moved to the Brdy–Wald training camp east of Pilsen in the Protectorate of Bohemia and Moravia. Formation of the **SS-Verfügungs-Division** began there. After less than two months the unit was ordered into the Würzburg area under the *XIV. Armee-Korps*.

While the units of the *SS-Verfügungstruppe* had seen action at the front, the **SS-Totenkopf-Verbände** had been given special assignments. The **1. SS-Totenkopf-Standarte "Oberbayern,"** together with the **3. SS-Totenkopf-Standarte "Thüringen,"** had been deployed in the rear of the *10. Armee* and in cooperation with the *Sicherheitspolizei* and SD executed many Jews and Poles. The **2. SS-Totenkopf-Standarte "Brandenburg"** was attached to *Einsatzgruppe III* in the rear of the *8. Armee*. On September 24, 1939, in reaction to the so-called "Bloody Bromberg Sunday"—about 1,200 ethnic Germans had been murdered by Poles there on September 3–4—it shot approximately 800 Poles in the Bromberg area alone. **SS-Heimwehr-Danzig,**

On November 4, 1939, Himmler inspected the formation of the *SS-Totenkopf-Division* in the Dachau concentration camp, which had been emptied for the purpose. Note the words on the left gate: "*Arbeit macht frei!*"

In February 1940, before the campaign against France, Himmler inspected the division again at Training Camp Münsingen.

made up of members of the *4. SS-Totenkopf-Standarte "Ostmark"* plus the *1. SS-Totenkopf-Standarte "Oberbayern"* and volunteers from Danzig, fought in and around the city of Danzig. At the end of September 1939, it was ordered to Dachau, together with the three *SS-Totenkopf-Standarten* which had taken part in the campaign in Poland. There, in the emptied concentration camp, they were to form the *SS-Totenkopf-Division*.

1940

After the campaign in Poland, in late 1939/early 1940, the *6., 7., 8., 9.,* and *10. SS-Totenkopf-Standarte* were formed with newly-recruited Reich German volunteers. While the *8.* and later the *10. SS-Totenkopf-Standarte* were stationed in Cracow, at the end of April 1940, the *6., 7.,* and *9. SS-Totenkopf-Standarte* were sent to Norway to act as occupation troops. Just prior to this, the *11., 12., 13., 14., 15.,* and *16. SS-Totenkopf-Standarte* and the *1.* and *2. SS-Totenkopf-Reiterstandarte* had also been formed.

In preparation for the coming campaign in Western Europe in 1940, the *Leibstandarte-SS Adolf Hitler* was moved into the Rheine area and on May 10, 1940, it took part in the attack on the Netherlands. Three days later, attached to the *9. Panzer-Division*, it saw action near Rotterdam and Delft. Following the rapid surrender, the reinforced regiment moved through Belgium into the Valenciennes area in France. Attached to the *1. Panzer-Division* on May 24, the SS troops saw fierce fighting southwest of Dunkirk. In the course of this, about eighty British prisoners of war were shot on May 28, 1940. The unit marched south through Cambrai into the St. Etienne area, meeting little resistance. After the ceasefire with France on July 4, 1940, it was ordered to Metz. There the *Leibstandarte-SS Adolf Hitler* was increased to brigade strength.

In January 1940, the *SS-Totenkopf-Division* was sent to Training Camp Münsingen for training. Ordered into the Korbach area for the campaign in the west, the division's troops went into action on May 19. They initially advanced towards Cambrai, then beginning on May 24, 1940, they saw heavy action at la Bassée Canal and suffered heavy casualties. After British troops allegedly shot at members of the division with "dum-dum" bullets, ninety-nine British prisoners of war were subsequently liquidated as a reprisal. Taken out of the main line of resistance on May 31, 1940, after two weeks rest the division was ordered south to Bordeaux via Lyon. It secured the area to the Spanish border, meeting little resistance. After the ceasefire, on July 13, 1940, the division was transferred to the Avallon area and in August back to Bordeaux. The division remained there until the end of the year.

At the end of 1939, members of the *Ordnungspolizei* formed the *Polizei-Division* at Wandern training camp. In January 1940, it was moved to the Westwall on the Kaiserstuhl area. From there it took part in the campaign in the west and southwest of Sedan it marched towards Vouziers. Initially marching behind the motorized units and seeing no combat, the division pursued French troops east of Bar le Duc to Neufchauteau and Besancon. There it received news of the ceasefire. As of July 10, 1940, the division was used as an occupation unit in St. Dizier, then on August 2, the troops were sent to Suippes training camp. There the unit was reorganized and renamed the *SS-Polizei-Division*.

Formation of the *SS-Division "Germania"* began in Bavaria in September 1940. In addition to Germans, the division was to include volunteers from Holland, Flanders, Denmark, Norway, and Finland. These high expectations were not met, however, and almost 90% of the division consisted of Reich German recruits from the 1918 age class and younger. In training until the end of the year, on December 21, 1940, the unit was renamed *SS-Division "Wiking."*

1941

The reinforced *Leibstandarte-SS Adolf Hitler* moved to Rumania in mid-January 1941, and nine weeks later to Bulgaria. From there the brigade—like the *SS-Division "Reich"*—took part in the campaign in the Balkans in April 1941. As part of the *XXXX. Armee-Korps (mot.)*, it

The automobile standard of the *Leibstandarte SS Adolf Hitler*.

The *Leibstandarte* was one of the first SS formations to receive field grey uniforms.

Members of the LAH at the Reich Party Congress in Nuremberg 1937.

Himmler inspects the *Leibstandarte SS Adolf Hitler* in Larissa (Greece) after the Balkans campaign, 1941.

fought Yugoslavian troops near Monastir on April 8–9, and on April 10, took part in the invasion of Greece. While the *SS-Division "Reich"* met no resistance while occupying Belgrade and then secured the area to Rumania and Hungary, the reinforced *Leibstandarte-SS Adolf Hitler* was involved in fierce fighting with Greek units at the Klisura Pass. After Greece's surrender, the *Leibstandarte-SS Adolf Hitler* was quickly brought up to division strength in Ostmark (Austria) in preparation for the coming campaign against Russia.

In an equally ad hoc fashion, the **SS-Division "Nord"** was formed from the earlier 6. and 7. *SS-Totenkopf-Standarte* in Norway. Thus the party troops—since 1940 designated *Waffen-SS*—went into the "struggle against Bolshevism" with a total of six divisions and about 120,000 men. Contrary to Himmler's wishes, however, these were not specially selected and led members of his "order." *SS-Hauptsturmführer* Ruoff, then 1st General Staff Officer of the *SS-Division "Nord,"* remembered the tactical value of his division:

> There were no signals communications with any command authorities nor from headquarters to *SS-Infanterie-Regiment 7*. I became aware of technical defects in the demeanor of the soldiers while on the ship. When I asked my *1. Ordonnanz-Offizier* (staff officer responsible for maps, war diary, and other official documents) about this, he replied: "Yes, don't you know that the men have not had any battle training at all […] the officer corps consists almost entirely of officers from the *Allgemeine-SS*, the NCO corps of NCOs from the same place. All retained their ranks when they transferred from the *Allgemeine-SS*."
>
> A map exercise laid on in the conference room revealed that the officer corps was unfamiliar with even the basic principles of tactics. This made it clear to me that the unit was unfit for use in the field. The commanding officer disagreed strongly with this. The views he expressed at the map exercise indicated that he was going to lead the battle group in action by means of orders issued to the officer corps at 1,000 each day. He responded to my vigorous opposition with complete incomprehension.

And the first action by *SS-Division "Nord,"* which began on July 1, 1941, turned into a complete fiasco. On that day the men attacked the Soviet fortress of Salla in Karelia (Finland) and were stopped in front of the well-fortified enemy positions. Heavy enemy fire led to chaos, which ultimately led to a near-panic flight back to the starting positions. Himmler was dismayed and gave a speech to replacement personnel of the division in Stettin on July 14, 1941, in which he stated that events like the one before Salla put the reputation of the *Waffen-SS* at risk.

Some of the other *Waffen-SS* divisions had also suffered heavy casualties, but in battle they had at least proved equal to units of the army. The *SS-Division* **Leibstandarte-SS Adolf Hitler** attacked from the area north of Lvov (Generalgouvernement) in the direction of Kiev as part of *Panzergruppe 1* and then turned south towards Odessa. After again turning east, on October 17, 1941, the division took Taganrog after fierce fighting. One month later, in temperatures of -30 degrees, the SS men attacked in the direction of Rostov, however they were forced to fall back to their starting positions, which ultimately became their winter quarters.

The **SS-Division "Reich"** was attached to *Panzergruppe 2* in the area east of Lublin and on June 28, 1941, advanced towards Minsk. While *SS-Infanterie-Regiment 11* (former *11. SS-Totenkopf-Standarte*) was tasked with combing the surrounding forests, the other units advanced across the Beresina towards the Dniepr. There they ran into the Stalin Line, which was to be the scene of very costly fighting. The division succeeded in crossing the river on July 11, 1941, and reached the Desna near Yelnya (approximately seventy kilometers southeast of Smolensk). Extremely heavy fighting developed and the Soviets, enjoying superiority in the air and outnumbering the Germans in men and materiel, inflicted very heavy casualties. The commanding general of the *XXXXVI. Panzer-Korps* praised the efforts of the German troops, which had been forced onto the defensive, in an order of the day:

> After one of the fierce defensive battles on Yelnya's northeastern front, the Förster Squad of *1./SS-Kradschützen-Bataillon*, whose assignment was to secure the company's left flank, was found as follows:
>
> The squad leader, *SS-Unterscharführer* Förster, shot in the head with his hand on the fuse cord of his last hand grenade.
>
> Machine-gunner *SS-Rottenführer* Klaiber, shot in the head, his machine-gun still pressed against his shoulder and a round in the chamber.
>
> Assistant gunners *SS-Sturmmann* Buschner, *SS-Schütze* Schyma, dead in the rifle pits.
>
> The solo dispatch rider, *SS-Sturmmann* Oldeboerhuis, dead by his motorcycle, kneeling with his hands on the handlebars, killed as he was about to deliver the final message.
>
> The driver, *SS-Sturmmann* Schwenk, dead in his foxhole.
>
> The only enemy seen were dead, lying in a semicircle around the position within hand grenade range.
>
> An example of the term "defense!" We stand in awe before such heroism!
>
> I have instructed that these names be published in the Honor Roll of the German Army.

In contrast to the disastrous to the disastrous action by *SS-Division "Nord"* in Karelia, such a battle was precisely in line with Himmler's wishes. After about 2,400 members of the *SS-Division "Reich"* had become casualties—killed, wounded, or missing—in barely four weeks, the unit moved south and took part in the final battles in the area of the Kiev Pocket. This was followed by actions to form a new pocket near Briansk and Vyazma beginning on October 6, 1941. After these successes the division was sent back to the Yelnya area, where it was supposed to breach the Moscow defense position and enter the Soviet capital. In temperatures as low as -45 degrees, the leading troops managed to fight their way to within about seventeen kilometers of Moscow. When the Red Army launched its big counterattack on December 5, 1941, the troops were forced to withdraw behind the Istra River and occupy winter positions.

The **SS-Totenkopf-Division**, which was attached to *Panzergruppe 4*, suffered even heavier losses. On June 24, 1941, it marched out of East Prussia and made for Dvinsk. On July 6, the division attacked from the Rosenow area to break through the Stalin Line near Sebesh. In four days of fighting, it lost just under 1,800 men killed and wounded. In those days, *SS-Oberscharführer* Weininger (*III./SS-Totenkopf-Artillerie-Regiment*) wrote a letter to his wife in which he expressed his thoughts about the sense of the Second World War, which were representative of those felt by most Germans:

> Once again I can devote a few free minutes to you and quickly tell you that I am healthy and doing well. This war here is very definitely—very different than the one against France and never before have I so desired peace and cleanliness as I do right now. It is simply impossible to describe the conditions here; one has to have seen everything with one's own eyes to be able to grasp it all! Yes, I can only tell you over and over again that I will be overjoyed when it is all over. Not that we are afraid of dying, for we have long since become accustomed to it and if it takes us there is nothing we can do about it; but the constant rush, the dirt and dust, the constant separation and loneliness, this confusion etc, over time makes one physically and spiritually ill. Thank God that at least we have the consolation that we are not fighting for nothing, because it is for our homeland and

through it we are ensuring a safe life for our loved ones. Even if many of us never get to see home again, everything we have endured and suffered here will not have been in vain, for our future is at stake! We must and do think that way—otherwise everything would be much worse! It's just beginning to get uncomfortable here again, another comrade has been killed and we have to go from this spot. But don't worry, somehow this war will also pass and we hope that we come home again in one piece.

At the end of August 1941, the *SS-Totenkopf-Division* reached Staraya Rusa by way of Opochka and Porshov. By that time the division had suffered an unbelievable total of 4,854 casualties. From then until the end of the year it engaged in further heavy fighting in the area south of Lake Ilmen—without proper winter clothing—and suffered further enormous losses.

On June 30, 1941, the **SS-Polizei-Division**, also part of *Panzergruppe 4*, marched out of East Prussia through Lithuania into Russia. Not until a month later, however, did it begin the attack towards Luga. The heavy fighting lasted until September 1, 1941. By the time the *SS-Polizei-Division* was able to cross the river of the same name, it had lost about 1,000 men killed, and more than 2,000 wounded. The unit was ordered north towards Leningrad and beginning on September 9, had to endure further fierce fighting near Krasnogvardeysk. The division's troops then moved into winter positions in the siege ring around Leningrad.

The **SS-Division "Wiking"** suffered lighter casualties. At the end of June 1941, it advanced out of the Lvov area towards Ternopol as part of *Panzergruppe 1* and from there advanced quickly eastward. Redirected south, on about August 20, 1941, the units reached the Dnepropetrovsk area. It had covered more than 1,000 kilometers in barely two months. After a fierce but successful battle for Dnepropetrovsk, at the beginning of November the division attacked towards Rostov. A bridgehead was established across the Mius, but this had to be abandoned after a few days because of fierce Soviet counterattacks. It subsequently occupied winter positions near Uspenskaya behind the Mius River.

The **SS-Kavallerie-Brigade**, formed from the two *SS-Totenkopf-Reiter-Standarten*, plus **SS-Brigade 1 (mot.)** created from the *8.* and *10. SS-Totenkopf-Standarte*, were directly attached to the *Reichsführer-SS'* operations staff and were initially used for special operations. These included pacifying the rear areas, which resulted in many mass executions of civilians plus suspected partisans, Jews, and Soviet prisoners of war.

1942

The year 1942 began very quietly for the **SS-Division Leibstandarte-SS Adolf Hitler** and remained so as it went on. In July 1942, the division was transferred to France, and on July 29, 1942, in Paris it paraded before *Generalfeldmarschall* Gerd von Rundstedt (December 12, 1875 – February 24, 1953), the Commander-in-Chief West. The rest of the year was spent reorganizing as an *SS-Panzergrenadier-Division*.

The year progressed in a similar fashion for the **SS-Division "Reich."** Unlike the *Leibstandarte*, however, it first had to endure several very difficult and costly defensive battles at Rzhev and Olino. Transferred to France in July, the division was rehabilitated and by the end of the year was reorganized as an *SS-Panzergrenadier-Division*.

The **SS-Totenkopf-Division** had to face equally fierce battles southeast of Lake Ilmen and in February 1942, it was part of a German force of 96,000 troops encircled by the Red Army in the Demyansk area. The fighting raged back and forth and this seriously delayed the division's withdrawal from action for transfer to France, where it was to be rehabilitated and reorganized as an *SS-Panzergrenadier-Division*. As for the first two divisions, the necessary orders had been issued in July 1942—however the last members of the *SS-Totenkopf-Division* did not leave Russia until mid-October. During the occupation of Vichy France, in November 1942, the unit moved to the Montpelier area on the Mediterranean coast. In mid-December the division was transferred to Angouleme for further training.

The *SS-Polizei-Division* was withdrawn from the Leningrad siege ring in mid-February 1942, and moved to the Volkhov sector. The Red Army had broken through to the west between the *16.* and *18. Armee*. The German troops succeeded in sealing off the breakthrough and by the end of June 1942, destroyed the enemy forces encircled in the primeval forest. The unit was subsequently ordered back to the Krasny–Bor–Kolpino area in front of Leningrad and there it experienced fierce defensive fighting at the end of the year.

The *SS-Division "Wiking"* remained in its winter positions until mid-July 1942, and then attacked Rostov a second time as part of the *LVII. Panzer-Korps*. *SS-Funker* Hans Erlewein described the quiet first half of the year in a letter to his mother:

> I am now finally back where I belong. We arrived at the company yesterday evening. The battalion commander was the first to welcome us. He recognized me immediately when I said my name. He has been promoted to *SS-Sturmbannführer* and has the German Cross in Gold. The journey was uneventful, only once did our flak have to go into action. The front is three kilometers away and we will be going forward this evening. Believe me, I am telling the complete truth, one doesn't hear a shot all day and all night. The front is as quiet as it is for you at home and it will probably stay that way for a few more weeks.

The unit took Rostov on July 23, 1942, and then marched almost unopposed across the Kuban south towards Maykop. Then in mid-September it was transferred to the area surrounding Mozdok on the Terek, about 350 kilometers away. There was fierce fighting there. In December of that year, the unit, by then designated *SS-Panzergrenadier-Division "Wiking,"* received marching orders for the Proletarskaya area, almost 500 kilometers distant. There it was to reinforce the *4. Panzer-Armee*, which had set out to relieve Stalingrad. The relief of Stalingrad was out of the question; however, the units were continuously attacked by the Red Army and forced to make a fighting withdrawal.

Things were easier for *SS-Division "Nord,"* which based on an order issued on January 15, 1942, was to be reorganized as an *SS-Gebirgs-Division*. Deployed in a secondary theater in Karelia, through all of 1942 the division did not even lose 300 killed from a total strength of more than 21,000 soldiers. In 1941, the *SS-Totenkopf-Division* lost far more many men in just four days of combat.

SS-Gebirgs-Division "Südost," made up of ethnic Germans from southeastern Europe, was formed in Serbia on March 1, 1942, and soon afterwards was renamed *SS-Freiwilligen-Gebirgs-Division "Prinz Eugen."* After about half a year of training, the unit was transferred from the Banat to southern Serbia to fight partisans.

The *SS-Kavallerie-Brigade* was expanded into the *SS-Kavallerie-Division*, also by recruiting ethnic Germans, in the spring of 1942. The first elements of the division received their orders to move to the Eastern Front in mid-August 1942, the remaining elements in October. First used to again secure the rear areas against partisans and to secure those fit for work and agricultural products, at the end of November 1942, it was sent to close a gap in the front north of Smolensk.

1943

The year 1943 brought a combined action in the Kharkov area by the *SS-Panzergrenadier-Divisionen "Leibstandarte-SS Adolf Hitler," "Das Reich,"* and *"Totenkopf."* All three were transferred from France to the Eastern Front at the turn of the year and there they took part in changeable, but ultimately successful operations. They helped the German side consolidate

Himmler inspects *SS-Kampf-gruppe* (SS Battle Group) *"Nord"* at Drammen, Norway on January 30, 1941. From left to right: *SS-Standarten-führer* Krüger, *SS-Oberführer* Voss (C.O. SS-T.I.R. 6), *SS-Gruppenführer* Wolff, *Reichsführer-SS* Himmler, *SS-Oberführer* Oberg, and *SS-Brigadeführer* Hermann (C.O. SS-T.I.R. 7).

Members of *SS-Gebirgs-Division "Nord."*

A Soviet deserter was obviously a special event for these SS members.

A photograph taken immediately after an action.

the precarious situation, but losses were again very heavy. The *SS-Panzergrenadier-Division "Leibstandarte-SS Adolf Hitler"* alone lost more than 4,500 men killed, wounded, and missing. The *SS-Panzergrenadier-Division "Das Reich"* suffered roughly the same number of casualties. The *SS-Panzergrenadier-Division "Totenkopf"* had 2,700 men killed, wounded, or missing in the spring of 1943. Because of these losses, the three divisions were rehabilitated in preparation for the German summer offensive in the Kharkov area. "Operation *Zitadelle*" began in the Kursk area on July 5, 1943. Because of poor weather conditions (steady rain), the Red Army's in-depth defense positions, plus the enemy's superiority in men and materiel, Hitler called off the offensive on July 13, 1943. The desired pincer operation by the *4. Panzer-Armee* from the south and the *9. Armee* from the north had proved impossible to achieve. The only positive outcome was the serious weakening of the Red Army in this sector, which made an offensive there unlikely. Once again, however, losses had been enormous. The *SS-Panzergrenadier-Division "Leibstandarte-SS Adolf Hitler"* had lost just less than 2,200 men killed, wounded, or missing. The numbers for the *SS-Panzergrenadier-Division "Das Reich"* were somewhat higher, while the *SS-Panzergrenadier-Division "Totenkopf"* suffered just under 4,500 casualties. After the Red Army took the offensive farther to the south, the SS units were immediately transferred to the area around Stalino, roughly 400 kilometers away. There they succeeded in stabilizing the Mius front.

At the end of the month the **SS-Panzergrenadier-Division "Leibstandarte-SS Adolf Hitler"** received marching orders for Italy, where the Italian king had dismissed the Duce (Benito Mussolini). Initially employed to disarm and intern the Italian military, further "clearance actions" in northern Italy followed, during which Jews were also liquidated. The period in Italy was also used to rehabilitate and reorganize the unit, which at the end of October 1943, was renamed the **1. SS-Panzer-Division** *"Leibstandarte-SS Adolf Hitler"* and ordered back to the Eastern Front. Attached to *4. Panzer-Armee*, the division was able to smash powerful Soviet forces west of Kiev, however it was unable to prevent the enemy from breaking through the German front on a broad front in the direction of Zhitomir at Christmas 1943.

After the Red Army again took the offensive near Kharkov, on August 4, 1943, the **SS-Panzergrenadier-Division "Das Reich"** was ordered back into the area. After fierce and ultimately unsuccessful fighting, on September 2, 1943, German forces began withdrawing through Poltava towards the Dniepr. The first elements of the division crossed the river near Kremenchug on September 25, and immediately moved northwest into the Kanev area. The Red Army had established a bridgehead there, which at least had to be sealed off. On November 6, 1943, the division marched into the Fastov area to join the *XXXXVIII. Panzer-Korps*, against which the Red Army had broken through west of Kiev. The ferocity of the fighting was evidenced by the casualties. Between early August and December 1, 1943, the *SS-Panzergrenadier-Division "Das Reich"* lost a total of 7,436 members killed, wounded or missing. Because of these losses, first elements of the division were taken out of action and sent to East Prussia for rehabilitation.

At the end of July 1943, the **SS-Panzergrenadier-Division "Totenkopf"** was transferred into the Stalino area and took part in the successful but costly stabilization of the Mius Front. Between July 30 and August 2, 1943, the unit lost almost 1,500 men killed, wounded, or missing. On August 5, 1943, the division moved back into the Kharkov area and on September 29, 1943, it pulled back beyond the Dniepr. When the Red Army broke through between the *8. Armee* and the *1. Panzer-Armee*, from October 22, 1943, the *SS-Panzergrenadier-Division "Totenkopf"* repeatedly engaged in contact missions as part of the *XXXX. Panzer-Korps*. When these were completed at the end of October 1943, the division was initially assembled as *Armee* reserve and from November 14, 1943, was again engaged in fierce defensive fighting. Altogether, the unit, which was renamed **3. SS-Panzer-Division "Totenkopf,"** lost an unbelievable 12,863 men killed, wounded, or missing between July 5 and November 22, 1943.

After the **SS-Polizei-Division** returned to the Leningrad siege ring, as of January 12, 1943, it was again involved in fierce defensive fighting. The weight of the Soviet winter offensive struck the division head on and in the space of about two weeks it was virtually destroyed. After taking approximately 3,000 casualties, it even fled in panic before the enemy. There was no possibility of the division being relieved, however, and it remained in the Kolpino area and suffered further heavy losses in the following offensives that began on February 10 and March 18, 1943. Not until April, after the Soviet attacks ended, could the units be withdrawn and transferred to SS Training Camp Heidelager. While one battle group remained with Army Group North and was ultimately deployed at the Volkhov once again, the units at the Heidelager training camp were employed against Polish partisans. With the change of government in Italy in the summer of 1943, the end of the German-Italian alliance was foreseeable. With this in mind, the units of the division—renamed **4. SS-Polizei-Panzergrenadier-Division** on October 22—were among the formations sent to the Balkans to fill the vacuum thought likely to develop there. Ordered to Serbia at the end of July 1943, in August the division was attached to the *XXII. Gebirgs-Korps* in eastern Greece (Thessaly). In addition to training, the division's troops also saw action against ELAS and EDES partisans.

Since the turn of the year 1942–43, the **SS-Panzergrenadier-Division "Wiking"** had been engaged in fierce defensive fighting in the Proletarskaya area (approximately 175 kilometers east of Rostov). The retreat by the *4. Panzer-Armee*, of which the division was a part, almost resembled a flight. By February 5, 1943, the units were in Rostov. Pulled back behind the Don, the division received orders to immediately move to the area north of Stalino. There, the unit destroyed a Soviet guards tank corps. It was subsequently employed along the Donetz in the Izyum area. Enemy attacks near Kharkov led to the *SS-Panzergrenadier-Division "Wiking"* being ordered to the *8. Armee*. After fierce defensive fighting west of Kharkov, the unit, as it had earlier in the year, had to retreat approximately 300 kilometers to the west. New positions were temporarily occupied in the Cherkassy area. Renamed **5. SS-Panzer-Division "Wiking,"** beginning on November 13, 1943, the formation became engaged in fierce defensive fighting during which the Red Army was able to take Cherkassy in mid-December 1943.

Like 1942, the year 1943 was a quiet one for the **6. SS-Gebirgs-Division "Nord."** SS-Brigadeführer Lothar Debes (June 21, 1890 – July 14, 1960), the division commander, described the conditions at that time very vividly but naively. His writings show, however, that operations in Karelia could not be compared with the other sectors of the front:

I liked the far north with its vastness, untouched by civilization, with its midnight sun, with its unique flora and fauna, the primeval forests and fish-filled lakes in summer and late spring. Winter was of course hard. At ten in the morning it slowly became light and by two in the afternoon it was already dark again! Even though I was only there for six months, I will never forget that time. Most unforgettable is the fabulous comradeship that prevailed up there in the far north in Russian–Karelia. Leader of the division's band platoon, which during quiet periods gave concerts in the division's service club on Wednesdays, Saturdays and Sundays, was the much-loved *SS-Hauptsturmführer* Nickel. The units were issued vouchers for the concerts. Some of the lucky ones then marched to the club, where sisters served coffee and cake. The rest marched to the cinema. The entry fee was a piece of wood for the big cinema stove (collected in the forest). Following the afternoon concert with coffee and cake, the first part went to the cinema, and the cinema-goers went to the service club where there was dinner with beer and an evening concert. Between the cinema and service club was the bookstore. The thing was so organized that everyone chosen on a given day could enjoy a concert with food and attend a movie and could also provide himself with intellectual fare for the shelter. And as 600 men had this opportunity each Wednesday, Saturday and Sunday, 1,800 men got to enjoy

Recruiting of volunteers for the *SS-Standarte "Westland"* began in May 1940. The poster includes references to sport and the strict exercise in the *Waffen-SS*.

German and Western European SS volunteers.

SS-Gruppenführer Gille, commander of the *5. SS-Panzer-Division*.

Hans Erlewein joined the *Waffen-SS* in April 1941, and from August 20, 1941, was a member of the *1./SS-Regiment "Westland."* In June 1943, he was transferred to to the *SS-Pz.Aufkl. Abt. 11* (SS armored reconnaissance battalion).

The German military cemetery near Modlin.

themselves each week. If one was about 4,000 kilometers from home, something had to happen in the northern loneliness! As well, now and then there was a stage show, which was put on in the cinema on the other days of the week. Admittedly the entertainment was limited to the time when the snow was deep and to the muddy period, times when the Ivan couldn't come. If one fished with a net, in half an hour one could catch a whole basket full of beautiful lake trout and those who were especially lucky could admire the huge northern elk in the hinterland.

The casualties suffered by the *7. SS-Freiwilligen-Gebirgs-Division "Prinz Eugen"* were also manageable. With about 20,000 men, at the beginning of January 1943, it was in the area south of Zagreb, and from January 20 to March 15, it took part in "Operations White I–III" against partisans and from May 15 to June 15, "Operation Black." It was then transferred to Dalmatia, where an Allied invasion was feared. From September 8, 1943, during the disarming and internment of Italian troops, there was fighting, in some cases heavy, in Split and Ragusa. In late October 1943, during the three-week "Operation Autumn Storm," the islands of Brac, Hvar and Korkula, and the Peljesac Peninsula were occupied. On December 2, 1943, fierce fighting broke out in the Sarajevo area against well-organized partisan divisions. These had launched a coordinated offensive from Bosnia with the goal of invading Serbia. The Germans responded with "Operations Ball Lightning and Snowstorm," which lasted until the end of the year. While these failed to destroy the partisans under Tito, they did degrade their cohesion considerably and cause significant losses in weapons and equipment.

After its action at the front in late 1942, at the beginning of 1943, the *8. SS-Kavallerie-Division* hunted Red Army stragglers and partisans in the operational area. On February 14, 1943, the unit was attached to the Senior SS and Police Commander "Russia-Center" for security duties in the rear area. Albert Schwenn was transferred to the *SS-Kavallerie-Division* in February 1943, and recalled his first actions:

> I volunteered for the *Waffen-SS* in 1940 and took my physical examination. Only eight of about fifty young men were accepted. None of the others met the entrance requirements still in use at that time—how this was later to change, when we received ethnic German comrades who were about 1.6 meters (5'3") tall! When my draft order finally came, I was initially very disappointed. Instead of the tanks or motorcycles, I had been assigned to the cavalry. My disappointment was only matched by my father's delight. He loved horses above all else and had no idea of the differences between civilian and military horsemanship. Then in October 1942, I became an *SS-Reiter* in the SS Cavalry Replacement Battalion. The training was not exactly ideal for instilling us young men with enthusiasm for the military life. From the start to the finish of our time as recruits we were always hungry, and we stole turnips from the warehouse and ate them raw.
>
> In February 1943, we were sent to the field unit. We were quartered in a former Russian cavalry barracks in Lapitschi near Osipovichi. We got up at four in the morning and at five rode off to hunt partisans. After three kilometers we dismounted and then walked for five kilometers—the horses had to be spared. At nine the motorized units, which had set out later, overtook us. Our comrades sat leaned back comfortably in their Kfz.15s and waved patronizingly to us "grooms."

From May 9 to June 10, 1943, the division took part in "Operation Vistula I" in the area between the Pripyat in the southwest, the Dniepr in the east and the Mozyr–Gomel rail line in the north. The principle objective of the operation was to requisition workers and cattle. "Operation Vistula II" began a few days later. After the Soviet attacks in the Kharkov area, in mid-August 1943, the unit was transferred to about 500 kilometers to the east to the *8. Armee*. As a result the units, which had not been conceived for modern motorized warfare, were deployed against the Red Army's masses of armor. The resulting actions were thus extremely costly and saw the *8. SS-Kavallerie-Division* move through Poltava and attempt to cross the Dniepr near Mischurin–Rog in order to ultimately reach Kirovograd on the Ingul River. The unit was virtually destroyed in the process and lost the bulk of its heavy equipment and armaments. Consequently on December 8, 1943, Himmler ordered the division to Essig (Croatia) for rehabilitation and reformation.

Many new divisions were formed during 1943, but saw no action that year. They were the:

9. SS-Panzergrenadier-Division "Hohenstaufen" in France
10. SS-Panzergrenadier-Division "Frundsberg" in France
11. SS-Freiwilligen-Panzergrenadier-Division "Nordland" at Training Camp Grafenwöhr
12. SS-Panzergrenadier-Division "Hitlerjugend" in Belgium
13. Kroatische SS-Freiwilligen-Division in France
14. Galizische SS-Freiwilligen-Division at the Heidelager training camp
15. Lettische SS-Freiwilligen-Division in Latvia
16. SS-Panzergrenadier-Division "Reichsführer-SS" in the Laibach area
17. SS-Panzergrenadier-Division "Götz von Berlichingen" in France

1944

For the *1. SS-Panzer-Division "Leibstandarte-SS Adolf Hitler"* the year began with heavy fighting as part of the *III. Panzer-Korps* to relieve the German troops encircled in the Cherkassy Pocket. On February 17, 1944, approximately 34,000 German troops were freed from the Soviet encirclement. This was followed by fierce actions as part of the *4. Panzer-Armee*, which was itself on the verge of being encircled by the Red Army. The *1. SS-Panzer-Division* was employed offensively and defensively in the Ukraine until the beginning of April 1944 and was then transferred to Belgium for rehabilitation. Surprisingly, not until four weeks after the Allied invasion of Normandy, was the division sent to the front in the Caen area on July 11, 1944. When the Allies broke through near Avranches, on August 7, the division was committed in a vain attempt to retake the strategically-important town. Ten days later the Allies succeeded in forming a pocket near Trun in which approximately 80,000 German troops were trapped. These included what was left of the *1. SS-Panzer-Division*, which on August 20, 1944, managed to break out to the east. Only about 20,000 members of the *Wehrmacht* and *Waffen-SS* reached the Seine near Rouen. While various battle groups remained in action, unusable elements were transferred to the Siegburg area for rehabilitation. The unit was then assembled in its entirety in the Lübbecke area near Osnabrück in mid-October. Despite the ferocity of the fighting in Normandy and the encirclement in the Falaise Pocket, the division's losses were surprisingly light. During two months of intense combat the division lost about 3,600 men killed, wounded, or captured.[31] After seven weeks of rehabilitation, the *"Leibstandarte-SS Adolf Hitler"* took part in the Ardennes offensive, which began on December 16, 1944. A well-known incident took place the next day near Malmedy, in which American prisoners of war lost their lives. If one compares the approximately eighty American victims with the civilian and military sacrifices in the Soviet Union, one can see the enormous differences in battle between the Western and Eastern Fronts.

On January 24, 1944, the *SS-Führungshauptamt* ordered the reorganization of the *2. SS-Panzergrenadier-Division "Das Reich,"* which became the *2. SS-Panzer-Division "Das Reich."* After the first elements of the division had been pulled out of action on the Eastern Front, the last troops still in action were withdrawn to East Prussia in the spring of 1944. On February 2, 1944, the men were first sent to Bordeaux (France), and on April 9, to the Montauban–Toulouse

The equipment and organization of the *SS-Kavallerie-Division* was more appropriate for use in the rear area than against heavy motorized enemy forces.

SS-Brigadeführer Fegelein, commander of the *SS-Kavallerie-Division*, with *SS-Standartenführer* Lombard, and *SS-Obersturmbannführer* Temme.

Gustav Lombard, Günther Temme, and Fredo Gensicke at a reunion in 1965.

area. There the division frequently saw action against the French Resistance. Following the Allied invasion in Normandy, the *2. SS-Panzer-Division "Das Reich"* was placed on alert in southern France and initially ordered into the Limoges–Tulle area and there were further actions against the Maquisards. These attacked German vehicles and units daily, and the German reactions became more violent. When sixty-four men from *III./Sicherungs-Regiment 95* were found dead, ninety-eight French hostages were hanged in Tulle. After an officer of the *2. SS-Panzer-Division* presumably fell into the hands of the partisans, the German reaction escalated even further. 180 civilians were killed in Oradour-sur-Glane. *SS-Obersturmbannführer* Otto Weidinger (May 24, 1914 – January 10, 1990) wrote about this event in his book *Kamaraden*:

> The tragedy that befell the French population of Oradour was frightful and from a human point of view the behavior of *Sturmbannführer* Diekmann cannot be excused and is incomprehensible to us all ... Oradour was solely the result of the failure of a single officer, who never received orders for such inhuman action. He acted contrary to the express order of his regimental commander, who was simply confronted with a fait accompli after his return.

The first of the division's units reached the invasion front at the end of June 1944, and in just three days of action in the Caen area lost almost 850 men killed and wounded. Further actions took place in the area St. Lo–Granville–Avranches, with the units committed mainly in battle groups. The division formed part of "Operation Lüttich," which was supposed to retake Avranches. The offensive failed, in large part due to the enemy's total control of the skies. The *2. SS-Panzer-Division* was then ordered into Viemoutiers area, thus escaping encirclement in the Falaise Pocket. After it was used to open the pocket, it carried out a fighting withdrawal towards the Westwall through Rouen, Montdidier, Hirson, and Stavelot into the area south of Prüm. There, too, there was changeable fighting, until the unit was transferred to the Paderborn area for rehabilitation. After barely six weeks the division moved into its starting positions for the Ardennes offensive. On December 21, 1944, five days after the start of this major offensive, it attacked from the Dasburg area through Luxembourg toward Liège.

The *3. SS-Panzer-Division "Totenkopf"* took part in at times heavy fighting in the Krivoy Rog area until mid-March 1944, and then was transferred to Rumania via Kishinev. Not completely operational after its heavy losses, at the beginning of May 1944, the elements of the division that were combat-ready saw action in the area west of Targul–Frumos. Two months later the OKW ordered the division to the *4. Armee*, to Grodno in the Bialystok area. The Red Army had driven through far to the west at the seam between the *2.* and *4. Armee*. Contact between the two armies could not be reestablished, but the situation was finally stabilized by withdrawing the *4. Armee*. On July 24, 1944, *the 3. SS-Panzer-Division "Totenkopf"*—which was probably the most powerful division in the *Waffen-SS* at that time—was sent to another crisis point. The Red Army was driving energetically towards Warsaw. The defensive battles in front of the Polish capital were dramatic. The division lost 5,000 soldiers killed and wounded by August 21, 1944. Its units were driven back towards the Vistula and on November 24, 1944, were assembled in the Nasielsk area as the *2. Armee*'s operational reserve. One month later the order reached it there to move to Hungary.

In Greece, the last troops from the Eastern Front reached the *4. SS-Polizei-Panzergrenadier-Division* in the spring of 1944. There the security duties assigned the division escalated steadily. When a reprisal resulted in the population of the village of Sistomon being liquidated, it led to an investigation of the responsible company and battalion commanders by a military court. The Red Army's advance to Serbia finally resulted in the transfer of the division to the area around Belgrade, approximately 600 kilometers to the north. From there the units marched to Rumania, where in late September 1944, they were supposed to retake Temesvar. Because of the true situation at the front, the division commander called off the attack on his own authority and the unit marched via Szeged into the Szolnok area in Hungary. In fierce defensive fighting, the *4. SS-Polizei-Panzergrenadier-Division* withdrew to the north and at the end of the year reached the Hungarian–Slovakian border.

In January 1944, the **5. SS-Panzer-Division "Wiking"** was encircled in the Cherkassy Pocket, and on February 16, 1944, it broke out to the west through enemy positions. Just 4,000 members of the division escaped, leaving behind all their heavy equipment and weapons. Initially transferred to the area east of Lublin, on March 16, 1944, the surviving personnel were transported to Kovel, approximately 140 kilometers to the east. As the Red Army encircled the transportation hub before the troops could get there, they assembled in the Maciejow area by March 21. The relief of Kovel, which began on March 29, was initially unsuccessful. Contact with the encircled troops was not made until April 4, 1944. After the front was stabilized, the division was transferred to Heidelager SS training camp for rehabilitation. The division was placed on alert in mid-July 1944 and sent to the Bialystok area, approximately 380 kilometers away. There it was drawn into the *2. Armee*'s chaotic retreat and in the space of two weeks marched about 160 kilometers to the southwest. On August 3, 1944, it launched an attack to restore contact with the *4. Armee* and afterwards took part in the fighting in defense of Warsaw. The *5. SS-Panzer-Division "Wiking"* recorded approximately 7,000 members killed, wounded, or captured by the end of August 1944. At the beginning of September, the unit, which was classified as "*conditionally defense capable*," was withdrawn behind the Narev. There, always committed in the main line of resistance, it suffered further losses to constant Soviet attacks. Nevertheless, at the end of December the division received orders to move to Hungary. The movement of units that had been virtually destroyed to other hotspots was an illustration of the status of the resources available to the German Reich at the end of 1944.

As in the previous years, 1944 was initially quiet for the **6. SS-Gebirgs-Division "Nord."** Because of the escalating, dramatic events, however, preparations for withdrawal were also begun in Karelia. When the Red Army launched its summer offensive in the area of the *20. Armee*, it began six weeks of fierce fighting which finally ended in early August with no great territorial gains for the Soviets. Then on August 25, 1944, the Finnish government signed a ceasefire agreement with the USSR and German forces had to leave the country immediately. Sometimes pursued by Soviet troops and finally attacked by its former Finnish allies, the *6. SS-Gebirgs-Division "Nord"* marched approximately 1,100 kilometers to the Finnish–Norwegian border. From there the SS mountain troops were transported by rail to Oslo and from there sent across to Denmark. On December 24, 1944, the first elements of the division ordered to the Pfalz.

In the Balkans, for the **7. SS-Freiwilligen-Gebirgs-Division "Prinz Eugen,"** 1944 began with "Operation Waldrausch" in the Travnik area, which commenced on January 4, 1944. The operation, which lasted two weeks in the high, snow-covered mountains, brought the troops to the limits of their physical endurance. Briefly deployed in the Split–Ragusa area, at the beginning of March 1944, the division was transferred to the Sarajevo area. In April, there was heavy but also successful fighting against Communist partisans trying to enter Serbia. Beginning on May 25, 1944, the *7. SS-Freiwilligen-Gebirgs-Division* took part in "Operation Rösselsprung," which was designed to capture Tito and his staff. Although this operation failed to achieve its goal, large partisan units were destroyed in subsequent actions until July 9, 1944. The advance by the Red Army in the summer of 1944, led to another large-scale action as part of "Operation Rübezahl." When Soviet forces reached the Serbian border, at the end of the September the unit was rushed to the front in the Nis area, about 300 kilometers away. There, the division suffered almost 8,000 casualties—killed, wounded, and missing—in August alone. A not inconsiderable number of the missing were ethnic Germans who wanted to be with their families living in Serbia in the coming difficult times. After fierce defensive fighting the units withdraw through Kraljewo and Uzice to Zvornik behind the Drina by December 13, 1944. The withdrawal was marked by frequent clashes with partisan units.

At the beginning of 1944, the **8. SS-Kavallerie-Division** was still undergoing reorganization in Croatia. On March 12, 1944, Hitler awarded the unit the title "Florian Geyer." One week later the division was employed in "Operation Margarethe," the occupation of Hungary. It resumed training there, until on August 20, 1944, orders were received to move to Transylvania (Rumania). After a rail journey of about 500 kilometers, the SS cavalry were unloaded near Neumarkt on the Maros and sent directly into action. When the Red Army launched an offensive on October 6, 1944, the division covered the retreat by German troops towards the Hungarian border. After a fighting withdrawal, at the beginning of November 1944, the units finally reached Budapest, the capital of Hungary. There they were encircled by the Red Army on Christmas Eve 1944.

The **9. SS-Panzer-Division "Hohenstaufen"** and the **10. SS-Panzer-Division**[32] **"Frundsberg"** had been formed at various training camps in France and in the spring of 1944 were with the *19. Armee* on the Gulf of Lyon. They were stationed there to defend against a possible Allied landing. When, however, the Red Army succeeded in encircling the *1. Panzer-Armee* between Ternopol and Kamenets Podolsk in the spring of 1944, on March 26, 1944, both units were placed on alert for transfer to the Eastern Front. At the beginning of April 1944, both SS panzer divisions were committed south of Ternopol as part of the *4. Panzer-Armee*, maintaining contact between the previously encircled German units and the German main line of resistance. Following the Allied invasion of Normandy, on June 11, they were transferred back to France. The units arrived in the Caen area at the end of June and took part in the fierce defensive battles there. After the front had somewhat quieted down in that sector, the SS units were ordered into the Chenodolle area, where the British army had broken through at the seam between the *7. Armee* and the *5. Panzer-Armee*. The two divisions were separate from each other in the actions that followed, consequently the *9. SS-Panzer-Division "Hohenstaufen"* was outside the Falaise Pocket while the *10. SS-Panzer-Division "Frundsberg"* was inside the pocket in August 1944. The two units, which were still relatively effective formations, attacked, one from the inside and the other from the outside, to free the approximately 80,000 encircled German troops. Despite this, approximately 50,000 were taken prisoner by the Allies which, given the overall situation, was probably not seen as a bad thing by many. For them the war was now over. At the beginning of September, the two divisions were ordered into the Arnhem area for "rehabilitation near the front." On September 17, 1944, they took part in the successful defense against the Allied airborne "Operation Market Garden." On September 22, 1944, by mutual agreement the *9. SS-Panzer-Division* took charge of about 1,200 wounded British soldiers. This was a humane action that probably could not have taken place on the Eastern Front. Whereas, after successful rehabilitation, the *9. SS-Panzer-Division* took part in the Ardennes offensive beginning December 18, 1944, the *10. SS-Panzer-Division* was deployed in the Linnich area from November 22 to December 6, 1944, and was then ordered to the Euskirchen area for further rehabilitation.

The **11. SS-Freiwilligen-Panzergrenadier-Division "Nordland"** had been formed in 1943 from the *Freikorps "Danmark,"* the *Freiwilligen-Legion "Norwegen"* and ethnic Germans from Rumania, and since the end of the year had been in action in the east in the Oranienbaum area (west of Leningrad). As a result of a Soviet offensive, within two weeks not only was the unit badly battered, it was also forced to move its positions about seventy-five kilometers to the west—along the Narva. Deployed between the Gulf of Finland and Lake Peipus, fierce and costly defensive fighting as part of *Armee-Abteilung "Narwa"* in Estonia followed, including in the Tannenberg Position. Hitler authorized the evacuation of the country in mid-September 1944, whereupon the division withdrew to Latvia. There the men took part in two so-called Battles of Courland until the end of the year.

The *12. SS-Panzer-Division "Hitlerjugend"* was formed in 1943 from seventeen-year-old volunteers from the Hitler Youth. After an about sixteen-month formation period in Belgium, in April 1944, the division moved to France, into the Bernay–Evreux–Chambois area. When the Allies landed in Normandy, the unit was immediately alerted and transferred to the Caen area. Two days later, after heavy fighting, 100 Canadian prisoners of war were unnecessarily shot. The division was in the thick of the fighting for Caen until mid-July 1944, and was finally broken up into battle groups and deployed south of the city. On August 17, 1944, it was trapped in the Falaise Pocket and only parts of it were able to cross the Seine near Elbeuf by August 26. Fighting a delaying action against American forces, but finally also against Belgian partisans, in mid-September the division's troops were taken out of action near Burbuy on the Ourthe and ordered to the Saarland, 200 kilometers away, for rehabilitation. In three months of action, the division had suffered casualties of about 9,000 men killed, wounded and missing, losses equal to 50% of its strength. In the roughly three months of rehabilitation that followed, the division received about 10,000 replacements and on December 13, 1944, it was transferred to Blankenheim Forest for the imminent Ardennes offensive. Despite fierce action, the division was unable to achieve its objectives and subsequently, at the end of the year, it was sent to the *5. Panzer-Armee* at Bastogne.

The *13. Waffen-Gebirgs-Division der SS "Handschar" (kroatische Nr. 1)*[33] was formed in 1943, first in France and then at SS Training Camp Wildflecken, and was made up primarily of Bosnian Muslims. In February 1944, it was transferred to back to Bosnia. Beginning in April 1944, the unit took part in numerous actions against Communist partisans under Tito. Because of societal conditions, many in Croatia did not think communism worth fighting. The division therefore only displayed a certain degree of reliability against Serbs. Its actions were frequently accompanied by the brutality typical of the Balkans. On September 19, 1944, the Commander-in-Chief "Southeast" described the situation within the division to the *Wehrmacht* Operations Staff:

> Disintegration of the *SS-Gebirgs-Division Handschar* continues despite outstanding deportment by the German cadre personnel (about 4,000). 2,000 cases of desertion and heavy losses in weapons (1,578 rifles, 61 submachine-guns, 61 MG 42 machine-guns etc.) in the last week. If the situation becomes more acute, which must be expected, further elements of the division will run away with their weapons or go over to the side they expect to be the victor. This is especially regrettable, as the *SS-Gebirgs-Division Handschar* is much better equipped than most of the German units under the Commander-in-Chief Southeast.

When frontline action against the advancing Red Army became predictable, the division's personnel was halved and reorganized. It was hoped that this would result in an effective unit. At the end of October 1944, the units were sent to the *LXIX. Armee-Korps* in Hungary to stabilize the front, however 600 more Bosnians deserted immediately. Consequently only battle groups saw action in the Batina – Apatin area behind the Danube. At the beginning of December 1944, remaining available remnants of the SS unit followed to Hungary and occupied positions west of Barcs.

A second unit whose personnel had been former members of the Hapsburg Monarchy of Austria-Hungary was the *14. Waffen-Grenadier-Division der SS (galizische Nr. 1)*. A battle group from the division first saw action against partisans in the Lublin area in February 1944. In response to the Soviet offensive in the direction of Lvov, the division was deployed southwest of Brody on July 15, 1944, and by the eighteenth, it was surrounded with large parts of the *XIII. Armee-Korps*. Most of the Ukrainian volunteers left their units while still in the pocket and

In April 1944, Fritz von Scholz (left), the commander of the *11. SS-Freiwilligen-Panzer-Grenadier-Division "Nordland,"* was promoted to *SS-Gruppenführer*. He had been awarded the Knight's Cross with Oak Leaves a few days earlier. To the right of Himmler is *SS-Obergruppenführer* Friedrich Jeckeln, Senior SS and Police Commander "Russia North."

Himmler eating a "one pot meal" with invited guests.

tried to go into hiding. The unit had thus been destroyed within a week. A battle group assembled at the Neuhammer SS training camp and from September 19, 1944, took part in the suppression of the Slovakian national uprising. The rest of the division followed into Slovakia, where training was supposed to continue, on October 18. In December 1944, units of the division were employed to construct defensive positions along the Waag and Nitra Rivers.

At the end of January 1944, the **15. Waffen-Grenadier-Division der SS (lettisches Nr. 1)** was transferred to the *16. Armee*'s front in the Staraya Russa area. On February 18, 1944, however, the division was forced to retire towards the Panther Position south of Ostrov. The units repulsed every Soviet attack until mid-April in fierce fighting. Nevertheless, despite receiving reinforcements, it was unable to effectively resist the Red Army during its summer offensive from July 10, 1944. As well, there were command errors, which resulted in the loss of almost all of the division's heavy equipment in three days. The troops crossed the Velikaya River, some by swimming. The division was destroyed. The Latvian SS volunteers fled into the forests or tried to reach their home towns. At the end of June 1944, the German command assembled what was left of the division in the area of Lubahn Lake. One month later it was transferred to the SS Training Camp Konitz in West Prussia, where the unit was supposed to be reformed by the end of the year.

The **16. SS-Panzergrenadier-Division "Reichsführer-SS"** had its origins in the *Begleit-Bataillon Reichsführer-SS* established in 1941. In 1943, it was moved to France and was enlarged to become the *Sturmbrigade Reichsführer-SS*. The brigade was briefly deployed to Corsica, after which formation of the division began in the late summer of 1943. Elements saw action at the Nettuno beachhead in the spring of 1944, while the bulk of the division was attached to the *LVIII. Reserve-Panzer-Korps* at the beginning of March, and took part in the occupation of Hungary. Transfer of the division to Italy began on May 18, 1944. Before it achieved full operational status, beginning June 18, the unit was deployed at the front along the Cecina River. On June 30, American forces attacked, and in the next fourteen days the unit lost nearly 2,000 men killed or wounded. The division was pulled out of the front on August 3, 1944, and ordered into the Bologna area. There it saw action against Italian partisans. Such was the disparity between its own casualties and those of the partisans, that many of the latter must have been victims of mass shootings of "civilian populations sympathetic to the partisans." At the end of September, for example, there was a cleanup operation in the Marzabotto area in which 718 enemy dead were reported against seven of the division's troops killed. In September, the unit again took over a sector of front opposite Bologna, then on December 20, 1944, the *16. SS-Panzergrenadier-Division* received new transfer orders and at the end of the month it occupied positions south of Lake Comacchino, behind the Senio River, as part of the *LXIII. Armee-Korps*.

The **17. SS-Panzergrenadier-Division "Götz von Berlichingen"** had been under formation in occupied France since autumn 1943. After about seven months of training, after the Allied invasion in early June 1944, the division was quickly transported from its quartering area south of the Loire to the *7. Armee* in the area west of Carentan. In four weeks of fighting, the unit was forced to withdraw towards the Mortain area. There it took part in "Operation Lüttich," an unsuccessful attempt to retake Avranches which began on August 7, 1944. Subsequently trapped in the Falaise Pocket, on August 21, only about 1,500 of the division's troops were able to regain the Germany main line of resistance. After rehabilitation in the Saarbrücken area, battle groups from the division saw action in Lorraine. The division subsequently took over a sector of front south of Metz. Fierce American attacks began in early November 1944, and the division was not able to move to the Saarland for rehabilitation until December 20, 1944.

The **18. SS-Freiwilligen-Panzergrenadier-Division "Horst Wessel,"** whose formation began in July 1944, also had a forerunner. The *1. SS-Infanterie-Brigade* had been formed from *SS-Totenkopf-Standarten* and was mainly employed on security and "cleanup" actions in the rear area of the USSR. Not only did these involve the requisitioning of workers and agricultural products, but also numerous mass executions of Jews and residents suspected of being partisans. Formation of the division could not be carried out at a training camp. Instead, short-term battle groups were formed, one of which took part in the occupation of Hungary in March 1944. The other saw action in the Ukraine as part of the *1. Panzer-Armee* from mid-July 1944. The latter was ordered into Slovakia at the end of August to help put down the Slovakian national uprising. The rest of the division also moved into Slovakia on October 5, 1944, and on November 2, was attached to the *4. SS-Polizei-Panzergrenadier-Division*, with which it participated in a disastrous action at the front. On November 9, 1944, Army Group South noted:

> In the *4. SS-Polizei-Panzergrenadier-Division*'s sector (*LVII. Panzer-Korps*), elements of the *18. SS-Division* failed completely, allowing themselves to be overrun and surrendering.

The unit's failure in action was in part due to lack of training and inadequate equipment, but also to the fact that the bulk of its soldiers were ethnic Germans from Hungary who lacked motivation. There was a repetition of this in the weeks that followed, and beginning December 16, 1944, the division was withdrawn from the area near the frontier into Slovakia.

Formation of the ***19. Waffen-Grenadier-Division der SS (lettische Nr. 2)*** began in Latvia on January 7, 1944. Latvian volunteers had previously seen action at the front opposite Leningrad and at the Volkhov and in the spring of 1943, had been combined to form the Latvian SS Volunteer Brigade. At the end of February 1944, this unit withdrew along the Velikaya towards the Panther Position. It was ordered into the Novorzhev area, where the remaining divisional units arrived. Now a complete formation, the *19. Waffen-Grenadier-Division der SS* was struck by the Russian summer offensive on July 10, 1944. As was the case with the *15. Waffen-Grenadier-Division der SS (lettische Nr. 1)*, command errors almost resulted in the disintegration of the division. Many Latvians deserted. Assembled in the area of Lake Lubahn (approximately 200 kilometers east of Riga), an attempt was made to resist the Red Army, first in the Modohn Position and finally in the Segewold Position. In any case, fighting on their home soil the Latvians were again motivated, and on September 30, 1944, the OKW was able to report:

> In the defensive battle in Latvia, the *19. Waffen-Grenadier-Division der SS* under the command of *Generalmajor der Waffen-SS* Streckenbach has fought magnificently in defense of its native soil.

From then until the end of the year the division took part in three so-called Battles of Courland.

Formation of the ***20. Waffen-Grenadier-Division der SS (estnische Nr. 1)*** likewise began—in Estonia—in January 1944. Here, too, there was brigade of volunteers which was expanded into a division. Elements had seen action near Nevel in January 1944, and then were ordered to the Narva Front in February. There was fierce fighting against units of the Red Army attempting to establish bridgeheads across the river that formed the frontier. As soon as new units were available, they were immediately ordered to the front. In the summer of 1944—by which time the unit was already in the hotly-contested Tannenberg Position—it finally reached its authorized strength. In August 1944, elements of the division saw action in the Dorpat area and then withdrew into the Rakke area, into which troops fighting in the Tannenberg Position to the northwest also flowed back. At the end of September 1944, orders were received for the unit to leave Estonia, which led to a major wave of desertions. Approximately 5,000 Estonian soldiers left their units and stayed in their homeland. The remaining troops were sent to Riga and from there by ship to Germany, where they assembled at SS Training Camp Neuhammer. There the division was rehabilitated and reorganized, a process that lasted until the end of the year.

Formation of the *21. Waffen-Gebirgs-Division der SS "Skanderbeg" (albanische Nr. 1)* began in April 1944. It was formed primarily to combat communist Tito partisan in Kosovo (New Albania). As some of its men had previously served in the Yugoslavian Army, in mid-June 1944, several units were committed against partisans in the Albanian–Montenegran border region with the *2. Panzer-Armee*. When the area of operations extended to Montenegro, however, the Albanian troops obviously lost their motivation. Already in the next month, during operations twenty times as many soldiers went missing as were wounded. It was obvious that most of the missing had deserted. Especially unsettling for the German side was the fact that the deserters took their weapons with them. Enough equipment for an entire battalion was lost in two weeks. It became apparent that, apart from the German cadre personnel, the division was not fit for use in the field. The division commander submitted a final evaluation report according to which the entire formation was a disaster. The evacuation of Albania began, as German units were withdrawing from the Balkans anyway. The remaining Albanian members of the division were discharged and replaced by about 1,800 members of the *9. Torpedoboot-Flotille*. At the beginning of November 1944, the *Kriegsmarine* men, together with the German cadre personnel, marched in the direction of Visegrad and from there to Zvornik. At that strategic crossing point there was particularly fierce fighting with the Tito partisans, who were tightly- and militarily-organized and led. On December 13, 1944, the unit, by then designated *SS-Divisionsgruppe "Skanderbeg,"* was attached to the *7. SS-Freiwilligen-Gebirgs-Division "Prinz Eugen,"* and with it occupied positions near Bijeljina.

The *22. SS-Freiwilligen-Kavallerie-Division* was supposed to be formed from ethnic Germans from Hungary beginning the end of April 1944. Formation, which suffered in particular from a shortage of heavy weapons, began about seventy kilometers west of Budapest. At the end of September followed the creation of the battalion-strength *SS-Kampfgruppe "Ameiser,"* which was attached to the *LVII. Panzer-Korps*. It was deployed near Sarkad in the Hungarian–Rumanian border region. The units were encircled by Soviet forces on October 2, 1944, and they subsequently attempted to fight their way back to Budapest in an, at times, very adventurous manner. There, together with other elements of the *22. SS-Freiwilligen-Kavallerie-Division*, they were used to seal of the Hungarian government quarter after Reich Administrator Admiral von Horthy announced that the country was quitting the war. At the end of that month, the deployed units moved to the *III. Panzer-Korps* in the Karola Position opposite the Hungarian capital. After brief fighting at the beginning of November, the unit was sent directly to Budapest. On December 13, 1944, it was attached to the *IX. SS-Gebirgs-Korps* in Buda, where it was encircled by the Red Army.

Beginning June 17, 1944, attempts were made to form a *23. Waffen-Gebirgs-Division der SS "Kama" (kroatische Nr. 2)*, however they failed miserably. Almost none of those conscripted obeyed the draft orders and the unit consisted mainly of German cadre personnel and ethnic German recruits. Following the mass desertion of Bosnian troops of the *13. Waffen-Gebirgs-Division der SS "Handschar,"* formation of the division was halted and concluded up on September 24, 1944.

The formation of the *24. Waffen-Gebirgs [Karstjäger]-Division der SS*, which was supposed to be formed from the *SS-Karstwehr-Bataillon* effective July 18, 1944, followed a similar path. Recruitment among members of the Adriatic Coastland (Northern Italy, Slovenia, and Croatia) was such that, practically, the division consisted of just one regiment. Efforts to at leach achieve brigade strength were unsuccessful, both for reasons of personnel and equipment. Used to combating partisans on the Udine–Laibach–Trieste area, the *SS-Karstjäger* were attached to the Senior SS and Police Commander Adriatic Coastland.

Following the failed declaration by the Hungarian head of state in October 1944, that his country was to immediately leave the war on the German side, the Hungarian military was supposed to be reorganized. This resulted in the creation of the ***25. Waffen-Grenadier-Division der SS "Hunyadi" (ungarische Nr. 1)***, which in November 1944, was transferred to Training Camp Neuhammer. As the troops could not even be completely clothed, formation in a broader context was out of the question until the turn of the year.

The division number "26" was reserved for a second Hungarian unit, however it was not formed in 1944.

The ***27. Freiwilligen-Grenadier-Division "Langemarck" (flämische Nr. 1)*** was established in the Lüneburg Heath beginning September 18, 1944. Its origins went back to 1941, when the *Freiwilligen-Legion "Flandern"* was formed for the eastern campaign. Formation of the division not only suffered from a shortage of personnel, but also from a lack of heavy equipment and armaments common at that time. As recruiting in Belgium was no longer possible, only collaborators already serving in German units (for example the NSKK) could be integrated into the units. They had little motivation or fighting capacity. During the German Ardennes offensive a regiment-strength battle group was moved into the Vor-Eifel district. To what extent a possible employment in Belgium itself was envisaged is difficult to determine. As the Flemings had actually only volunteered for service on the Eastern Front.

A second unit of Belgian nationals was the ***28. SS-Freiwilligen-Grenadier-Division "Wallonien" (wallonische Nr. 1)***. Orders for its formation were also issued on September 18, 1944, however only Walloons working in the armaments industry or serving in German organizations were available for its expansion. Quartered in the Gronau area, on December 20, 1944, one regiment was ordered to the Western Front and during the Ardennes offensive it even advanced into the area southwest of St. Vith. The units saw no action and in January 1945, withdrew to Gronau.

Plans existed to form the ***29. Waffen-Grenadier-Division der SS "RONA" (russische Nr. 1)*** from former volunteers of the Russian People's Liberation Army on July 31, 1944. Elements began helping put down the Warsaw uprising on August 2, 1944. As the men proved undisciplined and impossible to control and even their commanding officer, *Waffen-Brigadeführer* Kaminski showed no willingness to compromise on basic questions,[34] he was liquidated on Himmler's order on August 28, 1944. His unit was disbanded and the men integrated into the Vlasov Army (ROA).

At the same time, the ***30. Waffen-Grenadier-Division der SS (russische Nr. 2)*** was formed from Ukrainian, White Ruthenian, and Russian members of the *Ordnungspolizei*'s numerous *Schutzmannschaft-Bataillone*. With its previous experience in securing the rear area, the unit was supposed to be sent to Army Group G on August 4, 1944, to "combat terrorists." At the end of August 1944, there were several revolts in which the foreign members murdered their German superiors and joined the resistance. The division was immediately transferred from France to Alsace and by mid-November, was completely reorganized. On November 20, 1944, French forces established bridgeheads across the Rhone–Rhine canal, the unit received mission orders in the Larg Position. During a limited counterattack fierce street fighting developed in Hirsingen and Largitzen. Elements of the *30. Waffen-Grenadier-Division der SS*, at least, displayed a certain determination in battle while defending against French attacks on November 22, 1944. On that day the following entry was made in the war diary of the Commander-in-Chief West:

30. Waffen-Grenadier-Division der SS (russische Nr. 2)—commander: *SS-Obersturmführer* Siegling—has distinguished itself through its bravery and steadfastness during the fighting in the Burgundian Gate. It repeatedly repulsed heavy enemy attacks, destroying six enemy tanks. Request that it be named in the supplements to the *Wehrmacht* communiqué.

Developments in the situation soon brought about a reversal of this assessment. After the foreign volunteers had spent barely a week at the front in fierce combat, their strength disappeared rapidly. Given the events of August 1944, the division command feared that the men's reliability would fall again in this critical situation. And in fact, with the exception of one battle group attached to the *LXXXX Armee-Korps*, the bulk of the division was immediately transferred to Training Camp Münsingen, where it arrived on December 2, 1944. It was disbanded there on December 31. Many of its men were put to work building fortifications, while other entire units were sent to the two Hungarian *Waffen-Divisionen der SS* in Schieradz.

The **31. SS-Freiwilligen-Grenadier-Division** was created effective September 24, 1944, from ethnic Germans with Hungarian citizenship who were originally supposed to bring the *23. Waffen-Gebirgs-Division der SS "Kama" (kroatische Nr. 2)* up to authorized strength. Under training at least to the company level since April 1944, at the Sambor SS Training Depot, on November 1, 1944, the men were ordered to the Mohacs–Battaszeko area in response to Soviet advance to the Danube. When the Red Army then threw two bridgeheads across the Danube on November 9, the *31. SS-Freiwilligen-Grenadier-Division* was committed with the *LXVIII. Armee-Korps* in the *2. Panzer-Armee*. After the enemy launched a major offensive on November 27, stronger units were shattered in short time near Battaszeko. There was further heavy defensive fighting and what was left of the unit could not be withdrawn from the main line of resistance until December 21. It was sent to the Cilli–Marburg area for rehabilitation and to complete its formation.

1945

After costly fighting in the Bastogne area, later in January 1945, the **1. SS-Panzer-Division "Leibstandarte-SS Adolf Hitler"** was transferred to the Cologne area and from there ordered to Hungary. In mid-February 1945, during "Operation South Wind," the units successfully reduced in the Soviet Gran bridgehead and from March 6, 1945, took part in the so-called Lake Balaton Offensive from the area south of Stuhlweißenburg. After about a week it succeeded in crossing the Sio Canal in heavy fighting. The German attack had to be halted, however, after the Red Army launched its own offensive. In the days that followed, Soviet superiority in artillery, as well as in tanks and aircraft, resulted in enormous losses in men and materiel. Scarcely able to defend themselves, the troops' already flagging motivation—not only among the many soldiers seconded from the *Wehrmacht* to the "*Leibstandarte-SS Adolf Hitler*"—resulted in an almost hasty retreat by many units. Following this, on March 26, 1945, Hitler deprived the *Leibstandarte* of the right to wear his name, whereupon Himmler ordered *SS-Oberst-Gruppenführer* Sepp Dietrich that his men should remove their cuff titles. As the soldiers had already removed the cuff titles from their uniforms prior to the Hungarian action for reasons of security, it is possible that Himmler exercised a certain amount of "peasant cunning." Forced back towards Vezprem north of Lake Balaton, on April 1, 1945, the *1. SS-Panzer-Division* was already in the Wiener Neustadt area. There was further fierce fighting in the Berndorf area. The division subsequently withdrew via Annaberg–Scheibbs–Waidhofen into the Steyr area. There at the Enns River was the so-called demarcation line, which separated the territory of the western allies from that of the Red Army, and there the remainder of the unit surrendered to the Americans.

In heavy combat near St. Vith since December 24, 1944, on January 17, 1945, the **2. SS-Panzer-Division "Das Reich"** received orders to assemble behind the Westwall near Prüm. After about two weeks of rehabilitation, the division was transferred to the Farad–Csorna area of Hungary. Beginning March 3, 1945, the units moved via Raab to Stuhlweissenburg and from March 7, took part in the Lake Balaton offensive. Territorial gains were modest and as a result of the Soviet "Vienna Operation" which began on March 16, the troops had to be pulled back to their starting positions. On March 20, 1945, the *2. SS-Panzer-Division* was transferred to the area about fifteen kilometers south of Komorn to seal off an enemy breakthrough. Shortages of fuel and ammunition and Soviet air superiority made success impossible. The units flowed west, often in chaotic conditions, and on April 2, reached the area east of Lake Neusiedler. The men conducted a fighting withdrawal towards Vienna and held a small bridgehead at the Floridsdorfer bridge until April 13. The unit, which was disintegrating, then marched via Krems to Melk and from April 20, held a bridgehead over the Danube in Passau. From there the remnants of the division became prisoners of war.

When 1944 gave way to 1945, the *3. SS-Panzer-Division "Totenkopf"* was en route from Poland to Hungary. The leading elements of the division took part in "Operation Konrad" and as part of the *IV. SS-Panzer-Korps* were supposed to fight their way into the encircled capital of Hungary. Hampered by heavy snow and Soviet resistance, the unit was unable to accomplish its mission of reaching the Danube south of Budapest. The unit turned around, and on January 9, 1945, launched an effort to reach the Danube north of Budapest in "Operation Konrad 2." This successful advance was unexpectedly called off by Hitler four days later and the troops were moved to the Stuhlweissenburg area. "Operation Konrad 3" began there on January 18. This last attempt to reach the Hungarian capital failed due to the enemy defense and beginning counterattacks. The *3. SS-Panzer-Division* was forced to withdraw to its starting positions. On January 31, 1945, the division command reported its losses since June 22, 1941. According to this, a total of 17,069 of its men had been killed, 36,416 wounded, and 2,315 reported missing. The total of about 55,000 casualties illustrated the ferocity of the fighting in which this unit had taken part. On March 17, 1945, the units received orders to prevent the Soviets from breaking through in the area of "*Armeegruppe Balck*," the Soviet offensive that had begun the day before resulted in the collapse of the German defense. Lack of fuel and no air support, in particular, led to the loss of most of the vehicles and heavy weapons. Capable of only weak resistance, on April 6, the unit withdrew through Ödenburg towards Vienna, where there was fierce street fighting. The division was briefly rehabilitated in the Stockerau area in mid-April, after which it marched west through Krems towards Linz. While the Red Army was no longer on the offensive, at the beginning of May 1945, elements of the division engaged American troops in the area around Königswiesen. On May 7, 1945, the troops received the order to withdraw through Amstetten towards the demarcation line (the Enns River) and there to surrender to the western allies in the Gallneukirchen area. This was for nothing, however, for on May 14, 1945, the US Army handed them over to the Red Army.

In Slovakia, in January 1945, the *4. SS-Polizei-Panzergrenadier-Division* received orders to proceed to Pomerania, and beginning 16 February it took part in the German offensive there. Three days later—like so many German operations at that time—this was halted and on February 25, the division entrained in the Dirschau area. Halfway there the units were unloaded and had to engage Soviet forces that had broken through in the Rummelsburg area. At the beginning of March 1945, the division moved via Stolp and Lauenburg to Neustadt near Gotenhafen. The roads were completely clogged with refugee columns and *Wehrmacht* vehicles, making progress painfully slow. After defensive fighting near Neustadt, on March 12, the soldiers and civilians streamed towards Gotenhafen. Fighting went on there until the Red Army took the city on March 28. The remaining units of the division were evacuated to the Hela Peninsula on April 4, and from there were transferred by ship to the Oder Front from April 13. Various battle groups saw action in Mecklenburg from April 18. At the beginning of May 1945, the remnants of the division tried to reach the demarcation line near Schwerin–Ludwigslust by way of Kyritz and Perleberg and there surrendered to the US Army.

The *5. SS-Panzer-Division "Wiking"* was pulled out of action near Modlin at the end of the 1944 and transferred to Hungary. On January 1, 1945, the troops began advancing towards the Hungarian capital. After the attempt to reach the Danube south of Budapest failed, the division was sent to the area south of Gran. From there an advance towards Budapest began with good success, but on January 12, 1945, Hitler inexplicably called off the attack and ordered the unit into the Csajag area. One week later, German units tried to fight their way to Budapest from there but were unsuccessful. When the Soviets launched their own offensive at the end of January, not only was the *5. SS-Panzer-Division* forced onto the defensive, but was also forced to withdraw immediately. The German front began moving and in the process lost almost all cohesion. On February 4, the troops occupied positions in the Margarethe Position opposite Stuhlweissenburg. The front there remained quiet until March 16, 1945, when the Red Army began another operation with a heavy artillery bombardment. When it became obvious that Stuhlweissenburg was about to be encircled, the units pulled back without waiting for orders. Constantly pressured by enemy units, on March 29, the men reached the Raab bridgehead near Vasvar and were then supposed to occupy the Reich Defense Position southeast of Fürstenfeld. After several fierce battles, on May 7, 1945, the first elements of the *5. SS-Panzer-Division* left the main line of resistance to reach the demarcation line at the Enns River, approximately 160 kilometers away. By way of Graz and Radstadt the units reached the Klein–Arl Valley and surrendered to the Americans.

The first units of the **6. SS-Gebirgs-Division "Nord"** were ordered from Denmark to the *1. Armee* on the Western Front at the end of December 1944. There—always reinforced by other units—from January 24, 1945, they took part in "Operation Nordwind" from the Bärenthal area. The attempt to reach the Moder River near Ingweiler was called off after two days on account of heavy casualties inflicted by the American defense. At the end of February the division was sent into the area east of Trier. On March 6, the unit was supposed to cross the Buwer and advance into the area south of Trier. After two days and the loss of 500 men and almost all of its armored vehicles this operation, too, was called off. Divided, the division marched east through Boppard in the direction of Nuremberg. While, little by little, the bulk of the formation was captured by the Americans after minor battles, some smaller units ultimately reached the Neumarkt area and there were attached to the *38. SS-Grenadier-Division "Nibelungen"* on April 10.

After securing the Drina bridgehead near Visegrad, on January 13, 1945, the **7. SS-Freiwilligen-Gebirgs-Division "Prinz Eugen"** was transferred to the Syrmia Front to reopen the Vinkovice–Brcko line, which had been cut by partisans. From January 17, it took part in "Operation *Frühlingssturm*" from the area south of the Danube towards Erdevik. At the end of the month the unit was ordered into the area south of the Save near Virovitica. Beginning February 6, 1945, as part of the *LXXXXI. Armee-Korps*, the unit took part in "Operation Wehrwolf," attacking large partisan units. Committed in the role of fire brigade (*Feuerwehr*), in mid-February the division was sent to the *XXI. Gebirgs-Korps* in the area of Sarajevo in Bosnia and from March 1, took part in "Operation Feuerwehr." Constantly in action, on April 12, the unit marched into the Tuzla area. From there the division units moved to Agram and in the course of the surrender they reached southern Styria on May 11, 1945. On May 14, what remained of the division made its way into Yugoslavian captivity, during which the Communist partisans murdered many soldiers with unbelievable brutality.

The **8. SS-Kavallerie-Division "Florian Geyer"** had been encircled in Budapest since Christmas 1944, and initially fought on the east, then on the west bank of the Danube. Its casualties in January 1945, totaled 221 killed and 1,086 wounded.[35] After all relief attempts failed, an attempt to break out of the Budapest Pocket began on February 11, 1945. Of the total of about 30,000 encircled troops, just 785 reached the German lines, however. Then *SS-Rottenführer* Helmut Schreiber remembered those days in Budapest:

> I was born in 1924. On April 15, 1942, was called up and reported to the Ulan Barracks in Warsaw. From there I was sent to the SS Cavalry Replacement Battalion in Cholm near Lublin for basic training and after my time as a recruit to the so-called Heath Camp

in Debica for the formation of the *8. SS-Kavallerie-Division*. I was assigned to the artillery and served in that unit during my time with the division.

On Christmas Eve 1944, we were ordered to change positions, into the inner city of Budapest. In the early morning the hole was closed and the Russians sealed the pocket. As we had no ammunition for our guns (lFH 18 105-mm light field howitzers) anyway, we were immediately employed as infantry. I was initially assigned to the battalion command post as a forward observer. Our poor horses had already starved or been killed by enemy fire or bombs. This helped the hungry civilians, and the horses were butchered in no time.

From the Gellertberg, I was able to watch the blowing of the bridges over the Danube. At the beginning of January 1945, the rest of the battery personnel (supply train) were placed under me to form a small battle group.

Assigned to help me were an officer candidate and an NCO from the 2nd Battery who had lost his unit. There was almost no contact with other groups and each was more or less on its own, whether it was finding something to each or organizing ammunition.

I still remember well an occurrence in a house we occupied, near the post office on Vienna Street. While searching the house, we discovered a man in bed in an apartment. He claimed he was ill. His bed was in front of a door to a pantry filled with sausage, bread and other foods. What to do? We first satisfied our own hunger and then took a wash basket full to the hungry residents in the cellar. Later, after I was wounded, two women there dressed my wounds.

One night we were lucky. Our ammunition was almost gone, but the crew of a damaged armored troop carrier gave us some and we were at least able to defend ourselves again. Then, on January 30, 1945, I was wounded in the street fighting. First I was hit in the head, but fortunately it failed to penetrate my helmet, and ten minutes later I took a bullet in the area of my right collar bone. A comrade took me to the aid station, which was in the underground entrance to the castle. A temporary dressing took care of it. The cellar vaults were full of badly wounded men. There were no beds and they were lying on the ground, covered with paper. Rations consisted of a slice of bread and a cup of tea. Two days later my comrades came and collected me. Their reason: if we were going to go to the dogs, then we were going to go together!

On February 10, 1945, the order was given for all the wounded who could walk to assemble in the castle vaults, as the Swedish Red Cross was supposedly going to take charge of them. Nothing came of it. On the night of February 11–12, 1945, word went round that those who could still fight were going to try to break out. Many of the walking wounded went with them, but before long many came back distraught. The breakout had more or less failed. Then on February 12, the Russians brought us out of the cellars. What followed was hell. Those that could not walk were shot. During the march to Budafok we saw for ourselves the horror of the past few days. Everywhere lay small groups of German soldiers who had resisted, shot dead. We then went via Rumania and the Black Sea to Odessa. This was the beginning of almost nine years through half of Russia to the Urals.

Beginning January 3, 1945, the **9. SS-Panzer-Division "Hohenstaufen"** was supposed to occupy Bastogne, which had been fiercely contested since the end of 1944. After heavy losses in men and materiel, this plan, like so many others, had to be abandoned. After further actions, on January 23, 1945, the unit was pulled out of the front and sent into the area west of Coblenz for rehabilitation. On February 9, the unit began entraining to transport to Hungary and from March 6, it took part in "Operation *Frühlingserwachen*." From the area around Stuhlweissenburg the units attacked in the direction of Sarosd, however after heavy fighting and enemy counter-attacks, on March 17, they were forced to pull back to their starting positions. A chaotic retreat began and in late March there was further heavy fighting near Veszprem. On April 7, 1945, the remnants of the *9. SS-Panzer-Division* moved into the Reich Defense Position near Radkersburg. At the end of the month the division moved to the Amstetten area, and on May 8, it reached the Enns River and the demarcation line.

The *10. SS-Panzer-Division "Frundsberg"* took part in "Operation Nordwind," which began on January 17, 1945. The offensive in Alsace was supposed to take pressure off the German offensive in the Ardennes. The units advanced across the Rhine, initially without success, into the Brumath area and finally to Hangenau. After the offensive was called off, at the beginning of February, the division was transferred to Pomerania. There it took part in "Operation Sonnenwende," which began on February 15, 1945, from the Stargard area. Its objective was to cut off the Soviet forces that had advanced to the Oder. After five days the attack bogged down in the spring mud and fierce resistance and was called off. Struck by the major Soviet offensive in Pomerania, which began on March 1, 1945, after fierce fighting the division withdrew to the Oder bridgehead at Altdamm by March 8. After heavy attacks this position was also abandoned on March 20. Transferred to Stettin, at the end of the month the unit was ordered into the ear east of Görlitz. As a result of the Red Army's Berlin operation, which began on April 16, the *10. SS-Panzer-Division* was alerted and four days later was encircled near Spremberg. Contrary to Hitler's order to break through to the north to the *V. Armee-Korps*, the troops headed west towards Senfterberg. Division commander *SS-Brigadeführer* Harmel was dismissed by Hitler for disobedience. After final fighting near Moritzburg on May 3, two days later the remains of the unit marched to Teplitz–Schnau, following the general direction of retreat of the *4. Panzer-Armee* and when the surrender came broke up into small groups. The bulk of the division's troops were taken prisoner by the Soviets.

In Latvia the 4th Battle of Courland began on January 23, 1945, and the **11. SS-Freiwilligen-Panzergrenadier-Division "Nordland"** was roughly handled in the Priekule area. At the end of the month, it was shipped to Germany, where it was supposed to be rehabilitated. Two weeks later, however, it took part in "Operation Sonnenwende" in Pomerania. The German units succeeded in driving through to Arnswalde, which was encircled by the Red Army, and evacuating the garrison as well as the civilians. This was the only significant success of the so-called Pomeranian Offensive. When the enemy launched his own offensive on March 1, 1945, the German front collapsed in a matter of hours. Constantly on the move, on March 8, the unit reached the Altdamm bridgehead position. After immensely-powerful Soviet attacks the bridgehead was abandoned on March 20. By the end of March 1945, the *11. SS-Freiwilligen-Panzergrenadier-Division "Nordland"* had recorded a total of 2,939 killed, 10,272 wounded, and 1,278 missing since its formation. Most of the missing may have been captured by the Soviets. With a total of 14,489 casualties in total, the division had lost almost its entire personnel complement. On March 27, the units moved through Stettin into the Angermünde area. After the expected Soviet offensive along the Oder, the division was ordered into the area south of Frankfurt/Oder, but it never got there because of lack of transport and fuel shortages. Instead the transfer ended in the Strausberg area. The only tank battle on the way to Berlin took place there on April 19, 1945. Near Prötzel, *SS-Panzer-Regiment 11* was able to destroy around 100 enemy tanks. Exhausted, the troops withdrew to Berlin and ultimately saw action in the city center. On May 1, 1945, they, together with civilians, tried to fight their way through the Soviet encirclement, across the Weidendammer Bridge. All attempts collapsed under heavy enemy fire. At the beginning of May 1945, the remnants of the division were taken prisoner by the Soviets.

After the final battles at Bastogne, from January 10, 1945, the **12. SS-Panzer-Division "Hitlerjugend"** was withdrawn from the front and transferred to the area west of Cologne.

After a brief period of rehabilitation, on February 2, the division was transported to Hungary. There it took part in the battle for the Soviet Gran bridgehead beginning February 17. After this successful action, on February 25, the division was ordered to Stuhlweissenburg. From there the men attacked south on March 6, and on March 12, they were able to establish a small bridgehead over the Sio Canal. When, after fierce fighting and the start of the major Soviet offensive, the German offensive had to be called off, the *12. SS-Panzer-Division* was initially forced to withdraw to the Margarethe Position near Zircz, and on March 27, 1945, crossed the Raab in the direction of Odenburg. As the Soviets were already there, there was heavy fighting. Other stops included Rohr in the mountains and finally the Enns River, which formed the line of demarcation. The units surrendered to the Americans in the Linz area.

At the end of 1944, the *13. Waffen-Gebirgs-Division der SS "Handschar" (kroatische Nr. 1)* was already in Hungary and as part of the *LXVIII. Armee-Korps* occupied positions from south of Nagyatad to west of Barcs. During the relatively quiet period until March 1945, the division, from which thousands of Bosnians had deserted, was bolstered by members of the *Wehrmacht*. Soviet and Bulgarian troops attacked the German front at the end of March 1945, forcing the *13. Waffen-Gebirgs-Division der SS* from its positions. At the beginning of April 1945, the unit crossed the Mur south of Letenye and occupied its final positions south of Luttenberg. There were no major actions. Instead, on May 5, the last Croatians were released and three days later the German members set out to reach Judenburg. Not until May 12, were the men disarmed by the British Army and taken to the Rimini prisoner of war camp.

The *14. Waffen-Grenadier-Division der SS (galizische Nr. 1)* had been deployed in the Slovakian border region since the end of 1944, building positions. Then in February 1945, it was transferred into the Marburg area in Slovenia. There the division units took part in various operations against the partisan movement. As the division exhibited little fighting spirit, at the end of the month there were plans to disarm it. When the Red Army reached the Feldbach–Gleichberg area, where there were almost no troops, events developed rapidly. The *14. Waffen-Grenadier-Division der SS* was ordered to the front and there took part in the final battles with little motivation. In some cases German troops fired on the Ukrainians to keep them in their positions. During the surrender the unit marched to Spittal and from there to the prisoner of war camp in Rimini.

The *15. Waffen-Grenadier-Division der SS (lettische Nr. 1)* had been at SS Training Camp Konitz in West Prussia for reorganization since late summer 1944. When the Red Army reached Bromberg on January 23, 1945, the unit was placed on alert and ordered into the Bromberg area. It took part in heavy and confused fighting with the *XVI. SS-Armee-Korps* and finally in the retreat into the area around Neustettin. On February 15, the units again took the offensive and launched a counterattack. At the end of the month it was attached to *Korpsgruppe Tettau* which, on the verge of encirclement, ultimately fought its way back in small groups via Gramenz to Zedlin on the Bay of Pomerania. On March 11, 1945, the remnants of the *15. Waffen-Grenadier-Division der SS* reached the Dievenow bridgehead and marched into the Fürstenberg–Lychen area. From there it was employed building positions, first in the Neustrelitz area and then near Malchin. The unit was ordered into the Schwerin Forest, and there the Latvian SS volunteers surrendered to the western allies.

Still deployed in Italy at the turn of the year 1944–45, at the beginning of February 1945, the *16. SS-Panzergrenadier-Division "Reichsführer-SS"* was transferred to the Nagykanisza area in Hungary. In preparation for participation in "Operation *Frühlingserwachen*," the unit moved into an assembly area in Nagybojom and from there attacked towards Kaposvar on March 6. The unit failed to achieve the desired success and subsequently shifted the focus of its efforts south towards Kisbajom. There, too, it failed to achieve success and it was subsequently ordered to attack north towards Marczali. After equally futile efforts, further attacks were halted and the *16. SS-Panzergrenadier-Division* was ordered into the Pacsa area as mobile reserve. The division was split when the Red Army launched its major offensive at the end of March. The main body withdrew towards Nagykanizsa and tried almost hectically to cross the Mur at Alsolendva. On April 4, 1945, the troops were near Luttenberg and then marched into the hotly-contested area near Straden. At the beginning of May elements of the division were ordered into the area around Marburg and attached to the *XXII. Gebirgs-Korps*. When the surrender came, elements of the unit were captured by British forces in the Klagenfurt area and the others west of Graz.

The *17. SS-Panzergrenadier-Division "Götz von Berlichingen"* took part in "Operation Nordwind," which began on January 1, 1945, as part of the *1. Armee*. The offensive was called off just two days later, after American resistance and the enemy's complete control of the air made success out of the question. When American forces launched a counterattack in the Bitsch–Saargemünd area on January 6, elements of the division fled their positions—an indication of the level of motivation of the mainly ethnic German soldiers. After numerous defensive battles, at the end of March there was once again a panicky withdrawal, this time through Landau to Germersheim. In the process the unit lost almost all of its weapons and equipment. Nevertheless, the units took over the main burden of the defense in the *XIII. Armee-Korps'* area behind the Neckar near Neckarelz. At the beginning of April enemy pressure led to a retreat towards the Jagst and the Kocher. On April 13, 1945, the *17. SS-Panzergrenadier-Division* received orders to move into the Nuremberg area. Large parts of the division were smashed in fighting in the Middle–Franconian city. On April 16, the rest reached the area around Neumarkt in the Upper Pfalz. Constantly engaged by pursuing American forces the troops withdrew through Neustadt/Donau–Dachau–Kreuth to Jenbach am Inn. There the men surrendered to the Americans.

After its disastrous action in Hungary in late 1944, the *18. SS-Freiwilligen-Panzergrenadier-Division "Horst Wessel"* was in the Marburg area for rehabilitation and reorganization. While there many of the unit's officers were replaced. At the beginning of February 1945, the unit was sent to the Silesian front and occupied positions south of the Soviet bridgehead over the Oder at Cosel. The Red Army took the offensive in mid-March 1945, and created the so-called Oppeln Pocket, and the *18. SS-Freiwilligen-Panzergrenadier-Division* was among the units encircled there. A breakout to the German main line of resistance near Hotzenplotz began on March 19, 1945, and was achieved by at least some of the troops two days later. While several companies remained in the battle area, other units were ordered to the SS Training Camp Bohemia and Moravia, where they were to be reorganized. On April 10, however, they again received transfer orders for the front. The unit stayed in the Zobten area behind the Bober without seeing major action. When the surrender came it disengaged from the enemy and marched via Reichenberg in the direction of the demarcation line along the Elbe. During this time many members of the division were murdered by Czech partisans.

At the turn of the year the *19. Waffen-Grenadier-Division der SS (lettisches Nr. 2)* took part in the Third Battle of Courland. While the unit was only partially affected by the Red Army's attacks in the Fourth Battle of Courland, during the Fifth Battle of Courland, which lasted from February 12, to March 10, it was forced to withdraw its positions towards Tukkum. From March 17 to April 4, 1945, followed the Sixth Battle of Courland, which once again brought heavy fighting and casualties. The area held by the *19. Waffen-Grenadier-Division der SS* then remained quiet until the surrender. Only a small number of the soldiers became Soviet prisoners on May 8, 1945, however. The majority tried to hide themselves in the forests and a few lived in the wild as so-called "forest brethren" until the mid-1950s. When support from families slowly ended, they gave up their anonymity and partisan activities against the Soviet occupiers.

In the late summer of 1944, the *20. Waffen-Grenadier-Division der SS (estnische Nr. 1)* was at SS Training Camp Neuhammer, where it was to be reformed. When the Red Army reached the Oder in mid-January 1945, a battle group was formed from division members and marched off to the *17. Armee.* Deployed in the area northwest of Oppeln, following the Soviet major offensive, the troops were encircled in the Oppeln Pocket two months later. After the breakthrough to the German main line of resistance, the battle group had been reduced to battalion strength. All of its heavy weapons had been lost and the bulk of the troops had fallen into enemy hands. At the end of March all available elements of the division was transferred to Goldberg and there occupied their last defensive positions at the Katzbach. There was no major fighting, instead the units tried to reach the Protectorate of Bohemia and Moravia via Reichenberg and finally the demarcation line. The men surrendered to the Red Army in the Annaberg area.

Since the autumn of 1944, all that remained of the **21. Waffen-Gebirgs-Division der SS "Skanderbeg" (albanische Nr. 1)** was a battle group of German members of the *Waffen-SS* and the *Kriegsmarine.* Attached to the *7. SS-Freiwilligen-Gebirgs-Division "Prinz Eugen,"* the men marched fighting through Zvornik to Bijeljina. They held the positions there—sometimes encircled—until they withdrew in the direction of Brcko on February 16, 1945. Then *Oberstabsbootsmann* Ernst Schäfer remembered:

The visibility was poor, no-man's-land was shrouded in fog. There was no end to the small arms fire, the explosive bullets whizzed over our heads. Only by dashing in a zigzag pattern could we move backwards and forwards in our encircled pocket. When, after three major attacks on my position, the Tito partisans saw no chance, they tried to break open the Bijeljina Pocket somewhere else. They attacked about 500 meters from me, and the reserve platoon had to be committed. On February 11, 1945, our company made ready to counterattack. With extreme caution and without firing a shot, we reached the starting position. On the partisan side we found only lookouts, who gave themselves up. While combing the houses I couldn't give the orders fast enough. My SS non-commissioned officers were ready for anything!

When, after an hour and a half, we had occupied the entire village, the partisans came with reinforcements. During the hand-to-hand combat I remembered the promise I had given my mates. I told *SS-Hauptsturmführer* Knapp that I would not become involved in further house fighting, so as to avoid further casualties. After all, we wanted to get back home. Knapp agreed, we had taken the pressure off the next sector and accomplished our mission.

How long were we supposed to remain in Bijelkina? In the homeland there was fighting in Aachen and we were deep in the Balkans and could go no further. Sailors from my platoon approached me: away from the SS—home! They wanted me to go with them. I declined, we wouldn't get far. A group from one of the other companies tried it anyway. The next morning the partisans called to us: you can come and get your men. They're swinging from the trees!

On February 15, 1945, the mates of my platoon helped me celebrate my thirty-second birthday. An *SS-Unterscharführer* supplied a bottle of Raki. Another reason to celebrate was that German troops had arrived in the city at noon to get us out. We began our joint withdrawal on February 16, 1945.

At the end of February, the troops reached Brcko and were directed on to Brod. There the battle group was disbanded. While the navy personnel were sent to Waren an der Müritz, the remaining members of the *Waffen-SS* formed a battalion in the *7. SS-Freiwilligen-Gebirgs-Division "Prinz Eugen."*

Encircled in Budapest since Christmas 1944, from January 17, 1945, the **22. SS-Freiwilligen-Kavallerie-Division** fought in the Pest quarter. The situation that developed there was almost apocalyptic. With no food and medical care and under constant enemy artillery fire, growing apathy spread. When the order to break out of the encircled city was given on February 11, 1945, not even 100 of the division's men reached the German lines. In ten weeks of combat operations the division had been almost completely destroyed.

The *23. SS-Freiwilligen-Panzergrenadier-Division "Nederland" (niederländische Nr. 1)* was formed on February 10, 1945, by renaming the *4. SS-Freiwilligen-Panzergrenadier-Brigade "Nederland,"* which was made up of about 6,000 men. This was in keeping with Himmler's desire to fool enemy intelligence. In fact, Stalin and Tito had already designated smaller units brigades and larger ones divisions, even though these had nowhere near the strength of equivalent German units. By February 1945, however, there was no longer any need to fool enemy intelligence. From February 16, 1945, the troops took part in the Pomeranian offensive in the Reetz area. After fierce but unsuccessful fighting, from March 1, the division conducted a fighting withdrawal towards the Altdamm bridgehead. The units were almost destroyed by enemy artillery fire in that position. Because of general developments in the situation, on March 20, Hitler finally gave his approval for the abandonment of the exposed bridgehead. After assembling in the Garz area, on April 16, 1945, the *23. SS-Freiwilligen-Panzergrenadier-Division* received orders to proceed to the area around Frankfurt/Oder. Because of transport difficulties and lack of fuel, only elements of the division reached the *XI. SS-Panzer-Korps* on April 18, and there were trapped in the so-called Halbe Pocket on April 25. The attempt to reach the *12. Armee* was successful only for a very few. Assembled in the SS prepared position in Redekin, the rest became prisoners of the Americans as *SS-Kampfgruppe Wagner.*

The *24. Waffen-Gebirgs[Karstjäger]-Division der SS* was also created by designating an existing brigade a division without providing it with additional personnel and materiel. While elements were deployed to defend the coast at Marano Lagoon, other companies were used against partisans in the Udine area. The troops left the Gulf of Trieste at the end of April 1945, and marched north in the direction of Gemona. There they linked up with the units from the Udine area and secured the withdrawal route to Villach. In the process the town of Avasinis was burned down and about fifty inhabitants who had been captured were shot. From May 2, 1945, the unit was supposed to secure the passes through the Karawanks and then marched into British captivity.

The *25. Waffen-Grenadier-Division der SS "Hunyadi" (ungarische Nr. 1)* had been in formation at Training Camp Neuhammer since December 1944. When the Red Army neared the area, on February 6, 1945, the division command received orders to proceed to Training Camp Grafenwöhr. While the bulk of the division set off on foot, a battle group of trained soldiers attempted to cover the transfer. At the end of February, the Hungarians reached the area south of Nuremberg and there were issued weapons and equipment. When American troops advanced towards Nuremberg from the north on April 11, 1945, the *25. Waffen-Grenadier-Division der SS* was ordered to Neustadt an der Donau. Although action against the Americans would have been a great support, the Germans kept their promise to the Hungarians that they would only see action against the Red Army. And so the more than 12,000 Hungarian volunteers marched on to Landshut–Burghausen and by way of Salzburg reached Attersee on May 2. There they surrendered to the Americans.

The *26. Waffen-Grenadier-Division der SS "Hungaria" (ungarische Nr. 2)* was supposed to be formed at Training Camp Schieratz effective January 26, 1945. As happened so often, theory and practice bore little resemblance to one another, for by January 17, the Red Army was already nearing the training camp. The Hungarian volunteers quartered there were subsequently ordered to Sagan via Lissa. From there they were supposed to be transferred first to SS Training Camp Neuhammer, which was also overtaken by the rapid Soviet advance. On February 7, 1945, the units began marching towards southern Germany. Quartered in the Nuremberg area at the end of February, they received arms and equipment for two regiments.

Like its sister unit "*Hunyadi*," the *26. Waffen-Grenadier-Division der SS* left its quartering area when American troops reached Nuremberg from the north. The unit moved to Salzburg via Landau and Burghausen and on May 2, 1945, surrendered to the Americans in Attersee.

The *27. Freiwilligen-Grenadier-Division "Langemarck" (flämische Nr. 1)* was a division only on paper. It contributed just a regiment-strength battle group to the failed Pomerania offensive, which began on February 16, 1945, and this saw action in the Ravenstein–Reetz area. Like the other units committed there, on March 1, it was forced to withdraw towards the Alt-damm bridgehead. Relieved from its positions on March 20, 1945, what was left of the battle group marched to Prenzlau and was there reinforced by the units that had not seen action. On April 15, a mixed division group was formed from Flemish and Wallonian volunteers, and it was directed to stand ready in the Damitzow–Pomellen–Hohenholz area as reserve in antici-pation of the Soviet spring offensive. There was heavy fighting when the Red Army crossed the Oder on April 20. The German defense collapsed on April 25, and the Belgian troops fled in disarray, putting up little resistance. Instead they tried to reach the demarcation line south of Schwerin by way of Neustrelitz–Waren–Karow. Initially captured by the British, the Belgian volunteers were later handed over to Belgian authorities.

On January 30, 1945, the *28. SS-Freiwilligen-Grenadier-Division "Wallonien" (wallonische Nr. 1)*, which was quartered in the Gronau area, received the formation order for a regi-ment-strength battle group that was to be used in the Pomerania offensive. By February 6, 1945, the battalions were already engaging Soviet troops near Kremzow–Repplin. Three days later there was fighting at Lindenberg and on February 16, it took part in the attack towards Muscherin. The Red Army launched fierce counterattacks and the Wallonian volunteers were forced to withdraw towards Kremzow. The Soviet offensive, which began on March 1, led to the withdrawal of the physically and psychologically battered unit towards the Altdamm bridgehead. There it was relieved by a new Wallonian battle group and taken out of action. When the bridgehead was abandoned on March 20, 1945, the remnants of the battle group already in action assembled near Stettin with another from Gronau. On April 15, these, together with Flemish volunteers, formed the Belgian *SS-Divisionsgruppe "Müller."* After the fighting described in the account of the *27. SS-Freiwilligen-Grenadier-Division*, the Walloons tried to fight their way to Denmark. By way of Waren, they reached the area around Lübeck and there they were captured by the British on May 2, 1945. First interned in the Fallingbostel camp, gradually the men were handed over to Belgian authorities.

The *Waffen-Grenadier-Brigade der SS (italienische Nr. 1)* was formed using Italian volunteers in November 1944. Effective February 1, 1945, it was renamed the *29. Waffen-Grenadier-Di-vision der SS (italienische Nr. 1)*. While a regiment-strength battle group guarded supply lines in the area south of Piacenza against partisan ambushes from the beginning of February, the other half of the division, which only had about 4,500 men, was employed on security duties in the Piedmont. The division saw no action as a division and was disbanded when the surrender came.

Formation of the *30. Waffen-Grenadier-Division der SS (weißruthenische Nr. 1)* began on March 9, 1944, however it was halted by order of the OKW at the end of the same month.

When 1944 ended, the *31. SS-Freiwilligen-Grenadier-Division* was working up to opera-tional readiness in *Wehrkreis XVIII*. On February 16, 1945, the units began entraining for the roughly 500-kilometer journey to the area southwest of Hirschberg in Silesia. Then at the be-ginning of March, the troops took over a sector of front near Jauer. In the defensive fighting that followed, the division was all but wiped out in a few days. The survivors occupied new positions in the Strehlen area. While there was no significant fighting there until May 6, 1945, the retreat led to dramatic scenes. Bypassing Prague, the division was supposed to reach the Pilsen area more than 300 kilometers away, there to surrender to the Americans. In countless mixed columns of *Wehrmacht* personnel and civilians, the soldiers tried initially to reach

Königgratz via Braunau–Nachod–Josefstadt. Others marched via Trautenau west towards Paka. On the way there were frequent incidents with Czech partisans. Then *SS-Unterscharführer* Fredo Gensicke remembered:

> The Czechs raged against the defenseless German population and us soldiers. Then we were assembled in a large sports field. There individual SS members were seized by the legs, dragged over the running track on their faces and then shot! On the way to Teplitz, anyone who left the column to get something to drink or relieve himself was shot! It was terrible.

The *32. SS-Freiwilligen-Grenadier-Division "30 Januar"* was a unit at least nominally fully-formed in 1945. After the Red Army advanced through areas almost devoid of troops to Frankfurt/Oder, at the end of January/early February 1945, many SS training and replacement units were ordered to the front south of Frankfurt. Immediately committed against several Soviet bridgeheads, the units suffered horrific casualties. Almost 4,000 soldiers were lost—killed, wounded, or missing—in February–March 1945 alone. Despite this, by April 17, 1945, the *32. SS-Freiwilligen-Grenadier-Division* reached a strength of about 12,500 men. After the start of the Soviet "Berlin Operation" the day before, on April 20, 1945, the division was ordered from the Oder into the Erkner–Fürstenwalde area to prevent the encirclement of the *9. Armee*. While one battle group initially remained in the positions along the Oder, another marched into the new area of operations. Without having been able to influence the situation, the division and other units were encircled on April 21, 1945. Via Märkisch-Buchholz, the division and civilians reached Halbe and there tried to cross the autobahn to the *12. Armee* beginning April 28. Only a small part managed to reach the German main line of resistance near Dobbrikow by way of Kummersdorf, however. From there they were directed on to the demarcation line at Tangermünde and there were taken prisoner by the western allies.

Like several other *Waffen-SS* brigades, on February 10, 1945, the *Waffen-Grenadier-Brigade der SS "Charlemagne"* (französische Nr. 1) was elevated to a division. A few days later the *33. Waffen-Grenadier-Division der SS "Charlemagne" (französische Nr. 1)* received orders to join Army Group Vistula. Already on February 23, 1945—the units had not even been completely assembled—the available battalions was transferred to the front in the area around Hammerstein. Lacking anti-tank weapons, the division was ill-equipped to face the Soviet advance. And at the end of February the units were forced to withdraw towards Neustettin. The French volunteers were surrounded in Belgard on March 1, 1945. Organized into three battle groups, they tried to regain the German main line of resistance. Only the first of these succeeded, while the other two were almost completely destroyed by Soviet troops. In mid-March 1945, the survivors gathered in Neustrelitz, where the *33. Waffen-Grenadier-Division der SS* was supposed to be reestablished. On March 27, 1945, the division commander gave a summary of the fighting to date, completely ignoring reality:

> We have drastic days of bitter fighting and forced marches behind us. We have not fought as a small group within the German Army, but as an independent French division. With the name "Charlemagne" the French reputation for bravery and endurance has again been confirmed. The duration of our struggles has united us. [...]
>
> Everywhere we have helped hold back or stop the surging wave of bolshevism. This struggle could not be fought without serious losses and many of our comrades have not yet been able to make it back to our lines. We hope that General Puaud and with him other heroic fighters will soon be with us again. The struggle has welded us together. The fact that our division has been fused in glorious battles should be to our advantage, as we now form a block, a team.

Far from our homeland, we can add new glory to our banner. We know that all Frenchmen, who like us stand for the freedom of the motherland and for the new European order, view us with pride. [...]

The reputation of the L.V.F.[36] in the east, the success of the French SS Assault Brigade in the Carpathians, the battles fought by the militia in our motherland must create a block which, sealed by the French blood shed in Pomerania, must lead to the birth hour of a tradition that is worthy of the revolutionary idea for which we are fighting. Our belief in the victory of National-Socialism is unshakeable. It will become even more determined if the situation becomes more difficult.

At the side of our German comrades who are fighting for the same ideal, we follow the Führer, the liberator of Europe.

This order of the day, which is reminiscent of the outpourings of a National Socialist command officer, had little demagogic effect on the French volunteers. The bulk of the soldiers no longer had any motivation to fight and preferred to volunteer to construct anti-tank barricades in the Neustrelitz area. While the survivors withdrew via Malchin to Güstrow with the *3. Panzer-Armee*, in order to reach the demarcation line in the Bad Kleinen area, on April 24, 1945, the division commander received orders to take command of the *11. SS-Freiwilligen-Panzergrenadier-Division "Nordland"* in Berlin. About ninety Frenchmen accompanied him and took part in the final battles in Berlin.

The ***34. SS-Freiwilligen-Grenadier-Division "Landstorm Nederland" (niederländische Nr. 2)*** was created on February 10, 1945, by renaming the *SS-Freiwilligen-Grenadier-Brigade "Landstorm Nederland,"* which had been formed in November 1944. The unit's strength rose from about 5,400 men to about 6,000. Deployed in Fortress Holland, the units took over a sector of front in the line Rhenen–Tiel–Zaltbommel. Units were ordered into the area southwest of Zwolle in response to "Operation Plunder." When British units crossed the Waal, the companies of the *34. SS-Freiwilligen-Grenadier-Division* deployed there withdrew beyond the Rhine. This left the division holding a line between Rhenen and Vreeswijk. When the enemy crossed the river there, on May 4, 1945, the Dutch volunteers withdrew into the Veenendaal–Ede–Otterlo area. The next day they surrendered to the British Army.

The ***35. SS-Polizei-Grenadier-Division*** was formed from the former *Polizei-Brigade "Wirth,"* also on February 10, 1945. This, too, was nothing more than a renaming—the troops received no reinforcements and remained in their positions west of the Neiße between Oderzufluss and Guben. The Soviet offensive across the Oder resulted in the division being encircled with elements of the *9. Armee* and the unit was split into two battle groups. While one remained in its positions, the other moved to the southern edge of the pocket in the Lübben area. On April 23, 1945, the battle group which had remained at the Neiße also left its positions and tried to slip through to the west via Groß Leuthen and Groß Köris. The Red Army drove the German units before it, not just here but also in the area of Lübben. The units of the *35. SS-Polizei-Grenadier-Division* deployed there subsequently withdrew towards Schlepzig and assembled with the remnants of other divisions in the area east of Baruth. The bulk of the survivors were captured or killed by the Soviets during the attempt to break through to the *12. Armee*. Only a few managed to reach the German main line of resistance and ultimately surrender to the Americans at the Elbe.

The ***36. Waffen-Grenadier-Division der SS***, which was ordered formed effective February 14, 1945, had its origins in *SS-Sonderkommando "Dirlewanger"* formed in 1940. Originally assigned to guard a Jewish labor camp in the Generalgouvernement, from January 1942, it was employed to combat partisans in White Russia. Originally made up of convicted poachers and finally enlarged using career criminals, anti-socials, and political prisoners, the units spread fear and terror among the population. After helping to put down the Warsaw Uprising and the

Slovakian National Uprising, on February 12, 1945, *SS-Sturmbrigade "Dirlewanger"* reached Guben and from there attacked successfully in the direction of Naumburg. Russian pressure was such, however, that street fighting broke out in Guben ten days later. The units of what was now the *36. Waffen-Grenadier-Division der SS* subsequently occupied positions along the Neiße between Horno and Fürst. When the enemy took the offensive there on April 19, he quickly took about 1,000 prisoners. After Soviet forces encircled the *9. Armee*, the troops fell back from the Neiße on April 23, and marched via Burg to Lübben. The unit reached Schlepzig on April 26, 1945, and its disintegration began there. It did not take part in the breakthrough near Halbe on April 28, as a unit. Instead most members of the division tried to go underground and try their luck individually to reach their home towns.

In February 1945, the *37. SS-Freiwilligen-Kavallerie-Division* was ordered to Training Camp Lesser Carpathians in the Gajery–Malacky–Stupava area east of the March River for formation. While two battle groups from the division saw action, in mid-March 1945 the remaining elements moved to the Znaim area. The first battle group was transferred to the *96. Infanterie-Division* in the Bickse area in early March 1945, and in fierce defensive fighting at the end of the month it enabled other German units to withdraw across the Danube near Gran. It then made its own withdrawal through Slovakia—north of Bratislava—beyond the March River and on April 5, began assembling in the Marchegg area. After heavy fighting in the Stopfenreuth–Engelhartstetten area from April 7–9, the SS cavalry came back under its own division command, which had arrived from Znaim. The second battle group was not put together until March 26, 1945, and was sent to the *356. Infanterie-Division* on the Wiener Neustadt area. In costly actions the units withdrew through Ternitz and Puchberg to Schwarzau. On May 7, 1945, they tried to reach the demarcation line at Altenmarkt an der Enns. The division command, which from April 10, commanded one of its battle groups in addition to units of the *Wehrmacht*, took over a sector of front northeast of Vienna. One week later the *37. SS-Freiwilligen-Kavallerie-Division* was ordered back into the Znaim area to complete its formation. Elements of the division still saw action in the Freistadt area and there surrendered to the Americans on May 8, 1945.

Formation of the *38. SS-Grenadier-Division "Nibelungen,"* the last unit of the *Waffen-SS* to be established, began in the Freiburg–Feldberg–Todtnau area on March 25, 1945. When the western allies took the offensive on the Upper Rhine, beginning April 17, 1945, the division was sent to Training Camp Grafenwöhr. The 16- and 17-year-old recruits had not yet been issued uniforms and at best their Hitler Youth uniforms provided some degree of standardization. Not until April 19, 1945, were they issued *Waffen-SS* uniforms in Dachau. As the American advance made reaching Grafenwöhr impossible, on April 21, 1945, the unit received orders to occupy prepared positions in the rear at the Danube between Bad Abbach–Kehlheim–Neustadt and Vohburg for the *17. SS-Panzergrenadier-Division*, which was streaming back. When on April 25, that unit occupied the positions behind the Danube, the youths, who had only become soldiers a few days before, were incorporated into the defense front. Fighting with American troops began the next day. On April 28, the units received orders to pull back behind the Isar. There the *38. SS-Grenadier-Division* occupied its own positions between Freising–Moosburg–Landshut. On May 2, 1945, the young troops pulled back to Wasserburg am Inn, experiencing minor skirmishing. It then marched in the direction of Chiemsee and finally to Oberwössen near Reit im Winkel, where the division surrendered to the Americans on May 8, 1945.

CHAPTER 4
CHIEF OF GERMAN POLICE

Geheime Staatspolizei (Secret State Police)

Scarcely ten years after Himmler joined the NSDAP and became an insignificant party functionary, he was given his first state position when the National–Socialist Party assumed power. *Generalleutnant a.D.* Franz von Epp (October 16, 1868 – January 31, 1947), the Reich Commissar of Bavaria, named him acting chief of police of Munich. The former chief of police, *Oberregierungsrat* Julius Koch (January 29, 1881 – November 19, 1951) was initially placed on leave and then dismissed, because, "as chief of police in Munich he had waged all-out war against the national movement."

As soon as he took officer, Himmler began pursuing political opponents in Munich. Based on the "President's Decree for the Protection of the People and State of February 28, 1933," as acting chief of police he could, without judicial oversight, order people to be arrested and sent to so-called "protective custody camps." In addition to communists and social democrats, Jews were also arrested in large numbers, and on March 12, 1933, Himmler placated the population of Munich with the following astonishing declaration:[1]

> As there was great excitement in many places in the city and it was impossible for me to protect the individuals who had caused the excitement, I felt obliged to take this measure so that I could assume responsibility for health and life. I must emphasize one thing explicitly: to us a citizen of the Jewish faith is just as much a citizen as those who are non-Jews and his life and his property will be protected just the same. Here we know no difference. It is for this reason that protective custody is needed.

Himmler pacified the population by telling them that the prescribed protective custody—under which, for example, more than a few prisoners lost teeth while being "protected" by their SA guards—served the welfare of the imprisoned. This could not be worded more sarcastically.

In the days that followed, Himmler gave control of the political police, which had existed during the Weimar Republic as part of the criminal police, as well as the political auxiliary police to be formed from members of the SA and SS and the protective custody camps to the likewise newly-appointed acting minister of the interior in Bavaria, Adolf Wagner (October 1, 1890 – April 12, 1944). Himmler was replaced in his position as acting chief of police by *SA-Oberführer* August Schneidhuber[2] (May 8, 1887 – June 30, 1934).

To ensure comprehensive and centralized monitoring of opposition, not only outside but within the party as well, Hitler gave Himmler the task of exercising influence on the political police of the other German *Länder*. Himmler won over the former commanders of the political police battalions by giving them SS ranks and he initiated the installment of party-conforming police members in these positions. In October 1933, for example, *SS-Sturmbannführer* Bruno Streckenbach became chief of political police in Hamburg.

In December 1933, Himmler was himself named Chief of Political Police by the minister of the interior in Lübeck and Mecklenburg. Then, by May 2, 1934, Himmler succeeded in centralizing the political police of the German states—with the exception of Prussia—in the "Central Office of Police Commanders of the Länder." In Prussia, on the other hand, Hermann Göring—recently named prime minister of Prussia—also separated the political police from the criminal police and also placed them under a newly-created secret state police department (Gestapa). Although Himmler was named Inspector of the Secret State Police (Gestapo) and deputy chief of the Prussian Gestapo, Göring remained head of the Gestapo.

Nevertheless, Himmler had ensured that the political police in all of the *Länder* were either under his personal control or that of members of his SS. As the population—as in Munich, for example—were not uncritical of the Gestapo's actions, on October 11, 1934, before Gestapo officials Himmler issued the basic directive that, "the people [must] be persuaded that the feared secret state police is the fairest and most precisely-functioning authority in the new state."

Certainly this statement was not to be interpreted to mean that he was uncomfortable that his Gestapo was feared by the people, rather it surely displayed a certain pride that was also intended to impact his listeners. In addition to combating enemies of the regime, the Gestapo soon also began compiling regular assessments of public opinion.

When Himmler was promoted to Chief of German Police on June 18, 1936, the Gestapo and the criminal police were combined under the office of security police. Whereas the political police (now the Gestapo) had formerly been a component of the criminal police, both were now elements within the security police.

On July 1, 1937, Himmler issued a so-called "Separation of Functions Decree" which spelled out the different areas of responsibility of the Gestapo and the still independent and party-internal security service (SD). The Gestapo was responsible for combating political opponents, while the SD, as an intelligence service, was to assess the mood of the German population. Information it gathered about political opponents was passed on to the security police, which then initiated pursuance measures.

On September 27, 1939 the Security Police and the SD were combined to form the *Reichssicherheitshauptamt* (Reich Central Security Office),[3] and during the war it expanded its sphere of activity to new groups of people. The hundreds of thousands of prisoners of war and foreign workers had to be watched. In addition to the possibility of sabotage in the workplace, this also included, for example, unauthorized contacts with the German population. Escaped foreign workers were sent to concentration camps or even executed. The Gestapo was also active in the occupied territories, combating resistance movements there.

As well, during the Second World War, the Gestapo also took over crucial functions in connection with the persecution, deportation, and murder of European Jews as well as Sinti and Roma. Quite a few officials were assigned to the *Einsatzgruppen*.

In 1944–45, there were more than 30,000 policemen working in the Gestapo. Despite their comprehensive agent activities, they failed to prevent the assassination attempt against Hitler on July 20, 1944.

Ordnungspolizei (Order Police)

While Himmler had advanced to become the superior of about 6,000 German police (Gestapo officials), his rise in power grew exponentially three years later when Hitler named him Chief of German Police. Overnight he was suddenly in command of an additional roughly 100,000 police (*Schutzpolizisten* or Schupos) and gendarmes. In view of a centralization of the executive, on June 17, 1936, Hitler explained this step:

I. To unify the control of police duties in the Reich, a chief of the German Police shall be appointed within the Reich Ministry of the Interior, to whom is assigned the direction and executive authority for all police matters within the jurisdiction of the Reich and Prussian Ministries of the Interior.

II. (1) The Deputy Chief of the Prussian Secret State Police, *Reichsführer-SS* Heinrich Himmler, is hereby named Chief of the German Police in the Reich and Prussian Ministries of the Interior.

(2) He is personally and directly subordinate to the Reich and Prussian Ministers of the Interior.

(3) For matters within his jurisdiction he represents the Reich and Prussian Ministers of the Interior in their absence.

(4) His service title is: *Reichsführer-SS* and Chief of the German Police in the Reich Ministry of the Interior.

III. The Chief of the German Police in the Reich Ministry of the Interior will take part in the meetings of the Reich Cabinet in so far as matters within his jurisdiction are concerned.

IV. I hereby charge the Reich and the Prussian Ministers of the Interior with the execution of this decree.

Thus subject to the authority of the *Reichsführer-SS* were:

Ordnungspolizei Head Office (Order Police) with
Schutzpolizei (uniformed police)
Gendarmerie (village police)
Gemeindepolizei (municipal police)
Land- und Stadtwacht (rural and town guards)
Zollgrenzschutz (customs border guards, from 1937)
Feuerschutzpolizei (firefighters, from 1938)
Luftschutzpolizei (air defense police, from 1942)
and the *Sicherheitspolizei* (Sipo) Head Office with,
Kriminalpolizei (Kripo) (criminal police)
Geheime Staatspolizei (Gestapo) (secret state police)

There was another reason for the installation of Himmler as Chief of German Police, however, which he himself explained in a speech to *SS-Gruppenführer* on February 18, 1937:[4] With his appointment, the possibility finally existed, "to instill the police with an ideological content and for the first time to make it an instrument of an ideology."

Thus the police, which had always had to conform to the type of government in power, would be committed to National Socialism. To the extent possible, a personal union was to be created between the SS and the police. Members of the SS who were also members of the

Ordnungspolizei could and were expected to display their membership in the SS by wearing embroidered SS runes beneath the left breast pocket of their police uniform, and likewise SS men who were members of the Security Police could and were expected to wear their black SS uniform while on duty.

As a result of the return of the Sudetenland and the Memelland, as well as the incorporation of Austria into the Reich, by 1939, the *Ordnungspolizei* grew to about 125,000 active policemen. In addition to their usual peacetime duties, they had many other responsibilities in the event of war. To deal with these, in 1938, the so-called "*verstärkte Polizeischutz*" (enhanced police protection, renamed Police Reserve in 1940) was brought into being. With almost 100,000 men, it was almost as large as the active *Ordnungspolizei* at that time. The Police Reserve included members of all occupation groups (except police) from the 1901 to 1909 age classes, and they trained for possible police service on weekends or in one or two courses lasting several days. Training was limited primarily to the use of small arms, marching, guard duties and brief legal instruction.

When mobilization was announced on August 26, 1939, an initial group of about 30,000 police reservists was called up. As *Wachtmeister*, they provided the personnel for about fifty police battalions. Concerning the formation of the Police Reserve, a contemporary publication from 1942 noted:[5]

> The *Ordnungspolizei*'s peacetime strength was of course inadequate to meet all of its wartime responsibilities. All of its branches had to undergo massive expansion for the duration of the war and the Police Reserve was created for this purpose. Men from all stations and occupations were called up and even before the war they received instruction and training for their police tasks in wartime. Thus when war broke out the *Ordnungspolizei* was able to carry out the serious challenges it faced. In addition to carrying out police tasks, training of these men doing their war duty in the police continued. Today the members of the Police Reserve are doing their duty everywhere, whether on road patrol in the homeland, site defense or in the police battalions in Poland, in the occupied western territories and even in the far north in Norway. Side by side with their active-service comrades they are doing their duty and their zeal is unsurpassed by them.

In fact the formation of the Police Reserve and the police battalions formed from it had a special purpose. During the First World War the army had been solely responsible for securing the rear areas. Changing this practice made sense in National-Socialism's ideological goals. With his police battalions, Himmler could now act in the occupied areas independent of the *Wehrmacht*. They were thus to form an important executive authority of National–Socialist policy.

While roughly 60,000 police had been called up by the *Wehrmacht* in the course of general conscription in October 1935, in autumn 1939, a further approximately 16,000 trained policemen were used to form the army's so-called *Polizei-Division*. In return, the *Ordnungspolizei* received 26,000 untrained recruits from the 1918 to 1920, and 1909 to 1912 age classes. Of these, the approximately 9,000 men aged 19 to 21 were conscripted as so-called *Polizei-Anwärter* (police candidates), and the roughly 17,000 men aged 27 to 31 as so-called *Wachtmeister d.R.* (reserve technical sergeants). These men were used to form almost fifty additional police battalions.

On August 20, 1940, the German Police had a total strength of 244,500 members. It should be borne in mind that just four years earlier Himmler had been the superior of about 6,000 Gestapo officers. His police power potential had thus grown forty-fold! These included:

232,500 men of the *Ordnungspolizei*, including
176,000 active service members of the *Ordnungspolizei*, of which

16,000 policemen in the army's Polizei-Division
8,000 men in the *Wehrmacht*'s military police units
60,000 men in the approximately 100 police battalions
92,500 men in the village police, rural and town guards and the firefighters
56,000 police reservists and
12,000 men of the *Sicherhsitspolizei*

After the start of the campaign in Russia, in the summer of 1941, many volunteers from the conquered states of the Soviet Union came forward to carry arms on the German side. In addition to the formation of so-called eastern battalions within the *Wehrmacht*, the bulk of the volunteers were concentrated in the *Ordnungspolizei* in so-called *Schutzmannschafts-Bataillonen* (police battalions). About 200 of these battalions with a total of about 100,000 men were formed by the end of the war—especially in the Baltic States, White Russia, and the Ukraine. These police units were tasked mainly with guarding installations important to the war effort and combating partisans. A few also saw action at the front.

In his position as Chief of German Police, Himmler was thus the superior of a total of about 350,000 German and foreign police. Effective July 9, 1942, the police battalions deployed in the occupied territories were concentrated under twenty-eight regimental headquarters, "to ensure the standardized and effective command of the police and reserve police battalions." Initially this brought about no changes to the existing tactical or geographical attachments. The determining factor was probably Himmler's desire to demonstrate the power of the elements of the *Ordnungspolizei* serving outside the country, as well as to provide promotion opportunities for the former battalion commanders. For Himmler, who liked to see himself as a military man, control over twenty-eight police regiments also meant that he to some extent was performing the functions of the commander-in-chief of an army.

Not long afterwards, Himmler again showed his desire to bring about a merger of his SS with the police. In a decree dated February 24, 1943, Himmler awarded the police regiments the "SS" prefix "in recognition of your exceptionally brave and successful actions." As a result the units were now designated SS Police Regiments. The desired close ties between the SS and the police were also described in highly-propagandized form in the conclusion of the previously-mentioned contemporary publication of 1942:[6]

Through this book, many parents will come to know for the first time the immense fields of responsibility of the German police and will become convinced that service in it is truly service among and for the people, and many young people will perhaps make the decision to place all their strength and total being at the disposal of the German people, and therefore volunteer to serve in the *Waffen-SS* and the German Police.

After the heavy German losses at Stalingrad and in North Africa in early 1943, on March 29, orders were issued for the formation of eight so-called Police Rifle Regiment in which the 1st battalion would consist of German police members and the 2nd and 3rd battalions of European volunteers—mainly existing *Schutzmannschaft* battalions. As well, as during mobilization in 1939, there was another exchange of personnel between the *Ordnungspolizei* and the *Wehrmacht*. This time the *Waffen-SS* released about 7,500 untrained men (mainly older age classes or ethnic Germans) to the *Ordnungspolizei* and in return at least received younger, trained men from the police regiments. These were used to form new SS units or rehabilitate existing ones. In addition, the formation of police regiments using men from South Tyrol began that autumn.

Further transfers of members of the *Ordnungspolizei* to the *Waffen-SS* followed. For example, Latvian and Ukrainian police battalions were transferred to the Latvian and Ukrainian *Waffen-Verbänden der SS*, and on August 1, 1944, the bulk of the remaining Russian police battalions were used to form the *30. Waffen-Grenadier-Division der SS (russische Nr. 2)*. A second police division was formed on the Eastern Front using members of the German Police on March 16, 1945, and on April 8, it was attached to the *SS-Führungshauptamt* (Operational Headquarters SS). The first police division had already been transferred from the army to the *Waffen-SS* on February 10, 1942, becoming the *SS-Polizei-Division*.

During the war, therefore, in total almost 60,000 of the more than 350,000 German and foreign members of the *Ordnungspolizei* were ultimately transferred to the *Waffen-SS*.

Military Employment of the *Ordnungspolizei*[7]

In March 1938, five battalion- to regiment-strength march units formed from existing *Polizei-Hundertschaften* in the major cities took part in the entry into Austria. Then, during the occupation of rump-Czechoslovakia in March 1939, a total of ten police battalions were formed. Concentrated in two regiments, they were supposed to maintain order in the occupied areas and were transferred to Bohemia and Moravia.

During mobilization in the summer of 1939, seventeen more police battalions were formed and these were concentrated in *Polizei-Gruppen* (regiments). In the summer of 1939, the *Ordnungspolizei* began forming about fifty new battalions from police reservists and recruits in the *Wehrkreise* (military districts). The majority of these were so-called Reserve Police Battalions. The battalion numbers now reflected the military district to which the unit was responsible, with the exception of *Wehrkreis III* (Berlin). The resulting, in some cases high numbers undoubtedly deceived the enemy as to the actual number of German police battalions.[8]

After the end of the campaign in Poland, effective November 4, 1939, four new police regiments were formed for the four districts of the newly-created Generalgouvernement. A member of the *Schutzpolizei* wrote an informative report about police actions in the Generalgouvernement. He failed, however, to mention that Germans repatriated from the Baltic States and the Ukraine were resettled in the Warthe District after its Polish and Jewish inhabitants had been cleared out:[9]

There was a police regimental headquarters and several battalion headquarters in Warsaw. Here in Warsaw the police had set up several bases and also actively patrolled the city to maintain peace and order in this difficult-to-oversee city with its large and contorted ghetto. This ghetto was one of my first destinations. It was fenced in with barbed wire, at least they were beginning to fence it in at that time, and large signs alerted one to the danger of epidemic and forbade off-duty entry into this quarter of the city.

As strange as it sounds, in those March days of 1940, Warsaw was not only the most destroyed city in the east, but also the most in love with life. The streets, even where they passed through fields of ruins, were full of people. Unlike in the old Reich there was no blackout, the windows were lit, the streetcars ran and were overcrowded, the cafes were well-attended, and in addition to Polish cinemas there were police cinemas which were run by an Ufa projectionist from Berlin.

Before I finally left the east, I paid a visit to what was then Lodz. The purpose of my trip was first of all to visit the transit camps for the Germans from Volhynia and Galicia and in addition the city's ghetto.

In Przemysl I had had the opportunity to speak to the Galician Germans soon after they crossed the border, and in Lodz I was able to supplement and complete my material. My plan to also pay a visit to the new settlements in the Warthe District later in the spring came to nothing because of the action in Norway, which no one could have imagined at that time, but I saw a great deal in Lodz.

The peasant carts that had crossed the bridge in Przemsyl and been unloaded in Jaroslau sat outside Lodz in a vehicle park. The resettlement was in progress. On that

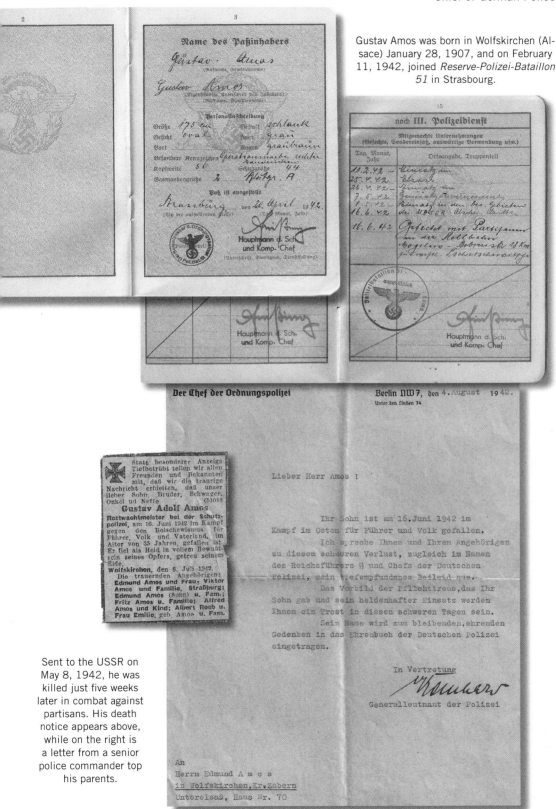

Gustav Amos was born in Wolfskirchen (Alsace) January 28, 1907, and on February 11, 1942, joined *Reserve-Polizei-Bataillon 51* in Strasbourg.

Sent to the USSR on May 8, 1942, he was killed just five weeks later in combat against partisans. His death notice appears above, while on the right is a letter from a senior police commander top his parents.

day families that had been assembled were called and taken to their new homes in buses. Other families sat in the different camps waiting to be called.

Until September the year 1940, was characterized by the training of the new police battalions, some of which were assigned occupation duties for a short time along with the "old" battalions. In addition to the police formations in the Protectorate of Bohemia and Moravia and the Generalgouvernement, after the end of the campaign in the west in June 1941, three police battalions were ordered to Alsace–Lorraine and Luxembourg. In addition to general police duties these also oversaw large-scale resettlements. The following report reflects the desired chauvinistic tenor desired by the state—in this case towards the French—at that time:[10]

Another time it was a German machine-gun sentry in Metz who was verbally abused by a Frenchman in a challenging way. Carrying out his duty, this sentry advised this questionable character—hands in his pants pockets up to the elbows, cigarette in the corner of his mouth and beret on his right ear—that he was crossing the road contrary to regulations. In reply, the words "*Sale Boche*" (German pig) came from the Frenchman's mouth. He then sat down before the policeman could give him a well-deserved boxing of the ears. Two passing members of the Wehrmacht heard the words and immediately gave the cheeky Frenchman an important lesson. Of course he did not escape his deserved punishment and subsequent deportation. All of this and much more, for example the use of the French language and unwillingness to adapt to the existing circumstances, resulted in the French elements, which had streamed in droves into this historically German region after 1919, having to be removed. There were major resettlement actions, whose main burden fell on the police. The many shining examples of the "chosen people" showed their true colors by singing the Marseillaise.

Parallel to the actions to resettle the French and Jews, the police also saw to the population of Lorraine which had been evacuated to the interior of France and saw to it that their return and the safeguarding of their belongings were carried out according to plan. A refugee forwarding office was set up in Metz for this purpose. It took care of more than 400,000 persons and was able to return them to their homes.

The report about Luxembourg also shows how the national policy of the day was subliminally transmitted to the public:[11]

As previously stated, pure German blood flows in the veins of the people of Luxembourg, for they belong to one and the same tribe as our Moselle states and they speak the very same dialect. But despite this, it would be presumptuous to claim that the people of Luxembourg immediately welcomed their new political situation with jubilation and true enthusiasm. On the contrary, at first they behaved very reticently and expectantly, which in the end was because about half of the country's inhabitants were well disposed towards France.

After German troops occupied Luxembourg and it became part of the Greater German Reich, a German administration was installed in this country and in Alsace–Lorraine. Units of the German police assumed responsibility for maintaining law and order and also guarded the country's borders with France and Belgium, as well as that with the Reich—customs had not yet been lifted. Monitoring of traffic into the Reich was solely for the purpose of product control, while the borders with France and Belgium were still sealed to prevent the immigration of Frenchmen and Jews. For this reason, therefore, it was necessary to transfer stronger police forces to Luxembourg.

One police battalion entered the city of Luxembourg itself shortly after the ceasefire with France. Many people lined the column's march route. Some were still very reserved and the majority had apparently come out of curiosity, to be present for the military spectacle of the arrival of the police unit in its green uniforms. Not too many raised their arm in the German salute.

The head of the column with the band had meanwhile reached the parade square, whose adjacent houses were decorated with the victorious flags of the Reich. A large crowd of people lined the festive square, and when the police battalion marched in smartly to the tune of a brisk German military march, then thousands of arms stretched and offered the police battalion the German salute, accompanied by lively shouts of *Heil!* The men in the green tunics were taken somewhat aback by this spontaneous demonstration. For all of the Reich and ethnic Germans from far and near had made their way to this square to attend a German hour of celebration.

At the same time, German police units were also dispatched to the Netherlands and Norway. Hans Richter wrote about the actions of the police in Norway in his publication:[12]

On Monday, the 22nd of April 1940, I learned by telephone that, not only had orders finally been issued for a deployment to Norway, but also that part of the headquarters staff had already left by aircraft for Oslo. Orders had been issued for the rest of the headquarters and the first battalion to be deployed to be transported out on the 24th of April. On the afternoon of the 23rd, the two police battalions stood in the barracks of the old Maikäfer on the Chausseestrasse in Berlin and were seen off by the commander of the *Ordnungspolizei, SS-Obergruppenführer und General der Polizei* Daluege. In his address to the men the general stated that conditions in Norway were not comparable with those in Poland. The Norwegians were a racially-related people to us and we had not entered the country to overrun it by force of arms, rather we did so to protect it from the much worse threat of a war which England wanted to bring to the peaceful north. The country had its own government, its administration and its own economic life, in which we wanted to interfere as little as possible. The German police should feel like friends and guests in Norway, but they should take hard but fair action wherever they encountered resistance. He concluded the speech with a *Sieg Heil* to the *Führer*.

Coming from Fredrikshavn (Denmark), in the evening set foot on Norwegian soil for the first time in Larvik. Larvik is a small port and also a beach resort. The reception was not overly friendly but also not outwardly hostile. Well, one could scarcely ask for more based on the stand the Norwegians had taken for hundreds of years.

Two schools had been prepared for the two battalions temporarily still in Larvik, and the offices of the commander of the *Ordnungspolizei* were initially in the Storthing, the building that housed the Norwegian legislature. When the battalions followed in the days that followed, they were immediately dispersed so that one battalion remained in Oslo while the second had to secure the Drammen area in the south. Soon there was a police guard at the Storthing, police patrolled the city, and after negotiations with the *Wehrmacht* the area for which the police were responsible was moved more and more to the north. An extremely important task was added to those of the police; guarding the Swedish border. This border is not a natural one, is formed neither by a river nor a mountain range, instead it runs through forest and generally can only be reached by cross roads. On the other side, Sweden had manned its border quite heavily, and to show them that we Germans had no offensive intentions of attacking Swedish territory, the military border guards were to be replaced by police ones.

Then the third battalion destined for Norway arrived in Oslo and was sent to Trondheim. There too, as everywhere, the stark contrast between war and peace. Up in Narvik, completely separated from the south, the small force of parachute troops and navy people was fighting the superior strength of the English, there was still a complete Norwegian division at Mo, and here in Trondheim there was peace. The city had certainly become different, even more than in Oslo the businesses were boarded up, but despite this the young people of Trondheim still strolled the streets exactly as before, all of the bars were full, and in the hotel's Wintergarten members of the *Wehrmacht* and Norwegians sat side by side in the beautiful tidy room and listened to the house band, which played every evening.

There were tragic incidents in the new "Eastern Provinces" of the German Reich (Wartheland and Danzig–West Prussia). In December 1939 and October 1940, there were two major waves of deportations of Jews and Poles from the two newly-incorporated Reich territories to the Generalgouvernement. In the process, approximately 160,000 Jews went to the Warsaw ghetto in autumn 1940.

For a number of police battalions, the year 1941, began with further resettlements and expulsions from the newly-incorporated territories. Himmler planned to deport a total of 831,000 Poles and Jews to the Generalgouvernement.

New assignments resulted from the Balkan Campaign in April 1941, and the war against the Soviet Union, which began in June. On the one hand the occupied areas—which included Carniola and Southern Styria in southern Europe and the Baltic States and White Russia in Eastern Europe—had to be guarded and elements of the population "resettled." In numerous cases the gruesome special tasks had to be carried out in keeping with the "ideological war." Various police battalions took part in the mass executions of several thousand Jews, with their tasks including guarding the Jews and transporting them to the execution sites, as well as sealing off the sites and participating in the actual shootings.

After the Red Army's first winter offensive was able to place the German forces in dire straits, in December 1941 police units were ordered from the rear area to the front to lend support. As the battalions had not been prepared for such a role and by then even the partisan war had assumed alarming proportions, the Commander of the *Ordnungspolizei* modified his training regulations and on January 16, 1942, issued the *Guidelines for Combat Training of Closed Units of the Ordnungspolizei for the East*. It was intended to provide more specific training for police members and improve their usability against the "treacherous Russian enemies." The men were to be instilled with, "an unconditional, tough fighting spirit, supplemented by flexibility in all situations and martial skills, especially the ability to employ all available weaponry. Those officers and NCOs without combat experience must adapt to the nature of this unconditional life and death struggle with a sound power of imagination [...] Training must be designed so that, after a certain time, the fighting men become accustomed to all situations and surprises and fully adapted to the new conditions in the east."

These pithy words show how badly the police battalions had been prepared for the coming operations in the east and simultaneously in southeastern Europe, and what improvised means were employed to take this into account. In addition to its previous tasks, during the course of 1942 the *Ordnungspolizei* increasingly also pursued measures of wartime economy. The collection of agricultural goods and the acquisition of labor (so-called *Ostarbeiter*) gained increasing importance.

From a political standpoint, the Wannsee Conference of January 20, 1942, and the final solution to the Jewish problem adopted there represented a special starting point for the *Ordnungspolizei*. Approximately 180,000 Jews were to be deported from the Reich to the Generalgouvernement or to Theresienstadt. To make room for the newcomers, large numbers of Jews—especially those living in the Warsaw ghetto—were murdered. At the end of April, Himmler also unveiled his General Plan East, which called for the Zamosch area in Poland to

Alexander Zahharov volunteered to serve in *Po-lizei-Bataillon "Ostland"* while in a Franconian resettlement camp for ethnic Germans from Estonia. Formed in Frankfurt/Oder in August 1941, in October it was renamed *Reserve-Polizei-Bataillon 33.*

also be cleared for ethnic German settlers. The resulting transports were almost all carried out by the *Ordnungspolizei*.

At the end of February 1942, various police battalions again saw action at the front. Five battalions were sent to Battle Group Jeckeln in Siverskaya, mainly by air. There they relieved elements of the *58. Infanterie-Division*, which were withdrawn from positions near Pushkin the siege ring around Leningrad.

In carrying out their duties, the other police battalions were located in the rear areas. After the creation of police regiments in the summer of 1942, they were deployed as follows:

Polizei-Regiment 1	The battalions were attached to the Senior SS and Police Commander Russia North, the SIPO in Ostland, and in Slovenia.
Polizei-Regiment 2	The battalions were deployed in the area under the Senior SS and Police Commander Russia Center and took part in numerous actions against partisans.
Polizei-Regiment 3	The entire regiment was stationed in the occupied Netherlands.
Polizei-Regiment 4	The battalions were deployed in occupied France.
Polizei-Regiment 5	The units were deployed in Serbia, some in Slovenia.
Polizei-Regiment 6	Individual battalions were attached to army security divisions with Army Group South.
Polizei-Regiment 7	The entire regiment moved to Norway at the turn of the year 1942–43.
Polizei-Regiment 8	Individual battalions were attached to army security divisions with Army Group Center.
Polizei-Regiment 9	Individual battalions were attached to army security divisions with Army Group North.
Polizei-Regiment 10	The battalions were deployed in the area under the general Commission Ukraine.
Polizei-Regiment 11	The battalions were deployed in the area under the general Commission Ukraine.
Polizei-Regiment 12	The regiment was employed in the Netherlands.
Polizei-Regiment 13	The battalions were deployed in the area under the Senior SS and Police Commander Russia Center and took part in numerous operations against partisans.
Polizei-Regiment 14	The battalions were deployed in the area under the Senior SS and Police Commander Russia Center and took part in numerous operations against partisans.
Polizei-Regiment 15	While one battalion was in the area under the Senior SS and Police Commander North, the other two were attached to the Senior SS and Police Commander Russia South.
Polizei-Regiment 16	The regiment was deployed in the Leningrad siege ring as part of Battle Group Jeckeln.
Polizei-Regiment 17	The battalions were deployed in the area under the Senior SS and Police Commander Russia North.
Polizei-Regiment 18	Initially used in Upper Carniola, it subsequently saw action in Slovenia.
Polizei-Regiment 19	The battalions were attached to the Senior SS and Police Commander Alpenland.
Polizei-Regiment 20	The regiment was deployed in Bohemia.
Polizei-Regiment 21	The regiment was deployed in Moravia.

Polizei-Regiment 22	The battalions were situated in the Generalgouvernement/Warsaw District.
Polizei-Regiment 23	The battalions were situated in the Generalgouvernement/Cracow District, however they also took part in operations under the command of the Senior SS and Police Commander Russia Center.
Polizei-Regiment 24	The battalions were situated in the Generalgouvernement/Radom District and took part in the transporting of thousands of Jews to the Belzec concentration camp. In the autumn it was transferred to White Russia.
Polizei-Regiment 25	The battalions were situated in the Generalgouvernement/Lublin District.
Polizei-Regiment 26	The regiment was on occupation duty in northern Norway.
Polizei-Regiment 27	The regiment was on occupation duty in southern Norway.
Polizei-Regiment 28	The battalions were deployed separately in France, Latvia, and the Ukraine.

At the end of 1942, many police units again saw frontline action, especially in the area of Army Group South. *Polizei-Regimenter 6, 8, 14,* and *15* were destroyed between the Don and the Donets in January 1943. The main reasons for this were the weak armament fielded by the police units, lack of combat experience on the part of the officers and men, and also the marked Soviet superiority in winter warfare.

In May 1943, more than 63,000 members of the *Ordnungspolizei* and roughly 4,000 members of the *Sicherheitspolizei* were in foreign service. They were deployed as follows:

Generalgouvernement	11,400 men of the *Ordnungspolizei*
	2,200 men of the *Sicherheitspolizei*
Senior SS and Police Commander Russia North	4,083 men of the *Ordnungspolizei*
	800 men of the *Sicherheitspolizei*
Senior SS and Police Commander Russia Center	7,000 men of the *Ordnungspolizei*
	750 men of the *Sicherheitspolizei*
Senior SS and Police Commander Russia South	12,900 men of the *Ordnungspolizei*
	2,000 men of the *Sicherheitspolizei*
France	2,000 men of the *Ordnungspolizei*
Finland	2,500 men of the *Ordnungspolizei*
With eight army security divisions	3,200 men of the *Ordnungspolizei*
Protectorate of Bohemia and Moravia	) total of approximately
Reich Commissariat for the Occupied Netherlands	) 20,000 men
Southern Styria/Southern Carinthia	) of the *Ordnungspolizei*

The individual units, now designated *SS-Polizei-Regimenter*, were deployed as follows in 1943:

SS-Polizei-Regiment 1	The battalions deployed on the Eastern Front and in Slovenia were transferred to the area surrounding Marseille, France in spring 1943, and there reformed *SS-Polizei-Regiment 14*, which had been destroyed on the Eastern Front. The battalion previously attached to the Sipo in Ostland was used to form *Polizei-Schützen-Regiment 36* in the summer of 1943.

SS-Polizei-Regiment 2	The battalions were deployed in the area under the Senior SS and Police Commander Russia Center and took part in many anti-partisan operations.
SS-Polizei-Regiment 3	While two battalions remained in the Netherlands, in January 1943 one was renamed *III./Polizei-Regiment 5* and transferred to Serbia.
SS-Polizei-Regiment 4	In the summer of 1943, the unit was transferred to the Zamosc area in the Generalgouvernement and took part in numerous anti-partisan actions.
SS-Polizei-Regiment 5	The regiment was attached to the Commander of *Ordnungspolizei* in Serbia.
SS-Polizei-Regiment 6	Committed during the Soviet winter offensive at the Don River at the turn of the year 1942–43 and destroyed there. The regiment was disbanded soon afterwards.
SS-Polizei-Regiment 7	The regiment was part of the Reich Commissariat for the occupied Norwegian territories.
SS-Polizei-Regiment 8	Committed during the Soviet winter offensive at the Don River at the turn of the year 1942–43 and destroyed there. The regiment was disbanded soon afterwards. What was left formed *I./Police-Schützen-Regiment 38*.
SS-Polizei-Regiment 9	In addition to security duties in northern Russia, in the autumn of 1943, the regiment saw action at the front in the Lepel area in the autumn of 1943.
SS-Polizei-Regiment 10	The battalions were deployed in the area administered by the General Commissariat of the Ukraine.
SS-Polizei-Regiment 11	The battalions were deployed in the area administered by the General Commissariat of the Ukraine.
SS-Polizei-Regiment 12	While one battalion initially remained in the Netherlands, in April 1943, one battalion formed *I./Polizei-Schützen-Regiment 31*. The *II. Bataillon* was transferred to to the Generalgouvernement in the summer of 1943. In October 1943, the last battalion also left the Netherlands and was attached to the SS and Police Commander Verona.
SS-Polizei-Regiment 13	The battalions were deployed in the area commanded by the Senior SS and Police Commander Russia Center and took part in many operations against partisans—including some in the Generalgouvernement. In the autumn of 1943, it saw action at the front in the Lepel area.
SS-Polizei-Regiment 14	Committed during the Soviet winter offensive at the Don at the turn of the year 1942–43 and destroyed there. In March 1943, what was left of the regiment was ordered to the Marseille area in France to reform. In the summer of 1944, the unit was transferred to to the border region between Croatia and Italy.
SS-Polizei-Regiment 15	Committed during the Soviet winter offensive at the Don at the turn of the year 1942–43 and destroyed there. The regiment was reformed in Norway in March 1943. In August it was transferred to northern Italy and attached to the SS

Members of *SS-Polizei-Regiment 19* in Slovenia. Note the older weapons (MG 08/15), and vehicles (Ford anti-aircraft), which were typical for units of the *Ordnungspolizei*.

	and Police Commander Upper Italy West.
SS-Polizei-Regiment 16	The unit was in the Leningrad siege ring as part of *Polizei-Kampfgruppe Jeckeln* and in autumn 1943, took part in the fighting in the Nevel area.
SS-Polizei-Regiment 17	The battalions of the regiment saw action in the Generalgouvernement.
SS-Polizei-Regiment 18	Transferred to the *20. Armee* in Finland. At the beginning of 1943, in the summer it was ordered to Greece.
SS-Polizei-Regiment 19	The battalions were attached to the Senior SS and Police Commander Alpenland.
SS-Polizei-Regiment 20	While two battalions were deployed in Bohemia, one battalion was ordered to Rome in October 1943.
SS-Polizei-Regiment 21	The battalion was deployed in Moravia.
SS-Polizei-Regiment 22	The battalions of the regiment were deployed in the Warsaw District of the Generalgouvernement. There they took part in the liquidation of the Warsaw Ghetto from mid-April to the end of May 1943, and in "Operation Erntefest" in November, in which the Jews from the Trawniki and Poniatowa labor camps were taken to the concentration camp in Lublin and for the most part shot.
SS-Polizei-Regiment 23	The battalions of the regiment were deployed in the Cracow District of the Generalgouvernement, however they also took part in actions under the command of the Senior SS and Police Commander Russia Center. In autumn 1943, the regiment saw action at the front at Nevel.
SS-Polizei-Regiment 24	In addition to security duties in White Russia, from March 1943, the regiment took part in fighting in the *2. Panzer-Armee*'s main line of resistance at Briansk. In autumn 1943, it saw action at the front at Nevel.
SS-Polizei-Regiment 25	The battalions of the regiment were deployed in the Lublin District in the Generalgouvernement and took part in many anti-partisan operations. Elements were also used in resettlement actions in the Zamosc area. On October 14, 1943, units took part in the suppression of the uprising in the Sobibor camp and in November in "Operation Erntefest," in which Jews from the Trawniki and Poniatowa labor camps were taken to the concentration camp in Lublin and for the most part shot.
SS-Polizei-Regiment 26	At the beginning of May 1943, the regiment was transferred from northern Norway to the Generalgouvernement, where it took part in numerous anti-partisan operations. In mid-August, it participated in the liquidation of the ghettoes in Bialystok and Glebokie, during which about 10,000 Jews were deported to Treblinka.
SS-Polizei-Regiment 27	The regiment served as an occupation unit in southern Norway.
SS-Polizei-Regiment 28	In March 1943, the regiment's battalions were assembled in Arnhem and in August transferred to Marseille, France. At the end of the year they were ordered into the area of Vichy and Dijon–Lyon.

Pol.-Schützen-Regiment 31	The regiment was formed in April 1943, for use by the Senior SS and Police Commander Russia Center. The unit's *I. Bataillon* was made available by *SS-Polizei-Regiment 12*. It took part in several major anti-partisan operations.
Pol.-Schützen-Regiment 32	The regiment was formed in April 1943, for use in Bialystok in the Generalgouvernement. The unit's *I. Bataillon* was provided by *SS-Polizei-Regiment 17*. It took part in numerous anti-partisan operations.
Pol.-Schützen-Regiment 33	The regiment was formed in April 1943, for use by the commander of *Ordnungspolizei* in the Ukraine. The unit's *I. Bataillon* was provided by *SS-Polizei-Regiment 20*.
Pol.-Schützen-Regiment 34	The regiment was formed in Bialystok in April 1943, with *SS-Polizei-Regiment 21* providing the *I. Bataillon*. Its actions included the liquidation of the Bialystok ghetto.
Pol.-Schützen-Regiment 35	The regiment was formed in Litzmannstadt in April 1943. *SS-Polizei-Regiment 24* provided one battalion. After use in the Warthe District, in December 1943, the unit was transferred to Galicia to bolster the *XIII. Armee-Korps*.
Pol.-Schützen-Regiment 36	The regiment was formed at the end of July 1943, for use in the area under the Senior SS and Police Commander Russia Center and White Ruthenia and it achieved operational capability in the autumn of that year.
Pol.-Schützen-Regiment 37	The regiment, which consisted entirely of Ukrainian police battalions, was formed at the end of November 1943, under the Commander of *Ordnungspolizei* Rovno.

After the disbandment of four regiments at the beginning of 1943, the *Ordnungspolizei* still had thirty-two regiments at the end of the year, of which:

13 were in action in the USSR,
5 were serving as occupation units in France, Norway, and the Netherlands,
5 were serving as occupation units in Serbia, Slovenia, Greece, and Italy,
6 were serving as occupation units in the Generalgouvernement,
2 were serving as occupation units in the Protectorate of Bohemia and Moravia,
1 was undergoing reformation at its home base.

The *SS-Polizei-Regiment "Bozen,"* made up mainly of men from South Tyrol, was a new formation which was deployed in Italy.

The year 1944 saw the beginning of the collapse of the German Reich. The Soviet winter offensive resulted in extremely heavy fighting along the entire Eastern Front, in which the *Wehrmacht* and the police formations attached to it once again succeeded in stabilizing the fronts in the spring. Police battle groups again had to be sent to the front during the Soviet summer offensive and these were often forced to withdraw to East Prussia in heavy fighting. The individual SS police regiments were deployed as follows:

SS-Polizei-Regiment 1	After the unit had been disbanded in the first half of 1943, in August 1944, it was reformed with personnel provided by *SS-Polizei-Regimenter 12*, *20* and *21*. In October 1944, however, two battalions were used in the reformation of *SS-Polizei-Regiment 6*. A second battalion, at least, was formed in Budapest from ethnic Germans.

SS-Polizei-Regiment 2	Initially deployed on anti-partisan operations in the area commanded by the Senior SS and Police Commander Russia Center, it saw action at the front during the Soviet summer offensive. Transferred to Brandenburg in October 1944, the regiment was ordered to the *XIV. SS-Armee-Korps* on the Upper Rhine.
SS-Polizei-Regiment 3	With just two battalions until autumn 1944, the regiment was deployed in the Netherlands and in September 1944, took part in the fighting in the North Brabant ("Operation Market Garden").
SS-Polizei-Regiment 4	The regiment took part in numerous anti-partisan operations in the Lublin area until summer 1944, and was then transferred to White Russia to defend against the Soviet summer offensive. From autumn 1944, the units were deployed at the front in East Prussia.
SS-Polizei-Regiment 5	Initially deployed in Serbia, from mid-March to mid-May 1944, it took part in the occupation of Hungary. Subsequently ordered back to Serbia, there followed actions in the Serbian–Albanian border area and Montenegro. At the beginning of October 1944, the regiment was sent to the *LXIX. Armee-Korps* at the front south of Belgrade. Attached to a variety of commands, the regiment withdrew to the Vinkovci area, in often heavy fighting.
SS-Polizei-Regiment 6	The regiment was reformed in October 1944, using personnel provided by *SS-Polizei-Regiment 1* and ethnic Germans.
SS-Polizei-Regiment 7	The regiment was deployed in the Reich Commissariat for the occupied Norwegian territories.
SS-Polizei-Regiment 8	The regiment was reformed after *Police-Schützen-Regiment 38* was disbanded in October 1944. At the end of that month elements saw action at the front north of Paks on the Danube with *LXXII. Armee-Korps*. In mid-November, it was attached to the *271. Volksgrenadier-Division* in the Dunavöldvar area.
SS-Polizei-Regiment 9	The regiment took part in anti-partisan operations in the Lepel area until summer 1944, and was then transferred to the front in the area south of Dvinsk in response to the Soviet summer offensive. The units were wiped out in the fighting. The survivors were sent to *SS-Polizei-Regiment 16* and *Polizei-Regiment "Alpenvorland."*
SS-Polizei-Regiment 10	The battalions saw action at the front in the Rovno area from January 10, 1944, and by May 1944, withdrew into the area around Brody. On July 18, 1944, the remnants were ordered into the Jablonka–Krasne area. From there the regiment reached Italy at the end of 1944, and was attached to the commander of the *Ordnungspolizei* in Trieste. There the unit took part in numerous large-scale anti-partisan operations.
SS-Polizei-Regiment 11	From January 10, 1944, the battalions saw action at the front in the Rovno area and by May 1944, had withdrawn to the area around Brody. What was left of the regiment was then ordered to the Jablonka–Krasne area and on July 24, orders

The average age in the police battalions was between thirty-five and forty-five years, and some members were even older.

	to see action with the *214. Infanterie-Division* in the area east of Ostrov. After heavy losses, the regiment was disbanded in November 1944.
SS-Polizei-Regiment 12	In northern Italy, one battalion took part in several anti-partisan operations, such as in Emilia Romagna in July 1944. The other battalion continued to operate in the Generalgouvernement.
SS-Polizei-Regiment 13	Because of losses in the Polotsk area, the *III. Bataillon* was disbanded in the spring of 1944, and its personnel divided among the other two battalions. The remaining battalions were transferred to Klagenfurt in April 1944, and attached to the Senior SS and Police Commander Alpenland. They subsequently took part in several actions against partisans in the Bleiburg–Solcava area.
SS-Polizei-Regiment 14	In Slovenia the regiment took part in numerous actions in the area southeast of Laibach.
SS-Polizei-Regiment 15	The regiment was assigned to numerous anti-partisan operations in northern Italy.
SS-Polizei-Regiment 16	Decimated after the fighting in the Nevel area, the remnants of the regiment were subsequently assigned other tasks, including guarding the ghetto in Wilna (Vilnius). In mid-June 1944, it was brought back to authorized strength through the addition of the remnants of *SS-Polizei-Regiment 9*, and from the end of July until August 1944, it took part in the fighting in the Dünaburg (Daugavpils) area while attached to the *132. Infanterie-Division*. It subsequently withdrew to Riga and in October 1944, was attached to the commander of the *Ordnungspolizei* in Ostland (the Baltic States).
SS-Polizei-Regiment 17	From January 16 to May 7, 1944, the regiment was encircled in Kovel and saw combat against regular Soviet troops. The retreat from White Russia toward Stolpce began in June 1944, and the following month the unit saw frontline action at Lida and Grodno. From there what was left of the regiment withdrew to East Prussia and until October, was deployed as part of the *VI. Armee-Korps*. In November 1944, it was transferred to Slovenia.
SS-Polizei-Regiment 18	After actions in the Peloponnese, in July 1944, the regiment was transferred back to the Greek mainland. In September 1944, it withdrew from Greece and this was followed by fighting in Belgrade in October. At the end of the month the battalions were already fighting off Soviet attacks in Hungary.
SS-Polizei-Regiment 19	In May 1944, the battalions were transferred from the Alpenland to the Mont Mouchet area of France. Following the Allied invasion in Normandy, they marched into the Paris area and saw action against the so-called Free Republic of Vercors. When the Allies landed in the south of France it was transferred to the Grenoble area. At the beginning of September Himmler ordered the regiment to protect

Petain and his administration in Belfort. Various units were sent to the *LXIV. Armee-Korps*'s main line of resistance in the Langres area. In October 1944, the unit saw action against the Americans in Alsace as part of the *16. Volksgrenadier-Division.*

SS-Polizei-Regiment 20   While one battalion was deployed in Bohemia, the *I. Bataillon* took part in various anti-partisan operations in the Roms district. In June 1944, it was ordered to northern Italy and in September to the area west of Milan. In October–November 1944, the battalion saw action against the Partisan Republic of Ossola in the Lago Maggiore area. The third battalion took part in the occupation of Hungary, which began in March 1944, and in August formed the new *I./SS-Polizei-Regiment 1.*

SS-Polizei-Regiment 21   While two battalions were deployed in Moravia, in March 1944, a battalion was sent to Hungary to serve as an occupation unit and in August 1944, formed *III./SS-Polizei-Regiment 1.*

SS-Polizei-Regiment 22   The unit was assembled in Warsaw in June 1944, and was sent into action in the Nalibocki Forest to bolster the hard-pressed Army Group Center. There it was immediately wiped out. What was left of the regiment was attached to *SS-Polizei-Regiment 2* on 12 July 1944, after which it was disbanded.

SS-Polizei-Regiment 23   Immediately after seeing action at Polotsk from autumn 1943 to mid-April 1944, the regiment was tasked with anti-partisan operations in the Ushachi area. At the end of 1944, the regiment was ordered to the the Orsha–Borisov area and Minsk for frontline action. In mid-July 1944, the units were again employed in anti-partisan operations in the Generalgouvernement. The *II. Bataillon* was disbanded there on account of heavy losses and its remaining personnel assigned to the other two battalions.

SS-Polizei-Regiment 24   After frontline action at Nevel, the regiment took part in various anti-partisan operations until June 1944. This was followed by the retreat to Lida, which lasted until the beginning of July. There what was left of the two remaining battalions was disbanded on July 12, and their personnel assigned to *SS-Polizei-Regiment 2*. The regiment was reformed in the Kattowitz–Hindenburg area in November 1944.

SS-Polizei-Regiment 25   The battalions took part in numerous anti-partisan operations in the Generalgouvernement. In March 1944, the *I. Bataillon* was transferred to to the Cilli–Laibach area and took part in various operations.

SS-Polizei-Regiment 26   From mid-January to the beginning of March 1944, the regiment saw action in a police battle group attached to the *263. Infanterie-Division* and later the *83. Infanterie-Division* of the *16. Armee*. The battalions were wiped out in the fighting withdrawal in White Russia in July 1944, and the remnants were attached to *SS-Polizei-Regiment 2*. After arriving in East Prussia they were ordered to Italy. There they were used to form *Polizei-Regiment Brixen*. *SS-Polizei-Regiment 26* was officially disbanded in November 1944.

SS-Polizei-Regiment 27	The regiment was deployed in southern Norway as an occupation unit.
SS-Polizei-Regiment 28	In February 1944, the battalions were transferred to Upper Carniola, where they took part in numerous security operations in the area of Laibach and Kamnik.
Pol.-Schützen-Regiment 31	The regiment took part in all the major anti-partisan operations conducted by the Senior SS and Police Commander Russia Center in the first half of 1944. The beginning of July saw the beginning of the retreat with elements of the *170. Infanterie-Division* and the *221. Sicherungs-Division*. There followed frontline actions at Lida and east of Grodno as part of the VI. *Armee-Korps* along the Bobr River. In November 1944, the regiment was attached to the *XXVII. Armee-Korps*, part of the *4. Armee* in East Prussia.
Pol.-Schützen-Regiment 32	The regiment took part in various anti-partisan operations in the Generalgouvernement and was disbanded in the summer of 1944.
Pol.-Schützen-Regiment 33	After heavy fighting at the front in Galicia, the regiment was disbanded on March 26, 1944. What was left of the *I. Bataillon* joined *SS-Polizei-Regiment 10*.
Pol.-Schützen-Regiment 34	The regiment was sent to the front northwest of Rovno in February 1944 and in March 1944, it was in the main line of resistance east of Brody with the *XIII. Armee-Korps*. At the beginning of August it was attached to *SS-Polizei-Regiment 17* and used at the front in the Grodno–Bialystok–East Prussia area in the *VI. Armee-Korps*, part of the *4. Armee*. Withdrawn from the frontline area, the battalions were immediately used to combat partisans in the Kielce area. Further actions followed northwest of Warsaw.
Pol.-Schützen-Regiment 35	The regiment suffered heavy losses at the XIII. *Armee-Korps'* front in Galicia in the spring of 1944, and was disbanded in April.
Pol.-Schützen-Regiment 36	The regiment took part in one more anti-partisan operation in the Uchaschi area in the spring of 1944, after which it and other police units withdrew across the Lida into the area east of Grodno. There it once again took part ion a costly frontline deployment opposite the East Prussia frontier as part of the *VI. Armee-Korps*. As a result, the regiment was disbanded effective August 30, 1944.
Pol.-Schützen-Regiment 37	In January 1944, the regiment was deployed at the front near Rovno as part of the *454. Sicherungs-Division*, resulting in its destruction. It was disbanded in April 1944.
Pol.-Schützen-Regiment 38	The regiment was supposed to be formed under the Senior SS and Police Commander Black Sea in August 1944. The collapse of Army Group South Ukraine prevented this, however, and in November 1944, it was entered as disbanded.

Chief of German Police

Paul Rieckmann was taken on by the *Schutzpolizei Hamburg* as an auxiliary police officer at the end of July 1940. In July 1942, he was assigned to the 2nd Company of the new *Polizei-Regiment 12* in Hamburg. In April 1943, the *I. Bataillon* formed the German cadre of *Polizei.-Schützen-Regiment 31*.

From spring 1944, *Oberwachtmeister* Rieckmann was attached to *Polizei.-Schützen-Regiment 31.* whose *II.* and *III. Bataillon* consisted of Ukrainian police. He took part in "Operations Cottbus," "Hermann," and "Kormoran."

After fierce fighting against partisans and regular troops, the summer of 1944 brought the end for the eleven SS Police and Police Rifle Regiments deployed in the USSR, which were wiped out and subsequently disbanded. At the end of 1944, therefore, the *Ordnungspolizei* was left with about twenty-four regiments, which were deployed as follows:

3 combined into Police Battle Group "Hannibal" in East Prussia
3 serving as occupation units in Norway and the Netherlands
12 serving as occupation units in Slovenia and Italy
4 serving as occupation units in the *Generalgouvernement*
1 serving as an occupation unit in the Protectorate of Bohemia and Moravia
1 undergoing reformation in Upper Silesia.

In addition, the Police Regiments "Brixen," "Schlanders," and "Alpenvorland" were formed for use in Italy, using mainly men from South Tyrol.

The spring of 1945, saw the majority of police units engaged in the struggle against the partisans, an effort that had become vital if supply lines to the various fronts were to be kept open. The individual SS Police Regiments were deployed as follows:

SS-Polizei-Regiment 1	After the regiment had been reformed in Budapest at the end of 1944, that December it was transferred to the Lausitz. There it was initially attached to Special Purpose Division Headquarters 608. On March 12, 1945, what remained was absorbed by the newly-formed *SS-Polizei-Regiment 29* and took part in the actions fought by the *35. SS-Polizei-Grenadier-Division*.
SS-Polizei-Regiment 2	Transferred to the Lausitz in January 1945, this regiment was also initially attached to Special Purpose Division Headquarters 608. Effective March 12, 1945, what remained was absorbed by *SS-Polizei-Regiment 29* and also took part in the actions fought by the *35. SS-Polizei-Grenadier-Division*.
SS-Polizei-Regiment 3	Deployed in Fortress Netherlands, on May 9, 1945, the regiment was captured by the British.
SS-Polizei-Regiment 4	At the end of January 1945, the regiment withdrew via Lyck, Arys, and Milken to the area south of Ltzen. There it was disbanded at the beginning of March 1945. Its remaining personnel were absorbed by *Pol.-Schützen-Regiment 31*.
SS-Polizei-Regiment 5	From the area northwest of Vincovci the battalions moved into the Kopreinitz area on the Drau River and at the end of April 1945, they marched through Belgrade towards the old Reich border, where they were captured by the western allies.
SS-Polizei-Regiment 6	At the end of January 1945, Army Group South requested the release of the regiment for an operation in the area of the *2. Panzer-Armee*. As a result, when the surrender came the battalions were in the area of the *XXII. Gebirgs-Korps* and were captured in the Marburg–Dravograd area.
SS-Polizei-Regiment 7	The regiment was in the Reich Commissatiat for the Occupied Norwegian Territories and there was captured by the British in May 1945.

SS-Polizei-Regiment 8	In January 1945, what remained of the regiment was transferred to the Protectorate of Bohemia and Moravia for reorganization and from there was ordered to Army Group Vistula. Together with the newly-formed *Polizei-Regiment 50*, it formed the *1. Polizei-Jäger-Brigade*, which was deployed at the Oder southwest of Stettin. Its use ended in a fiasco. On April 20, 1945, the enemy broke through the police positions, meeting almost no resistance. It subsequently headed west and surrendered to the western allies.
SS-Polizei-Regiment 9	In January 1945, *Polizei-Regiment Alpenvorland* was renamed *SS-Polizei-Regiment 9* and saw action in northern Italy until the surrender.
SS-Polizei-Regiment 10	From January 1945, the battalions were deployed in the Baccia Valley in the Görz Region, as well as in the Trieste area. At the end of April 1945, the regiment marched into the Villach area and at the beginning of May was supposed to be employed to expand defense positions in the Gemona area. It then surrendered to the western allies.
SS-Polizei-Regiment 12	In northern Italy the battalion was deployed in Campiglia Marittima in Tuscany until May 1945, and there surrendered to the British.
SS-Polizei-Regiment 13	Deployed in Slovenia, at the beginning of April 1945, the regiment was transferred into the area northeast of Graz where it took part in costly defensive actions against the Red Army. Elements of the *I. Bataillon* were still involved in anti-partisan operations, with one action against the Persmanhof, a partisan base in Eisenkoppel, gaining special public attention after the war. Civilians were shot for "assisting partisans." When the war ended, the battalions surrendered in the Villach area.
SS-Polizei-Regiment 14	Initially deployed in the Laibach–Cilli area, in March 1945, the regiment received orders to proceed to the *35. SS-Polizei-Grenadier-Division* on the Eastern Front and it took part in the division's final battles.
SS-Polizei-Regiment 15	Attached to the Senior SS and Police Commander Italy, in May 1945, the regiment surrendered to the British.
SS-Polizei-Regiment 16	Attached to the Commander of *Ordnungspolizei Ostland* in Libau, until the surrender it was employed to secure lines of communications in the rear of the Courland Pocket, after which it was captured by the Soviets.
SS-Polizei-Regiment 17	Deployed in Slovenia, the regiment marched through the Loibl Pass and across the Drau River with *SS-Polizei-Regimenter 18* and *28* and surrendered to the British north of Ferlach on May 9, 1945.
SS-Pol.Geb.Jäg.-Rgt. 18	Deployed in Croatia, in mid-February 1945, the regiment took over the positions on the Drau River in the Skopje area. At the beginning of April 1945, the battalions marched into the Koprivnica–Varasdin area and were attached to the *XV. Kosaken-Kavallerie-Korps*. They then withdrew to Austria by way of Marburg.

Members of
*SS-Polizei-Geb-
irgs-Jäger-Regiment
18.*

157

SS-Polizei-Regiment 19	Deployed in Alsace until the end of February 1945, at the beginning of March the regiment was transferred back to Slovenia, into the Cilli area. With other police units the regiment withdrew through Loibl Pass and across the Drau into the area north of Ferlach and there surrendered to the British.
SS-Polizei-Regiment 20	While one battalion remained attached to the SS and Police Commander Upper Italy until the end of the war, the other battalion was deployed in the Klattau area (Bohemia) until the surrender.
SS-Polizei-Regiment 21	The two remaining battalions initially remained in Moravia and then in April 1945 were mobilized for use against the Red Army in the Beskid Mountains.
SS-Polizei-Regiment 23	While one battalion was used to guard a labor camp in Warsaw, in mid-January 1945 a battalion was sent to the front in Upper Silesia, in the Hindenburg–Gleiwitz area. The regiment was effectively disbanded in March 1945.
SS-Polizei-Regiment 24	In spring 1945, the regiment was mobilized for action at the front together with *I./SS-Polizei-Regiment 23* in Upper Silesia.
SS-Polizei-Regiment 25	In the spring of 1945, the battalion deployed in Slovenia was transferred to Nove Mesto. It was ultimately captured by the British near Cilli on May 14, 1945.
SS-Polizei-Regiment 27	The regiment was in southern Norway when the surrender came.
SS-Polizei-Regiment 28	After constant action in the security areas in Slovenia, the regiment headed for Austria with the forces under the commanding general of Army Rear Area E. In mid-April 1945, it was deployed in the line Göttenitz–Gottschee to the Gurk River. By way of the Loibl Pass and the Drau River, the units surrendered to the British on May 9.
Pol.-Schützen-Regiment 31	The unit was pulled out of action at the end of January 1945, and marched via Lyck–Arys–Milken into the area southeast of Lötzen. In February 1945, it occupied positions near Grünwalde. There it was sent what remained of *SS-Polizei-Regiment 4* in mid-March. Attached to the *349. Volksgrenadier-Division*, the regiment was destroyed in the Heiligenbeil Pocket.
Pol.-Schützen-Regiment 34	The regiment was disbanded effective February 5, 1945, without seeing further action.
Polizei-Regiment 50	The regiment was formed from the remnants of various police units in the area of Army Group Vistula in February 1945. Deployed within the *Oder-Korps*, it was destroyed in its first day of fighting on April 20, 1945.

CHAPTER 5
THE TWELVE MAIN OFFICES (*HAUPTÄMTER*) AS HIMMLER'S ADMINISTRATIVE APPARATUS

Between 1936 and 1945, a total of almost 1½ million people were under Heinrich Himmler's command in his capacity as *Reichsführer-SS* and Commander of German Police. Twelve *Hauptämter* (main offices) were responsible for the administrative organization and control of this body. The expression already in use, that the chiefs of the head offices were Heinrich Himmler's twelve apostles, shows how Himmler's position was perceived.

The responsibilities of the main officers were coordinated, but in some cases they overlapped. Altogether they formed the structure which enabled the SS and the police to so successfully sustain National Socialism. Some of the main offices were directly linked to events that affected millions of people. When more than a million ethnic Germans were resettled from the Soviet Union—primarily in the Warthe District—the space required had to be simultaneously cleared of Poles and Jews. For the latter, these evacuations usually meant death in the camps at Belzec, Treblinka, and Sobibor. The survivors were sent to the concentration camps for labor service.

There, too, probably about a million prisoners lost their lives. Numerous main offices were involved in the above-named action: for example the SS Main Office of Race and Settlement, the Reich Security Main Office, the SS Economics and Administrative Main Office, plus the Head Office of the Reich Commissar for the Strengthening of the German People (RKF).

On June 30, 1944, the Statistical Research Institute of the *Reichsführer-SS* issued a report which included the number of SS men in the SS main offices. According to the report, 39,415 men were employed there as follows:

Main Administrative Office of the SS	9,349
SS Main Office of Race and Settlement	2,689
Personal Staff *Reichsführer-SS*	673
Heißmeyer Office	553
Office of SS Legal Matters	599
SS Personnel Office	170
SS Economics and Administrative Main Office	24,091
Main Office for Ethnic Germans	987
RKF	304

Total strength of the *Waffen-SS* at that time was 599,443 members, which meant that almost 7% were serving in the main offices. This was an indication of a large, but perhaps even a desired bureaucracy, which served to keep veterans ("*alte Kämpfer*") of the *Allgemeine-SS* in particular away from the fronts. It also conformed to Himmler's perfectionism, for as a rule his administrations always functioned smoothly.[1]

Missing from the above summary are the *SS-Führungshauptamt* (SS-FHA), the Reich Security Main Office (RSHA), and the *Ordnungspolizei* Main Office. The SS-FHA was probably included in the *SS-Hauptamt* total. The members of the RSHA and the *Ordnungspolizei* Main Office were probably not listed because they were members of the German Police and not the *Waffen-SS*. One can assume, however, that about 7,500 officials worked in these two main offices, which were administratively responsible for about 350,000 members of the security and order police. This was equivalent to about 2% of total strength.

In the summer of 1944, therefore, just about 50,000 men belonged to the twelve main offices of the SS and the police. The main offices will be described in more detail in the following text, with frequent reference to contemporary explanations by *SS-Standartenführer* Gunther d'Alquen (October 24, 1910 – May 15, 1998), chief editor of the magazine *Das schwarze Korps*, from his work *Die SS: Geschichte, Aufgabe und Organisation der Schutzstaffel der NSDAP*. At that time, there existed three main offices and five offices, which, while still not main offices, already had the features and scope of a main office:

In addition to the *Allgemeine-SS*, so to speak the mother of all other SS formations, there are the *SS-Verfügungstruppen*, the *SS-Totenkopfstandarten*, plus the Security Service and the Race and Settlement Organization.

The *Reichsführer-SS*'s supreme command post for the *Allgemeine-SS* is the *SS-Hauptamt* in Berlin.[2]

The supreme command post for the Security Service is the Reich Security Main Office in Berlin.

Supreme command post for the Race and Settlement organization is the SS Main Office of Race and Settlement in Berlin.

In addition to these main offices, there are the following offices, which are likewise directly under the *Reichsführer-SS* and have the characteristics of a main office:

Personal Staff of the *Reichsführer-SS*,

SS Chief Administrator,

Head of SS Personnel, these three in Berlin,

Chief of the SS Court, Munich, and
Chief of the *Ordnungspolizei, SS-Obergruppenführer General der Polizei* Daluege, with the rank of a main office commander.

1. The *SS-Hauptamt*

The leadership of the SS naturally grew in size in keeping with the growth of its membership. When Himmler took over the SS it had only about 280 members. The command staff, then called the *SS-Oberstab* or senior staff, was thus still very manageable. In the two years that followed, membership approached the strength of a German infantry division, and the SS leadership initially organized itself in a fashion similar to that of a division headquarters:

I a ....Organization, training, and security service
I b ....Motorization, transport organization
I d ....Clothing, rations, accommodations
II a ....Personnel section, staffing
II b ....Strength reports
III ....Matters of honor, legal matters
IV a ....Money management
IV b ....SS medical care (SS Reich Physician)
V ....Propaganda

In the summer of 1932, the growth of the SS—by then 25,000 members—resulted in its reorganization. The SS Office, SS Security Office, and the SS Race and Settlement Office were formed, in which the above departments were incorporated and expanded.

Because of the vast number of Germans applying to serve in his SS, on January 30, 1935, Himmler ordered another reorganization of the national leadership of the SS. The new *SS-Hauptamt* (SS Main Office) was divided into:

Hauptabteilung A with:
1.) Adjutancy
2.) Inspector of SS Guard Units and Concentration Camps
3.) Press Bureau
4.) Welfare Division
5.) Chief Registrar

Hauptabteilung B with:
1.) SS Command Office
2.) SS Personnel Office
3.) SS Replacement Office
4.) SS Legal Office
5.) SS Administration Office
6.) SS Medical Office

On June 7, 1935, *Hauptabteilung C* "Security Tasks" was created, raising the number of main departments in the *SS-Hauptamt* to three.

The first commander of the *SS-Hauptamt* was *SS-Gruppenführer* Curt Wittje (October 2, 1894 – March 16, 1947). Before the year was over, however, he was replaced by *SS-Gruppenführer* August Heißmeyer after being accused of having homosexual relations with fellow members.

Further changes followed by 1938. The *SS-Hauptamt* was then organized into the following offices:

Central Chancellery

I .... Command Office
II .... Personnel Office
IV .... Administration Office
V .... Medical Office
VI .... Registration Office
VII .... Office for Security Tasks
VIII .... Recruitment Office
IX .... Procurement Office
X .... Office for Physical Education
XI .... Signals Communications Office
XII .... Supply and Welfare Office
XIII .... Education Office

In early 1939, in his publication *Die SS: Geschichte, Aufgabe und Organisation der NSDAP*, *SS-Standartenführer*, Gunther d'Alquen described the *SS-Hauptamt* as follows:

The **SS-Hauptamt** consists of thirteen offices with the following responsibilities:
- The Central Chancellery (Zentralkanzlei or ZK) is the command post of the head of the SS-Hauptamt. It ensures that all of the offices under his command work together and examines management procedures within the *SS-Hauptamt*.
- The Command Office (I) deals with all matters pertaining to training, organization and the deployment of units of the *Allgemeine-SS*.
- The Personnel Office (II) deals with all personnel matters affecting all SS officers of the *Allgemeine-SS*, from *SS-Untersturmführer* up to and including *SS-Hauptsturmführer*.
- The SS Administration Office (IV) deals with all administrative matters affecting the *SS-Hauptamt*. It has the same ranking as the Administration Office S.D. and the Administration Office R.u.S. and together with them is subordinate to the Chief Administrator SS, the most senior administrative body of the *Schutzstaffel*.
- The Medical Office (V) deals with all processes associated with the *Schutzstaffel's* medical tasks and installations.
- The SS Registration Office (VI) handles the preliminary and final acceptance of SS applicants and candidates into the SS. It also controls transfers and discharges of enlisted men and non-commissioned officers as well as reenlistment processes. Its responsibilities also include the planning and introduction of all methods of registration, the maintenance of files containing personal data on all members of the SS plus the calculation of the total strength of the *Schutzstaffel* and the required drawing up of statistics.
- The Office for Security Tasks (VII) deals with the large-scale use of SS units on special occasions, for example during rallies attended by the *Führer* and state visits by foreign heads of government. It is also responsible for preparatory work for mobilization of the *Schutzstaffel*, which it carries out in cooperation with the *Wehrmacht* high command. This includes calling up SS-Totenkopfstandarten reinforcements for special exercises in peacetime and matters relating to the conscription of SS members.
- The Recruitment Office (VIII) is, as it name suggest, is responsible for the recruitment for all elements of the SS.

- The Procurement Office (IX) is responsible for procurement of equipment for the entire SS.
- The Office for Physical Education (XI), the Supply and Welfare Office (XII) and the Education Office (XIII) carry out the tasks expressed by their titles [...].

On April 1, 1940, *SS-Brigadeführer* Gottlob Berger (July 16, 1896 – January 25, 1975) took over the *SS-Hauptamt*, however this lost importance when individual offices were made independent main offices. The Recruitment Office remained the most important area of responsibility, however. *SS-Brigadeführer* Berger first began the recruiting of so-called "Germanic" SS volunteers and ethnic Germans. After the disaster at Stalingrad, this was followed by the creation of "foreign" units, whose personnel were neither so-called "Teutons" nor ethnic Germans. The list started with Muslims from Croatian Bosnia and Western Ukrainians living in Galicia (Generalgouvernement). In 1943, the Recruitment Office—subsequently expanded into *Amtsgruppe D* of the *SS-Hauptamt*—was organized as follows:

Amt D I: Germanische Leitstelle .... *SS-Obersturmbannführer* Dr. Franz Riedwig
Main Department D I/1: Planning
Main Department D I/2: North
Main Department D I/3: West
Main Department D I/4: Southeast
Main Department D I/5: East
Amt D II: Germanic Recruitment .... *SS-Obersturmbannführer* Max Kopischke
Amt D III: Germanic Education .... *SS-Oberführer* Dr. Rudolf Jacobsen

Further opportunities arose after Himmler became commander of the replacement army. Berger began recruiting additional foreigners, some of whom were already serving in the *Wehrmacht*. Russians, Hungarians, Cossacks, Turkmens, and Indians were taken into the *Waffen-SS*. Berger integrated practically all the human resources available to Germany. The only exclusions, apart from the Jews, were Poles, Lithuanians, and Greeks. This expansion of tasks resulted in one further reorganization of the *SS-Hauptamt*. After the main department D I/5: East was expanded into an independent office, D III[3] (*SS-Obersturmbannführer* Fritz Arlt), *Amtsgruppe D* of the *SS-Hauptamt* was organized as follows:

Amt D I: ....Planning
Amt D II: .... *Germanische Leitstelle*
Amt D III: .... *Freiwilligen-Leitstelle Ost*
Amt D IV: .... Administration
Amt D V: .... *Germanische SS*
Amt D VI: .... *Germanische Erziehung/SS-Leithefte*

Gottlob Berger planned one last modification to acquire stronger resources—this time from the German Reich—with the introduction of a central reporting office in the *SS-Hauptamt*. This was to be responsible for allocating draftees for the *Wehrmacht*, *Waffen-SS*, police, Reich Labor Service, Organization Todt, and the civilian labor sector. The constant disputes with *Wehrmacht* offices about the allocation of volunteers or non-volunteers and the selection of new age classes eligible for the draft had finally ended in the *Waffen-SS'* favor. The end of the war prevented its implementation, however.

2. The *SS-Führungshauptamt*

On August 15, 1940, Himmler ordered the expansion of Amt I (*Führungsamt*) of the *SS-Hauptamt* into an independent *SS-Hauptamt*:[4]

1) The *SS-Führungshauptamt* of the *Reichsführer-SS* and Chief of German Police is established effective 15/08/1940.

2.) As leader of the entire SS (*Allgemeine-SS* and *Waffen-SS*), the *Reichsführer-SS* uses the *SS-Führungshauptamt* as command center for the military leadership of the *Waffen-SS* (provided its units are not attached to the commander-in-chief of the army for special operations) and for pre- and post-military command and of the *Allgemeine-SS*.

3.) The *SS-Führungshauptamt* includes:

a.) The *Waffen-SS*[5] command with the previously-attached offices, inspectorates and departments:

      Waffen-SS medical inspectorate
      Waffen-SS weapons and equipment office
      Inspectorate of motor transport
      Inspectorate of concentration camps[6]
      Dachau garrison headquarters
      Prague garrison headquarters

b.) The SS Central Office[7] with attached offices

      Office for security tasks
      Office I

c.) The Office for Signals Communications

d.) The SS Administration Office

e.) The X-Ray Unit (*Sturmbann*)

The *Stabsstürme*

SS Garrison Command Berlin

4.) The offices, inspectorates and departments under a–e left the *SS-Hauptamt* effective August 15, 1940

The *SS-Führungshauptamt* (SS-FHA) thus became the central operations command of the armed SS. Initially, the SS-FHA was led *de jure* by Heinrich Himmler personally, but *de facto* by *SS-Obergruppenführer* Hans Jüttner (March 2, 1894 – May 24, 1965). On January 30, 1943, the latter took over as the new commander of the *Hauptamt* with about 450 employees.

The SS-FHA was soon reorganized, on October 23, 1940. Its organization is shown in full here to illustrate the Hauptamt's scope of responsibilities:

Chief of Staff with adjutancy
Office I: Command Office of the *Waffen-SS*
Officers and enlisted men
Disciplinary matters
Veterinary department
Inspectorate of concentration camps
Office II: Weapons Inspectorate (until November 1, 1941, then independent[8])
Department 1: Department I: Infantry
Department 2: Artillery
Department 3: Cavalry and bicycle units
Department 4: Motorized combat troops and motor pools
Department 5: Pioneers
Department 6: Signals units

Department 7: Motor transport
Department 8: Medical units[9]
Department 9: Armaments
Office II: Personal Staff (from 1 November 1941)
Office III: *Allgemeine-SS* Command Office (had existed since September 5, 1940)
Main Department I a (operations, command)
Main Department I O (organization)
Personnel Main Department
Intelligence Main Department
SS-Funkschutz (radio broadcasting station protection units) Main Department
Stabskommandant Berlin
Office IV: SS Administration Office
Budget
Pay
Clothing
Quarters
Barracks
Judicial system
Auditing
Savings association
Administration personnel
Clerk's office
Office V: SS Central Materials Office
SS Weapons Office
Office VI: General Office (until November 1, 1941)
Intelligence
Base matters
Press
X-Ray unit
Military history
Regulations
Clerk's office
Office VI: Inspectorate of Concentration Camps[10] (from November 1, 1941)
Office VII: Officer Training
SS Officer Schools (*Junkerschulen*)
Training courses for officers
Office VIII: SS Medical Office
Medical service
Junior staff
Pharmaceutical-chemical service
Scientific service

Whereas the *Allgemeine-SS* and the *Waffen-SS* had a total combined strength of about 200,000 members by the end of 1940, on November 26, 1942, the growth, especially of the *Waffen-SS*, made necessary another modification to the *SS-Führungshauptamt*. At that time almost 380,000 men were serving in the SS:

Office I: *Allgemeine-SS* Command Office
Office II: *Waffen-SS* Command Office
Office III: Central Office

Office IV: SS Administration Office
Office V: Personnel Office
Office VI: Cavalry and Bicycle Units
Office VI b: Veterinary Units
Office Group A (Supply)
Office VII: Supply Organization
Office VIII: Weapons Office
Office IX: Technical Equipment and Machines
Office X: Motor Vehicles
Office Group B (Training)
Office XI: Officer Training with Officer Schools
Office XII: NCO Training with NCO Schools
Office Group C (Inspectorates)
Inspectorate 1: NCO Replacements
Inspectorate 2: Infantry
Inspectorate 3: Cavalry
Inspectorate 4: Artillery
Inspectorate 5: Pioneers
Inspectorate 6: Armored Troops
Inspectorate 7: Signals Troops
Inspectorate 8: Ordnance and Repair Troops
Inspectorate 9: Supply Troops
Inspectorate 10: Motor Pools
Inspectorate 11: Replacement Training Units
Inspectorate 12: Motor Vehicle Technology
Inspectorate 13: Anti-Aircraft Artillery
Office Group D[11] (*Waffen-SS* Medical Service)
Office XIII: Welfare and Supply
Office XIV: Dental Service
Office XV: Medical Quartermaster's Office
Office XVI: Hygiene[12]
Office XVII: Medical Statistics
Office Group E
    War Reporting
    Chief Signals Officer
    Transport Officer
    SS-Standarte Kurt Eggers

In carrying out its assigned tasks, the SS-FHA was mainly responsible for new *Waffen-SS* formations. It was responsible for the training of officers and non-commissioned officers and the assignment of recruits acquired by the *SS-Hauptamt*. It also handled transfers of personnel or movement of units during or associated with the formation or replenishment of SS units. On June 30, 1944, the *Hauptamt* was responsible for about 160,000 members of the *Waffen-SS* out of a total strength of just under 600,000 men.

3. Personal Staff *Reichsführer-SS*

After he was named *Reichsführer-SS*, Himmler created his own office which was soon designated an adjutancy. From June 15, 1933, this was led by *SS-Hauptsturmführer* Karl Wolff (May 13,

1900 – July 15, 1984). A friendship developed between Himmler and his adjutant, who two years later rose to become chief adjutant with the rank of *SS-Oberführer*. Hitler called him his *Wölfchen*, or little wolf.

After Himmler was also named chief of German Police in 1936, on November 9, 1936, he issued orders for his chief adjutancy to become his personal staff:

1. Effective November 9, 1936, considering its size and the expansion of its range of duties during the year, the former *Reichsführer-SS* chief adjutancy is designated "The *Reichsführer-SS* Personal Staff."
2. I name *SS-Brigadeführer* Wolff chief of my personal staff.[13]
3. A department of the personal staff will form the new adjutancy of the *Reichsführer-SS*.

The responsibilities of the personal staff were described in a directive dated April 3, 1937:

The personal staff of the *Reichsführer-SS* is the office of the *Reichsführer-SS* responsible for those matters which do not fall under the fields of activity of the commander of the SS-Hauptamt, the SD head office, the Race and Settlement Main Office or the relevant central offices. For reasons of competence, the chief of the personal staff is to completely hand over to the commander of the *SS-Hauptamt*, the SD head office, the Race and Settlement Main Office or the relevant central office all matters that fall under their responsibility. The chief of the personal staff simultaneously maintains supervision of

the adjutancy of the *Reichsführer-SS*,
the *Reichsführer-SS*' point of entry,
the *Reichsführer-SS*' chamber.

Among the institutions which Himmler had managed by his personal staff were those SS business enterprises created in the 1930s, including:

Nordland-Verlag GmbH (SS publishing house),
Porzellanmanufaktur Allach (porcelain manufacture),
Photogesellschaft F.F. Bauer GmbH (photography),
Anton Loibl GmbH (funding source for the *Ahnenerbe* research branch and the *Lebensborn* eugenics program)
Gemeinnützige Wohnungs- und Heimstätten-GmbH (construction and maintenance of SS urban settlements),
Spargemeinschaft-SS, later SS-Spargemeinschaft e.V. (SS savings association),
Gesellschaft zur Förderung und Pflege Deutsche Kulturdenkmäler e.V. (maintenance of historic sites),
Externsteine-Stiftung (Externsteine Foundation)
König-Heinrich I.-Gedächtnis-Stiftung.

With the exception of the SS savings association, these institutions were organized under a "cultural department." This department was disbanded in 1938 when all business operations were organized into the SS Economic Administration of the *SS-Hauptamt*. One exception was the Porzellanmanufaktur Allach, which remained with the personal staff as the "Munich Office."

That same year Himmler elevated the personal staff to a main office and *SS-Gruppenführer* Wolff became *Hauptamtschef*. The Personal Staff *Reichsführer-SS* subsequently organized itself into the following offices:

Wewelsburg Office
Ahnenerbe Office[14]
Lebensborn Office[15]
Press Office/Department
Munich Office
Raw Materials Office
Office for Ethnic Questions
Central Institute for Maximum Utilization of Manpower
Headquarters Command Office with the following directly-attached main departments:
    SS Adjutancy
    Police Adjutancy
    Personal Department *Reichsführer-SS*
    Chief Responsible for
        Decorations and guests
        Administration
        Economic aid
        Personnel
    SS Judicial Liaison Officer
    Person responsible for service dogs, *Reichsführer-SS* and departments
    Decorations and orders[16]
    Records management and office
    Signals
    Transport service
    Commander of the Staff Department of the *Waffen-SS*[17]

In addition to these departments there were also smaller departments which were maintained within the Personal Staff. These included a nutritional science agricultural experimental station, and the Office of the Inspector for Statistics[18] founded in 1940. As well, at the Auschwitz concentration camp, research was carried out into natural rubber extraction. Göring had named Himmler "Special Representative for all Questions Concerning Plant Rubber."

When *SS-Obergruppenführer* and *General der Waffen-SS* Wolff was put out of action by a heart attack in February 1943, Himmler *de jure* personally took over leadership of the Personal Staff *Hauptamt*.

4. SS Main Office of Race and Settlement

The SS Racial Office was established under the leadership of *SS-Standartenführer* Walter Darré (July 14, 1895 – September 5, 1953) at the end of December 1931. The aim in doing so was to establish a standard "racial elite" in the selection of SS candidates. In addition to an Aryan family tree back to the eighteenth century, the SS men had to meet certain optical criteria, some of which were also used in the suitability guidelines for acceptance into the armed units of the SS. Himmler was convinced that, "blood alone determines history, civilization, law and economy." To him, "Germanic" blood was the guarantee of honor, loyalty, bravery, and ambitiousness.

In the summer of 1932, a settlement department was added to the racial office. This made plans for settling entire SS tribal communities (families)—some as so-called soldier peasants—in the hypothetical new "living spaces" (primarily in Eastern Europe). On January 30, 1935, the

Office of Race and Settlement was elevated to a main office. The SS Main Office of Race and Settlement (RuSHA) was thus one of the first three SS main offices to be created, along with the *SS-Hauptamt* and the *Sicherheits-Hauptamt* and was organized as follows:

- Adjutancy
- Organization and Administration Office
- Racial Office
- Training Office
- Clan Office
- Settlement Office

The previously-mentioned standard acceptance examinations of SS candidates and the training of the examination boards that carried them out were conducted by the Racial Office. After the start of the Second World War, racial-biological examinations of the native populations and the ethnic Germans living in Eastern Europe and the Balkans in particular were carried out. In keeping with Himmler's ideas, the Family Office was to assist in the creation of special tribal communities within the SS. To prevent his SS men from establishing families with women from undesirable elements of the population, on December 31, 1931, he issued a marriage order which was supposed to secure the future of the male order by establishing SS clans:

1. The SS is a body of German men of strictly Nordic descent selected according to certain principles.
2. In accordance with National Socialist ideology and in the realization that the future of our people rests upon the preservation of the race through selection and the healthy inheritance of good blood, I hereby institute the "Marriage Certificate" for all unmarried members of the SS, effective January 1, 1932.
3. The desired aim is to create a hereditarily healthy clan of a strictly Nordic German sort.
4. The marriage certificate will be awarded or denied solely on the basis of racial health and heredity.
5. Every SS man who intends to marry must procure for this purpose the marriage certificate of the Reichsführer SS.
6. SS members who marry despite having been denied marriage certificates will be stricken from the SS; they will be given the choice of withdrawing.
7. Working out the details of marriage petitions is the task of the "Race Office" of the SS.
8. The Racial Office of the SS is in charge of the "Clan Book of the SS," in which the families of SS members will be entered after being awarded the marriage certificate or after acquiescing to the petition to enter into marriage.
9. The *Reichsführer-SS*, the leader of the Racial Office, and the specialists of this office are duty bound to secrecy on their word of honor.
10. The SS believes that, with this command, it has taken a step of great significance. Derision, scorn, and incomprehension do not move us; the future belongs to us!

Nevertheless, Himmler realized that much of the population would react to such ideas with "derision and scorn." He declared his intention that the SS was not to be a pure men's league in a speech to SS officers in 1935:

Furthermore, we have not set the goal of bringing to life a men's league, which like all men's or soldiers' associations sooner or later falls apart, instead we have set the goal of gradually causing a true order to grow. I use the word order too often. It is thus not an order in the common sense of the word. I hope that in ten years we will be an order, and not an order just of men, but an order of clan communities. An order in which the women are just as vital a part as the men.

This was an expression of Himmler's great objective. The SS was to take a lasting and socially-leading place in Germany. The wording "gradually causing an order to grow" illustrates his thinking. He wanted to create an order following the pattern of several that had existed earlier in human history. In the fourth century, for example, Pachomios the Great (292–346) created a Christian community in Egypt after reaching the conclusion that only a union of many could guarantee the survival of individual Christians. The foundations of a religious order were fixed rules, such as, for example, joint property, obedience, and the willingness to work. Many orders were founded in reaction to emergencies of the times. Like other founders of orders (such as St. Francis of Assisi, 1181–1226), Himmler wanted to create a new lifestyle and gradually inculcate the National–Socialist ideology into the German and ultimately the European population.

The Training Office was responsible for racial-political instruction within the SS command and SS units and in the Settlement Office previous plans for the occupation of foreign territories were implemented. *SS-Standartenführer* Gunther d'Alquen described the basic tasks of the RuSHA prior to the Second World War in his previously-mentioned work:

After the Security Main Office, the next pillar of the SS Reich Command is the SS Main Office of Race and Settlement. In the Main Office of Race and Settlement, the Clan Office processes marriage applications by SS men. As is well known, no SS man can marry without obtaining permission from the *Reichsführer-SS*, on the basis of the marriage order of 1931. This requires a health examination of the man and woman. Guarantors are required for the bride's ideological and human relations. Furthermore a family tree—to 1750 for officers, and 1800 for non-commissioned officers—has been required until now. Presentation of a racial health certificate is likewise required.

To enable the rapid presentation of the necessary documents, clan care centers have been established or are planned in the SS foot Standarten. These are intended to assist both the SS man and the Race and Settlement Office in procuring all documents. All of this of course requires a huge amount of work and extensive organizational preparations, in order to as quickly as possible meet all requirements, which at the moment are very pressing as large numbers of people are again marrying.

The Settlement Office in the Race and Settlement Main Office is addressing and realizing the ideas of blood and soil through settlement of valuable SS families in conjunction with the new creation of German farming communities and homestead settlement.

The Race and Settlement Main Office continues to watch over the standardization of the racial acceptance examinations and the training of the specialists attached to SS units who are responsible for these acceptance examinations.

Between 1932 and 1945, four generals commanded the RuSHA. They were:

SS-Gruppenführer Richard Walter Darré (end of 1931 – August 31, 1938)
SS-Brigadeführer Günther Pancke (September 1, 1938 – July 8, 1940)
SS-Gruppenführer Otto Hofmann (July 9, 1940 – April 20, 1943)
SS-Obergruppenführer Richard Hildebrandt (April 20, 1943 – May 9, 1945)

Absender: _____
(Vor- und Zuname)

SS-Einheit: 8/58 SS-Nr.: 162951

Sip. Nr.:

O.U. den 20.6.44
(Wohnort) (Datum)
_____
(Straße und Hausnummer)

A

Betr.: Verlobungs- und Heiratsgesuch

Anlage:

An das

Rasse- und Siedlungshauptamt-SS
SS-Pflegestelle

Ich bitte um Erteilung der Verlobungs- und Heiratsgenehmigung mit

Fräulein / Frau _____

und übersende anliegend die umseitig angeführten Unterlagen.

Aus unten angeführten Gründen möchte ich meine Eheschließung bis spätestens _____ vollziehen. Ich bitte daher um bevorzugte Bearbeitung meines Antrages.

Gründe:

Eilt, Sofortvermerk

Vom RuS auszufüllen

Nach Erteilung der Verlobungs- und Heiratsgenehmigung bitte ich um Ausstellung des Eheeignungszeugnisses für das Ehestandsdarlehen

Ehestandsdarlehen ist beantragt,
wird beantragt,
wird nicht beantragt.
(Nichtzutreffendes streichen)

Vom RuS auszufüllen

M 8

Ich bin Schüler der **Ordensburg** und bitte, nach Erteilung der Verlobungs- und Heiratsgenehmigung an die Reichsleitung der NSDAP. — Hauptpersonalamt / Amt Führernachwuchs Nachricht zu geben.

Raum für sonstige Bemerkungen:

_____
(Unterschrift)
SS-Hauptsturmführer

Nicht zutreffendes streichen
zutreffendes unterstreichen
stark umrahmte Felder gelten nur für:
SS-TV, SS-VT, SS-Sammelstelle, Wachmänner,
Hauptamtliche und Ordensburgschüler.

Doppelt umrahmte Felder
werden nur vom RuS ausgefüllt.

Anmerkungen des RuS

Before becoming engaged or marrying, members of the SS had to submit an extensive application to the Race and Settlement Main Office.

171

Unterlagen:

Stück	von mir	Stück	meiner zukünftigen Ehefrau
1	RuS-Fragebogen	1	RuS-Fragebogen
	Familienbilder		Familienbilder
1	SS-Erbgesundheitsbogen	1	SS-Erbgesundheitsbogen
	SS-Sippenbogen (Frage- und Erbgesundheitsbogen zusammengefaßt)		SS-Sippenbogen (Frage- und Erbgesundheitsbogen zusammengefaßt)
1	SS-Untersuchungsbogen	1	SS-Untersuchungsbogen
1	ärztliche Zeugnisse zum UB		ärztliche Zeugnisse zum UB
1	Scheidungsurteil (wenn geschieden)		Scheidungsurteil (wenn geschieden)
1	SS-Ahnentafel	1	SS-Ahnentafel
1	Umschlag mit .... Urkunden .... Ahnenpässen .... Familienstammbüchern .... Schriftwechsel zum Ahnennachweis	1	Umschlag mit .... Urkunden .... Ahnenpässen .... Familienstammbüchern .... Schriftwechsel zum Ahnennachweis
	Bescheinigung über Mütterschulungslehrgang		Bescheinigung über Mütterschulungslehrgang
	Bescheinigung über Reichssport- oder BDM-Leistungsabzeichen		
	Antrag auf Ausstellung des Eheeignungszeugnisses für das Ehestandsdarlehen (VED.)		

Als Angehöriger der SS-VT. / SS-TV. / SS-Wach- und Grenzeinheiten / hauptamtlicher SS-Angehöriger (nicht zutreffendes streichen) füge ich noch bei:

Stück	von mir	Stück	meiner zukünftigen Ehefrau
1	Ehrenwörtliche Erklärung über Vermögen und Schulden		Ehrenwörtliche Erklärung über Vermögen und Schulden
1	Stellungnahme .... des Führers der .... (Einheit)		

Vorbedingungen

Ich darf als

a) SS-Wachmann / hauptamtlicher SS-Angehöriger
(nicht zutreffendes streichen)
erst nach Vollendung des **25. Lebensjahres**
heiraten und bin .... Jahre alt.

b) Angehöriger der SS-VT. / SS-TV.
(nicht zutreffendes streichen)
erst nach Vollendung des **25. Lebensjahres**
oder nach Beförderung zum SS-Oberscharführer / SS-Obersturmführer
(b. Führern)
heiraten und bin .... Jahre alt und im Dienstgrad ....

c) aus den SS-Junkerschulen hervorgegangener SS-Führer
erst nach Vollendung des **25. Lebensjahres**
und nach **zweijähriger Dienstzeit als SS-Führer** heiraten,
bin .... Jahre alt und wurde am ....
zum SS-Untersturmführer befördert.

Die **Vorbedingungen** zur Heirat sind also ~~nicht~~ erfüllt.
(wenn erfüllt, „nicht" streichen.)

a) Vorerst will ich mich nur **verloben.**

b) Aus nachstehenden Gründen ist **vorzeitige Heirat** notwendig:

Begründung:

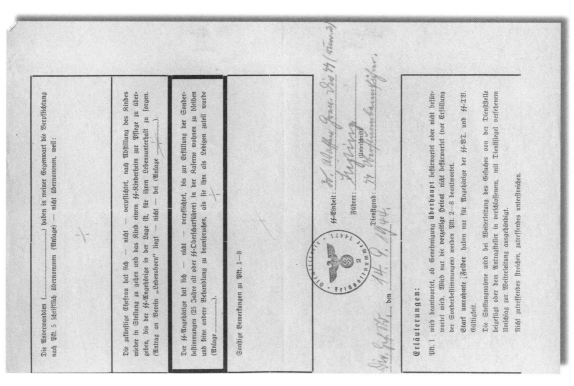

The SS member's immediate superior had to give a statement to accompany the engagement or marriage application.

5. Main Office *Dienststelle SS-Obergruppenführer* Heißmeyer

When the National–Socialists took power in 1933 they immediately began exerting influence on the upbringing of children. Government Centers of Education (Stabilas) were renamed National–Socialist Political Educational Institutions (*Npeas* or *Napolas*). The primary task of the *Napolas* was the, "bringing up [of the students] to be National–Socialists, ready physically and mentally to serve the people and state."

In the beginning the *Napolas* were under the Prussian Ministry of Culture. Then, from February 4, 1933, they were led by Bernhard Rust (September 30, 1883 – May 8, 1945), the *Gauleiter* of South Hanover–Brunswick. He issued a decree on December 27, 1933, which released them from the general school administration and created the State Administration for National–Political Institutes of Education. Joachim Haupt (April 7, 1900 – May 13, 1989) became the first inspector of the *Napolas*. His goal was, "to create a new type of school, in which the idea of a National–Socialist community education" would become a reality.

In 1931, Haupt had been suspended from the government center of education in Plön for having had homosexual relations with students, and in November 1935, he was discharged again. Reinhard Sunkel (February 9, 1900 – May 8, 1945) took over the post of inspector for a short time. As he had a Jewish grandmother, according to the Nuremberg Race Laws he was considered a Grade 2 "*mischling*" and consequently he too was suspended.

Himmler's efforts to have as many state functions as possible controlled using members of the SS resulted on February 1, 1936, in Bernhard Rust, the Reich Minister for Science, Education and National Culture, appointing *SS-Gruppenführer* August Heißmeyer, head of the *SS-Hauptamt*, as the new Inspector of National–Socialist Political Institutes of Education.

Until the outbreak of war, the *Napolas* represented political elite schools within the secondary school system. As such boarding schools basically required the parents to pay tuition, on April 2, 1936, soon after taking office, *SS-Gruppenführer* Heißmeyer declared in the newspaper Naumburger Tageblatt:

> In the future, I will strive to ensure that those who can afford to pay will no longer be the only ones to come to the national-political institutes of education, instead only those boys who have what it takes to later assume leadership roles in the state and party. Whether the training is paid for by the parents or from funds provided for this purpose will make no difference.

He again stated the basic intention behind the *Napolas*. The students would later assume leading positions in the state and party. At the end of 1938, there were fourteen institutions, of which eleven were in Prussia. By 1944, the number of these boarding schools rose to thirty-seven.

Effective April 1, 1940, the office of the inspector was elevated into an independent main office. *SS-Gruppenführer* Berger replaced *SS-Obergruppenführer* Heißmeyer as head of the *SS-Hauptamt* and the latter the new main office "*Dienststelle SS-Obergruppenführer Heißmeyer*," which had been named after him.

The office's expanded responsibilities resulted in talks with *Oberst* Johannes Frießner (March 22, 1892 – June 26, 1971), the Inspector of Army Education and Training. Frießner proposed that the students should be taught, "to think and act like officers following standard army principles." When Himmler learned of this he became very angry and on May 7, 1940, wrote to the new head of the *Hauptamt*:

> I have received your report of April 29, 1940, concerning expansion of the national-political institutes of education. A division of authority for education is out of the question.

I told *Oberst* Frießner this personally yesterday before the start of the inspection of 6,000 officer candidates by the Führer.

Oberst Frießner's proposal would result in the national-political institutes of education becoming nothing more than an army cadet corps which would turn all of its students over to the army.

Furthermore, I strictly forbid, and I emphasize this, that special emphasis be placed on education to think and act like officers according to standard army principles. I do request, however, that during the next negotiations you state clearly to the gentlemen that I determine the educational guidelines in the national-political institutes of education and not the army.

All arrangements with the Army High Command require my personal authorization.

In 1941, there were about 6,000 students at the *Napolas*, which during the war acted as "cadet schools." As a rule the students volunteered to become officer candidates for the *Waffen-SS* or *Wehrmacht*. In 1944, there were about 8,000 students in the National–Socialist political institutes of education, therefore elevation to the status of main office was justified.

6. *Reichssicherheitshauptamt* (Reich Security Main Office)

The Reich Security Main Office was formed on October 1, 1939, by combining the Security Police (Sipo) and Security Service (SD) main offices and was initially commanded by *SS-Gruppenführer* Reinhard Heydrich (March 7, 1904 – June 4, 1942). (*Note*: the Sipo has already been addressed in the chapter *Chief of German Police/Secret State Police*.) The tasks assigned to the SD will be documented in contemporary language using extracts from d'Alquen's work *Die SS: Geschichte, Aufgabe und Organisation der Schutzstaffeln der NSDAP*:

During the period of struggle, over the course of time the range of duties, which originally consisted of personal protection for the *Führer* and leading personalities of the movement, underwent an expansion. It was increasingly found that the exposure and recognition of hostile tendencies was an indispensible requirement in combating them.

From the constant monitoring of the party, the originally relatively simple task of protecting persons had developed into the problem of safeguarding the party and its diverse functions. For this reasons intelligence services were created in the party and all of its organizations with the task of counteracting the magnitude of hostile plans for attacks and destruction by investigating and assessing potential threats. There was, however, no standardized plan, and little effort was made to achieve a central summarization by the intelligence services.

At that time the SS had also created an intelligence service to assist in carrying out its tasks. In contrast to the other intelligence services in the party, a comprehensive, systematic political intelligence service developed from the so-called I c service, the later PI (press information) Service of the RF-SS from the period when the party was banned.

Built on the basis of the racial elite and ideological discipline in keeping with the general principles of the SS, immune to all sectional, immediate, and personal motivations—in combination with a comprehensive and objective goal, this intelligence service developed into a security service, first for the SS and the party and later for the people and the Reich.

After the assumption of power this became apparent when the Security Service of the *Reichsführer-SS* proved that, through the carefully-planned buildup of its organization, which stayed clear of personal dependencies, had registered all opponents and areas of life which were or could become of importance to the new National–Socialist state.

From the development in the areas of the party intelligence services, the representatives of the *Führer* then also reached the same conclusion. In his decree of June 9, 1934, he declared that "henceforth no party intelligence service may exist apart from the Security Service of the RF-SS."

Effective the issuance of this decree, the Security Service of the RF-SS is the only political intelligence service of the National–Socialist German Workers Party.

Through ongoing surveillance of open and secret opponents of the National–Socialist ideology, the Security Service of the RF-SS has reported on its findings concerning the situation and connections, and it has increasingly become an organ of protection for the state and people, working in close cooperation with the Secret State Police.

The apex of the Security Service of the RF-SS's organization is the [Reich] Security Main Office, which joins the other two main offices of the Reich command. The commander of the [Reich] Security Main Office is *SS-Gruppenführer* R. Heydrich, who was responsible for building the I c and PI Services and who is also chief of the Security Police.

Regional organization of the Security Service of the RF-SS, organized into higher and lower sections, closely follows that of the *Allgemeine-SS*.

Close surveillance of changes in the enemy's methods and his tactic of changing his manifestations, his ideologies and operating methods mean that the work of the Security Service of the RF-SS cannot be calculated by the hour, instead it is always contoured and farsighted.

As already described, the SD gained great importance in National–Socialism and in the summer of 1934, it was expanded into a main office. This was organized into the following offices:

Office I: Personnel and Administration
Office II: SD-Inland (Interior)
  Central Department II/1: Opponent Investigation
    Main Department II/11: Ideological Opponents
      Department II/111: Freemasons
      Department II/112: Jews
      Department II/113: Political churches
    Main Department II/12: Political Opponents
      Department II/121: Marxism
      Department II/122: Opposition
    Main Department II/2: Areas of German Life
      Department II/21: Culture
      Department II/22: Law and administration
      Department II/23: Economy
Office III: SD-Ausland (Abroad)/Counterintelligence

The merging of the SD Main Office with the Security Police Main Office to form the Reich Security Main Office in autumn 1939, created the central monitoring and investigative authority in the Third Reich. In addition to the general tasks of the criminal police, which remain the same today, this main office was responsible for a multitude of other tasks ranging from the ideological pursuit of individuals to genocide. Whereas the RSHA was organized as follows after the decree of September 27, 1939:

Office I: Organization, administration legal affairs
Office II: Investigation of opposition
Office III: Areas of German Life – SD-Inland
Office IV: Combating of opposition
Office V: Criminal Police
Office VI: SD-Ausland

After the war began there was a further expansion of its responsibilities and from 1941, it was organized as follows:

Office I (Personnel)
I A (Personnel Department)
   I A 1 (general personnel matters)
   I A 2 (Gestapo personnel)
   I A 3 (Kripo personnel)
   I A 4 (SD personnel)
   I A 5 (party and SS personnel)
   I A 6 (welfare)
I B (Recruiting, Education and Training)
   I B 1 (Ideological education)
   I B 2 (Nachwuchs)
   I B 3 (School curriculum design)
   I B 4 (Other curricula)
I C (Physical Education)
   I C 1 (General matters concerning physical education)
   I C 2 (Physical instruction and military training)
I D (Criminal Matters)
   I D 1 (Military criminal matters)
   I D 2 (SS disciplinary matters)
Office II (Organization, Administration and Law)
II A (Organization and Law)
   II A 1 (Organization of the Sipo and the SD)
   II A 2 (Legislation)
   II A 3 (Justice matters, damage claims)
   II A 4 (Reich Defense matters)
   II A 5 (Various: Determination of hostility to people and state, seizure of assets, loss of citizenship)
II B (Basic Questions Concerning Passports and Foreign Police)
   II B 1 (Passports I)
   II B 2 (Passports II)
   II B 3 (Identity Documents and Identity Cards)
   II B 4 (Basic questions for foreign police and border security)
II C a (Sipo Budget)
   II C 1 (Budget and pay)
   II C 2 (Supply and subject costs)
   II C 3 (Quarters and prisoners)
II C b (SD Budget)

II C 7 (SD Budget and pay)

II C 8 (Procurement, insurance, contracts, properties, construction and
motor transport)

II C 9 (Checks and audits)

II D (Technical Matters)

II D 1 (Radio, photography and film)

II D 2 (Teletypes and telephones)

II D 3 a (Sipo motor transport)

II D 3 b (SD motor transport)

II D 4 (Weaponry)

II D 5 (Aviation)

II D 6 (Management of Sipo and SD technical funds)

Office III (Areas of German Life – SD-Inland)

III A (Questions Concerning the Legal System and the Building of the Reich)

III A 1 (General questions concerning areas of life work)

III A 2 (Legal life)

III A 3 (Constitution and administration)

III A 4 (Rural life)

III B (National Values)

III B 1 (National values work)

III B 2 (Minorities)

III B 3 (Race and Racial Health)

III B 4 (Immigration and Resettlement)

III B 5 (Occupied Territories)

III C (Culture)

III C 1 (Science)

III C 2 (Education and Religious Life)

III C 3 (Folk Culture)

III C 4 (Press, Literature and Radio)

III D (Economy)

III D 1 (Food Industry)

III D 2 (Trade, Craft and Commerce)

III D 3 (Industry and Energy Sector)

III D 4 (Labor and Social Services)

Office IV (Opposition Investigation and Control – Secret State Police Office)

IV A (Opposition)

IV A 1 (Communism, Marxism and Auxiliary Organizations, War
Crimes, Illegal and Enemy Propaganda)

IV A 2 (Preventing and combating sabotage, political and police
intelligence representatives, political counterfeiting)

IV A 3 (Reaction, opposition, legitimacy, liberalism, emigrants,
matters of treachery not covered by IV A 1)

IV A 4 (Protection service, assassination report, surveillance,
special tasks, wanted squad)

IV B (Ideological Opponents)

IV B 1 (Political Catholicism)

IV B 2 (Political Protestantism, sects)

IV B 3 (Other churches, Freemasonry)

IV B 4 (Jewish matters, eviction matters)

IV C (Files)

IV C 1 (Analysis, main card index, personal file administration,
information center, A Files, foreign surveillance, visa center)
IV C 2 (Protective detention matters)
IV C 3 (Matters of the press and literature)
IV C 4 (Matters of the party and its organizations)
IV D (Occupied Territories)
IV D 1 (Matters concerning the Protectorate, Czechs in the Reich)
IV D 2 (Matters concerning the Generalgouvernement, Poles in the Reich)
IV D 3 (Anonymous reporting, foreigners hostile to the state)
IV D 4 (Occupied territories: France, Luxembourg, Alsace and
Lorraine, Belgium, Holland, Norway, Denmark)
IV E (Counterintelligence)
IV E 1 (General counterintelligence matters, preparation of reports
in cases of treason and high treason, factory security and
the security industry)
IV E 2 (General economic matters, economic espionage)
IV E 3 (Counterintelligence West)
IV E 4 (Counterintelligence North)
IV E 5 (Counterintelligence East)
IV E 6 (Counterintelligence South)
IV P (Dealings with Foreign Police)
Office V (Crime Prevention – Reich Criminal Police Office)
V A (Crime Policy and Prevention)
V A 1 (Legal issues, international cooperation and criminal investigation)
V A 2 (Prevention)
V A 3 (Female criminal police)
V B (Action)
V B 1 (Capital crimes)
V B 2 (Fraud)
V B 3 (Sexual offenses)
V C (Police Records)
V C 1 (Reich Police Records Central Office)
V C 2 (Manhunt)
V D (Security Police Forensics Institute)
V D 1 (Fingerprinting)
V D 2 (Chemistry and biology)
V D 3 (Document testing)
Office VI (Foreign Countries – SD-Ausland)
VI A (General Foreign Intelligence Office Tasks with seven specialists)
VI B (German-Italian sphere of influence in Europe, Africa and the East)
VI C (The East, Russian- Japanese sphere of influence)
VI D (West, Anglo-American sphere of influence)
VI E (Surveillance of ideological enemies abroad)
VI F (Technical aids for the intelligence service in foreign countries)
VI G ("Dr. Wilfried Krallert Office")
VI S (from 1943: Training, combating resistance)
Office VII (Ideological Research and Analysis – SD-Ausland)
VII A (Tracking Material)
VII A 1 (Library)

VII A 2 (Reporting, translation service, screening
    and evaluation of press material)
VII A 3 (Credit agency and liaison office)
VII B (Analysis)
  VII B 1 (Freemasonry and Jewry)
  VII B 2 (Political churches)
  VII B 3 (Marxism)
  VII B 4 (other hostile groups)
  VII B 5 (Scientific individual examinations of domestic problems)
  VII B 6 (Scientific individual examinations of foreign problems)
VII C (Archive, Museum and Scientific Special Missions)
  VII C 1 (Archive)
  VII C 2 (Museum)
  VII C 3 (Scientific Special Missions)

While Office I handled administrative matters concerning members of the RSHA and Office II controlled the organization and administration of the RSHA, Office III assessed the mood of the people in the German Reich and Offices VI and VII that in foreign countries. Office V was the Reich Criminal Police Office and was responsible for fighting violent and economic crime.[19] The Secret State Police (GESTAPO) formed Office IV and was responsible for the active pursuit of opposition domestically and of "*ideological enemies*" at home and abroad. Office IV B 4 under *SS-Obersturmbannführer* Adolf Eichmann (March 19, 1906 – July 1, 1962) rounded up the Jewish population as well as Sinti and Roma in Europe and interned the millions of deportees in ghettoes, concentration camps, and "death camps." The latter were set up in the Generalgouvernement as part of "Operation Reinhard." Even before this, the *Reichssicherheitshauptamt* had formed numerous *Einsatzgruppen*, which took explicit action against ideological enemies—Communists, Jews, Sinti, and Roma—primarily in the Soviet Union.

Einsatzgruppen

Whereas the Security Police and the Security Service were initially limited to regional activities within the borders of the German Reich, on March 13, 1938, the first mobile *Einsatzgruppe* (action group) made up of members of the SD was formed in response to the incorporation ("*Anschluss*") of Austria into the Reich. Under the command of *SS-Standartenführer* Franz Six (August 12, 1909 – July 9, 1975), its task was to arrest political opponents in Austria using previously-prepared wanted lists.

About half a year later on October 1, 1938, two *Einsatzgruppen* of the SD saw action during the incorporation of the Sudetenland into the German Reich. *Einsatzgruppe Wien* (Action Group Vienna) under *SS-Standartenführer* Jeinz Jost (July 9, 1904 – November 12, 1964) consisted of five *Einsatzkommandos* (companies), and *Einsatzgruppe Dresden* under *SS-Standartenführer* Walter Stahlecker (October 10, 1900 – March 23, 1942) of two *Einsatzkommandos*. The tasks assigned to these two *Einsatzgruppen* were to arrest persons "hostile to the Reich" whose names were on prepared wanted lists, or who were identified by Sudeten Germans.

When, after the Munich Agreement, the German military occupied so-called rump Czechoslovakia (Bohemia and Moravia) on March 15, 1938, two actions groups were formed: *Einsatzgruppe I "Prague" and Einsatzgruppe II "Brünn."* Split into several *Einsatzkommandos*, as during the previous two operations they arrested several thousand potential or actual members of the political opposition or agitators.

The Twelve Main Offices (*Hauptämter*) as Himmler's Administrative Apparatus

The Balkan Campaign resulted in the first large-scale encounters between SS units and Sinti and Roma peoples.

While the women and children were still often seen as "colorful" photographic subjects, the Sinti and Roma men were often given degrading tasks to perform as seen here: cleaning caterpillar tracks and the boots of German officers.

In the beginning the Jewish population also provided welcome subjects for photography ...

... which ultimately ended in the destruction of life and property.

On July 5, 1939, orders were issued for the formation of five *Einsatzgruppen*, usually consisting of two or three *Einsatzkommandos*. Each was assigned to one of the five armies envisaged for the Polish Campaign and placed under the Army High Command (OKH):

Einsatzgruppe I	*SS-Standartenführer* Bruno Streckenbach (February 7, 1902 – October 28, 1977)
Einsatzgruppe II	*SS-Standartenführer* Emanuel Schäfer (April 20, 1900 – December 4, 1974)
Einsatzgruppe III	*SS-Obersturmbannführer* Hans Fischer (August 21, 1906 – unknown)
Einsatzgruppe IV	*SS-Brigadeführer* Lothar Beutel (May 6, 1902 – May 16, 1986)
Einsatzgruppe V	*SS-Brigadeführer* Ernst Damzog (October 30, 1882 – July 1945)

The *Einsatzgruppen* were to carry out, "the fight against all elements hostile to the Reich and Germans in enemy territory behind the fighting troops." According to an order issued by Himmler on September 3, 1939, in addition to Jews this was to include all armed "Polish insurgents" encountered. These were often Polish stragglers, who were shot on the spot contrary to international law. On September 7, 1939, Heydrich ordered the *Einsatzgruppen*, "to render the leading social class in Poland harmless to the extent possible." Additional *Einsatzgruppen* were formed for this task:

Einsatzgruppen z.b.V.	*SS-Obergruppenführer* Udo von Woyrsch (July 24, 1895 – January 14, 1983)
Einsatzgruppen VI	*SS-Oberführer* Erich Naumann (April 29, 1905 – June 7, 1951)
Einsatzkommando 16	*SS-Sturmbannführer* Rudolf Trger (April 23, 1905 – June 18, 1940)

Each of the total of sixteen company-strength *Einsatzkommandos* consisted of 120 to 150 men, and thus had a combined strength of about 3,000 men. They are believed to have shot more than 12,000 Poles by the end of October 1939. The estimated number of executions rose to more than 60,000 by the spring of 1940. In addition to the "Polish intelligentsia," the victims included mainly Jews plus Sinti and Roma, plus patients from Polish mental institutions. As in Germany, the latter were killed by carbon-monoxide in gas trucks designated *S(onder)-Wagen* (Special Trucks)—modified trucks with larger bodies.

While RSHA offices were established in 1940, for the occupation of Denmark and Norway and during the campaign in the west, no *Einsatzgruppen* were formed. It was obviously assumed that the populations of these countries would comply with the German occupiers and there were surely doubts about carrying out mass executions in western and northern Europe, which would cast Germany in a bad light and possibly lead to a rise in opposition.

Things were different in the Balkan Campaign, which began in April 1941. *Einsatzgruppe Serbien* was formed in March 1941 under the command of *SS-Oberführer* Wilhelm Fuchs (September 1, 1898 – January 24, 1947). As the designation suggests, it was a formation focused on Serbia, which, unlike the other Yugoslavian countries such as Slovenia, Croatia and Bosnia, it was assumed would have a basically hostile attitude towards the German forces. The *Einsatzgruppe*'s task was again to eliminate suspected Serbian national and communist functionaries. Jews and gypsies were essentially to be liquidated. *SS-Gruppenführer* Harald Turner (October 8, 1891 – March 9, 1947), the head of the military administration of Serbia, described operations in a letter to *SS-Gruppenführer* Wolff on April 11, 1942:

Months ago I had all the Jews in the local country shot and all Jewish women and children placed in a camp [Sajmiste]. At the same time, with the SD's assistance I had a "delousing truck" made, with which the emptying of the camp will finally have been carried out in about fourteen days to four weeks. Since the arrival of Meyszner[20] and the handing over of this camp business over to him, it has been carried on by him. Then the moment came, in which the Jewish officers in prisoner of war camps under the Geneva Convention, like it or not, follow their relatives already gone, and this may easily lead to complications.

It is a paradox that the German agencies involved in the "final solution of the Jewish question" had reservations about breaking certain international agreements—in this case the Geneva Convention with respect to Jewish officers from Serbia held in German prisoner of war camps—while at the same time they were mass-murdering Jewish civilians. On August 20, 1942, *SS-Gruppenführer* Turner mentioned in a presentation to the *Wehrmacht* Commander Southeast that Serbia was the only country in which the Jewish and Gypsy question had since been resolved. It is believed that about 10,000 Serbians became victims of this "ethnic cleansing."

In Croatia meanwhile, enormous social problems developed between the political leadership and the largely penniless population, leading to growing unrest and communist agitation. As a result, *Einsatzgruppe E* under the command of *SS-Obersturmbannführer* Ludwig Teichmann (May 14, 1909 – January 24, 1947) was deployed there on August 2, 1941. It commanded five *Einsatzkommandos*. As before in Poland and Serbia, planned mass executions of Jews, accused of being "carriers of communist ideas" and held as scapegoats for attacks on German soldiers, were carried out.

The Security Police *Einsatzgruppen* had already shown in Poland and Serbia that they were capable of carrying out orders from Berlin without scruples, and in the conflict against the USSR they achieved a very different importance because of the much higher quality of the ideological foe. The following is from the *Wehrmacht*'s "Special Areas Guidelines for Directive No. 21" issued on March 13, 1941:

> In preparation for the political administration, the *Reichsführer-SS* will be given special tasks in the army area of operations on behalf of the Führer which are the result off a fight to the end between two opposing political systems. In the carrying out these tasks, the *Reichsführer-SS* will act independently and on his own responsibility. Moreover, this has no effect on the executive authority given by the commander-in-chief of the army and the offices mandated by him. The *Reichsführer-SS* will ensure that, in carrying out his tasks, operations are not interfered with. The OKH will arrange details directly with the *Reichsführer-SS*.

The arranging of details between the OKH and the *Reichsführer-SS* referred to was concluded between *SS-Gruppenführer* Heydrich and *Generalleutnant* Eduard Wagner (April 1, 1894 – July 23, 1944), the army's general staff officer responsible for supply and administration. They documented the tasks and the actions against the civilian population independent of the army. *Sonderkommandos* (special parties) of the *Einsatzgruppen* were to be deployed in the rear army areas near the front, *Einsatzkommandos* (action parties) in the rear army areas further to the rear:

> The carrying out of special security police tasks outside the field forces makes necessary the employment of special parties[21] of the Security Police and SD in the area of operations. [...]

1.) Tasks:

a) In the rear army area: securing of selected fixed installations (materiel, archives, card indexes of organizations hostile to the Reich or state, units, groups, etc.) prior to the start of operations as well as particularly important individuals (leading émigrés, saboteurs, terrorists, etc.) [...]

b) In the army group rear area: investigation and fighting of efforts against the state and Reich, provided they are not incorporated with the enemy's armed forces, plus general briefing of the commander of the rear army group areas as to the political situation. [...] The *Sonderkommandos* are authorized to take executive measures against the civilian population in the course of their tasks on their own responsibility. [...]

Thus elements of the *Einsatzgruppen* took over the informative work of the SD and other parts of the active executive measures—that is: shootings. Beginning May 1941, four battalion-strength *Einsatzgruppen* were formed at the border police school in Pretzsch from members of the Sicherheitspolizei, the *Ordnungspolizei* and the *Waffen-SS*:

Einsatzgruppe A [*SS-Brigadeführer* Walter Stahlecker] for Army Group A with:
  Sonderkommandos Ia and *Ib*
  Einsatzkommandos 2 and *3*[22]

Einsatzgruppe B [*SS-Gruppenführer* Arthur Nebe (November 13, 1894 – March 3, 1945)] for Army Group B with:
  Sonderkommandos 7a, 7b and *7c*
  Einsatzkommandos 8 and *9*

Einsatzgruppe C [*SS-Brigadeführer* Otto Rasch (December 7, 1891 – November 1, 1948)] for Army Group C with:
  Sonderkommandos 4a and *4b*
  Einsatzkommandos 5 and *6*

Einsatzgruppen D [*SS-Standartenführer* Otto Ohlendorf (February 4, 1907 – June 7, 1951] for the *11. Armee* (in the area of the Crimean Peninsula) with:
  Sonderkommandos 10a and *11b*
  Einsatzkommando 12

The *Einsatzgruppen* were originally supposed to operate independent of the army, however a modification was announced a few days prior to the start of the campaign in the east. In the OKW's "Guidelines for the Handling of Political Commissars" issued on June 6, 1941 (the so-called "Commissar Order"), the army committed itself to hand over captured commissars to the *Einsatzgruppen*.

The first use of an *Einsatzkommando* in the Russian campaign was representatively documented in a verdict by the Ulm District Court in the so-called *Einsatzgruppen* Trial on August 29, 1958. Especially shocking was the fact that some of the victims and perpetrators knew each other personally:

The village of Polangen [in the Memel District of Lithuania, author's note] was taken by German troops without a fight on June 22, 1941. In the very first days after the occupation defendant Böhme had the Jews of Polangen arrested by the Memel Police Department (GPK) and the Lithuanian police. The men were locked up in the local synagogue, while the women and children went to a children's home or a farm between Polangen and

Krottingen [present-day Kretinga, author's note]. While the shooting of Jews and communists was still going on in Krottingen I on June 26, 1941, defendant Hersmann suggested to defendant Böhme that they drive on to Polangen immediately after the executions, spend the night there and the next day shoot the Jews who had been arrested. Defendant Böhme did not agree, however. The two then agreed that the shootings should take place on June 30, 1941. Defendant Böhme originally wanted nothing to do with these shootings and wanted defendant Kreuzmann to carry them out. He abstained from this, however, because defendant Kreuzmann only held the rank of an SS-*Obersturmführer* and he did not wish to place him above defendant Hersmann, who held a higher rank, namely that of an SS-*Sturmbannführer*.

At the instigation of defendant Böhme, Dr. Frohwann, head of the GPK Memel, again asked defendant Fischer-Schweder to provide a Schupo party. Defendant Fischer-Schweder agreed to do so; by his order *Major* Gü. formed an execution squad, which in the main consisted of the same people as before, and again put defendant Schmidt-Hammer in command of it. The day before the shootings, defendants Böhme and Hersmann again divided their people. Defendant Sakuth was advised when the shootings were to take place by Dr. Frohwann, but possibly also by defendant Hersmann. Defendant Sakuth subsequently negotiated with the leader of a *Luftwaffe* unit in Polangen and was able to secure a platoon from that unit for the shooting.

On the day of the shootings, defendant Böhme and about twenty-five Gestapo members from the Stapo Tilsit drove to Krottingen, as did defendant Hersmann with about eight members of the SD from the SD office in Tilsit. Defendant Hersmann went ahead. When he arrived Dr. Frohwann and the members of the GPK Memel—including defendant Behrendt—and probably also with the members of the GPP Nimmersatt and defendant Sakuth of the SD branch in Memel were already there. Defendant Sakuth informed defendant Hersmann of the agreement made with the *Luftwaffe* unit leader, and defendant Hersmann reported this to defendant Böhme on his arrival. Defendants Böhme and Hersfeld then sought out the *Luftwaffe* officer. By that time the party provided by the *Luftwaffe* officer had already fallen in.

Stapo and SD members were then divided into small groups. As ordered, they and Lithuanian policemen again searched the houses for Jews. They found several and brought them together with the prisoners from the synagogue to the enclosed car station. The prisoners were all male Jews, with representatives from all age classes, from boys to old men.

The prisoners were subsequently taken to the execution site, which had been selected between bushes in the Polangen sand dunes. When the prisoners arrived, the Schupo detachment from Memel under the command of defendant Hammer was already there. It was camped in the pasture. The prisoners then also lay down in the grass next to the Schupo detachment, watched by the Gestapo people. A mutual conversation developed. Some of the prisoners, including the jeweler Segal and the pastry chef Gurewitz had previously lived in Memel and knew various members of the Schupo detachment, most of whom were reservists. Pastry chef Gurewitz was well known in Memel, and not only for his impressive girth. He was also known throughout the city for having a hole made in the ice of Memel Harbor in winter and bathing in the icy water.

It was clear to all of the participants, including defendant Schmidt-Hammer, that the prisoners were Jews. They were immediately recognizable as Jews from their typical racial features. After the arrival of the *Luftwaffe* platoon, defendant Schmidt-Hammer familiarized the men with the process and the firing command. He instructed the Luftwaffe men to likewise form up into two ranks next to the Schupo detachment and on his command to fire simultaneously with the Schupo men at the victims lined up in front of a trench. He told the air force men that the reason for the shooting was that the prisoners were snipers.

After handing over their valuables the prisoners had to dig trenches. As the ground consisted of loose sand, the walls of the trench repeatedly collapsed. This cause the Stapo and SD people supervising the action to drive the victims to work faster. The Jew Feinstein, who was handicapped by a club foot, was repeatedly struck in the presence of defendant Schmidt-Hammer. The Stapo and SD members knew from a reconnaissance in Garsden prior to the shooting, that the Jews were shot because of the clearance order. But defendant Schmidt-Hammer knew that the Jews were killed solely because of the race to which they belonged.

The shootings took place in the same way as the first two shootings in Garsden I and Krottingen I. In each case the victims were led from the nearby assembly place to the trench by Stapo and SD personnel in groups of ten men. There they had to stand facing the firing squad. Before giving the order to fire, defendant Schmidt-Hammer, as he had done in Garsden and Krottingen, declared to the victims line up at the trench: "You are being shot for crimes against the *Wehrmacht* by order of the *Führer*." After the salvo was fired, Stapo and SD men walked down the line and put another bullet into each victim. The next group of victims of course had to throw the bodies of those just shot into the trench, provided they had not fallen in themselves. When the body of the above-mentioned pastry chef Gurewitz did not fall into the trench, a Gestapo man ordered a particularly slender Jewish boy from the next group to throw the body into the trench. When the boy failed to do this immediately, an unidentified Gestapo man struck him, screaming: "Hurry up, the faster you are the sooner you can call it a day!"

Toward the end of the shooting, defendant Hersmann was informed that there was a Jewish pediatrician in a hospital in Polangen, where he was working alongside German medical personnel. Defendant Hersmann then gave orders to fetch the doctor. Despite protests by the German medical personnel, Stapo and SD people took the doctor away in a car, and he was shot in his white physician's coat.

Schnapps was passed out to the participants during the shootings, which was standard practice on such occasions. Defendant Hersmann, a *Luftwaffe* officer and Detective Superintendent Krumbach took photographs during the shootings. Witness Krumbach had to turn his film over to defendant Böhme, while the *Luftwaffe* officer's film was seized by defendant Hersmann.

When the shootings were over, in Polangen the Stapo and SD men ate a meal, which had previously been ordered by witness Pa. After this shooting in Polangen, defendant Böhme gave the leaders of the GPK and the officers of the GPP the authority to in future arrest small groups of Jews and communists on their own behavior and to shoot them and to make a report to him.

While the first mass shootings were justified by alleged "offenses against the *Wehrmacht*," Stalin's call for a partisan war behind the front provided a very welcome official justification. At a meeting at *Führer* Headquarters on July 16, 1941, Hitler declared:

The Russians have now given the order for partisan warfare behind our front. This partisan war also has its advantage: it gives us the opportunity to wipe out anyone who opposes us.

In addition to temporary secondments of units of the *Wehrmacht, Waffen-SS,* or *Ordnungspolizei* to the *Einsatzgruppen*, SS formations in particular were given independent missions to carry out mass executions when no Sipo detachments were available. On July 22, 1941, for example, *SS-Brigade 1 (mot.)* was sent to the Senior SS and Police Commander South in the Rovno area. Three days later elements of the brigade were committed to locate stragglers and Jews about forty kilometers to the south, between Ostrog and Shepetovka. As in Poland and Yugoslavia, troops separated from their units—no matter whether they were armed or not—were to be liquidated just like Jews. About 800 of the latter were shot by *SS-Brigade 1* "for favoring bolshevism."

After thus first action, the SS brigade, with the *56. Infanterie-Division*, was attached to the commander of Rear Army Group Area South. On August 4, 1941, elements of *SS-Infanterie-Regiment 10 (mot.)* shot 1,385 Jewish civilians in Ostrog, Hrycow, and Kunev. Then regional court director Otto Albert declared in a statutory declaration on March 29, 1947:

> During my time as a judge advocate with Military Administration Headquarters 787, in August 1941 our unit was in Ostrog right on the then Polish–Russian border. One day an SS battalion moved into Ostrog and began dragging all Jews out of their houses and into the town.
>
> *Major* z.V. Karl Behr, the military administration headquarter's *Major beim Stabe*, went round and learned that they planned to shoot the Jewish population, 6,000 to 7,000 people, on the spot.
>
> *Herr* Behr became extraordinarily upset about it. He contacted me in my capacity of judge advocate and immediately drove with me to the gathering place in order to stop the shooting if possible.
>
> At the gathering place we met the commander of the SS regiment, an *Oberstleutnant* (*Obersturmbannführer*), with whom we had a very animated confrontation. *Herr* Behr referred to the impossibility of what he was about to do and declared that it was no better than murder.
>
> The SS commander then declared that he was himself very uncomfortable about the matter, but he had orders from "high up" which he had to follow. After further negotiation he declared his readiness to let go all of the Jews employed by the military administration headquarters and their families, who we were supposed to identify. When we then gave him a very extensive list, he declared that there was not much point left in carrying out the action. In any case he kept his word and most of the unfortunate Jews were able to return to their homes, which had since been ransacked by the population. To my knowledge, because of our intervention only 400 to 500 Jews were shot that day.

Two days later *SS-Brigade 1 (mot.)* marched further northeast and combed the area south of Ovruch (rear area of the *XVII. Armee-Korps*). More than 300 Jews were shot in the wooded areas there. While elements of *SS-Infanterie-Regiment 8* were in combat against regular Soviet forces from August 20, 1941, *SS-Infanterie-Regiment 10* again saw action in the so-called "ideological war." On August 24, 1941, for example, 280 Jews were shot. Deployed to "overhaul" the area north of the Korosten–Belokorovichi military road, by September 12, 1941, the regiment shot more than 1,000 Jews and Red Army stragglers.

In keeping with German bureaucracy and Himmler's pedantry, the *Einsatzkommandos* had to submit reports about their actions to their superior authority, the Reich Security Main Office. In addition to Incident Reports USSR there were also weekly Reports from the Occupied Eastern Territories. These documents contained SD perspectives as well as the numbers of liquidations. It is unlikely that the totals in the reports often reflected reality, but they nevertheless provide shocking testimony concerning these actions.[23]

Sonderkommando 4 reported especially high execution numbers.[24] Incident Report USSR No. 97 of September 28, 1941 reported:

Advance Party *4a* with the fighting troops in Kiev since September 19. […] 150,000 Jews allegedly present. […] 1,600 arrests in the first action. Measures begun to arrest all of the Jews. Execution of at least 50,000 Jews envisaged. *Wehrmacht* welcomes measures and requests radical action. City commander Kurt Eberhard approved the public hanging of twenty Jews.

Incident Report USSR No. 101 of October 2, 1941 added:

In cooperation with group headquarters and two detachments from Police Regiment South, *Sonderkommando 4a* executed 33,771 Jews in Kiev on September 29–30, 1941.

The commander of *Sonderkommando 4a*, *SS-Standartenführer* Paul Blobel (August 13, 1894 – June 7, 1951) stated for the record before the International Military Tribunal at Nuremberg on June 6, 1947:

1. I was born in Potsdam on August 13, 1894. I attended the primary and continuation school in Remscheid until 1912. I subsequently completed my apprenticeship as a mason and carpenter and during 1912 and 1913 attended the building school in Wuppertal. I worked as a carpenter until the outbreak of the First World War. From 1914 to 1918 I was a pioneer in the field and I left the service in 1918 with the rank of *Vizefeldwebel*. I was unemployed until 1919 and lived in Remscheid. In 1919–20, I again attended the building school in Barmen. From 1921 to 1924 I worked for various companies, and in 1924, I settled in Solingen as an independent architect. During the bad times in Germany in 1928–29 I had no work and from 1930 to 1933 I received unemployment assistance in Solingen. After that time, I was hired by the city authorities to work in an office and remained there until spring 1935. In June 1935, I joined the SD-Oberabschnitt Dusseldorf, where I remained until May 1941. Finally I was sector leader for Dusseldorf. I was then ordered to the Reich Security Main Office in Berlin.

2. I became a member of the NSDAP on December 1, 1931. My membership number is 844662. I have been a member of the SS since January 1932, my membership number is 29100. I am also a member of the Reich Colonial Association, the Air Defense Association, NSV and for a time I was a member of the Reich Association of Fine Arts. My rank in the *Allgemeine-SS* is *Scharführer*, my rank in the SD since 1940 is *Standartenführer*.

3. In June 1941, I became commander of *Sonderkommando 4a*. This *Sonderkommando* was assigned to *Einsatzgruppe C*, which was under the command of Dr. Rasch. The area of operations assigned to me was in the area of the *6. Armee*, which was commanded by *Feldmarschall* von Reichenau. In January 1942, I was relieved as commander of *Sonderkommando 4a* and was transferred to Berlin for disciplinary reasons. I remained there unemployed for some time. I was under the supervision of Office IV under former *Gruppenführer* Müller. In autumn 1942, I was given the task of driving to the occupied eastern territories as Müller's representative to eliminate traces of the mass graves left by the executions carried out by the *Einsatzgruppen*. I had this job until the summer of 1944.

4. Afterwards I was ordered to the commander of Styria where I was supposed to be employed as liaison man between the Reich Security Main Office and *Gruppenführer* Rössner in the effort against the partisans, but I was never entrusted with this position.

I fell ill in December 1944, and from February to April, I was in a sanatorium in Marburg on the Drau. There I received orders to report to Berlin on April 11, 1945. I reported to Kaltenbrunner in April 1945, and drove to the Salzburg area. By doing so I avoided further orders. I and the rest of the group were captured in Radstadt in early May 1945.

5. During my service as commander of *Sonderkommando 4a* from the time of its formation in June 1941 until January 1942, I was several times given the task of executing communists, saboteurs, Jews and other undesirable elements. I can no longer recall the precise number of executed persons. Based on a cursory estimate, whose accuracy I cannot guarantee, I suspect that the number of executions in which *Sonderkommando 4a* participated was between 10,000 and 15,000.

I attended various mass executions and in two cases I was ordered to direct the executions. In August or September 1941, an execution took place near Korosten in which about 700 to 1,000 men were shot and at which Dr. Rasch was present. I had divided my unit into a number of thirty-man execution squads. The attached police of the Ukrainian militia, population and members of the *Sonderkommando* first rounded up the people and dug mass graves.

6. From the total number of persons selected for execution, each time fifteen men were led to the edge of the mass grave, where they were forced to kneel, their faces turned toward the grave. Clothing and valuables were not collected at that time. This was later changed. The execution squads consisted of men of *Sonderkommando 4a* and of police and militia. When the people were ready for execution, one of my officers who was in charge of the execution squad gave the order to fire. Because of their kneeling position at the edge of the grave, most of the victims immediately fell into the mass grave. I always employed larger execution squads to carry out the executions, as I rejected the use of specialists to deliver a shot to the back of the neck. Each squad fired for about an hour and was then relieved. The men waiting to be shot were gathered near the execution site and were guarded by members of the detachment not taking part in executions at that minute. I personally witnessed the execution described here and I saw that no physical abuse took place.

7. *Sonderkommando 4a* also shot women and children. In September or October 1941, I received a gas truck from *Einsatzgruppe C* under Dr. Rasch and an execution was carried out using the gas truck. It was a three-ton truck which was sealed completely air-tight and in which there was space for about thirty to forty people. After about seven to eight minutes all of those inside, who had been exposed to poison gas, were dead. I myself saw the bodies when they were unloaded from the gas truck.

8. During the last days of September 1941 *Sonderkommando 4a*, assisted by the headquarters staff of *Einsatzgruppe C* and two units of the police regiments stationed in Kiev, took part in the mass executions of Jews in Kiev. I regard the figure of 33,771 given me for the number of people executed, as too high. In my opinion no more than half of this number were shot.

9. As I was seriously ill and hospitalized in various places during the period from July 1941 to January 1942, I cannot be blamed for all of the executions carried out by *Sonderkommando 4a*. During my absence the *Kommando* was taken over by Dr. Rasch, *Hauptsturmführer* Waldemar von Radetzki and *SS-Hauptsturmführer* Dr. Beyer, and a number of mass executions also took place under their direction.

The following liquidation numbers were reported to the RSHA by the end of 1941:

Einsatzgruppe A: ....249,420 Jews
Einsatzgruppe B:...45,467 Jews

Einsatzgruppe C: .... 95,000 Jews
Einsatzgruppe D: .... 92,000 Jews

In addition to these just under 482,000 victims, the *Einsatzgruppen* also shot communist commissars of the Red Army and wounded and sick Soviet prisoners of war.

The establishment of the Reich Commissariat Ostland under Hinrich Lohse (September 2, 1896 – February 25, 1964) and the Reich Commissariat Ukraine under Erich Koch (June 19, 1896 – November 12, 1986) resulted in the creation of the regional administrations "Commander of the Security Police and SD" (BdS) and "Commandant of the Security Police and SD" (KdS). In some cases the leaders of the (previous) *Einsatzgruppen* took over new positions. So it was with the head of *Einsatzgruppe A*, *SS-Brigadeführer* Walter Stahlecker, who on September 29, 1941, became the Commander of the Security Police and SD in Riga; the commander of the security police and SD in Reval formed *Sonderkommando 1a*.

In addition to mobile *Einsatzgruppenkommandos*, there were also stationary authorities which also had special camps. One very special one was located in Maly Trostinets (approximately twelve kilometers south of Minsk). Under *SS-Obersturmbannführer* Eduard Strauch (August 17, 1906 – September 15, 1955), Commander of the Security Police and SD White Russia, from April 1942 500 to 1,000 Jews, mostly Germans, were employed in agriculture and various workshops in this former collective farm which was approximately 500 acres in size. In addition to this function as a labor camp, the collective farm also served as execution site for about fifteen deportation trains from Vienna and Theresienstadt. Approximately 15,000 people were shot or, from the summer of 1942, killed in gas trucks. Other victims came from the Minsk ghetto. Furthermore, in February of 1943, about 3,000 "suspected bandits" (elderly, women and children) who could not be employed as laborers were brought to Maly Trostinets from the Polotsk area. Beginning on October 27, 1943, the victims buried in mass graves were exhumed and burned. The remaining prisoners in the labor camps and prisons in the Minsk area were shot just before the Red Army retook the area in the summer of 1944. Probably more than 40,000 people in total were killed in this KdS camp.

The BdS Riga used the Bikernieki Forest (east of the Latvian capital of Riga) for mass shootings beginning on July 1, 1941. A total of about 8,000 Jews is believed to have been liquidated there. Of the roughly 28,000 German Jews deported to Riga, approximately 12,000 were likewise murdered after arriving in Bikernieki Forest and buried in numerous graves. Also interred in mass graves are about 10,000 members of the Red Army who died while prisoners of war in the hands of the Germans.[25] Beginning in 1943 an attempt was made to exhume and burn the bodies. This was only partly successful, in part because of the onset of saponification, and in addition to human ashes a Soviet investigating committee found bits of clothing, bones and body parts.

It is likely that units of the Security Police and SD killed another roughly 400,000 Jews plus partisans and suspected partisans between 1942 and 1944. If one adds to this the total of Jewish victims of the *Einsatzgruppen* in the second half of 1941, the total number of people murdered comes to about 900,000. Unfortunately, a detailed breakdown by origin and ethnicity is impossible. As well, many executions were carried out separate from the *Wehrmacht* and do not appear in incident reports. As well, the numbers that are contained in these reports often do not reflect reality.

Action Reinhard[26]

In autumn 1941, there was a change in direction in the policy towards German Jews. Whereas in recent months an—officially voluntary—mass emigration, assisted by numerous repressive measures, had been emphasized, in September 1941, Hitler imposed a ban on emigration and deportations. Instead the Jews were now to be concentrated step by step in the Generalgouvernement and after the victory over the USSR moved further to the east. With the entry of the USA into the war and the obvious failure of the blitz campaign against the USSR, however, the physical destruction of the Jews moved into the foreground.

While the *Einsatzgruppen* of the security police and the SD had been carrying out mass executions in the USSR since the summer of 1941, the overall exodus of Polish Jewry did not begin until the spring of 1942. In addition to the pragmatic concept of eliminating "useless eaters"—Jews who could not work—space also had to be created for the Jews arriving from the German Reich. When Germany was Jew free, the Generalgouvernement was to be cleared of the Jews still concentrated there.

Himmler gave this task to *SS-Brigadeführer* Globocnik (April 21, 1904 – May 31, 1945), the SS and Police Commander in the Lublin District. Not only was his district relatively central in the Generalgouvernement—all transports had to cover about the same distance to reach the camps—it also had very remote areas in the border areas with White Russia and the Ukraine. The mass killings could be carried out there with relatively little chance of detection.

Because of the enormous number of Polish Jews who were to fall victim to the so-called "Action Reinhard," a solution other than mass shootings was sought. Mass shootings as practiced by the *Einsatzgruppen* in the USSR would have meant that the entire operation would have taken a long time. Seen pragmatically, there was also the enormous requirement for pistol and rifle ammunition with which to shoot more than a million people, plus the required personnel and the associated risk of threatening secrecy.

And so the answer was the gassing of human beings, and the German personnel taking part already had experience with this form of mass killing. Since 1940, the perpetrators, about 120 members of the Security Police and the *Allgemeine-SS*, had murdered more than 70,000 patients[27] of German insane asylums with carbon-monoxide in the General Foundation for Welfare and Institutional Care.

Carbon-monoxide (CO) has extremely toxic effects on the human body and, depending on the concentration in the air and the inhalation period, leads to the following symptoms:[28]

0.02 % - 200 ppm	slight headache within 2 to 3 hours
0.04 % - 400 ppm	headache in the area of the forehead within 1 to 2 hours, spreading to the entire head within 2.5 to 3.5 hours
0.08 % - 800 ppm	dizziness, nausea and limb twitching within 45 minutes, unconsciousness within 2 hours
0.16 % - 1,600 ppm	headache, nausea and dizziness within 20 minutes, death within 2 hours
0.32 % - 3,200 ppm	headache, nausea and dizziness within 5 to 10 minutes, death within 30 minutes
0.64 % - 6,400 ppm	headache, nausea and dizziness within 1 to 2 minutes, death within 10 to 15 minutes
1.28 % - 12,800 ppm	death within 1 to 3 minutes

The "evacuation" of all Jews incapable of work (the elderly, the sick, and women with small children) from the Generalgouvernement to the first death camp in Belzec began in mid-March 1942. As Action Reinhard was supposed to be realized in the shortest possible time, a second camp (Sobibor) was put into operation in early May 1942. Here too members of the General Foundation for Welfare and Institutional Care were detached to the SS and Police Commander Lublin as an *SS-Sonderkommando* by their disciplinary superior, Viktor Brack of the *Führer* Chancellery. In a letter written on June 23, 1942, Brack informed Himmler of Globocnik's intention of promptly ensuring the murder of the Polish Jews by using additional camps:

Some time ago, upon instructions from *Reichsleiter* Bouher I made some of my men available to *Brigadeführer* Globocnik for the execution of his special mission. After receiving another request from him, I have now detached additional personnel. On this occasion *Brigadeführer* Globocnik declared that in his opinion the entire Jewish action should be carried out as quickly as possible, so that one day we would not be stuck halfway through should some sort of difficulties made it necessary to halt the action.

The nature of the difficulties that "could make it necessary to stop the action" first showed themselves when the stockpiling of supplies for the German summer offensive made it necessary to halt all deportation trains for about three weeks beginning June 19, 1942. After the resumption, on July 19, 1942, Himmler ordered that the "resettlement" of the entire Jewish population of the Generalgouvernement —including those capable of work—must be completed by December 31, 1942. To achieve this, a third camp—Treblinka—was put into operation in late 1942. As well, the gassing capacities of the first two camps were expanded and *SS-Hauptsturmführer* Christian Wirth (November 24, 1885 – May 26, 1944), the very rigorous former commander of *SS-Sonderkommando Belzec*, was named inspector of *SS-Sonderkommando "Einsatz Reinhard"* effective August 1, 1942. It was his job to see to it that actions in the three camps were efficiently run.

As a rule, the transports consisted of a goods train with twenty cars, each train carrying 1,000 to 1,500 people.[29] Shunted into a siding inside the respective camp, there the people were ordered to climb out and were told that they were being brought there for further work. With the exception of a few so-called *Arbeitsjuden* (work Jews), who were employed for at least a time either in the death facilities or the nearby labor camps, no one survived the transport. The victims had to undress, the women's hair was coarsely cut off and then the gassings took place—under the pretext of delousing. The bodies were buried in pits dug by an excavator, 50 to 60 meters long, 10 to 15 meters wide and 5 to 7 meters deep. To accelerate decomposition, caustic lime was spread over the bodies. The exhumation and burning of the victims began in November 1942, and continued until the end of Action Reinhard.

SS-Hauptsturmführer Christian Wirth reported the following figures to the Reich Security Main Office on December 31, 1942. The following numbers of Jews had been killed in the camps since mid-December in the course of Action Reinhard:

L [Lublin concentration camp]	12,761
B [Belzec]	0
S [Sobibor]	515
T [Treblinka]	10,335
Total	23,611

The total number of deportations since the start of Action Reinhard was:

L [Lublin concentration camp]	24,733
B [Belzec]	434,508
S [Sobibor]	101,370
T [Treblinka]	71,355 [actual total 713,555]
Total	1,274,166

One must assume that these numbers were almost synonymous with the death of the deportees. Various deportation trains continued to reach the camps in 1943, but the transport density of the previous year was never achieved again. Action Reinhard was concluded on October 19, 1943. *SS-Gruppenführer* Globocnik also went on to inform Himmler of the "economic" success of the action. This totaled:

Delivered funds	73,852,080.74 RM
Precious metals	8,973,651.60 RM
Currency in notes	4,521,651.13 RM
Currency in coin	1,736,554.12 RM
Jewels and other valuables	43,662,450.00 RM
Textiles	46,000,000.00 RM
Total	178,745,960.59 RM

By comparison: a German Panzer VI (Tiger I) tank cost about 250,000 Reichsmarks to manufacture. The total value of the "secured" Jewish assets was thus equivalent to approximately 730 Tiger tanks. In a reply, Himmler thanked Globocnik and expressed his gratitude for the great and unique merits he had earned for the entire German people in carrying out Action Reinhard.

If the murder of about 70,000 patients had been an unfathomable event, the killing of more than a million people in Action Reinhard was an incomprehensible act for a cultured nation like Germany. Most of the perpetrators also showed no remorse in the later postwar trials. To them the Jews, along with the Sinti and Roma, who were also victims of the death camps, were enemies of the German Reich who had to be "destroyed." In addition, they led a relatively comfortable life in the camps with many benefits and corruptive opportunities that they never had in civilian life. They obviously did not find it difficult to blank out the inhuman events they witnessed.

After the war the incomprehensible number of victims led to discussions as to whether there actually had been such mass murder or it was propaganda. During the trials before the jury court in Frankfurt am Main in 1950–51 (First Treblinka Trial), and the district court in Dusseldorf in 1964–65 (Second Treblinka Trial), and 1969–70 (Third Treblinka Trial), there was a very extensive hearing of evidence; as there was at the Sobibor Trials before the district courts of Berlin in 1950 and Hagen in 1965–66 and the Belzec Trial before the Munich I district court in 1963 to 1965. This documented the numerous transports from the Generalgouvernement as well as Germany and Western Europe to the camps of the *SS-Sonderkommando*. In a telegram for the end of the year 1942, the inspector of *SS-Sonderkommando "Einsatz Reinhard"* gave the figure of 1,274,166 "Jews smuggled through the camps" from the Generalgouvernement. The accused in the named trials did not deny the purpose of the camps. They did, however, invoke the fact that they had only been following orders and—provided that no individual actions could be proved against them—they were not legally prosecuted. Viewed morally, most of the trials were a fiasco for justice.

In addition to the postwar trials in Germany, in which the events of the time were reconstructed, a few years ago archaeologists examined the camps of Action Reinhard for evidence of mass graves. From 1997 to 1999, Prof. Andrzej Kola, lecturer for archaeology at the Nicolai Copernicus University in Toruń, conducted forensic examinations on the grounds of Belzec. A total of about 2,000 holes were drilled, revealing a total of thirty-three mass graves up to about six meters deep with a total volume of 21,310 cubic meters. In addition to human bones and ashes they also contained mummified body parts. At Sobibor, Professor Kola found mass graves with a total volume of 14,718 cubic meters.

Beginning in 2010, Caroline Study Colls, the forensic archaeologist for Staffordshire University, examined the ground at Treblinka. In contrast to the drilling at Belzec, Colls used non-invasive methods such as ground radar. She discovered ten mass graves, two of which were outside the former camp beside the railway station. The remaining eight graves had a total area of about 1,800 square meters which, with a depth of six meters, resulted in a volume of 10,800 cubic meters.

Statements by German members of the *SS-Sonderkommando* during the postwar trials as well as the mass graves confirmed in recent years, which are large enough for hundreds of thousands of bodies or their ashes, are sad proof of mass murder. The fact that "full" goods trains drove into the camps but that only empty trains carried on from there show that they were de facto not transit camps. The otherwise so necessary "theoretical" foot march of more than a million Jews across the border of the USSR (and to where there?) was organizationally impossible and is not described in any document or can be found in the recollections of eyewitnesses.

SS-Sonderkommando Belzec

Construction of the first camp at Belzec (approximately seventy-five kilometers northwest of Lvov) in the district office of Zamosch began on November 1, 1941.[30] Belzec was directly on the Lublin to Lvov railway line and therefore was easily reachable by transport. The transport trains drove over a spur of Belzec Station straight into the camp, in which there were two parallel tracks. About twenty goods trains could be shunted onto each of these tracks.

Commander of the *SS-Sonderkommando Belzec* was *Kriminaloberkommissar* Christian Wirth, former Inspector of the General Foundation for Welfare and Institutional Care, who was appointed *SS-Hauptsturmführer*. The camp had an area of about 265x275 meters[31] and was enclosed by fencing. To conceal the camp, pine branches were woven into the fence and these had to be replaced at regular intervals. Two wooden watch towers were erected near the tracks and these were later supplemented by two more.

The camp was divided into two zones, with the tracks in the southern sector. There were two barracks there for the, in the beginning, about sixty and later approximately 120 *Trawniki* men,[32] including a sick bay. They used another barracks as a kitchen and mess room. Then there were two undressing barracks for the victims and a fence, which was likewise made opaque with pine branches, to the second part of the camp to the north. It housed barracks for the Jewish work parties, the gassing rooms and the mass graves. From the undressing barracks a path approximately two meters wide and about 100 meters long led to the gas chambers in the second part of the camp. It was with barbed wire and was likewise made opaque with pine branches.

The first deportation train, from the Lublin ghetto about 130 kilometers away, reached the camp with about 1,400 Jews on March 17, 1942. Ten days later, by which time more than 20,000 bodies were already lying in the mass graves, Joseph Goebbels noted the following in his diary about the start of Action Reinhard:

> The Jews are now being deported to the east from the Generalgouvernement, beginning near Lublin. The procedure being used is rather barbaric and not to be described in more detail, and of the Jews themselves not much is left. On the whole it can be said that 60% of them are liquidated, while only about 40% can be put to work. The former *Gauleiter* of Vienna, who is carrying out this action, is doing it with considerable care and also with a procedure that does not attract too much attention. [...] The emptied ghettoes in the cities of the Generalgouvernement are now being filled with Jews deported from the Reich, and after a certain time the process will begin again there.

Within three weeks approximately 30,000 Jews were also brought to Belzec from the district of Galicia. Among them were about 15,000 Jews from Lvov, roughly 5,000 from Stanislau (approximately 110 kilometers southeast of Lvov) and approximately 5,000 from the Kolomya

The memorial on the former grounds of the Belzec camp.

(approximately 160 kilometers southeast of Lvov) ghetto. Despite these high numbers, no end to Action Reinhard appeared possible in the near future, and in mid-April 1942 *SS-Hauptsturmführer* Wirth was ordered to Berlin to report.

With more than a million Jews soon to be "evacuated" from the Generalgouvernement alone, with an average of about 10,000 persons murdered per week, this would have meant two years of daily action. But as Action Reinhard was supposed to be brought to a conclusion within half a year, more camps had to be put into operation and the capacity of the existing camps increased. After Wirth's return, the capacity of the camps was doubled from 3x32 square meters to 6x32 square meters. By mid-July 1942, the gas chambers, again designated delousing rooms, were ready for use. Carbon-monoxide exhaust from a diesel engine was fed by pipes into the individual rooms. The sizes of the rooms meant that the gassing process took about thirty minutes.

Following the resumption of deportations in mid-July 1942, and the naming of *SS-Hauptsturmführer* Wirth to Inspector of *SS-Sonderkommando "Einsatz Reinhardt"* on August 1, *SS-Hauptsturmführer* Gottlieb Hering (June 2, 1887 – October 9, 1945) took over command of *SS-Sonderkommando Belzec*.

The last shipment of Jews arrived in Belzec on December 11, 1942. According to a telex sent by Wirth, a total of 434,508 Jews had been deported to Belzec in the six months. Mathematically, this meant roughly 2,500 persons on two transport trains per day.

To save time and with the intention of carrying out the action as discreetly as possible, the victims were initially thrown into mass graves (on the camp grounds). When the first big phase of "Action Reinhard" ended in autumn 1942, they began reopening the graves with an excavator and until March 1943, the bodies were burned on the railroad tracks. Many of the bodies, of those killed in the spring of 1942, were in an advanced state of decomposition and could not be completely burned, however. It is possible that an order to halt further exhumations was also issued before their completion.

The camp was liquidated and still-usable components, such as the barracks for example, were taken to Lublin, and the grounds were planted with fast-growing spruce, fir and lupines.

SS-Sonderkommando Sobibor

The construction of a second camp in Sobibor (approximately eighty kilometers northeast of Lublin) with dimensions of about 600x400 meters began in early 1942. *SS-Obersturmführer* Franz Stangl (March 26, 1908 – June 28, 1971) was named commander of the camp, which had about thirty German personnel and 120 *Trawniki* men, in April 1942.

There were already several buildings in the selected area of forest and these were used as the camp administration building and military barracks. Sobibor Station had a siding approximately 800 meters long running parallel to the main track. From there an approximately 200-meter-long track was laid running the north, whose platforms could accommodate twenty freight cars. The platforms and the quarters of the German SS and Ukrainian *Trawniki* men were located in the so-called administration area (Vorlager). To the west of it was Camp I with the living and work barracks of the Jewish work force.

Northwest of the platforms was Camp II. Here the victims had to undress and turn over their valuables. In addition to the barracks for this, there was a small agricultural area with cows, pigs, and geese for the camp personnel, plus barracks for stowage of the clothing and other items taken from the victims. To the east to the rail line and northwest to Camp III, the camp, which was otherwise an open sandy area, was sealed off by a high wooden fence. The victims also had to pass through this on their way to the gas chambers.

Naked, the people walked down a roughly four-meter-wide and 150-meter-long path into Camp III. It was located in the northwest and consisted of the buildings where the victims were gassed, the burial pits and the barracks of the Jewish Sonderkommando. Like all subsections of the camp, it was also sealed off from the others by a barbed wire fence.

The gassing buildings each had three chambers measuring four by four meters, into which sometimes 100 people at a time were forced. The victims entered the chambers from a veranda running along the building. An engine delivered the carbon-monoxide, which was fed into the chambers by pipes. Opposite the entrance the dead were then pulled through hinged doors onto a ramp. From there a narrow-gauge railway took them directly to the burial pits. After undressing, the sick, invalids, and those who had died on the trains were taken straight to the pits, and there if necessary were shot.

The first deportation train from Oppeln arrived at the camp on May 5, 1942. Most of the transports came from the ghettoes in the Lublin District, the Protectorate of Bohemia and Moravia, Slovakia and Germany. On June 1, 1942, for example, a special train carrying 509 Jewish men and women left Hesse. The persons selected for the transport had been brought to Kassel one or two days earlier, registered in the gymnasium of the present-day Walter Hecker School and then deported to Poland. Another 500 Jews got on in Chemnitz and arrived at Sobibor on June 3, 1942.

While Belzec again became active in mid-July 1942, for Sobibor at the end of July 1942, there followed a phase during which no evacuation trains arrived because of work on the railway. During this time the gas chamber was expanded. When deportations to Sobibor resumed in October 1942, the exhumation and burning of previous victims from the pits also began. A total of 101,370 Jews was deported to Sobibor by the end of the first phase of Action Reinhard in December 1942. During the four-month operation this was equivalent to the destruction of an average of 850 people daily.

After an inspection of the camp on February 12, 1942, Himmler announced that additional transports would be arriving from Western Europe, Germany, and Slovakia. In March 1943, about 4,000 Jews arrived from France and about twenty transports with a total of 34,313 persons reached the camp from the Netherlands.

On July 5, 1943, Himmler ordered the erection of a new camp sector, in which captured munitions would be prepared for use by the German military. When captured Jewish Red Army soldiers were transferred to Sobibor as "work Jews," the underground committee planned a mass escape by all prisoners. While individuals had previously tried, on October 14, 1943, the militarily-trained prisoners were to lead an uprising. After several German members of the *SS-Sonderkommando* had been killed, 365 prisoners fled, of whom only about half reached the forest. The rest were cut down by the Ukrainian guard personnel, who immediately opened fire. Altogether, about fifty of them survived to see the end of the war.

After further transports from Lida, Vilnius, and Minsk, the camp was liquidated. It is believed that about 150,000 Jews from Poland and Western Europe died in Sobibor by October 1943. To prevent the resident Polish population from rummaging through the camp area, a farm was set up and maintained and a pine forest planted.

SS-Sonderkommando Treblinka

A third camp was set up in Treblinka (about eighty kilometers northeast of Warsaw). It was located on the Warsaw–Bialystok rail line, south of the town of Malkina Gora on the Bug River. Construction began at the end of May 1942 and was supposed to be completed by July 1, 1942. The camp's first commander was *SS-Untersturmführer* Irmfried Eberl (September 8, 1910 – February 16, 1948).

The camp was divided into three zones, which were separated from each other by barbed wire fences with interlaced pine branches to provide a screen. There were several roughly eight-meter-high wooden watch towers at the corners of the camp and in the actual killing areas. In the fore-camp (*Vorlager*), to which a 200-meter-long siding for twenty freight cars was laid

The memorial at the former grounds of the Sobibor camp.

from Treblinka Station, there were two barracks in which the men and women with children disrobed separate from each other. Later, however, the men's barrack was used for sorting the possessions left behind by the victims. The men were then forced to undress out of doors. Another barrack was used to store the Jews' possessions.

In the *Wohnlager* (administrative and residential compound) were the barracks for the Ukrainian guards (Max Biala Barracks[33]) and the Jewish prisoner-workers (three sleeping barracks and workshops). The so-called Upper Camp was situated on an area of about 200x250 meters on a slight rise, and it contained the original three gas chambers each with an area of sixteen square meters (total capacity just under fifty square meters) and the body pits. The Jewish Sonderkommando that worked there was housed in two additional fenced-in barracks.

The first transports rolled from the Warsaw ghetto to Treblinka on July 23, 1942. Himmler had ordered the deportations accelerated and gassing capacities were promptly expanded. The gas chambers were subsequently 16x20 meters in size (320 square meters) and in some cases approximately 1,000 people were squeezed in together. The sizes of the spaces meant that killing with carbon-monoxide, which was produced by two vehicle engines, took significantly more time than had been the case with the first gas chambers.

In the two months until September 21, 1942, it is believed that about 254,000 Jewish men and women were deported to Treblinka from Warsaw and approximately 112,000 from the area surrounding the city. This meant that about 6,000 people lost their lives daily. The fact that they could keep pace with the gassings and elimination of the bodies led to the replacement of *SS-Obersturmführer* Dr. Eberl, who was obviously "overtaxed" by his responsibilities, by *SS-Obersturmführer* Franz Stangl.

There followed transports with about 337,000 Jews from the Radom District, and by December 31, 1942, *SS-Hauptsturmführer* Wirth was able to report the unbelievable figure of 713,555 Jews deported to Treblinka. These were followed by Jews from Poland and other countries until the spring of 1943. It is believed that about 7,000 came from Slovakia, 8,000 mostly Germans from Theresienstadt, approximately 7,000 from Greece and about 7,000 from Macedonia. In addition to the Jews, approximately 2,000 Sinti and Roma were also deported to Treblinka.

After just a few transports arrived at Treblinka in April 1943, the unearthing and burning of bodies which had previously been interred in mass graves also began there. As the decomposition process was already well advanced, the effort was not a complete success. Nevertheless, the exhumation and cremation of the victims was considered concluded at the end of July 1943. The "*Arbeitsjuden*" doing the work reached the conclusion that they would now also be killed, and on August 2, 1943, they attempted to flee the camp. A total of about 250 inmates succeeded. Not least because of this, the Treblinka camp—after Jews from Bialystok were gassed on August 21, 1943—was liquidated. As at Sobibor, a farm was set up to prevent the Polish population from rummaging about. The unbelievable total number of victims during the approximately one-year existence of *SS-Sonderkommando "Treblinka"* was probably in excess of 750,000 people. Mathematically this was 2,000 people per day on average.

Excursus: *SS-Sonderkommando "Kulmhof"*

Almost simultaneously with the beginning of work on the Belzec camp in the Generalgouvernement, *SS-Sonderkommando* Lange became active in the Wartheland District. Under the command of *SS-Hauptsturmführer* Herbert Lange (September 29, 1909 – April 20, 1945), approximately twenty members of the Security Police and about eighty men of the *Ordnungspolizei* moved into an empty estate in Kulmhof (Polish Chelmno and Neren, approximately fifteen kilometers southeast of Kolo/German Warthbrücken) in November 1941. The site provided offices and quarters for the members of the *SS-Sonderkommando*, as well as storage spaces for the clothing and valuables of the victims. Initially the latter were Jews from the Wartheland incapable of work.

The first Jews from the surrounding area arrived on December 8, 1941. They were transported by truck from Kulmhof Station to the estate courtyard. There they were told that they were being resettled in a labor camp and first would be deloused. The victims then stepped into the interior of the manor house in groups of about fifty persons, undressed there and were led to a sort of ramp. There they climbed into specially prepared trucks. As, in contrast to the camps of Action Reinhard, there were no stationary gassing rooms, they were either killed on the approximately six-minute drive to the forest near Rzuchów two and a half kilometers away or on site by the carbon-monoxide exhaust gases from the engine. Finally the bodies were placed in a large pit.

From January 16–29, 1942, approximately 10,000 Jews from the Litzmannstadt ghetto were murdered at Kulmhof. In March 1942, *SS-Hauptsturmführer* Hans Bothmann (November 11, 1911 – April 4, 1946) took over the *SS-Sonderkommando* which, like the camps of Action Reinhard, was named after its location: *SS-Sonderkommando Kulmhof*. Under him approximately 34,000 persons were murdered between March 22 and April 2, 1942, and approximately 11,700 Jews were killed from May 4–15. Following actions between September 5–12, with a total of approximately 16,000 Jews, *SS-Standartenführer* Paul Blobel (August 13, 1894 – June 7, 1951), the former commander of *Einsatzgruppen-Sonderkommando 4a*, was given the task of having the bodies of the Jewish workers unearthed and burned. Rudolf Höß inspected the work in September 1942. Among the victims there were also deported Jews from Germany, the Protectorate of Bohemia and Moravia, Czechoslovakia, and Luxembourg.

As is evident from the Korherr report, 145,301 Jews were "smuggled through" the camps in the Warthegau. One must assume that the majority of these people were also murdered there. When the activities of *SS-Sonderkommando* Kulmhof initially ended in March 1943, Arthur Greiser, the *Reichsstatthalter* and NSDAP *Gauleiter* in the *Reichsgau Wartheland*, visited the men. On March 19, 1943, he wrote about his visit in a letter to the *Reichsführer-SS*:

> Several days ago I visited the former *SS-Sonderkommando Lange*, which is now under the command of *SS-Hauptsturmführer Kriminalkommissar* Bothmann, and which will terminate its activities as a *Sonderkommando* in Kulmheim, Warthbrücken District at the end of the month. I discovered a mood among the men of the *Sonderkommando* that I would not wish to fail to bring to your attention, *Reichsführer-SS*. Not only have the men carried out the difficult duty entrusted to them faithfully and well and in every respect consistently, they have also conducted themselves in the best military tradition.

The formulation that they had performed in keeping with the "best military tradition" shows the German virtue of unconditionally following orders. Stressing military tradition was intended to document the official nature of the action against the "enemies" (including Jewish children and the aged) of the German Reich. As there was no immediate use for the men but there was a desire to keep them together for possible future employment, they formed the *SS-Feldgendarmerie-Kompanie* of the *SS-Freiwilligen-Gebirgs-Division "Prinz Eugen."* They served there for about a year. When Himmler ordered the reduction of the Litzmannstadt ghetto, located about sixty kilometers southeast of Kulmhof, the *SS-Sonderkommando* was reactivated. On June 23 and July 14, 1944, it murdered more than 7,000 Jews from the ghetto. When the Red Army neared the Warthe in mid-January 1945, the *SS-Sonderkommando* was disbanded for good. It is likely that more than 150,000 people became its victims between December 1941 and January 1945.

A Summary of the Persecution of Jews in Europe[34]

Resentments against the Jews in Germany, as in other countries, were no invention of National–Socialism or fascism. Nuremberg will be used as an example to provide some benchmark data. In 1298, 628 Jewish men, women, and children—probably the entire Jewish community—lost their lives in a pogrom. In 1349, the Jewish synagogue in Nuremberg was destroyed, and the Church of Our Lady was built in its place. More than a third of the Jewish population, which numbered about 1,500 persons, was simultaneously slain and in some cases burned. All Jews were forced to leave the Frankish imperial capital in 1499, and the city council did not permit them to return until 350 years later. In 1852, however, just eighty-seven persons of the Jewish faith were living in Nuremberg. By the turn of the century that Jewish community had again reached about 1,700 people, several of whom made significant contributions to industrialization (Hercules bicycles, for example). Finally, 1,500 Jews from Nuremberg served as soldiers in the First World War, of whom almost 180 were killed.

The exclusion of the Jews in Germany, which the NSDAP had begun propagating in its 25-point program of 1920, was therefore nothing new. At that time rightwing circles also blamed Jewry for Germany's defeat in the First World War. The people, most of whom had little interest in or ability to question or criticize these claims, took little exception to the NSDAP's program and the state decrees enacted from 1933, which were supposed to lead to the destruction of the economic existence of the Jews and consequently their emigration. And those who aroused public attention about the issue possibly soon found themselves in the custody of the Gestapo. One so-called "*Flüsterwitz*" (a joke about a taboo subject) making the rounds at that time, shows how fear of the Gestapo restricted freedom of opinion:

> In a pub, several regulars greet one of their group who has just been released from the Dachau concentration camp. They ask him: how was it? He replies: simply wonderful. Breakfast at about 7:30, and there was a choice of coffee or tea as well as a soft-boiled or fried egg. Fresh bread and marmalade, and at ten there was another small meal … The regulars look at each other, shaking their heads, and say that Franz, who was also in Dachau, told a very different story! Whereupon the respondent says: well Franz is also now in Dachau again!

The deprivation of the rights of Germany's roughly 500,000 Jews began on April 7, 1933, with the Law for the Restoration of the Professional Civil Service, which forced Jewish civil servants to retire. Effective the same day, Jewish lawyers could have their certifications withdrawn. A few weeks later Jewish doctors and dentists lost their right to receive medical insurance payments and subsequently could only receive private payments for their services.[35] Then the 1st and 2nd Regulations of the Nuremberg Laws—the Reich Citizens Act of September 15, 1935—deprived German Jews of their civil rights. The Law for the Protection of German Blood and German Honor of September 15, 1935 made marriage between, "Jews and members of the state of German or kindred blood," or extramarital sexual relations between, "Jews and members of the state of German or kindred blood," punishable acts.

The repressive policies against the Jews with the objective of causing them to leave Germany did not go unnoticed outside the country. The USA initiated an international conference, which was held in Evian, France from July 6–15, 1938, in which thirty-two nations were to discuss how they could support Jewish emigration. The conference turned into a fiasco. Instead of a general willingness to accept German Jews, other states (for example Poland) suddenly expressed the desire to have their Jewish populations included in a possible migration agreement. Putting it euphemistically, however there was extremely little interest in accepting so-called *Ostjuden* (eastern Jews). The original humanitarian intention of allowing German Jews, with centuries of assimilation and economically integrated, turned into fear on the part of the conference participants of having to "deal with" millions of Jews from eastern and southeastern Europe. The congress therefore ended with the amicable but definite statement by the participants that raising the existing immigration quotas was unfortunately impossible.

In Germany, one week later another ordinance was issued, according to which the Jewish population had to show new identity cards identifying them as Jews. These identity documents had a large "J" in the center of the card. On August 17, 1938, another new law, the "Law on the Alteration of Family and Given Names," made it mandatory for Jewish men to bear the second fictitious given name Israel and Jewish women the given name Sara. A first step toward the recognition of the Jews in Germany—even though only toward public authorities at first—had been taken. As there was obviously a realization that most Jews in Germany looked little different than their Aryan neighbors—even though the caricatures in the anti-Semitic flyer "*Der Stürmer*" portrayed with respect to the so-called *Ostjuden*—by examining the identity cards, public authorities were supposed to see that these were third-class people.

On August 26, 1938, Josef Bürckel (March 30, 1895 – September 28, 1944), the Reich Commissar for the Reunification of Austria with the Reich, opened a central office for Jewish emigration in Vienna. His goal in doing so was to make the new *Ostmark* (Austria) Jew free as quickly as possible. Several weeks later an attempt was made to force this Reich-wide through the *Reichs-Kristallnacht* ("night of broken glass"). Not only were the injured Jewish parties forced to withdraw their insurance claims against the state and pay for the damages themselves, another economic burden soon followed on November 12, 1938. As a result the Jewish population was forced to pay a billion Marks to the German Reich for its "hostile attitude towards the German people and Reich." First they were smashed to pieces by the mob and then they were forced to pay a billion Marks as reparations. It was an act that should have caused any relatively critical contemporary to shake his head, provided he gained knowledge of it.

At the same time, the Jews in Germany were forced to sell off their businesses as well as their property—if necessary to trustees. Tenancy laws towards them were relaxed and the theoretical call-ups for labor or military service were definitively prohibited. This last decree probably saved the lives of more than a few half- and quarter-Jews in Germany who were not deported, as they neither had to serve as flak auxiliaries nor as soldiers in combat.

After a wave of immigration had been achieved in Austria, on January 24, 1939, the Reich Center for Jewish Immigration was founded for the entire German Reich. A required central registration of the Jewish population was created by the 10th Regulation of the Reich Citizenship Law of July 4, 1939, when the Reich Association of Jews in Germany was founded. This was subordinate to the RSHA and its purpose was to make preparations for the immigrations.

After the occupation of rump Czechoslovakia (Bohemia and Moravia), a similar central office was set up in Prague. At that time, immigration depended on the good will of other countries, and Germany was already looking for possible locations where it might settle the Jewish population, such as Palestine, Ecuador, Colombia, or Venezuela. With the victorious conclusion of the campaign in Poland, before September 1939 was over planning began to settle the Jews in a so-called Jewish reserve in the Lublin district. Construction of a barracks camp, which was to serve as a transit camp, began in Nisko (approximately eighty kilometers south of Lublin) in mid-October 1939. Three transport trains carrying about 3,000 Jewish craftsmen from Mährisch–Ostrau, Vienna, and Kattowitz reached the area on October 19–20, 1939. Two more transports carrying a total of 2,072 persons arrived from Kattowitz and Vienna one week later. The plan to concentrate the German Jews in the Generalgouvernement encountered stiff resistance from Dr. Hans Frank (May 23, 1900 – October 16, 1946), the local governor general. He declared that the Generalgouvernement was already overcrowded because of the influx of Polish Jews from the districts newly incorporated into the Reich (Wartheland and Danzig–West Prussia), and that the settlement of many thousands of Jews from the German Reich would lead to collapse. And even Hitler, in a conversation with the popular German author Colin Ross (June 4, 1885 – April 29, 1945), declared, "that the solution to the Jewish problem is just a question of space, which is very difficult for him to solve, as he himself has no space available. The formation of a Jewish state around Lublin would also never be a solution, for there too the Jews would live too close together."

The first deportation of German Jews to the Lublin region, approximately 1,000 persons from the Stettin area, took place in February 1940. On March 24, 1940, further resettlements were abandoned and in April the camp was liquidated and the Jews were transported back to Germany.

In May 1940, Himmler revived the earlier idea of the "immigration of all Jews to Africa or a colony somewhere else." In the same memo of May 15, 1940, dealing with the handling of the Slavic population in the east, he stated that, "the Bolshevik methods of physically destroying a people was, out of inner conviction, un-German and impossible" and should be rejected. It appears that he also implied this to the Jewish people, for on June 24, 1940, *SS-Gruppenführer* Reinhard Heydrich, head of the RSHA, wrote on this topic to *SS-Gruppenführer* Joachim von Ribbentrop (April 30, 1893 – October 16, 1946), the Reich Foreign Minister:

> Since my office took over this task on January 1, 1939, altogether more than 300,000 Jews have emigrated from the Reich. The entire problem—there are already about 3¼ million Jews in areas presently under German control—can no longer be solved through emigration; a territorial final solution is therefore necessary.

The plans were put into concrete terms and on August 17, 1940, Joseph Goebbels, Reich Minister of Propaganda, noted in his diary: "We intend to ship the Jews to Madagascar later [after the end of the war, author's note]. There they can establish their own state."

SS-Sturmbannführer Adolf Eichmann (March 19, 1906 – May 31, 1962), who was head of the Jewish Affairs and Evacuation division, forwarded the associated postwar plans to the Reich Association of Jews in Germany and representatives of the Jewish communities in Prague and Vienna. Otto Hirsach (January 9, 1885 – June 19, 1941), chairman of the Reich association, subsequently drafted a detailed memorandum about the preparatory measures for life on the tropical island.

Legationsrat Franz Rademacher (February 20, 1906 – March 17, 1973), the head of division for "Jewish questions" in the foreign office, drafted a memo with the title "The Jewish Question in the Peace Treaty." It referred to ratification of a potential but unrealized peace treaty with France that was supposed to follow the ceasefire that took place on June 21, 1940. He proposed that the island of Madagascar should become a "Jewish dwelling place under German sovereignty." To achieve this, the French Vichy government was supposed to cede its colony of Madagascar to Germany. The German Reich would be given the right to maintain an air and naval base in Madagascar and settle the Jews there. The conditions for the implementation of the Madagascar plan were never realized, however. After France refused to hand over its colony, and England showed no interest in a peace treaty, in September 1940, the Madagascar plan was shelved.

In October 1940, there was a second wave of deportations from Germany. Jews from Baden, the Pfalz, and the Saarland were deported to Camp de Gurs in France. In a letter to the foreign office, the chief of the RSHA noted on October 29, 1940:

> The *Führer* ordered the expulsion of the Jews from Baden by way of Alsace and the Jews from the Pfalz by way of Lorraine. After carrying out the action, I can tell you that 6,504 Jews were transported via Chalon-sur-Saône to the unoccupied part of France in agreement with local Wehrmacht authorities, without first informing the French authorities.

Seven transport trains left Baden on October 22–23, 1940 and two trains left the Pfalz on October 22, 1940.

Despite Dr. Hans Frank's hostile attitude, in spring 1941, about 5,000 Austrian Jews from the Vienna area were deported to the Generalgouvernement, allegedly because of shortage of living space. At the same time, the "voluntary" emigrations to other European countries or overseas went on. With the start of the campaign in Russia, a new territorial solution to the "Jewish problem" stepped into the focus of those responsible. It is likely that as early as spring 1941, plans were put into concrete terms for the establishment of a "Jewish reservation" in the far east after the expected lightning victory over the USSR.

While the *Wehrmacht* was still advancing through the Soviet frontier states, and the Sipo and SD *Einsatzgruppen* were rampaging there, in Germany the "Police Regulation on the Labeling of Jews of September 1, 1941" was issued. It decreed that all remaining Jews in Germany or under German sovereignty six years of age or older must wear a pocket-size Star of David on the left breast side of their clothing. Made of fabric, the star was to be yellow with a black outline and the word "Jew" in black letters and was to be visible at all times."

That same month Hitler forbade the emigration and deportation of further Jews so that they could be deported en masse further to the east after the quick end of the war with the Soviet Union—which was still expected at that time. As a consequence, in a decree dated October 18, 1941, Himmler prohibited any further Jewish immigration. According to the Reich Association of Jews in Germany, by that time 352,543 of its members had emigrated. The Israelite communities in Vienna and Prague also reported that 149,124 Austrian Jews had left, plus 26,009 from the Protectorate of Bohemia and Moravia.

New restrictions followed for those who had not emigrated: in autumn 1941, the working conditions for Jews were changed to "employment of a special nature," in which protection against dismissal was abolished. Finally the Jewish population was forbidden to use public telephones, public transport, electrical appliances, bicycles, typewriters, etc. Finally a decree was issued which stated that on the death of a Jew, his entire estate went to the German state instead of his family.

After it had been decided to carry out the mass killings of Polish Jews in autumn 1941, from mid-October to the beginning of November 1941, about 20,000 Jews were transported from the major cities of Vienna, Prague, Frankfurt am Main, Berlin, and Hamburg to the Litzmannstadt ghetto. Seven more transports were sent to the Minsk ghetto. When this ghetto became overfilled, in November 1941, five deportation trains were rerouted to the ghetto in Kaunas and from the end of November, another ten were sent to the Riga ghetto. When Riga also became unable to accept further deportees, those living there, approximately 27,500 Latvian Jews, were unceremoniously liquidated. On November 30, 1941, a train from Berlin arrived in the Latvian capital prematurely, whereupon all 1,053 Berlin Jews were immediately shot in Rumbula Forest. Also in Lithuania, in November 1941, *Einsatzgruppen* and their Lithuanian helpers murdered deportees from Berlin, Munich, Vienna, Breslau, and Frankfurt am Main in Fort IX in Kauen. A total of sixty-six evacuation transports is known for the period November 8–28, 1941, and these transferred at least 66,210 German, Austrian, and Czech Jews to the eastern territories. Of these transports forty went to White Russia, twenty-three to Latvia, two to Lithuania, and one to Estonia.

While the mass physical destruction of Europe's Jews had already become a reality by November 1941, it was not until December 13, 1941, that Dr. Joseph Goebbels noted it in his diary:[36]

Regarding the Jewish question, the *Führer* is determined to clean the table. He prophesized to the Jews that should they once again bring about a world war, they would be annihilated. These were no empty words. The world war has come, therefore the annihilation of the Jews has to be its inevitable consequence. The question has to be examined without any sentimentality. We are not here to pity Jews, but to have pity for our own German people. If the German people have sacrificed about 160,000 dead in the battles in the east, the instigators of this bloody conflict will have to pay for it with their lives.

The fact that Japan's actions resulted in a world war played just as little a role as did the fact that the "Jewish people"—including Jewish tradesmen (shoemakers, tailors, and barbers) in Poland or the Soviet Union, as well as Jewish pharmacists or doctors in Germany—were not responsible for it. America's entry into the war provided welcome cause, as a response to it, to officially turn the problematic question a territorial final solution in the form of a "Jewish reservation" into their physical destruction. Dr. Hans Frank delved into the new policy towards the Jews at a government meeting on December 16, 1941. As "his" Generalgouvernement had the greatest concentration of Jews in the entire area of German power, his statements are repeated in full. Although work on the Belzec camp in his area of power had been under way for six weeks, at this time he was obviously unaware of the use of gas as a possible method of destruction:

> One way or another—I will tell you that quite openly—we must finish off the Jews. The *Führer* put it into words once: should united Jewry again succeed in setting off a world war, then the blood sacrifice shall not be made only by the peoples driven into war, but then the Jew of Europe will have met his end. I know that there is criticism of many of the measures now applied to the Jews in the Reich. There are always deliberate attempts to speak again and again of cruelty, harshness, etc.; this emerges from the reports on the popular mood. I appeal to you: before I now continue speaking first agree with me on a formula: we will have pity, on principle, only for the German people, and for nobody else in the world. The others had no pity for us either. As an old National–Socialist I must also say that if the Jewish clan was to survive the war in Europe while we sacrifice the best of our blood for the preservation of Europe, then this war would still be only a partial success. I will therefore, on principle, approach Jewish affairs in the expectation that the Jews will disappear. They must go. I have started negotiations for the purpose of having them pushed off to the East. In January there will be a major conference on this question in Berlin, to which I shall send State Secretary Dr. Buehler. The conference is to be held in the office of *SS-Obergruppenführer* Heydrich at the Reich Security Main Office. A major Jewish migration will certainly begin.
>
> But what should be done with the Jews? Can you believe that they will be accommodated in settlements in the Ostland? In Berlin we were told: why are you making all this trouble? We don't want them either, not in the Ostland nor in the Reichskommissariat; liquidate them yourselves! Gentlemen, I must ask you to steel yourselves against all considerations of compassion. We must destroy the Jews wherever we find them, and wherever it is at all possible, in order to maintain the whole structure of the Reich … The views that were acceptable up to now cannot be applied to such gigantic, unique events. In any case we must find a way that will lead us to our goal, and I have my own ideas on this.
>
> The Jews are also exceptionally harmful feeders for us. In the Government-General we have approximately 2.5 million [Jews], and now perhaps 3.5 million together with persons who have Jewish kin, and so on. We cannot shoot these 3.5 million Jews, we cannot poison them, but we will be able to take measures that will lead somehow to successful destruction; and this in connection with the large-scale procedures which are to be discussed in the Reich. The Government-General must become as free of Jews

as the Reich. Where and how this is to be done is the affair of bodies which we will have to appoint and create, and on whose work I will report to you when the time comes.

In January 1942, nine more deportation trains with an average of 1,000 German Jews steamed to Riga. As well, between March and October 1942, more than 45,000 Jews were deported from the German Reich to transit camps at the eastern edge of the Generalgouvernement and to Warsaw. For a so-called "Jew exchange" the Polish Jews from Lublin were brought to Belzec to create space for "Reich Jews."

In May 1942, for the first time, and increasingly as of May 1942, Jews from Germany were sent directly or by way of Theresienstadt to the camps of "Action Reinhard." Between May and September 1942, seventeen transports went to the Minsk ghetto or straight to the nearby special camp at Maly Trostinets. Theresienstadt was the destination of many evacuation trains, and at the same time it was the departure point for numerous transports to Treblinka and Auschwitz. In 1942, five deportation trains also proceeded directly to the latter from Vienna and Berlin. The following numbers of persons were deported from the area of the Reich Association of Jews in Germany until the end of the big deportations in the spring of 1943:[37]

	Jan.	Feb.	March	Apr.	May	June	July	Aug.	Sept.	Oct.	Nov.	Dec.
1941										9,543	8,343	9.287
1942	5,175	–	3,369	6,985	6,956	6,731	14,039	9,927	12,346	3,272	2,144	2,426
1943	2,822	3,657	12,496	936								

On January 18, 1943, Himmler, wanting to maintain a statistical overview of the deportations, not only for himself but for Hitler as well, gave the record-keeping task to the *SS-Hauptamt*'s statistics department. The RSHA had previously had previously written memoranda based on reports by the individual offices and *Einsatzgruppen*, however these had not satisfied Himmler. He noted: "There is no need for the Reich Security Main Office to do any further statistical work in this area, for its previous statistical documents lack."

In fact Dr. Richard Korherr (October 30, 1903 – November 24, 1989), the *Reichsführer-SS*'s Inspector of Statistics, could only fall back on reports already available, so that the numbers could only be broken down better statistically. Dr. Korherr submitted his report on the "Jew balance sheet in Germany," which later became known as the Korherr Report, on March 23, 1943. Section V dealt with the "evacuation" of the Jews in the Generalgouvernement and the Soviet border states:

> The evacuation of the Jews superseded the Jewish emigration, at least in the territory of the Reich. This evacuation was prepared after the prohibition of Jewish emigration in autumn 1941 on a large scale and was carried out extensively in the entire Reich territory in 1942. In Jewish statistics this appears under the heading "emigrations." According to the figures of the Main Reich Security Office the following number of Jews had "emigrated" by January 1, 1943:[38]

from the old Reich with Sudetenland .... 100,516 Jews
from Ostmark (Austria) .... 47,555 Jews
from the Protectorate .... 69,677 Jews
Total .... 217,748 Jews

These figures also include the Jews evacuated to the ghetto for the aged in Theresienstadt.

The figures for evacuations from Reich territory including the Eastern Territories and also from territories under German control or influence between October 1939 and December 30 1942 are:

1. Evacuation of Jews from Baden and the Pfalz to France................................ 6,504 Jews
2. Evacuation of Jews from Reich territory, including the Protectorate and Bialystok area, to the east .... 170,642 Jews
3. Evacuation of Jews from Reich territory and the Protectorate to Theresienstadt .... 87,193 Jews
4. Transport of Jews from the eastern provinces to eastern Russia........... 1,449,692 Jews
Number passed through the camps in Generalgouvernement .... 1,274,166 Jews
through the camps in the Warthe District .... 145,301 Jews
5. Evacuation from other countries, namely:
France (as occupied before 10 November 1942) .... 41,911 Jews
Netherlands .... 38,571 Jews
Belgium.. 16,886 Jews
Norway.. 532 Jews
Slovakia .... 56,691 Jews
Croatia... 4,927 Jews
Total evacuations (including Theresienstadt and special treatment[39]) ..... 1,873,549 Jews
Without Theresienstadt .... 1,786,356 Jews
6. In addition there are the figures of the Main Reich Security Office for the evacuation of the Jews from the Russian territories including the former Baltic countries since the beginning of the Eastern campaign.[40]

The above figures do not include the Jews in ghettos and concentration camps. The evacuations of Jews from Slovakia and Croatia were carried out by these countries themselves.

At the beginning of 1943 a total of 297,914 Jews was living in the ghettoes, including:

Theresienstadt ....49,392 Jews[41]
Litzmannstadt .... 87,180 Jews
Cracow .... 37,000 Jews
Radom.. 29,000 Jews
Lublin .... 20,000 Jews
Warsaw.. 50,000 Jews
Lvov .... 161,514 Jews

In addition, there were 9,127 Jews in German concentration camps.

From May 1943, mainly so-called old people transports with 50 to 100 Jews were sent to Theresienstadt and so-called eastern transports with a maximum of about 400 Jews to Auschwitz. In January 1944, one last large transport with 353 Jews was sent to Theresienstadt. The monthly deportations were thus usually no more than fifty persons. Finally, in mid-1944, there were only about 14,500 people of the Jewish faith left in Germany.

Altogether more than 260,000 Jews were relocated from the German Reich—including Austria and the Protectorate of Bohemia and Moravia—the majority of whom lost their lives.

Deportations from Europe

Albania

To some degree Albania held a special position in "Europe under the swastika." At the beginning of the 1930s, less than 200 of this small country's total population of about 803,000 residents were Jewish. This figure rose to about 1,800 Jews by summer 1941, when the German Reich put an end to Jewish emigration. Under Italian occupation, restrictions were imposed on the Jewish population.

When Italy concluded a ceasefire with the Allies on September 8, 1943, the German military occupied Albania. A collaborative regime was formed, insofar as one can speak of a government capable of conducting negotiations. German attempts to initiate a deportation of the Jews failed after state officials provided the Jews with false papers for money and the Albanian population provided their Jewish fellow citizens with numerous hideouts.

Belgium

The western campaign began on May 10, 1940, and German troops marched into neutral Belgium. The Belgian Army surrendered eighteen days later. *General der Infanterie* Alexander von Falkenhausen (October 29, 1878 – July 31, 1966) was installed as military commander of Belgium and Northern France.

As in the German Reich, numerous decrees were issued against the Jewish population of Belgium. On October 28, 1940, an ordinance was issued requiring all Jews fifteen years of age and older to register in their place of residence. 56,186 Jews—the entire Jewish population was just under 70,000 persons at that time—were registered as a result. In the summer of 1941, Gerard Romsée (October 11, 1901 – April 14, 1975), appointed Secretary General of the Interior and Public Health in the summer of 1941, turned the Jewish register over to the German security police in Brussels. This led, on August 29, 1941, to the concentration of the Jews in Brussels, Antwerp, Liège, and Charleroi. In 1942, they were forbidden to leave the country, were ordered to wear the Jewish star and their assets were forfeited to the German Reich.

On July 15, 1942, orders were issued for the establishment of an SS collection point in Mechelen, where the Belgian Jews were supposed to be organized for labor in the east. The first deportation train soon left the camp, on August 4, 1942, carrying 998 persons. Five more transports followed that month. Five more transports followed in September 1942, and four in October. Like their predecessors, their destination was the concentration camp in Auschwitz.

In 1943, the organization of deportation trains was irregular. *General der Infanterie* von Falkenhausen may have been partly responsible as he is believed to have repeatedly delayed the evacuation measures. As a result, just one transport went from Belgium to Auschwitz in January, April, and July 1943. In December 1943, a total of 132 men and women reached the Buchenwald and Ravensbrück concentration camps.

January, April, May, and July 1944, each saw one transport with about 600 Jews[42] dispatched from Belgium to Auschwitz, and an additional thirty persons were sent to Bergen–Belsen in February, April, and June 1944.

In total, 24,916 Jews and 351 Sinti and Roma were deported from Belgian and the northern French Départements Nord and Pas-de-Calais. The majority of the deportees (about 20,000 Belgian and just under 5,000 German Jews) died in Auschwitz.

Bulgaria

After entering the First World War on the side of Germany and Austria–Hungary in 1915, on March 1, 1941, Bulgaria joined the Tripartite Pact (Germany–Italy–Japan). The agreement gave Germany the right to send military units through the country to reach Yugoslavia and Greece.

After the victorious German campaign in the Balkans, Bulgarian forces occupied Greek Thrace and Yugoslavian Macedonia. The Bulgarian occupation force also took part in the pacification of these areas.

Even before joining the Tripartite Pact, on December 24, 1940, the Kingdom of Bulgaria enacted a restrictive law against the Jews which required Bulgaria's approximately 50,000 Jews to register. In 1941, this was expanded to include the approximately 6,000 Jews living in Thrace, and the roughly 8,000 in Macedonia.

A "Commissariat for Jewish Questions" was founded in August 1942, and in cooperation with the German security police it was to make preparations for the "resettlement" of the Jews. In January 1943, German *SS-Hauptsturmführer* Theodor Dannecker (March 27, 1913 – December 10, 1945) arrived at the German embassy in Sofia as "Jewish advisor" and on February 22, 1943, he signed an agreement with the Bulgarian Commissar for Jewish Questions which called for a total of 20,000 Jews to be deported to eastern areas under German control. In addition to the entire Jewish populations of Thrace and Macedonia, this was to include about 6,000 Jews from old Bulgaria.

When these plans were announced at the beginning of March 1943, there were protests among the population as well as in the parliament in Sofia. In a speech on the subject, Vice Head of Parliament Dimitar Peshew declared: "We cannot believe that there are plans to send these people away from Bulgaria. Such an act would wrongfully stigmatize Bulgaria, morally and politically." This was followed by a petition against the deportation of the Bulgarian Jews. As a result, the government "only" had 7,122 Macedonian and 4,221 Thracian Jews deported, while the Jews in old Bulgaria were employed as forced laborers in the country. For the Jews from the newly-annexed areas, however, deportation meant death in Treblinka.

Although the Bulgarian government saved the lives of its own approximately 50,000 Bulgarians of the Jewish faith, it sent the Jews from the annexed areas to deportation and death.

Denmark

On April 9, 1940, the German military occupied Denmark to protect northern Germany. As Germany basically had no wish to interfere in the affairs of Danish government, German interests were represented by Reich Commissioner Cécil von Renthe-Fink (January 27, 1885 – August 22, 1964). In this way Denmark remained sovereign and in return supplied the German Reich, mainly with foodstuffs.

The previously stable situation changed in 1943, when the Danish resistance movement— supported and controlled by England—carried out numerous acts of sabotage against ports and transport routes. Various strikes also made it clear that the Danish population was becoming increasingly dissatisfied with the appeasement policy of its government.

Dr. Werner Best (July 10, 1903 – June 23, 1989) had been Reich Commissioner in Denmark since November 1942, and, contrary to his earlier approach, he showed great sensitivity in trying to influence policy. The results of this were negligible, however, and so on August 29, 1943, Hitler imposed a state of emergency, which was implemented by the commander of German forces in Denmark, *General der Infanterie* Hermann von Hanneken (January 5, 1890 – July 22, 1981). The measures adopted included disbandment of the Danish army and fleet.

Dr. Best tried to achieve a new German–Danish policy, but the Danes were disinterested. The arrest of 400 influential Danes on August 29, 1943, did not help matters. Another German reaction to the changed situation was the intended arrest and deportation of the Danish Jews. Police units were transferred from Norway to Copenhagen to carry out this task. As the Danish state had no special files on the Jewish population, the files of the Jewish community were seized.

This did not remain hidden from the Danish public and after the day of the arrests (October 2, 1943) had filtered through even to Sweden, Swedish radio broadcast that any Danish Jew in

Sweden would be given asylum. Following this an unusual rescue operation was organized in Denmark for its Jewish citizens. More than 7,000 of them were evacuated by night across the Öresund, the Kattegat, and the Danish Baltic island of Bornholm to Sweden. Only 481 of the total of about 7,500 Danish Jews were arrested and deported to the Theresienstadt ghetto.

And even here the country showed itself to be very active. While the other European countries had little interest in the subsequent fates of the deportees, Danish politicians demanded the integrity of their citizens. The deportees were subsequently better fed and visited by representatives of the International Committee of the Red Cross in Theresienstadt. Only about 10% of the Danish Jews ultimately died in the ghetto.

While this may have been because Denmark was not an explicitly hostile country and was also a Nordic people, this case does however also show what foreign politicians and populations could have achieved if they had wanted to.

While Dr. Best advised Hitler on November 3, 1943, that Denmark was Jew free, after the deportation the Danish government ultimately denied its cooperation and dissolved. Finally, after negotiations with the Swedish Red Cross, the evacuation of 430 surviving Danish Jews from the Theresienstadt ghetto began on April 13, 1945. The former deportees drove through Germany in so-called "white buses" of the Swedish Red Cross, crossed the Danish border near Padborg and were forwarded to Sweden.

France

After the German victory over France, a ceasefire agreement was signed in Compiègne Forest on June 22, 1940. As a result the country was divided. While, from October 1940, northern France and the French Atlantic coast as far as the Spanish border fell under the German military administration in Paris under *General der Infanterie* Otto von Stulpnagel (June 16, 1878 – February 6, 1948), a French government was formed in Vichy under Marshall Philippe Pétain which administered unoccupied southern France.

In September 1940 the Reich Security Main Office established the "Jewish Department in Paris" under *SS-Hauptsturmführer* Theodor Dannecker (March 27, 1913 – December 10, 1945). Soon afterwards anti-Semitism also began becoming a part of day-to-day politics in France. Numerous restrictions, including the choice of place of residence and profession, followed the formation of the General Commissariat for Jewish Questions (*Commissariat Général aux Questions Juives*) on 29 March 1941. It registered the approximately 30,000 Jews living in the north and south of France and passed the information on to the Gestapo.

While Soviets Jews had been liquidated wholesale in response to attacks on German soldiers, after attacks on German soldiers in France thousands of Jews were deported to the Auschwitz concentration camp. The end result was the same. While the actual assassins usually went unpunished, at least for Hitler the attacks brought a welcome pretext for the expiation campaign against the Jewish population.

The Drancy camp near Paris was the exit station for the deportations "to the east." Designed for 700 people, sometimes many times this number of people occupied the barracks. The first transport left for Auschwitz–Birkenau on March 27, 1942. Four more transports with a total of about 4,000 Jews left for Auschwitz in June 1942. Eight transports in July 1942, had the same destination. In August 1942, thirteen deportation trains, each with about 1,000 Jews, left France for Upper Silesia and exactly the same number followed in September. The evacuations ended for 1942 in November with a total of four trains. Thus a total of approximately 42,000 Jews had been deported to Auschwitz in the second half of 1942.

The deportations resumed in February 1943, with three transports to Auschwitz. Another followed in March 1943, while two proceeded to the concentration camp in Lublin and two direct to Sobibor. June 1943 brought one deportation and July two transports to Auschwitz. One train was dispatched to Auschwitz in September 1943, and two in October, each carrying approximately 1,000 persons. The year 1943 ended with two transports to Auschwitz, meaning that a total of about 16,000 Jewish people were dispatched from France.

The next deportation train left for Auschwitz in January 1944. Two transports left for Auschwitz in February, March, and April 1944, and in May one went to the Kaunas ghetto plus two to Auschwitz. After the invasion of Normandy, single trains proceeded to Auschwitz in June and July, and even in August 1944—a few days before the end of the war in France—single transports left for Auschwitz and Buchenwald.

A total of 75,721 persons were deported from France, the majority of whom lost their lives. Only about 30,000 of these were French citizens. About 26,300 Jews originally came from Poland, approximately 7,000 from Germany and roughly 2,500 from Austria. Approximately 4,500 had Soviet and about 3,300 Rumanian citizenship. The policies followed by the French politicians, who French President Jacques Chirac (November 29, 1932) acknowledged were responsible for the persecution of the Jews during the occupation,[43] had in fact helped protect the French Jewish population. Of the roughly 300,000 French Jews in France during the German occupation, "only" ten percent were deported.

Greece

Greece was occupied in April 1941 during the Balkan Campaign. In consultation with its ally Italy, the German Reich assumed responsibility for securing eastern Greece along the Aegean between Salonika and Piraeus. While the Jewish population of the Italian zone in western Greece initially remained largely unaffected until Italy's surrender in September 1943, in the German zone there was repeated pressure on the Jews. In addition, for example, to the introduction of compulsory labor, in January 1943, consultations took place in Athens between Dr. Günther Altenburg (June 5, 1894 – October 23, 1984), the Reich commissioner in Greece, representatives of the *Wehrmacht* and *SS-Hauptsturmführer* Dieter Wisliceny, head of the Special Unit for Jewish Matters ("*Sonderkommando für Judenangelegenheiten*").

As a consequence, on February 6, 1943, *Major* Max Merten (September 8, 1911 – September 21, 1971), War Administration Counselor attached to the *Wehrmacht* Commander Salonika–Aegean, ordered the identification and ghettoization of the Jews in Salonika. As well, on March 1, 1943, they were forced to submit a detailed declaration of assets, which was used to confiscate their property. Just two weeks later began the deportation of 43,850 of the just under 50,000 Jews from Salonika to the Auschwitz–Birkenau concentration camp, which lasted from March 15 to August 7, 1943.

One month later, Italy surrendered to the Allies, whereupon *SS-Brigadeführer* Walter Schimana (March 12, 1898 – September 12, 1948) ordered the arrest of all Jews in the former Italian occupation zone on October 3, 1943. While the Jews population fled into the mountains in many places, registration succeeded on the islands of Corfu and Rhodes and in the area around Joannina not least because of support from National Greek partisans. On March 25, 1944, the total of 1,725 Jews arrested in Joannina were deported to Auschwitz. The evacuation of 1,795 Jews from Corfu followed on June 17, 1944 and in mid-July 1944, the Jews from Rhodes were deported to Auschwitz.

Altogether, about 50,000 Jews were deported from Greece. The areas under Bulgarian occupation are not included in this number. The majority of those deported died in Auschwitz–Birkenau.

Italy

Fascism in Italy was far more liberal towards the roughly 50,000 Jews living in the country than was National-Socialism in Germany. For this reason almost 8,000 Jews relocated from Germany to Italy before the Second World War.

After the Grand Fascist Council had Benito Mussolini (July 29, 1883 – April 28, 1945) deposed and arrested on July 25, 1943, on September 9, German troops marched into northern Italy. German paratroopers freed Mussolini from imprisonment on the Gran Sasso on September 12, and he formed a fascist counter-government which, however, no longer had any sovereignty towards Germany. This ended the relative protection the Jews had previously had in Italy.

On September 10, 1943, *SS-Obersturmbannführer* Herbert Kappler (September 29, 1907 – February 9, 1978), the police attaché attached to Rudolf Rahn (March 16, 1900 – January 7, 1975), provisional German ambassador in Rome, was named Commander of the Security Police and SD in Rome. In this function, barely five weeks later, on the night of October 16, he had a total of 1,259 Jews arrested, of which 1,007 were deported to Auschwitz. This was probably a reaction to the reversal in Italy. As was so often the case, the Jewish population were made scapegoats for events over which they had no influence.

In November 1943, the new *Reppublica Sociale Italiana* (RSI) released its constitution, as a result of which the Jews lost their citizenship in its area of authority. On November 30, 1943, the Italian republic's ministry of the interior issued a directive that all Jews should be concentrated in camps and their assets seized. Those that could hid in the mountains with their families or tried to escape to Switzerland. The attitude of German authorities to the Italian mentality was shown by the offering of "per capita premiums" for the capture of these refugees.

Those that were captured went to local collection camps in northern Italy. These were initially under the oversight of Guido Buffarini (August 17, 1895 – July 10, 1945), the Italian Minister of the Interior. From there the Jews, as well as political opponents, were sent to the police custody and transit camp at Fossoli (approximately twenty kilometers north of Modena).

Deportations from there to Germany began on February 19, 1944. On August 2, 1944, the last of the total of seven transports left the camp, which was then liquidated. About 5,000 Jews were deported by way of the camp, with five transports sent to Auschwitz and one each to Bergen–Belsen and Mauthausen. The majority of the Jewish people were killed.

Croatia

After the Balkan Campaign, the Kingdom of Yugoslavia was divided into autonomous states. The largest was the so-called Independent State of Croatia under the leadership of Ante Pavelic (July 14, 1889 – December 28, 1959), whose politics were aligned with those of Italian fascism and German National–Socialism. Persecution of the country's population of roughly 25,000 Jews thus began almost immediately, on April 18, 1941. Placed in various concentration camps, probably about 15,000 Jews lost their lives in Jasenovac—a Croatian concentration camp on the border with Bosnia south of Novska—alone.

An initial German-Croatian agreement followed in mid-August 1942, according to which 5,000 Jewish men and women capable of work were to be deported from Zagreb to Auschwitz. Five months later the Croatian leadership planned to make the country practically "Jew free." On January 19, 1943, an order, "to remove all remaining Jews—with the exception of honorary Aryans and crossbreeds":

> The Jews held in Croatian concentration camps, provided they are not employed as labor forces, shall be released for resettlement to Germany. Jews living illegally in Croatia shall be arrested and sent to the Jasenovac camp. All Jews selected for resettlement shall be concentrated in the Gradiska camp.

In the course of this measure, approximately 2,000 Jews no longer fit for work were deported to Auschwitz via the satellite camp of the Jasenovac concentration camp—Stara Gradisla (approximately forty kilometers east of Jasenovac. The number of victims of the Jasenovac concentration camp can be read on the page www.haGalil.com, Jewish life online:[44]

Concerning the number of victims of this camp there are great differences in the historiography. While Serbian nationalists like Vuk Draskovic in Belgrade put the number at between 700,000 and 1.2 million, the latest research places the total number at about 85,000. According to historian Slavko Goldstein, this figure includes about 30,000 Serbs, 15,000 Jews, 20,000 Roma, and 20,000 members of the Croatian opposition.

The approximately 7,000 Jews who were deported to Auschwitz, the majority of whom died in the concentration camp, must be added to this figure.

Netherlands

With the end of the victorious German campaign in the west, on May 29, 1940, Arthur Seyß-Inquart was installed as Reich Commissar for the Occupied Netherlands. Preparation of a Jewish reporting protocol began under him in the summer of 1940 and on January 10, 1941, the "Reich commissar's decree for the occupied territories of the Netherlands concerning the reporting obligation of persons who are entirely or partly of Jewish blood." All with at least one Jewish grandparent were required to report to the local resident's registration office. The registration form went to the Reich Inspector of the Population Registry in The Hague and was a component of a central "Jew card index." The registration was finally completed at the beginning of July 1941. Of the 160,886 persons "of Jewish blood," about 19,000 were married to non-Jews and about 20,000 did not have a Dutch passport—most of the latter had emigrated from the German Reich.

In the course of the altered final solution to the Jewish problem, in 1942, deportations from the Netherlands began. The Jews were assembled in the "Westerbork Police Jewish Transit Camp"[45] and from there six transports, each carrying about 1,000 persons, were sent to Auschwitz. Nine more followed in August 1942, and eight in September. On September 24, 1942, *SS-Gruppenführer* Hanns Rauter (February 4, 1895 – March 24, 1949), the Senior SS and Police Commander attached to the Reich Commissar for the Occupied Dutch Territories, composed an interim report for Himmler. Not only did this provide detailed information about the category of persons who should be deported, it also showed that the Dutch police participated in the deportations "excellently"—obviously even more profoundly than the French police:

So far , with the Jews deported punitively to Mauthausen, we have sent a total of 20,000 Jews to Auschwitz. In all of Holland about 120,000 Jews will be deported, however this also includes the number of mixed Jews, who will remain here initially. There are approximately 20,000 mixed marriages in Holland. In agreement with the Reich commissar, however, I will also deport all of the Jewish parts of the intermarriages provided these have not produced any children. This will be approximately 6,000 cases, consequently 14,000 Jews from mixed marriages will initially remain here.

In the Netherlands there is a so-called "*Werkveruiming*," a work facility under the Dutch ministry for social affairs, which keeps Jews for various types of work in closed businesses and camps. So far we have not touched these *Werkveruiming* camps in order to let the Jews flee there. There are about 7,000 Jews in these *Werkveruiming* camps. We hope to get to 8,000 Jews by October 1. These 8,000 Jews have about 22,000 relatives in the entire country of Holland. On October 1, the relief works camps will be occupied by me at one blow and the same day the relatives outside them will be arrested and taken into the two large newly erected Jewish camps in Westerborknear Assen and Vught near Hertogenbosch. I will try to get hold of three trains per week in place of two. These 30,000 Jews will now be deported from October 1 onward. I hope that by Christmas we shall have got rid of these 30,000 Jews too so that a total of 50,000 Jews, that is half, will then have been moved from Holland.

For weeks already, the population registrars in the Netherlands have been doing preparatory work for the determination of the mixed marriages, meaning the delivery of proof that the Aryan parts of the mixed marriages are actually Aryan. These 13,000 mixed Jews will receive a note in their Jew pass that they are entitled to remain in Holland. Armaments workers still vital to the *Wehrmacht* will be processed in the same way, approximately 6,000 + dependents = 21,000 altogether. Included in this number are the diamond workers from Amsterdam, as well as photographic and NSB [National-Socialist Movement in the Netherlands] Jews.

On October 15, Jewry in Holland will be declared outlawed, that means that police action on a large scale will begin in which not only German and Dutch police organizations, but also the staff of the NSDAP, party organizations, the NSB, the *Wehrmacht* etc will be involved. Every Jew found anywhere in Holland will be put in the large camps. As a result no Jew, unless a privileged one, will be seen any longer in Holland. At the same time I will start the announcements according to which Aryans who hide Jews or help them over the border, and who have forged identity papers, will have their property seized, and the perpetrators will be taken to a concentration camp: all this in order to prevent the flight of the Jews which has started on a large scale. Of the Christian Jews, in the meantime the Catholic Jews have been deported, because the five bishops, led by Archbishop de Jonge in Utrecht, have not kept the original agreements. The protestant Jews are still here, and in fact we have succeeded in splitting the Catholic Church from this common front. Archbishop de Jonge declared at a conference of bishops that he would never again join a common front with the Protestants and Calvinists. The push by the churches, which began when the evacuation started, was badly shaken and has faded away. The new Dutch Police Hundertschaften are performing excellently in the Jewish matter and arrest hundreds of Jews day and night. The only problem that has appeared is that now and then one of the policemen slips up and helps himself to Jewish property. I have arranged presentations by the SS and police court before the assembled Hundertschaft.

The Jew camp at Westerbork is already complete, the Jew camp at Vught will be completed by October 10–15.

The Senior SS and Police Commander's disdain toward the Jews, which is obvious in this report, is shocking. It seems inconceivable that an educated man could express himself in this way.

While the Vught camp was being finished, in Westerbork nine deportation trains were loaded in October 1942, and seven in November. The year 1942 ended with three transports to Auschwitz. Altogether about 35,000 Jews had been evacuated from the Netherlands in the second half of 1942.

A total of nine transports to Auschwitz followed in January and February 1943. From March to July 1943, nineteen trains were sent to Sobibor. In April 1943, one train carrying emigrated German Jews went to the Theresienstadt ghetto. Sixteen more transports went to Auschwitz between August 1943, and September 1944. Seven deportations went to Theresienstadt and eight to the detention camp at Bergen–Belsen.

Of approximately 160,000 Jews, approximately 110,000 were deported from the Netherlands. The majority of them lost their lives in Auschwitz–Birkenau and Sobibor. There were protests and strikes against the deportation and treatment of the Jews, but also extensive collaboration, which in part made the deportations possible.

Norway

When Germany occupied Norway in April 1940, there were approximately 2,100 Jews living there. About 1,600 had Norwegian citizenship, while roughly 500 had travelled there from

Germany, Austria, or Czechoslovakia since 1933. In May 1940, even before the fighting in northern Norway had ended, the German security police requested the Norwegian police in the south of the country to confiscate radios from the Jewish population.

After the fighting ended the rightwing *Nasjonal Samling* party immediately began abusing Jewish businesses and individuals. While the majority of Norwegian citizens had no sympathy for these actions, in October 1941 German policy toward the Jews was instituted in Norway. *SS-Oberführer* and *Oberst der Polizei* Heinrich Fehlis (November 1, 1906 – May 11, 1945), combat missions of the security police and SD in Norway and also commander of the security police and SD in Oslo, requested the Norwegian ministry of police to systematically register the country's Jews.

After the Jewish population had finally been registered in January 1942, Vidkun Quisling (July 18, 1887 – October 24, 1945), who had been installed as Norwegian prime minister on February 1, 1942, issued a decree prohibiting Jews from residing in the country. The directive was not implemented, however, until the end of October 1942. After the Law for the Confiscation of Jewish Property passed on October 26, 1942, Karl Marthinsen (October 25, 1896 – February 8, 1945), chief of the Norwegian state police, gave all police agencies the order to arrest all male Jews over the age of fifteen the following day. While the men, mainly from the Oslo area—where the majority of Norway's Jews lived—were taken to the collection camp at Berg near Tønsberg, about half the Jews were able to emigrate to Sweden. Another wave of arrests followed at the end of November 1942, mainly affecting Jewish women and children.

Subsequently, on November 26, 1942, 532 Jews were deported from Oslo across the Baltic to Stettin. From there they were taken by train to Auschwitz, where they—at least the women and children—were killed on December 1, 1942. A second transport with 158 persons followed on February 25, 1943. They too were probably killed immediately after their arrival at Auschwitz–Birkenau.

Of the 700 Jews deported from Norway probably only thirty survived. In contrast to Denmark, however, the Norwegian officials showed little interest in the fate of their Jewish fellow citizens and so they acted like a typical bureaucracy, without active or passive resistance against the obvious wrong.

Poland

The German campaign in Poland began on September 1, 1939, and ended victoriously at the beginning of October. As a result, the country was divided between the German Reich and the USSR based on the German–Soviet Border and Friendship Treaty. Effective September 28, 1939, this left Germany in control of about two-million Jews and about 1.3 million under Soviet control.

On September 21, 1939, even before the end of the campaign, *SS-Gruppenführer* Heydrich issued guidelines for the future treatment of the Jews in Poland. These called for them to be concentrated in cities with rail connections in so-called Jewish residential districts. Jewish communities with less than 500 members were to be dissolved and their inhabitants moved to the next larger communities. Implementation of this guideline to form so-called ghettoes began in early October 1939, in large cities that had already been occupied.

On October 26, 1939, Dr. Hans Frank, governor-general of the newly-created so-called *Generalgouvernement* was named commissioner of the civil administration. One of his first official actions, on November 23, 1939, was the introduction of a Jewish star which had to be worn by all Jews over ten years of age. Jewish stores and businesses also had to be identified.

As the result of the start of the war with the Soviet Union in the summer of 1941, another roughly one million Polish Jews came under German rule. The Red Army had already deported about 300,000 Jews to Soviet labor camps, which left a total of approximately three million Jews under German influence.

According to the Korherr Report on the number of Jews in Europe, about half of (the total of 1,449,692 Jews) from the eastern provinces were "guided through to the Russian east" from March to the end of December 1942. In fact, only a small fraction of these people were used as workers—including in the construction of Through Road IV. For the majority, sooner or later "guided through" meant death by carbon-monoxide in the camps at Belzec, Kulmhof, Sobibor, and Treblinka or by the unleashed shootings in the ghettoes.

At the beginning of 1943 there were barely 300,000 Jews in the ghettoes of the *Generalgouvernement*. Only a small part survived the end of National–Socialism. If one adds to these the number of Polish Jews liquidated by the *Einsatzgruppen* of the security police and SD east of the former German–Soviet demarcation line, it is likely that more then two-thirds of the Jewish population of Poland lost their lives during the German occupation. Because of this dramatic figure, larger ghettoes with a tragic significance will be described briefly.

Warsaw Ghetto

The Polish capital surrendered to German forces on September 27, 1939. Just five days later a decree was issued calling for all Jewish residents to move to a district of the city located west of the center within six weeks. Beginning October 16, 1940, it was enclosed by barbed wire, paling fences, and solid walls. For just under two years, several hundred thousand Jews lived and worked in the ghetto, where in the beginning several companies continued to operate, mainly producing goods for the *Wehrmacht*.

The deportation to Treblinka of ghetto residents unable to work began at the end of July 1942. Despite new transports bringing Jews into the ghetto, in the course of Action Reinhard the number of inhabitants dropped steadily. It was finally designated a "remnant ghetto" and was no longer a cohesive residential area. At the beginning of 1943 about 50,000 Jews were officially still living in the ghetto. As well there was probably another roughly 5,000 people who had avoided the previous deportations but had no valid papers. When it became apparent that the remnant ghetto was also about to be liquidated, on April 19, 1943, the Jewish Resistance began opposing deportations by force of arms. *SS-Brigadeführer* Jürgen Stroop (September 26, 1895 – March 6, 1952), SS and Police Commander in Warsaw, initially believed that he could crush the uprising within three days and was visibly surprised by the strength of the rebel resistance. When the fighting finally ended on May 16, 1943, after about four weeks, *SS-Brigadeführer* Stroop reported:

> The former Jewish residential area of Warsaw no longer exists. The major action was brought to a conclusion at 2015 with the blowing up of the Warsaw synagogue. The total number of Jews captured and known to have been destroyed is 56,065.

Of these last approximately 56,000 Jews of the Warsaw ghetto, just under 7,000 were transported to Treblinka. Several thousand residents were liquidated in the ghetto or were killed in the fighting. The majority, however, were sent to the concentration camp in Lublin and most died there.

Litzmannstadt (Łódź) Ghetto

The second-largest Jewish residential district in former Poland was located in Litzmannstadt (Łódź), which was captured by German troops on September 9, 1939. In mid-June 1940, there were 160,320 residents there. Despite new arrivals of Jews from the German Reich[46] and the new eastern provinces (Wartheland and Danzig–West Prussia), the number of ghetto inhabitants dropped steadily due to the high mortality rate and the transports that departed during Action Reinhard, and later to Auschwitz. The numbers of residents were:

	1941	1942	1943	1944
Residents	145,992	103,034	84,226	75,551

In the course of the reduction of the ghetto through deportations—mainly people unable (or no longer able) to work—the following numbers were removed:

01/26/42 – 01/29/42 .... 10,003 to Kulmhof (Chelmno)
02/22/42 – 04/02/42 ....34,073 to Kulmhof
05/04/42 – 05/15/42 ....10,914 to Kulmhof
09/03/42 – 09/12/42 ....15,681 to Kulmhof

With the rapid Soviet advance westwards, evacuation of the Jewish residential area in Litzmannstadt began in June 1944. In the course of this the residents were moved as follows:

06/23/44 – 07/14/44 .... 7,196 (unfit for work) to Kulmhof
08/09/44 – 08/29/44 ....67,000 to Auschwitz, Sachsenhausen, and Ravensbrück

Bialystok Ghetto

Bialystok was initially occupied by German forces on September 15, 1939, but was then handed over to the Red Army, which incorporated it into the White Russian Socialist Soviet Republic. In the summer of 1941 the area was again occupied by the Germans and Erich Koch (June 19, 1896 – November 12, 1986), *Gauleiter* of East Prussia, was installed as head of the civilian administration of the Bialystok District.

Beginning August 1, 1941, the Jewish population, comprising approximately 60,000 people, was concentrated in a ghetto astride the Biala River. All Jews between the ages of 15 and 65 were employed as slave laborers, which at least provided a minimum level of nourishment. Many residents worked in armaments plants within the ghetto. Old and sick Jews were moved to the smaller camp at Pruzhany (approximately 100 kilometers southeast of Bialystok) and most died there.

The ghetto was reduced from February 5–12, 1943, in the process of which about 2,000 Jews were shot and approximately 10,000 deported to Treblinka. After Himmler ordered the dissolution of the ghetto, the deportation to Treblinka of those unfit to work, and to the Lublin concentration camp of those who could work began on the night of August 16, 1943—against armed Jewish resistance. Some of those sent to Lublin were subsequently sent to Auschwitz.

A remnant ghetto with about 2,000 Jews remained in Bialystok for about three weeks and these people were employed sorting and cleaning, after which they were transported to Lublin. They were probably all shot there during "Operation Harvest Festival."

Kielce Ghetto

Although the German military took Kielce on September 4, 1939, surprisingly it was not until March 31, 1941, that a Jewish residential area was created for the approximately 24,000 Jews living in the city and surrounding area. Since February 1941, this number had included 1,004 Jews from Austria.

The ghetto consisted of a large and a small area, and a paling fence divided it from the other parts of the city. Living conditions were catastrophic. Fearing the arising of a resistance movement, on the night of April 28, 1942, the security police and SD carried out an action against Jewish intellectuals, in which even specially important doctors were shot or sent to Auschwitz.

The reduction of the ghetto began four months later. On August 20, 1942, an initial group of 7,000 residents was deported to Treblinka. The deportation was difficult to surpass in crudity.

Im Namen des Führers

ernenne ich

unter Berufung in das Beamtenverhältnis
den

Johannes Vogelsang

zum Polizei - Wachtmeister

Ich vollziehe diese Urkunde in der Erwartung, daß der Ernannte getreu seinem Diensteide seine Amtspflichten gewissenhaft erfüllt und das Vertrauen rechtfertigt, das ihm durch diese Ernennung bewiesen wird. Zugleich darf er des besonderen Schutzes des Führers sicher sein.

Heidenheim (Brenz), den 25. Juni 1940

Für den Reichsminister des Innern

Major d. Sch.
und

Kommandeur des Ausbildungsbataillons

IM NAMEN DES FÜHRERS
UND OBERSTEN BEFEHLSHABERS
DER WEHRMACHT
VERLEIHE ICH
DEM

Oberwachtmeister d. Schutzpolizei
Johannes Vogelsang
II./ SS- Polizei Regiment 22

DAS

KRIEGSVERDIENSTKREUZ
2. KLASSE
MIT SCHWERTERN

Warschau, DEN 15.Juni 1943

Der SS- u. Polizeiführer
im Distrikt Warschau

SS- Brigadeführer u.
Generalmajor d. Polizei
(DIENSTGRAD UND DIENSTSTELLUNG)

For his actions during the clearing of the Warsaw Ghetto in April–May 1943, *Oberwachtmeister* Vogelsang was awarded the War Merit Cross 2nd Class with Swords from the SS and Police Commander in the District of Warsaw.

About 1,200 old, handicapped, or sick Jews were simply shot. Within just four days all Jewish persons, with the exception of about 2,000 young men capable of work, were taken to Treblinka and murdered there. The others were placed in a special camp within the old ghetto and had to clean the former Jewish district and sort through the valuables and possessions of the deportees.

The special camp existed until spring 1943, and was then liquidated. The Jewish work forces were sent to Auschwitz and Buchenwald or to the HASAG factories (Hugo und Alfred Schneider AG) in Tschenstochau.

Cracow Ghetto

Cracow was taken by German forces on September 6, 1939. It was originally planned that the Jewish population should be driven from the city beginning May 18, 1940, apart from approximately 15,000 Jewish craftsmen who would remain for economic reasons. On March 3, 1941, *SS-Gruppenführer* Dr. Otto Wächter (July 8, 1901 – September 10, 1949), the governor of the District of Cracow, ordered the creation of a Jewish residential area for "reasons of safety and hygiene." To which these remaining approximately 15,000 Jewish residents of Cracow had to move by March 20, 1941.

As in all ghettoes, living conditions were bad. In addition to inadequate hygiene and nourishment, the many thousands of Jews had to share 320 houses. When, effective September 15, 1941, another approximately 4,000 Jews from the area around Cracow were deported to the ghetto, there were in some cases eight people to a room.

The liquidation of the ghetto began on May 30, 1942 as part of Action Reinhard. More than 4,000 residents were deported to Belzec by June 8, 1942. During this and the second deportation action on October 27–28, 1942, which again involved more than 4,000 people, probably about 600 old and sick Jews were shot in the ghetto.

In December 1942, the ghetto was divided in two, with Area A for those able to work and Area B for Jews unfit for work. At the beginning of 1943, there were still about 37,000 Jews in the Jewish residential district of Cracow. In mid-March 1943, those that could work were sent to the concentration camps at Plaszow and the next day those unfit for work were either shot in the ghetto or killed at Auschwitz–Birkenau. Finally a Jewish work detail was employed in cleanup work and sorting the remaining Jewish property. This detail was subsequently likewise sent to the Plaszow concentration camp.

Lublin Ghetto

After German forces occupied Lublin on September 18, 1939, registration of the Jewish population began on October 25. This revealed a total of 37,054 Jews in the city, in which *SS-Brigadeführer* Odilo Globocnik was assigned as SS and Police Commander effective November 9, 1939.

In December 1939, he had the first labor camp for Jewish prisoners of war of the Polish Army set up and ordered the Jewish population concentrated in a separate residential area. As this was too small for the almost 40,000 people, about 14,000 had to be resettled. The residential district was designated a ghetto on March 24, 1941.

Jewish workers were detailed to construct the Lublin concentration camp in December 1941, and at the beginning of 1942, the ghetto itself was divided into two camps—for Jews fit and unfit for work. The deportation to the Belzec camp of those unfit for work began on March 17, 1942, as part of "Action Reinhard," while all of those capable of work were supposed to be sent to the Lublin concentration camp. In barely four weeks, by April 14, 1942, probably more than 15,000 Jews from the Lublin ghetto were killed at Belzec.

The ghetto was subsequently liquidated and the 6,000 remaining Jews were moved to the smaller quarter of Majdan Tatarski in Lublin. One week later, about 2,000 women and children were singled out and sent to the Lublin concentration camp or, as unfit for work, were shot in a nearby forest near Krępiec. Two more transfers occurred on September 2 and October 24, to Piaski ghetto eighteen kilometers to the southeast, and to the Lublin concentration camp.

The final liquidation of the ghetto took place on November 9, 1942. As in other ghetto liquidations, those who could not be moved (the elderly, sick and weak) were shot in their quarters, the hospital, or in the street. The survivors were taken to the Lublin concentration camp and most died there. Political prisoners were finally given the job of cleaning up and sorting the Jewish possessions left behind.

Radom Ghetto

German troops occupied Radom, where approximately 30,000 Jews lived, on September 8, 1939. *SS-Brigadeführer* Friedrich Katzmann (May 6, 1906 – September 19, 1957) was appointed SS and Police Commander there and he soon began concentrating the Jewish population in two separate ghettoes—a large one in the city center and a small one in the suburb of Glinice. The occupants had to work in the numerous armaments plants supplying the German military.

Just under three years later, first the ghetto in Glinice was liquidated in the course of Action Reinhard. While about 1,000 Jews able to work went to the large ghetto, the remaining approximately 4,000 together with about 2,000 more unfit persons from the large ghetto were deported to Treblinka and met their end there.

About ten days later, between August 16–18, the large ghetto in the inner city was also liquidated. About 400 sick and weak people were shot in the ghetto, and about 18,000 were deported to Treblinka. The remaining approximately 4,000 younger, fitter Jews were sent to the smaller Glinice ghetto, which became a labor camp. In December 1942 and January 1943, there was a selection of about 2,400 Jews, most of whom were sent to Treblinka. These included approximately 1,600 people who had been waiting—in vain—for visas to Palestine. The Glinice camp was finally liquidated on November 8, 1943, and the residents were sent with other Jews from the area to a barracks camp inside Radom. The inmates worked there until June 26, 1944, and were then transported to Auschwitz, where they initially continued working.

Lvov Ghetto

Lvov was one of the Polish areas occupied by the Red Army in 1939. The German military began operations against the USSR on June 22, 1941, and it was able to occupy the city on June 30. The setting up of a Jewish residential district in Lvov began on November 8, 1941. At times more than 160,000 Jews from the city and surrounding area would be concentrated there.

Deportations to Belzec began on March 14, 1942, as part of Action Reinhard. About 15,000 Jews were transported to certain death on ten trains by April 1, 1942. On July 24, 1942, about 8,000 Jews unfit for work were shot in the ghetto or transported to Belzec. Another deportation wave followed from August 10–23, 1942, and probably about 50,000 ghetto residents were evacuated to Belzec. This meant about two trains a day. On January 5, 1943, 10,000 Jews were transferred to the Piaski ghetto and most likely shot there.

The complete evacuation of the Jewish quarter in Lvov began on June 1, 1943, resulting in fighting with the Jewish resistance movement founded in the ghetto. In the end flamethrowers were used to clear the houses. With the liquidated of the ghetto in Lvov the resettlement of the Jews from the district of Galicia was considered virtually concluded. *SS-Gruppenführer* Friedrich Katzmann, the SS and Police Commander, wrote a final report on the Solution of the Jewish Question in the District of Galicia, which he sent to *SS-Obergruppenführer* Friedrich-Wilhelm Krüger (May 8, 1894 – May 10, 1945), the Senior SS and Police Commander East (General-gouvernement) on June 30, 1943:

In the meantime, further resettlement has been pursued vigorously, enabling all Jewish residential districts to be liquidated effective June 23, 1943. The district of Galicia is thus Jew free, except for the Jews in the camps under the control of the SS and police commander.

Isolated Jews who are still picked up will be specially dealt with by the respective *Ordnungspolizei* and military police posts. A total of 434,329 Jews were relocated by June 27, 1943.

Tschenstochau (Częstochowa) Ghetto

About 24,500 Jewish people resided in Tschenstochau, which was occupied by German troops on September 3, 1939. On April 9, 1941, a closed residential district was formed in the city, into which all the region's Jews—a total of about 48,000 people—were ordered to move. Living conditions were catastrophic, and inadequate nutrition and poor hygiene resulted in numerous epidemics which claimed victims.

The deportation of approximately 40,000 Jews to Treblinka, most of them unfit to work, began about 1½ years later in September 1942, as part of Action Reinhard. On January 4, 1943, during the final liquidation of the ghetto, there was armed Jewish resistance. This delayed the liquidation of the residential area only a little, however. The ghetto was deemed liquidated in March 1943.

Jews able to work and Jewish workers from the Kielce ghetto formed a special camp in Tschenstochau, producing *Panzerfaust* anti-tank weapons among other things. When the Red Army reached the city on January 16, 1945, it liberated the survivors.

Rumania

Although Rumania was historically closely tied to France and Great Britain, the occupation of Bessarabia, the Hertza Region and Northern Bukovina by Soviet troops on June 28, 1940, led to a political change of course. Ion Antonescu (June 15, 1882 – June 1, 1946), the former Rumanian defense minister, was named prime minister and on November 23, 1940, he signed Rumania's entry into the so-called Tripartite Pact with Germany, Italy and Japan.

After the fascist-oriented Antonescu took power, living conditions for the approximately 350,000 Jews living in the remaining Rumanian territory changed. While at first there were minor regulations, the day before the start of the war against Russia—June 21, 1941—he issued a decree that required the Jewish population to move from the country to the cities. The men were required to work, real estate and private property were forfeited and Jewish employees of the state were released.

After the outbreak of war with the Soviet Union, Bukovina, and Bessarabia, the territories occupied by the USSR in 1940, were soon retaken. For the Jews living there this meant assignment to concentration camps in Transnistria.[47] Of these roughly 190,000 Jews, more than half died from hunger, illness, and mass shootings. The Jews in the remaining parts of the country (Moldavia, Walachia, Dobruja, Banat, Transylvania, and the southern Crişana region) were not deported to the Transnistrian camps provided they were not active communists or refused compulsory labor service.

While the government thus behaved with relative restraint towards its own Jewish citizens, it acted brutally against the Soviet Jews. When sixty-six soldiers were killed in the bombing of the Rumanian headquarters in Odessa on October 22, 1941, Marshall Antonescu ordered 200 communists executed for every dead officer, and 100 for every fallen soldier. Like the Germans, the Rumanians used the attack as a welcome excuse to execute Jews. From October 23, 1941, it is estimated that members of the Rumanian Army liquidated 19,000 Ukrainian Jewish captives in the harbor area of Odessa. A further 20,000 were taken into custody and probably shot soon after.

SS-Sturmbannführer Gustav Richter (November 19, 1912 – unknown) had been active as police attaché with the German embassy in Bucharest since April 1941. There he functioned as "Advisor for Jewish Matters" and worked with the Rumanian commissioner for Jewish questions Radu Lecca (February 15, 1890 – 1980). On July 29, 1942, the pair discussed the deportation of more than 270,000 Rumanian Jews to Germany with Marshall Antonescu. While those able to work were probably supposed to go to Auschwitz, as part of the final solution to the Jewish question it was planned that those unable to work should be sent to the camp at Belzec. Manfred von Killinger (July 14, 1886 – September 2, 1944), the German ambassador in Bucharest, informed Hitler of the Rumanian government's commitment on August 11, 1942.

The deportation of the Jews to Germany or the *Generalgouvernement* was ultimately prevented, less for humanitarian reasons, than for the pragmatic plan to allow the Jews to travel to Palestine for ransom. In December 1942, Radu Lecca proposed allowing 70,000 Jews from Transnistria to travel to Palestine or some other place suggested by the western powers.[48] The proposal was directed towards the USA in particular, however it had absolutely no interest in such trade, consequently the plan was never implemented.

Rumania was the country that, after Germany, murdered the most Jews on its own initiative. Estimates place the number of victims at more than 150,000.

Slovakia

After the German military first occupied the Sudetenland and later rump-Czechoslovakia (Bohemia and Moravia), in March 1939, Slovakia formed an autonomous state. Dr. Jozef Tiso (October 13, 1887 – April 18, 1947) became prime minister and from October 26, 1939, state president.

In January 1939, even before the sovereignty of Slovakia, a "government commission for the solution of the Jewish question" was formed. There followed numerous regulations, which like in Germany placed limits on the number of Jewish doctors, pharmacists, journalists etc. The constitution of September 25, 1939, contained provisions for the Jewish population to be completely excluded, and from January 18, 1940, they were forbidden to serve in the army—which for many of them was not unpleasant. *SS-Hauptsturmführer* Dieter Wisliceny (January 13, 1911 – May 4, 1948) had been in Bratislava since September 1941 as representative of the Reich Security Main Office (Department IV B 4: Jewish Matters), where he worked as advisor to the Slovakian government in Jewish affairs.

One result of his "consulting" was that, after the start of the Russians campaign, the Jews were elevated to the "biggest tyrants of the Slovakian people." On July 4, 1941, a decree for temporary compulsory labor service for Jews and gypsies was issued and construction battalions formed, which were used to build roads, break rocks, or for drainage projects. As of September 1941, Jews were required to wear the yellow star on their clothing and were nearly banned from public life.

In February 1942, Hans Ludin (June 10, 1905 – December 9, 1947), German ambassador in Slovakia since January 1941, agreed with Slovakian representatives to send 20,000 Jews capable of work from Slovakia to Germany. The reason for this at that time was less the planned murder of people, rather it was Slovakia's duty to the German Reich to provide labor forces. Rumania also bore the costs associated with transporting the people.

The agreement was broadened even further, and Germany was now to take all of the Jews. On the key date of April 1, 1942, the figure was 88,951 Jews, some of whom were already concentrated in collection camps. The first transport carrying about 1,000 Jewish women aged 15 to 30 left the country on March 25, 1942, and the next day arrived at Auschwitz concentration camp. Six more transports with a total of 5,836 Jews capable of work arrived at Auschwitz by April 17. These were followed by six so-called "family transports" with a total of 5,799 persons, the majority of whom were probably killed immediately.

On June 25, 1942, *SS-Hauptsturmführer* Dieter Wisliceny reported that about 52,000 Jews had already been deported from Slovakia. Approximately 35,000 were still in the country because of various exemptions. On January 14, 1943, concerning the evacuation of the Jews the Rumanian ministry of transportation reported that between March 25 and October 20, 1942, fifty-seven trains with 57,752 Jews had left for Germany. Thirty-eight of these carrying 39,006 persons had gone to the Lublin concentration camp and the remaining nineteen with 18,746 Jews to Auschwitz.

The remaining Jewish population was supposed to be placed in concentration camps by April 1, 1944. This was accomplished only in part, however, partly because of the Slovakian national uprising that broke out in August 1944. New deportations began on September 30, 1944, however. Eleven transports with a total of 12,306 Jews followed by March 1945. Of these, 7,936 went to Auschwitz concentration camp, 2,732 to various concentration camps, and 1,638 to the Theresienstadt ghetto.

Altogether, of the roughly 90,000 Jews in Slovakia about 70,000 were deported, the majority of whom were put to death.

Soviet Union

Lithuania

When the German military marched into Lithuania on June 22, 1941, there were about 155,000 Jews[49] living there. As soon as Soviets troops withdrew, Lithuanian nationalists immediately began humiliating and even murdering them. Encouraged by the German side, Lithuanians carried out several such pogroms. The units of the German security police and the SD, meanwhile, busied themselves capturing the Jewish population. In addition to ghettoization in cities, the first mass shootings of thousands of Jews (as well as Soviet prisoners of war) took place in a forest near Paneriai (approximately ten kilometers south of Vilnius) in late summer 1941.

During the concentration of the Jews in the large cities, in July 1941, *SS-Oberführer* Hans Cramer (September 23, 1904 – April 15, 1945), the regional commissioner of Kauen, designated part of the city exclusively as a residential area for the city's roughly 30,000 Jews. The ghetto consisted of a small and a large area and on August 15, 1941, it was divided from the rest of the city by a fence. Residents capable of work had to work in the various German armaments factories that moved there. On October 28, 1941, there was a so-called "ghetto action" in which more than 9,000 Jews from the small ghetto, most unfit for work, were shot in the Ninth Fort—a fortification outside the city. After this the ghetto consisted of just the large camp, in which there were still about 15,000 Jews at the end of January 1942, according to a report by *SS-Brigadeführer* Stahlecker. When Himmler elevated the ghetto into a concentration camp in autumn 1943, the remaining Jewish prisoners worked there until the camp was evacuated. On July 14, 1944, with the Red Army approaching, they were deported to various German concentration camps.

On July 25, 1941, regional commissioner Hans Gewecke (July 17, 1906 – March 10, 1991) set up a Jewish residential district in Schaulen, which had been occupied by the *Wehrmacht* one moth earlier. At the end of 1941, approximately 5,000 people were living there and, whenever possible, they worked in German factories. In September 1943, the Jewish residential district formed an outer camp of the Kauen concentration camp. In July 1944, with the Red Army approaching, the inmates were evacuated to the Stutthof concentration camp.

On August 31, 1941, *SS-Sturmbannführer* Hans Christian Hingst, the regional commissioner in Vilnius, established two separate Jewish residential areas. The larger ghetto housed approximately 29,000 Jews classified as "able to work" and the smaller one about 11,000 unable to work. The latter were shot in Paneriai in early September 1941. During the reduction of the ghetto, between October 21–24, and on December 21–22, 1941, probably about 17,000 people were executed in Paneriai Forest. The bulk of the approximately 12,000 survivors continued to be employed in the German armaments industry. The Vilnius ghetto was finally liquidated on September 23, 1943. The remaining Jews were transported to Latvia and Estonia.

On January 31, 1942, *SS-Brigadeführer* Stahlecker, the commander of *Einsatzgruppe A*, reported that 136,421[50] Lithuanian Jews had been shot and roughly 20,000 confined in ghettoes. The combined total was roughly equal to the Jewish population of Lithuania when it was occupied by the *Wehrmacht* and indicates the probable total number of victims. Only a small part of the Lithuanian Jews in the labor and concentration camps survived the end of the war.

Latvia

A Latvian census taken in 1935 revealed a total of 94,479 Jews, whose number fell to about 74,000 as a result of emigration and deportations during the Soviet occupation in 1940–41. In the course of the German occupation these were rounded up and concentrated in various ghettoes.

In mid-October 1941, two ghettoes were set up in Riga for the approximately 32,000 Jews living there. In order to make "room" for the Jews from Germany, three so-called "actions" were carried out in the big ghetto. Thousands of Latvian Jews were shot in Bikernieki on November 8, 1941, and on December 8, in the forest near Rumbula. Acting on his own initiative, the officer responsible for the executions, *SS-Gruppenführer* Jeckeln, Senior SS and Police Commander Russia North and Ostland, also ordered all of the deportees on a train from Germany executed on arrival, the first time this had taken place.

In total, 15,073 Jews from the German Reich arrived in Riga from the end of 1941 until mid-February 1942, resulting in the expression "Reich Jew ghetto." *SS-Brigadeführer* Stahlecker, commander of *Einsatzgruppe A*, reported on January 31, 1942, that 35,238 Latvian Jews had so far been liquidated. In addition to the victims from the Riga ghetto, this number also includes those shot in the smaller ghettoes in Dvinsk (Daugavpils) and Libau.

In March 1942, about 1,900 Jews unfit for work were selected in the Riga ghetto. Under the pretext of being taken to Dünamünde (Daugavgrīva) for light work in fish processing, they were shot in Bikernieki Forest. About 13,000 Jews lived in the ghetto until 1943. Some worked in their own workshops, but the majority were employed outside in German war industries.

When, in 1943, Himmler decreed that the Jews still living in ghettoes in the *Reichskommissariat Ostland* should be brought together in concentration camps, he specified with respect to Latvia:

> As of August 1, 1943, I forbid bringing Jews out of the concentration camps to work. A concentration camp is to be set up near Riga, to which all of the clothing and equipment production sites that the *Wehrmacht* has outside are to be moved. All private companies are to be shut down. The unnecessary members of the Jewish ghetto are to be evacuated to the east.

A concentration camp was subsequently set up in Kaiserwald, a residential suburb of Riga, in which, in addition to German Jews,[51] Hungarian and Polish Jews from the Litzmannstadt ghetto were also concentrated.[52] While the "unnecessary members"—meaning those unable to work—including children under the age of fifteen, were deported "to the east," meaning to Auschwitz–Birkenau, the Riga ghetto was liquidated. The remaining inhabitants able to work were sent to the Riga–Kaiserwald concentration camp.

In May 1944, there were 11,878 Jewish prisoners in the main camp and its subcamps. The 6,182 men and 5,696 women produced mainly electrical equipment for AEG.

With the approach of the Red Army, evacuation of the inmates to the Stutthof concentration camp began in September 1944. Once again many Jews, mainly those unable to walk, were shot. The Red Army reached the Riga–Kaiserwald concentration camp on October 13, 1944.

Estonia

In the course of "Operation Barbarossa," on August 28, 1941, the *Wehrmacht* occupied Tallinn. In the 1930s, the overwhelming majority of the country's roughly 4,000 Jews lived in the Estonian capital. About 70% of the Jewish population fled to Finland or Sweden during the Soviet (1940–41) and then German occupations. The Soviets had deported another roughly 350 Estonian Jews to Siberia, leaving only about 1,000 under German control. They were subsequently forced to wear the Jewish star and disclose their possessions, which were then forfeited.

With the arrival in Estonia of *Einsatzgruppe A*, the majority of Jewish men over sixteen capable of military service were shot. *SS-Brigadeführer* Stahlecker, the commander of *Einsatzgruppe A*, informed his superiors on January 31, 1942, that, after the shooting of 963 persons, Estonia was "Jew free."

After Heinrich Himmler ordered on June 21, 1943, that all remaining ghettoes in the Baltic States were to be liquidated, the Vaivara concentration camp was established on September 19, 1943. Initially designated a reception and transit camp, the majority of the Jews able to work worked in the oil-shale extraction facilities of Baltöl (Baltic Oil).

Altogether about 20,000 Jews from the Riga, Kaunas, and Vilnius ghettoes and from Hungary and Theresienstadt were sent to Vaivara. The number of inmates reached its peak, 9,207 persons, in November 1944. While several subcamps were liberated by the Soviets, in September 1944, members of the security police and the SD carried out mass executions in the Lagedi and Klooga camps. The remaining inmates able to work were transported by ship to the Stutthof concentration camp.

Ukraine

In the course of "Operation Barbarossa," the *Wehrmacht* occupied all of the Ukraine by autumn 1941. The Reichskommissariat Ukraine, which encompassed about two-thirds of the country, was formed on September 1, 1941. The rest was under the commander of the rear army group area of Army Group South. During discussions on the final solution of the Jewish problem at Berlin–Wannsee in January 1942, it was estimated that 2,994,684 Jews lived or had lived in the Ukraine before the arrival of the Germans. As one can assume that almost 300,000 of them were serving in the Red Army and that the Soviets relatively soon evacuated large parts of the Jewish population—those able to work—to the east,[53] the total Jewish population that potentially fell under German mastery may have been 1.7 million.

This number diminished when on August 1, 1941, the Western Ukraine with about 450,000 Jews was incorporated into the *Generalgouvernement* as the Galicia District and Bukovina, Bessarabia, and Transnistria with about 250,000 Jews were occupied by Rumania. Of the remaining approximately one million Jews, in the end probably about 650,000 were in the *Reichskommissariat Ukraine* and were at the mercy of mainly *Einsatzgruppe C*. Immediately after the Jews were rounded up, it began liquidating most of the male Jews. This was followed by the shootings mainly of elements of the Jewish population unable to work (the old, sick, women, and children).

After German troops occupied Zhitomir in July 1941, the roughly 10,000 Jews remaining there were liquidated by September 1941.[54] Also in July 1941 the Germans took Pinsk. *SS-Kavallerie-Regiment 2* moved into the city in early August, and from the fifth to the ninth, shot the roughly 9,000 Jewish men who had been rounded up. On May 1, 1942, the surviving women and children were placed in a ghetto, which at times held up to 20,000 persons. The ghetto was liquidated on October 29–30, 1942 and the remaining approximately 16,200 Jews were shot inside the ghetto or outside the city.

In Vinnitsa, which had also been taken by the *Wehrmacht* in the summer of 1941, there were mass shootings of probably 10,000 Jews in September–October. A second "action" followed in April 1942, in which about 5,000 persons unable to work were murdered. The remaining men were separated in a work camp used to lay track. This camp existed until April 1944. It is likely that these Jewish workers were shot when the camp was liquidated.

One of the most famous mass murders took place in Babi Yar ravine near Kiev on September 29–30, 1941. On October 10, 1941, *Einsatzgruppen* incident report USSR No. 106 described it as an action desired by the Ukrainian population. An attack on the Hotel Continental on September 24, 1941, had caused a fire that resulted in many of the wooden houses in the area catching fire. A total of about 25,000 Ukrainians were supposedly left homeless:

> The population was extremely infuriated against the Jews, on the one hand because of their preferential economical status under Soviet rule and their service to the NKVD as informers and agents, and on the other the bombing and resulting fire. It could also be proved that the Jews had participated in arson. The population expected adequate reprisals from the Germans. For this purpose, in agreement with the city military command, all the Jews of Kiev were ordered to appear at a certain place on Monday, September 29, by six o'clock. This order was publicized by posters all over the town by members of the newly organized Ukrainian militia. At the same time, oral information was passed that all the Jews of Kiev would be moved to another place.

> In cooperation with group headquarters and two detachments of Police Regiment South, *Sonderkommando 4a* executed 33,771 Jews on September 29 and 30. Gold and valuables, linen, and clothing were secured. Part of it was given to the NSV (*National–Sozialistische Versorgung* = Nazi Welfare) for the ethnic Germans, and part to the appointed city administration for distribution among the needy population. The action was carried out smoothly and no incidents occurred. The population agreed with the plan to move the Jews to another place. That they were actually liquidated has hardly been made known. However, according to the experience gained so far, this would not meet with any opposition. The army has also approved the measures taken. The Jews that have not yet been caught or who return will be treated accordingly.

As was so often the case, attacks provided welcome justification to carry out reprisals against the Jewish population. As this was an internal report for the Reich Security Main Office, the author must not have exercised any euphemism, therefore the question arises whether he actually believed what he wrote.

On October 13, 1941, approximately 11,000 elderly Jews and children were shot in Dnepropetrovsk. On October 24, German troops took Kharkov. The Jews found there were immediately registered and in mid-December were concentrated in a tractor factory located outside the city. After the thaw, there began the systematic shooting in groups of 200 to 300 people.

While *Einsatzgruppe C* was deployed mainly in the *Reichskommissariat Ukraine*, *Einsatzgruppe D* followed the *11. Armee* and saw action in the Crimea. One especially extensive shooting action took place in the area of Simferopol, which was taken on November 1, 1941. The local Jewish population was initially registered and forced to wear identifying armbands, then from December 9–13, approximately 12,000 Jews were liquidated. Feodosiya was taken on November 3, 1941, and the Jewish population, 3,248 persons strong, was first registered and then, on December 1, concentrated in a ghetto. About 2,500 of them were shot there on December 4.

Additional large and small actions followed, in which *Einsatzgruppe D* alone shot a total of 17,645 Jews, 2,503 Krymchaks,[55] 824 gypsies, and 212 communists were shot. On April 8, 1942,

Einsatzgruppe D reported the unbelievable number of 91,679 Jews liquidated. In its reports *Einsatzgruppe C* claimed to have shot 95,165 people. According to the so-called Korherr Report, a total of 633,300 Jews were "evacuated" from the USSR by December 31, 1942. Deducting the official "evacuation numbers" from the Baltic States and White Russia, this meant about 400,000 victims from the Ukraine by the end of the year 1942.[56] A further approximately 50,000 people probably died in 1943–44 in the "liquidation" of the remaining ghettoes and labor camps, thus the Jewish population of the Ukraine probably lost about 450,000 killed.

White Russia

White Russia was occupied by the *Wehrmacht* by the end of August 1941. The security police and the SD assumed an original Jewish population of about 300,000 persons,[57] of which more than one third was believed to have fled. It was thus speculated that approximately 170,000 Jews were under German control there from the summer of 1941. As in the Baltic States, nationalist groups carried out pogroms after the withdrawal of Soviet troops and marked Jewish houses. More extensive measures followed by the German side: the Jews were no longer permitted to change their place of residence, from September 1941, had to wear a Jewish star and were required to work. The first mass executions began at the same time as the Jewish population was accused of collaborating with communists and partisans.

The White Russian capital of Minsk was taken by German forces on June 28, 1941, and immediately the authorities began concentrating the approximately 60,000 Jews living there in a marked-off area of the city. About 5,000 Jewish men were shot there on August 14, 26, and 31. A further approximately 12,000 Jews were liquidated on November 7 and 20, 1941, to make "room" for upcoming deportations from the German Reich. Between November 11 and December 5, 1941, about 7,000 Jews from Hamburg, Dusseldorf, Frankfurt am Main, Berlin, Brünn, Bremen, and Vienna arrived in Minsk. So-called "ghetto actions," in which several thousand Jews, mainly those unable to work, were shot were carried out on March 2, and 31, on April 3, 15, and 23, and once in May 1942. Gas vans were first used in an action on July 28–29, 1942. Afterwards there were still about 2,600 German and 6,500 White Russian Jews living in the ghetto. They too were all killed by the liquidation of the Jewish residential district in Minsk on October 21, 1943. Approximately 300 men used for cleaning and sorting duties were subsequently sent to the Lublin concentration camp.

On January 25, 1942, Gerhard Erren (March 4, 1901 – unknown), the regional commissioner of Slonim, wrote a representative and expressive report about his previous activities:

> Upon my arrival here there were about 25,000 Jews in the Slonim area, 16,000 in the actual town itself, making up over two-thirds of the total population of the town. It was not possible to set up a ghetto as neither barbed wire nor guard manpower was available. I thus immediately began preparations for a large-scale action. First of all property was expropriated and all the German official buildings, including the Wehrmacht quarters, were equipped with the furniture and equipment that had been made available … the Jews were then registered accurately according to number, age and profession and all craftsmen and workers with qualifications were singled out and given passes and separate accommodation to distinguish them from the other Jews. The action carried out by the SD on November 13, rid me of unnecessary mouths to feed. The some 7,000 Jews now present in the town of Slonim have all been allocated jobs. They are working willingly because of the constant fear of death. Early next year they will be rigorously checked and sorted for a further reduction.

Liquidation of the ghetto in Slonim began on June 29, 1942, and it encountered armed but ultimately ineffective Jewish resistance. Several had managed to come into possession of arms and ammunition while employed to overhaul captured weapons. Only a small part was left alive for cleaning and sorting work. In October 1942, regional commissioner Gerhard Erren reported: "I am glad to see the 25,000 Jews originally present in the region reduced to 500."

Reserve-Polizei-Bataillon 1 was employed in numerous executions of White Russian Jews. For example, on October 14, 1941, it shot roughly 1,300 Jews in Smilovichi and approximately 1,000 Jewish persons in Koidanov on October 21, 1941. The liquidation of the 3,400 Jews in Slutsk followed on October 27–28, 1941. This action moved regional commissioner of Slutsk, Heinrich Karl, to report to his superior Hinrich Lohse (September 2, 1896 – February 25, 1964), *Reichskommissar für das Ostland*:

> As far as the execution of the action is concerned, to my deepest regret I must point out that the latter bordered on sadism. The town itself offered a picture of horror during the action. With indescribable brutality on the part of both the German police officers and particularly the Lithuanian partisans,[58] the Jewish people, but also among them White Ruthenians, were taken out of their dwellings and herded together. Everywhere in the town shots were to be heard and in different streets the corpses of shot Jews accumulated. The White Ruthenians were in greatest distress to free themselves from the encirclement. Regardless of the fact that the Jewish people, among whom were also tradesmen, were mistreated in a terribly barbarous way before the eyes of the White Ruthenian people, the White Ruthenians themselves were also worked over with rubber truncheons and rifle butts. There was no question of an action against the Jews any more, rather it looked like a revolution. I myself with all my officials have been in it without interruption all day long in order to save what could yet be saved. [...]
>
> I was not present at the shooting before the town. Therefore, I cannot make a statement on its brutality. But it should suffice, if I point out that persons shot have worked themselves out of their graves some time after they had been covered.

The description of the events has an even more dramatic effect when one considers that the only crime of which the Jewish population was guilty was being Jewish. There had obviously been no objective selection according to "racial features," as a result of which some of the White Ruthenian population was also rounded up.

On January 31, 1942, *SS-Brigadeführer* Stahlecker, commander of *Einsatzgruppe A*, advised 41,828 Jews had so far been shot in White Russia and that there were probably about 128,000 Jews still living. Further actions against these followed in early 1942, in which about 15,000 Jews died. In February 1942, for example, the anti-partisan operation "Swamp Fever" was carried out, in which about 8,350 Jews were also shot in the area northeast of Minsk.

On July 31, 1942, Wilhelm Kube (November 13, 1887 – September 22, 1943), the commissioner general for White Ruthenia, submitted a report to the *Reichskommissar für das Ostland* concerning the "Jew actions" in his area carried out since mid-May 1942, and yet to be carried out:

> After in-depth discussions with *SS-Brigadeführer* Zenner and *SS-Obersturmbannführer* Dr. jur. Strauch, the very capable leader of the SD, we have liquidated around 55,000 Jews in White Ruthenia in the last ten weeks. Jewry has been completely eradicated in the countryside around Minsk. 16,000 Jews have been liquidated in the predominantly Polish area of Lida and 8,000 in Slonim. As the result of an encroachment by the rear army area, to which a report has already been sent, our preparations for the liquidation of the Jews in the Glebokie area have been disrupted. Without contacting me, the rear army area liquidated 10,000 Jews, whose systematic eradication we had already planned. In Minsk city, approximately 10,000 Jews were liquidated on the 28th and 29th of July.

6,500 of these were Russian Jews—mainly elderly, women and children—the rest consisted of Jews unable to work, most of whom had been sent to Minsk from Vienna, Brünn, Bremen and Berlin in November of the previous year by order of the Führer. [...] The Slutsk area has also been relieved of several thousand Jews. The same is true of Novogrodek and Vileyka. Radical measures are imminent for Baranovichi and Hanzevichi. There are still about 10,000 Jews still living in the city of Baranovichi alone, of whom 9,000 Jews will be liquidated next month. [...] There are 2,600 German Jews still in Minsk city. As well, there are 6,000 Jews and Jewesses still alive, who served as labor with the participating units during the action. Minsk will also see the greatest employment of Jews in the future, as the concentration of armaments companies and railroad tasks makes this necessary for the time being. In all other areas, the number of Jews coming for labor service has been set by the SD and by me at a maximum of 800, but possibly 500 if conditions permit. I and the SD would of course most like to see Jewry completely eliminated in the general district of White Ruthenia after the *Wehrmacht*'s economic claims are cancelled. For the time being the necessary claims by the *Wehrmacht*, which is the chief employer of Jewry, will be taken into consideration.

At the beginning of August 1942, therefore, there were probably fewer than 60,000 Jews[59]—some of them in hiding—in White Russia. Half of these were in the *Generalkommissariat Weißruthenien* and the other half in Army Group Center's rear army group area. Reduction of the Baranovichi ghetto followed in August 1942, and in December, it was liquidated after the murder of the last roughly 650 Jews. Of the approximately 170,000 Jews living in White Russian in the summer of 1941, probably more than 120,000 had been killed by the time the country was liberated by the Red Army.

Hungary

The Imperial–Royal Danube monarchy of Austro–Hungarian collapsed after the First World War and Hungary lost the majority of its territory. The revolutionary, unsettled situation in the country finally consolidated itself when the National Assembly named Admiral Miklós Horthy (June 18, 1868 – February 9, 1957) regent in place of the king.

As in many countries, there was also a latent anti-Semitism in Hungary, as a result of which Admiral Horthy issued a restrictive decree in September 1920.[60] Others followed, most out of touch with reality to a certain degree, for example a law which empowered the government to make preparations for "the emigration of the Jews." Had these plans been carried out, the economy and health system in Hungary would have completely broken down.

In terms of foreign policy the country, like Germany, tried to recover at least parts of the territory lost after the First World War. At the beginning of November 1938, it recovered areas in southern Slovakia with a Hungarian majority and in the western Carpathian Ukraine of Czechoslovakia. This did nothing to improve the "Jew problem." 67,000 Jews lived in these areas alone and another roughly 78,000 Jews came under Hungarian control after Hungarian troops occupied further parts of the Carpathian Ukraine in March 1939. On August 30, 1940, Hungary received northern Transylvania from Rumania, with the approximately 164,000 Jews living there. With these, and the thousands of Jews who had immigrated from Germany, Austria, the former Czech territories and Poland until 1940, according to a census there was a total of about 825,000 Jews living in Hungary in 1941. Thus, the country, which joined the Tripartite Pact on November 20, 1940, had the greatest number of Jews of any of the alliance partners.

When the Russian Campaign began in the summer of 1941, the Hungarian government saw an opportunity to rid itself of the so-called "*Ostjuden*" in particular. All Jewish persons without Hungarian citizenship were initially deported to Kőrösmező (approximately sixty kilometers southwest of Kolomyja) and from there to Kolomyja in southern Galicia. In this way about 18,000 Jews from Hungary were assembled in the Kamenets–Podolsk area by the end of August 1941. As this was based on a solely Hungarian initiative, which had not been discussed with its German ally, Military Administration Headquarters 183, for example, demanded that the Jews be sent back to Hungary, in part because of food shortages. When Hungary refused, *SS-Obergruppenführer* Friedrich Jeckeln (February 2, 1895 – February 3, 1946), Senior SS and Police Commander Russia South, took the pragmatic decision to liquidate the people in Kamenets–Podolsk. Hungary had thus evaded this problem. It is likely that there were many Jewish émigrés from Germany among the deportees, and the Hungarian government fundamentally also felt no responsibility for them.

When news of these mass shootings reached Hungary, however, Prime Minister László Bárdossy (December 10, 1890 – January 10, 1946) was forced to resign after numerous protests. The new government under the more centrist Prime Minister Miklós Kállay (January 23, 1887 – January 14, 1967) was installed on March 10, 1942. While in April 1942, Kállay announced the resettlement of the remaining Jews—at the same time as he authorized ethnic Germans to join the *Waffen-SS*—he did state that it could not be carried out until after the end of the war.

At the beginning of 1943, Hitler demanded that Hungary finally take part in an active phase in the solution of the "Jewish problem." Admiral von Horthy replied by asking what he was supposed to do with the Jews after he had more or less deprived them of all possibilities of living—he couldn't kill them! As there was already little enthusiasm for war in Hungary in 1941, and a growing desire to get out of the country's alliance with Germany, Prime Minister Kállay refused to carry out the requested actions against the Jewish population. They would also have been extremely counterproductive to a rapprochement with the western allies.

In order to prevent Hungary from leaving the alliance, Hitler finally ordered the occupation of the country. Units of the *Wehrmacht* and *Waffen-SS*, along with the security police and the SD, entered Hungary on March 19, 1944. Three days later, under German pressure, a new government was formed under Prime Minister Döme Sztójay (January 5, 1883 – August 22, 1946). On March 31, 1944, it ordered the wearing of the Jewish star. In mid-1944, there followed a German–Hungarian agreement, according to which 100,000 Jews able to work would be sent to Germany to construct armaments factories. At the end of April 1944, this plan was modified under the direction of *SS-Sturmbannführer* Adolf Eichmann and preparations were made to deport the entire Jewish population to concentration camps.

The transport of Jews to Auschwitz began on May 15, 1944. initially in the northeast of Hungary. According to *SS-Brigadeführer* Edmund Veesenmayer (November 12, 1904 – December 24, 1977), "Representative of the Greater German Reich in Hungary," a total of 437,402 Jews had been deported by July 9, 1944. While the Hungarian Jews able to work were used in the armaments industry, the elderly and women with children were probably murdered soon after their arrival at Auschwitz–Birkenau.

After reports about the terrible fate of the Hungarian Jews reached neutral and western countries in June 1944, on July 8, 1944, Reich Administrator von Horthy ordered a halt to the deportations. On August 29, 1944, he also asked Lieutenant-General Géza Lakatos, former commander-in-chief of the Hungarian 1st Army, to form a new government as prime minister. His efforts to reach a ceasefire with the western allies failed. When on October 15, 1944, Admiral von Horthy broadcast that he had asked for a ceasefire for Hungary, Ferenc Szálasi (January 6, 1897 – March 12, 1946), the fascist leader of the Arrow Across Party took over the affairs of government with German support.

SS-Sturmbannführer Adolf Eichmann returned to Budapest on October 17, 1944 to organize the deportation of the remaining approximately 220,000 Jews in the city. In November 1944, about 85,000 of them who were more or less fit for work were ordered to build the so-called southeast wall in Ostmark. The rest were surrounded in Budapest by the Red Army along with the German and Hungarian troops in the city.

Of the approximately 825,000 Jews registered in Hungary in 1941, more than half a million were deported from the country. For most of them this probably meant death in the gas chambers of Auschwitz–Birkenau.

7. Main Office SS Court (*Hauptamt SS-Gericht*)

In autumn 1932, Himmler tasked *SS-Standartenführer* Paul Scharfe (September 6, 1876 – July 29, 1942) with the creation of an SS jurisdiction as supreme disciplinary office within the SS. Initially under the *SS-Oberstab* as Department III, an SS Court Office (*SS-Gerichtsamt*) was established in the *SS-Hauptamt* when the *SS-Reichsführung* was reorganized in January 1935. In the summer of 1935, the SS Court Office was released from the *SS-Hauptamt* and was established in Munich as an independent office, SS Court, for all SS legal matters. Under *SS-Brigadeführer* Paul Scharfe it was organized as follows:

Main Department I

Department Ia	Disciplinary and complaint cases as well as matters of honor in the area of Senior Districts South and Main and appeals against decisions by the SS Court from the area of Department Ib.
Department Ib	Disciplinary and complaint cases as well as matters of honor in the area of Senior Districts Elbe and Southeast and appeals against decisions by the SS Court from the area of Department Ia.

Main Department II

Department IIa	Disciplinary and complaint cases as well as matters of honor in the area of Senior Districts Southwest and Rhine and appeals against decisions by the SS Court from the area of Department IIb.
Department IIb	Disciplinary and complaint cases as well as matters of honor in the area of Senior Districts West and Northwest and appeals against decisions by the SS Court from the area of Department IIa.

Main Department III

Department IIIa	Disciplinary and complaint cases as well as matters of honor in the area of Senior Districts North and Northeast and appeals against decisions by the SS Court from the area of Department IIIb.
Department IIIb	Disciplinary and complaint cases as well as matters of honor in the area of Senior Districts East and Center and appeals against decisions by the SS Court from the area of Department IIIa.

In autumn 1936, a main department was formed, which was supposed to pave the way for an internal military jurisdiction for the armed SS units. While this had so far been tied to the *Wehrmacht*'s military penal code, in May 1938, the justice minister gave his approval for the introduction of a special SS criminal jurisdiction. At a meeting of *Gruppenführer* in Berlin from January 23–25, 1939, *SS-Brigadeführer* Scharfe explained the introduction of sovereign SS jurisdictions as follows:

The SS man of course takes a special place compared to the simple party comrade, especially because he has to guard the movement and its leader, if necessary by giving his life. This special position [...] of course results in special treatment[61] of the SS man.

In judging cases, the rules given by the *Reichsführer-SS* were the only deciding factor and these were based on National–Socialist and military principles. The roles of the Main Office SS Court were documented by *SS-Hauptsturmführer* Gunter d'Alquen's publication mentioned earlier in the text:

> The SS Court, which is directly subordinate to the *Reichsführer-SS*, is the *Schutzstaffel's* supreme authority in all questions of disciplinary and honor court jurisdictions. Its primary activity, therefore, is handling disciplinary matters, in cases of a minor nature as an appeal body.
>
> Furthermore, the SS Court is alone responsible for handling pardons, both disciplinary and criminal in nature. As the supreme office of the SS disciplinary penal procedure, the SS Court is also a liaison office to all offices of the party and Reich with a professional relationship with its field of activity.
>
> A separate criminal jurisdiction is being introduced for the members of the *SS-Verfügungstruppen*, the *SS-Totenkopfverbände*, the SS main office security service and for the members of the *Allgemeine-SS* in the main offices responsible for these units.

With the introduction of an independent criminal jurisdiction for the SS and the police, on June 1, 1939, the office was elevated to the independent Main Office SS Court. Under *SS-Gruppenführer* Paul Scharfe it was organized into the SS Legal Department and the SS Disciplinary Office. In his capacity as supreme legal authority, the *Reichsführer-SS* reserved to himself final judgment on all court decisions. From April 18, 1940, he received the same powers as the commanders in chief of the three branches of the armed services. Not only judgments against officers of the SS and police required his ruling, but also all petitions for clemency, especially in death sentences.

As part of the process of an independent criminal jurisdiction, an SS and police prison camp was established at Dachau in May 1940. Initially it was still assigned to the SS Legal Department. Members of the SS and police sentenced to prison sentences were held in Section "G" and those to prison sentences with hard labor in Section "Z." The purpose of a separate prison camp for the SS and police was the desire to achieve educational ideals. At the end of March 1941, the clemency process and penal system were combined in one office. The Main Office SS Court was now organized into:

Office I...Law and administration of justice
Office II.........Organization, personnel and administration, disciplinary, and complaint
         systems
Office III.............................Clemency process, execution of sentence, and penal system

Setting up of the SS and Police Prison Camp at Danzig–Matzkau began in March 1941. All of those sentenced to prison would serve their sentences there, while those given hard labor were held at Dachau.

On August 15, 1942, *SS-Gruppenführer* Franz Breithaupt (December 8, 1880 – April 29, 1945) succeeded *SS-Obergruppenführer* Paul Scharfe, who died on July 29, 1942, as head of the Main Office SS Court.

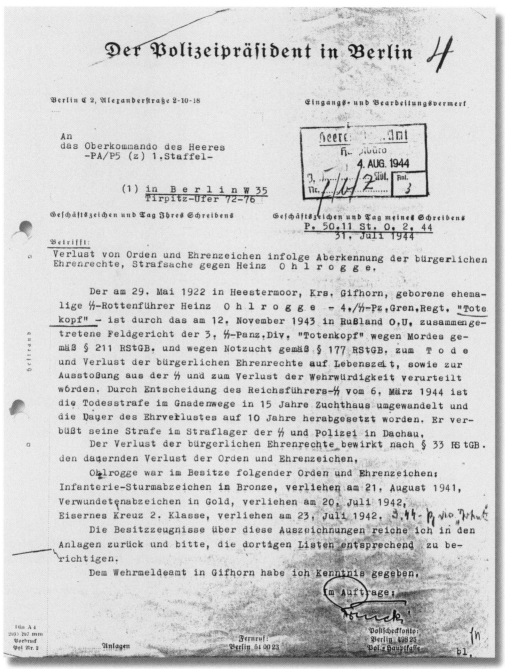

Der Polizeipräsident in Berlin 4

Berlin C 2, Alexanderstraße 2-10-18

Eingangs- und Bearbeitungsvermerk

An
das Oberkommando des Heeres
-PA/P5 (z) 1.Staffel-

(1) in Berlin W 35
Tirpitz-Ufer 72-76

Geschäftszeichen und Tag Ihres Schreibens

Geschäftszeichen und Tag meines Schreibens
P. 50.11 St. O. 2. 44
31. Juli 1944

Betrifft:

Verlust von Orden und Ehrenzeichen infolge Aberkennung der bürgerlichen
Ehrenrechte, Strafsache gegen Heinz Ohlrogge.

Der am 29. Mai 1922 in Heestermoor, Krs. Gifhorn, geborene ehema-
lige SS-Rottenführer Heinz Ohlrogge - 4./SS-Pz.Gren.Regt. "Tote
kopf" - ist durch das am 12. November 1943 in Rußland O.U. zusammengetretene Feldgericht der 3. SS-Panz.Div. "Totenkopf" wegen Mordes gemäß § 211 RStGB. und wegen Notzucht gemäß § 177 RStGB. zum Tode
und Verlust der bürgerlichen Ehrenrechte auf Lebenszeit, sowie zur
Ausstoßung aus der SS und zum Verlust der Wehrwürdigkeit verurteilt
worden. Durch Entscheidung des Reichsführers-SS vom 6. März 1944 ist
die Todesstrafe im Gnadenwege in 15 Jahre Zuchthaus umgewandelt und
die Dauer des Ehrverlustes auf 10 Jahre herabgesetzt worden. Er ver-
büßt seine Strafe im Straflager der SS und Polizei in Dachau.

Der Verlust der bürgerlichen Ehrenrechte bewirkt nach § 33 RStGB.
den dauernden Verlust der Orden und Ehrenzeichen.

Ohlrogge war im Besitze folgender Orden und Ehrenzeichen:
Infanterie-Sturmabzeichen in Bronze, verliehen am 21. August 1941,
Verwundetenabzeichen in Gold, verliehen am 20. Juli 1942,
Eisernes Kreuz 2. Klasse, verliehen am 23. Juli 1942.

Die Besitzzeugnisse über diese Auszeichnungen reiche ich in den
Anlagen zurück und bitte, die dortigen Listen entsprechend zu be-
richtigen.

Dem Wehrmeldeamt in Gifhorn habe ich Kenntnis gegeben.

Im Auftrage:

Din A 4
210 × 297 mm
Vordruck
Pol Nr. 2

Anlagen

Fernruf:
Berlin 51 00 23

Postscheckkonto:
Berlin 498 25
Pol. Hauptkasse

While serving with the *3. SS-Panzer-Division "Totenkopf"* in Russia, Heinz Ohlrogge raped and then murdered a woman. The death sentence handed down by the division court was, however, revised by Himmler
in his capacity as supreme authority of the SS and Police legal jurisdiction. Sentenced to prison, Ohlrogge was sent to the SS and Police punishment camp in Dachau. The above letter specifies that he was to
lose all of his decorations and awards, which are listed.

For Himmler, installation as commander of the Replacement Army and chief of Army Equipment just under two years later meant that he had command and judicial power over the members of the replacement army. Thus he now also had the powers of a disciplinary superior and judge over elements of the *Wehrmacht*, like those granted the commander in chief of the army.

This did not explicitly affect the Main Office SS Court, however the enormous growth of the *Waffen-SS* from eight divisions when *SS-Gruppenführer* Breithaupt took over the office to thirty-eight divisions at the end of the war did result in tremendous expansion. From January 30, 1945, until the end of the war, the main office was organized as follows:

Office I .... Legal Affairs and Personnel
I a .... Criminal law and criminal proceedings
I b .... Civil law, voluntary jurisdiction, and legal support
I c .... Court organization and judicial personal data
I d .... Technical personnel administration, non-judicial personal data, social care
I e .... Ongoing criminal matters and development of the law
I f .... Notarial recordings and offices
I g .... Coordination and control of preliminary proceedings[62]
SS and Police Special Court[63]
Office II .... Disciplinary and Complaint Systems
Office III .... Clemency Process, Execution of Sentence and Penal System
III a .... Right of Pardon and Rehabilitation
III b .... Execution of Sentence and Penal System
Office IV .... Legal Renewal and Legal Training
IV a .... Legal renewal – Legislative Preparatory Work
IV b .... Legal Support – Individual Cases
IV c .... Legal Training and Evaluation
IV d .... Legal Research
Supreme SS and Police Court
SS Judge's Office with the *Reichsführer-SS*

8. Main Office SS Personnel

When an operational headquarters (*Führungsstab*) for the SS was established in 1931, a Department II was formed which originally handled the personnel matters of all leaders (officers), from *SS-Untersturmführer* up to and including *SS-Sturmhauptführer*—from 1935, *SS-Hauptsturmführer*. Beginning in 1934, the department had printed "Seniority Lists of the *Schutzstaffel* of the NSDAP," in which at first all officers, but later only from *SS-Hauptsturmführer* upwards, were entered.

SS-Hauptsturmführer Walter Schmitt (January 13, 1879 – September 18, 1945) worked as personnel officer from March 1, 1934, and when the Personnel Office was formed he became office head with the rank of *SS-Oberführer*. As of January 30, 1945 the office was part of the *SS-Hauptamt*'s Main Department B. On January 30, Schmitt, by then an *SS-Brigadeführer*, became head of the SS Personnel Office, and one year later as an *SS-Gruppenführer* took over the Inspectorate of SS Officer Schools, and the SS Leaders' School at Munich-Dachau. Its function was described as follows in Gunter d'Alquen's contemporary publication:

The *SS-Personalkanzlei* is the office of the head of personnel of the SS. It handles all personnel matters of the officer corps of the entire *Schutzstaffel*. [...] It is responsible for the further training of the young officers coming from these schools. The *Allgemeine-SS* leaders' school in Munich–Dachau is also attached to the head of personnel.

In principle any member of the SS could apply for the officer career path, which also allowed him to select a special career, for example the security service (SD), administration service, service with the SS Main Office Race and Settlement or the *Ordnungspolizei*. After completing an entrance examination at an SS officers' school the SS officer candidate was made an *SS-Junker* (= *SS-Unterscharführer*). After passing an intermediate examination he was promoted to *SS-Standartenjunker* and after successfully completing the training course to *SS-Standartenober-junker*. Promotion to *SS-Untersturmführer* was granted by the *Reichsführer-SS* on the recommendation of the regimental commander. Although the SS always stressed in its recruiting that the officer path was open to anyone regardless of education, the standards of the SS officers' schools were so high that most applicants who had only attended elementary school failed to pass the intermediate examinations.

In June 1939, Department II (Personnel Office) of the *SS-Hauptamt* became an independent main office. At first *SS-Gruppenführer* Schmitt remained in command. He was thus still responsible for officer training until autumn 1940.[64] In November 1940, this responsibility was explicitly passed to the newly-created Office of Officer Training in the *SS-Führungshauptamt*. From November 1940, the Main Office SS Personnel was only responsible for already-trained officers and Himmler clearly defined its tasks with respect to the *SS-Führungshauptamt*:

1. Within its tasks for the entire SS, the Main Office Personnel is solely responsible for;
   a. all promotions and appointments to officer ranks,
   b. all transfers (transfer detachments) of SS officers,
   c. confirmation of all , […]
3. All applications for promotions to officer ranks, appointments, transfers and all are to directed to the Main Office SS Personnel by way of the responsible main offices.

When in 1939–40, many officers from the *Allgemeine-SS* and *SS-Totenkopf* units were transferred to the *Waffen-SS*, it became apparent that most lacked any strategic training and as a result were often completely overtaxed. One telling example is the failure of the officer corps of *SS-Gebirgsdivision* "Nord," which came from the *SS-Totenkopf* units, before Salla in the summer of 1941. After this, officers from the *Allgemeine-SS* serving in the *Waffen-SS* would be assessed by their company commanders and after about a year of service would be advised whether or not he thought they were suitable to attend an officers' school. Concerning this, former *SS-Sturmbannführer* Schmeißer recalled:

Often there were also requests from home to send men to officers' school because they were "old fighters" or something else. But they had no aptitude for school!

As a result of Schmitt's illness, on July 30, 1942, *SS-Brigadeführer* Maximilian von Herff (April 17, 1893 – September 6, 1945) was tasked "for the duration of the illness of *SS-Obergruppenführer* Walter Schmitt, head of the Main Office SS Personnel, […] with representing him and the management of business." Then on October 1, 1942, he was named new head of the Main Office SS Personnel. As a result of this promotion, until the end of the war Herff was responsible for a total of 22,000 officers of the *Allgemeine-SS* and *Waffen-SS*.

As the war dragged on, additional officers were0 transferred to from the *Allgemeine-SS* to the *Waffen-SS*. In the case of Amon Göth, commander of the Plaszow concentration camp—made famous in the motion picture *Schindler's List*—on July 23, 1943 the Senior SS and Police Commander East sent the following request to the Main Office SS Personnel:

Request that *SS-Untersturmführer (F)* Amon Göth be promoted to *SS-Hauptsturmführer*, as Göth's position is contingent upon a higher ranking or his promotion to *SS-Hauptsturmführer*. Given the very extensive and responsible scope of functions, in which Göth must show outstanding results, his promotion to *SS-Hauptsturmführer* is desired for reasons of authority.

SS-Obergruppenführer Herff subsequently promoted Göth, initially to *SS-Hauptsturmführer der Allgemeine-SS* and finally, on June 9, 1944, accepted, "qualified officer with the rank of an *SS-Hauptsturmführer (F)* of the *Allgemeine-SS* Göth as *SS-Hauptsturmführer der Reserve in the Waffen-SS*."

9. Main Office Order Police (*Ordnungspolizei*)

While the Secret State Police and the criminal police were initially under the Main Office Security Police and later, with the SD, the Reich Security Main Office, the Main Office Order Police, newly created in June 1934, under the later *SS-Oberst-Gruppenführer* Kurt Daluege (September 15, 1897 – October 24, 1946), was responsible for the:

Schutzpolizei
Gendarmerie (military police)
Gemeindepolizei
Land- und Stadtwacht
Zollgrenzschutz (from 1937)
Feuerschutzpolizei (from 1938)
Luftschutzpolizei (from 1942)

The Main Office *Ordnungspolizei* combined comparable tasks of several main offices in itself and was organized as follows:

Commander of the *Ordnungspolizei*
Counsel attached to the Commander of the *Ordnungspolizei*
Main Office

Administration and Law Department
Office Group V.u.R. I
Office Group V.u.R. II
Office Group V.u.R. III

Command Office
Office Group Command I
    Group Leader Organization
    Group Leader I a
    Group Leader I b
    Group Leader Training
    Group Leader Sp.
    Group Leader WE
    Group Leader War History
Office Group Command II (Personnel Office)
    Group Leader P

Group Leader P (Supply)
Group Leader P (Disciplinary)
Group Leader P (Welfare)
Group Leader P (War Victims)
Office Group Command III (Medical Services)
    Group Leader Med. 1 and 2
    Group Leader Med. 3
    Group Leader Med. 4
    Group Leader Head of Medical Services
Colonial Police Office
Volunteer Firefighters Office
Technical Emergency Help
Economic Administration Office[65]
    Office Group W I
    Office Group W II
    Office Group W III
    Office Group W IV
Legal Department
    Office Group R I
    Office Group R II

Inspector Generals
    Inspector General of the Uniformed Police
    Inspector General of the Village Police and Uniformed Municipal Police
    Inspector General of Police Schools
    Inspector General of Factory Firefighting Services
    Inspector General of Firefighters
    Inspector General of Accommodation
    Inspector General of Medical Services

Inspectors
    Inspector of Ideological Education
    Inspector of the Dental Service
    Inspector of Water Police (Harbors, Rivers)
    Inspector of Armaments and Equipment

Commanders of Schools and Institutions
    Border Police School Fürstenberg
    Commander Technical SS and Police Academy
    Ordnungspolizei Officers' School Eberswalde
    Ordnungspolizei Officers' School Fürstenfeldbruck
    Ordnungspolizei Officers' School Oranienburg
    Police Officers' School Berlin–Köpenick
    Police Weapons School I
    Police School for Administration Officials (Linz)
    Police School for Automotive Technology (Woisen)
    Police School for Physical Education (Spandau)
    Police School for Riding and Driving (Bendsburg)
    Police School for Riding and Driving (Rathenow)
    Police School for Technology and Communication

Police School for Administration Officials (Munich–Haar)
Hose Cart School Stetting

On August 31, 1943, *SS-Obergruppenführer* Alfred Wünnenberg (July 20, 1891 – December 30, 1963) took over command of the Head Office *Ordnungspolizei* from *SS-Oberst-Gruppenführer* Daluege, who had fallen ill. When Hitler relieved Himmler of all his offices in the last days of the war, Wünnenberg was named Chief of German Police.

10. Main Office SS Economics and Administration

On July 15, 1932, Himmler ordered the *Reichsführung-SS* Departments I d (clothing, rations, quarters) and IV a (money management) merged to form the SS Administration Office. Main Department B was then incorporated within the *SS-Führungshauptamt* under the leadership of *SS-Oberführer* Gerhard Schneider (April 6, 1890 – unknown).

In the beginning, the financial resources for administering the SS were provided almost exclusively by the membership dues of SS members and supporting members, who were not in active service in the SS but supported it with monthly contributions. Not until the "Law to Secure the Unity of Party and State" was passed on December 1, 1933, did the SA, and thus the SS, for the first time receive state funds from the Reich budget.[66]

Charged with embezzlement on March 24, 1934, office head Gerhard Schneider was demoted to *SS-Mann* and immediately kicked out of the SS. He was succeeded by Oswald Pohl (June 30, 1892 – June 7, 1951), who held the position until the end of the war. Under him, in April 1939, the SS Administration Office was elevated into a main office "Economics and Administration," which processed all SS financial and economic matters. Oswald Pohl, who was promoted to *SS-Gruppenführer* in 1937, was also named head of the main office "Budget and Construction" in the Reich Ministry of the Interior and there simultaneously managed Office II (Structures).

The constant growth of the *Waffen-SS*, the establishment of commercial enterprises and the immense concentration camp system led to the founding of the Main Office SS Economics and Administration (WVHA) on February 1, 1942. This combined the two main offices previously led by Pohl "Economics and Administration" and "Budget and Construction," and the new main office was organized into the following office groups:

Office Group A (Finance, Law, and Administration) ....*SS-Brigadeführer* Fanslau
Office Group B (Supply, Administration, and Equipment) .... *SS-Gruppenführer* Lörner
Office Group C (Buildings and Works) ....*SS-Gruppenführer* Kammler
Office Group D (Concentration Camps)................................*SS-Gruppenführer* Glücks
Office Group W (Commercial Enterprises).........................*SS-Obergruppenführer* Pohl

Two of these five office groups achieved special significance and will therefore be described in greater detail.

Office Group D (Concentration Camps)

On July 4, 1934, Heinrich Himmler appointed *SS-Gruppenführer* Theodor Eicke (October 17, 1892 – February 26, 1943), commander of the Dachau concentration camp, inspector of all concentration camps and the SS guard units stationed there. Initially based in Upper Bavaria, on December 10, 1934, he moved into new offices in Berlin and was attached to the Office of

Secret State Police. While it undertook the interrogation and release of, for example, members of opposition groups, as the central administrative and command authority the Inspectorate of Concentration Camps had power of disposition over prisoners. This included regulations concerning prison conditions including the penal code. After the IKL was moved from Berlin to Oranienburg in August 1938, on November 18, 1939, *SS-Brigadeführer* Richard Glücks (April 22, 1889 – May 10, 1945) took over Eicke's inspectorate, Eicke having been placed in command of the *SS-Totenkopf-Division*.

A fundamental shift in the field of concentration camps took place in late 1941. While the original intention was to use them to imprison in a concentrated way all potentially threatening opponents of the regime, pragmatism now stepped to the forefront and a decision was made to use the umpteen thousand prisoners concentrated in small areas explicitly as cheap labor (including in the armaments industry). When the Main Office SS Economics and Administration was created, the existing concentration camps were incorporated as Office Group D. Effective March 3, 1942, *SS-Brigadeführer* Glücks, the former Inspector of Concentration Camps, was named head of the office group. It was organized as follows:

Office DI (Central Office)..................................*SS-Obersturmbannführer* Liebehenschel
DI/1: Prisoner Matters
DI/2: Communications, camp defense, and guard dogs
DI/3: Motor transport
DI/4: Weapons and equipment
DI/5: Training of personnel

Office DII (Prisoner Work Assignments)............................ *SS-Standartenführer* Maurer
DII/1: Prisoner assignments
DII/2: Prisoner training
DII/3: Statistics and settlement

Office DIII (Medical Services/Camp Hygiene) *SS-Standartenführer* Dr. Lolling
DIII/1: Medical and Dental Care for the SS
DIII/2: Medical and Dental Care for the Prisoners
DIII/3: Hygienic and Sanitary Measures in the Camps

Office DIV (Concentration Camp Administration) *SS-Sturmbannführer* Burger
DIV/1: Budget, cash, and pay
DIV/2: Rations
DIV/3: Clothing
DIV/4: Quarters
DIV/5: Legal, tax, and contract matters

Altogether, probably about 2.5 million prisoners passed through German concentration camps. To the SS they represented a potentially-enormous source of labor which grew in importance as the war went on. The workers could be provided to private companies for a fee or employed in SS-owned operations. There were many reasons for imprisonment. Prisoners from the German Reich were roughly divided into seven categories, which wore identifying colored cloth triangles on their prison uniforms and later also on their civilian clothing:

Red..political prisoners
Blue...emigrants
Green..criminals

Black .... anti-social
Purple .... Jehovah's Witnesses
Pink ....homosexuals
Red-Yellow ....Jews

Foreigners working in the German Reich were also sentenced to concentration camps for the slightest offense. Otherwise, most foreigners in the camps were there for opposing the government, probable or suspected partisan activity, or for being members of the Jewish faith. While relatively few Jews were imprisoned in concentration camps in Germany, they formed a large percentage of the inmates in the camps set up in Eastern Europe in 1943. According to a report by the SS-WVHA, in August 1944, there were 379,167 male and 145,119 female prisoners in the concentration camps.[67]

As a rule, living conditions in the concentration camps were catastrophic. Physical and psychological mistreatment followed inadequate medical care and nourishment. Names like *SS-Unterscharführer* Oswald Kaduk (August 26, 1906 – May 31, 1997), report leader (*Rapportführer*) at Auschwitz, and *SS-Rottenführer* Stefan Baretzki (March 24, 1919 – June 21, 1988), a block leader (*Blockführer*) at Auschwitz, stand for unbelievable mistreatments and murder in the concentration camps.

The moral and educational qualifications of the SS guards were usually limited, and not just among the lower ranks. Those of the officer corps were on average also quite low. In 1939, the commander of the SS Leaders' School at Munich–Dachau made the following assessment of the then forty-year-old *SS-Sturmbannführer* Albert Sauer, who later commanded concentration camps in Mauthausen, Riga, and Ravensbrück:

Comprehension: limited
Level of education: simple school and craftsman training, little discernable life knowledge
Written form: adequate, poor spelling and syntax.

The overall assessment read:

Unclear, consumed character, who with downright babbling priggishness always looks for mistakes in others and is unwilling to take himself in hand. As he has so far not understood the necessity of educating himself and getting the necessary knowledge, his results are below average in all areas of training and knowledge. With exaggerated self-importance he believed he had been poorly treated by his previous superiors and therefore had absolutely no interest in paying attention during the course. Even more pointed suggestions failed to reach him.

It should be borne in mind that this was a man who had already been promoted to *SS-Sturmbannführer* and would later command large concentration camps.

The Concentration Camps

On March 13, 1933, six weeks after the National–Socialists took power, Himmler set up the first prison camp for his Munich Political Police in a former gunpowder factory in Dachau. Initially controlled by uniformed police, on April 11, 1933, installed the political auxiliary police to guard the camp. The Dachau camp, which ultimately represented the first German concentration camp, had to a certain degree a role model function in design and prisoner treatment for the camps that followed. As with all the pother camps, its administrations were organized as follows:

I .... Commander's Office
II ....Political Department
III .... Camp for Protective Detention Command
IV .... Administration
V .... Camp Doctor
VI .... Ideological Education

The camp commander usually held the rank of *SS-Sturmbannführer* or *SS-Obersturmbannführer* and was responsible for the running of the concentration camp. The guards, organized in an *SS-Totenkopf-Sturmbann* with up to twelve companies, did not belong to the commander's office organizationally, but in case of emergency the commander had full authority over them. In charge of the commander's office was the adjutant, usually with the rank of *SS-Hauptsturmführer*. He watched over all correspondence and was responsible for personnel matters (promotions, transfers, etc.).

The political department was not subordinate to the SS-WVHA like the other departments, instead it was under the Reich Security Main Office. It maintained the so-called prisoner index, which contained all the information about those held in the camps (arrest warrants, assignment to the camp, sentences, transfers to other camps, discharges, and death sentences). The interrogation of prisoners was carried exactly the same here as it was, for example, for executions ordered by the RSHA.

The protective detention camp officer (usually an *SS-Hauptsturmführer*) was responsible for order in the camp (for example, quarters, hygiene and rations) and in particular for work assignments by the prisoners in work parties in and outside the camp. This also covered inventory of prisoners, investigations of violations against camp order, and the execution of disciplinary penalties given to prisoners. The right hand of the protective detention camp officer was the First Report Leader—usually with the rank of an *SS-Oberscharführer*—who was the connective link between the camp command and the camp and whose responsibilities included the daily strength report. Beneath the Report Leader was the Block Leader. These were SS non-commissioned officers, whose duties included maintaining order and cleanliness in the barracks. They were present at morning and evening roll calls and also fulfilled the function of the so-called detachment leader, who supervised work parties. They were in constant contact with the prisoners and were unfortunately synonymous with sadistic treatment. In the postwar trials they provided the bulk of the accused from the concentration camps.

The administration handled all administrative matters dealing with quarters, clothing, and feeding of prisoners as well as the SS members. Under the leader, who usually held the rank of an *SS-Hauptsturmführer*, were the workshops, kitchen, laundry, gardens, storage items, and the crematorium.

So that the commander's office could control the many thousands of prisoners, self-administrations were set up which were responsible for smooth-running processes. Regarding this, the camp senior was the most highly charged prisoner and was directly responsible to the camp commander.

Under the Report Leader was the prisoner orderly room, which controlled the entire inner administration (maintenance of prisoner index, assignment to residential blocks, roll call preparation, allocation of food, etc.). In every block there was the block senior, who was nominated by the camp senior and conformed by the camp leadership. They were directly under the block leaders.

Under the commander's office detachment leaders, the prisoner *Kapos* were in control of work parties. The *Kapos* had foremen at their side but did not work themselves and for a long time came from the category of so-called career criminals. They integrated themselves into the brutal system of the concentration camp and scarcely treated their fellow prisoners any better or were even more bullying than the SS members of the commander's office. When the bulk of the German *Kapos* were sent to the SS Special Regiment Dirlewanger to prove themselves, as new members of the *Waffen-SS* they were then "comrades" of their former guards. Pragmatic as Himmler was, in response to heavy casualties among the comrades he promoted people he had previously considered the "dregs of society" and gave them a chance to rehabilitate themselves in his *Waffen-SS*.

With the idea of integrating the system of German concentration camps into the German armaments industry, the number of camps including subcamps as well as the number of prisoners grew disproportionately. While about 53,000 men and women were imprisoned at the end of 1940, by April 1943, the number had risen to about 203,000 and on January 15, 1945, the total of prisoners in the remaining fifteen concentration camps with their countless subcamps was 714,044 prisoners, of which about 90% were German. The hygienic and nutritional conditions were catastrophic. The residents of German cities were already suffering terribly from food shortages, so of course it was much worse in the concentration camps. Altogether, there were eighteen official concentration camps, which will be described briefly.

The **Auschwitz Concentration Camp** was set up in Upper Silesia in May 1940, in a former military barracks, initially for the imprisonment of members of the political resistance. Himmler inspected the concentration camp in March 1941, and ordered that it be expanded to hold 30,000 prisoners. He also directed that a camp for 100,000 inmates be constructed in Birkenau and another in Monowitz for 10,000 prisoners. In October 1941, the Auschwitz–Birkenau camp was established on the site of the evacuated village of Brzezinka (Birkenau), about three kilometers from the original camp. It subsequently housed for the most part Soviet POWs and Jews. The prisoners able to work were used by about fifty outside detachments from the concentration camp. The largest and best known worked in the IG Farben Factory, which was built in Monowitz about seven kilometers from Auschwitz–Birkenau.

On December 1, 1942, 22,391 male and 8,232 female prisoners were registered in the Auschwitz concentration camp. Five months later, there were 17,037 prisoners in the main Auschwitz camp, 11,671 prisoners in Auschwitz–Birkenau, 3,301 prisoners at AZ-Monowitz, and another 2,046 prisoners in the various outside detachments. In the following seven months, the number of prisoners almost tripled; on December 4, 1943, there were 87,773 prisoners in the Auschwitz concentration camp, of which 68,790 were able to work, and of which 44,869 had also been used for work.

The enormous occupancy rate led the camp command to make contingency plans for a possible prisoner uprising (Case A or "*A-Fall*"). The head of the SS-WVHA gave Himmler a detailed description of the situation in Auschwitz on April 5, 1944:

The extent and high occupation rate of the Auschwitz concentration camp led me last October to suggest a three way division of the camp. After your approval it has been carried out as of November 10, 1943. Therefore there are now three concentration camps in Auschwitz.

As to the security measures taken for Case A, I report as follows:
Camp I including the massive camp for men with a present strength of approximately 16,000 inmates.

It is surrounded with a fence and by barbed wire which, as in all concentration camps, is electrically charged. Besides there are watch towers, on the tops of which machine-guns are mounted.

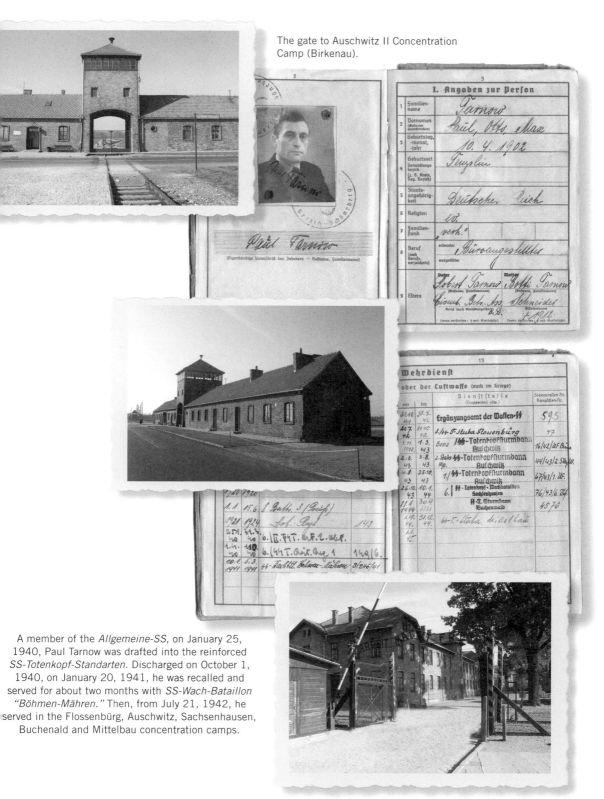

The gate to Auschwitz II Concentration Camp (Birkenau).

A member of the *Allgemeine-SS*, on January 25, 1940, Paul Tarnow was drafted into the reinforced *SS-Totenkopf-Standarten*. Discharged on October 1, 1940, on January 20, 1941, he was recalled and served for about two months with *SS-Wach-Bataillon "Böhmen-Mähren."* Then, from July 21, 1942, he served in the Flossenbürg, Auschwitz, Sachsenhausen, Buchenald and Mittelbau concentration camps.

Gate to the Auschwitz I Concentration Camp (main camp).

243

2.) Camp II is at a distance of about three kilometers from Camp I. It accommodates 15,000 male and 21,000 female inmates. Of a total of 36,000 inmates approximately 15,000 are unable to work. Camp II is also surrounded by an electrically-charged wire fence, there are also watch towers.

Camp III includes all subcamps attached to industrial establishments in Upper Silesia which, however, are located at considerable distances from each other. At present it consists of fourteen subcamps with a total number of approximately 15,000 male inmates. These labor camps are also surrounded by the usual wire fence and also have watch towers. The largest of these labor camps is in Auschwitz attached to the I.G. Farbenindustrie AG. It has at present 7,000 inmates.

[…] 2,300 SS men are available to guard the inmates of Camp I and II, including the staff of camp headquarters who are to be detailed to Case A. In addition there are 650 guards available for the subcamps of Camp III. *SS-Obergruppenführer* Schmauser will provide a company of police with about 130 men by the middle of this month. This company shall if necessary be used for additional security of Camp II. It will therefore be billeted in the close vicinity of this camp.

Apart from the direct security of Camp I and II by manned watch towers and by electrically chargeable wire fences, a line of bunkers has been constructed as an inner ring which will be manned by SS men. This line of bunkers is marked in red on the enclosed map.

In Case A, as a further security measure, the outer ring will be formed to be manned by the *Wehrmacht*. On the enclosed map this outer ring can be seen on the overlay indicating the field positions with the parts of the *Wehrmacht* earmarked for the operation. Inside the outer ring is also the labor camp at the I.G. Farbenindustrie AG with at present 7,000 inmates and the entire factory of the I.G. Farbenindustrie AG in which in addition to our inmates approximately 15,000 people are employed. Use of the *Wehrmacht* was decided upon a few weeks ago in Auschwitz by *SS-Obergruppenführer* Schmauser and the commanding general of the VIII Army Corps, *General der Kavallerie* von Koch-Erbach.

[…] The *Luftwaffe* units stationed in Auschwitz in the strength of 1,000 men are available provided the alert does not coincide with an air raid. These *Luftwaffe* units can, however, not absolutely be counted on. This has been taken into consideration in drafting the plan of operation.

Thus approximately 3,000 SS men were available to guard about 67,000 prisoners. Mathematically each guard faced about twenty-two inmates. The evacuation of the camp before the advancing Red Army began on January 17, 1945. The Soviets reached the area ten days later. By that time, the number of guards at Auschwitz Camps I and II stood at 2,474 men and fifty-six female auxiliaries, who guarded 15,325 male and 16,421 female prisoners. Auschwitz III concentration camp—sometimes also called Monowitz concentration camp—had 2,006 men and fifteen female auxiliaries guarding 33,037 male, and 2,044 female prisoners.

After the war, Auschwitz became a symbol of the mass murder of the Jewish population of Europe, as well as of Sinti and Roma. It is likely that more than a million people[68] lost their lives, especially in the main Auschwitz camp, but also in Auschwitz–Birkenau. Many were gassed with the pesticide Zyklon B, which was usually used to delouse the prisoners' clothing. The toxicity of Zyklon B to humans depended on its concentration in the air:

Weak concentrations	cause headaches, nausea, drowsiness, and vomiting
High concentrations	cause tachypnoea (rapid breathing and high breathing rate), then difficulty breathing, paralysis, unconsciousness, convulsions, and respiratory arrest

| 150 ppm | more than 30 to 60 minutes are life-threatening |
| 300 ppm | more than ten minutes are fatal. |

The first gassing experiments using Soviet prisoners of war were carried out in the basement of Block 11 of the main camp. Then, from autumn 1941 to December 1942, the mortuary of Crematorium I in Auschwitz was used as a gas chamber. With an area of just less than eighty square meters, up to approximately 750 people could be murdered simultaneously, which was equivalent to about ten persons per square meter.

After it was decided that the capacity of Crematorium I was insufficient for the expected transports of Jews, at Auschwitz–Birkenau work began to convert two farm houses so that mass gassings could be carried out there. So-called Bunker I had two gas chambers and accommodate a maximum of about 800 persons. It was first used in March 1942. So-called Bunker II had four chambers with a combined "capacity" of up to 1,200 persons and its use began in July 1942. *SS-Sturmbannführer* Rudolf Höss (November 25, 1900 – April 16, 1947) had been commander of Auschwitz since May 4, 1941, and with respect to this he recalled in his memoirs:[69]

Two old farmhouses, which were in a secluded location on the grounds of Birkenau, were sealed and fitted with stout wooden doors. The transports themselves were unloaded on a railway siding in Birkenau. The prisoners able to work were selected and led away to the camps, all luggage was set aside and later taken to the effects camps. The others, chosen for gassing, walked to the installation, about one kilometer away. The sick and the disabled were transported in trucks. All of those on transports that arrived at night were taken there by truck.

At the farmhouses everyone had to undress behind huge walls that had been put up. On the doors was "Disinfection Room." The duty non-commissioned officers had to tell the people through interpreters that they should pay close attention to their things, so that they could find them again immediately after delousing. This kept them from becoming unsettled. The undressed then walked into the rooms, 200 to 300 people depending on their size. The doors were screwed shut and one or two cans of Zyklon B were sprinkled in through small hatches; it was a granular mass of prussic acid. The effect duration, depending on the weather, was three to ten minutes. After half an hour the doors were opened and the bodies were pulled out by a party of prisoners, who were constantly working there, and burned in holes in the ground. Gold teeth and rings were removed before burning, firewood was layered between the bodies, and when a batch of about 100 bodies was in the fire was ignited with rags soaked in gasoline. When the fire really got going, the other bodies were thrown in. The fat that collected at the bottom of the holes was collected in buckets and poured back on the fire to speed up the burning process, especially in wet weather. The incineration process took six to seven hours. If there was a west wind, the stink of the burnt bodies could be smelled even in the camp. When the holes were emptied the remaining ash was pulverized. This was done on a concrete slab, where inmates pulverized the remaining bone with wooden pestles. What was left was then taken by truck to a deserted location and dumped in the Vistula.

At first the bodies were burnt in the open at Auschwitz–Birkenau, then in August 1942, construction began on Crematorium II. The purpose-built Morgue I in the building's basement was used as a gas chamber. It was thirty meters long and seven meters wide, with a surface area of 210 square meters. The height of the ceiling, which was up to 22 cm thick, was 2.41 meters. At the end of 1943, a partition was built, resulting in two chambers. This measure was carried out in order to minimize cleaning and the use of Zyklon B for smaller "transports." Morgue II served as the undressing room for the victims. The Zyklon B was poured in through openings in the ceiling and after death the bodies were transported by truck to the crematorium room with fifteen incinerators. The first gassing in Crematorium II took place on March 13, 1943. That day almost 1,500 people from the ghetto in Cracow were murdered.

Another crematorium (III), which was identical to Crematorium II, was used from June 1943. There too, it was possible to force as many as roughly 2,000 people inside. Construction of two more, smaller buildings began in November 1942. So-called Crematoria IV and V had no "body cellars"—there was a large undressing room on the left side of the building and on the right there were four gas chambers, two of which each had an area of about 100 square meters. The other two were only about twenty square meters in size and may have been used to delouse the victims' clothing. Once again, about 2,000 persons could be squeezed into each of the last two crematoria.

On October 7, 1944, there was a long-planned uprising in Crematorium III, when the Jewish *Sonderkommando* was assembled so that those unfit for work could be sorted out. Prisoners attacked the SS guards with axes and knives and set fires which badly damaged the crematorium. After spotting the smoke from Auschwitz–Birkenau, the prisoner *Sonderkommando* of Crematorium I in the main camp tried to overwhelm the SS guards. About 100 prisoners cut through the barbed wire and fled. The guards reacted immediately, however, and the escape failed. The last twelve prisoners hid in a barn about three kilometers away; it was then set on fire. In reaction to the uprising, 451 of the 661 members of all Jewish *Sonderkommandos* were shot. But at least the uprising had sent a message.

Crematoria II and III were blown up on January 20, 1945, and Crematorium V on January 26.

Camp Commandants:
SS-Obersturmbannführer Rudolf Höss (November 25, 1900 – April 16, 1947)
SS-Obersturmbannführer Arthur Liebehenschel (November 25, 1901 – January 24, 1948)
SS-Sturmbannführer Richard Baer (September 9, 1911 – June 17, 1963)

The **Bergen-Belsen Concentration Camp** was set up in April 1943, in a former camp for Soviet prisoners of war. Initially considered for the potential exchange of interned foreign Jews for German prisoners of war in England and America, and referred to as the Bergen–Belsen Civil Internment Camp, in June 1943, the camp was renamed Bergen–Belsen detention camp.

As the internment camp was initially not attached to any armaments factories, from March 1944, it also served as a collection site for prisoners from other concentration camps who were unable to work or seriously ill. These were housed in the so-called prisoner camp, which was euphemistically referred to as a so-called "recovery camp" by the SS-WVHA. With the erection of another camp—the so-called women's camp—in July 1944, followed the renaming as Bergen–Belsen concentration camp and the employment of the prisoners as labor. At that time the camp held approximately 6,400 inmates.

The first transports brought about 4,000 Polish women in August 1944. From the end of October 1944, about 4,000 prisoners from the women's camp at Auschwitz II also arrived at Bergen–Belsen concentration camp almost 600 kilometers away. On December 2, 1944, the total camp strength was 15,257 inmates, of which about half were in the so-called women's camp. A rapid increase in the number of prisoners resulted from the evacuation of the camps in the east.

On January 15, 1945, the occupancy number was 22,286 prisoners, which were guarded by 277 male and twelve female SS members. As a result of the influx of arrivals—in particular from Sachsenhausen—by March 1, 1945, there were 14,797 men, and 26,723 women in the concentration camp. Two weeks later, despite a high death rate this number had risen to 14,730 men, and 30,387 women. By April 6, 1945, hunger and disease caused camp strength to drop to a total of 39,789 prisoners. Two days later thousands of prisoners arrived at the concentration camp from the evacuated camps at Neuengamme and Mittelbau.

When British troops liberated the approximately 60,000 prisoners of the camp on April 15, 1945, they discovered a scene of horror. Because of the complete breakdown of supply and catastrophic sanitary conditions in the overcrowded concentration camp, a total of about 50,000 people had died in a few months—including about 13,000 after the British Army took over the camp. Then *Hauptmann* Nadolski described the handover of the concentration camp to the British troops:

On September 1, 1944, as a convalescent released from hospital, I took over leadership of the Luftwaffe's tank-destroyer courses which, economically subordinate to Army Tank School I in Bergen, were carried out at the Bergen training grounds. The commander of the training grounds was *Oberst* Harries. As I learned over time, the Belsen concentration camp was about four to five kilometers away. […] One day in March 1945, I saw a transport moving along the road by day. Emaciated figures in striped clothing, accompanied by SS guards, plodding wearily to the camp. Shocked by what I had seen, I informed our base commander. […]

In the first days of April, the Allied front moved forward to the Aller. As per orders, I had attached my training staff to the base commander, as we could not make contact with *Luftgau* Brunswick. On *Oberst* Harries' order we took up defensive positions at the Aller.

The commander of the British sector opposite us sent an offer to *Oberst* Harries to declare the training grounds including the Belsen concentration camp a neutral zone, as the English had no interest in seeing the inmates of the concentration camp break out of the camp while combat was going on and flooding the country that the English would later occupy.

When he sent an inquiry to the Reich government, *Oberst* Harries received orders to accept the offer of neutrality. […] The English demanded that the camp be handed over to them by the *Wehrmacht* and not by the SS. *Oberst* Harries informed *SS-Sturmbannführer* Kramer of the English demand and advised him that he would take over the concentration camp with a guard company and would have to arrest the SS. He fixed the 11th or 12th of April as the day of the takeover.

By order of *Oberst* Harries a *Hauptmann* of the armored troops school and I put together the guard company. With *Oberst* Harries the guard company marched to the Belsen concentration camp and we took over the camp. Kramer was waiting for us at the gate. We all, including *Oberst* Harries, were probably amazed to find Kramer still there. When asked, Kramer said that he had not received any orders from the Reichsführer and was remaining at his post. He was advised to remain in his barrack after the most necessary handover measures had been taken. There were still SS people in the watch towers. They were relieved by our Wehrmacht soldiers. After the handover there were still ten or twelve SS men in the camp, the others had disappeared the night before. Also still in the camp was Irma Gräss, head of the women's camp, with several SS girls, there were probably four or five.

Oberst Harries and we two watch officers then accompanied Kramer on a walk through the concentration camp. When we stepped through the second gate from the outer camp into the main camp, the scene was such that our breath stopped. Although it is difficult to describe the scene, I will try it with my words.

Over the camp hung a dense, malodorous cloud, produced by human uncleanliness, the overflowing drainage systems, and the dead bodies lying at the end of the camp, which we saw later. The individual sections of the camp were filled with starving people, who clustered at the section fences and stared at us with hollow eyes. There was also oppressive heat from a blazing sun. We walked along the camp's main street, everywhere the same scene. At the end of the camp we came upon two piles of bodies, about 12 to 15 meters long and as tall as a man, in some places less, showered with chlorine. We stood transfixed, surrounded by sweet stinking air. The shock froze every word in our throats, mute we turned away and walked back to the outer camp, behind us the seething mass of inmates in the fenced sections. On reaching the outer camp, *Oberst* Harries asked Kramer how such a thing was possible. *SS-Sturmbannführer* Kramer asked permission to explain. He described the development. [...]

Oberst Harries sent doctors and medics to lend help. As Bergen was now a neutral zone, food could be brought from *Wehrmacht* stocks and distributed in small portions, as befitted the weak stomachs. [...]

At about nine o'clock on April 15, 1945, the English arrived with armored cars, motorized infantry and a team of war reporters. Then we walked through the camp with the senior English officer, during which we also came to the two previously-mentioned heaps of bodies, which were immediately filmed. The English looked at us with angry and threatening facial expressions. [...]

During the handover on April 16–17, 1945 we German soldiers had complete freedom of movement within the neutral zone. On the evening of April 17, 1945, the German soldiers left the watch towers and total responsibility for the camp passed to the English. On that last day the captured SS men and girls were ordered to begin digging a grave for the two mountains of bodies...

Camp Commandants:
SS-Sturmbannführer Rudolf Haas (November 14, 1893 – May 1, 1945)
SS-Hauptsturmführer Josef Kramer (November 10, 1906 – December 13, 1945)

Buchenwald Concentration Camp as set up on the Ettersberg near Weimar for political opponents in July 1937. By the end of the year there were 2,561 inmates in the camp. During 1938, more than 3,000 so-called anti-socials were imprisoned at Buchenwald, plus several thousand Jews after *Reichskristallnacht*, and by December 31, the camp population was already 11,028. As a result of an amnesty on Hitler's fiftieth birthday, which included the release of the Jewish prisoners, the number of inmates fell to 5,523 by June 30, 1939. Thanks to the arrival of Austrian Jews and Czech and Polish political prisoners, it rose again to 11,807 by the end of December. The number of occupants dropped to 7,440 by December 31, 1940, mainly because of transfers to other concentration camps—for example 1,000 men sent to Mauthausen on March 4, 1940.

After an agreement between the *Wehrmacht* and the *Waffen-SS* the latter was supposed to take over a total of approximately 325,000 Soviet prisoners of war. Of these, in October 1941, 8,500—probably communist and Jewish commissars—arrived in the concentration camps to be shot.

Prisoner strength on December 31, 1941, was 7,911 (exclusive of the Red Army men), and on December 31, 1942, it stood at 9,517. By December 31, 1943, the number of inmates rose to 37,319, mainly because of prisoners from France, Italy, and the Balkans.

During the course of 1944, the number of inmates rose tremendously due to the arrival of thousands of French, Italian, and Danish prisoners, and 5,500 Hungarian Jews. After the former subcamp of Mittelbau became an independent concentration camp with 32,532 inmates on October 28, 1944, the number of prisoners in Buchenwald dropped from 88,024 to 55,492 persons. On December 31, 1944, however, there were 63,048 men and 24,210 women in Buchenwald concentration camp and its 129 outside detachments.

When about 20,000 prisoners from the evacuated concentration camp at Auschwitz arrived in Buchenwald at the beginning of 1945, the camp population rose to 83,906 men and 26,650 women. At that time the *SS-Totenkopf-Sturmbann KL Buchenwald* had a strength of 6,297 men and 532 female auxiliaries. By that point in the war some divisions had fewer soldiers.

At the beginning of 1945, Himmler ordered, to the extent possible, the German concentration camps evacuated before the arrival of allied troops. Thousands of prisoners were marched off towards the concentration camps in Flossenbürg and Dachau. On April 13, 1945, American troops reached Buchenwald concentration camp with 21,000 surviving prisoners. In total, approximately 200,000 people had been held in the Buchenwald concentration camp from July 1936 to April 11, 1945. Of these, probably 35,000 lost their lives.

Camp Commandants:
SS-Standartenführer Karl Koch (August 2, 1897 – April 5, 1945)
SS-Standartenführer Hermann Pister (February 21, 1885 – September 28, 1948)

Leo Wilm was wounded in Rumania in 1944 while serving with the *3. SS-Panzer-Division "Totenkopf,"* and after his recovery he was supposed to take over the function of a *Schirrmeister* (maintenance technical sergeant) in the Buchenwald concentration camp:

The gate of Buchenwald Concentration Camp.

Members of the *SS-Totenkopf-Sturmbann* Buchenwald Concentration Camp.

Leo Wilm (center) while serving as a dispatch rider with the *SS-Totenkopf-Division.*

After the end of my hospital stay I was astonished to learn that I was to report to Buchenwald. In fact my replacement unit was stationed in Warsaw—but because of the uprising there by the Polish Home Army, the convalescents were being sent to Weimar. When I arrived there I asked an *SS-Unterscharführer* at the station where Buchenwald was. He asked me if I wanted the barracks or the concentration camp and then took me with him on the bus heading there from the station. As we had some time until the bus left, we went into a bar at the station and had a beer. As we talked I became aware that the man was behaving rather strangely. I reported to the commander's office and at the same time requested convalescent leave. The leave was granted without further ado. When I returned to Weimar–Buchenwald about fourteen days later, I asked for a transfer back to my unit—I had no wish to serve in a concentration camp. But I was supposed to be a maintenance sergeant there. I was unable to build a good relationship with the non-commissioned officers and I always felt like an uninvited guest.

On August 24, 1944, the allies bombed the Gustloff–Werke and the SS barracks in Buchenwald. While no bombs fell on the concentration camp, the halls of the nearby *SS-Kraftfahr-Ersatz- und Ausbildungsbataillon* and the barracks were hit.

By 1945, I had abandoned hope of getting back to my original unit, but then in February, I received orders to take several men from the guard *Sturmbann* to the front at Stuhlweissenburg as replacements. At the end of February 1945, I was made a platoon leader in a battle group of the *9. SS-Panzer-Division "Hohenstaufen."* The company commander was Heinz Hannemann, an old friend from my youth and comrade from my time in the *SS-Heimwehr-Danzig*, who had since been promoted to *SS-Untersturmführer*!

Dachau Concentration Camp was set up in March 1933, in a former munitions factory near Munich for the imprisonment of political opponents, Jehovah's Witnesses, and so-called antisocials. The motto on the entrance gate next to the guard rooms and the commander's office became famous: "*Arbeit macht frei*" (Work Brings Freedom).

After *Reichskristallnacht* more than 10,000 Jews from all over Germany were imprisoned at Dachau for several weeks. From 1939, foreign political prisoners also went to the camp. Dachau concentration camp was emptied from October 27, 1939 until February 18, 1940, for the formation of the *SS-Totenkopf-Division*. During this time the inmates were TFF to other concentration camps.

As in Buchenwald, in the late summer of 1941, several thousand Red Army men were brought to Dachau and about 6,000 of them were liquidated at the Hebertshausen firing range from November 25, 1941. When Himmler issued orders at the beginning of October 1942, for all Jews held in German concentration camps to be deported to Auschwitz, the camp population was approximately 8,000 prisoners.

At the beginning of 1944, a camp for women was set up in addition to the men's camp. By January 15, 1945, the camp population rose to 52,596 male, and 2,651 female prisoners, who were guarded by 3,544 SS men, and sixty-two female custodians.

Following the evacuation of the Buchenwald and Flossenbürg concentration camps in April 1945, there were 67,665 prisoners in the concentration camp. Evacuation of the camp began on April 26, shortly before American troops reached Dachau on April 29, 1945. Only about 10% of the prisoners, however—6,887 inmates—were moved towards Tölz by way of Gauting–Berg–Wolfratshausen.

The total of about 200,000 prisoners held in the Dachau concentration camp were employed in 197 outside detachments—most in the armaments industrial or construction. According to files of the International Red Cross, 31,591 of these persons died.

Road sign showing the way to Dachau Concentration Camp.

Johann Ginner was called up to serve at Dachau Concentration Camp at the age of forty-five. He had previously served in the *Wehrmacht* from August 26, 1939 to September 23, 1940, and took part in the campaign in Norway. Released from active military service, he worked as a servant until December 1, 1944.

The gate of Dachau Concentration Camp.

251

Camp Commandants:

SS-Standartenführer Hilmar Wäckerle (November 24, 1889 – July 2, 1941)
SS-Gruppenführer Theodor Eicke (October 17, 1892 – February 26, 1943)
SS-Standartenführer Heinreich Deubel (February 19, 1890 – October 2, 1962)
SS-Obersturmbannführer Alex Piorkowski (October 11, 1890 – October 2, 1962)
SS-Sturmbannführer Wilhelm Weiter (July 18, 1889 – May 2, 1945)
SS-Standartenführer Hans Loritz (December 12, 1895 – January 31, 1946)
SS-Obersturmbannführer Martin Weiss (June 3, 1905 – May 29, 1946)

Former inmate Edgar Kupfer-Koberwitz recalled the SS guards in his Dachau diaries:[70]

January 19, 1944: The sentries now have orders to carry their rifles under their arm when escorting prisoner columns. This hadn't been the case in Dachau since 1939 (outbreak of war). [...]

The Italian troops here with the SS are hungry, they steal whatever they find. Several have even sold their uniforms for food. They also have it bad in other ways. The German non-commissioned officers kick and beat them. I have seen it myself. They would be better treated by the enemy. It is said that thefts are increasing and that they have shot two of them to serve as a deterrent. [...]

October 13, 1944: The new uniform worn by our guards is like an SS uniform, only with swastikas on the collar tabs instead of the "SS." One of the sentries said that he was no SS man. He had voluntarily joined the air force and he wanted to return to the air force. It is said that there was a big racket. Apparently he was reported twice. [...]

April 29, 1945: Suddenly the news: there are white flags on the towers! Everyone is delighted, that can only mean that the camp has surrendered. I myself don't believe it, I think it is just to make clear the borders of the camp. As well, the SS is still standing in the towers, there are still 200 SS men in the camp.

Suddenly outside shouting and running around: the Americans are in the camp, yes, yes, they are on the roll call ground! Everyone begins to move. The sick leave their beds, the almost healthy and the personnel run onto the block street, jump from the windows, climb over the wooden walls. [...]

Comrades come, come back, tell breathlessly: the Americans are on the roll call ground! They're shooting down all the SS. The camp is taken, we are free, free!

The Americans tell the guards to come down from the towers and out of the bunkers. [...] All were shot, the Americans don't leave alive any of the SS men who fell into their hands. One comrade who saw this then told me what he experienced, for it shocked him to see men being shot down despite raised hands, falling, bleeding and dying. [...]

The dead SS men are now lying everywhere in the camp area. Unfortunately there are nobodies among us who take the opportunity to go outside the wire to plunder and rob. Some of them take the wristwatches, cameras and even boots from the dead SS. Some of the bodies lie there like that, one even without trousers. But our joy escapes this as if it were nothing. As well, we have all seen too many dead. [...]

I even hear that excited prisoners snatched submachine-guns from the hands of American soldiers and shot SS men standing behind the electric fence with hands raised. Many comrades were disgusted by this. [...]

It was a beautiful and yet so bloody Sunday. Strange how everything ended the way it began. Everything began bloodily, and bloodily it ended.

The Americans entered the camp at 1145.

The memorial at the site of Flossenbürg Concentration Camp.

Members of the SS guards in front of the castle ruins at Flossenbürg.

The SS settlement at Flossenbürg for the guards and their families.

Floßenbürg Concentration Camp was set up in the Upper Pfalz Forest near a granite quarry to accommodate about 1,600 inmates, who were to work in the SS-owned Deutschen Erd- und Steinwerke GmbH. The first inmates were so-called asocials and criminals, who during the war were employed in ninety-seven outside detachments—most in the armaments industry. Approximately 1,000 Soviet prisoners of war were shot at Floßenbürg by 1942. The number of occupants first rose to about 3,000 and then to 5,000. Many of these were employed in the production of Messerschmitt fighter aircraft. Female prisoners were first used in outside detachments in January 1943, and a separate women's camp was created on March 14, 1945.

The numerous evacuation transports from the eastern concentration camps initially caused the camp population to rise to 8,000 prisoners at the end of 1944. On January 15, 1945, 2,564 male and 515 female custodians were employed to guard 28,737 male and 10,967 female inmates. On April 14, 1945, 45,813 prisoners were counted in the camp, which was originally built for 1,600 persons.

The evacuation of the camp began four days later with American troops approaching. About 10,000 prisoners set out on foot for Dachau. The US Army reached the concentration camp on April 23, 1945. All of the weak and sick inmates with care personnel had been left behind. 20,474 deaths had been registered from a total of approximately 100,000 prisoners. Other victims were the Soviet troops executed there and victims of the evacuation marches. Approximately 4,000 members of the *Waffen-SS* served in the *SS-Totenkopf-Sturmbann KL Floßenbürg*.

Camp Commandants:

SS-Sturmbannführer Jacob Weiseborn (March 22, 1892 – January 20, 1939)
SS-Sturmbannführer Egon Zill (March 28, 1906 – October 23, 1974)
SS-Hauptsturmführer Karl Fritzsch (July 10, 1903 – May 2, 1945)
SS-Obersturmbannführer Max Kögel (October 16, 1895 – June 27, 1946)
SS-Obersturmbannführer Karl Künstler (January 12, 1901 – April 1945)

Groß–Rosen Concentration Camp was built in August 1940, initially as a subcamp of the Sachsenhausen concentration camp in Lower Silesia. On May 1, 1941, it became an independent camp. The inmates were employed in 118 outside detachments—including in the quarry of the Deutschen Erd- und Steinwerke GmbH. All Polish inmates capable of work were supposed to be brought to the camp beginning December 24, 1943.

The number of inmates grew from an initial 6,500 to 51,977 male and 25,927 female prisoners by January 15, 1945. In mid-January 1945, there were 3,222 SS men, and 906 female wardens guarding the camp. Before the Red Army occupied the camp on February 13, 1945, inmates capable of work were evacuated to various concentration camps, including 9,559 to the Mittelbau concentration camp, 6,817 to Buchenwald and 2,514 to Dachau.

The total number of inmates including those in the satellite camps was approximately 120,000. Approximately 35,000 are supposed to have died, some during evacuation. Approximately 5,000 members of the *Waffen-SS* served in the *SS-Totenkopf-Sturmbann* at Groß–Rosen concentration camp.

Camp Commandants:

SS-Standartenführer Johannes Hassebroeck (July 11, 1910 – April 17, 1977)
SS-Standartenführer Arthur Rödl (June 13, 1898 – April 1945)
SS-Obersturmführer Wilhelm Gideon (November 15, 1898 – unknown)

Herzogenbusch Concentration Camp was built in 's-Hertogenbosch (Netherlands) in January 1943, to accommodate male inmates. Also set up at the same time was a transit camp, by way

The gate at the Groß–Rosen Concentration Camp.

View of the camp from the guard tower.

A *Rapportführer* (report leader) and two kapos.

The commander's office.

of which about 12,000 Jews were deported to Auschwitz and Sobibor, either directly or via Westerbork Concentration Camp. A camp for women was set up in 1943.

Some male prisoners worked in a so-called *Luftwaffe* detachment, disassembling crashed German and Allied aircraft. Others worked on farms or in a printing shop. The female inmates were used mainly in the production of gas masks.

The concentration camp was closed on September 5, 1944. The men were sent to Sachsenhausen, the women to Ravensbrück. About 30,000 people passed through the concentration camp and its thirteen outside detachments, and approximately 750 lost their lives. Approximately 150 members of the *Waffen-SS* were employed to guard the camp.

Camp Commandants:
SS-Sturmbannführer Hans Hüttig (April 5, 1894 – February 23, 1980)
SS-Sturmbannführer Adam Grünewald (October 20, 1902 – January 22, 1945)

Kauen Concentration Camp was established in the former Kauen (Kovno) ghetto in the General District of Lithuania. The reason behind this was the order issued by Himmler on June 21, of that year to concentrate all Jews still living in ghettoes in the *Reichskommissariat Ostland* in concentration camps by August 1, 1943. The Vilna, Kauen, and Schaulen ghettoes were liquidated, and of the approximately 35,000 inhabitants about 15,000 male and female

Jews capable of working were imprisoned in the concentration camp with its fourteen outside detachments. From there followed deportations, for example to work in the shale oil plants in Estonia or to Auschwitz and Lublin.

The evacuation of the approximately 8,000 surviving prisoners before the arrival of the Red Army began in July 1944. The women were sent to Stutthof and the men to Dachau. Those who could no longer work were sent to Auschwitz and probably died there. Soviet troops marched into Kauen. Kauen Concentration Camp was watched over by about 800—mainly Lithuanian—guards.

Camp Commandants:

SS-Obersturmbannführer Wilhelm Goecke (February 12, 1898 – October 20, 1944)

Lublin Concentration Camp was set up, initially for 5,000 prisoners, on the outskirts of the city of Lublin in September 1941. The camp was envisaged as the first construction phase for a large concentration camp with 50,000 inmates.

After negotiations with the *Wehrmacht*, at the end of 1941, the *Waffen-SS* intended to take over 325,000 Soviet prisoners of war from the Stalags, of which 150,000 were supposed to go to Lublin to the so-called "*Waffen-SS* Prisoner of War Camp." Plans called for a prisoner of war camp for 150,000 Red Army men to be built alongside the concentration camp for 50,000 prisoners. In fact, however, these large scale transfers never took place and only quarters for a total of 60,000 inmates and prisoners of war were built. A camp for female inmates followed in August 1942.

The inmates were used to construct an SS garment factory and then were put to work in it. Some also worked in the Deutschen Ausrüstungswerken (DAW) making ammunition boxes and lace-up shoes. The concentration camps had the highest revenue of any DAW facility in 1942.

A total of approximately 17,000 people were shot in the concentration camp during the Harvest Festival action—the liquidation of the Jewish labor camps in Trawniki and Poniatowa, and the Jews in the Lublin concentration camp—on November 3–4, 1943.

Evacuation of the camp began in March 1944, with the men sent to Auschwitz, Groß–Rosen, and Natzweiler and the female inmates to Auschwitz, Natzweiler, and Ravensbrück. The Red Army occupied Lublin on July 23, 1944.

After new research in 2006, Tomasz Kranz, director of the state museum in Maidanek, concluded that about 78,000 people, including 59,000 Jews, lost their lives in the Lublin concentration camp.[71]

Camp Commandants:
SS-Standartenführer Karl Koch
SS-Standartenführer Hermann Florstedt (February 18, 1895 – April 15, 1945)
SS-Obersturmbannführer Martin Weiss (June 3, 1905 – May 29, 1946)
SS-Obersturmbannführer Arthur Liebehenschel
SS-Obersturmbannführer Max Koegel

Mauthausen Concentration Camp was built as a subcamp of Dachau concentration camp in August 1938, five months after Austria was incorporated into the German Reich, near the small Upper Austrian town of Mauthausen. The male inmates were supposed to work the granite quarries of the SS-owned DESt. Made an independent concentration camp in March 1939, along with Groß–Rosen it had the worst conditions for prisoners.

In 1940, the concentration camp, together with the camp in Gusen built in May, formed the double camp of Mauthausen/Gusen. At that time about 3,600 prisoners were working daily

Guard tower ...

Josef Metzger was assessed as fit only for labor service and subsequently joined the concentration camp service as a member of the *Allgemeine-SS* in 1941.

... and barracks in the Lublin Concentration Camp.

SS-Sturmmann Metzger served almost four years at Mauthausen, Lublin, Buchenwald, and Mittelbau Concentration Camps.

in the DESt quarries. At the end of December 1940, the prisoner population was about 8,200 persons, just one year later approximately 16,000. A camp for female prisoners was set up in October 1943, and on December 31, 1943, the concentration camp reported a total population of 25,607 inmates.

On January 15, 1945, there were 5,632 SS men and sixty-five female custodians to watch over the camp's 72,426 male and 954 female inmates and its total of sixty-two outside detachments. As a result of the evacuations of other concentration camps, on March 7, 1945, there were 84,472 male and 1,043 female prisoners at Mauthausen/Gusen.

Approximately 20,000 inmates were evacuated by the time the concentration camp was turned over to the Vienna firefighter-police on May 3, 1945. When the US Army reached the camp two days later, there were still about 64,800 male and 1,734 female prisoners there. Of the total of approximately 195,000 prisoners, probably 70,000 died.

Camp Commandants:
SS-Sturmbannführer Albert Sauer (August 17, 1898 – May 3, 1945)
SS-Standartenführer Franz Ziereis (August 13, 1905 – May 24, 1945)

Mittelbau Concentration Camp had been a subcamp of the Buchenwald concentration camp since August 28, 1943, and in October 1944, it became an independent concentration camp with 32,532 inmates. Under the worst conditions the inmates built an underground system of tunnels in which the "long-range projectile in aircraft form" (Fieseler Fi 103), more commonly referred to as the V 1 (Vergeltungswaffe 1), and the so-called Aggregat 4, the V 2, were produced. In September 1944, the Mittelbau concentration camp organized itself into three camps with thirty-two outside detachments:

Mittelbau I (Camp Dora) – Main Camp
Mittelbau II (Camp Erich)
Mittelbau III (Camp Harzungen)

Most of the guards at the Mittelbau concentration camp were provided by the *Luftwaffe*. Effective September 1, 1944, these non-commissioned officers and enlisted men were considered transferred to the *Waffen-SS*. The officers—apart from the doctors—were sent back to their *Luftwaffe* replacement units.

On January 15, 1945, 3,319 guards were watching over 29,323 prisoners. Of a total of at least 50,000 prisoners, approximately 10,000 died or starved by April 3, 1945. Evacuation to Bergen-Belsen, Sachsenhausen, and Ravensbrück began on April 5, 1945. American troops reached the concentration camp one week later.

Camp Commandants:
SS-Sturmbannführer Otto Förschner (November 4, 1902 – May 28, 1946)
SS-Sturmbannführer Richard Baer

Natzweiler Concentration Camp was built in Struthof, Alsace (fifty kilometers south of Strasbourg) in May 1941. Initially, 1,500 male inmates were employed to quarry granite for the DESt. At the end of 1943, there were about 2,000 prisoners in the main camp. Of these only about 500 worked in the quarry, the rest overhauled aircraft engines. There was also a secondary camp in which attempts were made to extract crude oil from oil shale.

Including the fifty outside detachments, the number of inmates rose to about 14,000 by autumn 1944. On January 15, 1945, there were 1,626 SS men, and eighteen female custodians at the camp guarding 20,961 male, and 1,209 female prisoners.

Mauthausen Concentration
Camp.

Heinrich Himmler inspected the concentration camp on May 31, 1941, together with *SS-Gruppenführer* Eigruber (in the black uniform of the *Allgemeine-SS*), the Reich Governor of Upper Danube.

On the top step: *SS-Gruppenführer* Kaltenbrunner, the Senior SS and Police Commander Danube.

From left to right: *Reichsführer-SS* Himmler, *SS-Gruppenführer* Eigruber, *SS-Sturmbannführer* Ziereis, commandant of Mauthausen Concentration Camp, and *SS-Obergruppenführer* Wolff in the concentration camp's quarry.

An *SS-Scharführer* of the concentration camp guard is presented to Himmler.

A total of about 45,000 people were imprisoned by 1945, and probably about half of these lost their lives.

Camp Commandants:
SS-Sturmbannführer Egon Zill
SS-Obersturmbannführer Fritz Hartjenstein (July 3, 1905 – October 20, 1954)
SS-Sturmbannführer Hans Hüttig
SS-Hauptsturmführer Heinrich Schwarz (June 14, 1906 – March 20, 1947)
SS-Hauptsturmführer Josef Kramer

Neuengamme Concentration Camp was created in June 1940 from a labor camp opened in December 1938, on the grounds of a former brickworks near Hamburg–Bergedorf as an outside detachment of Sachsenhausen concentration camp.

In the spring of 1940, the prisoner population was approximately 2,000 persons. This doubled after the start of the Russian campaign and remained roughly constant until the summer of 1942. As in many concentration camps on Reich–German soil, Soviet prisoners of war suspected to be communists were shot there. At the end of 1942, there were more than 5,000 prisoners in the camp. By January 15, 1945, the inmate population, including the ninety outside detachments, grew to 38,230 male, and 9,934 female prisoners. The prisoners were mainly used in the armament industry or so-called construction brigades (for example for cleanup work after bombing raids).

While 600 guards were initially employed in November 1942, by mid-January 1945, this number rose to 2,130 SS men and 322 female custodians. Evacuation of the camp to Sandbostel, Lübeck and Bergen–Belsen began on April 20, 1945. British troops reached the concentration camp on May 4, 1945. There was a tragedy on May 3, 1945, when the RAF bombed the two ships *Cap Arcona* and *Thielbek* in Lübeck Bay. About 10,000 inmates from Neuengamme were on the ships and about 7,000 died in the attack.

Between 1938 and 1945, 87,000 men and 13,500 women were registered as inmates. There were also the Soviet prisoners of war and about 13,000 Jews and 500 Sinti and Roma, who were not registered. Probably about 35,000 people lost their lives at Neuengamme.

Approximately 4,500 members of the *Waffen-SS* served in the *SS-Totenkopf-Sturmbann KL Neuengamme*. The former *SS-Sturmmann* Helmut Uphoff joined the guards after he was wounded:

> After being wounded near Salla, at the end of August I was released from hospital to SS Replacement Battalion A in Goslar. As this no longer existed, I was ordered to SS Replacement Battalion Nord in Wehlau. There I initially belonged to the Convalescent Company and later to the 3rd Company. I was given convalescent leave in September 1941—the wound became inflamed on the trip back and I ended up in the reserve hospital in Posen.
>
> On October 15, 1941, I was back with SS Replacement Battalion Nord. Hanging on the blackboard there was a notice that they were looking for ten volunteers for the concentration camp in Neuengamme. As I had many relatives in Hamburg and felt no more need for the front, I volunteered with the others without actually knowing what I was getting myself into. We were only told that we would be employed as guards, and soon afterwards we were on the train to Hamburg.
>
> The entire Neuengamme concentration camp, including the guard camp, then consisted of wooden barracks. It was right next to the main camp. To my knowledge an entire *Sturmbann*, four companies, did guard duty on a four-day rotation. One company was always on duty, one in reserve, and two were off duty after noon. Also in the guard

The evacuation of the Neuengamme Concentration Camp began on April 20, 1945. Approximately 10,000 prisoners were supposed to be evacuated to Denmark. On May 3, the RAF bombed the ships *Cap Arcona* and *Thielbeck*, and about 7,000 prisoners died in the Baltic.

Helmut Uphoff served as an *SS-Sturmmann* in the *SS-Totenkopf-Sturmbann* KL Neuengamme from October 1941 to May 1942.

Memorial for the victims of the British air attack.

Memorial to those prisoners from Sachsenhausen Concentration Camp who died during the evacuation to northern Germany.

camp was the camp headquarters accommodation barrack. The headquarters office was there and probably that of the *Sturmbann* as well. The so-called block leaders also slept there. These were the "comrades" to whom we owed our bad reputation! Only they were allowed into the main camp. The guards were forbidden to enter the main camp and at best went into the divided area in front with medical facilities, for example to the dentist. And that required a pass.

Changing of the guard was always at twelve noon. Prior to this there was a briefing for the guard company which always ended with the *Reichsführer* order that any sentry preying on a prisoner would receive the same punishment. Our only contact was with the regular outside detachments, and most of them were Jehovah's Witnesses. They were harmless and never tried to escape.

The main camp was surrounded by an electrically-charged fence and to my knowledge there were eight to ten wooden towers around the camp. Each tower was manned by three men, who automatically relieved each other and whose free watch was below in the tower. We were armed only with rifles and there was a revolving searchlight atop the tower.

There were more barracks in the guard camp, whose function and location I can no longer remember. One could have been the food storeroom and there were also garages for the motor vehicles, of which we did not have many. We had an omnibus which took the men of the off-duty company to the station in Bergedorf, plus several trucks and automobiles. The kitchen, canteen, and dining room were in one of the barracks and then in another there were services, such as a barber, tailor, etc.

Our company had about 100 to 200 men—we ten from the combat units were the only active ones and the youngest in the entire battalion. We lived together in Room 10. All other members of the company, apart from the non-commissioned officers and officers, were reservists, old boys. Some had been NCOs in the *Kaiser*'s army and were now serving as simple riflemen.

Before every watch went on duty there was the infamous guard briefing, which we knew all too well. That was unless there was something new, and then the company commander took roll call. Then followed the mounting of the guard—the march from the guard camp to the main camp—and the changing of the guard. At twelve the next day the guard was relieved, marched from the main camp to the guard camp, lunch and free time. The commander of my 1st Company was *SS-Obersturmführer* Stötzler and the leader of the 1st Platoon *SS-Untersturmführer* Wendt. The *Stabsscharführer*'s name was Trautwein. The reservists were often members of the Allgemeine-SS—men who were too old for active service.

The prisoners were in the main camp at night. I don't remember exactly how many were there during my time—between 2,000 and 4,000—of whom about 1,500 were Soviet prisoners of war. As I recall, there were no Jews there during my time. Also there were no prisoners of war apart from the Soviets. Neuengamme was a labor camp. Each morning the work parties left under escort. The biggest work party worked in the clay quarry, located next to the guard camp and inside the klinker plant. I don't know of any other big work details, only the klinker plant detail and—the best of them all—the bakery in Zollenspieker. As the klinker plant had to operate day and night, the work detail was of course there at night and was watched by a group of sentries. I myself once had night guard duty.

At night the roll call square in the main camp was empty, and as soon as someone showed themselves outside we turned on the searchlight. Of course at night the camp was also lit by searchlights, some of which were on the fence, but they were more streetlights. We had orders to shoot if anything moved in the camp, but I cannot remember any shooting from the towers.

One time a prisoner succeeded in escaping from a work detail through the line of sentries and the old guard, who should have shot, was so befuddled that he forgot to shout and open fire. The prisoner was able to get away. The result: all work details were immediately recalled and the inmates were formed up on the roll call square until the inmate was recaptured. The sentry was sent to the bunker.

While the German prisoners went on work details, the Soviet inmates stayed in the camp. At the time—I was just twenty years old—I thought little about it one way or the other. Later I asked myself why the prisoners of war were actually there, they actually belonged in a Stalag. But at the time I knew precious little about it. In May 1942, all active members were sent back to the fighting troops. As I had a driver's license, I ended up with SS Replacement Battalion East in Breslau and from there was sent to the headquarters of the SS Panzer Corps in Bergen.

Concerning the concentration camp guards Max Pauly, the last camp commandant, declared before the International Military Tribunal in Nuremberg on March 15, 1946:

When I began my service as commandant of Neuengamme concentration camp in November 1942, all of the personnel were *Waffen-SS*. Later, in the summer of 1944, I began receiving individuals or even small units from the army and the air force who had been taken over by the *Waffen-SS*. They received new *Waffen-SS* paybooks and uniforms. In the summer of 1944, the camp also received SS female auxiliaries and custodians who were not members of the SS. In November 1944 total SS strength at Neuengamme was about 500 to 600 men. By summer 1944, the number had grown to about 2,500, and at the time of the surrender the number of SS troops in the camp and the outer detachments must have been about 2,500 to 3,000. The replacement personnel for Neuengamme came from every unit of the *Waffen-SS*, from 1944 many were ethnic Germans from Slovakia, the Banat, Danzig–West Prussia etc. The men were sent from every training and replacement battalion of the *Waffen-SS*, therefore it is impossible to name specific units. The growing requirements of the *Waffen-SS* fighting units resulted in a change of personnel, with the younger replaced by older age classes. This change affected approximately 500 to 1,000 men. During my period of service from November 1942 to April 1945, therefore, roughly 4,000 SS personnel served in Neuengamme and the outside detachments at one time or another.

Camp Commandants:
SS-Obersturmbannführer Martin Weiss
SS-Obersturmbannführer Max Pauly (June 1, 1907 – October 8, 1946)

Niederhagen Concentration Camp was built from a subcamp of the Sachsenhausen concentration camp which opened in January 1941. Located near Paderborn, it was the sole purely men's camp. With a population of about 3,300 men, it was the smallest independent concentration camp in Germany. From May 1943, Niederhagen was again listed as a subcamp of the Sachsenhausen concentration camp. The prisoners were used for the clearing of land and the planned expansion of Wewelsburg. An unusually high percentage of prisoners died in the process: 1,285 inmates lost their lives. After the expansion of Wewelsburg was halted, from August 1943, only forty-nine prisoners remained in the camp. About 200 SS men had originally guarded the prisoners.

Camp Commandant:

SS-Hauptsturmführer Adolf Haas

Plaszów Concentration Camp was formed in January 1944, from the Jewish labor camp of Plaszów in the Cracow District which opened in June 1941. The labor camp had ten outside detachments, including textile companies, quarries, and the Siemens Company. After the liquidation of the ghetto in Cracow, in June 1943, the inmate population (Plaszów labor camp) was 8,500 Jews and 500 Poles. The camp was supposed to be expanded in the second half of the year to accommodate an additional 8,000 prisoners.

During the Red Army's advance in the summer of 1944, the prisoners, whose number had risen to about 20,000, were transferred to other concentration camps. For example, 6,000 went to Auschwitz in August 1944, 5,000 to Mauthausen, and 5,000 to Flossenbürg. By September 1944, the camp population was still about 2,200 men.

On January 1, 1945, eighty-seven members of the SS were employed to guard the remaining 453 male and 183 female prisoners, who on January 15, 1945 were transferred to Auschwitz–Birkenau. The Red Army occupied Plaszów the next day. The camp became known through the motion picture Schindler's List. A total of between 25,000 and 30,000 prisoners passed through the camp, of which probably about 8,000 lost their lives.

Camp Commandant:

SS-Hauptsturmführer Amon Göth (December 11, 1908 – September 13, 1946)

Ravensbrück Concentration Camp was created in May 1939, by moving the former Lindenburg women's concentration camp to Fürstenberg (Brandenburg), initially for 867 women. By 1941, the camp population grew to about 3,600 female prisoners. In March 1941, the women's camp was joined by a men's camp for about 1,500 prisoners. The inmates were employed in the SS-owned Gesellschaft für Textil- und Lederverwertung GmbH and in forty-five outside detachments—most in the armaments industry.

In addition to Polish and Soviet foreign female workers who had broken laws, German political prisoners along with Sinti and Roma made up the bulk of the inmates. In 1942, there were approximately 7,000 women, in 1943, 10,000, and in 1944, almost 60,000. As in all the remaining concentration camps in Germany, these high numbers were the result of evacuations from the east from the summer of 1944. Whereas in 1941, there had been deportations "to the east," now people were being evacuated "from the east."

On January 15, 1945, there were 1,008 SS men, and 546 female custodians guarding 7,848 male, and 46,070 female prisoners. The percentage of guards to inmates was thus just 3%.

The evacuation of 24,500 prisoners to Mecklenburg began on April 23, 1945. As well, 7,500 prisoners were turned over to the Swedish Red Cross between April 22–28. The Red Army reached the concentration camp, which still held about 3,500 sick and their attendants, on April 30, 1945.

A total of 107,753 female and 20,086 male prisoners were registered. Probably about 25,000 died. In addition to the actual guard unit, the central training camp for female custodians was located in Ravensbrück. In his statement to the International Military Tribunal on March 19, 1946, Fritz Suhren declared:

I was commandant of Ravensbrück concentration camp from November 1942 until early May 1945. When I took over the post, in the camp there were approximately 250 men of the *Waffen-SS* serving in the guard battalion and 85 to 90 in the headquarters staff; the numbers at the end of April 1945 were 550 and 90 men. Over time, about half of these personnel were replaced by older age classes, men from regional defense units,

The Twelve Main Offices (*Hauptämter*) as Himmler's Administrative Apparatus

The gate of Ravensbrück Female Concentration Camp.

Himmler inspects Ravensbrück Female Concentration Camp on January 14, 1941.

The commander's office.

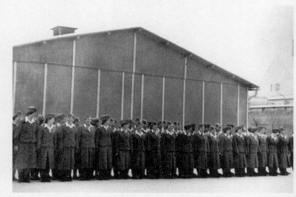

The female wardens of Ravensbruck Concentration Camp.

The camp commandant's villa.

air force members and ethnic Germans who had been taken into the *Waffen-SS*. Accordingly, during my time there approximately 950 men of the *Waffen-SS* served at Ravensbrück and outside detachments at one time or another.

Concerning the SS female auxiliaries, who were used as custodians, it should be noted that Ravensbrück served as a training camp, so that the vast majority were transferred after a short time. Accordingly, approximately 3,500 SS female auxiliaries served in Ravensbrück and outer detachments for a shorter or longer period while I was there. As far as possible, the camp headquarters staff was not replaced. Personnel were supplemented, in cases of transfers to the combat units, and occasionally there were also transfers to the guard.

Camp Commandants:
SS-Standartenführer Günther Tamaschke (February 26, 1896 – October 14, 1959)
SS-Obersturmbannführer Max Kögel
SS-Sturmbannführer Fritz Suhren (June 10, 1908 – June 12, 1950)

The **Riga Concentration Camp** was built in the General District of Latvia (Reichskommissariat Ostland) near the exclusive suburb of Riga–Kaiserwald in March 1943. It was set up for the inmates of the Riga, Vilnius, and Libau ghettoes, which were to be liquidated, who were considered able to work. Divided into men's and women's camps, the inmates worked in twenty-nine outside detachments, including in the repair shops of the army motor pool, the German State Railway, and the AEG. In March 1944, there were 6,182 male, and 5,696 female prisoners in the concentration camp. The evacuation of the remaining roughly 3,000 inmates before the Red Army began on August 6, 1944. The men who were evacuated went to Buchenwald and Dachau and the women to Stutthof.

Camp Commandant:
SS-Hauptsturmführer Eduard Roschmann (November 25, 1908 – August 8, 1977)

Sachsenhausen Concentration Camp was built for male prisoners near Oranienburg in July 1936. There were 2,523 inmates in the camp on December 31, 1937, and in December 1938, this figure rose to 8,309 through the arrest of approximately 6,000 so-called asocials (vagrants, con men, etc.).

During the course of the Polish Campaign numerous Polish and Czech citizens, plus Polish prisoners of war and 250 German soldiers serving military sentences (*Wehrmacht* disciplinary battalion) arrived at the camp, whose population reached 12,168 prisoners on December 31, 1939.

Almost 2,200 prisoners died in the first four months of 1940 because of poor living conditions. During the course of the year about 17,000 Polish prisoners arrived in the camp. Secondments went to Floßenbürg, Neuengamme, Dachau, and Groß–Rosen. Beginning September 1, 1941, 20,000 Soviet prisoners of war sorted out from Soviet prisoners of war camps arrived in Sachsenhausen concentration camp, of whom about 18,000 were shot by the end of the year. On December 31, 1941, the camp population, not counting the about 1,800 surviving Soviet prisoners of war, was 10,709 prisoners. One year later there were 16,577 inmates in the camp.

In 1943, the number of inmates grew to 28,224 through transports from Denmark, Norway, and France. In addition to smaller SS enterprises, the prisoners were employed in approximately 130 outside detachments—most in the armaments industry. Arrivals from Hungary and eastern concentration camps caused the number of prisoners to rise rapidly. On December 31, 1944, there were 47,709 prisoners in the camp.

After the concentration camps still to be evacuated from the east were figured into the total population of Sachsenhausen as of January 1, 1945, on January 15, the number of prisoners was: 52,924 men and 13,173 women, who were guarded by 3,632 SS men, and 361 female custodians.

The Swedish Red Cross took charge of the Danish and Norwegian inmates between March 16–18, 1945. As well, into April 1945, 20,000 prisoners were transferred to Dachau and Mittelbau concentration camps. On April 20, 1945, began the evacuation of the remaining 36,687 prisoners to northern Germany. Two days later the Red Army reached Sachsenhausen concentration camp. Of approximately 125,000 inmates, approximately 25,000 perished plus a further number during the evacuation marches. As well, approximately 18,000 Soviet prisoners of war were shot.

Camp Commandants:
SS-Gruppenführer Hans Hellwig (September 25, 1881 – August 24, 1952)
SS-Standartenführer Karl Koch
SS-Standartenführer Hermann Baranowski (June 11, 1884 – February 5, 1940)
SS-Oberführer Hans Loritz (December 21, 1895 – January 31, 1946)
SS-Sturmbannführer Walter Eisfeld (July 11, 1905 – April 3, 1940)
SS-Obersturmbannführer Rudolf Höss
SS-Standartenführer Anton Kaindl (July 14, 1902 – August 31, 1948)

Stutthof Concentration Camp was created in January 1942 from the civilian internment camp for men built on September 2, 1939, on the site of a former nursing home approximately thirty-five kilometers east of Danzig. One year earlier—in January 1941—a civilian interment camp for women had also been built. Both were designated SS special camps (*SS-Sonderlager*) on November 5, 1941.

After a visit by Himmler in January 1942, Soviets prisoners of war and prisoners from Western Europe and the Baltic States were delivered to the new camp. At the beginning of 1942, the average camp population was 3,000 prisoners. At the beginning of 1943, a new camp for 25,000 prisoners was built alongside the old camp. The inmates were employed in a total of 146 outside detachments, primarily in the DAW, camp workshops, brickworks and agriculture. The second half of 1944, the saw the arrival of large evacuation transports from Riga, Kaunas, and Schaulen, but also from Auschwitz. The makeup of the inmate population changed to about 70% Jews.

On January 15, 1945, 943 SS men and 108 female custodians guarded an inmate population that had grown to 18,436 male, and 30,199 female prisoners. Evacuation of the camp to Lauenburg began ten days later. Of the about 48,500 prisoners, approximately 10,000 moved in columns of about 1,000 men, each guarded by just forty men. In winter conditions without proper supplies, many prisoners died of exhaustion. Others were sent towards Königsberg. In April 1945, the last prisoners were transported by ship via the Hela Peninsula. Of a total of about 106,000 prisoners probably about 50,000 died between 1939 and 1945.

Camp Commandants:
SS-Obersturmbannführer Max Pauly
SS-Sturmbannführer Paul Hoppe (February 28, 1910 – July 15, 1974)

Vaivara Concentration Camp was built in Estonia in September 1943, with one camp for female and one for male prisoners working in the shale oil plants (Baltöl). First to arrive at the camp and its twenty-seven outside detachments were about 7,000 Jewish prisoners from the liquidated Vilnius ghetto and about 2,000 from the Kaunas ghetto.

The gate at Sachsenhausen Concentration Camp.

Klemens Altmann, an ethnic German from Rumania, volunteered for service in the *Waffen-SS* in 1941. He served briefly with the *SS-Kavallerie-Brigade*, after which he was employed at Sachsenhausen Concentration Camp.

Stutthof Concentration
Camp.

At the end of 1944, Vaivara concentration camp was evacuated to Stutthof and in part to Auschwitz. Of the total of about 12,000 prisoners, *SS-Hauptsturmführer* Bodmann, the camp doctor, registered 1,506 dead. In the course of the evacuation of Estonia in late August/early September 1944, all prisoners still in subcamps were sent to Klooga. While elements of *Waffen-Grenadier-Ausbildungs- und Ersatz-Regiment der SS 20* sealed off the camp, personnel of the Commander of the Security Police in Estonia liquidated prisoners unable to work. Then *Waffen-Unterscharführer* Alexander Zahharov remembered:

> In early 1944, while the *Estonian SS-Panzergrenadier-Battalion Narva* was on its way to the *5. SS-Panzergrenadier-Division Wiking* at the front near Cherkassy, I came down with a severe case of neuritis. After treatment in hospital I was sent to the SS rest home in Zakopane and finally to the *Waffen-Grenadier-Ausbildungs- und Ersatz-Regiment der SS 20* in Klooga. There we were quartered near a subcamp of the Vaivara concentration camp. In mid-September 1944, elements of our unit were ordered to seal off the Klooga labor camp. We were told that we would be guarding several thousand Jewish prisoners who were to be evacuated. When our battalion fell back before the Soviets soon afterwards, I and several non-commissioned officers remained behind as the cleanup detachment. Out of curiosity, several comrades and I went into the evacuated Klooga camp. What we saw there was terrible … The barracks were all open and prisoners who had been shot lay everywhere. Now we were soldiers and had seen dead men and were familiar with death and decay … But the shooting of defenseless people left behind a bad impression that remains to this day!

Camp Commandants:
SS-Sturmbannführer Hans Aumeier (August 20, 1906 – January 24, 1948)
SS-Hauptsturmführer Helmut Schnabel (August 26, 1912 – unknown)

Amtsgruppe W (Commercial Enterprises)

In the context of Himmler's visions, companies were formed before the war which were supposed to improve the SS' budget and further the *Reichsführer-SS'* cultural and ideological passions.

While the latter hobbies only achieved marginal importance because of the outbreak of war, until the end of the war the prisoners in the concentration camps in particular represented an enormous potential source of cheap labor. In addition to the "rental"[72] of prisoners to companies of the free economy, on April 29, 1938, Himmler founded the *Deutsche Erd- und Steinwerke DEST* (German Earth and Stone Works Company, in part for the quarries in the Flossenbürg, Groß-Rosen, and Mauthausen concentration camps) and in May of the following year the *Deutschen Ausrüstungswerke* (German Equipment Works or DAW), which took over production sites in the Dachau and Auschwitz concentration camps, some of which already existed.

In July 1940, the existing SS companies were combined under the *Deutschen Wirtschaftsbetriebe GmbH* (German Enterprises). Managing director of the DWB GmbH was Oswald Pohl, who wanted and was supposed to become active in continuously new fields of business. In developing the Economic and Administrative Main Office, from February 1942, it formed Amtsgruppe W. Like *SS-Obergruppenführer* Pohl, the SS officers of this office group had a dual function. They were shareholders and trustees of the various SS companies and, as members of the *Waffen-SS*, were also members of the SS-WVHA. Despite lacking experienced leaders and specialists, plus resistance from competitors in private industry, in 1943, Amtsgruppe W had annual revenues of 134.5 million Reichsmarks. That same year Oswald Pohl founded

Ostindustrie GmbH (OSTI), which employed about 10,000 Jewish prisoners in eight factories in the *Generalgouvernement*. In the end, however, this employment did nothing to save the Jews from their inevitable fate. Carried out in November 1943, "Operation Harvest Festival" further drastically reduced the Jewish labor forces in the *Generalgouvernement*, and the workers of Ostindustrie GmbH were among the victims.

Office Group W was organized into eight offices:

Office W I Stone and Earth (Reich) ....*SS-Sturmbannführer* Mummenthey
W I/1: Deutsche Erd- und Steinwerke GmbH
W I/2: Deutsche Erd- und Steinwerke GmbH
W I/3: Porzellan-Manufaktur Allach GmbH, Bohemia–Keramische Werke AG, Porag-Porzellan Radiatoren GmbH, Victoria-Porzellan AG

Office W II Stone and Earth (East) ....*SS-Obersturmbannführer* Dr. Bobermin
W II/1: Ostdeutsche Baustoffwerke GmbH
W II/2: General Trustees for Manufacturing of Building Materials for the Districts of Styria and Carinthia
W II/3: Russia Firms

Office W III Food Companies .... *SS-Hauptsturmführer* Rabeneck
W III/1: Sudetenquell GmbH, Heinrich Mattoni AG, Apollinaris Brunnen AG, Rheinahr Glasfabrik AG
W III/2: Freudenthaler Getränke GmbH
W III/3: Deutsche Lebensmittel GmbH

Office W IV Wood Processing Companies................... *SS-Sturmbannführer* Opperbeck
W IV/1: Deutsche Ausrüstungswerke GmbH
W IV/2: Deutsche Heimgestaltungs GmbH
W IV/3: Deutsche Meisterwerkstätten GmbH

Office W V Agriculture, Forestry and Fishing   *SS-Obersturmbannführer* Vogel
W V/1: German Research Institute for Nutrition and Food GmbH
W V/2: Forest Management
W V/3: Fishing Industry

Office W VI Textile and Leather Use ....*SS-Sturmbannführer* Lechler
W VI/1: Gesellschaft für Textile- und Lederverwertung GmbH

Office W VII Books and Pictures ....*SS-Hauptsturmführer* Dr. Mischke
W VII/1: Nordland-Verlag GmbH
W VII/2: Deutscher Bilderdienst

Office W VIII Special Tasks .... *SS-Sturmbannführer* Klein
W VIII/1: Society for the Promotion and Care of German Cultural Monuments
W VIII/2: Externsteine-Stiftung e.V., King Heinrich Memorial Foundation, Convalescent and Rest Homes
W VIII/3: Cultural Buildings

While Amtsgruppe W might have formed the basis for a later nationalization of private industry—following the NSDAP's original socialist thinking—its effect on the overall German war economy was minimal. It was not even able to equip its own troops of the Waffen-SS. When Himmler ordered the introduction of a service coat for the Waffen-SS, which was to have just five buttons, it was only possible to equip a few units with it. The majority retained the army model with the obligatory six buttons.

The Waffen-SS did make probably about 250,000 prisoners (mainly from Poland and Eastern Europe) available to the external armaments industry in 1944–45, almost three times as many as were employed in the SS' own companies. In 1944, for example, a total of about 40,000 concentration camp inmates were working in the factories of the DESt and DAW.

11. Main Office for Ethnic Germans, and Staff Main Office of the Reich Commissar for the Strengthening of German Nationhood[73]

The Ethnic Germans and Their Settlement Areas

In order to be better able to describe the functions of these two main offices, it makes sense to shed some light on the story of these emigrants. The term "ethnic German" was coined in 1933 in the form of the so-called "Ethnic German Council"[74] created that autumn and it replaced the terms "border and foreign Germans" previously used. The so-called borderland Germans were the German minorities that had come under foreign rule as a result of the border changes after the First World War, while the so-called foreign Germans were those who had lived in their own settlement areas abroad, often since the Middle Ages.

The most extensive wave of outmigration from German principalities took place in the 18th century. After the end of Turkish sovereignty in eastern and southern Europe, tens of thousands of so-called colonists were recruited by the Russian and Austro–Hungarian monarchies to resettle the areas that had been won back. On July 22, 1763, the Russian Czarina (of German origin) Catherine the Great announced that she would permit foreigners to settle in the thinly-populated area of the empire along the Volga in the Saratov area. To promote interest in settling the empty area, she offered special incentives, such as:

freedom of religion
freedom from taxation and levies for 5 to 30 years
interest-free loans for all purchases
freedom from military service "forever"
independent local government and school administration
free allocation of 30–80 dessiatines of land (1 dessiatine = roughly 3 acres) per family, and,
payment travel costs in case of need.

Approximately 27,000 settlers from Hesse, the Pfalz, Northern Bavaria, Northern Baden, and the Rhineland responded to this appeal. The main reasons were on the one hand freedom of religion and on the other, after the numerous wars, of a pragmatic economic and political nature.

Czar Alexander I issued a decree on February 20, 1804, authorizing German settlement in the area of the Black Sea. In contrast to the manifest of 1763, the German emigrants had to have at least 300 Gulden in assets plus a good character reference and good agricultural knowledge (especially in viticulture) or be able to prove training as an artisan.

Alexander II ended the incentives previously offered German colonists with a decree on June 4, 1871. With military service now obligatory, the pacifist Mennonites emigrated (mainly to North America). According to a census, in 1897 there were approximately 1.8 million Germans living in Russia. The German population is said to have grown to a total of 2.4 million by 1914. As there had been no more settlers from Germany, obviously significantly more identified themselves with Germany than had been the case seventeen years earlier. With about 3,000 colonies, the main settlement areas were on the Volga, in the Ukraine, the Crimea, the Trans–Caucasus and Bessarabia. An impressive 300,000 Germans served in the Czarist military during the First World War. The Russian Revolution of 1917 led to numerous changes in politics and society. The new minority policy, for example, resulted in the founding of the Autonomous Socialist Soviet Republic of Volga Germans on February 20, 1924.

In southeast Europe, in the twelfth century, the Hungarian King Geysa II recruited German colonists to guard against incursions by Mongols and Tatars and to develop the area economically. As in Russia, the settlers were offered various incentives, such as:

free election of judges and ministers,
jurisdiction according to their own common law,
exemption from duties and
free markets.

In return the German immigrants committed to pay the king an annual percentage rate of charge and, if necessary, to do military service. After settling in the Transylvania area, for a long time they enjoyed autonomous status. This autonomy finally ended in 1867 with the establishment of the Austro–Hungarian double empire.

When in 1716, after more than 150 years of Turkish rule, the Banat, also located in southeastern Europe, became a German nation of the Holy Roman Empire, German Emperor Karl VI settled about 15,000 German farmers and artisans in the area. They were supposed to make the barren region fruitful again. During the subsequent rule of Empress Maria Theresia, a further roughly 22,000 German settlers resided in the Banat. A third wave of colonization under Emperor Josef II brought another roughly 30,000 Germans to the Banat.

Terms like "Banat Swabians" and "Transylvanian Saxons" did not, however, describe the residents true origins and were only used as collective terms for the colonists. Most in fact came from the regions of the Rheinpfalz, Rheinhesse, Triers, and Lothringen (Lorraine) on the west side of the Rhine and from Franconia. Smaller numbers came from Bavaria, Swabia, and the Austrian Alpine lands. The colonists were given several more years of freedom from levies in the 18th Century and were permitted to elect their own administrations and judges. After Banat was incorporated into Hungarian territory in 1778, however, more restrictive policies and Hungarianization followed.

Also in the eighteenth century, "Sathmar Swabians" settled in northwestern Rumania. In addition to voluntary settlers, Protestants from the Austrian provinces, the so-called Landler, were forcibly resettled in Transylvania for religious reasons.

The Danube Monarchy fell apart after the First World War. In 1919, the Transylvanian Saxons and Banat Swabians voted to join the Kingdom of Rumania. The new Rumanian state did not leave the minorities with many privileges, but it was much more liberal towards the ethnic Germans than, for example, the regime in Hungary. Lower Styria, Southern Carinthia and Upper Carniola became part of the newly-created kingdom of the Serbs, Croats, and Slovenians, which took a chauvinistic line against the German minority.

After losing World War I, the German Reich's borders were also reduced. It lost Alsace–Lorraine to France, West Prussia (minus Danzig), and the province of Posen and Upper Silesia to Poland. Eupen–Malmedy went to Belgium, the Memelland to Lithuiania, and the Sudetenland to Czechoslovakia.

In 1935, the German Foreign Institute in Stuttgart published statistics, according to which[75] there were living:

66,000,000 Germans in the German Reich
400,000 Germans in Danzig
6,500,000 Germans in Austria
150,000 Germans in Belgium with Eupen–Malmedy
5,000 Germans in Bulgaria
60,000 Germans in Denmark with Northern Schleswig
23,000 Germans in Estonia
6,000 Germans in Finland
1,700,000 Germans in France with Alsace–Lorraine
2,000 Germans in Greece
20,000 Germans ion Great Britain
250,000 Germans in Italy with South Tyrol
70,000 Germans in Latvia
10,000 Germans in Lichtenstein
120,000 Germans in Lithuania with the Memel Region
290,000 Germans in Luxembourg
100,000 Germans in the Netherlands
5,000 Germans in Norway
1,371,000[76] Germans in Poland, including
    383,000 in Posen–Pomerelia
    390,000 in Upper Silesia
    40,000 in the Teschen Region
    60,000 in the Olsa Region
    360,000 in central Poland
    67,000 in eastern Poland
    71,000 in Galicia
2,000 Germans in Portugal
800,000 Germans in Rumania
6,000 Germans in Sweden
2,950,000 Germans in Switzerland
15,000 Germans in Spain
700,000 Germans in Yugoslavia
    33,000[77] in Lower Styria
    17,000 Gottschee
    20,000 in Bosnia
    170,000 in Croatia and Slovenia
    460,000 in the Vojvodina (Banat, Bačka, Syrmia)
3,500,000 Germans in Czechoslovakia
600,000 Germans in Hungary
1,000,000 Germans in European Russia.

In consultation with victorious powers of the First World War, National–Socialist policies, using almost democratic means, achieved the recovery of many smaller territories that had been lost in the Treaty of Versailles. The Sudetenland was returned to Germany in 1938, and the Memelland in 1939. The incorporation of Austria in March 1939, however, brought the addition of a region and a people that had been an autonomous state before the First World War and, seen historically, had frequently been at war with Prussia.

After the so-called Pact of Steel between Hitler and Mussolini, on June 23, 1939, an agreement was reached for the resettlement of the more than 200,000 ethnic Germans living in northern Italy. By December 31, 1939, a total of 185,085 ethnic Germans from South Tyrol, Trentino, the Kanal Valley, and Belluno registered for resettlement and were pooled in the Association of Optants for Germany.[78]

The resettlement of Baltic Germans from Latvia and Estonia also began in October 1939. Although this was less than popular there—most Germans had established themselves and achieved a high standard of living—the fear of the imminent exertion of Soviet influence was so great that most decided on resettlement. Heinrich Bosse wrote frankly in his book *Der Führer ruft*:[79]

> On October 9, 1939, the country's German newspapers announced the appeal for resettlement. No one was prepared for this. The more fervent and passionate the commitments to the nation had been, the more understandable had been the intertwined demand to hold onto the outpost that had been entrusted to us by the German people. Now, from one day too the next, all this no longer meant anything.

On November 16, 1939, Hitler also agreed with Stalin that the ethnic Germans living in the areas of eastern and southern Poland recently annexed by the Soviet Union could also leave the country. Hereupon about 58,000 ethnic Germans left Volhynia and approximately 40,000 the Narva area around Bialystok. Further resettlements followed from September 1940, after Rumania ceded Bessarabia and northern Bukovina to the Soviet Union after an ultimatum issued on June 26, 1940. Approximately 90,000 ethnic Germans left Bessarabia and 45,000 from northern Bukovina subsequently left their homes. After the conclusion of a treaty between Germany and Rumania, 14,500 ethnic Germans were also resettled from Dobruja, near the Black Sea in the Rumanian–Bulgarian border region, and 45,000 from southern Bukovina. The next group was the German minority in Lithuania, with about 35,000 members. Altogether about 420,000 ethnic Germans were settled in the Warthegau, Silesia, and West Prussia in the space of one year.

After the end of the western campaign, on May 18, 1940, Eupen–Malmedy and Moresnet were reincorporated into the German Reich. The mainly German population approved. Before May was over, Hitler announced the reunification of the Eupen-Malmedy and Moresnet area with the German Reich. Section 2 of the decree read: "The residents of German or related blood […] become German citizens subject to further specific provisions. The ethnic Germans become citizens of the Reich in accordance with the Reich Citizenship Law."

Alsace and Lorraine were occupied by German troops from June 19, 1940, during the western campaign and subsequently attached to the district of Baden. After Hitler decreed on October 18, 1940 that, "the Alsace and Lorraine areas […] will be regained by the German nation in a very short time," orders soon followed for French elements of the population to leave. Alsace and Lorraine were not, however, incorporated into the German Reich but instead were only annexed by it. The resettlement of an initial group of roughly 70,000 ethnic Germans from the occupied part of France to Lorraine began on May 14, 1941. Three months later on August 23, 1941, the law concerning citizenship in Alsace, in Lorraine, and in Luxembourg was issued: "Those German Alsatians, Lorthringer and Luxembourgers who a) have been or are subsequently called up by the *Wehrmacht* or *Waffen-SS*, or b) are acknowledged as proven Germans, become entitled to citizenship by law."

On May 15, 1941, after the campaign ion the Balkans, a treaty was signed between Germany and Croatia according to which southern Styria, Upper Carniola and southern Carinthia were

Heinrich Himmler

"HONOR THE DEAD AND PRAY FOR THEM!
ERECTED TO THE ETERNAL MEMORY OF
THOSE WHO REST HERE, FOREFATHERS
OF THE CHILDREN RETURNING TO THEIR
MOTHERLAND
DORNA WATRA NOVEMBER 1940
THE GERMAN RESETTLERS"

Impressive memorial to the 2,555 ethnic
German resettlers from Dorna Watra. They
were among the 52,350 returnees from
South Bukovina in Rumania.

The former German Catholic cemetery in Jakobsdorf, Hermannstadt District in Transylvania.

annexed by the German Reich. This was followed by formation of the *Steirischen Heimatbund* and the *Kärntner Volksbundes*. They registered about 820,000 residents and divided them into "peoples lists." With the Law for the Group Nationalization of Members of the German Race in Southern Styria, Southern Carinthia, and Upper Carniola of October 14, 1941, German citizenship was issued according to the peoples lists. It could be issued with the "right of withdrawal," which meant that it could be denied again within ten years. The resettlement of the German minority from Gottschee (Italy) to southern Styria began two weeks later. At the same time about 80,000 "undesirable" Slovenes were moved out.

The number of settlers from areas of the USSR (including those since occupied by the *Wehrmacht*) in the Wartheland had already reached almost 500,000 by the end of 1941.[80] In July 1942, 120,000 of these were still in, in some cases, very improvised resettlement camps. The majority of the others had taken over towns evacuated by the Poles. An initial total of 364,665 Poles and Jews had been moved out of the *Generalgouvernement* by March 14, 1942. A total of more than 630,000 Poles and Polish Jews were deported from the Wartheland alone, and most of the latter were liquidated in Action Reinhard.

The Staff Main Office of the Reich Commissar for the Strengthening of German Nationhood announced the following resettlement figures in a report on July 1, 1942:

Estonia and Latvia	72,643
Lithuania	50,744
Volhynia and Galicia	134,655
Narev Region (eastern Generalgouvernement)	30,631
Bessarabia	93,548
Northern Bukovina	43,538
Southern Bukovina	52,107
Dobruja	15,072
Rumania (old kingdom)	9,732
Gottschee (city)	14,270
Laibach and scattered settlements in Laibach Province	15,072
Bulgaria	848
Rump Serbia	1,575
Ingermanland (area between Estonia and Leningrad)	4,344
Greece	144
Total number	523,851

When the Red Army recaptured large parts of the Ukraine including the Crimea in early 1944, the approximately 125,000 Black Sea Germans not deported to Siberia by Stalin in the summer of 1941, were evacuated from Transnistria to the Wartheland.[81] Arthur Greiser (January 22, 1897 – July 21, 1946), the *Gauleiter* there, together with *SS-Brigadeführer* Heinz Reinefarth (December 26, 1903 – May 7, 1979), the Senior SS and Police Commander "Warthe," welcomed the 1,000,000th resettler to his *Gau*. Although by then the resettlements were only a flight from the Red Army, the National–Socialist press euphemistically declared:

> More than a million German resettlers in the Wartheland. In connection with the racial securing of German living space in the east begun four years ago by bringing home the outside German ethnic groups and their settlement within the expanded Reich borders, the Reichgau of Wartheland has put a significant part of its national-political work behind it. In these days *Gauleiter* and Reich Governor Greiser has been able to report to the *Führer* and to the *Reichsführer-SS* as Reich Commissar for the Strengthening of German Nationhood that, in the course of the ongoing resettlement of the Black Sea

The three stations of the resettlers:

Ethnic Germans leave their former settlement area in Eastern Europe to find new homes in the Warthe District and West Prussia.

On March 16, 1944, Arthur Greiser, *Gauleiter* of the Wartheland, welcomes the 1,000,000th resettler.

In the photo in the center is Heinz Reinefarth, Senior SS and Police Commander Warthe.

The flight before the Red Army began in the late summer of 1944.

Germans, the number of Germans in the Wartheland has passed the one million mark. Following the arrival of the Black Sea Germans still on their way, the German population in the Wartheland will rise to 1.1 million.

After Rumania changed sides on August 23, 1944, from mid-September until the beginning of October 1944, 100,000 ethnic Germans fled the Banat and Transylvania. Those who remained, believing the leadership of the ethnic group who declared that the German military would soon take care of the threatening situation or reluctant to leave their homes and possessions, were subsequently exposed to rape, dispossession, and deportation. All over Europe, ethnic Germans under foreign authority suffered. Dispossession and forced labor were reactions to Himmler's racial policy at the cost of other people, not just in eastern and southeastern Europe.

Main Office for Ethnic Germans

The *Volksdeutsche Mittelstelle* was formed in January 1937, from the *Volksdeutscher Rat* formed four years earlier by Rudolf Hess. The office was headed by *SS-Obergruppenführer* Werner Lorenz (October 2, 1891 – March 13, 1974), who in particular was responsible for the resettlement of the ethnic Germans from the Soviet Union in 1939–40.

In view of the further resettlements and the creation of new settlement areas, in June 1941, the office was elevated to become the Main Office for Ethnic Germans. As its area of responsibilities often overlapped those of the Staff Main Office of the Reich Commissar for the Strengthening of German Nationhood, on September 9, 1942, there was a clear delimitation of powers.

The Main Office for Ethnic Germans was now explicitly responsible for the leadership and welfare of the German ethnic groups, as well as for transport and supply of the resettlers in the so-called resettlement camps. This included public relations work at home and abroad with political influence on the ethnic Germans. The main office therefore had the following eleven offices:

Office I: Headquarters..*SS-Obergruppenführer* Werner Lorenz
Office II: Organization and Personnel...*SS-Sturmbannführer* Konrad Radunski
Office III: Finances, Economics and Administration..........................*SS-Sturmbannführer* Heinrich Lohl
Office IV: Information ....*SS-Obersturmführer* Waldemar Riemann
Office V: Germanness Education ....*SS-Hauptsturmführer* Willi Puls
Office VI: Ethnic Germans within the Reich................................*SS-Hauptsturmführer* Heinz Brückner
Office VII: Ethnic Germans in the New Eastern Areas..............................*SS-Oberführer* Horst Hoffmeyer
Office VIII: Culture and Science ....*SS-Obersturmbannführer* Wilhelm Luig
Office IX: Political Office of German Ethnic Groups ....*SS-Obersturmbannführer* Hans Weibgen
Office X: Ethnic Germans Economic Management...........................*SS-Hauptsturmführer* Lothar Heller
Office XI: Resettlement...*SS-Standartenführer* Walter Ellermeier

12. Staff Main Office of the Reich Commissar for the Strengthening of German Nationhood

While the nation still promoted German nationality abroad—with a view towards colonization—around 1900, this policy changed under the Third Reich. The former colonists were now urged to abandon their homes of many years and return home ("*Heim ins Reich*"):

Heinrich Himmler

Identity card of a member of a resettlement team in the German Racial Assistance Main Office.

Book of remembrance for members of the *8. SS-Totenkopf-Infanterie-Regiment* tasked with the resettlement of Volhynian and Galician Germans.

Identity card for an Alsatian SS volunteer who served in the German Racial Assistance Main Office.

Propaganda print for "The *Führer*'s Resettlements" 1941.

The abandonment of worthless or no longer tenable foreign posts represents a gain for Germandom as a whole: first it will bring new strength to core Germandom, which cannot be strong enough for the tasks envisaged for Germandom in Europe; but then such Germans, who for centuries have demonstrated their colonizing abilities, will be used especially to strengthen Germandom in the newly-won areas in the east.

So the resettlements were actually a concentration of the Germans in Europe. Influenced by Germany's successes, which were exploited for propaganda purposes, hundreds of thousands willingly answered "the Führer's call." On September 10, 1939, Hitler named the *Reichsführer-SS* the Reich Commissar for the Strengthening of German Nationhood. From the former Central Office for Immigration and Remigration[82] he created an office with the same name under the command of *SS-Brigadeführer* Ulrich Greifelt (December 8, 1896 – February 6, 1949).

Its areas of responsibility in part overlapped those of the Main Office for Ethnic Germans. In particular, the members of the German ethnic minorities or the mixed population of occupied or annexed areas were supposed to be categorized in so-called "people's lists" to quantitatively determine integration capacities. Undesirable elements of the population—for example Poles or Jews—were to be moved out:

> Cleansing the annexed eastern territories of persons of foreign race is one of the most important aims that must be achieved in the east. This is the cardinal racial-political task that the Reichsführer-SS, Reich Commissar for the Strengthening of German Nationhood, must accomplish in the annexed eastern territories.

In September–October 1939, approximately 930,000 ethnic Germans from Poland entered their names on the Reich Commissar for the Strengthening of German Nationhood's people's lists. They were divided into four categories:

I .... Ethnic Germans who in the past had stood up for Germandom,
II .... Ethnic Germans who could prove their Germanness but had not been active,
III ....Ethnic Germans who had entered relationships with non-Germans, such as children from this relationship and
IV ....Ethnic Germans who had acted against Germandom (communists or social democrats)

The office staff initially assigned 340,000 people to People's List I and II, 535,000 to People's List III and 55,000 to People's List IV.

In response to the beginning of the war with Russia, in June 1941, the office was elevated to the Staff Main Office of the Reich Commissar for the Strengthening of German Nationhood. It was organized as follows:

Office Group A
Office Z – Central Office
Office I – Resettlement and Cultural Identity
Office II – Labor

Office Group B
Office III – Economy
Office IV – Agriculture
Office V – Financial administration

Office Group C
Office VI – Planning
Office VII – Buildings
Office VIII – Central Land Office

The office's responsibilities were again clearly laid out in the 1943 edition of the NSDAP's organization book:

> The Staff Main Office of the Reich Commissar for the Strengthening of German Nationhood is responsible for all settlement and expansion planning and execution of these plans inside the Reich and in the areas under the jurisdiction of the Reich, including all administrative and economic questions associated with settlement, especially the use of people for the purpose of settlement.

As these fundamentally new tasks could not be carried out by existing Reich agencies, Himmler established new offices which were subordinate to the Staff Main Office of the Reich Commissar for the Strengthening of German Nationhood. The two most important were the Deutsche Umsiedlungs-Treuhand GmbH, which was supposed to assist the resettlers in matters of property rights, and the Deutsche Ansiedlungsgesellschaft, which took charge of seized property (from Poles, for example) and leased it to resettlers.

Due to overlapping functions and responsibilities, several main offices were involved in the resettlement of ethnic Germans:

- Main Office for Ethnic Germans, which carried out the actual resettlement work.
- Reich Security Main Office, which was primarily responsible for the political assessment of the ethnic Germans.
- Race and Settlement Main Office, which carried out racial checks.
- Staff Main Office of the Reich Commissar for the Strengthening of German Nationhood as command staff.

In addition, as later Reich Minister of the Interior, Himmler issued citizenship certificates for the resettlers.

After the victory over Poland, the planning department of the Staff Main Office of the Reich Commissar for the Strengthening of German Nationhood outlined the settlement of former Polish areas in West Prussia and the Wartheland. Altogether, about 4.3 million (ethnic) Germans were to be moved in and approximately 560,000 Jews and about 3.4 million Poles removed. These plans could not be completely realized, however.

The drawing up of a so-called General Plan East, which was supposed to create new large settlement areas, began at the same time. One was located between Lublin and Lvov in the Zamosc area in the *Generalgouvernement*, and another in the area around Zhitomir in Volhynia in the Generalkommissariat Ukraine. On November 22, 1942, during a speech to officer cadets at the *SS-Junkersschule* in Bad Tölz, Himmler declared that the occupied territories in the east were, "colonies today, settlement territory tomorrow, empire the day after tomorrow!"

The reality already looked quite different. On July 30, 1941, during a visit to Lublin, Himmler had ordered *SS-Brigadeführer* Odilo Globocnik, the local SS and police commander, to create, "a large settlement territory in the area of the existing ethnic German colonies near Zamosch."

Ethnic German resettlers from Bessarabia.

Kommando book for a member of the German Racial Assistance Main Office. *Sonderkommando* "R" (Russia) was responsible for registering the ethnic Germans in Transnistria, which had been under Rumanian administration since 1941.

To achieve this, about 110,000 Estonian Poles were supposed to be moved out and approximately 60,000 ethnic Germans moved in from Poland. In reality, however, only about 9,000 ethnic Germans were settled there. National Polish partisans, who created constant unrest, were largely responsible for hindering further settlement efforts, which were ultimately halted in August 1943.

In late 1942, efforts began to create a German settlement area around Zhitomir. Located about two kilometers south of the city, it was called Hegewald. By March 1943, 10,178 Volhynian Germans were resettled there from areas threatened by partisans. 7,327 ethnic Germans occupied about twenty-seven villages along the Zhitomir–Berdichev road, from which 10,623 Ukrainians had previously been deported to Dnepropetrovsk. A further resettlement action followed in the Chernyakhov area at the beginning of 1943. About 3,242 ethnic Germans were resettled in the area, which was renamed Försterstadt. Roughly 4,000 Ukrainians were driven into the surrounding districts (rayons). When the Red Army advanced into the area one year later, the unlucky settlers were evacuated again, to Wartheland. *Generalplan Ost* thus ended in failure.

CHAPTER 6
REICH MINISTER OF THE INTERIOR

On August 20, 1943, Hitler removed Wilhelm Frick (March 12, 1877 – October 16, 1946),[1] the Reich Minister of the Interior, after various differences. The main reason may have been Hitler's feeling that Frick no longer possessed the mental flexibility and strength to hold the position in times of total war. While Frick took over as Reich Protector of Bohemia and Moravia, a rather representative function, effective August 26, 1943, Hitler installed the *Reichsführer-SS* as the new Reich and Prussian Minister of the Interior. On August 26, 1943, *SS-Oberst-Gruppenführer* Kurt Daluege, who had been placed on leave on August 17 after a second heart attack, wrote the following letter to his good friend Himmler:

> It was with great joy that I learned, unfortunately by radio, of your long-overdue and much strived-for appointment to Reich Minister of the Interior and Plenipotentiary for Reich Administration. You know, dear Heinrich, how great is the joy and pride of so many of the best *Gauleiters* at this your great calling to this so difficult but vital position. I only regret that I shall not be able to help you personally with all my strength. I consider myself the best authority on the old Prussian and present Reich ministry of the interior. Should you need me in important matters, then call me. My most fervent wish, however, remains that you can fulfill this new and tremendous task in the best of health.

Himmler, who had previously held the executive position as Chief of German Police, now also combined the legislative in his person. As a dynamic organizer, he was supposed to bring quiet to the people, who were becoming war weary, and at the same time mobilize forces for the struggle. Through a rigid simplification of the administration, in the interior ministry alone he was able to halve the original number of about 800 officials and employees.[2] Not a few of these were simultaneously drafted into the armed services. In order to win back the population's sympathies and trust in the National–Socialist state, among the measures taken by the new Reich Minister of the Interior was an order that it must be made clear to all officials that they were there solely to help the people and had to sacrifice, which meant putting in extra hours, to achieve this. They were to, "instruct doubters, fortify the wavering, and counter the malicious with energy and impose on them the justified punishments."

Because of the many responsibilities he had taken on, Himmler was unable to explicitly worry about the ministry, and so he did what he practiced in many areas. He launched a vigorous program of reorganization and modification (for example remaking officialdom and the bureaucracy) and left the main area of responsibility to a subordinate. This was Wilhelm Stuckart (November 16, 1902 – November 15, 1953), who probably felt himself to be Frick's legitimate successor. Regarding this, on August 21, 1943, Josef Goebbels noted in his diary: "Stuckart is somewhat depressed about developments in the Reich Interior Ministry. I can understand that; he actually deserved to take over the administration."

Stuckart[3]—a member of the SS since 1936—had wide-ranging freedom of action. On January 30, 1944, Himmler appointed him *SS-Obergruppenführer* and "permanent representative of the Minister of the Interior."

This was in keeping with Himmler's strategy of bringing members of the SS into key positions. Stuckart worked with great devotion and was seen as a "man of great ability and quite different from the dime-a-dozen upstarts" from the ranks of the NSDAP, and not just by Himmler. The latter made no influential decisions after taking over the Reich Ministry of the Interior. He was, however, responsible for the naturalization of the ethnic Germans resettlers.

CHAPTER 7
COMMANDER OF THE REPLACEMENT ARMY

I n reaction to the Stauffenberg assassination attempt on July 20, 1944, and the presumable involvement of *Generaloberst* Fromm (October 4, 1888 – March 12, 1945) in the plot, that same day Hitler named Himmler the new commander of the Replacement Army (DdE). This appointment was probably only the result of events, for all the powers in questions of education, National–Socialist command, disciplinary criminal law and jurisdiction for the so-called *Volksgrenadier* Divisions of the twenty-ninth and following waves had already been given over to Himmler on July 15, 1944.[1] This already meant that he had a not inconsiderable influence on the powers of the BdE. Fromm would probably have been removed in the second half of 1944, because of his repeated calls to end the war with the Soviet Union.

On July 21, 1944, Himmler for his part named *SS-Obergruppenführer* Jüttner, head of the *SS-Hauptamt*, his permanent deputy as BdE and in Berlin gave his inaugural speech to officers of the head of Army Equipment and commander of the Replacement Army and of the General Army Office. A few days later followed further addresses to officers of the new *Volksgrenadier* divisions at the Grafenwöhr and Bitsch troop training grounds. In his typical way Himmler declared to the officers of the *Volksgrenadier* divisions:

> I give to you the authority to seize any fellow who is hanging around and if necessary tie him to a train wagon. Put in the divisions' most brutal, energetic and best officers who will immediately catch fellows such as these and put against the wall any who resist.

Himmler saw his main task as BdE as the mobilization of all available forces. In his speech to the *Gauleiters* in Posen on August 3, 1944 he expressed himself as follows (in part)—the speech is documented in its original length in appendix 3:

> You can be sure about one thing: I will never need an order from the *Führer* to form new divisions. I will constantly form them, and when they have got their weapons, I will go to the *Führer* and ask: Where do you need a division? That's the way I see the duty of the commander of the Replacement Army.

There was another reason why Hitler named Himmler to the post of Commander of the Replacement Army. The *Reichsführer-SS* was supposed to reform the *Wehrmacht* from the ground up. He was not only supposed to influence training of officers but of new recruits in particular. Goebbels noted in his diary on August 4, 1944,[2] "that Himmler is now carrying out the urgently-needed reform of the army with a firm hand. He will undertake to build up the army according to National–Socialist principles, as he has built up the Waffen-SS."

On January 5, 1945, Hitler elevated Himmler's position to commander-in-chief of the Replacement Army. This acknowledged the fact that the Replacement Army had reached a strength of over two-million men.

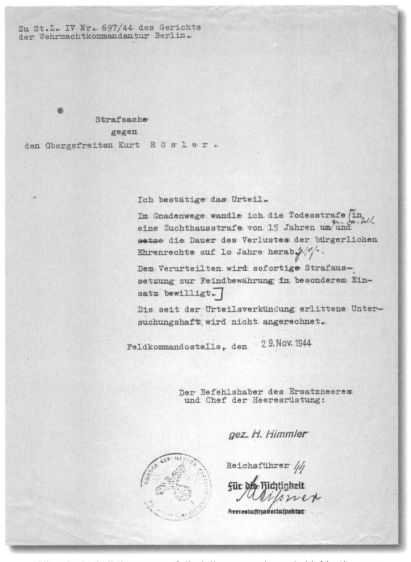

Himmler had all the powers of disciplinary superior and chief justice over the members of the Replacement Army.

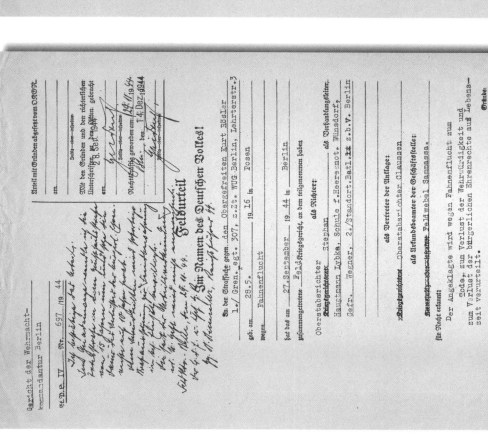

Gericht der Wehrmacht-
kommandantur Berlin

St.P.L. IV Nr. 697 /19 44

Im Namen des Deutschen Volkes!

Feldurteil

In der Strafsache gegen den Obergefreiten Kurt Kösler
1./Gren.Rgt. 307, z.Zt. WUG.Berlin, Lehrterstr.3

geb. am 28.5. 19.16 in Posen

wegen Fahnenflucht

hat das am 27.September 19 44 in Berlin zusammengetretene Feldkriegsgericht, an dem teilgenommen haben

Oberstabsrichter Stephan als Richter
Schöffen:
Hauptmann Lybka, Schule f/Heeresmot. Wünsdorf.
Gefr., Wegner, 2./Standort.Batl.z.b.V. Berlin

als Vertreter der Anklage:
Oberstabsrichter Claussen
als Urkundsbeamter der Geschäftsstelle:
Feldwebel Sammassa.

für Recht erkannt:

Der Angeklagte wird wegen Fahnenflucht zum Tode, zum Verlust der Wehrwürdigkeit und zum Verlust der bürgerlichen Ehrenrechte auf Lebenszeit verurteilt.

Gründe.

G r ü n d e.

I.

Der 28 Jahre alte verheiratete Angeklagte ist der Sohn eines Rohrlegers und Installateur. Der Beruf seines Grossvaters väterlicher und mütterlicherseits ist nicht bekannt. Er besuchte die Volksschule bis zur 8.Kl. und war dann Laufbursche bei verschiedenen Firmen. Arbeitslos geworden, kam er 1934 zur Landhilfe. 1934/35 befand er sich im freiwilligen Arbeitsdienst. Nach seiner Entlassung war er in verschiedenen Stellen als Gelegenheitsarbeiter tätig. 1937 legte er die Prüfung als Schwimmeister ab, nachdem er zuvor schon als Bademeister beschäftigt worden war. Am 28.8.1939 wurde er Soldat. Er nahm an den Unternehmen in Norwegen teil, war in Finnland und zuletzt in Lappland bei einem Inf. Regt. eingesetzt. Ihm wurden das E.K.II., das Inf. Sturmabzeichen in Silber und die Ostmedaille verliehen.

Der Angeklagte wurde 1937 wegen unbefugten Grenzübertritts zu 30.-RM Geldstrafe verurteilt. Disziplinarisch ist er nicht bestraft. Er wird wie folgt beurteilt:

"Geistig rege, gute Skiläufern sonst jedoch nicht allen körperlichen Anforderungen gewachsen.

Im Winterkrieg auf Grund seines sehr guten Skilaufens voll bewährt, sonst jedoch nur ausreichend, ist nicht in das National.sozialistische Ideengut eingedrungen.Führung genügend."

Der Partei oder einer ihrer Gliederungen gehört er nicht an. Sein Tauglichkeitsgrad ist k.v.--

II.

Der Angeklagte hatte vom 27.5.--22.6.1944 Urlaub nach Berlin. Dieser wurde bis zum 25.6.1944 verlängert. Am 4.6.1944 besuchte ihn der Grenadier Siegfried A b e l von der gleichen Einheit, der bis zum 2.6. Urlaub gehabt hatte. Bevor beide auf Urlaub gingen, hatten sie bereits in Erwägung gezogen, vom Urlaub nicht mehr zu ihrer Einheit zurückzukehren. Abel hatte geäussert, dass er Schweizer Franken besitze und man in die Schweiz fliehen könne. Darüber unterhielten die beiden sich

-3-

wieder, als Abel bei dem Angeklagten zu Besuch war.
Abel fuhr sodann nach Bunzlau, wohin seine Familie evakuiert
war und forderte den Angeklagten auf, ihm mit seiner Frau zu
folgen. Am 6.6. trafen der Angeklagte und seine Frau in Bunzlau
ein. Dort wurde endgültig beschlossen, in die Schweiz zu fliehen
Der Angeklagte liess sich von Abel gegen Hingabe von 1.000 RM
700 Schweizer Franken geben. Da die Ehefrau des Angeklagten
jedoch von Frau Abel in Erfahrung gebracht hatte, was die
Beiden vor hatten, kehrte der Angeklagte mit seiner Frau wieder
nach Berlin zurück. Diese bat ihn, unter allen Umständen zu
seiner Einheit zurückzukehren. Der Angeklagte wollte sich aber
darauf nicht einlassen und bemerkte, dass sie ja doch einmal
abgeschnitten werden würden.   Auf weiteres Drängen seiner Ehefrau verprach er dieser dann schliesslich, doch, zur Einheit
zurückzukehren. Am 25.6. begab sich der Angeklagte mit seiner
Frau zum Bahnhof, fuhr jedoch nicht ab, sondern begab sich
in die Wohnung der Zeugin Klimmeck, in Berlin, wo er sich
mit Abel ins geheim verabredet hatte . Bei Frau Klimmeck
hatte der Angeklagte bis zu seiner Einberufung gewohnt. Er sowie
Abel erklärten ihr, nicht mehr zur Front zurückkehren zu wollen
und zu versuchen, in die Schweiz zu gelangen. Bei dieser Gelegenheit verbrannte der Angeklagte seine Uniform. Am 26.6.
fuhren die Beiden noch einmal nach Bunzlau und von dort
am 27.6. mit Personenzügen über Dresden nach Lindau.
Nach einigen Tagen dort angekommen, begaben sie sich zu Fuss
in Richtung Bregenz, um an die Schweizer Grenze zu gelangen.
Da ihnen diese zu stark bewacht erschien, führten sie ihr
Vorhaben nicht aus, sondern kehrten um. Der Angeklagte fuhr
nach Berlin zurück, wo er am 1.oder 2.7. eintraf, während Abel
sich schon vorher von ihm trennte. Der Angeklagte begab sich
aber nicht in seine Wohnung, sondern hielt sich in der Folgezeit in der Umgebung von Berlin auf. Am 16.7. traf er sich mit
seiner Ehefrau, um sich Geld und Wäsche geben zu lassen. Am
29.7. nahm er Wohnung bei der Zeugin Klimmeck, der er erklärte, dass die Flucht nicht geglückt sei, er aber erneut
versuchen wolle, in die Schweiz zu gelangen. Am 30.7.1944
entwendete er gelegentlich eines Besuchs eines Bekannten aus
einer in einem Schrank hängenden Jacke einer Bekannten mit
Ausweisen, um diese gegebenenfalls einmal zu benutzen.

-4-

Am 1.8. traf er sich in der Wohnung der Klimmeck wieder mit
seiner Frau, wurde jedoch alsbald nach deren Erscheinen daselbst
festgenommen.

Dieser Sachverhalt beruht auf den Angaben des Angeklagten,
der Aussage der Zeugin Klimmeck und den verlesenen Aussagen
des Gren.Abel und der Ehefrau des Angeklagten.

III.

Der Angeklagte gibt zu seiner Entlastung folgendes an:
Er sei nun schon mehrere Jahre an der Nordfront eingesetzt
und habe keine Lust mehr gehabt, dorthin zurückzukehren.
Deswegen habe er sich früher schon nach Afrika und auch
zur Fallschirmtruppe gemeldet. Er habe insgesamt nur 4 mal Urlaub
gehabt. Er sei meistens zur Jagdkompanie kommandiert worden
und deswegen mit Urlaub schlechter dran gewesen als diejenigen
Kameraden, die dieser nicht angehörten. Er fühlte sich ungerecht behandelt. So habe er einmal keine Marketenderware
(Likör) erhalten, weder von der Jagdkompanie noch von seiner
eingentlichen Einheit. Wenn er der Jagdkompanie fertig
höriger der Jagdkompanie sich zu einem Unternehmen fertig
zu machen, so sei er darüber hinaus auch noch zum Arbeitsdienst worden. Furcht vor neuen Einsätzen habe
er nicht gehabt. Nicht richtig sei die Aussage des Abel,
man habe deswegen fahnenflüchtig werden wollen, weil zu der
damaligen Zeit starke Angriffe der Russen erfolgt seien.
Um in den Besitz der Branzosen Nachkampfsprange zu gelangen,
hätten ihm nur noch 3 Sätze gefehlt. Nicht richtig sei,
dass er und Abel wegen zu starker Bewachung der Grenze umgekehrt seien. Vielmehr habe er schon auf der Fahrt nach Lindau
starke Bedenken gehabt. Diese hätten ihn dann veranlasst,
von der Durchführung des Planes Abstand zu nehmen. Nach der
Schweiz zu gehen, habe er überhaupt völlig aufgegeben. Wenn
er noch eine Uniform gehabt hätte, dann hätte er sich auch
wieder gestellt.

—5—

IV.

Unglaubhaft ist, dass der Angeklagte nicht wegen der starken Bewachung der deutsch-schweizerischen Grenze wieder umgekehrt ist. In seiner ersten Vernehmung am 1.8. hat er ausdrücklich erklärt, dass das Überschreiten deshalb nicht möglich gewesen sei, da diese zu stark bewacht war. Weiterhin hat er der Zeugin Klimmeck, wie diese durchaus glaubhaft bekundete, erklärt, dass der Plan, in die Schweiz zu gelangen, nicht geglückt sei und er erneut versuchen wolle, in die Schweiz zu gelangen. Die Zeugin Klimmeck kann sich zwar an diese Äusserung nicht mehr genau erinnern, hat diese aber so aufgefasst, wie sie in ihrer Vernehmung am 4.8.1944 von ihr wiedergegeben worden ist. Hinzu kommt, dass der Angeklagte die 700.-Franken dem Abel nicht zurückgegeben hat, was durchaus nahegelegen hätte, wenn er die Absicht, nach der Schweiz zu gehen, restlos aufgegeben hätte. Bezeichnend ist in diesem Zusammenhang, dass der Angeklagte sich noch am 30.7. durch Diebstahl falscher Papiere verschafft hat.

V.

Der Angeklagte hat sich der Fahnenflucht gemäss § 69 MStGB schuldig gemacht. Die Tat war bereits in dem Augenblick vollendet, als er in Buchs den festen Entschluss gefasst hatte, in die Schweiz zu gehen und daraufhin keine Anstalten mehr machte, zu seiner Truppe zurückzukehren.

VI.

Bei der Bemessung der Strafe lagen die Richtlinien des Führers vom 14.4.1940 zu Grunde. Wenn auch gewisse Anhaltspunkte dafür vorliegen, dass der Angeklagte aus Furcht vor persönlicher Gefahren gehandelt hat, so hat dies das Gericht nach dem persönlichen Eindruck des Angeklagten und nach seinen bisherigen kämpferischen Leistungen nicht für erwiesen erachtet. Die Tatsache, dass der Angeklagte bereits mehrere Jahre an der Nordfront eingesetzt war, mag in der Hauptsache für ihn bestimmend gewesen sein. Die Todesstrafe war jedoch deswege geboten, weil es sich sowohl um eine gemeinschaftliche Fahnen-

—6—

flucht als auch um eine versuchte Flucht ins Ausland handelt. Aus diesem Grunde konnte selbst dann, wenn der Angeklagte sich dienstlich falsch behandelt gefühlt haben mag, eine Zuchthausstrafe nicht als ausreichende Sühne angesehen werden. Der Verlust der Wehrwürdigkeit folgt aus § 31 MStGB.

Oberstabsrichter.

Berlin, den 28.9.1944.

Kommandeur des Streifendienstes
im Wehrmachtstandort Groß-Berlin
Berlin NW7, Prinz-Friedrich-Karl-Straße 1
Vernehmungsabteilung
Az.14/ Schl Br.Tgb.Nr. 45460/44

Berlin, den 1.August 194
Fernsprecher: 42 59 36 App.230
Querverh.:

Betrifft: Strafverfahren gegen den Obergefreiten Kurt R ö s l e r wegen Fahnenflucht, Diebstahl, Urkundenfälschung, falsche Namenführung und Verstosses gegen die Verbrauchsregelungsstrafverordnung.

An das
Gericht der Wehrmachtkdtr. Berlin

Berlin NW 40
Lehrterstrasse 58

In der Anlage wird der Tatbericht gegen den Obergefreiten Kurt R ö s l e r
1./Gren.Rgt.307 - Fp.Nr. 07 295 B

zur weiteren Veranlassung übersandt. — Gem. § 62 H.Dv. 3/9 wird um Mitteilung des Straftenors, des Tages der Verurteilung und des Aktenzeichens oder des Gerichts, an das der Vorgang weitergeleitet wurde, gebeten.

1 Tatbericht mit
5 Anlagen

Oberstleutnant u.Kommandeur

3 AUG 1944

II. Beweismittel

1. Eigenes Geständnis des Beschuldigten (s. anl. Vernehmungsprotokoll des Vernehmungsoffiziers)
2. Zeugen: —
3. Soldbuch, Wehrmacht-Führerschein, Postausweis, U-Bahnkarte, Karte des Wehrmeldeamtes.

III.

Der Beschuldigte ist am 1.8.1944 um 18.oo Uhr, von der Heeresstreife — Stfw. Fuhrmann — vorl.festgenommen worden.

Als Anlagen werden beigefügt:
1. Vernehmungsprotokoll des Vernehmungsoffiziers.
2. Begl. Abschrift der Einlieferungsbescheinigung des Wehrmachtuntersuchungsgefängnisses vom 1.8.1944.
3. Durchschrift der Nachricht an die Truppe vom 1.8.1944.
4. Meldung der Heeresstreife vom 1.8.1944.
5. Beweismittel gem.II.3

Der Beschuldigte war nach seinen Angaben

vom		bis	Soldat in der alten Wehrmacht
vom		bis	Soldat in der Reichswehr
vom	28.8.1939	bis jetzt	Soldat in der neuen Wehrmacht

und war ernannt bzw. befördert

am 1.12.1942	bei 1./G.R.307	zum Obergefreiten
am	bei	zum

Nach seinen Angaben hat er keine — solche — militärischen oder sonstigen Strafen erhalten.

Oberstleutnant u.Kommandeur

2B 2000. 2.44 Commern-Druckerei, Berlin SO 16

Kommandeur des Streifendienstes
im Wehrmachtstandort Groß-Berlin
Vernehmungsoffizier

Aktenz.: Schl 14/ Br.Tgb.Nr.45460/44

Berlin NW 7, den 1.8. 1944
Prinz-Friedrich-Karl-Straße 1
Fernsprecher: über Wehrmachtkommandantur Berlin
und 42 59 36

Verkürzter Tatbericht

gegen den Obergefreiten Kurt B ö s l e r
von 1./Gren.Rgt.3o7 — Fp.Nr. 07 295 B
geb. am 28.5.1916 zu Posen/Warthegau
wegen Fahnenflucht, Urkundenfälschung, falsche Namensführung, Diebstahl und Verstoßes gegen die Verbraucherreglungsstrafverordn.

I. Tatbestand und Verdachtsgründe:

Der Beschuldigte hat sich schuldig gemacht:

1.) der Fahnenflucht gem.§ 69 MStGB,
Indem er seinen bis 25.6.44 befristeten Urlaub nach Berlin bis zu seiner am 1.8.1944 erfolgten vorl.Festnahme überschritt in der Absicht, sich dem Wehrdienst für dauernd zu entziehen;

2.) des Diebstahls gem.§ 242 RStGB;
Indem er am 30.7.1944 in der Wohnung des Willi Schmize,Berlin, Koloniestrasse 130 einen Briefumschlag mit Postausweis,U-Bahn-karte,Wehrpass und Karte des Wehrmeldeamtes — alle Ausweise ausgestellt auf den Namen Erwin Knoblauch — stahl;

3.) der Urkundenfälschung gem.§ 267 RStGB,
Indem er sich mit den unter 2.bezeichneten Ausweisen der Heeresstreife gegenüber am 1.8.1944 auswies;

4.) der falschen Namensführung gem.§ StGB 132a,
Indem er sich als Erwin Knoblauch ausgab;

5.) eines Verstoßes gem.§ 2 der Verbraucherregelungs-Strafverordnung in der Fassung vom 26.11.1941,RGBl I.S.734;
Indem er laufend Zigaretten,die er von seiner Feldeinheit mitgebracht hatte,und Rauchermarken,die er auf seinen Urlaubsschein erhalten hatte,gegen Lebensmittel und Lebensmittelmarken eintauschte und diese Marken für sich verbrauchte.

Der Beschuldigte ist geständig.Er gibt an,er habe keine Lust mehr Soldat zu sein und habe schon den Versuch unternommen,in die Schweiz zu flüchten,jedoch sei ihm diese Flucht nicht gelungen,da die Grenze zur Schweiz zu stark bewacht sei.Der Beschuldigte hat seine Uniform in den Tegeler-See geworfen,und sich damit selbst die Möglichkeit genommen,wieder freiwillig zur Wehrmacht zurückzukehren.Er hat sich aus der Volksgemeinschaft ausgeschlossen und sein Leben verwirkt.

19 2000. 2.44 Commern-Druckerei, Berlin SO 16

CHAPTER 8
MILITARY COMMANDER

Commander-in-Chief Upper Rhine

On November 12, 1944, the American 6th Army Group (Lt. Gen. Devers) launched an offensive against *Heeresgruppe G* (Army Group G, *General der Panzertruppen* Balck) on both sides of the Vosges. One week later, the French 1st Army (General de Lattre de Tassigny), advancing along the Swiss border by way of Belfort, reached the Upper Rhine near Mühlhausen. Further north, on November 23, 1944, the American 7th Army (Maj. Gen. Patch) also reached the Rhine near Strasbourg. As it did so it turned north and pushed the German *1. Armee* (*General der Infanterie* Obstfelder) back towards the north. As a result, the German *19. Armee* (*General der Infanterie* Wiese) was isolated in a bridgehead position in Alsace.

The Commander-in-Chief West, *Generaloberst* Rundstedt, informed Hitler that these positions in the rest of Alsace could not be held by the badly-weakened units there, which had been in combat for weeks without replacements. If the bridgehead was to be held at all, he advised, it would require the dispatch of two panzer divisions and a total of three infantry divisions to Army Group G. Because of the planned offensive by Army Group B in the Ardennes, however, Hitler initially only approved the transfer of two infantry divisions from the Netherlands to Alsace.

Hitler did, however, instruct Himmler in his capacity as BdE in the Black Forest[1] to transfer all available forces from *Wehrkreise* (Military Areas) V, VII, VIII and IX to the front and secure the Upper Rhine and the Westwall. This was a utopian idea given such poorly-trained forces fielding few heavy weapons. When the commander-in-chief of Army Group G requested permission to withdraw the 19th Army behind the Rhine, Hitler relieved him of command, and without further ado on December 2, 1944, he made Himmler responsible for the defense of the Upper Rhine.

For this new task Hitler gave Himmler the powers of the commander-in-chief of an army group. Himmler thus commanded all forces of the *Wehrmacht* and the *Waffen-SS* between Bienwald and the Swiss border. In addition to replacement units, the *Volkssturm* was also mobilized, in order to occupy those parts of the Westwall still in German hands. A National–Socialist political officer (NSFO) attached to Army Group G described the personnel situation on December 1, 1944, as follows:[2]

The longer one regarded the 19th Army in its heavy actions in Alsace, the more one's respect rose for a fighting unit whose character was not that of a well-trained army, but essentially a random collection of fighting men. Despite this, combat has succeeded in turning this mob into a unit. Today, however, it is an almost completely exhausted unit. The best intentions, which are demonstrated by the outstanding actions performed by individuals, is being exhausted by the unbroken combat. Many individuals have reached the end of their strength. Things would be completely different if they could be given two day's sleep.

Hitler directed Himmler first to hold the line in the Alsace bridgehead, unsettle Allied forces with local attacks, and to amass sufficient men and materiel for an offensive from the bridgehead. Following this, on December 12, 1944, Himmler ordered the *LXIII. Armee-Korps* (*Generalleutnant* Schack), which was under his command, to launch a regional offensive in upper Alsace. The *189. Infanterie-Division*, which a short time earlier had been formed from the *189. Reserve-Division*, launched "Operation Habicht" between Kaysersberg and Ribeauville. Its objective was to destroy the Allied forces that had advanced through the Vosges there.[3] As in the entire area of *Oberkommando Oberrhein*, "considerable numbers of officer candidates, reserve officer candidates, non-commissioned officer courses and other elements of the replacement army, the army and the *Waffen-SS*" had been moved up. The combat report also noted that, "although there could be no proper preparation due to the short lead time, [...] the attack was begun with these scarcely or completely untested and tossed-together units. Consequently the relatively significant initial successes on the first day were achieved at the cost of such heavy casualties that the attack had to be called off on the second day."

After this failure, on December 13, 1944, Himmler, who had previously voiced his dislike for the *Wehrmacht* generals, not least in his speech in Posen, relieved the commanding general of the *LXIII. Armee-Korps*, *Generalleutnant* Friedrich-August Schack (March 27, 1892 – July 24, 1968) and replaced him with *General der Infanterie* Erich Abraham (March 27, 1895 – March 7, 1971). Two days later he also relieved *General der Infanterie* Siegfried Rasp (January 10, 1898 – September 2, 1968), commander-in-chief of the 19th Army, for alleged incompetence.

On December 16, 1944, Army Group B began the Ardennes offensive in Belgium and Luxembourg. In response American and French forces were withdrawn to the north, weakening the forces facing Army Group G, in favor of the German side. After the Rundstedt offensive in the north became bogged down, "Operation Nordwind" was launched in Alsace on December 31, 1944. This was a combined operation between Army Group G with the 1st Army and *Oberkommando Oberrhein* (*Reichsführer-SS*) with the 19th Army.

While the 1st Army was supposed to break through to the south towards Zabern and then turn east, the 19th Army was supposed to establish bridgeheads north and south of Strasbourg and drive west. The troops that broke through north of Strasbourg were then supposed to link up with the 1st Army in the Hagenau – Brumath area and encircle the US VI Corps. The units attacking south of Strasbourg were to retake the city.

At that time the 19th Army was organized as follows:
LXIV. Armee-Korps   16. *Volksgrenadier-Division, 189.* and *198. Infanterie-Division, 708. Volksgrenadier-Division* and *Panzer-Brigade 106.*
LXIII. Armee-Korps   159., 259., 338. and 716. *Infanterie-Division* and,
XIV. SS-Armee-Korps   553. *Volksgrenadier-Division* and *Division 405.*

During the night of January 5, 1945, the *553. Volksgrenadier-Division* (*Generalmajor* Hüther), which had been badly battered in the previous fighting, succeeded in establishing a bridgehead near Gambsheim. As the American units withdrew strong elements into the 1st Army's attack area, the *Volksgrenadiere* were able to cross the Rhine in their assault boats almost trouble free. The bridgehead was quickly expanded towards Herlisheim and Offendorf, and additional forces were ferried in to hold it. On January 4, 1945, the *Wehrmacht* Operations Staff (*Oberst i.G.* Meyer-Detring) noted of the fighting to date in Alsace:[4]

> In slow and fierce fighting, in the northern Vosges our troops have advanced almost to the end of the mountains. The inadequate training of the troops has made itself felt, especially in the interplay of weapons. In addition to the physical exhaustion of the forces employed because of the previous fighting, it was evident that our forces, from mid-level command down to the common soldier were inadequately trained.
>
> The operation was designed in such a way that the right wing was supposed to make the main thrust at the Saar, in order to then clear the area to the east. This wing of the advance became bogged down, however; by contrast the battle group in the forested wing made good progress. The focus of the attack was subsequently shifted to the east in order to seek a decision there. To this end the *Reichsführer-SS* was supposed to carry out a secondary advance with a weak division at his disposal. Since the day before yesterday (January 2) it transpired that the enemy was shifting forces into the western attack area, denuding the front north of Hagenau and at the Rhine. The forces of the *553. Volksgrenadier-Division* that crossed today have encountered no resistance. The *269. Infanterie-Division* is now also attacking north from the Schlettstadt area.

On January 8, 1945, the 19th Army launched its "Operation Sonnenwende." Deployed between the Rhine and Ill Rivers, the *198. Infanterie-Division*, elements of the *269. Infanterie-Division* and *Panzerbrigade 106* attacked from the Alsace bridgehead towards Strasbourg. The units succeeded in forcing the French behind the Ill. On January 12, 1945, however, the German attack spearheads bogged down and even after repeated attacks were unable to reach the actual objective, Strasbourg. Himmler reacted immediately by relieving one of his generals. *Generalmajor* Schiel, commander of the *198. Infanterie-Division*, was replaced by *Generalmajor* Konrad Barde (November 13, 1897 – May 4, 1945) on January 18, 1945.

After the German forces bogged down south of Strasbourg, an effort was made to take the offensive to the north, from the Gambsheim bridgehead. To achieve the strategic objective, the encirclement of the American VI Corps, *the XXXIX. Panzer-Korps* (*General der Panzertruppen* Decker) was sent to the *Oberkommando "Oberrhein."* The *10. SS-Panzer-Division "Frundsberg"* reached the bridgehead during the night of January 14–15, and on the seventeenth, attacked in the direction of Brumath. The units were pulled back to their starting positions that evening, however, after suffering heavy losses to enemy air activity and artillery.

Himmler subsequently ordered another attack from the Gambsheim bridgehead by the *10. SS-Panzer-Division "Frundsberg,"* this time further north in the direction of Hagenau. He was not present to witness the attack, however. After the collapse of Army Group Center Hitler had named him commander-in-chief of new army group, which was to be formed ad hoc, on the Eastern Front. On the evening of January 20, 1945, he handed his *Oberkommando*[5] over to *SS-Oberst-Gruppenführer* Hausser and during the night travelled in his special train to Berlin.

Commander-in-Chief Army Group Vistula

On January 12, 1945, about four months after its successful 1944 summer offensive, the Red Army launched its winter offensive. Striking from the Baranov bridgehead at the seam between the *4. Panzer-Armee* (*General der Panzertruppen* Gräser) and the *17. Armee* (*General der*

Infanterie Schulz), by evening the 1st Ukrainian Front (Marshall Konev) had gained about 20 kilometers in the direction of Litzmannstadt.

On the same day, the 3rd White Russian Front (Marshall Chernyakhovsky) launched its offensive from Lithuania against the *3. Panzer-Armee* (*Generaloberst* Raus), and the *4. Armee* (*General der Infanterie* Hoßbach) in East Prussia. The fourteenth of January also brought the attack by the 2nd White Russian Front (Marshall Rokossovsky) from the Narev bridgehead in the direction of Elbing and Graudenz against the *2. Armee* (*Generaloberst* Weiss), and the 1st White Russian Front (Marshall Zhukov) south of Warsaw from the Magnuszew and Pulawy bridgeheads, in the direction of Posen against the *9. Armee* (*General der Infanterie* Busse) and *4. Armee*.

Although the German troops had made every possible preparation to meet the coming offensive by the Red Army, outnumbered as much as ten to one in materiel and personnel, there was little they could do. With powerful artillery, air and tank support, the enemy broke through the in-depth defense positions. Ultimately the enemy forces advanced faster than the German units, lacking fuel for their vehicles and heavy weapons, could withdraw. So-called fortresses, like Posen and Schneidemühl for example, were set up around vital transportation junctions and were supposed to prevent the Red Army from using the railroads. As well, many German units were simply overrun.[6]

The Red Army drove into an area almost devoid of enemy troops, from which the terrified civilian population fled in great haste in ice and snow. Within two weeks the parts of the Generalgouvernement still in German hands and the Wartheland District had been lost. The enemy was at the Oder in the west and in the north was approaching the Frische Haff at Elbing. The encirclement of the *3. Panzer-Armee* and the *4. Armee* in East Prussia was imminent.

The Soviets had smashed Army Groups Center and A even more quickly than in the summer of 1944, and had gained another 400 kilometers of ground to the west. The rapid advance to the west and northwest created a gap of several hundred kilometers between *2. Armee* in West Prussia and *9. Armee* in Silesia. A new army group was supposed to close this gap. The Chief of the Army General Staff, *Generaloberst* Guderian, announced this decision by Hitler on January 22, 1945:[7]

1.) By order of the *Führer*, the *Reichsführer-SS* is assuming command of the newly-formed Army Group Vistula

2.) Its mission is:

a) Close the gap between Army Groups A and Center, stop the enemy from breaking through in the direction of Posen and Danzig and thus prevent the isolation of East Prussia, and secure the massing of new forces being moved up.

b) Organize the national defense behind the entire Eastern Front on German soil.

3.) Troops:

Attached to Army Group Vistula are:

a) *9. Armee* (with all army units), (timing will be included in a separate order),

b) *2. Armee* (with all army units),

c) 300 tank-destroyer teams (provided by the Generals of Anti-Tank Defense of all arms,

d) Military Districts 2, 3, 20 and 21 including the *Gneisenau* and *Volkssturm* units being formed in these military districts,

e) Orders will follow for further attachments.

4.) Boundaries (Map 1 : 1 Million)

a) To the right to Army Group A (later Center):

Fortress Glogau–Krotoschin–Ostrowo–Petrikau (towns on the Vistula),

b) To the left to Army Group Center (later North):

Elbing (Vistula)–Osterode (Center)–Willenberg (Center),

c) Army Group Vistula will report timing of readiness to work and possible assumption of command.

d) The headquarters of Army Group Vistula is being formed from the *Waffen-SS* and army as per closer arrangements by the *Reichsführer-SS*. Details to be determined by the Org Abt directly with the *Reichsführer-SS*. Quartermaster General will set his senior quartermaster staff in direct consultation with the *Reichsführer-SS* and will regulate the delivery of necessary transport capacity.

e) Chief of Army Signals will determine allocation of signals units.

f) Headquarters: Schneidemühl.

The installation of Himmler as commander-in-chief of Army Group Vistula on January 21, 1945, was an affront to the German generals. While the use of Himmler to secure the Upper Rhine could be explained by his position as Commander of the Replacement Army—the forces there were not named Army Group Upper Rhine until after he had handed command over to *SS-Oberst-Gruppenführer* Hausser—the *Reichsführer-SS* was now the commander-in-chief of an army group, which was of an entirely different order geographically, strategically, and in terms of personnel. As a rule he had no access to the generals and senior officers under his command and he worked almost exclusively with pressure and threats. As had been the case when he was the Commander-in-Chief Upper Rhine, senior unit commanders were discharged on a regular basis.

Goebbels wrote in his diary that Hitler had been, "extremely satisfied with Himmler's work [*Author*: in Alsace]." In fact Himmler had achieved the tasks he had been given—bolstering the Upper Rhine front and launching attacks to improve the situation—in cooperation with Army Group G. Considering the tasks assigned on January 21, 1945, the naming of Himmler as commander-in-chief of Army Group Vistula was obviously planned primarily for organizational matters. Goebbels wrote in his diary that this was, "mainly attributable to the fact that the units flooding back from the areas into which the Soviets were advancing, had partly collapsed, and a strong hand was needed to make them into a solid fighting contingent again."

Hitler, the former First World War corporal, had become the commander-in-chief of the armed forces, and now a man who had not even completed an officer candidate course in 1918, was in command of the most important army group of early 1945. Both obviously trusted in intuition, which they believed enabled them to correctly assess military situations and react strategically to them. Both mistrusted the *Wehrmacht* generals—especially after the twentieth of July assassination attempt—and both desired the metamorphosis of the *Wehrmacht* into a people's army, in which the spirit of National–Socialism prevailed, as he propagated (but had not yet achieved) in the *Waffen-SS*.

After leaving Berlin in his personal train *Steiermark* (Styria) at 0700 on January 21, 1945, at about 1300, Himmler reached Schneidemühl. At 1400 he had a meal with *SS-Gruppenführer* Gebhardt (November 23, 1897 – June 2, 1948), and then at about 1630 left for Marienburg (south of Dirschau). In the castle there he gave a typically pathetic speech to political and military leaders. Dr. Hans Leeser, the former mayor of the city of Elbing in West Prussia, remembered:[8]

On the evening of Sunday, January 21, 1945, the district commander of the *Volkssturm*, the well-known Knight's Cross holder, and U-boat commander *Kapitän zur See* Hartmann, called and told me that there was no cause for any sort of unrest among the population in Elbing, as there was going to be a fundamental change in the military situation in a few days. He had just come from a meeting in Marienburg, at which the *Reichsführer-SS* had been present and had stated that he was the new commander of the new Army Group Vistula and that everything would be in order again in a few days.

Here I would like to note the following: In spring 1946, I spent a short time with the former *Gauleiter* Forster in the Fallingbostel internment camp. I asked him about the meeting with Himmler in Marienburg. He told me the following:

Himmler lied to us terribly. He moved panzer armies around on a large map, giving us the impression that the situation would soon change. Afterwards, it turned out that these panzer armies hadn't existed at all.

Concurrently, in his capacity as BdE, Himmler ordered the dispatch of the alert units, which had been in formation since the release of codeword *Gneisenau* on January 13, 1945. These were units of the Replacement Army in which the recruits were supposed to have at least four weeks of training. And so 16- and 17-year-olds who had just received their uniforms were sent into action.

The headquarters staff of the new Army Group Vistula was formed from the former staff of the Commander-in-Chief Upper Rhine (Chief of the General Staff: *SS-Gruppenführer* Lammerding) and was supposed to take over command of troops yet to arrive on an approximately 300 kilometer length of front. Soon afterwards, in the Posen area the 1st White Russian Front crossed the Warthe (the so-called C Line) on both sides of Fortress Posen, which was encircled. Armored vanguards reached the Tierschtiegel barrier and the Netze River near Kreuz. To the northeast they crossed the Netze and advanced northwest. About all that was present in the area west of Posen and north of the Netze was alert units (training and replacement units, plus schools and *Volkssturm*) and fragments of Army Groups Center and A with no unified command, corps headquarters were at first rushed to the front:

a) Headquarters, **V. SS-Gebirgs-Korps** from the Balkans to the Tirschtiegel barrier east of Meseritz.

b) Acting Headquarters, **III. Armee-Korps** from Berlin, in the Oder–Warthe position between Landsberg and Crossen.

c) Acting Headquarters, **II. Armee-Korps** from Stettin, which was to lead alert units from Kreuz to Schneidemühl. In fact it was unable to offer resistance until the Pomerania position.

d) Headquarters, **XVI. SS-Armee-Korps**, formed from Operations Staff Baltic Coast, which was supposed to take over the Fortress Schneidemühl–Fordon (east of Bromberg) sector.

The addition of Headquarters, *9. Armee* with the *XXXX. Panzer-Korps*,[9] which was engaged between Wollstein and Lissa, followed on January 27, 1945. All additional units, including corps headquarters, the Oder–Warthe salient, and the Netze River line, were to be subordinated to the Fortress Schneidemühl.

In addition to the task of forming the personnel for the new Army Group Vistula and establishing a continuous front from the Oder–Warthe Position to Elbing, far from reality Himmler tried to regain the initiative by immediately launching attacks of his own. That same day he instructed the headquarters of *V. SS-Gebirgs-Korps* and the headquarters of the newly-attached *XXXX. Panzer-Korps*:[10]

It is vital for subsequent operations by the army group that the C Line be retaken as soon as possible and Fortress Posen freed. As prerequisite for this, *V. SS-Gebirgs-Korps* must halt the units fighting their way back out of Posen in the general line Pinne–Neustadt–Neutomischl–Wollstein. Should these troops have already been absorbed into the Tirschtiegel Barrier, they must be shifted to the east in this line at an early stage while conducting powerful armed reconnaissance. The use of tank-killing teams is especially promising for this purpose.

Himmler's orders, like Hitler's, could not be carried out. Armed for the most part with small arms, it was almost impossible for the German troops to hold the lines they had just occupied against the masses of Soviet armor. Counterattacking to retake the Vistula Line would have had some chance of success, if the German troops had had sufficient fuel and tanks, plus an air force capable of operations and sufficient ammunition for their artillery. None of these were available, however.

On January 28, 1945, Headquarters, *X. SS-Armee-Korps* (*SS-Obergruppenführer* von dem Bach) was formed from the former Headquarters of Anti-Partisan Units and attached to the *9. Armee* in the Woldenburg area. Deployed between the *XVI. SS-Armee-Korps* and Acting *II. Armee-Korps* to command various alert units in an area almost devoid of troops, *X. SS-Armee-Korps* was supposed to take the offensive in the next few days:[11]

AOK 9 [Headquarters, 9. Armee] shall conduct an offensive operation against the Woldenburg area on the one hand and the Hochzeit crossing on the other, with the objective of driving into the flank of the enemy forces advancing in a generally western

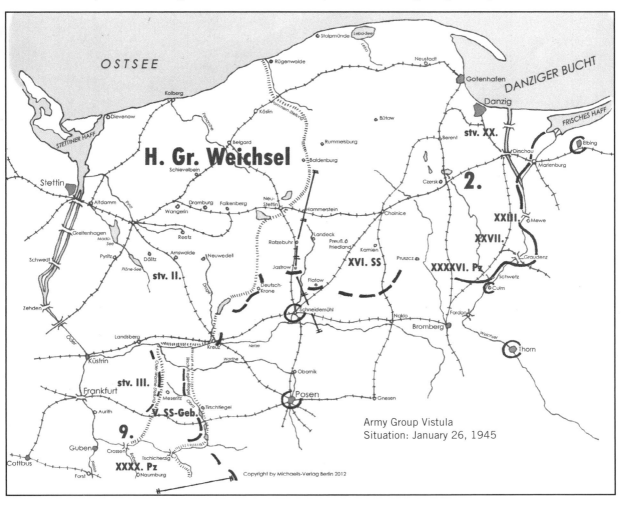

Army Group Vistula
Situation: January 26, 1945

direction and cutting off their communications with the rear. *X. SS-Armee-Korps* will command the operation. The commander of *Panzer-Jagd-Brigade 104* is at the *X. SS-Armee-Korps*'s disposal for consultation.

Before the *X. SS-Armee-Korps* launched its attack, however, the order was recalled. This was symptomatic of the pace of events in Pomerania. On January 30, 1945, Himmler issued a directive for the conduct of operations by the units under his command (AOK 9, AOK 2 and Acting Headquarters, *II. Armee-Korps*) in the coming days:[12]

1. It is vital that the army group use all available means to prevent the enemy from advancing further to the west. Holding even minor strongpoints, which split the enemy drive, becomes of even more importance. Only under these conditions will the army group be able to properly employ the large units which are on their way.
2. To this end, the *9. Armee* must at all costs defend the Lissa–Odereck line and the Oder–Warthe Position on its right wing. Enemy armored groups that have broken through are to be hunted down and destroyed by assault guns and tank-killing teams. Landsberg, which is a pillar, is to be reinforced. The enemy must be prevented from breaking through to Küstrin. Enemy armored forces that have broken into the gap between the *V. SS-Korps* and *X. SS-Korps* are to be engaged and destroyed where they are found. This calls for the utmost daring and mobility. On the army's northern wing Schneidemühl, which is a breakwater, in particular must be held. In this sector strengthening of the security garrison in the Pomerania Position is important.
3. The focal point of the defense for the *2. Armee* remains on its two wings. On its southern front the army must wage mobile warfare to prevent a further breakthrough to the northwest. This will create the conditions necessary to firm up this sector by commiting the *32. Division.* Breakout by the garrison of Fortress Thorn as per special voice command.

As was often the case, Himmler's typical rhetoric ignored reality. The situation was deteriorating steadily. While he was using inflated words to spur his thrown-together units to fight, but with no actions to back them up, from January 31 to February 2, troops of the Soviet 2nd Guards Tank Army were establishing three bridgeheads over the Oder at Kienitz, Genschmar and Güstebiese. The Soviet 1st Guards Tank Army also broke through the *9. Armee*'s Tirschtiegel Barrier and the Oder–Warthe position, and on February 1, 1945, established a bridgehead over the Oder at Aurith. Farther south, the Soviet 33rd Army gained a bridgehead—also against the *9. Armee*—at Tschicherzig. The Red Army had thus achieved important objectives of its winter offensive.

With just two army headquarters to command the troops occupying a length of front that by now had grown to about 500 kilometers, and delays in releasing Pz.AOK 3 (Headquarters, *3. Panzer-Armee*) from East Prussia, on February 2, 1945, *Armee-Oberkommando 11* (Headquarters, *11. Armee*) was formed. Temporarily created from the staff of Headquarters, *III. (germanisches) SS-Panzer-Korps*, under the command of *SS-Obergruppenführer* Steiner, the army headquarters assumed command of the area between Kolmar (*2. Armee*) and the junction of the Finow Canal and the Oder (*9. Armee*).

With the deployment of this army headquarters, the organization of Army Group Vistula was seen as complete. Organizationally, Himmler had succeeded in forming a complete army group in ten days. Smaller and larger units were continuously fed in—mainly from the Western Front and the homeland. Viewed nominally, these were impressive reinforcements. In fact, however, almost none of the divisions were anywhere close to their authorized strengths in men or materiel. This was especially true of the armored units, most of which were not even

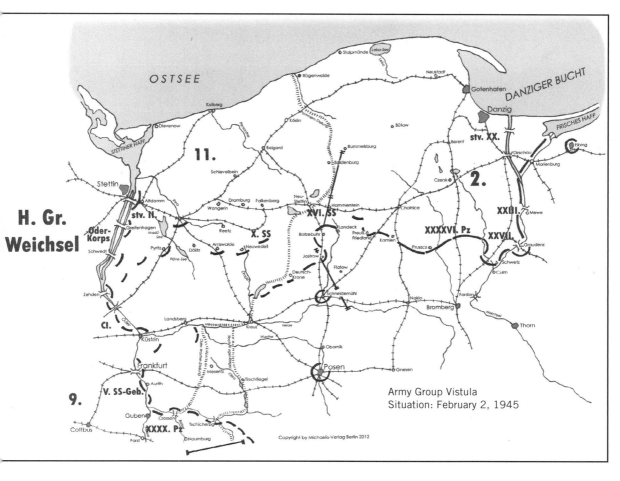

Army Group Vistula
Situation: February 2, 1945

at 50% of their authorized strengths and had fuel for a maximum of three day's operations. The new formations were for the most part made up of young recruits and convalescents, while some of the "old" units had been decimated in previous battles. The designations of some divisions alone were deceptions. The *27.* and *28. SS-Freiwilligen-Division*, for example, were not even at regiment strength.

With morale falling, that same day Himmler advised *SS-Obergruppenführer* Carl Oberg (January 27, 1897 – June 3, 1965), the Senior SS and Police Commander France and now commander of the blocking and rear defense lines, that:

In every case in which shirking and cowardice clearly exist,[13] whether officer or enlisted man, I wish you to intervene with summary court justice. The sentences are to be carried out before the assembled personnel of the company in question or the battalion in question.

I wish for a report to be sent to me each evening by telex about the number of officers and men caught, and about the soldiers from the deployed personnel replacement transfer battalions who belong to specific divisions and were truly separated from their units in action. Simultaneous notification of Permanent Deputy *Ob. D.E. SS-Obergruppenführer* Jüttner, so that he can immediately take steps so that the remaining soldiers separated from their units can be retrained to again become soldiers, which can then be sent back to the army group. Your daily reports should also include all court-martial sentences or death sentences.

After the Red Army reached the Oder north of Küstrin in late January/early February 1945, the opportunity existed, at least in principle, to drive from the north into the 1st White Russian Front's extended flank. As per the previously-mentioned OKH directive of February 2, 1945, the newly-formed *11. Armee* was therefore, "to strike the Russian 2nd Guards Tank Army advancing towards the Oder (…) and thus eliminate the direct threat to the Reich capital."

In addition to the formation of Headquarters, *11. Armee*, for which about ten brigades and divisions were being sent, the Chief of the Army General Staff also planned to transfer the *6. Panzer-Armee*[14] from the Western Front to Army Group Vistula:[15]

> Headquarters, *6. Panzer-Armee* with army units will transfer to the Frankfurt/Oder – Fürstenwalde area as OKH reserve and on arrival will be subordinate to Army Group Vistula in matters of supply. It is intended to attach units being brought in from the west to *Pz. AOK 6* by special order and with these attack from the Odereck–Crosen area through Meseritz–Zielenzig and reach the Warthe on both sides of Landsberg, and in cooperation with forces of the *9. Armee* attacking through Frankfurt–Küstrin destroy the enemy forces that have advanced into the bend of the Oder. Army headquarters: Cottbus.
>
> *Pz. AOK 6* to report plan of attack and deployment of forces to OKH Operations Dept. as soon as possible.

His plan was to destroy the Red Army forces at the Oder with a pincer movement by the *11. Armee* from the northeast in the direction of Landsberg and the *6. Panzer-Armee* from the area east of Guben. Hitler made new arrangements and ordered the *6. Panzer-Armee* which had just taken part in the failed Ardennes offensive, to Hungary.[16]

Himmler was ordered to Berlin on February 7, 1945, to discuss the upcoming offensive. There he had talks, not just with Hitler, but with *Reichsleiter* Bormann and *Generaloberst* Guderian as well. The next day, after discussions with Hitler, he issued the following directive:[17]

1. In keeping with my directive *Ob. Kdo. H. Gr. Weichsel [Vistula] Ia 15/45 g. Kdos. Chefs*, in view of the changed enemy situation[18] it is vital to protect our buildup area in the general line Bahn–Pyritz–north tip Plöne See–Arnswalde–Neuwedell–Pomerania Position astride Deutsch–Krone.
2. To this end, in keeping with the request made by AOK 11 on February 8, 1945, in addition to the "*Wallonie*" and "*Langemarck*" Divisions, I release the *Panzer-Division "Holstein"* and the *Führer-Begleit-Division*. But I expect that these valuable fast units will be committed at the focal points, sharply concentrated in an offensive role. With the overall objective in mind, the release of further units from the forces being assembled must be avoided at all costs. This would only be justified by an absolute emergency and then a request with justification would be submitted to me.
3. [...] AOK 2 will carry out a drive with the *5. Jäger-Division* and the joining *32. Division* through Ratzebuhr into the deep flank and rear of the enemy advancing north of Deutsch–Krone at the earliest possible time. For this purpose AOK 11 must drive towards it with a group of mobile forces, in a generally northeast direction. The objective of this operation must be to reach the Deutsch–Krone–Jastrow–Landeck road, in order to ultimately establish contact between the two armies. The operation will be carried out in close cooperation between the two armies.

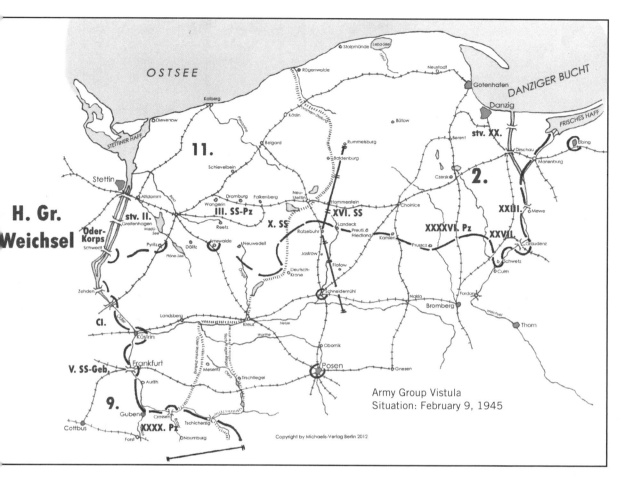

Army Group Vistula
Situation: February 9, 1945

On February 10, 1945, Himmler was again in Berlin, two and a half hours away, for further talks. *Generaloberst* Guderian, the Chief of the Army General Staff, wanted the offensive to begin as soon as possible, but Himmler rejected the idea because the necessary ammunition and fuel had not yet arrived. As Guderian clung to the idea of an early start, he asked Hitler for the transfer of *General der Infanterie* Wenck to the army group headquarters staff, as he believed that he would comply with his plans. After the *Reichsführer-SS's* lack of strategic knowledge was pointed out, Hitler intervened and placed *General der Infanterie* Wenck, Chief of the Operations Staff in the General Staff, in operational command of the offensive. Guderian had gotten his way. Guderian's memoirs contain an account of the conversation from his subjective point of view:[19]

> *Guderian*: *General* Wenck must be ordered to the *Reichsführer's* staff, otherwise there is no guarantee that the attack will succeed.
> *Hitler*: The *Reichsführer-SS* is man enough to carry out the attack alone!
> *Guderian*: The *Reichsführer* … does not have the experience or the qualified staff to carry out the attack independently. The presence of *General* Wenck is indispensible for its success.
> *Hitler*: I forbid you to reproach me [by saying] that the *Reichsführer-SS* is not equal to his task.

Guderian: I must insist that *General* Wenck be ordered to the army group staff in order to properly lead the operation.

Hitler to Himmler: Very well, Himmler, *General* Wenck will join your staff this night and lead the attack.

Oberst i.G. Eismann, Army Group Vistula's 1st General Staff Officer, remembered the haste demanded by Guderian and imposed on *General der Infanterie* Wenck:[20]

He (Wenck) spoke frankly to me about the plan of operations and its chances. He agreed with me in a series of serious objections and misgivings. Fundamentally he favored attacking at all costs and as soon as possible. Not everything he heard during these trips (to the frontline troops) was confident and positive, however. He also saw the major difficulties. In particular, he undoubtedly realized that the requested timing for the start of the attack could simply not be met.

After a meeting between Himmler and Guderian on February 14, 1945, Guderian came into Wenck's room, where I just happened to be. The fierce struggle with Himmler had taken its toll on *Generaloberst* Guderian, and he looked completely worn out. There he again made Wenck and I swear that we would do everything in our power to see to it that the attack began at the time planned. Despite this, *Generalleutnant* Wenck clearly expressed his serious concerns about the attack, which he sought to confirm through his own experiences with the troops. *Generaloberst* Guderian wanted to hear nothing of it. Even when Wenck said that he was in the wrong place at the army group and asked to be relieved, Guderian merely replied: "The attack must be carried out. Everything depends on it." *Generalleutnant* Wenck was very depressed after this conversation.

Back in Pomerania, Himmler turned to administrative matters. For example, on February 11, 1945, while *General der Infanterie* Wenck was planning the coming offensive, the *Reichsführer-SS* was handing out the first four Anti-Partisan Combat Badges in Gold to members of the *24. Waffen-Gebirgs[Karstjäger]-Division der SS* and afterwards dined with the recipients.[21] As well, he again took action to counter the signs of disintegration that were becoming apparent:[22]

Several days ago I announced that von Salisch, the former *SS-Standartenführer* and chief of police of Bromberg, had been executed by firing squad for cowardice. As well, a court martial found *Oberst* von Hassenstein guilty of deserting the post entrusted to him without orders and with no apparent urgency. I confirmed the sentence and he has also been shot.

I expect every officer to be an example of bravery and firmness and lead the way for our brave soldiers. If the officer is at the front, his men will not leave him. However, in cases where one or another falls victim to human weakness, cowardice or momentary panic, the officer shows himself to be unworthy of the rank awarded him and his shoulder straps.

At the same time that the fiercest fighting was taking place on Army Group Vistula's front, Himmler, in his own way, was looking after a multitude of things simultaneously. An order issued on February 14, 1945, not only illustrates this, it is also a reflection of the conditions at that time:[23]

There is a rising chorus of complaints from the population that German troops are looting houses abandoned by their owners and that the poor people's possessions are being stolen or destroyed. All commanders of every rank are responsible to me to see to it that such disgraceful incidents are stopped with all force and that discipline and order are maintained.

Anyone caught looting is to be shot immediately.

The lot of the people forced to leave their homes is hard and sad enough. As soldiers, it is depressing to know that thousands of villages have fallen into the hands of the Russians, who plundered and destroyed them. Decency demands that in villages in which there are German soldiers, not the smallest thing is stolen from abandoned houses or anything willfully destroyed. This is a crime against ourselves and German families.

Furthermore it is the unbreakable will of the army group and its armies to liberate the areas that have fallen into Russian hands as quickly as possible and place them in the firm guardianship of the German armies. This order is to be distributed to the company level and passed on to every soldier.

The *11. Armee* in Battle

Meanwhile, *Generaloberst* Guderian and *General der Infanterie* Wenck had worked out plans for the offensive in Pomerania. The *11. Armee* would be divided into three groups of forces for "Operation *Sonnenwende*" (Solstice): the *XXXIX. Panzer-Korps*, the *III. (germanische) SS-Panzer-Korps,* and *Korpsgruppe Munzel*.

The impressive-sounding titles belied the actual fighting strengths of these units. No units were at authorized strength and none of the corps had more than about 20,000 men—the strength of an infantry division at the start of the war. On February 16, 1945, *III. (germanische) SS-Panzer-Korps* was supposed to attack across the Ihna River south of Zachan and break through to encircled Arnswalde. The next day *XXXIX. Panzer-Korps* was to attack east of Madü Lake and initially gain the narrows between Madü Lake and Plöne Lake. If breakthrough was not achieved on the first attempt, the panzer corps was to block the narrows and regroup. The next attack would be made east of Plöne Lake close to the center group (*III. SS-Panzer*-Korps). The latter unit, which formed the attack's spearhead, was initially supposed to advance out of the area north of Arnswalde toward Berlinchen and later drive towards Neudamm–Küstrin. *Korpsgruppe Munzel* was to attack from the area south of Nörenberg, closely aligned with the center group at first, and then swing southeast in the direction of Friedberg and later Landsberg–Küstrin.

Because of developments in the situation, *Generaloberst* Guderian ordered offensive action to begin on February 15, 1945. Exploiting the element of surprise, the *III. (germanische) SS-Panzer-Korps* was able to break through to encircled Arnswalde. When the other attack formations set off the next day, however, they ran into a prepared enemy with powerful anti-tank defenses. The west wing of *XXXIX. Panzer-Korps* became bogged down east of Madü Lake, while the east wing advanced through Brallentin to Dölitz. *Korpsgruppe Munzel* fought its way into Reetz. Despite Soviet counterattacks which began immediately, *XXXIX. Panzer-Korps* succeeded in establishing a bridgehead near Blumberg and reached the line Sallenthin–Muscherin–Dölitz. The *III. (germanische) SS-Panzer-Korps* held the Arnswalde area and was able to advance to Liebenow.

The ferocity of the fighting and the immediate start of Soviet counterattacks quickly showed, however, that the offensive was probably not going to achieve the success that was hoped for it. In addition to the enemy, the surface conditions—thawed ground which quickly turned into mud—hampered the necessary rapid movements by the motorized attack units. After the German forces were able to gain little ground, Himmler reproached the leadership of the *11. Armee*. *Oberstleutnant i.G.* Dankworth, 1st General Staff Officer of AOK 11, responded on February 17, 1945:

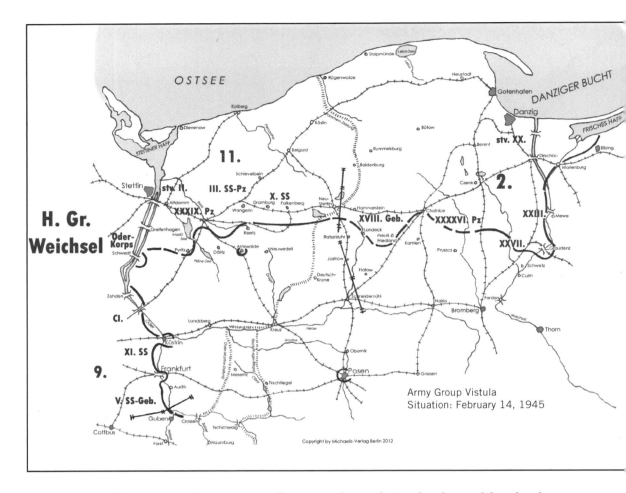

Army Group Vistula
Situation: February 14, 1945

Headquarters, *11. Armee* energetically opposes the conclusion that the attack has already bogged down. It was a foregone conclusion that this drive to the south would meet a prepared enemy and that breaking through the established security zone would take some time.

Events to date have shown that the western group is advancing slowly and that the main drive must be made further to the east. The decision as to where the offensive forces will be concentrated must be made this afternoon between 1500 and 1600. The intention is to send armored forces from Dölitz, where at present the blown bridge is being rebuilt, west against Lübtow, while the main forces advance south in the direction of Bernstein. In Arnswalde, as in Reetz, enemy resistance proved too strong, consequently, for the time being it has only been possible to tie up the enemy forces there, while the actual drive through Nantikow will be made further south in the direction of Sellnow.

SS-Obergruppenführer Steiner emphasizes once again the comments made above and expresses firm confidence that, despite all pessimistic responses, the attack by the eastern group at least will be carried out in the next two days.

Himmler, who had intentionally stayed away from the execution of the offensive and on February 16, 1945, in Bernau demonstratively presented sixteen German soldiers with the Close Combat Badge in Gold, and one with the Sniper Badge, responded to *SS-Obergruppenführer* Steiner, the commander-in-chief of the *11. Armee*, by telex:

I come back to my telephone conversation and repeat: it is important that *XXXIX. Panzer-Korps* attempt with all available means to open Dölitz from Blumberg. Planned destruction of enemy forces north of Plöne Lake only pins us down and is not battle-deciding. In doing so we tie up three divisions: *Holstein, 10. SS-Panzer,* and *4. SS-Polizei-Panzergrenadier-Division.* This plan to destroy the enemy forces is therefore to be set back and the units added to the main attack.

However neither reorganizing the units nor energetic orders brought the hoped-for breakthrough of the enemy front. Instead, on February 18, 1945, AOK 11 was already losing ground. After *General der Infanterie* Wenck was injured in an automobile accident that day and put out of action,[24] in the evening *SS-Obergruppenführer* Steiner decided on his own initiative to call off "Operation Solstice." The evacuation of about 7,000 civilians through the approximately one-kilometer-wide corridor began on the evening of February 19. The former garrison of Arnswalde under the command of *Generalmajor* Hans Voigt (February 21, 1896 – April 26, 1969) joined the evacuation. This was virtually the only visible, but also sensible success of "Operation Solstice."

On February 20, 1945, Hitler reached the same conclusion as Steiner and ordered the operation halted. As the 1st Ukrainian Front had at the same time placed the *4. Panzer-Armee* (Army Group Center) in serious difficulty, there followed not only the cessation of further attacks, but also the withdrawal of several units, weakening the *11. Armee. General der Infanterie* Krebs, acting chief of the Army General Staff, advised Army Group Vistula that:[25]

The *Führer* has decided to call off the attack by the *11. Armee.*

In the course of the following unit transfers, on February 22–23, 1945 *Panzer-AOK 3* (*Generaloberst* Raus) took over the overall command of the units of Headquarters, *11. Armee.*[26] *Generaloberst* Raus remembered:[27]

When the fighting in the western part of Samland stopped after the encirclement of Fortress Königsberg, my army headquarters and I were relieved and ordered to Pomerania with no explanation. Several members of my staff and I went ahead. Aboard a minesweeper, we sailed along the Frische Nehrung past the battleship Scheer, whose three-gun salvoes were thundering over the lagoon towards Elbing, into mine-filled Danzig Bay and from there by rail to the site of the new army headquarters in Rummelsburg. The bulk of the staff and all the equipment followed the next day on a steamer from Pillau to Gotenhafen, then by rail to Rummelsburg. An immediate inquiry to Army Group Vistula, to which the headquarters was attached, brought no clarification of the purpose of the move. But I was certain that my personal report to Himmler in his headquarters in a camp in the Prenzlauer Forest, scheduled for February 13, would provide clarity as to the subsequent fate of the army headquarters.

On February 13, 1945, accompanied by several members of my staff, I went by train via Kolberg and Stettin to Prenzlau. After my arrival at Himmler's forest camp, an SS officer escorted me to the operations staff barracks. There one of Himmler's advisors, a senior general staff officer, briefed me on the situation and the army group's intentions. There I learned that the offensive would soon begin from the area southeast of Stargard, its objective being to eliminate the powerful enemy forces gathered in the area east of Küstrin. […]

Himmler listened to my report and asked me to attend a discussion in his living quarters at 2200. He referred to the briefing by his advisor and declared that both he and the *Führer* were convinced that the outcome of the offensive at Stargard would decide the war in Germany's favor. As an experienced commander of armored forces, I and my staff had been ordered there on behalf of Hitler to command this offensive. After the fighting in East Prussia delayed my departure from there, *SS-Obergruppenführer* Steiner, the former commander of the *III. SS-Panzer-Korps* had been given this task. […] I left Himmler's office at three in the morning without having received my orders and on February 14, I returned to Rummelsburg.

When I arrived there I resumed my familiarization trips at the front. They mainly covered the area of the *X. SS-Korps* (*Generalleutnant* Krappe) and the positions held by the completely improvised troops of *Korps Tettau*. The former was in a fifty-five-kilometer-wide lake and forest position and consisted of an infantry division that I was familiar with, which was at half strength and had no supply installations, and the 5th Württemberg Division, an outstanding unit with 75% of its normal combat strength. Some of the terrain in its defense sector was open and passable by tanks. Neither the *X. SS-Korps* nor *Korps Tettau* had tanks or assault guns. The weakest unit was the Pomerania Division. It consisted of a colorful mixture of construction pioneers, *Luftwaffe* ground crew, navy ranging units, *Volkssturm* battalions and various other units. It had neither a signals battalion nor artillery, nor anti-tank weapons (other than *Faustpatrone*), nor supply installations. Even some of the regiment and battalion commander positions were still unmanned. In terms of the head count, however, the division was strong, but it had only rifles and a few machine-guns. It didn't receive its last unit leaders until after the fighting had started. They were from a group of men returning from leave who were trying to get back to the trapped Army Group Courland. The army commander personally stopped them on the road and drove them to the unit in his car. This division of the Korps Tettau was not deployed in the front, instead it held the Pomerania Position, a blocking position set up during the war against Poland which extended to the Baltic Sea east of Köslin.

The *2. Armee* in Battle

The heavy fighting in other sectors of the front of course went on during the Pomerania offensive. On February 15, 1945, Army Group Vistula reported the *2. Armee*'s situation to the Army High Command:

> The situation on the army group's left wing has deteriorated further today. The enemy extended his attacks to the Preußisch Friedland area and tried, with some success, to break through the flanking barrier set up in the area south of Konitz by attacking from all sides, in order to create the conditions for a strategic breakthrough to the north and northwest. Simultaneously, he continued his attacks with powerful forces against the *2. Armee*'s southern front on both sides of Tuchel, and in the difficult wooded terrain of the Tucheler Heath, which enabled him to bring up forces unchecked, achieved considerable penetrations. The army has no forces left with which to seal off or eliminate these. […]
>
> The fighting power of our units, which in this sector have been in the heaviest fighting for days, has been weakened considerably. In particular, the two panzer divisions (*4.* and *7. Pz.Div.*), which are bearing the main brunt of the fighting in the area around Konitz, have between them a total of thirty-six serviceable tanks and twelve assault guns. If the enemy should succeed in driving the *XXXXVI. Panzer-Korps* further into the Tucheler Heath, which at present cannot be prevented with the forces available, the danger exists that the *2. Armee* might be split in two, resulting in the collapse of the Vistula Front.

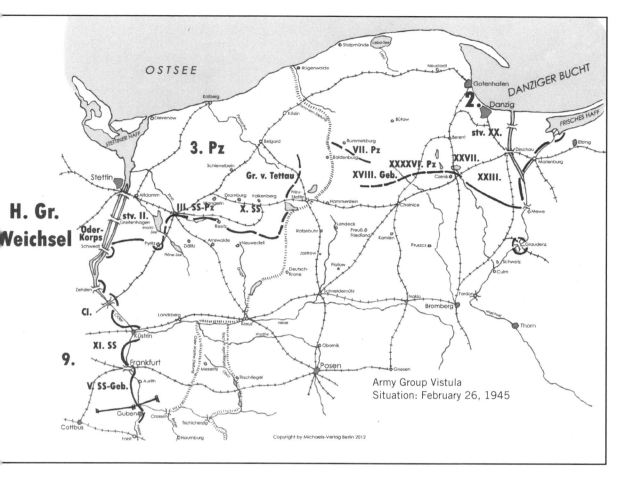

Army Group Vistula
Situation: February 26, 1945

To prevent the encirclement of a large group of German forces in Fortress Graudenz, the bulk of the garrison left the fortress on the night of February 16–17, 1945, and took up new positions to the northwest. While it remained relatively quiet on the *2. Armee*'s left wing along the Vistula and the Nogat and on the right wing held by the *XVIII. Armee-Korps*, as previously mentioned the Red Army continued offensive action against the *XXXXVI. Panzer-Korps* and *XXVII. Armee-Korps*. Conducted on a broad front, the armored attacks resulted in loss of contact with Fortress Graudenz and the German units were soon pushed back to the north. Nevertheless, the bulk of the fortress garrison had not been encircled.

As the *XXXXVI. Panzer-Korps* had nothing with which to counter the enemy advance, on February 19, 1945, it was pulled out of the area and temporarily took over Gruppe Rappard's quiet sector southeast of Danzig. It was replaced by the *VII. Panzer-Korps*, which now commanded in the area between *XVIII. Gebirgs-Korps* and *XXVIII. Armee-Korps* in the Konitz (Chojnice)–Tuchel area. The *2. Armee*'s southern front now ran in a line from Mewe through Czersk to Chojnice.

On February 22, 1945, the Soviet 19th Army attacked further west, at the boundary with the *3. Panzer-Armee*, and broke through the positions held by the *XVIII. Gebirgs-Korps*. Mauled by the enemy tank units, the units—some split into small groups—fell back to the northwest. The next day Soviet troops reached Baldenburg and advanced on Bublitz and Pollnow.

Himmler thereupon ordered the *VII. Panzer-Korps* to assemble near Rummelsburg in order to restore contact with the *3. Panzer-Armee* from there. At the same time the *XXXXVI.*

Panzer-Korps received orders to return to the *2. Armee*'s southern front. It was replaced in its positions on the left wing of the army by the *XVIII. Gebirgs-Korps*. The Red Army, whose objective was the Baltic Sea, then turned east and attacked the *VII. Panzer-Korps* in the Rummelsburg–Neustettin area. Neustettin fell to enemy troops on February 27–28.

2. Armee's situation became ever more critical. In *VII. Panzer-Korps*'s sector, Rummelsburg changed hands several times by March 3, 1945, and then remained in Soviet hands. While it was quiet in the *XXXXVI. Panzer-Korps*'s sector southwest of Barent, the enemy was able to break through the *XXVII. Armee-Korps* and especially the *XXIII. Armee-Korps* south of Stargard, on a twelve-kilometer width of front on a line from Czersk to Mewe, penetrating up to ten kilometers. The remaining troops in the encircled Fortress Graudenz also had to fight off powerful attacks and on March 6, 1945, were forced to surrender.

On March 8, 1945, Soviet armored forces reached the Barent area in *XXVII. Armee-Korps*'s sector. With a breakthrough to Danzig imminent, the entire right wing of the army (*LV. Armee-Korps*, *VII.* and *XXXXI. Panzer-Korps* and *XXVII. Armee-Korps*) was pulled back toward the Gotenhafen–Danzig defense area. This was done to, on the one hand, prevent the army from being split apart, and on the other to shorten the front and free up forces. In fact chaos reigned at and behind the front. The front was constantly in motion and the Red Army tank units had gained an enormous amount of territory since mid-February 1945. Columns of refugees initially moved west, and when the enemy reached the Baltic between Kolberg and Rügenwalde, back to the east again. The rear-echelon service of the frontline units constantly moved back with the refugees and the roads were continuously clogged with vehicles, wagons pulled by teams of horses and oxen and soldiers and civilians.

On March 10, 1945, the *2. Armee*'s front ran from east to west as follows: after the Red Army established a bridgehead across the Nogat, the *XVIII. Gebirgs-Korps* held a line from the Frische Haff in a southwesterly direction to the Vistula. It linked up with the *XXIII. Armee-Korps*' front, a semicircular path through Dirschau to Löblau. From there to the Zuckau area was the *XXVII. Armee-Korps*. West of Zoppot to south of Gotenhafen the *XXXXVI. Panzer-Korps* tried to hold the positions against the masses of Soviet armor. Then followed the *VII. Panzer-Korps* to Hela, where alert units of the *LV. Armee-Korps* were deployed.

The next day, the OKH issued the following order:[28]

1. It is the task of the *2. Armee* to defend the ports of Danzig and Gotenhafen, which are of vital importance for the supply of Army Groups Courland and North, from a position advanced far to the west and south and prevent its front from being split into two bridgeheads.

2. Firm control is to be maintained over the link between Army Group North and the *2. Armee* over the Frische Haff. Conduct of operations on the Frische Haff is transferred to Army Group North. Army Group North is to keep one battalion at the ready at the Frische Nehrung's starting point east of Danzig for boundary protection.

It was already becoming apparent that, tactically, the *2. Armee* was more aligned with Army Group North than Army Group Vistula. When *Generaloberst* Weiß, the *2. Armee*'s commander-in-chief, was placed in command of Army Group North on March 12, 1945, his former army was also attached to the army group. It was no longer part of Army Group Vistula. The units withdrew through Danzig to the Frische Haff in fierce fighting and there surrendered to the Soviets on May 9, 1945.

The *3. Panzer-Armee* in Battle

While Headquarters, *3. Panzer-Armee* was taking over the affairs of the *11. Armee*, on February 22, 1945, enemy tanks broke through *Korps Tettau* at the boundary with the *2. Armee* and reached Baldenburg in the area of the Pomerania Position. The only troops there were about sixty, fifty-year-old members of the Pomerania Division who had been stationed there as blocking sentries. Facing Soviet tanks for the first time, the men in fact succeeded in destroying three tanks with *Panzerfaust* anti-tank weapons and delayed the advance until the next day. Then the enemy overran them and almost all of the older men were killed.

On February 23, 1945, weak units of *Korps Tettau* were able to briefly restore contact with the *2. Armee* between Bublitz and Rummelsburg. Elements of *Panzer-Division Holstein* were then supposed to attack and with the *VII. Panzer-Korps* advancing towards it from the east were supposed to close the gap in the front. However after the Red Army simultaneously advanced towards Köslin and other elements attacked *VII. Panzer-Korps*, contact between the two German armies could not be established. In fact, by reaching the railway line from Stargard to Danzig the enemy also severed the last major line of communication between the two armies. Köslin was defended practically only by about 2,000 recruits with no heavy weapons and it subsequently fell on February 26, 1945. By then Korps von Tettau's front extended to the Baltic Sea, where Hitler had already declared Kolberg a fortress as a precaution.

On February 28, 1945, the Red Army launched an offensive against *X. SS-Armee-Korps* positioned south of *Korps Tettau*. The *5. Jäger-Division* held its sector for a day and was then overrun by the masses of Soviet armor. Contact with the neighboring *III. (germanische) SS-Panzer-Korps* was severed. The Soviet tactic envisaged breaking through the main line of resistance between the armies, then between the corps and finally between the divisions, after which pincer movements would encircle and destroy the units. In addition, to establish another bridgehead across the Oder, enemy forces drove through the *12. Luftwaffe-Feld-Division* towards Greifenhagen on both sides of Pyritz in the area of Acting Corps Headquarters, *II. Armee-Korps*.

On March 1, 1945, Soviet tanks reached the Falkenburg–Dramburg area at the seam between *X. SS-Panzer-Korps* and *III. (germanische) SS-Panzer-Korps*. From there elements turned against the *SS-Panzer-Korps* and others advanced in the direction of Kolberg. As a result *X. SS-Armee-Korps* was encircled in the area south of Schievelbein. *Korps von Tettau* also lost all contact and was encircled south of Belgard.

Not only had the Red Army succeeded in driving through the front within a few days, it had already isolated individual German army corps. When Himmler realized that even his pithy orders had done nothing to change the imminent end of the war, he at least tried to demonstrate that he had commanded his troops with all hardness. In his eyes this deflected a failure as an army commander and in fact no other commander-in-chief could have done much to change the outcome. Hitler saw it differently: the Red Army was eighty kilometers from Berlin. He made his "faithful Heinrich," who in his opinion had paid too little attention to Army Group Vistula, responsible for it. In any case, in addition to this function Himmler had looked after his other offices. After the *Reichsführer-SS* went to the SS hospital in Hohenlychen for treatment of angina pectoris, Hitler ordered the installation of a second chief of the general staff. He was supposed to assist the first, *SS-Brigadeführer* Heinz Lammerding (August 27, 1905 – January 13, 1971), in commanding the army group. On March 3, 1945, *Generalleutnant* Eberhard Kinzel (October 18, 1897 – May 23, 1945), the former commander of the *337. Volks-grenadier-Division*, was added to the army group headquarters as Second Chief of Staff.

Himmler had known the convinced National–Socialists since he was named commander of the Replacement Army and on March 5, 1945, he wrote an enthusiastic report to the *Waffen-SS* liaison officer in *Führer* Headquarters, *SS-Gruppenführer* Hermann Fegelein (October 30, 1906 – April 29, 1945), which in his divorced-from-reality style read like a justification to a subordinate:

Dear Fegelein!

General Kinzel, who is now with my army group, commander of the *337. Volksgrena-dier-Division*, reported to me that his division still has a ration strength of 3,200 men. Of his division's seventeen unit commanders, he has lost 14 of 17 killed or wounded, and 42 of 45 company and battalion leaders.

In the last fourteen days he has pronounced and carried out fifteen death sentences in his division, which has fought bravely, including one against an officer. In his opinion the reason for the men's failure was not ill will, but rather unprecedented exhaustion. As this must be broken at all costs, he had the mentioned death sentences carried out.

I am sharing these lines with you only to give a picture of the unprecedented severity of the fighting which the army group, especially the *2. Armee*, has had to endure in the past weeks. Of the tanks that attacked *2. Armee* today, 37 of 90 were knocked out by the units.

The statement that death sentences were pronounced and carried out to break the state of exhaustion is shocking. Himmler's respect for this shows an abstruse and inhuman morality, to demand and endorse without reservation even the sacrificing of his own people, as long as it served to prolong the existence of the National–Socialist regime.

At the *3. Panzer-Armee's* front, the *10. SS-Panzer-Division "Frundsberg"* had been given hopeless assignments. Hitler's fervent imagination believed that contact could be restored to the *2. Armee*. Because of the enemy advances, the division was now committed to at least rescue the two separated corps from Soviet encirclement. Setting out via Naugard, on March 2, 1945, the *10. SS-Panzer-Division "Frundsberg"* was able to gain kilometers kilometers, but after the Soviets counterattacked it was itself forced to withdraw. The enemy simultaneously took the offensive on the left wing of the *III. (germanische) SS-Panzer-Korps* south of Dramburg, and the main line of resistance had to be withdrawn towards the line southern end of Madü Lake–Freienwalde. The next day the *SS-Panzer-Korps* withdrew behind Stargard.

There was also heavy fighting in the area of Acting Headquarters, *II. Armee-Korps*, which had been renamed *Korps Hörnlein*, between Madü Lake and the Oder near Greifenhagen. There the Red Army tried to eliminate the still existing German bridgehead and establish one of its own. At the same time, the *III. SS-Panzer-Korps* was forced to withdraw towards Gollnow in fierce defensive fighting. On March 5, 1945, the German units of *Korps Hörnlein* and *III. SS-Panzer-Korps* had already been forced back into the roughly twenty-five-kilometer-wide Stettin–Altdamm bridgehead and the area around the Greifenhagen bridgehead.

On March 7, 1945, even this bridgehead had to be evacuated before the enemy masses. The *25. Panzer-Grenadier-Division*, however, successfully hindered the Soviet attempt to drive from the Greifenhagen area into the rear of the German units positioned around Altdamm. An attempt by the Red Army to occupy the island of Wollin by way of Dievenow also failed. Naval units were committed there.

On that day Propaganda Minister Goebbels visited *Reichsführer-SS* Himmler in the SS hospital in Hohenlychen. About this he wrote in his diary:

There is a very pleasant, modest and absolutely National–Socialist atmosphere around Himmler, which has an extraordinarily soothing effect. One can only be pleased that the old National–Socialist spirit still prevails, at least in Himmler.

Korps Tettau and *X. SS-Panzer-Korps*, practically encircled by Soviet units since February 28, 1945, had conducted a fighting withdrawal to the northwest by way of Greifenberg, and on March 10, they launched an attack to break through the Soviet lines to the west. The next day elements at least of these units regained the German lines.

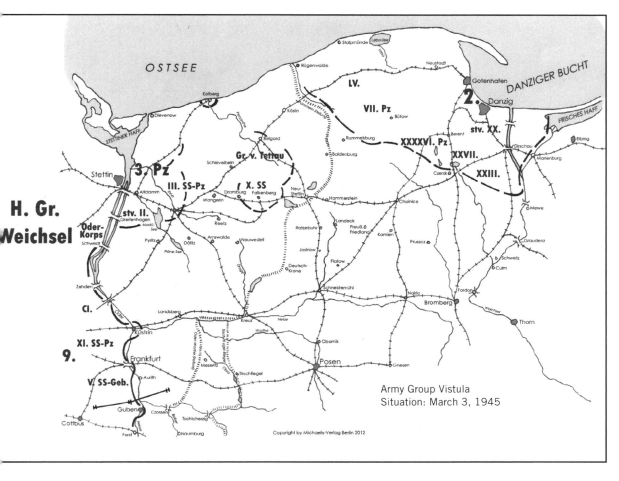

Army Group Vistula
Situation: March 3, 1945

Like a rock amid the waves, Fortress Kolberg held out against the Soviet attacks until March 18, 1945. This was less for strategic reasons than simply an attempt to evacuate the approximately 85,000 civilians (of whom about 50,000 were refugees from the east). In his order of the day of 1 March 1945, *Oberst* Fritz Fullriede (January 4, 1895 – November 3, 1969), who had been named commander of Fortress Kolberg, declared:

> For us the defensive battle only has purpose until the refugees and the population trapped in the city have been rescued by sea. You all are defending not this city of Kolberg, but the people living in it. That is our task.

With Hitler's agreement to give up the bridgehead near Stettin on March 19, 1945, the last troops withdrew across the Oder to the west. This left just three large German bridgeheads in the area of Army Group Vistula: Küstrin, Frankfurt/Oder and Glogau.

The *9. Armee* in Battle

All of these bridgeheads were in the area of the *9. Armee*, whose length of front was about 130 kilometers. On the army's left wing between Zehden and the Hohenzollern Canal was *CI. Armee-Korps* (*General der Artillerie* Berlin). Next was the *XI. SS-Panzer-Korps*

(*SS-Obergruppenführer* Kleinheisterkamp) through Fortress Küstrin (*SS-Gruppenführer* Reinefarth) to Frankfurt/Oder. In Frankfurt, which Hitler had declared a fortress, were troops equivalent to a weak division under the command of *Oberst* Bieler. To the south as far as the area north of Guben was the *V. SS-Gebirgs-Korps* (*SS-Obergruppenführer* Jeckeln).

The thawing of the Oder, with the associated high water, led to a quiet period in the area of the front. As well, the Red Army had suffered heavy losses and undertook extensive regroupings.

After Himmler's state of health had improved after the angina pectoris, on March 15, 1945, Hitler ordered him to Berlin. The day before Himmler's advisor in the Personal Staff noted in a letter:[29]

> The *Reichsführer-SS* has not been particularly well in recent weeks. He has too much to do and has also had to deal with a protracted flu. For about twelve days, the *Reichsführer-SS* was so ill that he had to stay in bed.[30] Happily, his condition has improved and he is almost his old self again.

After his meeting [with Himmler] Goebbels wrote in his diary:

> The Führer is shifting much of the blame directly onto Himmler. He says that he asked Himmler again and again to move our troops into Pomerania. Himmler allowed himself to be misled by repeated reports by Department Foreign Armies East, believed in the drive on Berlin and deployed accordingly. […] Himmler bears the historic guilt for allowing Pomerania and much of its population to fall into Soviet hands.

What Hitler said was paradoxical. In his charges he forgot that he had ordered 6. *Panzer-Armee* to Hungary, that Himmler had ordered all available units to Pomerania, and that Guderian was responsible for the *Sonnenwende* offensive and had *General der Infanterie* Wenck plan it.

The consequence of this was that the *Reichsführer-SS* was relieved of command of Army Group Vistula on March 20, 1945. Hitler named *Generaloberst* Heinrici (December 25, 1886 – December 13, 1971) the new commander-in-chief and Himmler concentrated on his unofficial attempts to conclude a separate peace with the Western Allies.

APPENDICES

Himmler's surviving speeches provide a wealth of information about his thoughts and actions, as well as developments in National–Socialist Germany and the constantly-worsening military situation. Marked by boyish camaraderie, they were supposed to demagogically commit the listeners further to the party line. In the end the speeches are a call to hold out and they express the true facts only very euphemistically. The appreciations expressed by Himmler in his speeches must always be viewed from the perspective of National-Socialism. It is quite apparent how far distanced from reality were his visions of "life and struggle" that he wished to impart to the German people.

APPENDIX 1

Speech on the Installation of *SS-Gruppenführer* Dr. Kaltenbrunner as New Head of the Reich Security Main Office in Berlin, on January 30, 1943

My SS Leaders! Comrade Kaltenbrunner!

I have ordered and summoned you, the closest personnel of the Reich Security Main Office, you who hold the senior positions of responsibility, to this room, just as in June of last year, 1942, when your commander had been killed. I gathered the department heads in this room and held the first meeting here, with the full and clear awareness that the creator of the Reich Security Main Office, the Security Service, and the Security Policy, *Obergruppenführer* Heydrich, created this tasteful and beautiful room as one of his last accomplishments in life, which spoke for him and his nature, and which should always speak for the nature of this Aryan security service of the Germanic nation. In the same way, the entire security service and the entire security police bore his stamp, were of his nature, of his character.

For ten years now we have been a National Socialist state. In an hour or two it will be ten years since we marched through the Brandenburg Gate. I believe Heydrich was also part of that march back then. Let me look back one more time, so that we may then look toward the future. In 1930, it was necessary for the party to set up an intelligence service in order to get a picture of the communist, Jewish, Masonic, and reactionary opponents. At the recommendation of then *Gruppenführer* von Eberstein, I acquired the retired *Oberleutnant zur See* Reinhardt Heydrich. Getting him was actually based on a misunderstanding, which is something very few people know about. It was said that Heydrich was an information officer. Back then, in 1930, I didn't pay much attention; I thought an information officer was a man who procures information. Heydrich was an information officer in the sense of an information devices officer; he was a radio officer who used communication devices as his trade. He came to see me in the small house in Waldtrudering at the time and explained to me: "Well, *Reichsführer*, I am not at all the person you are looking for; I was a radio officer." I looked him over: tall and blond with decent, keen, and kind eyes. I said to him: "Look here, that doesn't matter, it doesn't bother me at all; sit down in the room, I'll be back in fifteen minutes, and write down how you picture an intelligence service of the NSDAP." In those fifteen minutes he wrote down what he had in mind. I said: "Yes, I agree; alright, I'll take you." Then the salary was set for this head of the security service, as we called him. The 4th Regiment in Schleswig–Holstein undertook to pay 80 Reichsmarks a month; that was the first part. From the rest of the budget I took, I believe, another 40 Reichsmarks. In the initial period he also got something from the navy. I told myself, you'll be able to help him out in the immediate future; at any rate, we'll give it a try. *Untersturmführer* Heydrich began with the 120 borrowed marks after he had joined the SS in Hamburg, had hung around the port with the Hamburg boys who were jobless, had done his service honestly, and had settled down splendidly as a former lieutenant. Then we began the work. It was very strange. At the time, I had on my staff a *Sturmbannführer*, a retired *Major*, H. Heydrich had barely shown up when, six or eight days later, the *Münchener Post*, the social democratic paper, reported that an intelligence officer was present. Heydrich was very suspicious and told me back then, with the nose he always had: "H. did that." I would not allow it. I said: "You can't get started by attacking one of my staff." Heydrich wrote his first name with "dt" at the end; he (H.) wrote "Reinhard" with only a "d." Later, in 1933, it became known that H. did indeed work for the Munich police, I think for 100 Reichsmarks a month. He then hanged himself in his cell.

We then worked together for a year. The security service grew out of the smallest, smallest of means. Today, hardly anyone suspects just how much it grew from privation, how many sacrifices there were along that road. Hardly any of the chaps who later joined had an inkling. That is why you must tell those who are councilors and chief-inspectors today. We lived through the difficult years of 1931 and 1932. Who today still knows—as Dr. Goebbels said very rightly today—how desperate we were in 1932! The party lost a lot of its followers after the August elections. The priests, the Center Party, and the reaction were trying to break us through elections. We did not become part of the government in which Papen was chancellor. The driftwood we had collected was washed away again. At that time, only the *Schutzstaffel* grew. The subsidies, the donations, and a lot of dues from the party were no longer coming in. There was less and less. We supported the *Schutzstaffel*—today it is alright for me to say this—at the central office as well as outside in the various regiments (today's *Oberabschnitte*) of Weichsel, Sepp Dietrich, and Daluege, by contributing 350 Reichsmarks from our Reichstag allowance of 550 Reichsmarks, from which we lived. Christmas 1932 was so bad that the men, those who worked for the security service at the time, could only be given installments of one mark, two marks, three marks. Mrs. Heydrich, who courageously and boldly suffered and fought by our side, cooked a thick soup for all so that the men got some food once a day. Christmas 1932 we had enough money to let the men travel home. We didn't have the money to allow them to travel back, let alone pay them their salaries for December or January.

With this small team we arrived at January 1933. By that time things were already getting a little better. There was the election campaign in Lippe, and we got a boost. We then proceeded to the capture of power. Now, at the time, we were tied to Munich; for us, Munich was crucial. In Munich we didn't get around to it until March 12—I never dwelt on it and I never gave it a thought of my own—I became police president of Munich and took over police headquarters; Heydrich was given the political section in Munich, Department 6a. And that is how we started. During these beginnings we acquired a few infinitely brave and hard-working collaborators, above all, you, my dear Müller, and your deceased comrade Flesch, who recently died after a long [period of] suffering. We turned the political division of police headquarters into a Bavarian Political Police. The political police grew in the *Länder* like mushrooms after a rain. I became a unique legal specimen—someone can earn a doctorate by examining this question in the future—by combining in one person all the German citizenships that existed at the time. I was a Bavarian, Badener, Württemberger, and so on; I was at home everywhere. I acquired the citizenships by becoming the commander of the political police in Hesse, Bremen, Lübeck, Lippe (both Lippes), Anhalt, and so on, and became a civil servant there. In Munich we created a central office: the commander of the political police of the states. With this there arose a kind of security police.

A year later, on April 20, 1934, the then-Prussian Minister President Göring, following a long meeting of us old party comrades, made me the deputy chief of the Secret State Police. Heydrich became inspector. With this, the political police of the states in all of Germany were in one hand, and we could slowly begin to create a Reich apparatus. It grew in various organizational forms. It was in part the SD, in part the Security Police; at the time it was called the Stapo.

I will not neglect to mention June 30, 1934, with its bitterness, the bitter necessity, the bitter duty. The event had repercussions and brought the attempt by Jewish and other opponents to stir up enmity between us and the *Wehrmacht* and the party. The *Wehrmacht* was supposed to break us. At the time, strong nerves, restraint, and intelligence were required, in ample measure, to manage the situation. We managed it.

There came the year 1936, when, on June 17, I became chief of the German police, with the title *Reichsführer-SS* and Chief of the German Police. Back then, Daluege, now *Oberstgruppenführer*, was truly generous in handing the criminal police under his authority over to Group Leader Heydrich as inherently related to and an indispensable part of a security police. That year, the entire criminal police headed by Nebe came to us. Now the total apparatus was growing. The state apparatus and the SS apparatus grew together more and more. The number of faithful members rose. Together we really managed things very well in the first few years. I spoke for many, many hours with *Obergruppenführer* Heydrich about all the problems. As the years went by he knew my views, knew the path I wanted to take, knew the goal I had for the organization, how I envisaged the SS as a whole.

Especially during the war years, Heydrich grew into greatness, which I was able to confirm in his obituary to you before the entire German nation and before the public. His greatness—and this I would like to highlight here once more—lay in the fact that he was always first a German and a Teuton, that he approached all things as a National Socialist, that for all the ambition and responsibility he had for his Reich Security Main Office, he had all the faithful qualities of a comrade, in that he stood up for you and the men. Let me say that I was not happy about some things. I knew exactly that this person or that person messed something up. Perhaps you are not yet aware today what a loyal boss you had, what he took upon himself. There were cases where I said: "Heydrich, I don't believe that." He didn't lie to me. But at all times, he first, and with infinite chivalrousness, stepped in front of you men. For all the ambition he had for his security police and his Reich Security Main Office, he saw things first of all from the perspective of the total SS. Over the years, he weighed everything very wisely so that this entire apparatus above all never became misanthropic – something that such an apparatus should tend toward by its nature. We always see people only from the negative side. When someone comes to us, he does not come to recount something nice that has happened, but he wants to recount something ugly that has happened. Second, it must be that this entire service—to use this expression for once—of the German nation is never pessimistic, that we will never allow ourselves to be overwhelmed even by bad news—we get practically no good news—and by negative things, that everything will remain solidly locked within our chests. We must be absolutely clear that there can be 1,000 negative things. Everything negative, everything harmful you must report to your commanders, who in turn will report it to me. But when you report something, please, never report it with a tear-choked voice and a downcast head: something terrible has happened; the world has more or less broken apart; National Socialism is destroyed and is already lying in fragments on the ground; we are the only shining bearers of the grail; we still have the grail of the National Socialist world view in our pure hands, but all others are really swine. Instead, carry on in the style that Heydrich introduced and with which he corrected a good deal in you; you know that yourself. The bad, the defeats, the setbacks that exist will be soberly recorded and soberly reported, without a downcast head and without priesthood. In reports you say: this I consider probable, that exaggerated; conclusion, this or that situation outside is probably such-and-such; my suggestion for change is this and that. Or: I have no suggestion to make, I merely feel obligated to make this report. But you should not report: the entire movement is in danger, or something else is in danger. We will survive the war. We shall, and of this you may be assured, overcome all our enemies, be they priests or Jews. In this Europe we shall survive the difficulties: that is my firm conviction. Things will still get insanely difficult for us. But we will get through it, and in the end there will be a Germanic Reich.

Another thing that was so incomparable in Heydrich—and he trained you in this spirit—was that he always stood, that he never yielded, and that he had an indomitable will and indomitable aggressiveness. We stepped up, and we shall—I know that is no different with you new leaders—step up again and again, spiritually and in actual fighting, just like our divisions on the front line. We shall attack. And if we have attacked ten times, we'll attack for the eleventh time. If we have attacked seventy times, we will also attack for the seventy-first time. I am not just picking a random number, but I am taking a case that happened with one of our divisions, which, over the course of one year, launched seventy-two attacks led by its commander. And if it is necessary to attack a seventy-third time, it will be done. As long as one man can bend his finger on the trigger, the trigger will be pulled and there will be fighting. If one fights and attacks in this way, one is unconquerable. The same is true for all of us SS men spiritually. An immense number of problems will appear. Problems are appearing today. I know the problems of the economy, the problems of plutocracy. I know the problem that our *Volk*, raised the wrong way in some things, does not have the right attitude toward work, that in some areas we spoke too much of rights and too little of duties, that we must address the whole question of religion, that the negative is not enough, that we must beware of introducing any kind of new priestly service after the war. I know that the question of whether we are a dying or a growing people has in no way been resolved, that child subsidies, tax relief, houses, etc., have never helped in this area, that only a religious attitude toward these things, an inner transformation, can help. Rest assured, should we live to be seventy or eighty years old, if fate lets us live that long, we must step up again and again in every year of our lives.

Here, the security service, the chief political office of the SS, must march at the front, but without ever doing anything rashly, without ever engaging in politics itself. Instead, it must always only work politically as it is commanded. Within itself, it must educate the men that Heydrich began to educate, that Kaltenbrunner will continue to educate, men who are ready on the ideological level, who never deviate from the line, but who are never stubborn and inflexible in implementation, who are stubborn in will, stubborn in their goals, but who never give up a single component of our ideology. Therefore, we will never become Jesuits; because we condemn that. We will never become sectarians. We will be generous, as generous as an old pagan can be. We believe in a God and will be as generous as only the person who believes in a God can be. This is how you were raised by Heydrich and me over the course of twelve years.

It has now been almost three-quarters of a year since Heydrich was torn from his work at a young age. He was a man of the future. You cannot do anything about fate, it is what it is. In the months up to now, I myself assumed leadership of the Reich Security Main Office, because I wanted to let some time pass. The year ahead will ask a lot of us. The bridge must be manned on every ship. Therefore, I thought for a long time about whom I should make commander of the ship. After long, careful considerations, my choice fell on one of my oldest men, on *Gruppenführer* Kaltenbrunner. We have known each other for much longer than he has been wearing the SS uniform officially. I know him, and we know each other from the time when he set himself apart from the many unknown National Socialists in Austria as the leader of the illegal SS. It is always a good lesson for a *Reichsführer-SS* and for a main department head of the SS—but especially for a head of the Reich Security Main Office—to be illegal for a good long while. I believe, Kaltenbrunner, that the time when you were really tested in Austria, tested in your endurance, in your character and your strength, was one of our best schools of life and—unbeknownst at the time—the best preparation for the new task that you are now taking on.

Kaltenbrunner, you are taking over a tried-and-true leadership corps, immaculately trained, spotless and pure in its spirit and character. You are taking over excellent department heads and group chiefs. I know that these men of yours are getting an equally good main division chief. And I know that you will lead this Reich Security Main Office, which was created over the course of twelve years by someone who is now dead, in the spirit of the SS and by continuing the legacy of our comrade Heydrich, so that the SS and the *Führer* will have in the Security Service an instrument as good as—though better in its character than—what England trained over centuries and has in its service. With this, Kaltenbrunner, I present to you the document in which the *Führer* appoints you Main Office Chief [*Hauptamtschef*] of the Reich Security Main Office, and I hand the Reich Security Main Office over to you. Lead it well!

APPENDIX 2

Speech at the *SS-Gruppenführer* Meeting in Posen, on October 4, 1943

Honoring the Fallen

In the months which have passed since we last met in June of 1942, many comrades have fallen and given their lives for Germany and for the *Führer*. First and foremost—and I ask you to stand in his honor, and in honor of all our dead SS men and dead German soldiers, men and women—first and foremost, from our ranks "let us honor" our old comrade and friend, *SS-Gruppenführer* Eicke. […] Please be seated.

I have considered it necessary to call you all together, the High Leadership Corps of the SS and Police, now at the beginning of the fifth year of the war, which will be a very difficult war year. Down to earth, as we always were, in a spirit of respect for the truth[1] with regards to ourselves, there are several things which we wish to discuss at this conference of *Gruppenführer*. Just as I was accustomed to do in long years of peace, I wish to describe the situation as I see it, in as few words as possible, with regards to our responsibilities and that which we have already achieved and accomplished, as well as with regards to that which stands before us to be accomplished in the future.

The Russian Leadership

First, the military situation. I will begin with Russia. When—I believe it was in 1937 or 1938—the great show trials were being held in Moscow, and the ex-Czarist officer and later Bolshevik general Tukhachevsky and other generals were shot, we were, at that time, all over Europe, even in the Party and the SS, of the opinion that the Bolshevik system, and therefore Stalin, had made one of its most serious mistakes. We were absolutely mistaken in this judgment of the situation. We can state this, once and for all, in a spirit of full respect for the truth. I believe that Russia could not have withstood the two years of war—it is now in the third year of war— had it retained its ex-Czarist generals. It turned—I'll discuss this first of all—its political commissars into generals, it sought out those who had grown up through the Red Army as commanders, as generals, so that they could simultaneously act as political commissars. The stubbornest bearers of the will of the Bolshevik—doctrine, I should like to call it, not ideology—is, in Russia, simultaneously a commander and leader.

The Attack of 1941

In 1941, the *Führer* attacked Russia. That was, as we now know, shortly, perhaps a quarter or half year, before Stalin launched his great thrust into Central and Western Europe.[2] I can sketch out this first year with very brief strokes. The attack was effective. The Russian army was driven together into great pockets, destroyed, taken prisoner. We did not then value the mass man as we do now, as raw material, as manpower. Which is not a shame in the end, if one thinks in terms of generations, but it is regrettable today due to the loss of manpower: the prisoners died by the tens of thousands or hundreds of thousands from exhaustion, from hunger.[3]

The Winter of 1941–42

Then came the summer and autumn of 1941, the series of victories which took us almost to Moscow, and the winter of 1941–42. The winter of 1941–42, with its consequences, was, on the one hand, the work of fate, which hit us hard for the first time; on the other hand, however, it was also the work of the political commissars, the "politruks," whose severity and relentlessness, whose fanatical, brutal will drove the raw material of the Slavic, Mongolian mass man to the front, and didn't let him get back out again.

1942

In early 1942, we again went over to the attack, in the Crimea, across the Donetz to the Don and to the Volga. The arc of front held by Germany and its allies was drawn taut. The war could have been brought to a close for Russia in 1942 if all had held out. Since according to all calculations, and in all probability, which must not be left out of consideration in war, with which one must still reckon after all, the Caucasus would have fallen into our hands sooner or later. Russia would have been cut off from its chief sources of petroleum, and hunger would have handled its people even more roughly than is the case today. Then came the collapse of our allies. First came the breakthrough among the Rumanians, then the breakthrough among the Italian Army, which was already of very little value even then, then the breakthrough and retreat of the Hungarian units: the total loss of approximately 500 kilometers of front. This loss required the withdrawal of the German front, in order to be able to close it again at all. This loss made the sacrifice of Stalingrad necessary from the point of view of fate. It is not our intention to reflect upon every detail here today. I am personally convinced that this sacrifice—that sounds dreadfully harsh when I say so now—was necessary, since, without the link-up of enemy forces around Stalingrad, it would no longer have been possible to close the German front. That will, I am convinced, be the finding of military historical research 10, 15, or 20 years after the war. At the same time, a very belated consolation.

1943

The first great battle for Kharkov followed early this year. Kharkov was evacuated under sometimes—this is known to every one of our units out there—very peculiar circumstances. At the right time, then, upon the order of the *Führer*, the tank corps arrived in Kharkov under the leadership of our old comrade, *SS-Obergruppenführer* Hausser. The deliberate evacuation of Kharkov was also carried out by Hausser using the tank corps. A glorious campaign of several weeks then began, carried out by this corps in an unusually mobile manner in the open field, a manner I consider truly correct and absolutely true to type for motorized and tank units. Our tank corps drove the enemy; Sepp Dietrich was the first to break into Kharkov with his *Leibstandarte*. Kharkov was retaken, and the German front was re-established.

In late spring and summer of this year, we replied to the attacks of the Russians with a big counterattack at Belgorod. We can report with pride that the only corps which really penetrated the deeply entrenched system of Russian positions was our *SS-Panzer-Korps*, led by the *Standarte "Deutschland"* of the old *"Das Reich"* Division. The Russians had built a position seven kilometers deep, a model and an example such as we Germans ought never to forget: to work hard, to dig in, and build positions. Because the hard work, the sweat poured out in so doing, will save the lives of tens of thousands. We Germans have still not really learned this after four years of war. If we had to give a grade for this like in school, the best the Germans could get for building their positions would be between 4 and 5 [i.e., D or F]. I must acknowledge one thing here: our SS Divisions have learned a great deal over the past two years, and generally build their positions very assiduously.

In the middle of this operation on the eastern front came the necessary withdrawal of a great number of divisions to Italy. That was why we could not counter as forcefully as necessary the Russian attack, which we could have terminated with a catastrophe for the Russians if we had had ten more tank divisions, purely on the grounds of strength.

The Human Potential of the Russians

Here I would like to say a few words on assessing the total strength of the Russians. An element basic to an overall assessment is the question of Russian population numbers. That is the great riddle. Population estimates for that country, which has been hermetically sealed off for decades, range from 170 to 250 million. I have taken a lot of trouble with this question, and have had studies prepared starting with the first Czarist censuses, that is, the first censuses ever carried out in Russia. At that time, the Bolshevik tendency to conceal everything from Europe and the world—from the building of a street which is not indicated on any map, to the concealment of large industries manufacturing tanks and airplanes, and which are shown to the European info-tourist as "tractor factories," while tanks are built in the next hall—did not yet exist. I had census figures brought to me which were not gathered under this law of camouflage and concealment, decades before the Bolshevik administration. These figures enable one to perceive a certain increase, a gradual growth. We came to the conclusion through our calculations that Russia must have two hundred million people, maybe two hundred twenty million at the very most. To describe the calculations in detail at this time would take too long and might also be too boring. I came to the conclusion that the Russians, in addition to the divisions on their western front, that is, the divisions standing directly opposite us today, have squeezed an additional four million soldiers out of the body of their people early this year and over the course of the year. That means 400 times 10,000 men, or 400 new divisions. I calculate this in approximately the following manner: the Russians have already drafted all men born in 1926, and some of the men born in 1927. It is a tragedy according to the laws of nature that Russian men born in 1925 to 1927 amount to 1.5 and 1.8 men respectively, while our men born in the same years amount to only 500,000 to 600,000, that is, a third of the Russian number. In addition, the Russians have undoubtedly added a lot of people to their companies by drafting even younger men, men born in 1928. The *"Das Reich"* Division reports that, in some cases, the divisions opposing us contained whole companies consisting of 14 and 15 year olds. That is entirely indifferent to the Russians; to them, only the masses count; the masses must be trampled, stuck, and slaughtered. They are—to use a really brutal expression—like a pig which has been stuck and must slowly bleed to death. The Russians have doubtlessly further reinforced their army by an additional 1 million men through the incorporation of auxiliary forces, that is, chiefly women and boys in the military and supply units, general staffs, and as auxiliary machine gunners. The Russians have apparently not received any Chinese. They have, however, recruited another 1 million men from their small splinter nationalities, such as the Afghans (two to three million people), Mongols from Outer Mongolia (two million people), and Kirghis; these people are perhaps not yet exhausted in terms of military purposes. I believe that all in all they have raised another four million men for their offensive army. With regards to the situation as a whole, I am, as you know, an optimist. I know that we will win the war. That is a law of nature. But I have always been rather conservative in my calculations, and I think I can show that I have never made a mistaken prophecy in these matters. I therefore believe that the Russians have lost approximately two million men in dead, prisoners, and disabled. We must therefore expect one more desperate total winter offensive by the Russians, with a strength of 200 divisions, that is, approximately two million men. We must and will hold off this attack and this clash. Absolutely nothing is endless on this earth; the potential of the Russians is not endless either. When these Brusilov offensives, to use this comparison, are finally over, the potential of the Russians will therefore be approaching its natural end. Hunger is a serious problem among the Russians. It is interesting that the Russians consider it correct, with the mass man, to keep the officers and commissars physically strong and in a good mood by feeding them an American diet, while little Ivan is fed very shabbily with a bit of bread or similar rubbish. They are fighting the whole war through their brutally trained leadership strata of political officers; officer-commissars or commissar-officers; politruks or subordinate officers; subordinate officers or politruks; it has gradually come to be all one and the same.

The Partisan War

Now I come to another aspect of the war in Russia, of which there is so frightfully much talk. When you arrive in the East, in the high staff headquarters, a map on a scale of 1 to 1 million is usually spread out in front of you. Every mine found on a certain date anywhere along railroad tracks thousands of kilometers long is diligently entered with a squiggle on this map on a scale of 1 to 1 million. Every attack, whether an attack on a munitions transport or a cattle theft usual in the district, is entered with a cross or something similar. The result is that a map like that looks all red. One is tempted to say: "It's hopeless! Give up! There's nothing we can do." But if you transfer the same data to a map on a normal scale, and compare it to the criminal cases in our sheltered German fatherland, still richly supplied with policemen even today, then it sinks to an unpleasant minor matter. But they all tell you—if you will listen to it—all the lowest ranking staff members, especially in the communications zone, "It's dreadful! Army Group Center is cut off from the fatherland by a 400-kilometer belt of partisans."

When somebody tells you that, just hand him your handkerchief so he can dry his tears. I always ask such people the question: "Has the Army Group Center suffered from hunger so far?" Answer: "No." "Has their ammunition been cut off?" "No, they've received everything." Of course, the trains are delayed for hours, half a day. Has the supply of people suffered as a result? No, the army group has received them.[4]

The Vlasov Hullabaloo

Then you hear the next prayer. This goes: "We we're wrong about the Russians." This song is usually sung by men from some eastern province, who were over there in their youth, some of whom have written very good books and had a Russian mother, too, and now they tell stories. It is also sung by the little political vagabonds whom we first came to know in the eastern struggle against Poland, whom we rejected at home, and who have now been drafted as soldiers, officers and majors, and are still peddling their intellectual poison under cover of the uniform of our decent German army. Goaded on by this propaganda tendency—I can't call it anything else—they tell you so many stories, or write them home by military post (and the stories then trickle down from top to bottom): "Yes, we were wrong about the Russians. The Russians are not at all these robots"[5] (this is the expression used most frequently) "that we thought they were in 1941. Now that we're over here in the East, our eyes have been opened. The Russians are a noble people, and so on and so forth, a collection of all virtues. We just have to educate them as National Socialists, the best thing would be to create a Russian National–Socialist Party or something similar. Then they would"—this is the next bit—"form the army of liberation under General Vlasov." Then comes the following, which is a constant claim of General Vlasov: "Russia can only be freed by Russians. Germany has so far never been able to defeat the Russians." So give Vlasov 500,000 or 1,000,000 Russians, arm them well, train them insofar as possible according to German principles, and Vlasov is so noble, that he'll go off against the Russians and kill them for us. People can say a great deal of rubbish and nonsense; that wouldn't be so dangerous. But when a piece of nonsense like this has the end effect that a glorious army, looking back on hundreds of years of tradition like the German one, begins to doubt its own strength due to the gossip of politically untrained little officers of higher or lower rank—the little bundle of proverbs who talks like this doesn't even notice how devastating it is when he says: "We cannot beat the Russians, they can only do that themselves"—then that is dangerous. Everybody you ask, "How's the Russian infantry?," will tell you, with pathetic thoughtlessness (since the two things don't go together logically, after all): "The Russian infantry is garbage. We are vastly superior to them." But: Russians can only be defeated by Russians. I wouldn't have had any objections, if we had hired Mr. Vlasov and every other Slavic subject wearing a Russian general's uniform, to make propaganda against the Russians. I wouldn't have any objections at all. Wonderful.

Brigadeführer Fegelein and the Russian General

Our comrade Fegelein once captured a Russian general like that. Look, they're cheap. They're Slavs. Full of humor, as he is, Fegelein told his staff: "We'll treat this one real good. We'll act like we're going to recognize him as a general. So, when he comes in, stand up, stand at attention, keep quiet, say 'General Sir, this' and 'General Sir, that,' show him how much respect you have for him." Of course, this worked. You don't need to give a Russian general any political ideas, political ideals, or political plans for the future. You can get them cheaper than that, gentlemen. The Slavs are known for that. The Slav is never able to build anything himself. In the long run, he's not capable of it. I'll come back to this later. With the exception of a few phenomena produced by Asia every couple of centuries, through that mixture of two heredities which may be fortunate for Asia but is unfortunate for us Europeans—with the exception, therefore, of an Attila, a Genghis Khan, a Tamerlane, a Lenin, a Stalin—the mixed race of the Slavs is based on a sub-race with a few drops of our blood, blood of a leading race; the Slav is unable to control himself and create order. He is able to argue, able to debate, able to disintegrate, able to offer resistance against every authority and to revolt. But these shoddy human goods are just as incapable of maintaining order today as they were 700 or 800 years ago, when they called in the Varangians, when they called in the Ruriks. Every Russian, every Slav, likes to hear himself talk. An old story. If you encourage them: "Please tell us, we place the highest value on your opinion. After all, we can only learn from you," then you won't find a single Russian commissar who won't fall for this; it's like tickling them with a peacock feather, just like this. Our Fegelein treated his general that way, and his general told us everything that such a brave, courageous commander really shouldn't ever tell at all, everything from his battery positions to his divisional marching plans and orders (he had a whole offensive army). He gave us everything ripe for the slaughter. It was clear in his mind that after all his blabbering—he was never asked anything directly, not with a single word—that he really couldn't go back to Little Father Stalin, even though he wore the Order of Stalin number seven hundred and something, a sort of Great Knight's Cross from over there, which he then gave Fegelein as a gift. Fegelein gave the medal to the *Führer*, and the *Führer* gave it back to Fegelein in a very nice silver box. Just thought I'd mention it.

Vlasov Again

When Fegelein told me the story of the general, I said, "Sure, we can do everything. The man gets promised everything and he'll get it, too. He gets the pension of a German lieutenant general (he's a Russian lieutenant general). He gets good food, liquor, women." That's really disgustingly cheap. A torpedo costs, what do I know, 10,000 marks, as soon as we fire it. The preliminary concentrated artillery fire for a single division or corps costs many hundreds of thousands. We don't even know whether the fire will be as effective in every case as when we buy just one cheap Russian general. Of course, it doesn't go like that formally; you don't say, "You get 100,000 marks down, now betray everything to us." Of course, he won't do it. Comrade Slav has a few points of honor here. You have to go about it differently. Let's figure it out. How much pension does he get? 1,500 marks a month, that's 18,000 marks a year. Let him live ten years, that's 180,000 marks. Miscellaneous expenditure is 20,000 marks. That's 200,000 marks total. It's really cheap if you get a Russian offensive army for it. You can do that with every Russian general, every one. We really shouldn't take them so seriously. If we could do that, then things would go right. But we Germans handle it so badly, I must say, in the state and the armed forces, that even many a Party comrade has fallen for this and gotten caught. Mr. Vlasov has made speeches in Paris, in Brussels, in Berlin. At his feet sat astonished members of the German leadership corps; their mouths hang wide open, their noses fall right down into their mouths out of sheer astonishment: "Golly! That Bolshevik can do simply everything." And they let that butcher's assistant tell them so. I took the trouble to read his whole speech once. I'll write an opinion on this speech, and send it to you in the near future. Mr. Vlasov says: "It's a shame how the Germans treat the Russian people. We Russians abolished corporal punishment decades ago." (Sure, they abolished it. That's why they shoot them now instead. That's just another kind of incentive.) "You Germans re-introduced corporal punishment, oh, how barbarous, how low-down." Everybody in the audience feels ashamed. A few minutes later he claims: "How nationalistic the Russians are, you must appeal to their nationalistic soul." Can't you just see how the victor over Field Marshal Paulus, General X (I no longer recall his name), who was locked up by the GPU for years, beaten, whipped, and tortured, so that he suffers from hip pain even today and has a severe head injury, was victorious over Paulus at Stalingrad out of pure nationalism? Nobody contradicts him. I thought the Russians had abolished corporal punishment. Apparently, among the Russians, only the generals are beaten, to get better results out of them. This Vlasov hullabaloo has gone around Germany without contradiction. Instead of skillfully making propaganda out of it, to disintegrate the Russian army, this propaganda has been turned against us, and has to some extent paralyzed the strength of resistance and the will to resist of our own ranks through errors and false notions.

Ruling With a Minority

I have felt obligated here to speak of these things quite openly here, with absolutely no rancor against anyone. All the things that we are still doing wrong, that we still can't do right, that is, how to act with regards to foreign peoples, the domination of masses of foreign blood by a small minority of the upper crust, all these things just have to be learned. We of the old Reich, I'm speaking of Lesser Germany, have only been a Reich for seventy years. We have not yet had the opportunity to rule large political minorities, or even majorities, with a German minority, like the Ostmark in Old Austria, with its minority of twelve million Germans, ruling 40 to 50 million members of foreign races in the Balkans. Nor have we had the opportunity to learn to rule millions, hundreds of millions, with a minority, as England does, having learned how for 300 years. We must take things as they are. We will learn that too; and if we could rise from the dead again in 100 years, we would see that our grandchildren and great-grandchildren will already be better at it than we are. I wish to instruct the SS in all these things. I believe that we are best protected from error through our self-assured racial attitude. We must also learn a great deal ourselves. We'll do it, I believe, to put it modestly for once, the least badly, relatively speaking, and with the fewest mistakes.

Psychology of the Slavs

Now, back to the Slavs! I consider it necessary to speak to each other about this once again. Whether it's Peter the Great or the late Czars, whether it's Lenin or Stalin, they know their own people. They are perfectly well aware that the concepts of "loyalty," "never betray anyone," "never conspire," have no place in the Russian vocabulary. Whatever people may tell you about the Russians, it's all true. It's true that some of the Russians are fervently pious, and fervently believe in the Mother of God of Kazan or someplace else, it's absolutely true. It's true that the Volga boatmen sing beautifully; it's true that the Russian of today, in modern times, is a good improviser and good technician. It's true, for the most part, that he's even a lover of children. It's true that he can work very hard. And it's just as true that he is stinking lazy. It's just as true that he is an uninhibited beast, who can torture and torment other people in ways a devil would never permit himself to think of. It's just as true that the Russian, high or low, is inclined to the perversest of things, even devouring his comrades or keeping his neighbor's liver in his lunch bag. It's all part of the scale of feelings and values of the Slavic peoples. It's often purely a matter of chance which lot he draws; and to people who don't know the beast, he is often a very great riddle: what is the fellow up to now? The Russians themselves know each other very well, and have invented a very practical system, whether it was the Czars with the Okhrana, or Mr. Lenin, and Mr. Stalin with the GPU or the NKVD. When four Russians get together, with little father, little mother, and their little children, not one of the four or five knows who is betraying whom at the moment: which one is the informer betraying the father now: is it the mother, or the daughter? And who, in return, is betraying them? In doubtful cases there may be two, even three, informers in this family. I am not exaggerating. This remark is entirely accurate with regards to the city. In the countryside, our comrades who have been over there in the East can confirm that there are still twenty or thirty NKVD informers and agents in every village, even after the withdrawal of the Bolsheviks. This ensures, to an absolute certainty, that no conspiracy can get started, because everything will still be reported to the top by means of this informer apparatus. Then comes the pistol or deportation, and that is how this entire people must be governed.

Heart in the Wrong Place

It is basically wrong for us to project our whole harmless soul and heart, all our good nature, our idealism, onto foreign peoples. This applies to Herder, who wrote the "Voices of the Peoples," probably in a drunken hour, and caused us, in later generations, such boundless suffering and misery. That applies to the Czechs and Slovenes, to whom, after all, we brought their national feeling. They themselves were absolutely incapable of it; rather, we invented it for them.

For the SS Man, one principle must apply absolutely: we must be honest, decent, loyal, and comradely to members of our own blood, and to no one else. What happens to the Russians, the Czechs, is totally indifferent to me. Whatever is available to us in good blood of our type, we will take for ourselves, that is, we will steal their children and bring them up with us, if necessary. Whether other races live well or die of hunger is only of interest to me insofar as we need them as slaves for our culture; otherwise that doesn't interest me. Whether 10,000 Russian women fall down from exhaustion in building a tank ditch is of interest to me only insofar as the tank ditches are finished for Germany. We will never be hard and heartless when it is not necessary; that is clear. We Germans, the only ones in the world with a decent attitude towards animals, will also adopt a decent attitude with regards to these human animals; but it is a sin against our own blood to worry about them and give them ideals, so that our sons and grand-children will have a harder time with them. When somebody comes to me and says, "I can't build tank ditches with children or women. That's inhumane, they'll die doing it." Then I must say: "You are a murderer of your own blood, since, if the tank ditches are not built, then German soldiers will die, and they are the sons of German mothers. That is our blood." That is how I would like to indoctrinate this SS, and, I believe, have indoctrinated, as one of the holiest laws of the future: our concern, our duty, is to our people, and to our blood. That is what we must care for and think about, work for and fight for, and nothing else. Everything else can be in-different to us. I wish the SS to face the problem of all foreign, non-Germanic peoples, partic-ularly the Russians, with this attitude. Everything else is soapsuds, a fraud against our own people, and an obstacle to earlier victory in the war.

Russian Soldiers on Our Side

One thing is a matter of course in this war: it is better for a Russian to die than a German. If we use the Russians, then they must be mixed with Germans in a ratio of 1:2 to 1:3. The best thing is to use individual Russians; then you can drive with them in a tank. One Russian with two or three Germans in a tank, magnificent, nothing wrong. But you must never let one Russian meet other tank-driving Russians, otherwise the Russians will conspire. But if for some reason you wish to have Russian-only companies then be careful, gentlemen—and that is not just a thought, gentlemen, that is an order—they must have their informer apparatus, their NKVD, in this company. Then you can sleep in peace. Otherwise, this is one of the earliest warnings I've issued, take care that these sub-humans always look at you; they must always look their superior in the eye. It's like with animals. As long as an animal looks his tamer in the eye, he won't try anything. But have no doubt about one thing: he is a beast. We will able to utilize the Russians with this attitude; with this attitude we shall be superior to the Slavs at all times. But not with any other attitude.

The Russian Theater of War Today

Now back to the military situation! We are in a curtailed position today. It is a shame that we had to give up the Donetz Basin. We have given it up. That will in no way decide or influence the outcome of the war at all. It is advantageous to us to have a short, straight front in this way; it will be extended, and must be extended, with all our strength; it will then form our east wall with the shortest, straightest connections to the rear. All in all, this offers one very great advantage. The enemy has now regained the great area which we previously had to conquer, large expanses of which we seriously damaged. I view the offensive of the Russians this winter with calm. I am convinced that we can hold off this last great lunge of the desperate beast. And then, he wouldn't be a Slav if he didn't suddenly show signs of very severe exhaustion, and I mean intellectual exhaustion.

The Italian Theater of War

Now for Italy, the other theater of war! There must be no doubt in our minds that the weakness of this people lies in their blood, in their race. In considering this problem, we must distinguish between that which is comfortable or uncomfortable for us today, and that which will be comfortable or uncomfortable for us in the future. Italy was a weak ally, beginning with Greece and Africa, and ending with Russia. There is, after all, no nation which hasn't thrashed the Italians, from whom the Italians haven't taken a beating. The Italians, we can see this right now, will be considered the most contemptible people in the world; no one, no Albanian, no Montenegrin, no Frenchman, no American, no Englishman, no Russian, no German, will have any respect for them, since they have proven themselves everywhere to be cowards, as soldiers, as men. That is the most contemptible judgment that one can hand down against a people and a race. We must therefore distinguish between that which is comfortable for us today and that which would be comfortable for us in the future. If the Italians were a neighbor truly related to us in terms of inner qualities, then it would be magnificent if Italy had remained strong. But with a consistently weak neighbor who has no resistance to anything, the situation as it is, I must say, is much better. It is considerably better. At the moment, it is uncomfortable; it came at an inconvenient time. If the betrayal had come a quarter of a year later, it would have been better for us. But you can't hope for that in war. Fate simply doesn't ask what you want. It throws you heavy punches. In the long-distant future, we will be thankful to fate and to God that it happened as it did.

The Failure of the Italians

I've already said that the Italians have failed everywhere. Pantelleria, to take only one characteristic example, capitulated with 12,000 men after the loss of thirty-six killed and 120 wounded over the course of six weeks. They had enough water—the report of the honorable commander of Pantelleria was not true—for the garrison of 12,000 men, probably for another ten to twelve days. I personally believe they had enough water for even longer. The island could simply not be taken, every expert says so; even the airplane hangars were underground, built into rock casemates. They simply couldn't be gotten out of there. Something must be said here: the surrender of Pantelleria was tragic insofar as the Duce consolidated the island, exactly as he built the Italian air force, exactly as he created the Italian navy. That navy was his work, his navy. But these people, one can really say, are still Italians after all; the Duce is the only one who embodies and bears in himself the great Roman tradition.

The Italian army in Sicily didn't defend itself. It showed the white flag everywhere, right away. Then came the betrayal. That was very hard for us, since we were in the midst of transporting our divisions. Based on news reports, I was already convinced of the disintegration of Italy one and half years ago. The army was infected with Communism and was sympathetic to the Anglo-Saxons. We couldn't carry out the counter stroke before sufficient German divisions had been sent over the Alps.

The Liberation of the Duce

Next came the real implementation of the armistice. And then came the—how should I say—bold stroke by our SS men and the men the *Luftwaffe*, the liberation of the Duce. I was very happy that the work of the Security Service could be mentioned for once, after all these years, since it is precisely the task of the Security Police and Security Service to work in silence. Their work is never mentioned, cannot be mentioned. Their men die as bravely as our men do at the front, but their work must not be mentioned. That which they provide in terms of important information and documents, the importance of that which they do, can never be mentioned. Thus, it pleased me greatly that the Security Service—the work of our friend Heydrich, which is being carrying on in a dignified and forceful manner by his successor Kaltenbrunner—was able to show for once, in public, that it is strong and gets results.

The liberation of the Duce, insofar as I could tell everywhere, met with an unprecedented response in our people, and gave them an unprecedented boost. But it was also interesting because it was taught us that virtues like loyalty and comradeship are values of the mind which are profoundly rooted, not only in the German people, but in the entire European group of peoples.[6] Let us never underestimate the value, the unique eternal value, of this ideal. The manner in which our people reacted to this act of comradeship and loyalty was therefore a shining example and a gleaming proof of this fact.

The Balkans

I will briefly list the individual nations of the Balkans. Croatia, for the moment in serious disorder, is a state made up of 6 1/2 million men, of whom 3 1/2 million are Croats. Two million are Bratislavs, that is, a kind of Serb, and one million are Bosnians. It is a state with very large minorities. Its national leader, Poglavnik, entered office as a result of the difficult conditions imposed upon him by the Italians, and placed at a disadvantage by the fact that he was forced to renounce the largest and most valuable parts of his country. It was obvious that he did not enjoy any authority in this manner. Most of the country was occupied by the Italian army. The bands under Mr. Tito—he has become a sort of popular hero there—and Mr. Draža" Mihailović—Tito is the Communist man, Draža" Mihailović is the Yugoslavian–English–American man—dominated the situation.

The situation in Slovenia is similar. Albania's independence was now recognized by us. Serbia is naturally the hotbed of conspiracy in the Balkans, yet it is relatively quiet. Greece is also somewhat quieter for the moment.

It is clear that we must concentrate large numbers of troops to the Balkans in order to shield and protect this part of Europe exposed by the collapse of our ally. We must expect attacks there by the Anglo-Americans. It is naturally of interest that the Balkans are one of the principal objects of strife between Russia and the Anglo–Americans. Russia says: that's my sphere. And the Anglo-Americans say: that's our sphere. The best fruits for us will grow out of the perpetual strife between our noble allies.

The Other Occupied Territories

France, the Netherlands, Norway, Denmark, Belgium, Poland, Bohemia, and Moravia—the situation is known. We must be on the lookout everywhere, that is clear. We must expect acts of sabotage, paratroop attacks, minor rebellions, strikes, insubordination, and diffidence everywhere, even among the favorably-minded elements of the population. In the Germanic countries, one thing is quite clear to me: the majority of the people in these Germanic countries, in the bottom of their hearts, will only be won over when the die has been cast in the present struggle between the two Germanic Empires, that is, the German and British empires, when it is seen who is the stronger. They will then fall to the stronger. It is disagreeable to us that they do not come to us with open hearts. But it cannot be denied that the political preconditions for this did not exist. There were no great figures—this is the tragedy of the renewal movements in Holland, in Flanders, in Norway, and in Denmark—able to win their people over to us and lead them into the Germanic political community today, according to their own political laws. It is perhaps—even probably—best, from a historical point of view, that this is so difficult. The select few who come to us, and fight in our Germanic volunteer units, in our Germanic corps (in the *III. SS-Panzer-Korps*) are naturally some of the most valuable members of the Germanic nations. These men, who fought their through to us from out of thirty million Germanic people, who were trained among us, will be the old fighters of the greater Germanic community.

The Sabotage War

We must, of course, anticipate an increase in the most unpleasant forms of sabotage, the use of poisons, explosives, in short with everything. These are things that we have to pay attention to, which must be taken seriously down to the minutest detail, but whose objective—wearing down our nerves and spoiling our good humor—must never be permitted to succeed. I say this in full awareness that every detail must be taken seriously in this war. But we must consider nothing a tragedy, since all these things do not kill us. They cannot kill us; they are pinpricks, they are unpleasant, they hem us in here and there; but they cannot wound us mortally. Mortally—I would like to emphasize this here for the first time—there is only one thing that can hurt us: a weakening of our will to resist. He who, in spirit and determination, refuses to give in, cannot be defeated, unless he can be starved out, which is not the case with us, if he stays strong, as a man and as a soldier, if he has his weapons, and cannot be overcome with these.

The Air War

Since the *Luftwaffe*, which in the first years of the war possessed absolute mastery of the air, has had to stretch itself out to great theatres of war all over Europe, it has naturally had to be spread thinner. Since we had to intervene in Italy in battles involving the heaviest sacrifices to protect the security of our supply lines, since neither the Italian fleet nor the Italian air force could protect our supply lines to Africa to any significant degree, we have suffered much attrition in Italy. The terror attacks on our country have doubtlessly hurt us badly in many places. I am firmly convinced, I would like to say that I can state definitely, that the worst is over, that we have found a tactic to break these air attacks, that, through work, we can multiply our aircraft production and improve our weapons. I am firmly convinced that we will have overcome the chief dangers of the situation by the end of this year or the beginning of the next year, that we will be active again during the coming year.

The War at Sea

We truly had some bad days for a time this year. Fate tested us once again. Just when problems were appearing on the eastern front, just when treason was raising its ugly head in Italy, when the air attacks were getting terrible, the U-boat war was interrupted, too. As always in war, things go back and forth. Sometimes offensive weapons are stronger, sometimes defensive weapons. We just went through a period during which the defensive weapons of the English were stronger, were technically superior to ours. For months, therefore, the U-boat war had to be restricted to a minimum. As you have seen from the reports of the last fourteen days, we are now active again. Offensive weapons have once again recovered and surpassed the enemy's technical lead, and offensive weapons are now once again at an advantage. That is an example and a lesson that one must never give up, that a cause is only lost—technically, militarily, spiritually—when one gives up. If the *Reichsmarschall* in the air force, if *Großadmiral* Dönitz in the navy, had said, after the low point, "There's no point, the others are too powerful, they're better equipped technically, the U-boat is out of date, or our air force, or some technical development or other, is out of date," then the enemy would have triumphed. When one does not give in, but rather, as happened here in both cases, gives the order: "Ready for action!"—then, this example, in both the Air Force and the navy, shows that things can also go forward again. You just have to have the nerves for it.

The Home Front

I now come to another aspect of this war, the home front. Some of the German people, namely the older men drafted, are now serving in their second four-year world war. The German people were already very tense years before the war, because of rearmament, the Four Year Plan, the recovery of Austria, the Sudetenland, and the occupation of Bohemia and Moravia. There can be no doubt that hostile propaganda is now streaming and trickling into the German people from many sides. We are unfortunately unable to screen off hostile broadcasters entirely, or in any manner worth mentioning. The temptation has grown to listen to hostile broadcasters, who achieve better psychological effects than we do, sometimes, unfortunately, very good ones. As in all cases in which a prohibition or law cannot be given the emphasis of enforcement by executive authority and punishment, the effect of the prohibition is harmful to authority; that is true in this case as well. We have, of course, prohibited listening to hostile broadcasters, but we were not, and are not, able to punish violations of this prohibition in any meaningful way. Today we pay somewhat more attention to it to some extent, since, when Mr. Badoglio committed his piece of piggery, when treason ran amuck in Europe, the result was naturally a wave of defeatism in Germany. Shortly before, after the air attacks on Hamburg, a mood of crisis prevailed in many cities, which were, particularly our beloved capital of Berlin, almost panicky for days, until the mood calmed down and leveled off again. As a result of listening to foreign broadcasters, talk then circulated through the channels which always exist, even in a great people, "Oh God, we can no longer win the war. Wouldn't it be better therefore," etc. etc. Then came this highly interesting remark: "Ah, a Duce can be arrested, how interesting." When the Duce was arrested I said to myself, now we've really got to watch it. The people who think that's so interesting, they interest me. Since that time, as you may note from the reports from the Reich Ministry of Justice, and you will continue to note over the coming few weeks, Mr. Administrative Advisor so and so, and Mr. Factory Owner so and so, and Mr. Waiter, and Mr. Chauffeur, and Mr. Plumber, and Mr. Employee, have all had their pretty little heads cut off and placed between their feet for damaging the morale of the German people as defeatists, for disintegrating the powers of resistance of the German people, and for treason. It's really not important for us to kill anyone. If we really had to shoot as many people as all that, or as many as I'd have to, it would get increasingly difficult to sign a death sentence. When I was appointed Reich Minister of the Interior, everybody said (since it's so awfully easy to say), "Sir, hit hard, stay tough. The German people expect terrible severity from you." I'm already severe, I don't need any admonitions. It's very easy to say something like that, but: a death sentence means eternal misery for a whole family; it means bringing shame on a name which was once honorable. Imagine for a moment what it will mean to the children and grandchildren of that family, when it is later said (you must always visualize these things as they will look ten or fifteen years after the war): "The father of this family was beheaded for high treason during the Great War, which involved the fate of the Germanic nation." (In the distant future, everything we do today will look heroic. Human weaknesses will then be forgotten. All the cowards will have died off in the meantime, and in the end everybody will be considered a hero). Such a family will be shamed for all time. I know all that. I know how hard it is; and I therefore try to restrict the necessary educational measures. I know that there's a great deal of theft in Germany, that the concept of private property has been much weakened by suffering, and by the relaxation of all moral standards such as always happens in war, or due to a poor upbringing of the German people in this regard. I can't catch every thief, I'll never catch them all. I don't even want to catch them all, otherwise I'd have to arrest too many thousands of people. I'll never catch every defeatist. I'm perfectly well aware that, in one or two years, when the divisions and regiments withdraw into their garrisons—some of the older veterans having been wounded up to 7, or 8, or 9, or 10 times, while the rest no longer march with us because they lie under the grass; when, I hope, a still decent part of the old SS once again marches back to Germany, I know that many thousands will applaud us then, and perhaps feel themselves to have been much more heroic than we were, or—we don't think of ourselves as heroic—more decent than we were. It will always be like that. I don't mind. We shouldn't mind either. We should never lose our sense of humor. It is, however, necessary to set an example for the number of cowards who can be found among every people. It is, God knows, unfortunately true that these cowards are always found in the upper, rather than the lower or middle, ranks of a people. Intellect obviously ruins the character in some manner, at least as regards the formation of will and energy. It's enough for me, for such education, if I always grab one out of 100 of the defeatists who later cry "hurrah," and lay his head between his feet, then the others will shut up for a quarter of a year. Then all the little mommies will say, "For God's sake, don't get yourself killed, don't make us unhappy. Somebody we know was recently beheaded. It's in the newspapers. So just keep quiet, cry 'hurrah' very loud." Good, let him; we've achieved our objective. We could never storm a fort or a front line position with a person like that anyway. We know that anyway. But the main thing is to keep them from hurting our decent people. Insofar as is necessary, action will be taken brutally and mercilessly. None of us enjoys that. Although we don't like it, you must act mercilessly, gentlemen, without regard to family relationships, or acquaintance, or class, or possible previous earlier service; without regard to whether he is a party comrade or not, when the fate of the nation so requires. Always go after a big fish rather than a little one who's stupid and has been fooled. The domestic front will always be in order if we have the nerve to keep it in order, although it gives us no pleasure to take action personally.

Foreigners in the Reich

We must be also clear in our minds that we have six or seven million foreigners in Germany. There may even be eight million. We have prisoners in Germany. They are not all dangerous, as long as we strike hard at the smallest minor problem. It's a small matter to shoot ten Poles today, instead of maybe having to shoot tens of thousands in their place later, and compared to the fact that shooting those tens of thousands would cost German blood, too. Every little blaze must be immediately stamped out, smothered, extinguished; otherwise, just as in a real fire, a veritable prairie fire, politically and psychologically, may break out among the people.

Communists in the Reich

I don't believe that the Communists will dare try anything, because their leaders, just like most other criminals in our country, are in concentration camps. Something must be said here: only after the war will it be seen what a blessing it was for Germany—all humanitarian drivel to the contrary notwithstanding—that we locked this whole criminal underclass up in the concentration camps—I'll take care of that myself. If they were running around loose, it would be much harder for us. Particularly since the sub-humans would then have their subordinate officers and commanders; they'd have their workers' councils and soldiers' councils. But this way, they're all locked up, and are making grenades, artillery shells, or other important things, and are very useful members of human society.

The Situation on the Enemy Side

Now I would like to give a short overview of the other side. We Germans always see-saw between extremes. Either we are totally exhilarated and applauding enthusiastically, and we can't wait until we have reached all our objectives in a lightning war of 18, 16, or even 15 days; or we let our jaws hang down and whine: "Yes, the enemy is wonderful in everything. The English are doing great. The Russians are doing great; we're the only ones that aren't." At the same time, we completely forget that, on the other side, like everywhere else, they can't do the impossible either.

Russia

I would like to list our various enemies quite briefly. Once again, Russia. Here, I can sum up quite briefly. Russia will, in my opinion, when the next great offensives are over, have just about exhausted its human potential. One can, of course, draft sixteen year olds, they can make an early grab at fifteen year olds—I am absolutely in favor of us doing the same, if the fate of the nation so requires, since it is better for fifteen years to die than for the nation to die[7]—but one cannot continue endlessly in this direction, since, in the end, with thirteen year olds and twelve year olds one can no longer wage war. Human potential is, in my view, one of the weakest points of the Russians, although it was once their greatest strength. In addition, in my conviction, unprecedented famine now prevails among the Russians, something which can never be correctly evaluated by us. The front line is, however, still better fed than the people behind the front. Nevertheless, it is still very bad in many cases even at the front. The Russian has had great transport difficulties for a long time. These, too, are not yet overcome. I don't believe that the Russians are weak in a material sense; rather, I believe that they will die of hunger and loss of blood.

England

England has been waging war for four years now. So far, it has suffered no very great losses in blood. In England, however, the constant fear—the very correct fear—prevails that, when the U-boat war sets in again with full force—and it will do that for months now, in my view—the whole equilibrium in food, supplies, and landing possibilities will fall to pieces. For all the military operations that England and America wish to carry out, will stand or fall on tonnage. The landing operations that they carried out at Salerno doubtlessly cost them half a million tons. I very much doubt whether England can permit itself many such landing operations over the long term. I nevertheless believe that England will undertake landing operations, perhaps even this fall—they don't have much time left for this—but certainly early in the year. But there is another thing I believe: when the war for England—and this applies even more so for America later—really becomes a matter of the blood of their sons, the war in England and America will be more unpopular that it is already.

America

America is waging a war on two fronts, even moreso than England: the Pacific war against Japan, which, fortunately, is a stronger, more warlike ally, and the war in Europe, or the Atlantic. I do not believe that the conditions in America are for the best. One must keep in mind that America still has a great number of Jews, and a brutally plutocratic form of economics. It is hardly conceivable how they push and shove in America. I believe we were still babes in the woods by comparison in 1918. The difficulties and misery gradually appearing before the population in America are furthermore inconceivable. In addition, we have taken Mr. Roosevelt's best electoral propaganda point—he will certainly be reelected next year—away from him through the liberation of the Duce. A "show trial" of Mussolini and fascism was in fact intended to be the central point of his electoral propaganda. The following applies, however, to both countries: the war will become fearfully unpopular in England and America the moment England and America have to fight somewhere in Europe, whether in Italy, the Balkans, or even France, Denmark, or Norway. This applies especially to America. England fought the last world war using its own people. America, on the other hand, had, I believe, 60,000 to 70,000 dead in the World War. That was, unfortunately, far too few. I am convinced that if the Americans had suffered 500,000 dead in the World War, they wouldn't have entered the war this time. It will be a difficult psychological point for those gentlemen when the number of dead exceeds that of the World War. Once the number reaches the hundred thousand mark or climbs into the hundreds of thousands, then enormous difficulties will set in for the Americans. The Americans are in fact by no means as brave as they act. On the contrary: the American is by no means a brave soldier; he is well armed, he has very strong artillery, he is well equipped in all things, but he is not a good infantryman.

Political Problems on the Enemy Side

Now come the great political difficulties. England and America are not united. England says: America, you must help me more in Europe. Naturally, in doing so, each swindler wants to cheat the other. Each is seeking to exploit the strength of the other. America wants England to help defeat Japan. England is trying to exploit the Americans in order to defeat Germany. England is in a situation which is becoming increasingly difficult. Mr. Churchill can't hide this from his countrymen. What is England really fighting for? And then come the difficulties with Russia. Stalin, a brutal, ice-cold, power politician, says: I am bearing the chief brunt of the war. Therefore, I want to have the say in Europe. Poland, the Balkans, Latvia, Lithuania, Estonia, are in my spheres of interest. Germany, when it is defeated, will also be in my sphere of interest. Now they are starting to have a hard time on the other side. The war with Germany really started because they gave guarantees to Poland. That's why Mr. Sikorski had to die too, I believe—because he clung to this old fairy tale. This naturally caused frightful difficulties for England. So England has now issued an Atlantic Charter as well. But England is in even greater need of Russia as an ally. It is, in fact, its strongest ally on the continent. So while Bolshevik Russia wants to have the say in Europe, England would dearly like to maintain—as it is so beautifully called - the "balance of power" in Europe, and not let the Bolsheviks into Europe, for God's sake. It is a chaotic jumble of interests and views, of intentions and plans. Each one wants to exploit and swindle the other for his own plan, and then bring home the harvest for himself. That is a system which will, of course, hold together for a while, but which will certainly collapse one day. The moment the alliance collapses, the power of our enemies will, of course, still be considerable, but not threatening. The war will be won by the side that continues to hit back, and keeps hitting back, who never surrenders. For us, the end of the war—once Russia is exhausted and drops out one day, and the war becomes a burden for England and America, will confirm our position as a world power. Because we can really say by comparison—though there are problems with every comparison—that the Seven Years War brought Prussia's confirmation as a great European power. That war was carried on for seven years to ensure that the already conquered province of Silesia would remain part of Prussia. This war will ensure that everything annexed to the German Reich, to Greater Germany, and then to the Germanic Reich in the years since 1938, will remain ours. This war is being carried on to keep the path to the East open; so that Germany may be a world power; to found the Germanic World Empire. That will be the meaning of this war, whether it lasts 5, 6, perhaps even 7 years. We don't know how long it will last. We don't even ask how long. It will be carried on by us for as long as it lasts, and it will be carried on with determination and good humor by us for as long as it lasts. It will be won by the side that stands, that doesn't give up or give in, even in the most difficult situations. To ensure that this never happens, is our principal task.

The SS in the War

Now I come to our own development, to the development of the SS over the past few months. The development was, when I look back over the entire war, unprecedented. It has gone ahead at a truly astonishing pace. Let's take a look back at the year 1939. Then we were a couple of regiments, 8,000 to 9,000 men in police units. We were armed, of course, but only received our artillery regiment as the heavy branch of service to all practice purposes two months before the start of the war. Let us recapitulate the tasks, duties, and missions entrusted to us over the past 4 1/2 years. First, however, I would like to list and once again describe some still further external changes.

Personnel Changes

The following changes have been made in the Main Offices: The successor to our fallen comrade and friend Heydrich is our comrade *SS-Obergruppenführer* Kaltenbrunner. He is unfortunately sick today. He has phlebitis, but it is not, however, dangerous, thank God. That is why he could not come.

Our old friend Daluege has such a serious heart problem that he is taking a cure, and must now withdraw from active service for 1 1/2 to 2 years. I would like to send a teletype or telegram this evening to our two friends, namely Daluege and Kaltenbrunner, on behalf of all of us. We hope that Daluege will be well again and able to go into action on the front line again in, as I say, approximately two years. On his behalf, *SS-Obergruppenführer* Wünnenberg, who previously led the Police Division, and was then designated to lead the *4. SS-Panzer-Korps* as commanding general, who is a general in the *Waffen-SS* and the Police, will head the *Ordnungspolizei* as Chief of the Order Police. *Gruppenführer* Breithaupt, as the chief of the SS Court, has succeeded our old comrade and friend, Scharfe of the SS. *SS-Obergruppenführer* Hofmann has changed posts. He has given up the Race and Settlement Main Office, and has become the Senior SS and Police Commander Southwest.

SS-Gruppenführer Hildebrandt has given up his *Oberabschnitt* Weichsel and has become chief of the Race and Settlement Main Office. *SS-Obergruppenführer* Schmidt has given up the Personnel Main Office at his own request, and has entered my personal staff for Special Tasks. His successor is *SS-Gruppenführer* von Herff. One of my closest and oldest associates, *SS-Obergruppenführer* Wolff, after a severe illness which seriously endangered his life (operation for kidney stone) has, thank God, gotten well again, and is now—it is the first time anyone has held this position—the Supreme SS and Police Commander for all of occupied Italy. He is therefore responsible for a region with 25 to 30 million inhabitants. He has *SS-Gruppenführer* Globocnik as the Senior SS and Police Commander for the coastland, as well as several other SS and Police leaders under him. He could not come today.

Senior SS and Police Commanders have since then been assigned as follows: in Croatia, Kammerhofer, who, at the request of the Croats, is not called Senior SS and Police Commander there, but rather the Representative of the *Reichsführer-SS*; this was formerly Meyszner's title in Serbia; it is now Stroob's title in Greece—I would like to say right away that I am reassigning him to Schimana. You will become the Higher SS and Police Leader in Greece; you will not, therefore, lead the SS Volunteer Division for Galicia. *SS-Gruppenführer* Hanke will become Senior SS and Police Commander in Denmark.

Corps and Brigades

In the *Waffen-SS*, since we saw each other last, we have progressed to the next stage of organizational development. At that time, 1½ years ago, we were just forming the 1st SS Panzer Corps led by *SS-Obergruppenführer* Hausser, who is now leading operations in the Italian littoral.

In the meantime, the following corps have been created or are being formed:

The *I. SS-Panzer-Korps* under *SS-Gruppenführer* Sepp Dietrich, consisting of the *SS-Panzer-Division "Leibstandarte-SS Adolf Hitler"* and the *SS-Panzer-Division "Hitler-Jugend,"* which is now being formed;

The *II. SS-Panzer-Korps* under *SS-Obergruppenführer* Hausser, consisting of the *SS-Panzer-Division "Das Reich,"* and the *SS-Panzer-Division "Totenkopf."*

The *III. SS-Panzer-Korps*, the Germanic panzer corps, under *SS-Gruppenführer* Steiner, consisting of the *SS-Panzer-Division "Wiking,"* now in the East, plus a new unit now being formed, the *SS-Freiwilligen-Panzer-Grenadier-Division "Nordland,"* and the *SS-Freiwilligen-Panzer-Grenadier-Brigade "Nederland."*

The *IV. SS-Panzer-Korps* under *SS-Gruppenführer* Krueger, who previously led the *"Das Reich"* Division, consisting of two new divisions, namely, the existing *SS-Panzer-Division "Hohenstaufen,"* which was raised by *SS-Obergruppenführer* Berger as the *9. Division*, together with the *10. Division*, in February of this year over a period of five to six weeks, and trained and formed by *SS-Obergruppenführer* Jüttner. That was a masterpiece, I can tell you, the greatest piece of daring. It was the most fearful situation that I had seen for several weeks. The old panzer corps, consisting of *"Das Reich," "Leibstandarte,"* and *"Totenkopf,"* left France. In the second half of December came the order from the *Führer*: on February 15, two new SS divisions are to be recruited in France out of the labor service camps from youths born in 1925. You could write a book about it later, and tell the whole story about how difficult that was, but it was done nevertheless. Those recruits were trained with live ammunition from the very first day, since we never knew whether the English were coming. After eight weeks, they were already considerably better, and now they have become magnificently good divisions. At the moment, we have been ordered to form the 16th and 17th SS Divisions by January. We are already mutually occupied with this hard work. The *IV. SS-Panzer-Korps* will be formed from the *SS-Panzer-Division "Hohenstaufen"* (the 9th Division), and a new division is to be formed, to be called the *SS-Panzer-Grenadier-Division "Reichsführer SS."* It will be formed from the *"Reichsführer SS" Brigade* which, we hope, has succeeded in getting out of Corsica today with the last man.

The *V. SS-Gebirgs-Korps* under *SS-Obergruppenführer* Phleps, consisting of the *SS-Freiwilligen-Gebirgs-Division "Prinz Eugen"* and a Bosnian Mountain Division (*SS-Freiwilligen b.h. Gebirgs-Division [Kroatien]*), now being formed.

The *VI. SS-Gebirgs-Korps*, the Latvian corps, under *SS-Gruppenführer* Pfeffer-Wildenbruch, consisting of an already-formed Latvian brigade which fought very well on the Volkhov, and a Latvian division now being formed and soon to be at full strength.

The *VII. SS-Panzer-Korps*, which is now being formed, with an existing SS panzer division (the 10th Division) in France, which has been given the name "*Frundsberg*," and the *17. SS-Panzer-Grenadier-Division*, which was initially given a next very strange sounding, but—when correctly understood—very defiant name: "*Götz von Berlichingen.*" "*Frundsberg*" and "*Götz von Berlichingen*": these names are a declaration of defiance made by us against our enemies, both domestic and foreign.

In addition, we have formed still more brigades and assault brigades. In the future, when everything squeezed out of the *Waffen-SS*, and the manner in which the *Waffen-SS* gave of itself, can finally be described in detail, it will seem a considerable performance.

Commander of the Anti-Partisan Units

In the meantime, I also created the office of the Chief of the Anti-Partisan Combat Units. The Chief of the Anti-Partisan Combat Units is our comrade *SS-Obergruppenführer* von dem Bach. I considered it necessary that the *Reichsführer-SS* should be the commanding officer, in keeping with his authority, for all these actions, since I am convinced that we are in the best position to concern ourselves with the outspokenly political struggle carried on by our enemy. We've been successful insofar as the units available to us, and formed by us, weren't repeatedly taken away to plug up gaps in the front.

It should be noted that the creation of these offices, in the sequence of division, corps, army, has led to the next stage, namely, that of Supreme Command of an army or even of a group, if you want to call it that, for the SS.

Order Police and Security Police

Now briefly on the tasks of the Order Police and Security Police. They have remained within the same framework. What was achieved, I can only say, is enormous. We have formed approximately thirty police regiments out of police reservists and older "police soldiers," or police officials, as they were formerly called. The average age in our police battalions is no less than in the Security Battalions of the *Wehrmacht*. The performance is magnificent, surpassing all praise. We have also formed police regiments by combining previously formed police battalions of "native peoples." That is, we no longer left these police battalions by themselves, but we mixed them in a ratio of 1:3. That is why we have achieved much greater stability with them than with any of the other domestic or native units, precisely in the present time of crisis. The tasks of the Security Police, just like those of the Order Police, have grown with the expanding geographical territory. It is precisely in this connection that we will only be able to talk about our accomplishments after the war. It will certainly be entertaining to be able to speak to our counterparts in the [British, author's note] Secret Service and lay our cards on the table on both sides. The other side is not making life easy for us. At the same time, you should never forget that the fortunate situation in which we now find ourselves, in having occupied many parts of Europe, also involves the disadvantage of having millions of people, and dozens of foreign nationalities, under us, and therefore against us. Everyone who is a convinced Communist is automatically against us; every Freemason, every democrat, every convinced Christian, is against us. These are the ideological enemies opposing us all over Europe, all of whom the enemy has for himself. Nationalism, correctly or incorrectly understood—in France, Norway, Denmark, the Netherlands, or Serbia—is against us. The enemy can therefore exploit this ground, which has been magnificently well prepared for him, for his acts of sabotage and parachute activities at any time. We didn't have these problems until now, except in the Caucasus and in Iran, which is very far away. Our dear English and American adversaries are already on the continent. They have southern Italy, we have northern Italy. Now we'll see some fireworks. I'm glad of it. It will be a wonderful opportunity for us to show what we are capable of in this area. It will be our first chance to meet the English in this field with the same weapons for once. The only foreign people the English have under them are the Irish. The Irish, however, are so Catholic, and so preoccupied with religion, that despite their national hostility to England they are kept calm, neutralized by the Church, so that we cannot use them. An opportunity is now appearing for the first time. You can be sure we will not fail it to make use of it.

Tasks as Reich Minister of the Interior

In addition to everything else we've achieved in this time, I cannot keep silent about the fact that I have become Reich Minister of the Interior. I have a little bit more work. I view my responsibilities as falling into the following major categories:

1. Restoration of the authority of the Reich, much of which has been lost;
2. Decentralization of tasks not of importance to the Reich. To keep the Reich in hand, while calling upon all the creative powers slumbering in the German people under German self-government;
3. Radical elimination of corruption or misconduct throughout this entire apparatus and in every case. I will proceed ruthlessly. If somebody has done something wrong and if I catch him, big or little he's coming before the Khadi court, since such a case, exorcised and carried out in public, does not harm respect for the state and party, but strengthens it, because then everybody says: "All kinds of respect."

If somebody's a blackguard, throw him out. That applies equally to us within the SS. I am now coming to a few things which, as is my custom, I will state clearly. It is quite clear that human shortcomings are found everywhere. Organizations distinguish themselves only through the following: one organization conceals them and thinks it has to cover them up with the famous blanket of Christian brotherly love, so as not to hurt its prestige. Another organization cleanses itself brutally. It says, "He was a swine, we've shot him," or "We've locked him up," or, in any case, "We threw him out." Then they say: "Now, get busy and blabber about it or do something else." That gives them the right to say: "If anybody else among you is a swine, then he's going to get the same." As *Reichsführer-SS*, as Chief of the German Police, and now as Reich Minister of the Interior, I would have no moral right to proceed against any racial comrade, nor could we bring forth the strength to do so, if we did not take care to cleanse our own ranks brutally. You can be sure that I will do this as Reich Minister of the Interior. You can also be sure that I will not go off at a madman's clip, and then maybe pull the bridle so hard that the nag falls down on his hindquarters; rather, the bit will be pulled slowly and gradually, so the horse will be brought to a decent pace again.

SS Economic Enterprises

I'm now coming to a few other individual areas of major responsibility, which you must all know something about. We have gigantic armaments industries in the concentration camps. That is the responsibility of our friend *SS-Obergruppenführer* Pohl. We put in many millions of man hours on armaments each month. We tackle the most ungrateful problems, and I must admit that whether it's in Pohl's concentration camps or his economic operations, whether outside among the Senior SS and police commanders or in the factories of the SS Administrative Main Office, one thing is obvious: we are SS men wherever we are. If something is in a bad way, get right down to it. Educate every subordinate in this direction for me. We want to help without being hindered by jurisdiction, for after all we want to win the war. Whatever we do, after all, we're doing for Germany. Whether it involves the building of a street or tunnel that isn't going ahead somewhere; whether it's an invention which can't come into existence due to sheer bureaucracy, or whether it's something else: wherever we can lend a hand, we're going to do it. Whatever we achieve in our armaments factories will be a considerable accomplishment, one which is worth seeing, even if we can only describe and estimate it at the end of the war.

The Evacuation of the Jews

I want to mention another very difficult matter here before you in all frankness. Among ourselves, it ought to be spoken of quite openly for once; yet we shall never speak of it in public. Just as little as we hesitated to do our duty as ordered on June 30, 1934, and place comrades who had failed against the wall and shoot them, just as little did we ever speak of it, and we shall never speak of it. It was a matter of course, of tact, for us, thank God, never to speak of it, never to talk of it. It made everybody shudder; yet everyone was clear in his mind that he would do it again if ordered to do so, and if it was necessary. I am thinking now of the evacuation of the Jews, the extirpation of the Jewish people. It is one of those things that's easy to say: "The Jewish people will be extirpated," says every Party comrade, "that's quite clear, it's in our program: elimination of the Jews, extirpation; that's what we're doing." And then they all come along, these 80 million good Germans, and every one of them has his decent Jew. Of course, it's quite clear that the others are pigs, but this one is one first-class Jew. Of all those who speak this way, not one has seen it; not one has lived through it. Most of you know what it means when 100 bodies lie together, when 500 lie there, or if 1,000 lie there. To have gone through this, and at the same time, apart from exceptions caused by human weaknesses, to have remained decent, that has made us hard. This is a chapter of glory in our history which has never been written, and which never shall be written; since we know how hard it would be for us if we still had the Jews, as secret saboteurs, agitators, and slander-mongers, among us now, in every city—during the bombing raids, with the suffering and deprivations of the war. We would probably already be in the same situation as in 1916–17, if we still had the Jews in the body of the German people. The riches they had, we've taken away from them. I have given a strict order, which SS Group Leader Pohl has carried out, that these riches shall, of course, be diverted to the Reich without exception. We have taken none of it. Individuals who failed were punished according to an order given by me at the beginning, which threatened: he who takes even one mark of it, that's his death. A number of SS men—not very many—have violated that order, and that will be their death, without mercy. We had the moral right, we had the duty to our own people, to kill this people which wanted to kill us. But we don't have the right to enrich ourselves even with one fur, one watch, one mark, one cigarette, or anything else. Just because we eradicated a bacillus, after all, doesn't mean we want to be infected by the bacillus and die. I will never permit even one little spot of corruption to arise or become established here. Wherever it may form, we shall burn it out together. In general, however, we can say that we have carried out this most difficult task out of love for our own people. And we have suffered no harm to our inner self, our soul, our character in so doing.

The Attitude of the SS Man

In describing what we have done in this one year, in a—I would almost like to say—statement of accounts, for all of us, and before us all, there is one thing I must neither overlook nor neglect: the significance of the SS man's attitude. Here, I believe, we have endured decently, generally and on the whole, as in all other things as well. The attitude of our brave leaders and men was proper in desperate situations at the front, where they, in the darkest hours, in the very darkest hours, grew beyond themselves, in life and in death, in this heroic great death, which has continued over the last 10 weeks. The attitude of our men was, generally and as a whole, good throughout the partisan war, even in the remotest areas. Their attitude was also good in the homeland.

For my attitude means more than what I say. The people, the little man in the misery of his heart and with fear in the pit of his stomach, is already looking at our attitude in many cases today, asking: How does the SS man stand? What's his facial expression? Does he look miserable? Does he let his jaw sag? Or: How does this SS battalion march to the front? Or: How did the police guard act in some dump in the Balkans or in Russia? Or: How does the SS man act during an air raid? Does he stick around, or does he take to his heels? Is he the one who prevents a panic and helps dig people out? Or contrarily: Is there an SS officer or SS man who claims special rights, who travels by car where he isn't entitled, who lives better than other people, who does no extra duty and takes every Sunday off, whose wife makes endless demands, who gets herself in a twist and won't do this and won't do that, and makes unreasonable demands while others are being bombed? Or are our wives the hardest-working, the most modest, the bravest, those who never criticize, who hold their heads high at all times? In general and as a whole, our attitude was good. There is still room for improvement in our ranks. To say this is part of the duty of a commander or group leader. I would like to head this chapter with the words "We, Ourselves."

The Principle of Selection

We have arisen through the law of selection. We have selected from the average of our people. Our people arose through the dice game of fate and history in long-ago primeval times, over generations and centuries. Foreign peoples swept over this people and left their hereditary material in them. Channels of foreign blood flowed into this people; yet this people has nevertheless, through horrifying misery and frightful blows of fate, still had, in their blood vessels, the strength to endure. Thus, this entire people has been drenched in, and is held together by, Nordic–Gaelic–Germanic blood; so that in the end one could, and still can, continue to speak of a German people. Out of this people, the result of diverse mixtures of hereditary factors, such as was available after the collapse which followed the years of the struggle for freedom, we have now consciously attempted to select the northern Germanic blood, since we could assume that this part of the blood was the bearer of the creative and heroic, of the life-maintaining qualities of our people. We examined the outward appearance on the one hand, and then revised that outward appearance in terms of new requirements on the other hand, through more and more samples, both physical and intellectual, both of character and soul. We repeatedly sought out and rejected that which was not suitable, that which did not adapt to us. As long as we possess the strength to do so, this order will remain healthy. The moment we forget the law of the racial foundation of our people, the law of selection and severity with regards to ourselves, then the germ of death will lie within us; in that moment we will perish, just as every human organization, every prime of life in this world, comes to an end at last. To enable this flourishing and bearing of fruit to continue for as long and as blessedly as possible, and—don't be alarmed—for as many thousands of years as possible, must be our aspiration and our inner law. For that reason, it is our duty, whenever we meet and whatever we do, to remember our principle: blood, selection, toughness. The law of nature is precisely this: what is hard, is good; what is strong, is good; that which endures out of the struggle for existence, both physically and in terms of will and soul, is good—always viewed from the vantage point of time. Naturally, somebody can rise to the top for a while—this has often happened in history—through swindling and cheating. For nature, for the fate of the earth, for the fate of the world, that doesn't matter. Reality, that is, nature, fate, purges the swindler after a time—not viewed in the ages of men, but in the ages of the world. Never to deceive ourselves, but rather to remain genuine at all times, that must always be our endeavor; that is what we must advocate and inculcate in ourselves, in every young man, and in every one of our subordinates, over and over again.

The SS After the War

One thing must be clear, one thing I would like to say to you again today: the true forging together of our order, this order which we built up over ten long years, the fundamental principles of which we founded ten years before the war, and in which it was educated, will only begin when the war is over. That will still remain to be accomplished by us—if I may say so, we, the old fighters—in twenty exhausting years of hard work after the end of the war, to create a tradition of 30, 35, 45 years, that is, a generation. This order will then march into the future, young and strong, revolutionary and effective, to fulfill its task of providing the Germanic people with a superior stock capable of binding this Germanic people and this Europe together and holding them together, producing the intellects required by the people in economics, farming and politics, and as soldiers, statesmen, and technicians. In addition, this superior stock must be so strong, so filled with life, that each generation will be capable, without question, of sacrificing two or three sons from each family on the battlefield, yet nevertheless ensure the passing on of the bloodline.

The Virtues of the SS Man

I now wish to speak of the most important virtues which I began to preach and to inculcate in this order, this entire *Allgemeine-SS*—since that is the foundation of the order—years ago, and which are of such decisive meaning and importance, especially now in the fifth year of the war:

1) Loyalty

So far, thank God, no case has occurred in our ranks in which a reputable SS man was disloyal. Let one thing be the guideline here: should anyone in your circle of comrades ever be disloyal to the Führer or the Reich, even if only in thought, you must ensure that he is expelled from the order, and we will ensure that he loses his life. Everything, I already said this and I'll repeat it once again today, everything can be pardoned in this world, but there is one thing which cannot be pardoned among Germanic people, and that is disloyalty. It would be unpardonable, and it is unpardonable. Cases like the Badoglio affair in Italy should, and never will, happen in Germany. The name Badoglio will in the future be a term of abuse for bad dogs, for four-legged mongrel curs, just as in ancient times Thersites was a term of abuse for traitors. We can only say one thing, and say it again and again: let the German people, every one of its men and every one of its women, prove, through unprecedented, unconditional loyalty, that this German people is worthy of living in the era of an Adolf Hitler, for which people the Führer arose and dedicated his life, filled with care, filled with responsibility, and filled with work for our Germanic German people.

2) Obedience

Obedience is required and given in the soldier's life, morning, noon, and night. The little man always obeys, or almost always. If he doesn't, he's locked up. The question of obedience among the bearers of higher honors in the state, party, and army, and even here and there in the SS, is more difficult. I would like to state something here clearly and unequivocally: that the little man must obey is a matter of course. It is even more a matter of course that all SS high-ranking SS leaders, that is, the entire corps of *Gruppenführer* [group leaders], should be a model of unconditional obedience. If anybody believes that a command is based on mistaken perceptions on the part of a superior or on mistaken information, it is a matter of course that he—that is, every one of you—has the duty and the responsibility to speak out, stating his reasons manfully and truthfully, if he is convinced that they mitigate against the command. But once the involved superior or *Reichsführer-SS*—in most cases, it the corps of *Gruppenführer* which is concerned—or, even the *Führer*, has decided and has given an order, it must be carried out, not just to the letter and to the text, but in keeping with the intent. Whoever carries out the order must do so as a loyal trustee, as the true representative of the authority giving the order. If you ever believe that an order is mistaken or even wrong, then there are two possibilities: if you don't believe that you can take responsibility for an order, then you must state honestly: I cannot take responsibility for it, I wish to be discharged from carrying out the order. In most cases, you will be ordered to carry it out anyway. Either that, or your superior will think: His nerves are shot, he's weak. Then he might say, Alright, you can retire from service. But orders are holy. If the generals obey, then the army will obey, too, as a matter of course. The holiness of an order becomes more and more important with the increasing size of our territory. To enforce an order in our little Germany isn't at all difficult. To carry out an order when we have garrisons in the Urals—as we will have one day, of that I am convinced—that will be a good deal harder. In this case, it will not always be possible to verify that the order has been carried out. Verification, among us, must not and never will consist of enforcement by a commissar, as in Russia. The only commissar we have must be our own conscience, our faithfulness to duty, loyalty, obedience. If you set this example, gentlemen, then every subordinate will follow your example. But you will never be able to demand obedience if you do not first show the same obedience to authority yourselves, unconditionally and without limitation.

3) Bravery

I don't think there is much need for admonitions on bravery among us, since our officers are brave, and our men are brave. For curiosity's sake, however, I would like to give you a contrasting example: an example of how things are done among the Russians; I would also like to express a few thoughts in this regard. I heard the following story from an Estonian officer who was forced into the Red Army with his Estonian company, but who succeeded in escaping: a unit of the Red Army carried out an attack which was repulsed by the Germans. Afterwards, the unit commissar ordered the officers to a conference. The officers had had to report to the dugout, in a prescribed manner, that is, at attention. The commissar kept on working quietly and let the officers stand at attention for a long time. When one became restless and began to fidget, the commissar just looked up and said, "You seem quite tired." Then he asked, "Does anyone of the gentlemen have anything to say about the attack?" One officer replied that the German resistance was too strong, that attack at this position was impossible. The commissar drew his pistol, shot the officer, and then simply asked, "Does anyone else have any comments"? Half an hour later, they carried out another attack. Look, that's an example of the kind of bravery we don't want, and that we don't need. The "commissar" ordering us to attack must be our own courage, our own loyalty, our own obedience. There is an enormous difference.

In our ranks, we live according to our Germanic laws, one of which, a really beautiful one, says, Honor is compulsion enough. With foreign peoples, we must apply Asiatic laws. We must never lose sight of that. If we have one of our blood before us, a Norwegian or Dutchman of good racial stock, then we can only win his heart over to us according to our, that means his and our, totally Germanic laws. With a Russian or Slav, from a racial point of view, we should never even try to apply our holy laws to them, but rather the tried and tested laws of the Russian commissar. I would like to bring up another issue here, which is part of the topic of bravery. I mean moral courage, which is sometimes not quite as it should be. I know really a lot of my best SS leaders, who would storm any bunker, any fort, unconsciously, automatically, without thinking about it, but who, if they had to demote a subordinate, for example—I think I already mentioned this earlier in my remarks—they do this for me to see; but then when the time for enforcement comes, they act like astonished Central Europeans and say, "Quite incomprehensible, my dear fellow. Dreadfully sorry. I'll have to speak to Berlin about it right away. Another mix-up by the Personnel Main Office. Of course, in Berlin, it's all theory." It would be better to have moral courage beforehand, and say, "You, you're demoted, get out." No, gentlemen, it doesn't work like that. In the future—I think I already said this once—I'll have to send all such people back to the commander involved and say: "Ah, that was your mistake; the demotion was an error. Now you get your valuable employee back again." This is, in fact, an element of bravery, so-called moral courage. And I would like to educate my leadership corps in it where it is lacking. Part of bravery also consists of faith, and here, my group leaders, we won't be outdone by anyone in the world. Faith wins battles, faith gets victories. We don't want men in our ranks who are pessimistic, who've lost their faith. It doesn't make any difference what his job is, whether he's a member of the *Allgemeine-SS*, in economic life, in a government position, somewhere in the *Waffen-SS*, on the front (that doesn't usually happen), or whether he's headquarters staff at the front, or somewhere else in the communications zone, in the homeland, in the police, or in the Security Police or Order Police. People who are so weak that they've lost their faith will be rejected by us, we don't want them. He who has lost the strength to believe shall not live among us in our ranks.

4) Truthfulness

I come now to a fourth virtue, which is very rare in Germany, truthfulness. One of the greatest evils, one which has become widespread in the war, is untruthfulness in communications, reports, and data sent by subordinate positions in civilian life, in the state, party, and army, to superior positions. The communication, the report, is the basis for every decision. It is really true, that, in the war, one can now assume in many sectors that 95% of all reports are lies, or only half-truths, or are only half-correct. This begins with troop strength reports. I'll take an everyday example. If somebody is asking for reinforcements, then in his strength report he gives his "troop strength." If he's even cleverer, he'll give the "trench strength." Of course, that's even less: "I have only 200 men left." Frightful! Only 200 men. If anybody is sly enough to say, "What's your ration strength?," he'll see that there are 1,300 men eating in the regiment concerned. I must say: these are remarkable ratios. Very odd. 200 men are fighting, while 1,100 men are the huge tail wagging behind this little head. How peculiar.—If somebody wants weapons, on the other hand, he says, "I have a troop strength of 3,000 men, but not nearly enough weapons. I need vehicles and weapons." If somebody needs material, mines or anti-tank cannons, for his position, then the position becomes 25, 30, 35 kilometers long. It stretches out like a rubber band. But if he's supposed to occupy it and somebody says, "Your division is so strong, you could occupy at least twenty-five kilometers," then the division shrinks, and suddenly he says, "I can only occupy seven kilometers." Then there are the famous communications "for military reasons." It used to be that when somebody closed a Jewish company or took away a Jew, a Mr. Paymaster So and So reported, "What, do you want to impair the defensive strength of the German people? You're sabotaging the war effort." In reality, the Jew bought off the paymaster with a fur coat. Today, if we take 800 Jewish women away from a company, along comes a gentleman and says—so as not to insult him, let's call him by a title which doesn't even exist—Mr. "War Advisor," who's just had a pair of brand new boots made by the company, and he says, "I must report that you have seriously harmed war production."

Or: sometimes, when I see proposals for promotions and decorations, there's no activity anywhere which isn't decisive to the war effort. It's astonishing. Look here. I believe, if we want to be able to look each other in the eye, we must succeed in obtaining absolute and unrestricted honesty. Otherwise, management becomes impossible. Nothing can be managed if, for example, every Senior SS and Police Commander, and every division and corps commander, conceals 500 or 1000 men from us. If seventeen divisions each have 1,000 men too many today, then the German people are being deprived of a division. If every division has just 300 trucks too many per division, then two divisions could be motorized out of the surplus. These are things we can't be responsible for. I now come to another matter on the subject of truthfulness. In both war and peace, it must be so—and this will be a particular object of education in peacetime—that we SS men no longer need to make written contracts; but rather, among us, just as in former times, a man's word and handshake must be equivalent to a contract; an SS Man's handshake, if necessary, must be of greater value than a surety for one million or more. The handshake or given word of an SS man, if necessary, must be proverbially safer than a mortgage on the most valuable property of another man. It must be so! If we make contracts, we must keep them. If I make a contract with an agent, even if he is a contemptible character, then I keep the deal. I stand for this attitude without condition. When I decree that anybody in the Generalgouvernement who informs on a Jew concealed in some hideout gets one third of the Jew's fortune, it often later happens that a Secretary Huber or an *Untersturmführer* Huber, a person who—if he can get away with it—indulges in unauthorized private travel, who orders anything from a new pencil to a new telephone, that is, somebody who never saves, suddenly starts to save for the German Reich. He says for example, "The Jew has 12,000 RM. Why should I give 4,000 RM to the Pole who turned him in? No, I'll save the money for Germany. The Pole gets 400 RM." In this manner, a subordinate goes off on his own and breaks the word of a whole organization. These are things that must be impossible.

If we give our word, it must be kept. If the *Reichsführer* promises somebody protection for his organization—as is often the case in the Balkans—then this promise must be kept. We, precisely we of the SS, must earn a reputation for contractual loyalty all over the world such as to gain the greatest value for Germany in so doing, that is, faith through trust. Many people will then come to us who won't go to official agencies. There's always a lot of confusion in the Balkans. That's really our big advantage. If they were united, it would be terrible. There's confusion in the Caucasus, there's confusion in Russia. We can only—and that's only part of the lesson—take constant care that the territories occupied by us, and the peoples governed by us, never unite, that they remain disunited at all times: if they united, they would, of course, only be against us. So if we promise protection to a splinter group which comes to us, then it must be out of the question for any member of the SS or the police, that is, the order as a whole, to go and break our given word. Our word must be holy.

Justice! Gentlemen, it is always very important to me that justice must never be to the letter alone, but unrestricted justice, in terms of intent, not words or form. At the same time, I'm coming to a matter which is not quite right among us. To our sorrow, as you know, many regrettable legal matters come before me in legal cases. I have every judgment against a SS officer or police officer laid before me, and sometimes I note the manner in which my officers judge each other, time after time. You know the proverb of the crow that tried to cover itself with another bird's feathers... It's such a habit for an officer not to hurt another officer. Gentlemen, Germany could learn from the old Prussian army in this regard. An organization remains healthy as long as it feels an unwavering pressure, an irresistible drive, to keep itself clean. A corps must be trained and educated to say to someone who has done something wrong "You must turn yourself in." Or, if it's more serious: "You must be punished for the sake of justice. You don't belong here in our ranks, or at least not in your present position in our ranks. It's wartime; you can go off and clear your name by serving as a common enlisted man and rise up through the ranks again. But you don't belong in our ranks in your present position." Now, instead of this impulse—one cannot really call it by any other name—to cleanse one's own ranks, as was still the custom in the old army under Wilhelm I, an impulse to act like a bunch of lawyers has spread throughout all organizations in Germany. There's no more talk of cleansing, expelling, purging anyone; rather, everybody is somebody or other's lawyer; it's like a trade union. Everybody acts on the principle of: "Well, you never know, you might do something wrong yourself one day. So just be careful! If you cover up for him, he'll cover up for you." It's a great setup. You can falsify history like that for a while, gentlemen; you can manipulate your way upwards like a con-man. But one day, when tough times come along and there's pressure from fate, then an organization like that collapses because of it. So I want you as judges, and you as senior officer corps of the SS, to ensure that such things are no longer covered up. If a little man and a big man are on trial or involved in some legal matter, I don't want to see the little man get punished and then hear people say of the big man, "He was only marginally involved." Of course, the officer is only marginally involved. In a case like that, you should say, "You have the higher rank, therefore you have the greater insight. Consequently, you must be more strictly and severely punished." It's the little man who is marginally involved. If he hadn't had his superior's example, he wouldn't have done it. There's another thing I want. I want clear responsibility. That's another element of truthfulness. I always feel sick when I ask "Who decided that?" and I get an answer like, "Oh, the so and so Ministry Main Office." So I say, "OK; and who, pray tell, is Mr. Ministry?" That's what I want to know. I was born that way, I've got great curiosity. I want to know which *Untersturmführer*, *Obersturmführer*, *Hauptsturmführer*, *Sturmbannführer* was it? Who was it in the Main Office? Was it Mr. Meyer, or Mr. Huber? Who made the decision? Of course, a lot of people say, "I've got a great boss, my Main Office boss or my Senior SS and Police Commander is a real good man. Since he's so decent, he always covers up for his subordinates." And since all these little wretches look so tremendously brave behind their superior's back, they say, "The Old Man will look out for us, he'll go off like a big tiger and fight for us before the *Reichsführer*." So I no longer want to read that the "So and So Main Office So and So has decided"; rather, gentlemen, I want to know whether it was Mr. *Sturmbannführer* Meyer or Lehmann. If the decision was correct, then he can only be proud not to be just a government employee someplace in the background.

We don't want to see just the big ones covering themselves in glory. The little man should get some glory, too. Besides, there's also a really positive side too. You and me, we'll sometimes become alert to someone who never attracted any attention at all, who has never even been noticed for all his hard work, and we'll be able to say: "Damn! That was really a great job! The report is concise, but it means something. That man must have eyes like a hawk. I'll have to take a closer look at him." We'll discover a lot of good brains in our ranks this way; we'll be glad to have opened the way for somebody with talent, maybe sometimes even a genius. If a decision is wrong, though, then I don't want the top-ranking commandant to cover up a piece of nonsense out of sheer frivolity and maybe fight a battle to the death with his comrade from another Main Office or Upper Division, just because he says: "It's our jurisdiction. That the decision is nonsense, makes no difference. If it was my Main Office that made the mistake, then it has to be defended." I also want us to act correctly with regards to other offices, gentlemen. I believe that I can say of myself that when I go ahead, I set a good example. If I'm wrong, I say so, I'm wrong. My God, our authority can't be so small-minded that we can't admit that. We all have so damn much work to do, that out of one hundred decisions a certain percentage of wrong, badly thought out, or half-baked decisions must be made. That's human. I'd rather have the work get done, and the decisions be made; rather than one man making five perfectly correct decisions, I'd rather have somebody else make one hundred decisions in the same period of time, of which five may be wrong; since the other ninety-five are still correct. Since mistakes may be made, I admit them; I don't defend nonsense "for the sake of Germany." You say: "Yes, we made a mistake. That will be improved or corrected, without any loss of our prestige." That's how it's got to be with us; and we want to go ahead and set a good example. I've also given orders to this effect in the Ministry. The individual should stand forward by name; we're not a joint-stock company. Because of the Jews, it became a habit with us to do all business in the form of joint-stock companies; but nobody knew who the joint-stock company was, or which Jew was "Mr. Ltd." or "Mr. Inc." I don't want a "Mr. Ministry," but I do want administrative advisors, secretaries, etc., and, among us, I want SS officers, *Untersturmführer*, or *Obersturmführer*, or maybe even a *Standartenführer*, if he's clever enough. But I want to know them all by name. So let's all start doing that. We want to eliminate anonymity, and substitute clear responsibility. Whatever I do, I am responsible for it: we must educate even the lowest-ranking Unterscharführer to this, but we must start with the higher leadership.

5) Honesty

I now come to a fifth point: sanctity of property, honesty, sincerity. I must say that these things have gotten very murky in Germany; we have become—if I say this now in a closed room, it's because it's only intended for this small group of people—a very corrupt people. We should not, and need not, however—I want to mention this—take it so tragically, so pessimistically. Many people say, "Oh, the Finns are an honest people." Yes sir. Do you know why they're so honest? Not because they've got simply fantastic moral inclinations, but because they had laws for 300 years, that anybody who stole one Finnish mark should have his hand hacked off. And that was so painful and so distressing that the whole people, as a result of such measures and such education, gradually became honest. We're not going to start doing that here, but, gentlemen, we must always take care to begin with ourselves. We will never succeed in bringing the pestilence called corruption under control, not even within our own ranks—it's not so bad yet—unless we persecute all signs of incipient corruption in our ranks without exception and without restriction, without asking "Who is it?," and without saying "But ... but ..." We must persecute them with barbarous severity, demoting all corrupt men, depriving them of office and decorations, and exposing them before their subordinates.

At the same time, that which really deserves the name of corruption is not so bad in our ranks. There are, however, little things that nobody notices any more and which are now called "getting something organized." For example, a family lives in the East. They've got more than enough workers already. They grab this Russian, that Russian, maybe a Russian girl. That's terrific, really magnificent. The missus doesn't have to do anything any more, she no longer cooks or beats carpets. What for? We're a master race. Nobody asks who pays for these workers; they'd be better utilized in an armaments factory. For a while, at first, before *Obergruppenführer* Pohl got them—Eicke had already gone into front line service—this was true even in the concentration camps, due to the confused relationships of authority. A lot of families had a prisoner here, and a prisoner there; other families even got all new furniture and I don't know what all else. We've still got old cases pending, and we're going to clear these old cases up, right down to the last detail, without mercy. Because it's stealing to claim workers to which one is not entitled, when the work isn't really a necessity of life. 100 men used solely on the grounds of comfort in such work today, are a loss for German armaments. But from what I have said, uncertainties about these questions arise from the state of emergency we lived through in 1936–37. Since that time, we no longer have all the necessary consumer goods which the human heart desires, and which we would like to have, such as silk, stockings, chocolate, or coffee. Hazy conditions are the result. We don't want to be hangmen here. There's a lot of temptation: can you buy it, can't you, maybe you can get it in France, or Belgium, or someplace else if you pay extra. These are things which make education difficult, of course. So I'm not concerning myself with all these moot questions which many people take for granted in this epoch of misery. I'm simply saying today that that the strictest conceivable standards will be established for the SS the moment normal conditions are restored after the war. If we do that for twenty years in peacetime, we'll achieve a faultless attitude on all these matters in the future through education. I'd like to mention one more thing. To me, it's obvious that the old fighters, the longer they have fought for the movement, the greater is their duty to act decently in all things. When somebody comes to me and says, "But he's an old fighter," then I must answer, "Sir, please excuse me, but did we really fight for the Third Reich just so we could wreck it ourselves, destroying through violence the respect that the people once had for us?" It is precisely the old Nazi who, when he slips, must be caught and punished; who, in really serious cases, must pay with his life. We can take no account of past service. If we punish him, and the others talk about it, we save ninety-nine others. But if we look the other way, saying, "He's an old Nazi," "He's an old SS officer, you can't sentence officers," then the next ninety-nine will be guilty in the same case, and the whole organization will gradually suffocate because of it.

6) Comradeship

The word "comradeship" is used with great frequency. Comradeship is generally quite good among us, especially among the frontline troops. I would, however, since I am speaking of comradeship, like to all one thing: avoid any disputes amongst yourselves. Disputes are unproductive. Differences of opinion are productive, if they are managed factually. Disputes, rancor, anger, and backbiting are unproductive, and paralyze the strength which we owe the Fatherland. They cost strength of nerve, which we need for other things, namely, for the fulfillment of our duties.

I must perhaps make another request, that disputes between higher leaders not be carried out at my expense. In many cases, the *Reichsführer* has to play postman, since the two gentlemen are no longer speaking to each other. So one of them writes a letter to the *Reichsführer-SS*, then the other one writes a letter, too. Then the Reichsführer has to write to both of them, and so on. It would save stamps, and be much simpler, it would save us all time, if the gentlemen would write to each other, and sit down together for once. In most cases, almost all cases, it turns out that if they speak their mind, if they take the time to discuss it, the matter is settled. If they don't take the time for it, if one says, "I don't have time, I can't see him this afternoon, besides, we can't agree on whether he visits me or I visit him, let's meet someplace neutral, the best thing is to meet by an old oak tree, or something like that." If they can't reach an agreement like that, since these are all matters of prestige—a man has his prestige after all, especially when his person is involved—then they can never even discuss the matter. But then they write letters to each other for weeks and weeks, months and years, just to get mad every time and wait for the other man to do something. Then some little wretch comes along and says, "I've got a real great relationship with my Old Man, if I tell him the other guy was in the wrong again, he'll say: he's representing my interests, he's a good *Untersturmführer*, he's in the right." I'd like to tell you something: beware of such subordinates, beware of such comrades. Let us all beware of men who kindle disputes and don't advise reconciliation between German people. Everybody who decorates himself with cheap laurels in this manner, as especially brave representatives of their ministry, their section, their division, would best be removed from office immediately for encouraging quarrelsomeness and character defects. These are things—I would like to draw your attention to this—that we want to eradicate from our entire officer corps.

7) Readiness To Undertake Responsibility

I have already briefly spoken on the subject of readiness to take responsibility. Situations will arise in this war requiring tremendous readiness to take responsibility. At this point, I'm not thinking of what I said before, that responsibility must be clearly stated, that the individual must stand up and be counted instead of remaining anonymous; rather, I am now thinking of another kind of responsibility, namely, a willingness to take responsibility even when, gentlemen, it really has nothing to do with you. I would like to say something here about the famous matter of jurisdiction. Our friend *Obergruppenführer* Wolff, in Italy, has just introduced something in the local Italian office: he said, "The man with jurisdiction is the man who can get it done." That's really true. In particular, there are men who say, "Of course, I'm responsible for that, but I can't get along with the person I have to deal with, he doesn't like me, he turns me down. So I'd rather see that nothing gets done in this matter." Somebody else who isn't competent, of course, could certainly get something done, because he's friends with the man on the other end. But he's not allowed to negotiate. The man with the authority would rather do nothing for the SS than see something get done by somebody who doesn't have the authority. I think you understand what I mean. Look, we must be generous here, right up to the hilt. The main thing is, something's got to be done. It's the same thing in battle: if an important hill has to be taken, it doesn't matter whether the 995th Division or the 998th has authority to do it. The main thing is, it has to be taken; then afterwards, they can always say, "OK, it's in your sector now; of course, we took it, but please be so kind as to occupy and hold it; don't let it be taken away again, or else we'll have to take it again." That which must be accomplished for Germany and for the SS must be accomplished by the person who is able to do it, whoever can get it done, and that person must possess an uttermost love of responsibility.

8) Industry

I would like to say another word about hard work. Let's teach all our men, today during the war and later in peacetime, that no work is undignified. It often happens that, as soon as one becomes, let's say, an Unterscharführer, of course, he can't carry suitcases any more, he can't do this and he can't do that any more. He can only stand around and supervise. That's the way it is now. For example, if an officer goes out with his wife, of course, he can't carry a package in uniform; it's better to let his wife do it. It's almost like in the Orient with us. Maybe we should make it a law that the wife with the package should also walk three steps behind. These attitudes have already become really traditional, and I don't want to see them adopted by us. I would like us to issue a motto for us, namely this, that for men and women of this order, this racial community of the SS, the word "work" will be writ large; that no work done for Germany is shameful, be it with axe or spade or with the pen, whether in agriculture, in the home or factory, or whether with the sword or plough. I am of the heretical opinion that we will be a poor people after the war, thank God. I find that downright encouraging. If we were really rich and well-off, we would probably not last long. We would collapse from sheer megalomania. We wouldn't know whether we were coming or going from sheer conceit. Because the war costs a lot of money, and because we must finance everything ourselves, I therefore truly believe that we will be a poor people. We will therefore have to work again. Above all, we must keep people from saying: "Servant girl, oh, no, no German girl can do that, that's for foreigners." We would end up like the ancient Romans, bringing over slave nationalities by whom we would be racially contaminated. These are some of the great problems which are already weighing down upon me and which concern me more than a lot of things in this war. The war must be carried on to the end; we'll win it after all, we just don't need to make mistakes. The other questions, however, winning the peace, winning over people's hearts again, letting them relax again after the war, and then getting them back to work immediately, educating them; these questions will be much more difficult at times. I believe, as I said, that the German people, at the end of the war, will be, not pauperized, but poor; that we will have to be very productive and work very hard. I hope we won't be so rich that we can only gobble meat until our teeth fall out, and commit other acts of nutritional stupidity; but rather, that all these things will be regulated by life itself. I also believe that the evils of the bombing war will lead to a dispersion of the great cities, so that we will be driven out onto the land a bit by our gracious God. Many people will then say: "It's not so bad on the land at all; I've got a goat, somebody else has a pig, we've got a few potatoes." That would be a very good start. Besides, we won't suffer so many hard knocks. That's really good for the immediate future. We would never have been willing to spend the money required to tear down the cities. Now they've been torn down by fate, and we will probably rebuild them more rationally with more open spaces. We must recognize these things in time, and apply education correctly from the outset. When you, as officers, discover childish military vices such as an Unterscharführer thinking that he doesn't have to work, then you must intervene. Sometimes it goes so far—not, thank God in our divisions—that soldiers no longer dig in. They seem to think: a Master Race doesn't dig in. It allows itself to be killed, but it doesn't dig in. I want these things to be rooted out as radically as possible among us, so that they cease to be a habit.

9) Avoid Alcohol

We really need waste no words on the subject of alcohol, we know that. With the hundreds of thousands of men that we're losing in the war, we can't afford to lose still more men, physically or morally, through addiction to alcohol and self-destruction. Here as well, the best comradeship which you can extend to your subordinates is the greatest, most merciless severity. Crimes committed under the influence of alcohol must be punished twice as severely. Leaders who allow their subordinates to hold drinking parties in their companies will be punished. I must request that this be carried out everywhere.

Practical Tasks

Now to the practical tasks, and then I will finish. Beginning with myself, I already told you that, in the Reich Ministry of the Interior, I see the practical work before us as consisting of strengthening the authority of the Reich, and in defending domestic morale and conduct. In the field of the *Waffen-SS*, the main thing is to train officers and non-commissioned officers in sufficient numbers for the purpose of new formations, since I see that we will have to intervene on an increasing basis among foreign nationalities. We will therefore need officers and non-commissioned officers. These new formations will be the responsibility of the *SS-Hauptamt* during the initial recruiting stage; during the second stage of training and armaments, they will be the responsibility of the *SS-Führungshauptamt*. Another task, of particular concern to our *Obergruppenführer* Pohl, will be the increasing and strengthening of our armaments works and armaments efforts; the task of the Order Police will be to mop up the East, since the reduction in territory involved will release gendarmerie and staff strengths, even if we only cover the territory using the present strengths. The main thing is to mop up mercilessly, completely. Many will weep, but that doesn't matter; there is a lot of weeping already. We must economize on strength, since we will need intervention reserves here and there in this troubled Europe. The work of the Security Police will increase in significance, since the war of nerves, of psychological warfare, will reach a climax in the fifth and sixth years of the war. For the Senior SS and Police Commanders, in terms of practical tasks, I see a task which also applies in particular to the *SS-Hauptamt*. To me, the Senior SS and Police Commander is the representative of the *Reichsführer-SS* in his area. Woe, if the SS and Police ever have a falling out. Woe, if the Main Offices ever become independent from each other with regards to their subordinates through well a well-intended, but incorrect, notion of their responsibilities, each with its own hierarchy of authority. That would, I firmly believe, be the end of the SS, if anybody ever shoots me out of hand. It must and shall be, that even under the decimated *Reichsführer-SS*, this Order of the SS, with all its branches – its foundation the *Allgemeine-SS*, *Waffen-SS*, Order Police, Security Police; the general economic management, training, ideological education, the whole genealogical question—shall form one block, one body, one order. Woe, if we fail to bring that about. Woe, if the individual main offices, the individual chiefs, ever get a false idea of their tasks here; if they believe they are doing good, when in reality they are taking the first step towards ruin. We have come a long way on the path towards fusion. In the bitterest hours of the hard struggle of this year, the *Waffen-SS* was merged together from the most diverse divisions and units, out of which it formed the *Leibstandarte*, the *Verfügungstruppe*, the Death's Head units, and finally the Germanic SS. When in recent weeks our Divisions "*Reich*," "*Totenkopf*," the Cavalry Division and "*Wiking*" fought together, everyone knew: Wiking is with me, *Das Reich* is with me, *Totenkopf* is with me; nothing can happen to us, thank God. And so, as it is and must be within the *Waffen-SS*, the Order Police and Security Police, the *Allgemeine-SS*, and *Waffen-SS* must now gradually merge. This is already happening in the area of appointments to office, recruiting, training, economic affairs, and medical treatment. I'm always doing something to accomplish this purpose; over and over again, a band is being wrapped around this bundle of shoots, to allow it to grow together. Woe, if these bands should ever loosen, since everything—you may well believe it—would sink back into its old meaninglessness in a generation, in the shortest period of time. One could then say: that wouldn't be a shame; if it is incapable of living, let it die. That is true. Nor would I ever wish to keep anything alive, even my—our—SS, which is so dear to us, if it is incapable of living. I simply believe, however, that we could not bear responsibility for it before Germany, before the Germanic world; because this Germanic Reich needs the Order of the SS. It will need it for at least the next few centuries. Another form for it will certainly be found in one hundred, a thousand, two-thousand years. When we're finished, some remnant will be saved and maintained by us, together with a few basic ideas. Something new will arise from that remnant, just as we held out our hand to grasp the torch held out to us, here and there, from the age of the Germanic tribes, from the age of chivalry, from the Vehmic organizations [*Translator's note*: secret medieval courts similar to American vigilante committees; anti-French resistance organizations under the occupation of the Rhineland], from the Prussian army; we are now the bearers of that torch, for the purpose of kindling a great Light. Thus shall it be in later times. Today, I believe, we cannot afford to allow anything to happen to this SS. I therefore urge one thing to you all, you, my Main Office Chiefs, my Senior SS and Police Commanders, to the entire corps of *Gruppenführer*, to the highest level of hierarchy of the Order of the SS: always look at the whole, always see the Order as a whole, never just look at your own sector, never just look at your own Oberabschnitt, but always look at the SS, and above that, the Germanic Reich, and above that, our *Führer*, who created this Reich and who is still creating it.

Party and *Wehrmacht*

Unity, which is more important than ever in Germany today, must be a sacred commandment to us, even if we may get angry over something or other once in a while. We need complete unity with the Party and with all its institutions. Fortunately, unity with the SA already exists. The new Chief of Staff Schepmann also views the creation of peace and harmony between old party organizations as his most important task. We need unity with the armed forces. We know that, as political soldiers, we think that many things in various units of the armed forces are out of date, unattractive, or incorrect. Always look at the positive; consider it your task to win men over; be a missionary. Don't look at the negative; don't look at what you don't like, but try to win men over who are often thirsting for a message. Try to make them understand the meaning of the war, and of the tasks that you are carrying out. Teach them about the racial question. We are, after all, fortunate enough to be able to say that we know all about that. That is what gives us our strength, that which makes us invulnerable to crisis. Take the trouble to communicate and propagate these thoughts. Every company commander to whom you communicate our ideas will become stronger, and his company will become stronger. Every division commander not rejected or insulted by you, but rather won over, will be a relentlessly uncompromising fighter in this war, with 15,000–20,000 men behind him. That means he'll hold the front; because it's the heart that holds the front; not the body, not the weapons, not the cannons.

SS Female Auxiliaries

There is another point I want to mention here. We have already thinned our ranks very seriously. Where we can still spare a man, we want him out. After long hesitation, I have agreed that *SS-Obergruppenführer* Sachs, who came to me with this plan, should create a school for SS female auxiliaries in Oberehnheim. I must say that this newest institution of the SS is also making very good progress so far. I have set myself the task in this respect of creating a mold which was neither an institution for clerks, nor one for merry-making. The German people, with all its values, must after all succeed in calling into being an institution similar to the Finnish Lottas. We must attempt to achieve—through a selection of these girls, so that truly the most valuable will come to us, as well as through an awakening of their feeling of honor—that which cannot be achieved through compulsion, not through curfews, punishments, and all other kinds of bans. In this connection, *Obergruppenführer* and *Gruppenführer*, it is your job, each of you, to make an effort to send us every valuable young girl of your acquaintance or from among your blood relatives, just as we used to recruit men for the *Waffen-SS* and candidates for the officer career path. Our comrade and friend Waldeck has behaved ideally in this regard, and has sent us his daughter. He is now going to send us his second daughter. The *Oberabschnitt* which has helped the most in this new area has been Hoffmann's *Oberabschnitt Südwest*. This will help us achieve one thing: every girl that we can use, will replace one man. A bit of nonsense occurred in one office, since soldiers and SS Men are, after all, very stubborn. There, the commander said: "I'll let these girls train SS Men as communications assistants in the communications service, then I'll send the girls away; I don't want girls in my unit." That is, of course, not really the purpose of the institution; rather, the purpose is the other way around, to use the girls to replace the men. But I think that generally that will all be straightened out. I am now asking you to treat these girls with all your chivalry, all your sense of justice, all your concern; take care that this institution remains sacred; act with all the nobility which, in other respects, really exists in our ranks. I don't want any jokes here; these are our daughters; they're the sisters of SS men, and are intended to be the brides of younger SS men and officers. When I met these girls, I said that when a man wants to marry one of them and he finds out she was an SS female auxiliary, he mustn't say: "No, for God's sake, it's out of the question." Rather, when a man wants to marry one of them and he finds out she was an SS female auxiliary, he must say, "Yes, I can marry her, she's all right." That's how it must be. That is how the girls must behave; that is how you commanders must look out for them, and enforce this attitude with regards to your subordinates.

The Future

The immediate future will, I believe, bring very heavy burdens; we will have a hard winter, a hard spring, before us. The assault in the East will be bitter as never before. The partisan war will increase. As soon as the thaw permits, landings and air attacks by the English and Americans will increase as well. This winter, the motto must be: "Stand, believe, hit back, fight, never give up." That is the main thing. Whatever it takes to end the war and achieve victory, one thing must be clear in our minds at all times: a war must first be won spiritually, in terms of will and soul; after that, physical, bodily, material victory is only a result. Only he who capitulates, only he who says, "I've lost my faith, my will to resist," can lose; because he has laid down his weapons. He who fights and resists stubbornly, until an hour past the conclusion of peace, has won. We need all the stubbornness we possess, all the obduracy that distinguishes us so absolutely; all our tenacity, all our obstinacy, all our pig-headedness. We want to show the English, the Americans, and the Russian sub-humans that we are tougher; that we, precisely we, the SS, will be those who stand forever. We wish to be the ones who return to fight again and again, whenever the opportunity arises, even in the fifth and sixth years of the war, with good humor; not with faces as bitter as the dead, but with good spirits, will, and drive. If we do that, many others will follow our example, and will stand as well. In the last analysis, we must have the will, and we have it, coolly and soberly to kill anyone who, in any position, no longer wishes to go on fighting in Germany—that can happen under stress. It is better to put a certain number up against the wall than to allow a breach to be opened anywhere in our lines. If we are prepared spiritually, in terms of will and intellect, then we will win the war according to the laws of history and of nature; because we incorporate the higher human values, the higher, more powerful values of nature. As I said already, our work will begin after we've won the war. We don't know when the war will be over. It can happen suddenly, it can take a long time. We'll see when it happens. But I am already predicting to you today, when armistice and peace suddenly come along, let no one believe that he can simply fall back and sleep the sleep of the just. Make sure all your commanders, chiefs, and SS officers understand this: because, gentlemen, if we once relax, a great many others will fall into the same sleep as well. I'm going to wake up the SS so thoroughly, and keep it so wide awake, that we can go straight to work building Germany. The Germanic work will then begin immediately in the Allgemeine-SS; the harvest is ripe, and ready to be carried to the granary. We'll recruit the young by conscription. We'll put all our *Waffen-SS* units in top shape in terms of armaments and training. For the first half year after the war, we'll work as if the big attack were coming the very next day. It will be decisive for Germany to have an operational reserve of 20, 25, or 30 intact SS divisions at the negotiations for peace or an armistice. When the final peace comes, then we'll be ready to proceed with our great work of the future. We will colonize; we will educate the young in the laws of the Order of the SS. I consider it absolutely crucial to the life of our people that concepts such as "ancestors," "grandchildren" and "future" not be taught as external matters, but that they become a part of our being. It must be a matter of course for us to have children, without question, without the need for offer premiums and material incentives. It must be a matter of course that the greatest number of descendents should issue from this Order, from this, the racial upper stratum of the Germanic people. We must be truly capable of supplying the leadership stratum for all of Europe in twenty or thirty years. If the SS, together with the farmers, if we, together with our friend Backe, then colonize the East, in bold strokes, without inhibition, not inquiring about traditional methods, with revolutionary drive and impetus, then we'll be able to extend the racial borders of the Reich by 500 kilometers to the East in twenty years.

I asked the *Führer* today to grant the SS—if we fulfill our tasks and duties until the end of the war—the privilege of maintaining the outermost German border to the East in a military sense. I believe this is the only privilege in which we need fear no competition. I don't believe that anyone will dispute us this privilege. There, we will be able to train every age group in the practical use of weapons. We will dictate our laws to the East. We shall burst forth and press gradually onwards to the Urals. I hope that our generation succeeds in enabling every age group to fight in the East, so that every division spends a winter in the East every two or three years. Then we'll never grow soft; we'll never have uniform-bearers who only come to us because it's comfortable, because the black uniform naturally looks very attractive during peacetime. Everybody will know that if he joins the SS, there will always be a possibility of getting killed. He'll know he won't be dancing in Berlin or celebrating Carnival in Munich every other year; rather, he'll be stationed on the Eastern border in an ice cold winter. This will ensure us a healthy selection for all time. This will enable us to create the preconditions for the entire Germanic people and for all of Europe, led, ordered, and trained by us, the Germanic people, over generations, to resist the fateful struggle with an Asia certain to break forth once again. We don't know when that will be. When the "mass man" arises on the other side with 1 to 1.5 billion people, then the Germanic people with its, I hope, 250 to 300 million people, together with the other European peoples, for a total of 600 to 700 million people, on a perimeter extending the Urals, or, in one hundred years, extending over the Urals, will carry on its battle for life against Asia. Woe, if the Germanic people should fail to prevail in this struggle. That would be the end of beauty and culture, of the creative power of this earth. That is the distant future. That is what we are fighting for: it is our duty to pass on the heritage of our ancestors.

We see into the future because we know the future. That is why we do our duty more fanatically than ever, with greater faith than ever before, more bravely, more obediently, more decently than ever before. We want to be worthy of being the *Führer* Adolf Hitler's first SS men in the long history of the Germanic people, a history which stands before us.

Now let us honor the *Führer*, our leader Adolf Hitler, who created the Germanic Reich, and who will lead us into the Germanic future.

To our *Führer* Adolf Hitler
Sieg heil! Sieg heil! Sieg heil!

APPENDIX 3

Speech to the *Gauleiters* in Posen on August 3, 1944

Dear Party members!

At the beginning of my presentation and my report I would like to state the following: I consider it necessary that we, in this select governing body of the Reich and the Party, have total clarity over what happened. However, I would like to ask you to communicate to the outside world only those facts which will be made known through the judgments and verdicts of the People's Court in the coming weeks and months. This speech is what we need for our own guidance and clarification.

With this assassination attempt on July 20, for the first time in our history a German officer violated his oath and laid his hand on the commander-in-chief to whom he vowed his loyalty. But this was just the final outward expression of a lengthy development.

I must go back here quite a ways with a few sentences. The German general Staff acquired its fame and reputation thanks to the first Moltke. Regrettably the second Moltke—I am taking great leaps along general lines—the original chief of the general staff in the Great War, distinguished himself with a fit of hysteria and weeping upon the beginning of that war, as he was desperate and convinced that defeat was inevitable. Strange things happened during that war. Strange phenomena occurred, which are difficult to explain. It is hard to explain the Battle of the Marne. How to explain the fact that the German side failed to learn of the mutiny of the entire French army and that a general offensive was not undertaken. According to most optimistic assessments only three or four divisions were not involved in this mutiny. It is strange that such an enormous breakdown, such a catastrophe in the ranks of an army went undetected by the enemy.

Another fact that the *Führer* once highlighted: that in 1918 several hundred naval guns which, as they said at that time, were suitable for defeating attacks by tanks, were mounted on suitable all-terrain trucks. However they never made an appearance at the front through all of 1918, instead an invisible hand inserted them here and there behind the front. But they never came forward to the front lines.

Finally, the very fact of the collapse. There is no doubt—as Nazis we know this very well—it was a communist, Bolshevik, social democratic revolution. It is common knowledge to us. It was partly an uprising of the disappointed, decent German soldiers—though only a very few—partly of the disappointed and ill-treated workers, but for the most part it was the uprising of the sub-humans, the uprising of the deserters, the Jews, the asocials, the criminals. It goes without saying that we push these facts to the foreground in our propaganda, in our entire enlightenment of the people. But we in this narrow circle must be absolutely clear that all this would not have happened had the senior commanders had any value, and if the senior commanders had kept their oath they had sworn and which embodied centuries of tradition, or at least its letter. Had the generals and the members of the general staff not lost their nerve, the revolution, the uprising and the soldiers' councils could not have taken place. We have to say this—and history is as unmerciful as it is unsentimental—that the generals left their supreme commander in the lurch and gave him the advice to flee the country.

This collapse and this terrible defeat led to what I might call the years of insurrection: the Ruhr, Munich, the Soviet Republic etc., everything that we witnessed, and the building of the new *Reichswehr*. It was largely rebuilt by the old general staff. And it is known to us that, not by accident, many capable officers who later have become known as national socialists, had to disappear from the army.

It is further to be noted that in this army of 200,000 and later 100,000, a systematic negative selection was taking place. While the Navy has learned a lesson from the collapse and mutiny of 1917–18 and, small as it was, rebuilt itself with people from the *Freikorps*, and therefore became sound, the army, on the other hand, built on the most unsound part of the "intellectual" general staff.

We need to be clear that those we have considered our national heroes and national generals, as Schobert, Dietl, Hube, Schörner, were suppressed for years, were not promoted, got no command. They were loathsome to that particular clique, considered unreliable to them as outsiders. One could describe in detail how difficult it was, even at the time when the *Führer* was already supreme commander of the armed forces, to give a man like Schobert his first division, then a corps, then a higher command; how difficult it was to get a man like Dietl out of oblivion, how difficult it was to give to a man like Schörner—that "never promoted" *Oberstleutnant* at the age well over forty—that was in 1940, he must have been forty-four by then—a mountain division. That same Schörner—I know that today—was summoned before the commander in chief of the army, and had to answer to *Herr* von Brauchitsch, because I once visited him in Pontarlier in the Jura. He was summoned to Berlin and had to answer for how it came to this unlawful, illegal visit by a notorious Nazi.

That's how this army was formed. The young who joined had good will. They learned a lot, they worked diligently. But the belief in a large-scale rearmament was not present in this army. I think the *Führer* could tell you a lot, how hard it was, now that the army finally had a government that wanted to do everything for them, to carry out anything so that they finally could get a new cannon or some more divisions. The army became complacent, became an end in itself. These 100,000 men, who would be a decisive factor as the only armed body in the country in a civil war scenario. For that reason they had the enormously inflated and bloated military district staffs with very strong Ic staffs (intelligence), the clandestine structures for the event of a civil war. It was outwardly an apolitical army, but in reality it was, in the General Staff at least, a highly politicized army.

The year 1933–34 began well. The army could not resist the momentum. The man at the head of the War Ministry or the *Reichswehr* Ministry, Blomberg—I have to say today exactly as I said it in all previous years—is decent, loyal and faithful. But he was soft, could not enforce anything and acted foolishly in private life. But he was decent and loyal to the *Führer*. That's why he had enemies in his own ranks.

In 1934, in my opinion, great opportunities were available. It was the time of rearmament where we went over to the People's Army, the introduction of general conscription, for one year, later for two years. Then in 1934, Röhm, had he not had his unfortunate disposition, his ill-fated aspirations, his unfortunate infidelity, could have gained some influence on the army with the SA. June 30, 1934 destroyed this possibility. The army emerged from it as loyal, faithful and brave.

Herr Fritsch was the supreme commander of the army. After him—I can summarize it here—come Mr. von Brauchitsch. The chief of staff is Mr. Beck, later Mr. Halder. The characteristics of these gentlemen, especially the latter, I would like to reserve for later.

Many participated only reluctantly in the march into Austria in 1938. Only hotheads like Schobert and a brave man like *General* Weichs of Nuremberg were enthusiastic. Of course, they obeyed the command. That is very clear. Outwardly one never directly disobeys an order. That is not possible. They are ruled too well by conventions. One will never compromise oneself, one will never be rude. One will justify everything and everything was justified. And they were intoxicated themselves with that cheap and bloodless war, they were the big victors.

Nervous fits began during the Czech crisis. Mr. Beck gets his usual hysterics at the thought that we should go against the Czechs. Another, his deputy—the name I forgot at the moment— gets a memory disorder and crying fits. One played the role of the blessed Moltke the Second. Further, Mr. Beck—I can describe him here—is certainly a very intellectual man. I have in all the years disrespectfully called him the Moltke impersonator. Because he, pinching the lips razor-sharp, leaning slightly forward, in a distinguished, military way, attempted to bring out some words, phrases and witty bon mots, and there was never anything in the way of content. It was all meaningless. He should have become an actor. It would have been a wonderful performance.

The march into the Sudetenland succeeded. Again there was no need to fight, no need to go into action. Then came the spring of 1939 and then in 1939 the war finally came. The Polish campaign and the western campaign were lightning wars. Our fabulous *Luftwaffe*, established by *Feldmarschall*, later *Reichsmarschall* Hermann Göring, was effective, as were the revolutionary tactics of the armored troops, pushed through by the Führer despite great opposition.

And further: compared to the western armies we were a little less calcified. Compared to the west we were the more revolutionary. Our army was the more revolutionary. That's why we won, among many other reasons: the national socialist attitude of men, NCOs and many officers. That was probably the main reason.

Then in 1941 came the war against Russia. In these circles there was much hesitation. They said: "We don't need the war with Russia. Stalin would have never done anything to us." But merely the fact that *Herr* Stalin massed 20,000 tanks at the border speaks for itself. What we found at the border speaks for itself. I recently told someone: "You know, it is clear, you're absolutely right, that Stalin put his army together just to play a little war game, that's why he needed those 20,000 tanks and the huge air force."

Again and again we can say: what a stroke of luck! Even if we should not keep a square meter of Russia, as it looks today. But we'll get back many thousands of kilometers. No doubt about it. (*Applause*)

But even if we should not keep a square meter, this decision of the *Führer* in 1941was the salvation of Germany and Europe. (*Lively applause*)

In the beginning of the Russian campaign in 1941, the lightning victories took place thanks to the bold, revolutionary, Blitzkrieg strategy and tactics of the *Führer*, and the generals are duly enthusiastic. But already at that time, I was beginning to see some problems and errors which I have been trying to remedy, especially in the training of my officer corps. I am talking primarily of moral shortcomings of that once excellent officer corps.

I will randomly highlight a few examples for you which I experienced painfully for years as *Reichsführer-SS* and leader of the *Waffen-SS*. In 1939, for example, the Oxhöfter Kempe near Danzig was being stormed. The attacking battalion was part of the *SS-Heimwehr Danzig*. We had the misfortune that the regimental commander had been wounded, or had an accident the day before, and was therefore absent. From the famous Pomeranian *Landwehr* Division, which at that time had a very reactionary officer corps, they received Graf Rittenberg as a temporary battalion commander, and they stormed the Oxhöfter Kempe with him. And afterwards it was reported: The umpteenth Pomeranian *Landwehr* Division led by *Graf* Rittenberg has taken Oxhöfer Kempe. This was in the *Wehrmacht* communiqué.

I was in Zoppot and said: *Mein Führer*, that's not true at all, that was my battalion. And the *Führer* says to me: That was the battalion of *Graf* Rittenberg, what are you talking about? I said: *Mein Führer*, I can prove it; our dead are lying around there, it suffices to take a look. So they asked back (at the Wehrmacht): Yes, of course, they responded, it was a battalion of the SS, but on that day it was placed under the command of the Division, and the battalion is of course named after the commander – that was not necessary – and that's why it was called *Graf* Rittenberg's battalion.

I've seen this same phenomenon in hundreds of thousands of cases with—I cannot call it otherwise —Romanesque phraseology. We have got used to this phraseology which is not much different from the Italian. The same things we experienced already in the western campaign, but especially since 1941, for example, the double counting of prisoners. All these things, my dear party members, I have seen for myself. In the years 1941, 1942, 1943, I have been travelling a lot by car, saw the withdrawals from Kiev to Kharkov, and have seen all the mess. I watched that too during the advance. There was a knocked-out tank with the inscription: 111th Division. Then another division comes by and one crosses it out and writes: 78th Division. So it was already captured twice. Then comes the next, the 11th Division and the tank is counted three times. The soldiers had the nerve to lie and say: we destroyed or conquered this or that tank, while in and of itself it's the task of booty collection units with some brave fifty or sixty year old men to haul the tank away. We have deceived ourselves about our exploits in many cases. I will not diminish anything. There has been an untold number of real soldierly deeds and exploits. But we put up with too much in this army, and the army has developed a habit to "organize" those heroic deeds.

One could go on with this endlessly. This is indecency. And everything comes out of it. If people are indecent among themselves, they behave no better against others. For example, those regiments or battalions which were transferred from other divisions—I can sing a song about it—were sent to all the miserable tasks and the riskiest attacks, and used according to the principle: This battalion does not belong to our division, so we want to "use it up" first. Of course there were many exceptions! There was a number of decent battalion commanders. But in general no attention was paid to these things. And that was clever! They were allowed to take the worst attacks, they were sent into miserable situations, they were given less awards, and they were given, of course, no canteen articles. I sometimes got those battalions which were treated in this way transferred to me, when they only had one officer and ten men left. Then it was said: The *III. Battalion Regiment "Totenkopf"* transferred back to the *"Totenkopf"* or some other division. Once I received a company back where there was one NCO and one man left. I had given it away with 150 men, that is – not given, it was taken away from me. The day before there still were ten men and one NCO there. This one officer and ten men still had to go patrol all day, until there were just nine NCOs and one man left. Then came an order from the army staff that this company of the umpteenth division shall be sent back again.

Do not think that I have experienced this only once. That has been the thorns and ordeal of our brave SS men for many years. I am not complaining here. I am not used to complaining. I have only had the opportunity to get a deep insight into the characters of people and see those who are really decent, and who are not. Many treated our SS men decently, no matter whether it was fashionable or not. I have had a great opportunity to really get to know the characters well, especially at the time when it was unfashionable to have good relations with the SS or even with me, but where you could earn a little cross by treating us as badly as possible.

In the winter of 1941, began the first major crises in the staffs. It required the unprecedented energy of the *Führer* to bring the front to a halt. Everybody wanted to clear out, everyone wanted to—this word be cursed—resign, or in plain German—to run away. Winter clothing had been neglected completely. I must tell you an example of this. I knew that the Russian campaign would come. In February 1941, I visited party comrade Terboven in Norway and talked to him, and he was kind enough to show me around and organize everything and we flew together up to Kirkenes and Vardo and the Vadsoe. I wanted to get experience in winter war, in winter clothing and all the things you need for the winter. With this experience, both from the Finns and the Norwegians—rich experience—I came back and ordered that winter clothing be made for the then five or six SS divisions. *Obergruppenführer* Pohl and his men had to apply for the foreign currency to buy all these skins and furs. In May we still had none. In June we received them, and with an occasional inquiry from the generals, for what we needed the winter clothing, we received the classic answer: The German soldier does not need winter clothing, he does not freeze. In September–October, *Herr* Brauchitsch showed to the *Führer* ten or twelve men in fine winter clothing. They, however, existed only in the models, otherwise not. That's just a part of the hustle and bustle of this clique in these years. I always talk only of this clique but all that has rubbed off, of course, on the others who had been taught those bad habits. It's all part of the tone that a decent officer could allow himself. It was normal in those years that in the moments where the front was falling apart and there were gaps, the *Führer*, in his anxiety "where can I get one division, where can I get a regiment" very often got this answer from the Home Army or the commander-in-chief of the army: "We have no more regiments, we must fall back."

It militated against this that the front had been advanced so far towards Moscow that the enemy had much shorter lines of supply and sources of aid from the big city. Very soon after the offensive of October 3, it was realized that our forces were insufficient. The enemy also immediately launched his counterattack. The overextended, completely linear front with no depth found itself in a dangerous situation. The breakthroughs became a strategic threat to Army Group Center. Hitler's decision to hold was nevertheless in keeping with the restraints of the situation and was appropriate. But the all too strict application of this essentially correct decision in this predicament misled him to an inappropriate ban on all movements, even tactical ones, even when they were urgently necessary for the self-preservation of the troops. This resulted in unnecessary heavy losses and worsened the acute danger in which the overextended front and the exhausted and suffering troops found themselves. In fact, enemy breakthroughs forced some of those tactical withdrawals, which, if they had been carried out in time, would have improved the front, relieved pressure and caused much lighter casualties in men and materiel.[8]

Then, really through the entire year, the *Führer* kept asking me: "Do you have a police regiment, do you have anything at all?" I really had the ambition to never, or almost never, say no to the Führer. When I did say it, I really had nothing more. For these reasons I had to pull more and more police, which you, dear party comrades, as *Gauleiters* and Reich Governors, indeed felt, because you often had no police for the most urgent tasks. It was always a balance: Should I say "no" to the *Führer*, while I know exactly that he cannot get anything from the army, and should I allow that a disaster happens at the front, or I should take it on my hump and say: Yes, I still have a police regiment? Those regiments had an average age of thirty-nine or forty years. I gave away regiments with an average age of forty-six years to the front. In most cases I have been denied the armor-piercing weapons for them. It was terribly difficult for the *Führer* in all these years. It was hard to understand what was going on. You could feel it but you could not grasp it, and you could not prove it. But we in the SS knew, of course, exactly: This one is decent, that one not, he belongs to the clique, that one does not belong to it. We knew that when we came to an army corps. I was free to travel and have seen the whole German front from the Fischer Peninsula to Taganrog. I knew them all in the years 1941–42. I was in most army headquarters, knew them all, knew that here it was one way, here it was another. But in all cases I lacked proof. Something was clear: in the years 1941, 1942, and 1943, growing defeatism trickled from the staffs and down. But the front was in good shape. And when a brave front commander came to a headquarters, there appeared a chief of staff (do not take it amiss), in many cases a member of this Masonic "Schlieffen Association," which we did not dissolve in 1933–34, or one of those typical general staff-types, who with a worried face explained to this brave front-line soldier on the map, how hard it was, how perilous and tense the situation was. They have those beautiful expressions that are part of their vocabulary. It was explained that, naturally, due to tactical reasons we should take this line, the Gustav–Dora–X line, but unfortunately, of course, you can not talk about it, it's an order from headquarters—against all military rules we must not do it. But of course, we are soldiers and we obey. Sometimes I was about to explode out of rage when I looked at all this and could not comprehend it, could not grasp it. Once I caught such a pig. I could prove that the major had spoken in defeatist terms, in the crudest form. Of course, I fetched him and reported him to his service. He was then to be interrogated by an appropriate judge. But Mr. judge did not interrogate him to determine what happened, but said to the major: You should say: I did not say this-and-this in this company—you have to add to your statement the following: "The foreign newspapers say so"—then you can not be punished. The major took the advice, and naturally came out unpunished. I got a letter that the attitude of the major was proper, because he was an impeccable man, an impeccable officer. Now, most embarrassingly, the major and the judge sit together in one prison cell. *(Applause)*

Such things could always happen to us in those years if one called attention to such things. Then when I was free to reclaim and ask for the return of police regiments which I had sent with 2,000 men, but which now had 300 men, I could get the response: Of course if you want to take responsibility for the fact that the front collapses here, then of course, we will give it to you, but militarily it is irresponsible and the regiment must stay—even if it's only 300 men. In the end it was always so: I gave them something, and in the end I had to apologize even if I demanded the return of the rest of what I had given them.

It was so even in smallest details. The *Leibstandarte* was with Army Group South under Field Marshal Manstein, the Marshal Lewinski. His name is Lewinski, not Manstein. He is a born von Lewinski and has only later changed name to von Manstein. I say this, so here is clarity regarding him. With the *Herr* Marshal von Lewinski it was common when the *Leibstandarte* was used, that even our highly trained technical people were sent to battle, and not until the last battalion of these technical people had kicked the bucket before they were pulled out. This is the reason why we have those above average losses in the SS, and why so many SS commanders lie beneath the grass.

We never wanted to speak about it, even when it would have made sense in many cases. But when we saw that all was in vain, when we watched that some malevolent people had the intention to kill this uncomfortable troop off, and get it out of the way for possible future developments, then I must say, we were bitter when we saw this best blood flow.

In these staffs, for example, foreign press reports—especially the negative foreign press reports —were systematically copied and passed down, although it was forbidden. Foreign broadcasters were not only listened to, but listened to, written down and disseminated. Orders were very often transmitted with twenty-four hours' delay—all things we almost never learned about. They were sent in a meaningless form, although the transmitter of the command knew exactly that this was not was intended. But if you are a hair-splitter or word-splitter, of course, you can make any order into something else. It was sometimes impossible not to see these things. But try and prove that this order was deliberately sent twenty-four hours too late. You cannot prove it, because those involved will say: I have sent it to so-and-so many but there was line noise, sorry. Or: I tried to radio him, but his radio station was down.

Or: We wanted to radio him, but our radios were out of service. Or: I have sent over an officer with the Storch but he got lost, I'm sorry. When the division then goes west because both neighboring divisions had already cleared out and it pulled back too late, it is embarrassing. Then they say: I am terribly sorry, but such things happen in war. It is curious just where this happens.

But it happens and it is unbelievable.

In many cases the concept of duty in the staffs was disastrous.

I am speaking quite openly about the officer corps, which I am now responsible for raising and training. I tell them: For all of us, all the soldiers and officers, I can wish only one thing:

that no military historian ever publishes a book showing where the positions were in this campaign, with photographs of the Russian and German positions. If he publishes several volumes on the Don, Donets, Dniepr, Volkhov, or wherever we were, just with aerial photos, for one could easily say: those are the Russian positions. For they had many positions. The German positions are only few, a couple of rifle pits, because the gentlemen officers had to live in the village in a Russian house, with Russian women at the time, because they were not forward with their men, and, of course, if the officer is not forward, the men are not there either. They just dug a few pits, and after the Russian preparatory artillery fire, the men, the vehicles, the tanks were hit where they stood, or killed in the pits, and the Russian infantry went to the attack supported by tanks. If a man has no tank foxhole then, of course he gets overrun or flees even before they start the attack. In this way many front collapses begin. With great difficulty one could here and there iron out the break-in again. So it was still in the years 1941–42, sometimes in 1943, where the infantry still had some punch. But all this unnecessarily cost the men's lives. And afterwards they lay down again in new foxholes.

They would, of course, not treat the Russian population badly if they lived with them and amused themselves with them. When we said: Bring the Russian women forward so that they build positions, they said: We cannot treat women of another nation in this way. Once when I was in Mariupol I said: Why have you not built a road to Taganrog long ago? In this mess all vehicles break down! They responded: We have no workers. I say: But you have the whole city of Mariupol, take those people. Yes, but who will organize the food for the workers? I said: Do you think that the Russians organized catering for them? You should say: Starosta or Commissar of the city, be here at six o'clock in the morning with 10,000 women and men with spades, pickaxes and shovels and if not, you all go to Siberia, a camp at the Arctic Ocean or somewhere else. You just have to say to the women: here you dig a machine gun pit, there—this-or-that. They will do it better than any sapper officer. They can do it; they got a great education from the communists. Then an officer told me this in Mariupol: Yes, in fact you are right, the Russians have built a great tank ditch twenty kilometers away from here. They made the population of Mariupol dig it. They marched away at three in the morning, were on the spot at six or seven, and in the evening they marched back. They had to bring their own food. I said: Of course, the Russians can do it and we can't. Instead we let our vehicles break down, and then we have no tanks to put in the front line, and no supplies either. We build, as I said, no positions. At the beginning the break-ins (breaches, openings in the line) occurred, and had to be repaired with blood and blood again. Later, the break-ins were beyond repair. A regiment was rolled up, then a division, and then armies were rolled up, in no small part because the mood was carried down from the top, from these defeatists, these despondent people, so that the officers became neglectful. They were not arrested and no positions were built. Everybody had his eye on the rear: we're falling back again, withdraw again, and so on. Another thing was typical. Wherever things went well, then it was the *Herr* Commander of the umpteenth army, the *Herr* Commander of the Army Group so-and-so who has achieved the victory. Generous as the *Führer* was, he said: Oh, let it be, it's OK. If something went bad because a great command was performed miserably, or was carried out wrongly or disobediently, then they said: This is what the *Führer* ordered. They went so far that they—that was almost normal—in every tiny issue and decision and responsibility always said: We have to ask the *Führer*, he has to decide. They pushed on him all responsibility where it was natural that the officer, the one in command should do it himself. Conversely, they used to say maliciously: The *Führer* interferes in everything, in the command of each battalion, you cannot lead in this way; Mr. Beck and Mr. Höppner, those brilliant people would not do such a thing!—I believe that. Then came the fatal trend where they said: The war is unwinnable. They were fanatical, I might almost say, insane defeatists and pessimists because they fanatically spread this notion. This defeatist wave reached its apex in August 1943, when the Badoglio treachery took place in Italy and the Duce was arrested. Then it was said in these circles: Wonderful, fascism came to an end, terrific, they arrested the Duce, why not arrest the *Führer*, that would be nice if it happened here, why should it not happen here? The Duce was then liberated and when I became the minister of the interior, we took down a number of those people. And it immediately became quieter. The following took place at that time and it has never been spoken of before. I can openly tell you about it in this circle. In the security police we were on track of these reactionary conspiracies for a long time. The first stage in such things is that one feels: There is something rotten here. This is the first stage in anyone who later turns out to be swine. Heydrich, for example, was classic in these things. In our circles we called him jokingly our "creator of suspicions of murder." But he really had a nose. I imagine he is enjoying himself in his grave, as he now realized that all these pigs which we had recognized as pigs for years, decided to expose themselves and that there still is justice and that all of them come before the court. At that stage, we had the conviction that the reaction was going to do something. Here I must remind you of something which caused our party member Stürtz a lot of grief. Backe too had a lot of grief with it. Such a little thing will show you a lot, my dear comrades. Sometimes I suddenly demand something without justifying it. Even when I know that something causes problems and inconvenience, and I do it anyway, then there has to be a reason. But I often cannot tell about the reason. Recently I required a military training area near Berlin. On all sides it was said: Why? There are so many areas already here. You can borrow it from the army. I said: No, I cannot. I could also prove that all those military training areas were full to capacity in recent months. The units of SS were already training at the Army area near Neuhammer, and at another with 8,000 or 10,000 men. There was no room for more. I then said to myself that for this coming coup I need a military training area near Berlin where troops can wait, without attracting attention, where I am the master of the house, where no one can peep. For, better safe than sorry, and more is better; I did not want to be surprised. That was a good ground for the military training area, which I had acquired in Lausitz, among the, excuse me, the swine-people there. This was a very communist district at the time—it's there in the middle of a reactionary area—and in February 1943 they were already saying: But it's no use, the Russians are coming soon anyway. They told us this! There was another clue. A strange man, a minister Popitz, who tried for many months to get in touch with me. I had been told by a middle man that urgently wanted to speak with me. We let this middle man talk and he told us the following: It would be necessary to end the war now, we must come to an understanding with England and the condition would be that the *Führer* should retire to an honorary post of president. He said that his group was aware that they could not do it against the SS, so he hoped that I would be a sensible German, do it for Germany of course and not for selfish reasons, and that I would participate.

When I heard this for the first time, I immediately went to the *Führer* and said: I'll kill this fellow right away, it's outrageous of him to expect something like this from me. The *Führer* laughed and said: No, you will not kill him, but listen, let Popitz come see you, and let him say what he wants. That's interesting, and if he exposes himself at the first interview, then you can arrest him immediately. I said: I must have plein pouvoir (full powers) so that I can arrest him at once or later. There will of course be a terrible wave of complaints back and forth. There were some other gentlemen involved. One of them went now to the Catholic side and is sitting in Switzerland, and another, a high clergyman, we have already arrested. There was also a man from the Foreign Office involved here who is already sentenced to death, Envoy Kiep. He was also in this thing. We definitely had the right circle here.

Herr General Halder was there too. We had to use aliases for all these people. The whole problem went under the code name "Baroque" because it was so baroque. Mr. Halder went under the name "Reservist" because he kept himself in reserve to take over the German army. There were several candidates for this, you see. The first discussion with Mr. Popitz was very interesting. It was my first act as Minister of the Interior, how strange. We have recorded the conversation. He came and visited me at the Ministry of the Interior. But he dared not be quite as open as I would have liked. Soon he asked for another meeting. At that time it seemed to me too early to arrest him. I went to the *Führer*, explained the situation and said: it's too early, the case is too immature. If we take him out now, we will in the best case catch a couple of small fish together with him. Popitz is far from the center of this. He has a small part in this and the important figures are somewhere else. They are to be found in the circles around *Herr* Halder. At that time I at least brought in the middle man, however, and left Popitz to dangle under observation. He looked increasingly sick. Those who saw him said he was white as paper, a walking bad conscience. He kept calling me and asking about the middle man but I left him in uncertainty about my involvement in his arrest. I knew that he was too great a coward to escape and also to do anything. He was just too afraid. And he didn't.

Nor did we arrest *Herr* Halder. We just watched him. He was close by, in Aschau, and drove around bravely in a car that he had, with an honor guard of NCOs.

One, who without a doubt was dangerous, was the degraded *General* Höppner. I then encountered the whole "Baroque" complex, which included the old Excellency Solf, the widow of ambassador Solf, and a von Zarden family, a really reactionary bunch. Many of them have already been sentenced. All of them have been arrested. Unfortunately, we did not have enough proof to implicate the Army in this. You can imagine how impatient we were, but we just did not have enough material.

Then came the collapse of Army Group Center. In this connection you have to understand that something incredible happened here. You cannot explain this in a logical way that an army group of twenty-eight divisions disintegrates just like that. The units were unsettled internally, on the one hand by the non-existent or defeatist hand of the senior leadership, the corps and army commanders, and on the other by the habit, or bad habit, of surrendering and playing with *Herr* Seydlitz and the Russian generals. The soldiers were in fine shape. If challenged by a frontline officer and told: My dear fellows, turn around and come with us,—then that was absolutely possible, then he did it.

The officer corps, however, sometimes presented an awful picture. It is a tragedy when one considers the following fact. Three of my units got out of the collapse at Minsk. One was a Russian unit, the Kaminski Brigade, with 6,000 or 7,000 men, led by a Russian. I had to listen as the German command staff told me how many cigar boxes filled with Iron Crosses First and Second Class they had picked up as souvenirs after finding them lying at the roadside, thrown away.[9] All my units came back well-outfitted when there was a collapse. I once told the *Führer*: it is terrible, but our SS divisions and my units do best when there is a collapse somewhere, as we pick up clothing and canteen wares, everything they could dream of. We always return with more tanks than we left with. We just have to gather what others had thrown away or left behind. We always return with more guns, more weapons than we had had at the outset. We only have to pick them up.[10] A second unit was under a young *Obersturmbannführer* and *Oberstleutnant der Schutzpolizei* Siegling. The man had had 2,000 or 3,000 Russians in his unit. During the retreat he picked up 9,000 or 10,000 men, all excellently clothed. I asked: where from? He said: the clothing depots were all at the front. We just had to walk or drive there. The Russians had not arrived yet and the Germans were also gone. The administrators were still there, and for a couple of bottles of spirits we managed to change uniforms and take all the new weapons and ammo we could bear before they put everything on fire.

The third unit we brought back was the Dirlewanger unit. In 1941, I'd set up the Dirlewanger Poachers Regiment. Dirlewanger is a good Swabian, wounded ten times, an original. I had asked the *Führer*'s permission to recruit from Germany's prisons all poachers who had hunted with shotguns. I got around 2,000 of them. Out of these good people[11] only 400 are still alive. I have then been replenishing this regiment with SS men on probation. You see, we have in the SS a very tough jurisdiction. Our people get years of prison for a couple of days' AWOL. In this way the troop remains sound. The battalion that parachuted on Tito's headquarters consisted exclusively of people on probation, excluding the officers, naturally. All those 800 soldiers were restoring their reputation in this way. They jumped into Tito's headquarters. I released several hundred of these. When that was not enough, I told Dirlewanger: Pay attention, I want you to choose suitable career criminals from the thugs in our concentration camps. The tone in this regiment is often, as you can imagine, pretty rough, pretty mediaeval. We use whipping for punishment. Or if someone begins to doubt whether we can win this war, he can pretty soon fall dead under the table with a round in his head. This is the only way to handle such types. These guys, many of whom had been sitting in concentration camps a mere six weeks before, came back from this famous collapse, marching in good order, with brand new uniforms and weapons, as well as 1,000 Asiatic Soviet prisoners, after having broken through the Soviet front. I am describing for you these three examples just to show you what a profound collapse, what a terrible internal breakdown has happened in the Army. On the one hand it happened because the staffs were increasingly defeatist and failed, on the other, because the Soviets have been sending agents from the Seydlitz–Committee to our side. Those people infiltrated our units and, in best Jewish style, called on soldiers to shoot their officers, or transmitted conflicting orders. It led to soldiers demanding paybooks from each other all the time. This was a total breakdown with a great loss of weapons and withdrawal of tanks. Those who were at the eastern border, *Gauleiter* Koch and the other eastern *Gauleiter*, can confirm what a calamity this was. A kind of interaction developed: From the staffs the defeatism permeated down to the front. And when the front began to crumble, this in itself increased the defeatism in the staffs, and they said: See, the Eastern Front is collapsing! We have to have a ceasefire or peace or something else.

And now we come to the Beck Committee. He was to become governor general of the German Reich. An interesting detail about *Herr* Beck. We know this because we interrogated his maid. She, a brave girl, said that she had wondered why the bedclothes of *Herr* Beck were soaking wet the five nights prior to the July 20. The revolutionary was sweating from anxiety. And then—and this detail is also interesting—he went to the Bendlerstrasse, the central command, and later shot himself. I shall return to this later. I'll tell you later how this happened. All this sounds like a cheap criminal novel, quite miserable.

Another one was *Herr* Höppner. In my eyes—I had never met him before—a disgusting, indecent man, who had been expelled by the Army itself; he'd been degraded from the rank of general. Unfortunately, I was unable to arrest him because we had to respect the psyche and psychology of the army.

And there was also a man like *Herr General* Olbricht, who had a key position in Army's Main Office. When one tries to reconstruct the whole organization, the whole mechanism, one can only come to the following conclusion: This was a typical mechanism of civil war. A secretive, complicated structure where most members didn't even know what its purpose was, and which was meant to have a key place in the State, just like in the times of the 100,000-man army when they were practically the only real executive force in the State.

Then there was quartermaster general Wagner. From the very beginning I disliked that eastern lumphead. Always false and unable to ever keep a promise. His role was difficult to assess. He fell victim of the recent epidemic of suicides. He shot himself as well.

Another one was the bow-legged intelligence general Fellgiebel, about whom I made two separate reports in 1942 and 1943. Already in 1942, he spoke very defeatist in Vinnitsa, and it repeated itself three or six months later at a hotel in Berlin. He spoke of these things to complete strangers, one of whom was quite accidentally an *SS-Oberscharführer* in civilian clothes. "This war cannot be won, this is ridiculous" etc. It turned out that *General* Fellgiebel belonged to a quite large circle of gentlemen who believed that the *Führer* should be violently murdered. I believe that this circle comprised several dozen people.

Another one was a small poisonous dwarf, a man whom I would have been ashamed to have as an aide. It's the *Herr General* Stieff. He always appeared to me to be a debased version of the Italian king: high heels and high cap, so that people could notice him at all, dark skin, a really fine figure. This man had known for at least a year that an attempt was being prepared. Within this circle he was considered very wise and cunning. He wanted to show the *Führer* a new model of uniform and a new rucksack. He had this incredibly cunning plan to put explosives into the rucksack on the back of some poor soldier and detonate it during the show for the *Führer*. *Herr* Stieff waited with the undertaking for at least nine months, as far as I understood, only because he wanted to be present at the explosion, because he might be killed as well. As far as I can see, this was the only reason. (…) *Herr* Stieff was asked if he was prepared to do this. He declined indignantly, as he said. But then he told others about *Herr* Staufenberg's question. It must be said that of the others, none took the opportunity to put on his helmet, strap on his belt and report to his supreme warlord or report the affair to some superior. *Herr* Gördeler, from Mutschmann's district, was chosen to become Reich Chancellor.

We are looking for him, with a price of 1 million Marks on his head. *Herr* von Witzleben was supposed to become the commander in chief of the *Wehrmacht*. A morphine addict who was already a sick man in 1938–39, so much so that during an inspection of the West Wall with the Führer he was unable to crawl out from a bunker. The *Führer*, in his generosity, made him a marshal after the campaign in the West. This man, this mummy, this spiritual and mental corpse, was elected to play the role of the commander in chief. When we came to arrest him on the second day, I saw him in the car: he was crying in the car. Among many, many others there was one *Generalmajor* von Treskow, chief of staff of one of the most important armies in Army Group Center. He'd been in the conspiracy for 1½ years. Supposedly—and I repeat this with all caution—he was killed or killed himself on the July 21.

One *Graf* Lehndorf from Steinort, East Prussia was his contact. He was in a horse depot near Bialystok, where the brother of *General* Fellgiebel was in command, or who always drove there and went on to see *Herr* Treskow in army headquarters. He was certainly noteworthy: the personal details of the general staff rest in the general staff itself, it has no chief of personnel. It is also remarkable how cleverly all the posts in the general staff were filled. The clique had their men in all important positions.

Several figures from the civilian side also took part. President of the Reich *Graf* Schulenburg, the son of our old, decent general and *SS-Obergruppenführer*, the man who was the only one to keep his oath to the commander in chief in the Great War. The son desecrates the memory of his father. For many months, *Graf* Schulenburg tried to get a job at my Ministry. I had an aversion against him and said No, I don't want him here. He was trying his best. He was to become a state secretary or Minister of the Interior. Now I understand why he wanted to get in here so much.

Now to something really sad. In this company there was a Party member, *Graf* Helldorf. He was in this treasonous conspiracy for 6 months to a year. He, of all the people! This is most paradoxical. He complained that the Party had become a party of fat cats. His interrogator—this was *Gruppenführer* Müller—replied to him that he himself was one of the fattest cats. Dr. Goebbels and I had to pay his debts two or three times. (Dr. Goebbels: "80,000 marks, and he now owns four apartments in bombed out Berlin!")

District President *Graf* Bismarck—he was more or less a not so important participant—in Potsdam also played a role. A major role in the Popitz–Kiep–"Baroque" complex was played by our old friend *Herr* Werner von Alvensleben who—I can promise you this—is now going to break his neck. Our old friend Alvensleben. (Dr. Goebbels: "The former liaison to Schleicher?")

Yes! Now he is breaking his neck. What I am telling you here can only be a short overview, gentlemen. You can be sure that there is much more in other branches. Another player was

General Stülpnagel in Paris, and with him an *Oberstleutnant* von Hofacker, the fanatical defeatist and pessimist, whom I met before. I honestly believe that he is a pessimist out of religious conviction. Sadly, he is so fanatical he really understands how to attract others with his pessimism. We should understand the simple fact that many of those who took part in this were initially pulled into it without any ill will. As apolitical officers they simply didn't understand it. They were presented with clever, supposedly wise, logical arguments and they were unable to escape the conclusions. Until they lost their reputation, broke their oath and now are going to be shot. The city commandant of Berlin absolutely played a role in it too. It does not follow that if his name is *Haase* (rabbit), than he knew nothing. He definitely knew something.

The role of *Generaloberst* Fromm is interesting. I can describe him as follows: he is so smart and cunning that we cannot prove that he took part in this stupid revolution. However, we can easily prove that he has not believed in victory, that he was neglectful in the discharge of his duties and lazy. Thousands of people can confirm it. The first impression I and Dr. Goebbels got of the man was strange. I have to mention here that at 2330, young officers were arresting their generals outside of the Bendlerstrasse complex. Their attitude, as well as the attitude of the guard battalion, which Dr. Goebbels contacted, were gratifying. But the moment *Herr* Fromm, who had been arrested by Olbricht and other officers, was released, a strange, kitschy movie-like scene played itself out. It looked like a bad movie. Nobody would believe that something like this can happen in reality. And therefore it is very interesting: *Herr* Beck is sitting there. Commanders of military districts call and want to talk to Fromm. But the great revolutionary *Herr* Höppner is sitting where Fromm usually is. Then this or that military district commander says, no I won't do it. Whereupon the revolutionary Höppner responds: Well then leave it, it makes no difference anyway. The one who was really fanatical, who wanted to see it through doggedly and obstinately and who was the driving force, was Stauffenberg.

Then Fromm enters the room where the future German government was sitting. Then *Herr* Beck, who was sitting there in civilian clothes, stands up and says: Excuse me. He has a gun in his hand and he shoots himself. First shot in the eye. The second shot also unsuccessful. Upon which *Herr* Fromm administers the coup de grace with his own gun. Excuse me!

Then Herr Fromm did something strange. At 2330, when everything was clear, he organized a drumhead court-martial in Berlin and condemned *Herr* Olbricht, *Herr* Stauffenberg, Mertz von Quirnheim and *Oberleutnant* von Haeften, Stauffenberg's adjutant, to death on the charge of high treason and breach of oath, AND on the suspicion of the participation in the assassination attempt on the *Führer*. As is well known, nobody can be condemned to death on a suspicion. There was, above all, no need to shoot them at 2330. It was enough to just arrest them. I must say that I cannot avoid the impression that what went on here was a liquidation of, if not witnesses, so at least unpleasant conversation partners. They were buried so quickly that *Herr* Olbricht and the other gentlemen were interred with Knight's Crosses on their breasts. The next day they were dug up again and their identity was once again established. I then gave the order that their bodies be cremated, and the ashes strewn in the fields. We do not wish to make for these people any kind of graves or monuments. The *Reichsmarschall* put it right: it is too decent to scatter it over the fields. Strew it into a sewage plant.

As a small side effect, I was alerted by *Gauleiter* Bürckel to the person of *General* Graf Sponeck. He sat in the fortress in Germersheim and enjoyed himself. This is a general who in the Crimea in 1942, shamefully ran from his own division, and only later pulled the division back. At that time, the *Reichsmarschall* put the greatest effort in organizing a court martial and only with extreme difficulty he succeeded in bringing the associate judges—generals—to condemn the coward to death. The *Führer*, in his goodness, commuted the sentence. I said to some officers of the army: You know, I'll tell you something, if a big or even smaller man in the SS would do something like that, you can be sure that his comrades within the first twenty-four hours would bring the gun and say: Now it is time that you disappear, deliver us from your presence. Or they would send him a gun, and he'd have an hour or two, and then he'd disappear.

We learned this in the old German army as decent German soldiers.

I kept it in the SS, and we want to introduce it in the army. You can be sure I will bring back all the good old customs. But no one came to *Herr* Sponeck. On the contrary, he is a devoted Catholic. They would write letters to him: "We suffer with you, you endure for us, we wish and congratulate you for having had the courage to take a stand," which is to say to disobey orders again, etc. *Herr* Sponeck was cared for in Germersheim with particular love. On the night of the twenty-first I asked the *Führer*: Can't I have him shot right away? The first thing I did early the next morning, at seven armament on the twenty-first, was issue the order during a telephone conversation: Shoot him and call me back when it's done. Then he was dead.[12]

Of course this had a very cautionary effect in all these circles. Because what I do, this is not petty revenge. The time is too serious and I have no taste for that. I know you believe me. But we need to educate the army in the toughest and kindest form again to what it once was, especially the officer corps. We must bring in this concept of unconditional loyalty again, a loyalty that keeps the oath, just as it was in the time of Friedrick the Great, so that a man, even if he is degraded, standing on the sand pile (before execution) would shout: Long live the *Führer*! *Heil Hitler*! We must bring such loyalty and such obedience in again. Because that has made us great. We must also bring in truthfulness, a sense of honor, hardness against oneself. All these things we have to bring in by all means necessary, and all means of education will be used.[13]

I would now like to summarize what has happened so far. What will the punishment be, and how shall we carry on?

First. Next week the first major trial before the People's Court will begin. I went ahead and asked the *Führer* about making the trial go ahead before the People's Court, because some of the perpetrators are members of the Army. Only a few, one or two are members of the Air Force, there is a couple from the Navy, as well as a few from the police, Helldorf among them, unfortunately. For Helldorf and maybe one more person one would have to have a trial before the Supreme SS and Police Court. And all the civilians, Schulenburg, Gördeler, Bismarck etc. will have a trial before the People's Court. You cannot hold several trials and fragment the whole thing. The German People have the People's Court and it was my request that all the trials take place before it, and it was approved.

Secondly, and I think this is very important. We need to understand that even though we are unhappy about many things in the Army, it is still a German People's Army and we need it, with these seven million that are in it today, to win the war. We will later transform it and develop something new, about which I can tell you later. But is a prerequisite for the transformation that the army eliminates these people, the traitors, by itself. Thank God, they took this opportunity, or Fortune has so ordained, that they took care of things in their own ranks, and we on our part—Dr. Goebbels and I—saw to it that no one from the Air Force or the Navy, no one from the SS and police, intervened. The Army had to do it itself. And it is important that it continues in this way. It was always my intention and plan that the Army takes this as an opportunity to cleanse itself. I suggested creation of a court of honor of a few field marshals and generals, which would ask the *Führer* to degrade *Feldmarschall* Witzleben and transfer him, and some other generals etc., to the People's Court. Some other officers, where the case is not so clear, would be dismissed from the army and transferred to the People's Court too, and only if they are acquitted, would they be readmitted to the Army.

We must follow the great historical example of another army which was totally compromised by treason and corruption. This was the Prussian army in the years 1797 to 1806, from the cannonade of Valmy till the capitulation of the fortresses. This army could be resurrected only due to the fact that the *Immediatkommission* was created, and that there were people at that time who had the strength of soul to do so. These were young people, Gneisenau, Scharnhorst, Clausewitz, and a few outsiders, thrice cursed and insulted outsiders, who were able to assert themselves. And the army had to disband approximately two-thirds if not three-quarters of the old regiments of Frederick the Great, and to degrade the generals who were guilty, and thus have the army cleaned up.

The big trial will most certainly be followed by a number of smaller trials, because I am determined to take care of every smallest root in the ministries and offices. There will be some interesting dismissals followed by new ramifications. I am convinced that we will find branches in business and in the Foreign Office, in the various ministries. We will probably find them everywhere, and with diligence and hard work we will take care of everything. It was because of this that the revival of the army took place, because of this that a really improvised and poorly-armed army achieved the victories of 1813, 1814, and 1815.

As a German people we want to keep the German army, which is precious to us. For how many battles has it fought, and how much glory has it tacked to its banners, whether they were Prussian, Austrian or Bavarian. It has a glorious tradition. We who always have an army, who will always want to have and must have an army, are interested in creating the necessary conditions for it. This condition can only exist if we carry out part of the process in the political-propaganda form, which makes things clear to the people and to the world: we have struggled with blood poisoning, and now we are in great shape because we have given the army the opportunity to clean itself and not be cleaned or have to be cleaned from the outside.

The big trial will undoubtedly be followed by a number of smaller trials. For I am absolutely determined to go after every tiny root that leads into this or that ministry or only that branch. There will be interesting small or larger roundups, with which we then dig up these bifurcations. I am convinced that we will find these bifurcations in industry, in the Foreign Office, in the various ministries. We find them everywhere, and with industry and hard work we will get them all out. There will be a number of smaller trials, each a difficult one, and based on its quality each ministry can get its little extra.

Second. We will introduce absolute clan liability. We have pursued this before and acted according to it. I have a following view. When a man distinguishes himself, no matter, a small soldier or a statesman, the state will reward him, as they have been rewarded by the old German or Austrian states. They were often rewarded with a piece of land. We are planning to reward our front-line soldier generously. He will get a farm of seventy-five acres, no luxuries but pretty decent, and almost debt free. Some great general or a great soldier will receive a sum of money or a respectable estate. When a soldier or a general is rewarded with a farm or an estate, not only he receives it but it becomes the family estate. If the family lives, it still has it four or five generations later. So, in reality, it is awarded to the whole clan, and the whole clan gets strengthened in their prosperity and their property. When a bearer of the Knight's Cross falls, then, apart form the normal, generous assistance, the family receives particular help from the Office of the *Führer*, financial and otherwise. When we are doing it on the positive side, we should, I think, absolutely do it on the negative side too. No one will come to us and say, that's Bolshevik what you're doing. No, do not take it amiss, that's not Bolshevik, but a very old tradition of our ancestors. You need only read the Germanic sagas. If a family was banished or declared outlawed, or when there was a blood feud in the family, they were extremely consequential. If a man has committed treason, his blood is evil because there is treason in it, it had to be cut off. And in a blood feud an entire clan was exterminated to the last member. The family of *Graf* Stauffenberg will be wiped out to the last member. *(Applause)*

For it must become a unique cautionary example. Furthermore, all in Germany who are so unlucky as to bear the name of this traitor and scoundrel Stauffenberg, will be able to request a name change. We will confiscate the estates of all the families, whose member has been involved in this treason. But it must happen in an—I will here use a good Austrian expression—optically flawless fashion. It must not be said: "What a great Hitler Youth hostel or a fine Party school." No, everything has to go to the Reich Commissioner for settlement and be reserved for soldiers of this war. In this connection I have a plea to the Reich Minister of Agriculture to do it flawlessly. Nobody should be able to say: "Aha, the Party or some Party member benefits from the whole thing, of course, this is revenge." No, we are doing this for our front-line soldiers. If we now confiscate some thirty or forty such estates, then we will see some more fidelity and loyalty! What some other people are now showing in the way of faithfulness and loyalty is incredible! It is my firm conviction that we will have conditions just like the Prussian kings. For, the Prussian kings did not treat their nobility with silk gloves. Once in a while a noble was losing his head. Once in a while an estate was confiscated, which was a great way to boost loyalty and obedience to the warlord, so it was a pure joy to see. He could then drill them and they had great accomplishments. We don't want to be unfair. Our nobility has contributed in this war too. You can now be sure the last Aunt Frieda will say to her nephew, or her son: You keep your oath, son, otherwise you'll place the whole family in danger. In this way we will do well.

Thirdly, I will do the following. Fortress Germersheim is now under my orders. This is now my recovery home for certain people. People on whom we do not have direct incriminating evidence, but of whom we know that not everything was all right. Those whom we will now retire. Because in this final year of the war I do not want to have a bunch of discontented nobles running around. They are going to keep each other company at dinner parties. I even have a candidate for the table elder on my mind. They will have all the time in the world to discuss things, and some will be lucky to have such an illustrious company. Many more will have to retire. And I want to tell you here that the Office of Personnel under the seriously injured Schmundt and his deputy Burgdorf are doing a great job. They coined a fine slogan: An officer of whom we have to think, what to do with him, should retire. And I want to tell you something: The strength of the former army was in that one never knew if one would get promoted to captain, to major or to colonel. One never knew if one was not going to get thrown out. This was a well considered means of selection. It was not always handled quite fair, but it was a balanced means of selection and of obedience, of absolute discipline and allegiance. It is also a very honorable thing to become a major. I remember from my days as a young boy, when someone was a retired major or captain. For us he was a respectable person.

Not every captain must necessarily become a colonel. They will make an extra effort when they know that not everyone is going to make it.

In order to be sure that those retired are going to be useful to society, I made sure that the Office of Personnel will inform their district employment offices and their respective *Gauleiters* of their retirement. And I'd like to ask you to be prudent and wise in these cases. I do not want somebody to say that we are taking petty revenge at the employment offices. Do not say to them: You were colonel, now we have to teach you a lesson, but: We need you. We do not have a director job for you, but now in the war, while this holy people's war is aflame, everyone must join in, please come to the factory, you can take over the supervision of twenty Russians and twenty other foreigners. You will fit in, you can do it. I believe that a positive word will in many cases influence people who otherwise have a negative attitude. Such people can have a decent fellow in them and can still do something useful. After some time, he will get to know the German worker for the first time, he will see his faith and decency, and it may even happen that some of those families will change their attitude. I would like to ask you, in those cases where the man is neither good nor evil, that no petty revenge takes place. Do not, for example, say to them: You want to work in this factory? No, you are going to that one, three hours away, you can walk. You should say instead: Naturally, you can start here tomorrow. You should not say: This is the dirtiest job, you go there. I request that you treat these people reasonably. Generally, I am asking you to help me with this job which the *Führer* has given me. I am asking you for help, my old Party comrades. We need to be aware of another thing, and it is the impression shared by many decent officers. As one general told me: This army and this officer corps are not going to recover after the blow of the July 20. I said: What are you talking about? He said: I am convinced that the German People will find something new, and something new will be born. This Army, built on the foundation of that 100,000-man *Reichswehr* is destined to go to its grave. He is probably right and he said it well.

Another characteristic example. The Army has a small volunteer contingent. I think 36% of the volunteers are assigned to the Army. But they do not get even this number. It was very interesting yesterday when I heard that only 10% of cadets from officer schools reported for active service as an officer in the Army, while 90% have not reported and are reserve officers. In the *Waffen-SS* I probably have three times as many. Of course there must be recruitment. One has to tell them: Come to us. The very fact that a huge army of seven million does not get the 70,000 volunteers which it needs, that it no longer gets the candidates for the active officer career path, is an obvious sign that this institution has no inner attractive power, no inner life anymore. On the other side, we are going through the greatest crisis of this war. And there are no pauses. We can not afford to be radical or rough, to hit them really hard. Because we have to win this war with this Army, good or bad. It would be much easier in peacetime when there's an army of one million people. Today the army is a body of seven million people, over-bred, bloated and watered down.

Now we are slowly recuperating after the collapse of Army Group Center. The *Führer* has ordered the formation of fifteen new divisions which will be under my command. That was actually the first step which was taken even before July 20. He gave me all the rights that the commander in chief of the army has with the exception of tactical and strategic leadership at the front. I now travel from division to division, from one officer corps to another, let me introduce each officer, and speak to them for 1½–2 hours. Sometimes I feel like in the years 1933–34, when I talked to every *SS-Standarte* just before the Röhm crisis, and spoke to them about the basic concepts of loyalty, obedience and comradeship. I must now, ten years later, deal with these same basic concepts. I do not need to tell you that this is very troublesome, beside all my other duties. I do not need to explain to you how much energy this requires. Because these divisions must succeed, and I must succeed in awakening in their officer corps the old concepts of honor, obedience, steadfastness and faithfulness, and in lighting in their hearts the fire of the holy People's war. And here, dear Party comrades, I'd like to ask you, wherever you can, speak to these soldiers, above all to the officers, try to influence them, so that they do not run away, do not resign, so that they again have that holy fire and the code of honor in their hearts, never throw the weapons, so that the officer never lets his men down, etc.

This is, of course, difficult. You can imagine what a fury I sometimes have in my heart when I see all the mess which they have left behind, which now has to be made up with hard work. It is hard but we must not show these things on the outside. We are doing this for Germany, and above all for the man whom we all love, who has the hardest task on Earth, for our *Führer*.

We need to be clear, that one-third or one-fourth of the officer corps is very good. They are totally determined, they are heartbroken over this. Then, there are those 50–60% in the middle, as it always is in life, neither evil nor particularly active. When properly approached and educated, they willingly participate and do a decent job. They were not actively resisting the rot. But in a decent corps they will function well. When the corps is honorable again, they feel three times better than before. The issue is: when. They have to be encouraged, so that they can say: Great, finally things are ok. The large center must be shaken up, and we must explain things to them, but we must not hurt or offend them. Because the company commanders and battalion commanders are the most important; this is the great mass.

Then there are the 5–15% who are real swine, those who belong to the clique. We want them out, and, if hostile, we will judge and convict them. I am now the highest authority for those units and they are going to feel it. They all know it. I am getting on my table every sentence and I won't tolerate those typical officer verdicts where one colleague covers for the other. And I am not talking just about judges. The judges are in many cases the toughest, tougher than the associate judges who will never seriously punish a colleague from another branch, those who typically will convict to three months fortress or six weeks house arrest. You have to really punish. I said: When a soldier does something, he will be punished; if an officer does something, he will be punished twice or three times as hard.

When Brauchitsch or Fritsch were commander-in-chief, the entire officer corps was never really addressed by their former superiors—the commanders of the armies and army-groups. It is my goal that they clean their own house. The *Führer* took command years ago. However, what he lacked was the loyal and capable people who can say to their officer: You have acted indecently, you have to go. Or: I forbid you to speak about the commander-in-chief in these terms; how dare you! Führer can not do anything about things like that, can not see such things from where he is.

I'd like to ask you to understand that, when I'm at the training grounds, I never invite the *Gauleiter*, or the Higher SS and Police Leader to these speeches; these things have to be spoken of without outside observers. For I am now the commander-in-chief of this army,[14] and I want to speak to them of those unpleasant things—and there are plenty—and I can't reprimand them while the highest dignitaries of the state are present. The situation is very serious, and each of these divisions has to go now and close the gap in the East, and stand on its own.

The second responsibility given me by the *Führer* on July 20, was the Home Army, the Replacement Army, and the responsibility of the chief of armaments of the Army. We have immediately delivered the forty trained replacement battalions which the chief-of-general staff needed; more than that – we put in the field another six new brigades. It was an improved performance of Valkyrie; because everything ran under the name of Valkyrie. They kept all these troops at home in order to have a civil war army. The first, unsuccessful Valkyrie performance was on July 20, and I have now made an improved one, namely I have formed the six "Valkyrie brigades" and immediately sent them to battle.

You can be sure about one thing: I will never need an order from the *Führer* to form new divisions. I will constantly form them, and when they have got their weapons, I will go to the *Führer* and ask: Where do you need a division? That's the way I see the duty of the commander of Replacement Army. (*Applause*)

Here I must ask for another thing. The production of weapons is more important than ever before. There is a false impression that we had many weapons in stock. At least until now, I have unfortunately not discovered anything in armories, etc., with which I could arm new divisions. During this combing through of warehouses we are finding a great deal individual things and pieces of equipment. Unfortunately, I have discovered very few weapons, and it is difficult to arm new divisions today. Therefore it is extremely important that the production continues at the highest gear. I need your help in this process.

I now have a third mission, which I'll probably get transferred tomorrow through *Führer*'s signature: the reorganization of the whole quartermaster office and administration of the Army and simplification of all its institutions. I think I will be able, firstly, to retrieve many people for the front, and, secondly, to send the older ones, who are unable to bear weapons, to the armaments industry, and in the way of exchange, to get the younger men, the cohort of 1918 and younger, from the factories to the front. Those guys, who are unable to do anything when we remove them from the staffs, will at least stop bothering others with their unnecessary writings.

You have read my order of the day. I have written in it everything I considered necessary, and informed my warriors of everything I want done. But I am asking you—I must say it again and again —not to expect miracles or magic from me. You will certainly—and for that I am grateful—give me a wealth of tips, about what is rotten in the country. I am sometimes unable to react immediately, because, as I said, the machine of the State must run constantly for the front. But I will roam constantly and through the work for the front, automatically be everywhere, cut, move, dissolve staffs, and even though I can't be everywhere at the same time, I will tackle one problem after another. I have hired *Obergruppenführer* Jüttner as my chief of staff who is in charge of my main office in Berlin.

I am so grateful to you when you inform me of particularly poor and miserable people, just as I am grateful when you inform me of good people. But I prefer above all when you tell me: He is an old, brave Nazi but unsuitable for leadership positions. We cannot afford to place all the old Nazis in places where they are going to fail professionally. It would be a mistake. But when I know that this or that captain is a great guy and a good adjutant at the military district command, I will take him to me, also as an adjutant, and I will thus have two more loyal eyes. I must not make the mistake in taking him to a battalion commander office, or at a higher position in a staff, where he fails; I am asking you to take this into account.

The next important thing which I will suggest to the *Führer* is to place under my command the supervision of prisoners of war. Please do not think I want to rob you. I have enough to do as it is.

The mission, which the *Führer* gave me, to rebuild and reorganize the Army, requires that I have power over many areas. The next thing I will look into is the prisoners of war, with the exception of the English and Americans. Now, perhaps including the English and Americans, because I can now do it as commander-in-chief of the army and commander of the Replacement Army.

I am firmly convinced that during our combing of the "indispensable" positions we will make many interesting discoveries. If think that we are going to discover here some 150,000–200,000 men —the most skilled shirkers on Earth. You know how it is: The son of *Herr* so-and-so, who had invited the district commander for hunting and supplied him with meat and liquor, becomes suddenly an experienced metal worker without ever having had a file in his hand, and thus becomes indispensable for the war effort. I firmly believe that we will find the most tenacious shirkers who managed to escape our attention for the last four or five years. We are not going to put them all in one division. We will distribute them in existing divisions and march battalions. Others will go to new divisions.

One thing you can take for granted from me. My command will be clear and rigorous. I have written about my wishes and instructions in the order of the day. (…) I am unfortunately unable to be everywhere and see everything, I do not have enough time for this, but I pay sudden visits in garrisons. The other day a commander of a battalion came to me and said: I cannot get rid of my recruits. For three months I have been offering 400 well trained soldiers, but nobody wants them. I am sure that such things happen quite often. (…)

Again, please, do not expect any magic from me. I need months to change things. To complete the reconstruction will require years. Gradually, we will grow a new Army. In my order of the day I mentioned how I imagine this Army's name could be: National–Socialist People's Army. I asked the *Führer*—and the *Führer* agreed—that the new divisions which are being formed, be called *Volksgrenadier* divisions. We are moving away from the concept of *Reichswehr* and everything connected with it. We have to find a name which will express the National–Socialist character of this holy war which this army must win.

Concluding, I would like to tell you that we had hardly ever been happier than on the evening of the July 20. Because the consequences, had the attempt been successful, would have been horrible, had God not helped us on that day. It would have been the end of our Greater

German Reich and of our German Nation. The danger was great. When we now read the orders of the conspirators, we are wondering over the extent of their idiocy. I will give you a couple examples: overtaking of concentration camps, disarmament of guards and promise of the release of the inmates. We have now 550,000 inmates, of whom 450,000 are foreigners. That would mean to have a half million of worst bitter political and criminal enemies, political enemies of the Reich and criminal enemies of any social order, spilled over the whole land. That would have meant that within the next two or three weeks we would have had chaos in the streets. What they prepared for us is clear from their plans: arrest of district governors, *Gauleiters*, liquidation of every Party office, in Berlin—overtaking of the High Command of the SS, of the Main Office of Security, arrest of Dr. Goebbels, etc., etc. They went after the whole Party, the whole movement. After the death of the *Führer*, the whole Party was to be liquidated. This was the plan and purpose of these people who said they did it for Germany, but who, on the one side were criminally stupid, on the other side—I am convinced, were in the service of the enemies of Germany, secret agents of the Jesuits and Freemasons. As always with secret agents, they have been activated precisely when the war entered the decisive phase, in order to tip the balance.

For us there is one lesson from this experience: we have to stand together, more than ever before. When we now think of all our problems and someone sees some ridiculous differences of opinion, some conflict of competences etc., it is all unimportant, we have to bury it, it doesn't matter. Everything depends on our unity in the final stage of this struggle. Because this is a final stage. Sooner or later, when the final round is over, the coalition will disintegrate, it can not hold. And the moment the coalition is broken, we have won this war. When it becomes clear that nobody in this coalition, or the coalition as a whole, is able to conquer us, we have won.

I came to understand one more thing. I have already decided this, also for the SS. When somehow a ceasefire comes, I will work on the army and the SS like never before. I will create a new army with 30–40 panzer divisions and a number of active infantry divisions, which will be trained in everything, from basic training till ideological training, from antitank tactics to surviving in -40 degree temperatures. Further, twelve SS panzer divisions and thirty European divisions which, as we have seen at Narva, are able to fight quite well. When then someone begins to talk of peace, when someone on the other side gets weak, then the *Führer* will have good arguments in his hand in order to be able to decide the conditions of this peace. And we do not need to talk now when we are going to reconquer those hundreds of thousands or a million square kilometers which we'd lost in the East. This is obvious. The program is unchangeable. It stands fast that we will move our national border 500 kilometers to the east. That we will settle the area. It is unshakable that we will create the Germanic Reich. It stands fast that thirty million Germanic peoples will join our ninety million, so that our racial basis will grow to 120 million. We will be the force of order in the Balkan and in Europe in general. We will organize the whole continent militarily, politically and economically. We will fill the East with our settlements and create a garden of Germanic blood. We will move our security border far to the East. Because we can be sure that, unless our Luftwaffe has its bases on the Ural, our children or grandchildren will lose a war in one or two generations. Those who do not have a security margin of 2,000 or 3,000 kilometers in a future air war, will lose it.

Besides, I find it wonderful that already today we understand our economical, political, human and military tasks in the gorgeous East. If the Cossacks could conquer the whole area to the Yellow Sea for the Tsars, our sons will do it for us. And year after year, generation after generation we will equip and send treks of settlers a couple of hundreds of kilometers further, create new bases, settle new areas and push out the others. This is our task.

In the East, we will have our training areas where we will practice each winter, with so-and-so many divisions, in ice and snow and cold. Just like their fathers in 1941, the children will practice here in later years, they will live in Finnish tents, and every generation will practice sharp shooting, will show their worth, so that the danger which every victory brings with itself, the danger of becoming soft and comfortable, will be averted in the coming decades and centuries.

Also, I find it excellent that fate is so kind and so hard to us at the same time. It melds us together, we are more united than ever.

It gives us the ability, after the gloomy July 20, to fill with our beliefs and educate those organizations which up till now did not share our beliefs. It showed us all our weak points. It eliminated all those who were weak. Weak psychologically, health-wise, those who were unable to bear the burden any longer. Excellent that they are folding together. This is a selection process of nature. And, as always, those who are stronger in this fight remain. And we have only one ambition: When the history of this time will be written, one dogma will be expressed: Adolf Hitler was the greatest Aryan, not only the greatest Germanic, leader—and they will say about us, his henchmen: His Paladins were faithful, obedient and steadfast, they were worthy to be his comrades, to be his paladins. *Heil Hitler! (Long-lasting, stormy applause)*

APPENDIX 4

Rank Comparisons

Waffen-SS	deutsche Polizei	Schutzmannschaft	Heer
SS-Grenadier	Anwärter	Schutzmann	Grenadier
SS-Sturmmann	Unterwachtmeister	Unterkorporal	Gefreiter
SS-Rottenführer	Rottwachtmeister	Vizekorporal	Obergefreiter
SS-Unterscharführer	Wachtmeister	—	Unteroffizier
SS-Scharführer	Oberwachtmeister	Korporal	Unterfeldwebel
SS-Oberscharführer	Zugwachtmeister	Vizefeldwebel	Feldwebel
S-Hauptscharführer	Hauptwachtmeister	Kompaniefeldwebel	Oberfeldwebel
SS-Untersturmführer	Leutnant	Leitenant	Leutnant
SS-Obersturmführer	Oberleutnant	Starschy	Leitenant Oberleutnant
SS-Hauptsturmführer	Hauptmann	Kapitan	Hauptmann
SS-Sturmbannführer	Major	—	Major
SS-Obersturmbannführer	Oberstleutnant	—	Oberstleutnant
SS-Standartenführer	Oberst	—	Oberst
SS-Oberführer	kein vgl. Rang	—	kein vgl. Rang
SS-Brigadeführer	Generalmajor	—	Generalmajor
SS-Gruppenführer	Generalleutnant	—	Generalleutnant
SS-Obergruppenführer	General	—	General
SS-Oberstgruppenführer	Generaloberst	—	Generaloberst

ENDNOTES

Foreword

[1] Eugen Kogon coined this expression in 1946 in his book, *Der SS-Staat: Das System der deutschen Konzentrationslager*, Frankfurt, 1946.

Chapter 1

[1] As it was clear to Hitler that he would never achieve influential power without the generous financial support of German industry, not only did he abandon the pursuit of this socialist goal, he also opposed those within the party who had a different view.

[2] Electoral alliance between the DNVP, *Stahlhelm* and *Landbund*.

[3] Hafner, Sebastian: *Anmerkungen zu Hitler*, Munich, 1978.

Chapter 2

[1] Heinrich was the son of Prince Arnulf von Bayern, and his wife Therese Princess von und zu Liechtenstein.

[2] On November 28, 1918, Wilhelm II finally officially renounced the Royal Crown of Prussia and the Imperial Crown of Germany.

[3] This was equivalent to a *Feldwebel* who was an officer candidate.

[4] Letter from Himmler to *SS-Gruppenführer* Oswald Pohl, head of the SS Economics and Administration Office, dated November 29, 1941 in: Heiber, Helmut, *Reichsführer!*, Munich, 1970.

[5] In contrast to Hitler, Gregor Strasser wanted to socialize Germany. He wanted to completely break the power of the capital of industry. After Strasser, along with Ernst Röhm, became a powerful opponent, Hitler had him shot in Munich on June 30, 1934, during the putting down of the so-called Röhm putsch.

[6] He initially also remained deputy when Dr. Goebbels was named (Reich) Propaganda Leader in 1930.

[7] While this was about 500 Reichsmarks monthly, by 1942, Himmler had a net monthly income of 1,992.10 RM. In 1943, when he became Minister of the Interior, this rose to 2,636.92 RM. This was equivalent in buying power to approximately 11,000 Euros, equivalent to a present-day federal minister.

[8] "Supporting Members of the SS" were persons who for various reasons did not want to officially take part in serving in the SS, or who quite simply promised themselves social or economic advantages by becoming one. One well-known supporting member was the clothing maker Hugo Boss. In 1932, there were already about 13,000 supporting members, who donated about 17,000 RM annually to the "Heinrich" Special Account at the Dresdner Bank. One year later this number had risen to 170,000 supporting members, who paid in about 357,000 Reichsmarks annually.

[9] On September 8, 1933, the chief-of-staff of the Supreme SA Commander, Ernst Röhm, announced an order, according to which the *Reichsführer-SS, SS-Obergruppenführer* Himmler, was to be addressed as *"Mein Reichsführer."*

[10] Gerhard von der Ahé was born on July 21, 1928. After his father was killed in street fighting on February 19, 1933, the Himmler family accepted him as a foster child. Initially very welcome, it became apparent that after being separated from her husband Margarete Himmler had little pedagogical effect on the boy. From 1940, Gerhard von der Ahé attended the Napola in Berlin–Spandau and at the end of 1944, the sixteen-year-old volunteered for service in the *Waffen-SS.* He was inducted by *SS-Panzergrenadier-Ausbildungs-und Ersatz-Bataillon 10* and when the war ended he was captured by the Soviets while serving with the *10. SS-Panzer-Division* "Frundsberg." Back in Germany in October 1955, Gerhard von der Ahé temporarily lived with Margarete Himmler in Bielefeld. He moved to Lübeck in 1956, and last worked for the Lübecker Nachrichten. In 2001, during an interview by the *Lübecker Nachrichten*, he remembered his childhood as a "peaceful idyll." Gerhard von der Ahé died in a senior care facility in Lübeck in December 2010.

[11] In the foreground were archaeological, anthropological and historical research and expeditions. The *Ahnenerbe* was finally attached to the Personal Staff of the *Reichsführer-SS* as Office A.

[12] Son Helge was born on February 15, 1942, and on June 3, 1944, daughter Nanette Dorothea was born.

[13] Heiber, Helmut (ed.), *Reichsführer!*, Munich 1970, p. 299.

[14] Heiber, Helmut (ed.), *Reichsführer!*, Munich 1970, p. 364.

[15] Heiber, Helmut (ed.), *Reichsführer!*, Munich 1970, p. 368.

[16] *SS-Obergruppenführer* Berger had been named *Stabsführer des Volkssturmes* (Staff Leader of the *Volkssturm*) at the beginning of October 1944.

[17] Himmler's final circle probably included:
> *SS-Obergruppenführer* Prof. Dr. Karl Gebhardt,
> *SS-Brigadeführer* Otto Ohlendorf, head of Department III in the RSHA,
> *SS-Standartenführer* Dr. Rudolf Brandt,
> *SS-Obersturmbannführer* Werner Grothmann, personal adjutant,
> *SS-Obersturmbannführer* Werner Linnemayr, personal adjutant of the head of the SS Personnel Office,
> *SS-Sturmbannführer* Josef Kiermayer, personal secretary, and
> *SS-Sturmbannführer* Heinz Macher.

[18] Chavkin, Boris and Kalganov, A.M. (ed.), *Die letzten Tage von Heinrich Himmler*, Cologne, 2000.

Chapter 3

[1] Based on Section 1 of the Law for the Implementation of Article 177/178 of the peace treaty of March 22, 1921, as a result of the ultimatum by the Allied governments of May 5, 1921, the citizen's militias within the Free State of Bavaria were declared disbanded. Persons who participated in one of the disbanded organizations as members were liable to a fine of up to 50,000 Marks or a prison term of up to three months or imprisonment in a fortress for the same duration.

[2] Quoted from the Civil Servant's Calendar 1936, Berlin, 1936.

[3] Offices and Main Offices later developed from these.

[4] The Reich Interior Ministry gradually took over the financing of the concentration camp guard units (*Totenkopfverbände*) (in 1936) and the concentration camps themselves (1938).

[5] The relationship between the SS and SA had limited the SA command to about 10% of its own strength. The numerical ratio between the NSDAP, which by then had about 850,000 members, and the SA, with half a million members, was interesting.

[6] A short time later the *SS-Stabswache Berlin* was renamed the *Leibstandarte-SS Adolf Hitler*.

[7] This was responsible for the *Allgemeine-SS*, the *Leibstandarte-SS Adolf Hitler*, the *Politische Bereitschaften/SS-Verfügungstruppen* and the concentration camp SS Guard Units/ *Totenkopfverbände*.

[8] These functionaries were of less importance in Germany as they were in the occupied territories. There the Senior SS and Police Commanders—especially in anti-partisan activities—the actual overall command of the deployed SS and police formations and attached *Wehrmacht* units.

[9] Even today, an order is defined as a community in which the members take a vow to the order and bind themselves to a lifestyle by following very specific rules and thus lead an almost spiritual life in this community. In fact the difference from a cult is almost fluid.

[10] The individual *Stürme* or *Sturmbanne* often had only a fraction of their former strengths and so the peacetime obligations, such as regular meetings, participation in large functions or sporting activity were usually no longer opportune.

[11] Following National–Socialist racial theory, in 1934 Philipp Depdolla published the book *Erblehre, Rasse und Bevölkerungspolitik*. According to it the following racial divisions existed:

- Pure Nordic Race, those whose living area is in the lands around the Baltic and North Seas, in particular therefore in Northern Germany, in England and Scotland and in Scandinavia. The Nordic Race is characterized by its tallness, 1.74 meters on average, with long limbs and slender build. The head has a so-called index of less than seventy-five, meaning that its width is less than 75% of its length, as the rear of the head bulges more to the rear. Forehead and lower jaw are narrow; the chin prominent. Hair colors were blonde, reddish-blonde or dark blonde. Eye color ranged from deep blue to blue-grey or grey.
- Primarily Nordic or Gaelic Race, those who live in the western area of the Elbe, Holland and Denmark. They resemble the Nordic people but are taller and more powerfully built.
- Alpine and Ostish Race, people who are spread from the Western Alps and France through Southern Germany to Bohemia and Eastern Europe. Head index and hair and eye colors resemble those of the Dinarian Race. Average height is only 1.63 meters, however.
- Dinarian Race, those whose main area of distribution is in the Dinarian Mountains (western southeast–European peninsula) – especially in Dalmatia and Bosnia. Because of their straight, flat rear of the skull, their head index is between 85 and 87. The nose is large and often curved. Hair and eye colors brown to almost black. Average height is 1.73 meters.
- Mediterranean or Western Race, those who live on the Mediterranean peninsulas including North Africa. Average height is 1.61 meters. Eyes and hair were dark brown to black.

[12] The minimum height for the *Leibstandarte-SS Adolf Hitler*, however, was 1.78 meters.

[13] The army also had special requirements for different branches of service, for example:

- Cavalry: weight not greater than 65 kg, height between 1.60 and 1.72 meters, slim.
- Artillery: powerful, slim

- Pioneers: if possible not under 1.65 meters, muscular or round body shape
- Signals Units: should not be color-blind
- Motor Transport Units: good vision, good hearing, unhindered nose breathing, only exceptions for glasses wearers and color-blindness

[14] According to the *Wehrgesetz*, every German man was liable to military service from the end of his eighteenth year to age forty-five. The circle of persons could be expanded during time of war. While *Wehrpflicht* initially meant only registration of the men, *Dienstpflicht* was active service in the *Wehrmacht*. According to the *Wehrgesetz, Dienstpflicht* for every German male fit for service as a rule extended from the end of his twentieth year to age forty-five. This meant that young men were initially inducted at the age of 20–21.

[15] AHA = *Allgemeines Heeresamt* (General Army Office).

[16] 234,000 of these came from armaments companies.

[17] Concerning the history of the ethnic Germans please see the chapter German Racial Assistance Main Office and Office of the Reich Commissar for the Consolidation of German Nationhood.

[18] The people received German citizenship when they were issued the Citizenship Certificate of the Reich Minister of the Interior (*Reichsführer-SS* Himmler).

[19] For returnees, this meant that they generally had to do their military service in the army, the air force or the navy.

[20] Himmler also had special influence on the leaderships of the ethnic groups in his capacity as Reich Commissar for the Consolidation of German Nationhood.

[21] The Deutsche Mannschaft was equivalent to the SA, the *Einsatzstaffel* to the SS.

[22] Including those called up in 1940 and 1941.

[23] The small number of about 22,000 Hungarian ethnic Germans in the *Waffen-SS* on December 28, 1943, is calculated as follows: about 17,000 men were taken in in 1942. In about a year and a half of action until the end of 1943, about 4,000 were killed or were wounded and discharged. From September to December 1943, about 10,000 men were inducted into the *Waffen-SS*. The remaining roughly 12,000 men followed from January to February 1944.

[24] Diary No. 106/44 g. Kdos. of February 8, 1944.

[25] Wilhelm Hintersatz served in the First World War as an officer and in 1919 converted to Islam. From then on his name was Harun-el-Rashid Bey.

[26] This included those whose loyalty was not certain. Because of time pressure during the transfer to the west, however, the division command was unable weed out all the unreliable men.

[27] Galicia had been attached to the *Generalgouvernement* as its fifth district on August 1, 1941.

[28] After obligatory labor service was introduced in Galicia, the men could or must choose whether they wished to join the SS Volunteer Division, the construction service in Galicia, the *Ordnungspolizei*, or work in the armaments industry in Germany.

[29] The recruiting effort was carried out under the title of a Hungarian panzer-grenadier division.

[30] See: Michaelis, Rolf: *Die Waffen-SS: Mythos und Wirklichkeit*, Berlin, 2006.

[31] If one compares the number with the unbelievable figures at the start of the Russian campaign, it is apparent that the leaders of the division led their units with much more care than was the case at the beginning of the war.

[32] Both divisions were still designated *9. SS-Panzergrenadier-Division* until October 26, 1943.

[33] This was the official designation from May 15, 1944.

[34] Kaminski was fundamentally opposed to fighting nationalist partisans, preferring instead to fight only communist "bandits."

[35] In the end the daily rations for the more than 11,000 wounded inside the fortress was only fifteen grams (half an ounce) of legumes and half a slice of bread.

[36] *Legion Volonter Francaise* = Army French Infantry Regiment 638.

Chapter 4

[1] See *Münchner Neueste Nachrichten* of 13 March 1933.

[2] Schneidhuber, whose first marriage was to a Jewess, repeatedly clashed with Himmler. Rather a moderate politically, he became a victim of the so-called Röhm Putsch because of existing discrepancies with Himmler. Although he was not a member of Röhm's inner circle and fundamentally rejected his homosexuality, Schneidhuber was shot in Munich on June 30, 1934. Himmler thus demonstrated his determination to even liquidate party members who did not conform to his own line.

[3] See chapter 5.

[4] Himmler's speech to the *SS-Gruppenführer* in Tölz on February 18, 1937, in: BA, NS 19/4004. Himmler declared: "The police must safeguard the German people, as an organic body, its life force and its installations against destruction and degradation. No restrictions can be placed on the powers of a police force entrusted with these tasks." Himmler, Heinrich, *Aufgaben und Aufbau der Polizei des Dritten Reiches*, in, *Dr. Wilhelm Frick and His Ministry*, edited by Hans Pfundtner, Munich, 1937.

[5] Rumler, Günther and Holzmann, Otto: *Freigemachtes Grenzland*, Berlin, 1942.

[6] Rumler, Günther and Holzmann, Otto: *Freigemachtes Grenzland*, Berlin, 1942.

[7] See Michaelis, Rolf: *Der Einsatz der Ordnungspolizei 1939–1945*, Berlin, 2008.

[8] For example:

Berlin (*Wehrkreis* III)	*Polizei-Bataillone* 1, 2, 3, 4 and 5
Wehrkreis II	*Polizei-Bataillone* 21 and 22
Wehrkreis XVII	*Polizei-Bataillone* 171 and 172

[9] Richter, Hans, *Einsatz der Polizei*, Berlin, 1943.

[10] Rumler, Günther and Holzmann, Otto, *Freigemachtes Grenzland*, Berlin, 1942.

[11] Richter, Hans, *Einsatz der Polizei*, Berlin, 1943.

[12] Richter, Hans, *Einsatz der Polizei*, Berlin, 1943.

Chapter 5

[1] *Oberst* i.G. Eismann, Army Group Vistula's operations officer, recalled that he had never known a better-functioning staff than the one Himmler created in his capacity as commander-in-chief of Army Group Vistula.

[2] The *SS-Hauptamt* was also the supreme command authority for the SS Guard Units/ *SS-Totenkopfverbände* and the *SS-Verfügungstruppen*.

[3] The *Freiwillige-Leitstelle Ost* was responsible for more vigorous recruitment among the Soviet people.

[4] *Reichsführer-SS* Berlin, August 15, 1940, Diary No. 1107/40 secret.

[5] The *Waffen-SS* command had been set up on June 1, 1940.

[6] The Inspectorate of Concentration Camps (KL) was renamed Office VI / SS-FHA on 1 November 1941.

[7] The *SS-Zentralamt* (Central Office) became the command office of the *Allgemeine-SS* on 5 September 1940.

[8] On April 10, 1940, the *Waffen-Inspektion* became the *Amtsgruppe Inspektionen* (Office Group Responsible for Inspectorates) on April 10, 1942, with: In 1 NCO Schools; In 2 Infantry; In 3 Cavalry and Motor Vehicles; In 4 Artillery (and from 10/04/1942: *Flak*); In 5 Pioneers; In 6 Motorized Troops; In 7 Signals Troops; In 8 Armaments.

[9] The department became independent on November 15, 1940 as Office VIII.

[10] On March 16, 1942, the inspectorate was placed under the Economic and Administrative Main Office.

[11] Office Group D was formed from the former Office VII / Medical Services on November 26, 1942.

[12] The office only existed from August 1–31, 1943 and was then placed directly under the *Reichsarzt-SS* as Office III.

[13] Wolff had been promoted to *SS-Brigadeführer* with an effective date of November 9, 1935, and on January 30, 1937, to *SS-Gruppenführer*.

[14] The Ancestral Research and Teaching Society (Ahnenerbe) was founded in Berlin in 1935, to research "Germanic" prehistory and German folklore. During the Second World War the research mission was broadened to include more pragmatic things.

[15] The *Lebensborn e.V.* was established in Berlin on December 12, 1935, to assist the wives and partners of SS members, later also women from occupied "Germanic" countries who were expecting the child of a *Wehrmacht* member. In addition to medical examinations there were various maternity homes. Initially a main department of the Clan Office in the SS Race and Settlement Main Office, in 1938 the *Lebensborn e.V.* was then attached to the Personal Staff *Reichsführer-SS*.

[16] It was attached to the SS Adjutancy and processed high decorations for members of the *Waffen-SS* and Police.

[17] This was responsible for the command and welfare of all members of the *Waffen-SS* transferred to the Personal Staff.

[18] From January 1944, its title was: Statistical Scientific Institute of the *Reichsführer-SS*. It was directed by Dr. Richard Korherr and was tasked with carrying out statistical work for Himmler. Of interest is the so-called "Korherr Report," a statistical summary of "Jewish evacuations" in Europe until the end of 1942.

[19] In April and June 1938, for example, the Reich Criminal Police Office conducted an operation called "*Arbeitsscheu* (Indolent) *Reich*." In two waves of arrests, more than 10,000 persons (homeless, beggars, vagrants, "gypsies," and welfare cheats who had obtained state welfare by fraud) were sent to concentration camps. It was a process that was largely welcomed by the population.

[20] *Einsatzgruppe Serbia* was dissolved in January 1942, and its tasks passed over to *SS-Gruppenführer* August von Meyszner (August 3, 1886 – January 24, 1947), the Senior SS and Police Commander in Serbia.

[21] No explicit distinction between *Sonderkommando* and *Einsatzkommando* is mentioned here. The *Sonderkommando* and *Einsatzkommando* did not differ in numbering. Instead they were numbered consecutively.

[22] After a reorganization in 1942–43, the *Einsatzgruppe* commanded the *Einsatzkommandos* 1a, 1b, 1c and 1, 2 and 3.

[23] Himmler decried, for example, the exaggerations made by *SS-Brigadeführer* Nebe, who according to the magazine *Spiegel* (issue 5/1950) always added a zero to the shooting numbers.

[24] The originals are held by the Federal Archive in Berlin–Lichterfelde under the number R 58/214-221.

[25] Not to be forgotten in this context are the roughly three-million Soviet prisoners of war who perished miserably in transit and collection camps in 1941–42. In contrast to the treatment of western-European prisoners of war, the OKW had different directives from Hitler and carried them out without complaint.

[26] The official title was, *The SS and Police Commander in the Lublin District – Action Reinhard.* It was also referred to as *Aktion Reinhardt*.

[27] They were patients suffering from schizophrenia, epilepsy, dementia, paralysis, and senile dementia.

28 In cases of carbon-monoxide poisoning, the amount of oxygen absorbed by red blood cells is very restricted and enzymes are blocked in the muscles and nerves. The symptoms of this are headache, dizziness and nausea, convulsions, and difficulty breathing. The interval between the first symptoms and loss of consciousness is very short. Bodily functions fail rapidly and independent action becomes impossible.

29 The sum of 1,000 persons can be reconstructed for many of the transports. According to timetable order No. 565 of the General Directorate of the Ostbahn, Cracow on August 26, 1942, a "special resettlement train" from Lukow to Treblinka via Siedlce weighed 400 tons full, and 300 tons empty. The weight transported was thus 100 tons. For 1,000 people this resulted in 100 kg per person (body weight including clothing and luggage).

30 A labor camp for Sinti and Roma from Germany had existed there since May 1940. The "gypsies" were moved out in the summer of 1940, and about 10,000 Polish Jews were put to work digging the so-called "Bug trench." These were anti-tank ditches built to border the Soviet occupation zone. The camp was liquidated in October 1940.

31 By comparison: a modern soccer field has a surface area of 90x120 meters, making the camp equal in size to six soccer fields (two in length, and three in width).

32 Most were former Soviet prisoners of war who were Ukrainian nationals. They were trained for guard duty at SS Training Camp Trawniki in the Generalgouvernement.

33 This title was an homage by guard personnel to *SS-Unterscharführer* Max Biala, who was fatally stabbed during a deportation on September 11, 1942.

34 Like other numbers in this book (for example the German minority groups abroad), those as a consequence of the persecution of the Jews in Europe are hypothetical, although as far as possible they are based on original documents.

35 The Fourth Regulation of the Reich Citizenship Law of July 25, 1938, forbade Jews from practicing medicine, while the Fifth Regulation of the Reich Citizenship Law of September 27, 1938 forbade them from practicing law.

36 The USA and Japan had been in a state of war since December 8, 1941. Three days later, upholding his pact with Japan, Hitler declared war on the United States. The European War had escalated into a world war.

37 See BA R 8150/26.

38 These were the numbers as of October 1941.

39 This is how Action Reinhard was rewritten.

40 This total was based on reports by the Sipo and SD *Einsatzgruppen* and included the shootings of most Jewish population elements in the conquered territories of the USSR. Although Himmler repeatedly criticized the numbers provided by the RSHA, Dr. Korherr accepted them, having no alternative.

41 Of these, 24,313 came from Germany and 25,079 from the Protectorate of Bohemia and Moravia.

42 On the transport on January 15, 1944, there were also 351 Sinti and Roma who were also in Mechelen.

43 Chirac commented: "These hours of darkness sully our history forever. They are a reproach to our past and to our traditions. The criminal madness of the occupiers was supported by Frenchmen, by the French state."

44 See: http://www.hagalil.com/archiv/99/03/jasenovac.htm

45 After 1933, many German Jews emigrated to the Netherlands. To control an unchecked influx, the Dutch government closed the borders. As well, it concentrated the emigrants in collection camps. The largest was the Central Refugee Camp in Westerbork, where Jewish men had to work in the surrounding peat farms under less than ideal conditions. On July 1, 1942, the Central Refugee Camp Westerbork was renamed "Police Jewish Transit Camp Kamp Westerbork."

[46] During 1942, just under 20,000 Jews from Germany and the Protectorate of Bohemia and Moravia came to the ghetto.

[47] The Province of Transnistria encompassed the area east of the Dniestr (Rumanian Nistru) and the southern Bug.

[48] Ironically, after the war Radu Lecca, who could be characterized as thoroughly corrupt, tried to portray himself as the savior of Rumanian Jews because he did not deport them to Germany.

[49] See Reitlinger, Gerald, *Die Endlösung*, Berlin, 1961. He gives the number of 153,743 Jews based on a census in 1935.

[50] The total of 136,421 shot Jews does not include those who had previously gone to one of the three big ghettoes, while covering those who, for example, were executed immediately after leaving the deportation trains, or the liquidated Jewish communities in the countryside.

[51] A total of about 27,000 German Jews were deported to Riga. A very few of them survived.

[52] For the prisoners this meant separation from their family members, the wearing of blue and white prisoner clothing, removal of their hair, and the loss of their remaining private space.

[53] The evacuation fell victim to pragmatism, the desire to retain the maximum possible work force for German armaments.

[54] When the Red Army retook the city on December 31, 1943, a committee investigating National–Socialist crimes exhumed the mass graves and counted 9,263 bodies.

[55] This was a Turkish-speaking minority of the Jews living in the Crimea.

[56] Peter-Heinz Seraphim (September 15, 1902 – May 19, 1979), the "Jewish Expert" in the Institute for German Work in the East, assumed at the end of 1942, that there were still about 200,000 Jews in the Reich Commissariat Ukraine. Others lived to the east in the rear army area or had "gone into hiding."

[57] The Poles had occupied areas of Lithuania and White Russia in 1920–21. The USSR reoccupied these areas in 1939, and according to an estimate by the Security Police and the SD there were about 820,000 Jews in this entire area. Of these, about 500,000 were living on Polish territory. If one assumes that about 20,000 Jews lived in occupied Lithuanian territory, the resulting number for the actual White Russian areas was about 300,000 Jews.

[58] These were volunteers. Attached to the *Ordnungspolizei*, they ultimately formed *Schutzmannschaft-Bataillone* (police battalions).

[59] Of the approximately 128,000 Jews thought to be in White Russia at the end of January 1942, about 70,000 died by the end of July 1942.

[60] These limited the number of Jewish students to 6% of all those studying. Thus the number of Jews who in future could hold high-ranking positions in the state or the private enterprise was roughly equivalent to the Jewish portion of the population. After this regulation was lifted in 1928, ten years later—in 1938—followed a law according to which the existing percentage of Jews in private occupations and the economy was supposed to be limited to 20%. This quota was lowered to 6% in May 1939. This was a plan that could not be implemented, as Jews represented more than 50% of doctors, about half the lawyers and more than a third of businesspeople.

[61] In this context, the words "special treatment" had a positive meaning—as they generally imply. From 1941, at least among the German leadership, the term became a synonym for the murder of sick people, members of the opposition, Jews, Sinti, and Roma.

[62] Main Department I g was set up in May 1944, as part of enhanced investigations of corruption and concentration camp crimes. It was supposed to carry out the function of a public prosecutor's office and centrally coordinate and control investigative proceedings within the entire SS and Police jurisdiction.

[63] Like the army, which had a central court, the Main Office SS Court formed a Special Purpose SS and Police Court, which was responsible for criminal cases of special importance.

[64] A total of approximately 16,000 SS members passed through the *SS-Junkerschulen* (officer schools) by 1945.

[65] In January 1944, the office was initially placed under the Economic and Administrative Main Office and then ultimately taken over.

[66] The Reich Interior Ministry took over in stages the financing guard units (*Totenkopfverbände*) of the concentration camp (1936) and the concentration camps themselves (1938).

[67] In addition, 1,930,000 prisoners of war and 5,976,673 foreign workers were employed in the German armaments industry.

[68] According to Piper, Franciszek, *Die Zahl der Opfer von Auschwitz*, a probable total of 1,305,190 people were deported to Auschwitz:

> 438,000 Jews from Hungary
> 300,000 Jews from Poland
> 69,000 Jews from France
> 60,000 Jews from the Netherlands
> 55,000 Jews from Greece
> 27,000 Jews from Slovakia
> 25,000 Jews from Belgium
> 23,000 Jews from the German Reich
> 10,000 Jews from Yugoslavia
> 7,500 Jews from Italy
> 690 Jews from Norway
> 34,000 Jews from other concentration camps
> 46,000 Jews from the Protectorate of Bohemia and Moravia
> 23,000 Sinti and Roma
> 15,000 Soviet prisoners of war
> 25,000 other deportees

[69] *Rudolf Höss: Kommandant von Auschwitz*, 1958.

[70] Kupfer-Koberwitz, Edgar, *Dachauer Tagebücher*, Munich, 1997.

[71] The first figure quoted after liberation in 1944 was 1,700,000 victims. In 1948, it was suspected that 360,000 people died in the Lublin Concentration Camp (Maidanek). Later estimates put the total at 235,000 victims (110,000 of them Jews); according to these estimates the number of victims killed in mass gassings at Maidanek was less than 50,000. The latest research reflects the numbers of the Director of the State Museum.

[72] At the end of 1942, 0.30 Reichsmarks was calculated for each prisoner per day. This rate rose to 1.50 Reichsmarks by 1943.

[73] See Michaelis, Rolf, *Die Volksdeutschen in Wehrmacht, Waffen-SS und Ordnungspolizei*, Berlin, 2011.

[74] The Ethnic German Council itself was supposed to represent a centralization of German racial policy and was the forerunner of the *Volksdeutsche Mittelstelle*.

[75] These were not always Germans. In some cases they were persons who had German ancestors. For Switzerland this number included the German-speaking people, who de, however, had no facto ties to Germany.

[76] This number reflects the state in 1939.

[77] Lower Styria and Gottschee were also called Drau–Banat.

[78] By October 1940, about 56,000 persons had left their homes and the majority settled in Austria. The number of South Tyroleans and residents of the Kanal Valley willing to resettle rose to 222,018 by mid-1942, the number of those who had already left to 76,824 persons. Of these, to date 55,768 had been placed in the districts of Ostmark, especially in Tyrol–Vorarlberg (27,308), and the rest in the Old Reich. At the end of 1942, there were also about 6,000 ethnic Germans from the southeast plus 600 from South Tyrol in the "Protectorate

of Bohemia and Moravia." As a result of Italy's defection to the Allies, on October 1, 1943, the provinces of Belluno and Trentino were concentrated into Operations Zone Alpenvorland and the remaining roughly 135,000 ethnic Germans were left in the area as a minority group under Peter Hofer. The *Gauleiter* of Tyrol–Vorarlberg took over the administration of the region. At the same time the so-called Wendish, who lived in the Kanal Valley, were recognized as ethnic Germans after lengthy discussions with Italy.

[79] Bosse, Heinrich, *Der Führer ruft*, Berlin, 1941.

[80] For the ethnic Germans in the incorporated areas, on April 25, 1943, Hitler introduced "citizenship with right of withdrawal." For the ethnic Germans (especially in the Wartheland and later in Northern Italy and Slovenia) this meant that while they were immediately liable to military service, after the war their German citizenship could be denied.

[81] A process that was to be repeated in Southeast Europe, where not all of the ethnic Germans joined the fleeing refugees. Socially even close to the communist party, they hoped (in vain) that they might keep living in their previous settlement areas despite the defeat of Germany.

[82] This had been founded in June 1939, for the resettlement of South Tyrolean optants (those who opted for Germany).

Chapter 6

[1] Frick issued the Racial Health Laws and the Nuremberg Race Laws. He was convicted of war crimes and executed on October 16, 1946.

[2] In the course of which Himmler also dissolved the existing office of the Interior Minister and reassigned its functions to his personal staff.

[3] It is not understandable that a politician who assumed such responsibility in the Third Reich could be de-nazified as a "hanger on" by the German authorities in 1950.

Chapter 7

[1] See BA, NS 19/3910.

[2] Goebbels, Joseph, *Die Tagebücher, Band 13*, Entry dated August 4, 1944.

Chapter 8

[1] His field headquarters (Special Train "Heinrich") was at Triberg Station.

[2] Schramm, Percy E. (ed.), *Kriegstagebuch des OKW, Teilband I 1944/1845*, p. 425.

[3] Division Order of December 11, 1944, and Battle Report of December 14, 1944, Militärarchiv Freiburg, RH 20-19/145.

[4] Schramm, Percy E. (editor), *Kriegstagebuch des OKW, Teilband II 1944/1845*, p. 990.

[5] The command was renamed Army Group Upper Rhine on January 22, 1945.

[6] In some cases they simply perished, were captured or were able to regain contact with larger formations or the front.

[7] Telex OKH/GenStdH/Op Abt. (I a), Nr. 450 037/45 geh. Chefsache.

[8] *Zentrum gegen Vertreibung* (Center against Expulsion): Report by Dr. Hans Leeser, former Mayor of the city of Elbing in West Prussia, of May 29, 1952.

[9] Deployed at the border with Army Group Center, initially only the remnants of the *25. Panzer-Division*, the headquarters of the 608th Special Purpose Division and alert units were present.

[10] Headquarters, Army Group Vistula, *Oberst* i.G. Eismann for the Chief-of-Staff, Operations Officer Diary No. 51/45 Secret Command matter, of January 27, 1945.

[11] Headquarters, Army Group Vistula, *Oberst* i.G. Eismann for the Chief-of-Staff, Operations Officer Diary No. 111/45 Secret Command matter, of January 29, 1945.

[12] Headquarters, Army Group Vistula, *Reichsführer-SS* Himmler, Dept. Operations Officer Diary No. 139/45 Secret Command matter, of January 30, 1945.

[13] The following is from a letter to the commander-in-chief of Army Group Vistula: "The overall impression I gained in recent days, which I can truly characterize as my most difficult and worry-filled, is that we in the *Wehrmacht* find ourselves in a crisis of leadership on the largest scale. The officer corps no longer has a firm grip on the forces in the field. There are the worst signs of disintegration in the units themselves. Soldiers are taking off their uniforms and trying everything in their power to obtain civilian clothes so that they can get away, and these are not isolated occurrences. It has also been determined that soldiers in civilian clothes are hiding in many civilian vehicles so as to escape with the refugees."

[14] Like the *11. Armee*, the *6. Panzer-Armee* was not referred to as an "SS" army, at least not in the written language then in use.

[15] OKH/Army General Staff/Operations Section (1 a), *Generaloberst* Guderian, Nr. 450 073/45 secret command matter, of February 4, 1945.

[16] With the last usable sources of oil located in Hungary, the *6. Panzer-Armee* was deployed there to secure this vital resource.

[17] Headquarters, Army Group Vistula, *Reichsführer-SS* Himmler, Dept. Operations Officer, No, 27/45 Secret Command Matter, of February 8, 1945.

[18] Concentration and preparation of the attack forces was not possible at that time, however. Instead, elements of the envisaged units were tied to the front by extensive enemy attacks—for example, the Polish 1st Army attacked at the border between Headquarters, *11. Armee* and Headquarters, *2. Armee* in the Deutsch Krone–Ratzebuhr area in the direction of Kolberg.

[19] Guderian, Heinz, *Erinnerungen eines Soldaten*, Stuttgart, 1994.

[20] *Oberst* i.G. Eismann: Records.

[21] See Michaelis, Rolf, *Die Träger des Bandenkampfabzeichens in Gold*, Berlin, 2013.

[22] Appeal by the *Reichsführer-SS* and commander-in-chief of Army Group Vistula Himmler of February 11, 1945.

[23] Commander-in-Chief of the Replacement Army, Stab Ia 647/45, of February 14, 1945.

[24] Wenck required convalescence well into April. After the disastrous outcome of his "Operation Sonnenwende" the accident may have been opportune.

[25] OKH, Army General Staff, I a Operations Dept. Nr. 450 134/45 Secret Command Matter, of February 21, 1945.

[26] It was originally supposed to be brought in from East Prussia during the formation of Army Group Vistula as its operations staff. After this was delayed, however, AOK 11 (Headquarters, *11. Armee*) was formed—from *III. (german.) SS-Panzer-Korps*—as an interim solution for about four weeks.

[27] Raus, *Generaloberst* (Rtd.), "*Die Pommernschlacht und Abwehrkämpfe an der Oder*," in *Militärwissenschaftliches* Nr. 3, March 1951.

[28] OKH/Army General Staff/Operations Section (1 a), Nr. 450 181/45 secret command matter of 11 March 1945.

[29] Heiber, Helmut, *Reichsführer!* Document 386, Page 391, Munich, 1970.

[30] In fact, Himmler probably used his stay at Hohenlychen—at a time when the army group was engaged in fierce defensive fighting—primarily to carry out exploratory discussions with Swedish Count Bernadotte.

Appendices

[1] This statement shows that Himmler, for opportunistic reasons, was not so particular about the truth when it came to outsiders. In fact his maxim was: "The end justifies the means;" however he also applied this to his subordinates, who he in some cases placated with euphemisms, but sometimes also demagogically swore to be loyal to the party line.

[2] The question of whether the German campaign in Russia was a preventive strike, or whether this claim was merely a justification, was a controversial one. Like the formation of the Security Police and SD *Einsatzgruppen*, adherence to the old National–Socialist goal of "living space in the east" showed that it was an ideological war and not a preventive strike. It is noteworthy that in its history the USSR almost never began an offensive war. When the USSR occupied Finnish Karelia in the winter of 1939–40, it was to regain an area in which primarily Russians lived. One can also see the occupation as a strategic operation, which created a buffer for a potential Finnish attack on the important Murmansk Railway.

[3] Probably about 3.5 million Soviet prisoners of war died of starvation. Many thousands were shot for being communist functionaries, some of them in German concentration camps.

[4] Here Himmler was explicitly trying to calm his listeners, and probably hoped that by doing so the effect would be transmitted to subordinate offices and the German people.

[5] The origins of the word robots lie in the Slavic word "*robota*," which means "work." In a play by the Czech playwright Căpek, in 1921, a race of humanoid helpers takes over the work of humans—and ultimately rises up against them.

[6] A few sentences earlier he had declared that Mussolini was the only one in Italy with any honor.

[7] Himmler finally ordered this as BdE in the spring of 1945, when he had recruits with about four week's training sent to Army Group Vistula!

[8] Whereas there had been little objectivity in the speech so far, this statement and open criticism of Hitler's rigid adherence is an extraordinary remark.

[9] This in itself insignificant statement does, however, show the freedom Himmler took in his position. In contrast to American soldiers, some of whom were big souvenir hunters and even traded cigarettes for Iron Crosses, this was neither the case with the Soviet volunteers serving with the Germans nor the Red Army troops. Their only interest in memorabilia was wristwatches.

[10] Based on twenty years of research into the history of the *Waffen-SS* and more than thirty publications, this statement with the generalization "always" can likewise be classified as pure invention.

[11] That's why they were in prison, because they were so upstanding and brave.

[12] Himmler described this as his first action after becoming BdE, which made him the master of the courts responsible for the Replacement Army and as well commander of *Wehrmacht* penal institutions.

[13] Comparing the Third Reich with the period of Frederick the Great was more than paradoxical. Comparing Hitler to the Prussian King was presumptuous. It obviously never occurred to Himmler that the officer corps' criticized lack of loyalty toward Hitler was caused by his criminal orders since 1933—and exponentiated since 1939.

[14] Himmler was commander of the Replacement Army and not commander-in-chief of the army, but he certainly would liked to have been. The formulation as commander-in-chief of this army could, however, also have been legally interpreted as a description of the function of the BdE.

BIBLIOGRAPHY

Bundesarchiv Berlin: NS 19   Personal Staff *Reichsführer-SS*
                            NS 32   *SS-Hauptamt*
                            NS 33   *SS-Führungshauptamt*
NS 3: SS Main Office Economics and Administration
RS 1: Headquarters and Senior Commands of the *Waffen-SS*
Bundesarchiv/Militärarchiv Freiburg: Files of the army groups and armies
Bundesarchiv Koblenz: Files of the *Reichsführer-SS*
Central Office Judicial Administration Ludwigsburg: Various investigation and trial files

Ackermann, Josef. *Heinrich Himmler als Ideologe*. Göttingen: 1970.
Angrick, Andrej. *Besatzungspolitik und Massenmord. Die Einsatzgruppe D in der südlichen Sowjetunion, 1941–1943*. Hamburg: 2003.
Birn, Ruth. *Die Höheren SS- und Polizeiführer*. Tübingen: 1985.
Bonifas, Aimé. *Häftling 20801*. Berlin: 1976.
Bornemann, Manfred. *Geheimprojekt Mittelbau*. Bonn: 1994.
Breitmann, Richard. *Der Architekt der Endlösung: Himmler und die Vernichtung der europäischen Juden*. Paderborn: 1996.
Cüppers, Martin. *Wegbereiter der Shoah. Die Waffen-SS: der Kommandostab Reichsführer-SS und die Judenvernichtung, 1939–1945*. Darmstadt: 2005.
Dallin, Alexander. *Deutsche Herrschaft in Russland*. Dusseldorf: 1958.
Research Center for Contemporary History (published by). *Der Dienstkalender Heinrich Himmlers, 1941/42*, Hamburg: 1999.
Frießner, Hans. *Verratene Schlachten*. Hamburg: 1956.
Gerwarth, Robert. *Reinhard Heydrich*. Munich: 2011.
Goguel, Rudi. *Cap Arcona*. Frankfurt am Main: 1982.
Hackett, David (ed.). *Der Buchenwald-Report*. Munich: 1996.
Hausser, Paul. *Soldaten wie andere auch*. Osnabrück: 1966.
Heiber, Helmut (ed.). *Lagebesprechungen im Führerhauptquartier*. Munich: 1964.
Heinemann, Isabel. *Rasse, Siedlung, Deutsches Blut: Das Rasse- und Siedlungshauptamt der SS und die rassenpolitische Neuordnung Europas*. Göttingen: 2003 .
Herbert, Ulrich (ed.). *Europa und der Reichseinsatz*. Essen: 1991.
Klietmann, Dr. Kurt-G. *Die Waffen-SS*. Osnabrück: 1965.
Kolb, Eberhard. *Bergen–Belsen*. Göttingen: 1996.
Krausnick, Helmut and Wilhelm, Hans-Dietrich. *Die Truppe des Weltanschauungskrieges*. Stuttgart: 1981.
Kupfer-Koberwitz, Edgar. *Dachauer Tagebücher*. Munich: 1997.
Lagergemeinschaft Buchenwald–Dora (published by). *Buchenwald: ein Konzentrationslager*. Frankfurt/Main: 1984.
Langbein, Hermann. *Menschen in Auschwitz*. Munich: 1995.
Longerich, Peter. *Politik der Vernichtung. Eine Gesamtdarstellung der nationalsozialistischen Judenverfolgung*. Munich and Zurich: 1998.
Manstein von, Erich. *Verlorene Siege*. Munich: 1979.
Meissner, Gustav. *Dänemark unterm Hakenkreuz*. Frankfurt am Main: 1990.

Michaelis, Rolf. *Die Waffen-SS: Mythos und Wirklichkeit*. Berlin: 2006.

Michaelis, Rolf. *Der Einsatz der Ordnungspolizei, 1939–1945*. Berlin: 2008.

Michaelis, Rolf. *Die Volksdeutschen in Wehrmacht: Waffen-SS – Ordnungspolizei*. Berlin: 2011.

Neubacher, Hermann. *Sonderauftrag Südost*. Göttingen: 1956.

Neulen, Hans Werner. *An deutscher Seite*. Munich: 1985.

Reitlinger, Gerald. *Die SS: Tragödie einer deutschen Epoche*. Munich: 1957.

Sauer, Karl. *Die Verbrechen der Waffen-SS*. Frankfurt/Main: 1977.

Schiller, Berndt. *Raoul Wallenberg*. Berlin: 1993.

Schneider, Ulrich (ed.). *Auschwitz: Ein Prozess*. Cologne: 1994.

Schramm, Percy (ed.). *Kriegstagebuch des OKW*. Munich: 1982.

Schulte, Jan Erik. *Zwangsarbeit und Vernichtung*. Paderborn: 2001.

Smith, Bradley and Peterson, Agnes (ed.). *Heinrich Himmler. Geheimreden 1933 bis 1945 und andere Ansprachen*. Frankfurt am Main: 1974.

Stein, Georg. *Geschichte der Waffen-SS*. Dusseldorf: 1967.

Steiner, Felix. *Die Freiwilligen*. Rosenheim: 1992.

Tuchel, Johannes. *Die Inspektion der Konzentrationslager, 1938–1945*. Berlin: 1994.

Wildt, Michael. *Generation des Unbedingten. Das Führungskorps des Reichssicherheitshauptamtes*. Hamburg: 2002.

Heinrich Himmler